GOVERNING CHINA

ALSO BY KENNETH LIEBERTHAL

Coeditor with Shuen-fu Lin and Ernest Young, *Constructing China: The Interaction of Culture and Economics*

Coeditor with David M. Lampton, *Bureaucracy, Politics and Decision Making in Post-Mao China*

Coeditor, *Perspectives on Modern China: Four Anniversaries*

Coauthor, with Bruce J. Dickson, *A Research Guide to Central Party and Government Meetings in China, 1949–1986*

Coauthor, with Michel Oksenberg, *Policy Making in China: Leaders, Structures, and Processes*

Coauthor, with Nicholas Lardy, *Chen Yun's Strategy for China's Development: A Non-Maoist Alternative*

Revolution and Tradition in Tientsin, 1949–1952

Sino-Soviet Conflict in the 1970s: Its Evolution and Implications for the Strategic Triangle

Central Documents and Politburo Politics in China

Kenneth Lieberthal

Governing China

From Revolution
Through Reform

Second Edition

W • W • NORTON & COMPANY

NEW YORK • LONDON

W. W. Norton & Company has been independent since its founding in 1923, when William Warder Norton and Mary D. Herter Norton first published lectures delivered at the People's Institute, the adult education division of New York City's Cooper Union. The Nortons soon expanded their program beyond the Institute, publishing books by celebrated academics from America and abroad. By mid-century, the two major pillars of Norton's publishing program—trade books and college texts—were firmly established. In the 1950s, the Norton family transferred control of the company to its employees, and today—with a staff of four hundred and a comparable number of trade, college, and professional titles published each year—W. W. Norton & Company stands as the largest and oldest publishing house owned wholly by its employees.

Copyright © 2004, 1995 by Kenneth Lieberthal.

The text of this book is composed in New Baskerville with the display set in Weiss and Tiger Rag.

Composition by Binghamton Valley Composition.

Manufacturing by Maple-Vail.

Book design by Martin Lubin Graphic Design.

Production manager: Roy Tedoff.

Library of Congress Cataloging-in-Publication Data
Lieberthal, Kenneth.
    Governing China: from revolution through reform / Kenneth Lieberthal.—2nd ed.
        p.   cm.
    Includes bibliographical references and index.
    ISBN 0-393-92492-0 (pbk.)
    1. China—Politics and government —1949– 2. China—History—20th century.   I. Title.
DS777.75.L557   2003
951.05—dc22
                                                                2003060937

W. W. Norton & Company, Inc., 500 Fifth Avenue, New York, N.Y. 10110

W. W. Norton & Company Ltd., Castle House, 75/76 Wells Street, London W1T 3QT

TO JANE

Contents

Tables, Charts, and Maps

MAPS

Preface

The first edition of this book appeared in early 1995, but the writing was completed in December 1993. In the decade since, such far-reaching developments have taken place that this second edition, while maintaining the broad outline and approach of the original, does far more than provide updates of chronology and data. This edition addresses the major issues China confronts from the perspective of the country in 2003. This has required very extensive revision of many chapters and at least some changes in each. This second edition also lists the pertinent secondary literature that has been published since 1993.

China in 2003 is a far livelier, wealthier, more open society than it was in 1993. It has during the intervening decade put in place an advanced telecommunications system, with one of the most extensive wireless networks in the world. Computers and access to the Internet have become widespread in major cities. The consumer revolution has blossomed to the extent that major east coast cities now boast middle classes that enjoy many of the comforts and tastes of their Western counterparts, and private ownership of houses and cars is beginning to take hold. In the overall economy, the state sector has shed jobs, while the private sector has become the major generator of new employment. Foreign direct investment in China has mushroomed to where the country is fast becoming seen as the future manufacturing center of the world. And China is now a member of virtually every major multilateral regime, including the World Trade Organization, which it joined in December 2001.

The past decade has witnessed enormous population migration from rural to urban areas and from the interior to the coast. This vast population shift is now accelerating into one of the most massive movements of people in human history. The resulting problems are in some places compounded by ongoing environmental degradation, which puts enormous strain on the ability of various localities to sustain current activities.

These sectoral changes, population movements, and environmental developments have created vast new demands on China's political system. To put it simply, the institutional and regulatory arrangements of the early 1990s no longer suffice to meet the requirements of large sectors of the population. Other fundamentals, such as relatively strong state control over access to information, have also changed. This second edition details both these new challenges and the responses of the political system to them.

As when the first edition of this book appeared, there are lingering questions about the country's future. China's political system has time and again confounded expectations about its strength and stability. Political changes of enormous consequence punctuated nearly every decade of twentieth-century

Chinese history: the fall of the millennia-old imperial system in 1912; the May Fourth movement in the late 1910s; the unification under the Nationalists in the late 1920s; the Japanese occupation of the late 1930s; the Nationalist collapse and communist victory of the late 1940s; the Great Leap Forward and the ensuing famine, perhaps the deadliest in human history, at the end of the 1950s; the ideologically driven, faction-ridden bloodshed of the Cultural Revolution in the late 1960s; the adoption of far-reaching post–Mao Zedong reforms in the late 1970s; and the Tiananmen student protests and resulting massacre at the conclusion of the 1980s. The 1990s proved the most politically stable and economically prosperous decade in a century, but as this revised edition explains, it is too early to say that China has arrived at a fully secure path to success.

The periodic political upheavals in China's long history reflect inherent weaknesses in the Chinese polity. Two stand out. China's leaders have been adept at organizing complex governing bureaucracies, but have not been able to elaborate political processes and institutions to prevent their own power struggles from disrupting the entire system. Despite myriad laws and regulations, therefore, the Chinese system has remained at its apex—among the top twenty-five to thirty-five leaders—an arena in which each leader's activities are restricted primarily by the attitudes and resources of the group's other members. But major conflicts and resulting instability at the top reverberate throughout the system, disrupting the entire polity. China's first timely and peaceful leadership succession in 2002–03 is evidence of gradual progress toward greater acceptance of rules of behavior among the elite, but the system remains far from stable and well institutionalized.

In addition, the Chinese population has not been given the opportunity to develop regular means of political participation. The state has for millennia operated on the premise that it must dictate the terms of political activity. It may conditionally entrust the administration of such activities to state-approved organizations such as guilds as long as those bodies stay within the boundaries determined by the political authorities. Chinese state administrations from imperial times to the present have often used ruthless means to suppress groups and organizations seeking to escape this political straitjacket.

Despite the recent flowering of civic and professional associations and far greater freedom to pursue personal desires, the people of China still have not experienced meaningful, sustained political participation based on stable, autonomous institutions. Political authorities have often mobilized the people to exert themselves for state-directed ends and, in the process, to engage in ritualistic rites of loyalty to state leaders. But truly autonomous political efforts directed toward shaping the policies and/or selecting the personnel of the state have been confined overwhelmingly to illegal underground organizations such as secret societies or to sporadic outbursts of popular protest through demonstrations and street violence. Such protests have occurred repeatedly, causing China's leaders to feel that radical instability—even chaos—always lurks just beneath the surface calm of society.

The outbursts take place either when people sense that paralyzing conflict among the leaders is rendering the state's repressive mechanisms ineffective, or when individual Chinese leaders encourage popular protest to serve their interests in power struggles at the top. The former occurred in the 1989 Tiananmen protest movement; the latter took place in 1978 and 1979, when Deng Xiaoping supported the Democracy Wall movement for several months before suppressing it. These outbursts erupt, in short, when the political system gives "space" to the population for such initiatives. Chinese citizens have not had the day in, day out opportunity to develop skills in the organization of autonomous groups and associations as vehicles for political participation. Popular political participation has, therefore, remained sporadic and destabilizing rather than evolving into a conventional means of relieving tensions and mitigating conflict in the system. It would take years to develop the attitudes and skills necessary to enable the latter types of participation to work well. Acts of popular protest—strikes, demonstrations—have increased in number virtually every year over the past decade.

These weaknesses at the top and the bottom of the political system may bode ill for China's future stability. But all long-term observers of this remarkable country know that there are few places in the world for which the phrase *plus ça change, plus c'est la même chose* ("the more things change, the more they stay the same") more aptly applies. Almost all first-time visitors to China marvel at the rate of change they see and hear about. Yet the past still weighs heavily on the present in such areas as the organization of the state, basic ideas about the nature of political leadership, the nature of the state's role in the economy, and many deep-rooted notions regarding the state's relations with society. It is important to understand not only what has changed due to China's many upheavals, therefore, but also what has proved enduring. Ideas and approaches that have evolved slowly over centuries cannot be jettisoned overnight, regardless of the political rhetoric that might fill the air during times of excitement and unrest.

Present-day China is thus a product of its deep imperial past and of its twentieth-century revolutions, both Nationalist and communist. It carries forward powerful legacies that inform basic ideas and practices. It also shapes its policies in the crucible of the largest bureaucratic structures in the history of the human race, structures that reflect both the imperial era's legacies and China's wide-ranging emulation of the Soviet Union in the early 1950s. New leaders taking the helm in 2002–03 again bring the potential for significant change in China, as the country pursues unprecedented integration into the international economic system and seeks to cope with the social and political consequences. The legacies and institutions of the distant and the more recent past will in varied, cross-cutting ways shape the future.

The challenge of understanding China is heightened by the fact that its experience does not fit neatly into many of the conceptual models of Western social science. It is, for example, simultaneously urban and rural, a member of the industrialized global North and of the unindustrialized global South. Parts of the country have become modern metropolises, while other areas remain very undeveloped. Also, China's middle class is itself deeply intertwined with the state, rather than growing up in opposition to the power of the state as in the West. This country of unprecedented vastness and variety is inevitably developing its own unique blend of attitudes and conditions.

The obstacles to understanding China make it tempting to view the country in relatively simple images. In the past five decades, Americans have, for example, variously imagined the People's Republic of China as a communist totalitarian society, a modernizing country, and a utopian revolutionary society. We have at times waxed eloquent over the marvelous similarities between Americans and Chinese, pointing to the shared traits and aspirations that give us a special feeling of friendship for each other. At other times we have regarded the Chinese as "the other"—Oriental, strange, and lacking the individualism that defines American character. When the United States reestablished political relations with China in 1971–72, popular images of the Chinese shifted almost overnight from an "army of the blue ants"[1] to what might be termed "eight hundred million protestants practicing their ethic." When China's leaders unleashed their army against peaceful protesters on the streets of Beijing in June 1989, American public opinion toward China veered from positive to negative in the largest single change ever recorded by polling in just a few short months.

This fragility in public perception reflects our tendency to focus on immediate developments, which sometimes change very rapidly, rather than on the forces that shape China's long-term evolution. This book is written to take full account of these underlying historical, institutional, and cultural forces, exploring their dynamics and implications in detail. It then applies the insights gained from this effort to the analysis of current issues and challenges. The distant past thus is not presented here as mere description; it is used to provide insight into the present and future.

This volume is organized around the four major components molding China in the 1990s:

☐ the legacies of the imperial system and its demise (Chapters 1 and 2);

☐ the effects of the particular ways in which the Chinese Communist party developed, including its struggle for power, elite political conflicts, and past policy initiatives (Chapters 2–5);

☐ the organizational structure and operational dynamics of the post-1949 Chinese state (Chapters 6 and 7); and

☐ the difficult issues facing contemporary China and the political resources available to the state in addressing them. These challenges include sustaining economic growth, coping with environmental problems, and managing relations between the state and society (Chapters 8–10).

The concluding chapter (Chapter 11) considers not only internal developments but also issues around China's periphery in analyzing the prospects for change in the country's domestic system and international posture.

I have written this volume for both students and general readers. I have done my best to avoid jargon and to provide enough background information in each section to enable readers to evaluate the arguments being made. The chapters collectively treat "politics" in broad enough fashion to make this volume pertinent to those interested in Chinese economics, history, and society.

The volume has been shaped by my experiences both in China itself and in teaching courses on China. Drafts of this manuscript were used in four courses I taught, and the current version reflects comments made by my students.

During my various research experiences in China over nearly thirty years I have interviewed people at all levels of the system: Politburo members, advisors to the top leaders, ministers, bureau chiefs, provincial personnel, county officials, city cadres, urban entrepreneurs and intellectuals, and peasants, among others. These contacts have included people at all points on the political spectrum from leading reformers to some of the noted conservatives discussed in this volume. Although the identities of these sources must remain confidential, their insights are present throughout this book.

During my more than seventy-five trips to the PRC, I have conducted research in nearly every major part of the country, as well as in Hong Kong and Taiwan. I have had the pleasure of developing deep personal ties with a number of Chinese in various walks of life. These friendships have not only immensely enriched me over the past three decades; they have also afforded me opportunities to appreciate the long-term perspectives of intelligent Chinese as they have grappled with many of the challenges addressed in this volume. My travels have also permitted me to sample directly the mood of the country in almost every year since the late Maoist era. I felt the excitement of the milling crowds and talked with dissidents at Democracy Wall in early 1979, and personally witnessed the Tiananmen Square protests and the massacre that followed on the morning of 4 June 1989. Since my first visit to Beijing toward the end of the Cultural Revolution, China has undergone startling change. My main purpose here is to convey an understanding of the dynamics of change and continuity in the Chinese system.

The end notes (pages 435–56) primarily guide the reader to the secondary English-language literature on the subjects discussed in the text. Chinese-language materials are cited only when they provide the sole source for important information in the narrative. The text employs pinyin romanization, the standard form currently used in China, for transliteration of all Chinese names and terms except a very few for which other spellings are well known (such as Chiang Kai-shek).

To help readers keep track of individuals, a Glossary of Selected Individuals (pages 337–47) provides basic identifying information on the key persons cited. Chinese terms are used only when they provide insight into how China works. The use of abbreviations has been minimized but not eliminated. A list of abbreviations is included in the front matter.

The appendices in this volume consist of three important Chinese documents. The first is then-party General Secretary Jiang Zemin's speech to the Sixteenth Party Congress in November 2002. This speech lays out officially the tasks confronting the party and its goals. The second is the Chinese Communist Party constitution adopted at the Sixteenth Congress. The third is the State Constitution as revised in March 2003. These three documents provide a good basis for understanding official views on the issues China currently confronts, how to deal with those issues, and the structure and formal obligations of the political system itself.

Acknowledgments

The many opportunities I have had over the years to talk to Chinese about China have improved my feel for the country, added to the joy of studying it, and in important ways affected my judgments about it. I owe them a profound debt. Colleagues and students over the past two decades have considerably sharpened my understanding both of China itself and of how best to teach about it. I am grateful for these experiences and the pleasure they have given.

I want to extend particular thanks to individuals who took the time to read all or part of this book in manuscript and to give me the benefit of their suggestions and corrections. Professors William Kirby (Harvard University), Steven Levine (University of North Carolina), and Andrew Nathan (Columbia University), as well as an anonymous reviewer, carefully read the entire volume; their copious comments and insights strongly influenced the first edition. Professors Albert Feuerwerker (University of Michigan), Abigail Jahiel (University of Delaware), Nicholas Lardy (Institute of International Economics), Ching-kwan Lee (University of Michigan), Donald Munro (University of Michigan), Albert Park (University of Michigan), Ernest Young (University of Michigan), Ezra Vogel (Harvard University), and the late Michel Oksenberg read selected chapters of the first and/or second editions and saved me from errors, both conceptual and factual. I very much appreciate the willingness of all these colleagues to contribute their time, energy, and wisdom to this effort.

Another group of individuals played a very important role in producing the final outcome. Shunyao Jin, Gil Krakowski, Dan Lynch, Andrew Mertha, Bettina Schroeder, and Kaja Sehrt, all doctoral candidates in political science at the University of Michigan when they worked on this book, and Wang Rongjun and especially Zhao Mei of the Institute of American Studies of the Chinese Academy of Social Sciences, provided outstanding support as research assistants on the first and present editions.

I had the pleasure of working on parts of the first edition manuscript for five weeks during the summer of 1993 as a resident scholar at the Villa Serbelloni, the Rockefeller Foundation's study center in Belaggio, Italy. I again want to express my sincere gratitude to the Rockefeller Foundation for inviting me to hold this position. I also thank the Institute of American Studies of the Chinese Academy of Social Sciences for hosting a research stay in Beijing that was very helpful to my work on the second edition, and the University of Michigan for granting me leave in the fall of 1991 to begin work on the first edition and in the winter of 2001 to focus on producing the second edition. The university's Center for Chinese Studies provided research assistant support for the first edition.

Both editions have benefited from the deft editorial hand and astute substantive judgments of Steven Forman, my editor at W. W. Norton. He proved to be the ideal editor, knowledgeable about both the subject matter of the volume and the editorial demands of such a project. His contributions have considerably exceeded those of the typical editor, and I feel lucky to have had the opportunity to work with him.

My wife Jane has made many accommodations to this writing effort. I suspect that having the opportunity to share the Bellagio experience and a summer in Beijing made up for some of these, but I am keenly aware of how much I owe her. This book is dedicated to her.

Despite the best efforts and strongest admonitions of all of the above individuals, poor judgments and specific errors undoubtedly remain in the text. By appreciation for their advice and help, I do not mean to suggest that any of the above individuals agrees with everything in this volume. For this final text, I assume sole responsibility.

Abbreviations Used in the Text

APC	Agriculture Producers Cooperative
CAC	Central Advisory Commission
CCP	Chinese Communist party
Comintern	Communist International
FDI	Foreign Direct Investment
GATT	General Agreement on Tariffs and Trade
GDP	Gross Domestic Product
GMD	Guomindang (Nationalist party)
GNP	Gross National Product
GONGO	Government organized nongovernmental organization
IFI	International Financial Institution
IMAR	Inner Mongolian Autonomous Region
IMF	International Monetary Fund
MPR	Mongolian People's Republic
NGO	Nongovernmental organization
NPC	National People's Congress
NRA	National Revolutionary Army
PLA	People's Liberation Army
PRC	People's Republic of China
ROC	Republic of China
SMA	Standard Marketing Area
SOE	State-Owned Enterprise
WTO	World Trade Organization

Pinyin Pronunciation Table

Chinese characters are one syllable long, and the pronunciation of each is made up of "initial" and "final" letters. Pinyin letters generally are pronounced like their English equivalents, with a few notable exceptions. Those that often create difficulties for the native English speaker are the following:

INITIALS:

PINYIN	ENGLISH
c	*ts*
qi	*ch*eek
x	*hs*
z	*dz*
zh	*j*ack

FINALS:

PINYIN	ENGLISH
a	f*a*ther
ai	b*ye*
ao	n*ow*
e	b*u*t
i	*see* [*note:* after the initials "ch," "sh," and "zh," the "i" is pronounced "r"]
iu	*yo*
ou	s*o*
u	l*oo*t
ua	tr*ois* (French for "three")

Chinese names: In Chinese, the surname is first, then the given name. In most instances, the surname has one character, and the given name has two. English convention provides for capitalization of the first letter of the surname and of the first letter of the first character of the given name. Thus, the late Chairman Mao's full name is Mao Zedong.

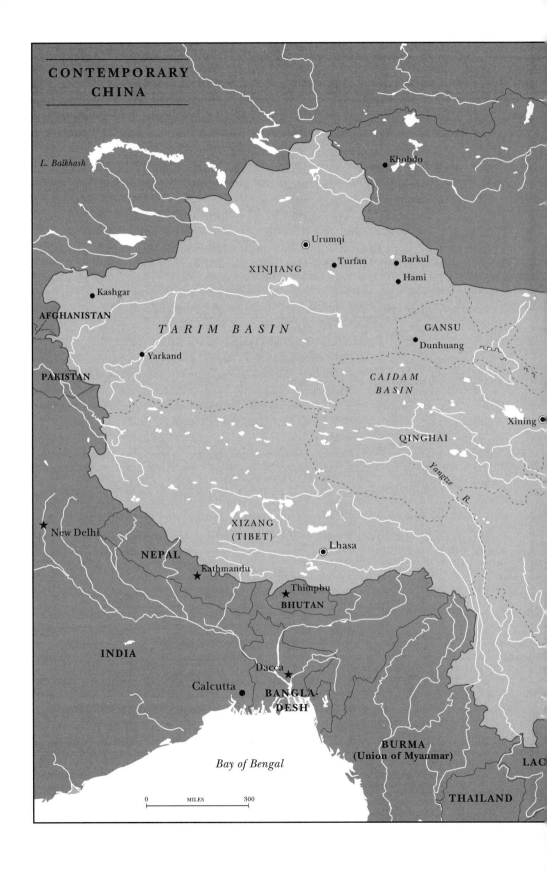

CONTEMPORARY
CHINA

L. Balkhash

Khobdo

Urumqi

XINJIANG   Turfan   Barkul

Hami

Kashgar

AFGHANISTAN

TARIM BASIN

GANSU

Dunhuang

Yarkand

PAKISTAN

CAIDAM
BASIN

Xining

QINGHAI

Yangtze R.

XIZANG
(TIBET)

Lhasa

New Delhi

NEPAL

Kathmandu

Thimphu

BHUTAN

INDIA

Dacca

Calcutta   BANGLA-
DESH

BURMA
(Union of Myanmar)

LAO

Bay of Bengal

THAILAND

0   MILES   300

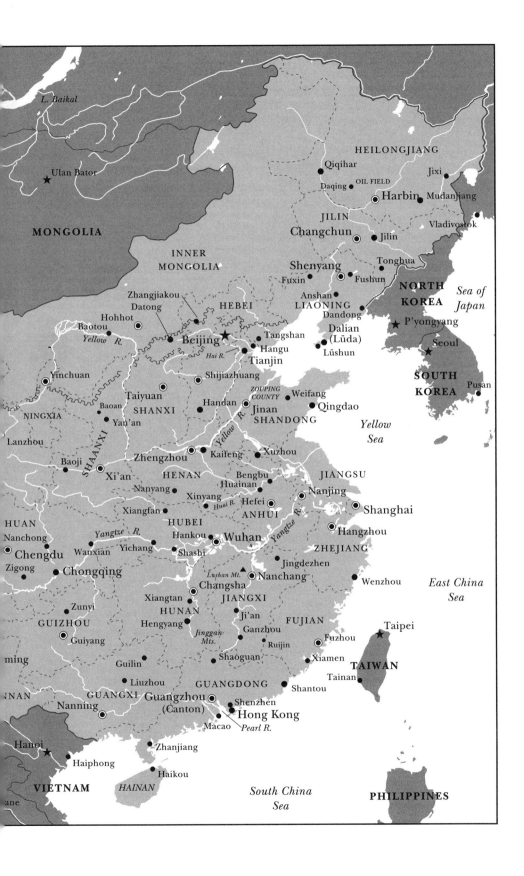

Part One
LEGACIES

1
The Legacies of Imperial China

The post-1949 Chinese communist state* under Mao Zedong conveyed the impression that it could transform China's society almost at will. It repeatedly convulsed the multitudes with huge political mobilization efforts at the same time it marshaled this agrarian country's scarce resources for a prodigious push toward rapid industrial development. Until the launching of the Cultural Revolution in 1966, the People's Republic of China (PRC) seemed to epito-

---

* Throughout this volume, the term *state* is used to include all the governing organizations and the bodies they directly control. In reference to the post-1949 Communist era, *state* thus encompasses the Communist party, the government, the military, and the social organizations that are either owned by the state, such as state enterprises, or under its direct control, such as state-sponsored "mass organizations" like the trade unions and the Women's Federation. When only the government or the Communist party is meant, the text uses the terms *government* and *party* rather than *state*.

mize worshipful loyalty to Mao, disciplined implementation of political decisions, a pliable population driven by ideological fervor, and disdain for the rest of the world.

Both this image and the more complex reality underlying it reflected the imprint of China's imperial past, a system of rule that began roughly two thousand years ago and evolved gradually up to the beginning of the twentieth century. For example, the imperial tradition nurtured the idea of basing the state system on ideological commitment, strong personal leadership at the apex, and impressive nationwide governing bureaucracies. The assumption in modern China that the government's influence should be pervasive because the government sets the moral framework for the entire society is also a product of the imperial era.

Additionally, the imperial system bequeathed contradictions and weaknesses that bedeviled Maoist China. The very majesty of the emperor's position, for example, produced tensions between the ruler and the bureaucracies of the government administration. The emperor's personal entourage often clashed with bureaucratic officials. No national tax collection agency extended into the localities. Rather, taxes were collected by county magistrates, and each governing level (county, prefecture, circuit, and province) siphoned off a certain percentage as these revenues filtered up through the national bureaucracy. The central government's revenue base remained, therefore, sharply constrained. At the village level, moreover, a key stratum of local leaders referred to as the "gentry" divided their loyalties between the state and their own immediate constituencies. Although the specifics changed, each of these and other underlying problems of the imperial era found their analogs in the Maoist period.

Within two years of Mao Zedong's death in 1976, Deng Xiaoping began an effort to reform the Maoist system. Deng's own initiatives, though, were also shaped in many ways by the complex legacies of the imperial era. His post-Mao reforms addressed some problems, such as the need to elaborate a national tax bureaucracy. But in other areas, such as assuring the loyalty of local officials, the reforms initiated by Deng have highlighted the continuing difficulties rather than provided solutions.

Imperial China had a monarchical system of governance and a patriarchal social system. The society was given a very distinctive style and aura by the official ideology of state Confucianism, but in many details it paralleled the multilayered dependent relations, sources of status, and modes of behavior found in Western monarchical societies of the premodern era.[1] The Chinese system distinguished itself from the others primarily by its enormous size, its relatively modern bureaucratic structures of state administration, and its explicit, detailed state ideology. It also lasted an extraordinary length of time. It is almost as if, in Western terms, the Roman empire had evolved but nevertheless survived into the twentieth century.

This past both shapes and haunts China. Many Chinese observers since the late nineteenth century have blamed traditional ideas for their country's inability to defend itself against foreigners whose military strength had grown along with industrial power. These critics have felt China must reject traditional culture to become a wealthy, strong nation. They have argued, for example, that the traditional system discouraged the types of investment behavior and technological change that modern economic growth requires. They have a point. As far back as the Han dynasty (206 B.C.–A.D. 220), Confucian scholars posited, "When profit is not emphasized, civilization flourishes and the customs of the people improve. . . . To open the way for profit is to provide a ladder for the people to become criminals."[2] This attitude did not prevent the emergence of flourishing commerce in China, but it did sustain a view of commerce as a low-status occupation that alone did not qualify one for prestige or power.

In imperial Chinese society, moreover, the superiority of the civilization eclipsed the idea of nationalism based on ethnicity. The Chinese referred to their empire as *tian xia* ("all under heaven"). *Guojia* ("nation-state") replaced this term only in the modern era.[3] As a consequence, foreigners could gain legitimacy as rulers of China if their actions conformed to the norms of Chinese civilization. When the Manchus conquered China and set up the Qing dynasty in 1644, for example, they resumed holding the traditional imperial examinations in the Confucian classics the very next year. During its final one thousand years, imperial China was under foreign rule for approximately half the time.

Nationalism has developed as a strong force in the West only since the 1700s. Western nationalists embrace their past as a source of pride, and more than a few have developed myths of a deep past in which to root themselves. By contrast, Chinese intellectuals have been wrestling with China's past since the end of the nineteenth century, and many have tried to forge a sense of patriotism by rejecting that past. Tensions over what it means to be Chinese have therefore troubled the country's politics throughout this century; these tensions draw variously on the notions of ethnic, or Han, Chinese, *hua ren* (people who are culturally Chinese), and *zhongguo ren* (citizens of the Chinese state).[4]

The Imperial Chinese System

The traditional Chinese state was an awesome political achievement, the most advanced such governing body in the world. Featuring a centralized bureaucratic apparatus begun over two thousand years ago by Qin Shi Huangdi (r. 221–210 B.C.), the first emperor of the Qin dynasty (221–206 B.C.), China's system of governance evolved through the rise and fall of various dynasties until the early 1900s.

There is no reason to try to capture the evolution of the imperial Chinese system over this period of roughly two millennia. It changed a great deal. But fundamental features of that system provide great insight into contemporary China's style, capabilities, and discontents.

The imperial system in China lasted so long in part because of its own self-confident sense of greatness. The *philosophes* of the European Enlightenment considered China's the ideal system, with rulers chosen for their intellectual strengths and virtue. China's emperors needed no convincing on this score. Their mentality at the height of the last dynasty, the Qing (1644–1912), is captured in a letter written by the Qianlong emperor, who reigned from 1736 to 1796.

The Qianlong emperor wrote in response to an effort by King George III of England to gain China's consent for establishing diplomatic relations between the two countries and for developing trade ties. In 1793 the king sent an extraordinary mission to Beijing, headed by Lord Macartney. The Macartney mission brought England's best manufactures, along with skilled craftsmen and scientists, to impress the Qing court. The Qianlong emperor responded as follows to George III:

[T]he territories ruled by the Celestial Empire are vast, and for all the envoys of the vassal states coming to the capital there are definite regulations regarding the provision of quarters and supplies to them and regarding their movements. . . . How can we go as far as to change the regulations of the Celestial Empire . . . because of the request of one man—of you, O King? . . . The Celestial Empire, ruling all within the four seas, simply concentrates on carrying out the affairs of government properly, and does not value rare and precious things. Now you, O King, have presented various objects to the throne, and mindful of your loyalty in presenting offerings from afar, we have specially ordered the Yamen to receive them. In fact, the virtue and power of the Celestial Dynasty has penetrated afar to the myriad kingdoms, which have come to render homage, and so all kinds of precious things from "over mountain and sea" have been collected here. . . . Nevertheless, we have never valued ingenious articles, nor do we have the slightest need of your country's manufactures. . . . You, O King, should simply act in conformity with our wishes by strengthening your loyalty and swearing perpetual obedience so as to ensure that your country may share the blessings of peace.[5]

The Qianlong emperor had reason to be smug. He was certain that Chinese civilization existed on a higher plane than any other. The Chinese believed that even those who achieved superior military power (such as, at times, the nomadic tribes to China's north) would inevitably adapt to their ways. The erosion of this confidence during the nineteenth century rocked Chinese society to its foundations.

Overall, the imperial system did a remarkable job of ruling a vast country while employing only a modest number of officials (at the height of the last dynasty, the Qing, about twenty thousand in the formal bureaucracy, supplemented by many staff assistants). To understand the strengths as well as some of the more problematic legacies of this system, five key components warrant more detailed scrutiny: the ideology; the institution of the emperor; the bureaucratic structure; the society; and the economy. It is usually more useful to look first at a country's governing structure and then at the political ideology employed by its leaders to bolster their power, but in China the ideological underpinnings of the governing structure were so fundamental by the time of the Qing dynasty that they must be examined to explain the rest of the system.

CONFUCIANISM AS IDEOLOGY

Confucius (551–479 B.C.) was an itinerant philosopher who lived during the Warring States period, a time of incessant turmoil and warfare. He traveled from state to state, advising leaders on how to ensure order and prosperity in their realms. Because he based this advice on fundamental precepts he devised concerning human nature, cosmology, rules of correct conduct, and principles governing social relationships, his teachings are called a "philosophy." But Confucianism also became a state ideology and, like Marxism and other political ideologies, it evolved over time in response to the changing political needs of its believers. As political ideology, Confucianism by the late imperial era had three core features.

First, it was a strongly conservative governing ideology. It aimed primarily at preserving order and looked not to the future but to a mythical state in the past to identify the ideal society (it therefore regarded anything "new" or "progressive" as untrustworthy). Long experience was the criterion of worth, and the wisdom of the ancients stood as the highest form of understanding. Confucius proclaimed that wise men "revere the words of the sages." Confucian officials sought to perfect the present by eliminating defects that had crept in since the ancient past.

Second, Confucianism valued hierarchy in both political and social spheres. It assumed that in the political sphere citizens were not and should not be equal. As Mencius, a disciple of Confucius, summed it up, those who worked with their minds were fit to rule, and those who worked with their hands were not. Working with the mind required literacy first of all (no mean task itself with a language comprising over forty thousand characters, of which perhaps 10 percent were often used) and then mastery of the Confucian classics. Success required long years of study, and only a small percentage of the population ever succeeded. The ruling group thus remained small, and admission to it required learning a doctrine that justified the right of the few to rule the many. The only democratic component of the system was that, in theory, anyone who could master the ideology could join the ruling elite. Confucianism did not base rule on hereditary factors. But those from elite backgrounds had far greater access to the resources and support necessary to meet this key qualification for joining the political elite.[6]

Confucius taught that social relationships should be hierarchical as well, and that the key to social harmony lay in every person's understanding the mutual obligations that characterized each set of social ties. Typically, the lesser party—son, wife, student, subject—must show loyalty and obedience, while the superior party—father, husband, teacher, ruler—must reciprocate with empathy and acts of assistance.

Third, it was the essence of Confucianism that people should understand the "correct" conduct demanded by each type of relationship and should act accordingly, as this provided the key to a harmonious society. Indeed, although Confucians wanted everyone to understand the bases of the doctrine, they were on balance practical enough to recognize the even greater importance of correct conduct, whether or not it was grounded in profound learning. Following the rules of conduct, including the protocols of speech, became central to social harmony and might, over time, actually nurture correct thinking.

The Confucian emphasis on correct practice led naturally to an emphasis on ritual, the formal expression of the correct way. In the words of one student of this phenomenon, the Chinese stressed "orthopraxy" (that is, engaging in prescribed practice) over "orthodoxy" (that is, conforming one's thinking to prescribed ideas).[7] Confucians felt that correct practice would itself shape ideas over time. Correct practice, in addition, conveyed one's acceptance of the prevailing official ideology and its associated social theory conveying legitimacy to the government that promulgated and enforced this ideology. One of the six ministerial bodies in the Qing was the Board of Rites.

In China even today, mouthing "correct" formulations is viewed as socially responsible even if all concerned know that there is little relationship between those formulations and the thoughts of the people using them.[8] This situation makes it potentially easier for Chinese leaders to elicit formal support and compliant behavior from the populace. It also makes it difficult for the leaders to know the real state of mind of their own citizens and of their political subordinates.

The superior-subordinate relationships defined in Confucian doctrine largely stripped youths of initiative and generally placed social power in the hands of the older, more conservative segments of the population. Students deferred to teachers, children to parents, subjects to leaders, and all to the emperor. The emperor, as the key link between heaven and earth, secured prosperity for his country through right conduct toward his[9] subjects and through correct performance of the rites that propitiated heaven. No formal laws could bind the emperor, but, as explained below, most who held this position felt constrained to conform to correct conduct as prescribed by basic Confucian doctrine. The emperor's virtue in mastering and practicing this doctrine, it was felt, assured the prosperity of the country and thus secured his mandate to rule.

During the imperial age, the Chinese made fidelity to Confucian precepts the defining characteristic of civilized society. Those further from the center of imperial power, who had less regard for Confucian norms, were considered less civilized. The Chinese tried to broker relations with foreign peoples by fitting them into a ritualized system of exchange of goods and pledges of loyalty that Westerners dubbed the "tribute system."[10] This system of diplomatic relations and foreign trade was managed on the Chinese side by the Board of Rites. It was structured so that the conduct of relations with neighboring peoples would utilize rituals that would bolster China's official political cosmology. For example, the kowtow, which was performed by both Chinese and foreigners, required those having an audience with the emperor to kneel down and knock their foreheads on the ground three times, and then to repeat this act for a total of "three kneelings and nine knockings of the head on the ground." In this as in other ways in the imperial era, form became as important as substance in maintaining the ideological base of the system.[11]

Yet, in this as in so many spheres, surface appearances concealed a more complex reality. During the Qing dynasty, Confucian forms were in fact fully utilized only in the core Han regions. In more peripheral areas, the ruling Manchus, much like the Ottomans, established something closer to a loose confederation in which the empire allowed very different forms of government to exist, in conformity with the traditions of the various subject peoples. The Manchu court intervened in complex ways in these local polities in order to ensure leverage in each locality. Their rule in Tibet, for example, took full account of local Buddhist traditions while interjecting the court into the selection of the Dalai Lama.[12] The non-Han minority people consequently saw themselves as loyal to the Manchus, rather than to the Han Chinese.[13] The resulting legacy is a myth of a highly integrated Confucian polity that has tended to obscure the historical reality of necessary flexibility to keep a geographically extensive, ethnically diverse empire viable.

Even in its core territories, Confucianism was not the only ideology that influenced China's traditional polity. At various times, Buddhism (which came from India, and reached its golden age in China during the Tang dynasty [A.D. 618–907]), Daoism, and other strands of thought have had significant impact. China's imperial history is also replete with tales of political intrigue, military skulduggery, bureaucratic degeneration, and social upheaval. These phenomena reflect in part another important political and philosophical doctrine called Legalism. This approach advocated extensive use of material rewards and physical punishments to obtain desired behavior. Legalists premised their approach on the assumption that people are inherently selfish. For much of China's history over the past two millennia, while Confucianism was the official ideology, actual practice also made substantial use of Legalism. The Legalist philosophy was applied most fully during the reign of Qin Shi Huangdi. One of imperial China's most powerful figures, the first emperor of the Qin dynasty acquired power through astute military campaigns and political treachery. He then established a central bureaucratic state that engendered the imperial Chinese system.

The first Qin emperor's approach to governance differed fundamentally from that of Confucius. The Sage (Confucius) believed that people are educable, and therefore that the state should stress education and rule by example. Qin Shi Huangdi and his notoriously cruel minister Li Ssu, by contrast, adopted the Legalist view that people are inherently selfish and boorish, and respond only to the blatant manipulation of rewards and punishments.

Qin Shi Huangdi's achievements suggest a man larger than life. In his reign there rose major parts of the defensive barrier in the north known as the Great Wall.[14] He ordered the production of a huge army of nearly ten thousand life-size terra cotta figures installed near his massive tomb in Xi'an to protect him in his afterlife. His use of power was as startling in its scope as were all his other activities. He created a society characterized by widespread torture and political knavery. He decreed such excruciating types of execution that it became common for a condemned individual to plead for clemency in the form of a swift death (being beheaded with a broadsword) instead of a slow one (such as being quartered by four oxen pulling one's limbs in different directions).[15]

Qin Shi Huangdi's empire survived his death by less than four years, but his notion of powerful rewards and punishments—of the use of extraordinary violence to achieve the goals of the state—became an integral part of Chinese governing practice. As a result, China's subsequent political system both extolled rule by virtue and example and made ready resort to cruel punishment. To put it differently, the traditional system wedded lofty Confucian ideology and tough Legalist measures into an integral whole.[16] A similar dichotomy between lofty rhetoric and hard nosed coercion characterized imperial China's approach to dealing with external security threats.[17]

This blend of ideologically defined moralism and hard-edged coercion has long survived the destruction of the imperial Chinese system that spawned it.

THE EMPEROR

The notion that the political system headed by the emperor provided moral guidance for the society was fundamental to traditional Confucian thought. As the "son of heaven" and the "ruler of all under heaven," the emperor assumed responsibility for maintaining "civilized" society and for mediating the relationship between that society and heaven. "Heaven" was not identified with an anthropomorphic deity as in Western religions but rather was more akin to some combination of history and fate.

Confucian principles were not entirely supportive of imperial power, however. These principles envisaged a central role for the emperor; however, in Confucian thought the emperor was accountable for his actions, which would be measured against the standards of the ideology. Those who could claim the most thorough grounding in the ideology were the Confucian scholar officials, not the emperor himself.

On the other hand, the ideology placed such emphasis on obligations to family that these officials were themselves confronted with some daunting dilemmas. Should they criticize the emperor when such criticism might bring severe retaliation against their entire clans? How much loyalty should they accord to the emperor and to their bureaucratic duties on his behalf when their families could benefit from a less strict approach to office?

The emperor headed not only the bureaucracy through which he governed but also an extended family and the life of the court itself. The tensions between the bureaucrats (the outer court) on the one side and those involved in the emperor's personal life (the inner court) on the other have been a perennial source of trouble for the political system.[18] Admission to the outer court was based largely on rigorous training in Confucian doctrine. Admission to the inner court, comprising imperial relatives and attendants, was based on blood ties (in the case of relatives), attractiveness (in the case of concubines), and surgery (in the case of eunuchs).

Typically, the early years of a dynasty saw a powerful inner court, as a new ruling house consolidated its power against officials held over from the former dynasty whose loyalty was suspect. The middle years were characterized by the relative flourishing of the outer court, which managed a complex and thriving society. The final decades usually saw the inner court reassert itself. Inbreeding produced weak emperors, and a dissolute life in the imperial palace, the Forbidden City, further eroded discipline. Intrigues among eunuchs, concubines, and court retainers contributed significantly to the decline of a number of dynasties. Underlying tensions between the leaders' personal relations and the formal governmental organs continue to rankle the Chinese system today.

Because the emperor was to mediate between heaven and earth (and thus assure heaven's beneficence), the Chinese considered him personally responsible not only for actions under his direct control, such as government discipline, but also for those events over which he exercised only indirect or no control, such as floods and droughts. These latter were taken as signs of imperial incompetence or decay. When the emperor fell short, however, there were no clean political solutions. The emperor's position was so essential to the system (especially in the later dynasties) that no statutory limits could be placed on imperial power.

Among the scholar officials, a particular group, called "censors," was designated to ferret out problems in the political system. These members of the outer court were supposed to call the emperor's attention to poor performance of any officials, including the emperor himself. But since no official had an independent base from which to circumscribe the power and activities of the emperor, criticism had to take the form of remonstrance. The censor could only hope to make the emperor understand his problems and focus attention on correcting them, all the while affirming the emperor's moral superiority. This type of criticism thus bolstered the position of the emperor at the same time that it sought to change his behavior.

Imperial performance so abysmal that nothing could bring improvement occasionally produced large-scale social unrest. Official corruption bled the population through excessive taxation; failure to maintain granaries and dikes invited disasters. Military forces lost their effectiveness through corruption and sloth, and court rivalries sapped the ability of such regimes to galvanize their energies in support of renewal. Under these circumstances, unrest often began in the peripheral areas of the country, where restless groups threw off the relatively weak yoke of imperial control. That unrest then spread to more central areas, sometimes abetted by strong outside military forces.

The successful overthrow of an emperor was understood as a sign that through poor conduct that emperor had lost the "mandate of heaven." The succession to a new leader and a new dynasty could then be considered legitimate. Should the challenge to the empire fail, however, the emperor retained the "mandate of heaven" in the popular view. Since all failed challengers had defied the most fundamental strictures on obedience and civilization, they suffered terrible retribution.

The imperial system thus left a legacy of strong personal rule at the top, unbounded by formal law or regulation. The emperor's role as propagator and personifier of the official Confucian ideology bolstered his right to rule. This system was rife with tensions between the emperor and the governing bureaucracies, the inner and outer courts, and those who would reform an emperor gone astray versus those who would let a willful emperor have his way. This system provided no resolution to the contradiction between a powerful leader whose personal virtue was thought to anchor the entire system and a powerful administrative bureaucracy seeking to enhance its own rights and privileges and to assure stability and prosperity.[19] This contradiction became a crisis when the leader became highly erratic and/or unusually willful. Contemporary China still wrestles with striking a balance between the authority of the core political leaders and the need for effective institutions.

THE BUREAUCRACY

Over a period of centuries, the bureaucratic system initiated by the Qin dynasty took on characteristics that are associated with modern bureaucracy in the West: highly defined offices, merit-based appointments, clearly articulated reward structures, considerable specialization in functions, highly developed formal systems of communications, detailed rules concerning proper lines of authority, regularized reporting obligations, formalized structures for monitoring compliance and deviance, and so forth. Specific codes of dress and conduct reflecting the status of various bureaucratic positions buttressed this system.[20]

In theory, the bureaucracy administered the empire so as to assure harmony in accordance with the Confucian precepts. County magistrates, for example, periodically gave public lectures on Confucian morals to the populace.[21] The system thus relied on a strong, ideologically motivated bureaucracy to lay a firm basis for a civilized, harmonious society. Officials might not live up to their obligations under this system, but the remedy would be their removal from office. The classical liberal preference for diffusing power and limiting the "reach" of the government in society is directly antithetical to the fundamental tenets of the traditional Chinese polity.

As in every bureaucratic system, reality departed to some extent from formal prescriptions, but overall the Chinese bureaucratic system was extraordinary in its scope, capabilities, and "modernity." It was a profoundly nonpluralistic system, based squarely on the notions of hierarchy, centralization, and the state as the propagator of the correct moral framework for the society. This centuries-long tradition of centralized bureaucratic rule was one of China's most extraordinary accomplishments. In this sphere, the legacies of China's past remain particularly strong.

Even China's concrete administrative system today bears a strong resemblance to its imperial forebear. During the Qing dynasty, the administration consisted of three hierarchies: the civil, the military, and the censorate. The civil administration in Beijing had six ministries, called boards. These took charge, respectively, of personnel; revenue; rites; war; punishments; and public works. Beneath these there were four levels of administration: counties or cities; prefectures; circuits; and provinces (there were twenty-two provinces in 1899). The total size of the civil administration remained small, however. As noted above, in the 1800s roughly twenty thousand individuals held official positions in the civil bureaucracy, less than 1 percent of the number of officials in 2003. Since the Qing dynasty was ruled by the alien Manchus, each board had both Manchu and Chinese heads and deputy heads.[22]

The military consisted of Manchu troops organized into banners, plus a Chinese professional army called the Army of the Green Standard that was held over from the Ming period and served as a constabulary force. The banner system, so called because each force had its own pennant, grew out of a Manchu institution from the period before the Manchus conquered all of China. The emperor was considered the head of the military.[23]

The censorate attached officials to the six boards and to fifteen circuits in the provinces. Censors scrutinized the administration at all levels and reported problems to the emperor. When censors felt compelled to criticize the emperor himself, they proceeded at enormous personal risk.

Within the ranks of the imperial bureaucracy, mastery of the Confucian classics became increasingly important for admission to and advancement through the official hierarchy. By the later dynasties, the official examinations that largely determined elite recruitment and promotion concentrated overwhelmingly on mastery of Confucian ideology. This body of knowledge may have had only limited utility for teaching officials how to handle flood control, revenue collection and transfers, and the myriad other duties they would assume when appointed to office. But there were distinct political benefits to making mastery of political orthodoxy the core stepping-stone in a relatively meritocratic bureaucratic system.

The mature Confucian system required politically ambitious younger people as well as those already in office to devote a great deal of time to preparing for the next round of official examinations. People with political ambition, therefore, exerted much of their energy throughout their careers on immersing themselves in the highly conservative ideology that buttressed the regime, and this bound scholars and officials to the state rather than making them independent of it.

The examination system also created a common culture shared by officials who came from diverse parts of a large country. Even the official spoken language of Mandarin Chinese, based on the Beijing dialect, added a sense of unity and distinctiveness to the small official class and the larger number of people who aspired to be a part of that class. The larger group of aspirants, moreover, generally assumed informal leadership positions in their local communities and helped to bridge the gap between a distant officialdom and the localities. As of the early nineteenth century, approximately 1.1 million people (out of a population of over 300 million) had obtained the lowest level official degree and thus formed the lower gentry.[24] Altogether, the examination system was highly effective in indoctrinating the elite and the politically ambitious in the conservative values of the regime. Its legacy is the view that ideological indoctrination of officials is both natural and necessary.

CHINESE SOCIETY

Chinese society displayed the characteristics embraced by Confucian philosophy: it was hierarchical, family focused, and ritualistic. The overwhelming majority of people made its living off the land, with village size and organization varying considerably in different parts of the country. In south China, single-lineage villages tended to be more common than in the north, and therefore prohibitions on marrying within the village were especially strong in the south. In many cases, clan organizations played powerful roles in the village economy and ritual life.

Since each county had only one official member of the national bureaucracy (the *zhixian,* or county magistrate), the system made extensive use of intermediate elites. The most important group consisted of those who were trained for the official examinations but who currently did not have an appointment to the national bureaucracy. This group included two types of individuals: those who had passed the exams and were awaiting appointment, and those who held appointments but were in the midst of the mandatory three-year mourning period for each parent, which required that they stay home without official assignment for that period. Given the often close relationships between such people and the larger landholders in the locale—official office often brought with it the means to obtain land; owning land brought with it the resources to study for the official examinations—this group of trained individuals typically had prestige and power in the villages.[25]

The county magistrate often depended on this intermediate stratum of individuals for advice about local conditions and for assistance in assuring order and managing the economy. These individuals could speak the official language and were literate. They shared the magistrate's training in Confucian political ideology. They identified, on the whole, with the national elite and formed a privileged and important segment of the nonofficial population. At the same time, they were integral to their own villages, subject to the strong social expectations of their relatives and friends. They thus had dual roles as informal extensions of the state apparatus and as protectors of their own locales from the demands of the central state.

In a land-holding agricultural economy, land ownership formed a major base of social stratification. Studies have made clear, though, that land was considered a commodity and was not held intact from generation to generation. China did not have a system of primogeniture, wherein the eldest son inherited all the land of the father. Rather, the death of a father would trigger a division of the land holdings among the sons. This system brought continuous social mobility, and huge concentrations of land in the hands of particular families tended not to last more than two or three generations.[26]

In this society, women were severely repressed. In the later dynasties a practice called footbinding became popular. When a girl reached about age six her mother would wrap her feet tightly, curling the toes under the ball of the foot. Keeping the feet tightly bound over the ensuing years produced bones that broke and curled under, so that the overall length of the foot ideally would not exceed three inches. The resulting "lily feet" were considered attractive and a sign of status, and only non-Chinese minorities and very poor women who had to work in the fields all day had natural feet. Footbinding was extremely painful, and it sharply limited the physical mobility of women.

Most women were kept out of sight in the women's quarters of the home. Their duties varied with the wealth and status of the family, but in general they were subservient to their husbands and their grown male children. Women were betrothed by their fathers and typically had barely met their husbands before the marriage. While wealthier men might have more than one wife (or a wife and a number of concubines), a widow was expected to remain chaste after the death of her husband, even if this occurred when she was still very young.

Wives lived in the husband's household and were under the authority of the mother-in-law, which often made for tense, miserable relations. Because women left the household while males brought new people (their wives and children) into the household, there was a very strong preference for male offspring, and female infanticide was not unknown. Women, indeed, were held in such low regard that often girls were not given names. (They were merely called "second daughter" or something similar.) Grandparents would not count the offspring of their daughters among their grandchildren. As in many patriarchal societies, female suicide was common.[27]

From the 1920s to the 1940s, the communists sought to harness female resentment to the cause of the revolution. The slogan they used was "Women hold up half the sky." Gender relations have changed greatly in China, as elsewhere, during the twentieth century but, as Chapter 10 explains, gender equality is still far from a reality.

The most enduring legacy from traditional society is the pattern of social obligations created by the Confucian value system. As noted above, Confucian doctrine placed tremendous emphasis on knowing the proper behavior—that is, the mutual obligations—attendant on each type of social relationship. The Chinese language itself reflects this emphasis, with its unique nouns to distinguish seemingly marginal degrees of relationship—such as "third cousin twice removed on the maternal side."

The Confucian understanding of human nature and society contrasts strongly with American thinking. The latter holds that each person owes every other person a general social obligation because of the very humanity shared by all. Underlying this view is the idea that every individual has a soul and therefore some inherent value. Although this tradition has often been more honored in theory than in practice, it has been quite fundamental to the development of American and modern Western society and culture.

Confucian society lacks this notion of abstract social obligation. Its obligations are concrete and determined by specific social relationships. An individual, indeed, never stands independently as Ms. Li or Mr. Zhao, but is always part of a web of social relationships: wife, mother, daughter, sister, husband, son, student. One deals with others through these personal connections, and one's social strategy is based to a considerable extent on building supportive webs of personal ties.[28]

This specificity of social obligation helps explain a paradox often observed by Westerners in China. A poor family living at bare subsistence level will take in any distant relative who shows up at their door needing help. The relative may live in the family's cramped quarters, share their food, and eventually find a modest job with their aid. This same family, though, would pass a starving beggar on their street every day and refuse to give him any money.[29] How could the same people appear solicitous in the one instance and callous in the other? The family's defined social obligation toward the distant relative and lack of obligation toward the beggar on the street explain this paradoxical behavior. A stranger without any "connection" (the current Chinese term is *guanxi*) is simply of no concern to the family.

Such sights remain common in contemporary China, even though Confucian ideology no longer holds sway. A traffic accident quickly draws a crowd, but only police officers help the victims. A guide to behavior developed for Chinese visiting the United States in the early 1980s advised the visitors not to stand by and laugh if they saw someone injured in an accident. Rather, the guide explained, Westerners expect you to empathize and to offer help in such a situation. In other cases where Westerners would feel obligated to extend help, Chinese feel no such pressure and, indeed, actually shy away from involvement lest any assistance *create* a relationship with someone whose character is unknown. At the same time, *specific* relationships in China now, as in the past, engender very strong loyalties and powerful displays of mutual obligation. This fundamental nature of social obligation has been one of China's major obstacles to developing a sense of citizenship, as Chinese see themselves more as parts of specific webs of relations than as common members of a single nation.

The Confucian notion of social obligation shifted attention away from the individual's personal rights and interests as the object of political thought. The pluralist notion of society as an arena of contending groups with social policy emerging from the interplay is fundamentally at odds with the principles and practice of China's historical governance. Rather, in Confucian ideology, proper governance maintained harmonious relations through correct policies and appropriate moral guidance. The "natural" state of society is thus one of harmony rather than contention. Since everyone has a common interest in enjoying the fruits of a well-governed, harmonious society, moreover, there are in theory no fundamental clashes of interests between individuals and groups. The basic assumption on which the edifice of representative government rests in the West is completely missing from China's tradition.[30]

Chinese society in the late imperial era was, nevertheless, richly varied. Domestic commerce flourished, and local cultural traditions varied greatly. Some regions, such as the lower Yangtze, produced a very cosmopolitan urban life.[31] Others, such as the loess soil region of northern Shaanxi, remained poor and extremely backward.[32] The Qing dynasty, moreover, witnessed a great upsurge of local social and economic activity.[33] This local vibrancy did not, however, produce major changes in the political system itself until the very end of the Qing.

THE ECONOMY

China's economy was overwhelmingly agrarian, characterized primarily by small peasant producers. These farmers showed considerable ability to obtain high yields by careful adaptation to local ecological conditions. Nevertheless, one remarkable feature of the agricultural economy was a lack of technological change from the Ming through the Qing dynasties (from the 1300s to the early 1900s). During this long period of basic technological stagnation, agricultural output increased substantially, but this increase was gained primarily by more intensive cultivation, applying traditional inputs, bringing new land under the plow, and introducing new crops such as sweet potatoes.[34]

Two general explanations have been given for this overall dearth of technological development. In one view, China's huge population made the man-to-land ratio so adverse that there were never sufficient resources to allow for technological experimentation. In addition, the high population density provided very few incentives to find labor-saving ways of increasing output. The other explanation points instead to the role played by extractive elites, who obtained the rural surplus (through taxes, land rents, usurious loans, corruption, and so forth) and then spent the surplus on consumption rather than on investment in improved methods of production.

As is often the case in historical explanation, the discrepancies between these two positions remain unresolved. There is evidence that the man-to-land ratio increased over this period, but different scholars disagree over the relevant figures.[35] In similar fashion, there appears to have been a rural surplus that was successfully captured by a small elite (perhaps 4 percent of the population), but explanations of their behavior and of regional variance are very inexact.[36]

Scholars agree that China's economy during the Ming and Qing was highly commercialized, with a substantial portion of farming households producing at least part of their output for the market. An extensive system of local "periodic" markets convened on a fixed schedule every few days, leading into progressively higher levels of marketing nodes in county towns and larger cities. This system has been described most thoroughly in the works of G. William Skinner.[37]

Skinner's research suggests that by the Qing dynasty, China actually consisted of nine regional economic systems, called macroregions, each of which had its own core and periphery.[38] The nine macroregions were connected to each other by commercial and political ties, but their distinctiveness outweighed their relationships. Each macroregion had its own economic and accompanying social dynamics.[39] Skinner argues that for most analytical purposes one should think of China more in terms of these regional systems than in terms of the standard administrative divisions of counties and provinces. For the throne, the most important macroregion for revenue purposes was the lower Yangtze, with north China the second most important.[40]

The extensive commercial activity of late imperial China naturally involved a large group of specialized merchants. Although the Confucian ideology assigned high status to farming and low status to commercial activity, in fact commerce was a major source of individual wealth. Successful merchants often used a part of their wealth to gain respectability and security. They could do so in several ways: purchasing land and becoming absentee landlords; hiring tutors for their offspring so that they might take the official examinations and enter the government; or directly purchasing a government title and/or office, as at various times the government sold titles and offices to raise money.

Merchants sought security because their interests were vulnerable to state intervention in the economy. Debates over such issues as whether to maintain government monopolies on the salt and iron industries go back to the first century B.C. In economic as in other areas, there were no clear limits to the potential scope of state activity, and during periods of relatively strong governance the bureaucracy's reach extended far into the economy. At the height of the Qing, for example, the government exercised monopolies in the sale of ginseng, the trade with Japan in copper (needed for coins), salt, textiles, and porcelains from the imperial factories in central China, with customs bureaus throughout the empire.[41]

The state apparatus, moreover, based itself from early times onward in the major cities and thus rather easily and naturally intervened in urban production and commerce. Indeed, Skinner's research indicates that the Qing administration carefully placed administrative offices in the core city of each macroregion, presumably in order to maximize effectiveness in extracting revenues. But the boundaries of political administrative units (provinces, counties, and so on) partly cut across those of the macroregions, rather than completely conforming to them. This arrangement probably helped prevent merchants from acquiring too much power by making them focus their political activities on units that did not coincide with the sphere of their economic activities.[42] Unlike Europe, where cities grew up largely outside the rural-based feudal system, in China an independent bourgeoisie never had a chance to develop beyond the effective reach of the state.[43]

In sum, imperial China's rural economy was efficient in terms of output per unit of land but not in terms of output per unit of labor, regionally diverse, relatively commercialized, and technologically stagnant. A small elite extracted much of the agricultural surplus and consumed it rather than improving production. Although conditions varied greatly across the country, those with adequate property holdings generally became absentee landlords instead of managerial landowners who might seek to increase production so as to maximize profits. The state itself felt free to intervene massively in the commercial sector of the economy.

LIMITS OF THE IMPERIAL STATE

For all its grandeur, the imperial Chinese state, like its counterparts elsewhere, undertook a minimal range of functions compared with modern political systems. It propagated a political ideology that delineated no clear boundaries to the state's intervention in the society, but its leaders in fact evidenced more concern over controlling their own administrative apparatus than over expanding the government's roles in the economy and other spheres.[44] Even though China's territory and population grew greatly over the final six hundred years of the imperial system, for example, the authorities kept the number of county-level units at a relatively constant number (about 1,400 to 2,400), thus restraining the size of the formal bureaucracy they had to control.

The imperial government restricted its actual efforts to a few rather circumscribed spheres. These included propagating ideology, suppressing rebellion (in other words, protecting its own power), maintaining national defense, gathering revenues to sustain itself, selecting its successors, and constructing public works.

China's extensive public works focused on the management of water that flowed from the high western reaches of the country eastward to the sea. The major river in the north, the Yellow River, is highly silted. It overflowed its banks so often and with such catastrophic results that it was called "China's sorrow." In the southwest, virtually all water available for agriculture in western Sichuan Province on the populous Chengdu Plain still comes via a remarkable set of waterworks constructed more than a millennium ago. In southeast China, wet-paddy rice cultivation required careful control of water flow for irrigation. Water management was so crucial, indeed, that one school of scholarship portrays the imperial system as shaped primarily by the need to control water resources. Karl Wittfogel called imperial China a "hydraulic society."[45]

Even a state of this great capacity nevertheless falls dramatically short of a modern state that seeks to foster economic development, manage social change, provide for basic welfare, and in myriad other ways penetrate and organize the economic, educational, and social lives of the populace. The imperial Chinese state could be highly successful as long as demands remained limited. When new challenges stemming from the spread of the Industrial Revolution required such changes as new levels of revenue extraction, new types of economic development, and new approaches to education, this state system proved inadequate to the task and perished as a consequence. But it left enduring legacies for the current Chinese political system.

Imperial Collapse

The imperial system formally ended on 12 February 1912, when the six-year-old Qing emperor Pu Yi abdicated his throne in response to pressures from the republican revolution of the previous year. This marked the end of more than two thousand years of the imperial Chinese system of rule. Previous dynasties had experienced periods of growth and decline with sufficient regularity to warrant scholarly use of the notion of a "dynastic cycle."[46] But only the Qing dynasty's fall produced an actual revolution. Two factors combined to account for this unprecedented outcome: traditional forces of dynastic decline, such as a succession of weak emperors, widespread corruption, frequent floods, and local rebellions, that prevailed until the 1890s and substantially weakened the Qing court; and the impact of the industrializing West and Japan, which confronted China with an unprecedented set of demands and resulting crises.

DECLINE OF THE QING

After reaching its peak in the late eighteenth century, the Qing dynasty began a gradual decline. Traditional factors contributed to this turn for the worse. Prosperity produced relatively rapid population growth, from approximately 125 million in 1650 to 225 million in 1750 to 410 million in 1850.[47] However, few changes occured in agricultural technology to expand food production apace with population. The result was a thinner margin to cushion hard times brought on by natural and human-caused disasters.

Natural disasters became deadlier as corruption spread in the ranks of the government. Here, the incumbency of Heshen (1750–99), an aide to the aging Qianlong emperor from 1776 to 1796, marked the turning point. Qianlong put Heshen in charge of revenues and personnel and also assigned him to suppress the White Lotus Rebellion in central and western China. Heshen and his friends siphoned off so much money and so corrupted the bureaucracy that the rebellion continued until after Qianlong's death and Heshen's removal. When the Qianlong emperor's successor, the Jiaqing emperor, forced Heshen to commit suicide and confiscated his estate, Chinese records noted that the estate included 60 million ounces of silver, seventy thousand furs, a silver service of 4,288 pieces, and other items worth more than $1.5 billion in modern money.[48] Funds that should have been used to strengthen dikes and ensure the proper management of granaries were diverted to other, personal, outlets. The empire was weakened as a result.

Weak successors, some dominated by stronger relatives, followed powerful initial dynastic leaders. Two of the first four emperors of the Qing were towering figures who reigned for sixty years each (the Kangxi emperor from 1661 to 1722,[49] and the Qianlong emperor from 1736 to 1796), whereas three of the last four emperors each governed for fewer than fourteen years (the Xianfeng emperor from 1851 to 1861; the Tongzhi emperor from 1861 to 1875; and the Xuantong emperor from 1908 to 1911). The long ostensible tenure (thirty-three years) of the Guangxu emperor (r. 1875–1908), moreover, is somewhat misleading. He ascended the Dragon Throne at age three, "ruled" under the formal regency of Empress Dowager Ci Xi until 1889 and under her strong influence through 1897, asserted his own programmatic preferences for only a period of months in 1898, and then suffered effective arrest until his death in 1908.

Weak rulers, corrupt officials, population pressures, thin resources, and other traditional maladies produced unrest, first in border areas and then among the disaffected in the more populous parts of China. The White Lotus Rebellion noted above rocked central and western China from 1774 to 1804. During the mid-1800s, four great rebellions—each with its own dynamics— brought the empire almost to its knees. These were the Taiping Rebellion (1850–64), the Nian Rebellion (1853–68),[50] the Southwest Muslim Rebellion (1855–73), and the Northwest Muslim Rebellion (1862–78).[51]

Of these, only the Taiping Rebellion had any real connection with the Western impact on China that would subsequently transform the Qing's dynastic decline into a revolutionary upheaval. Hong Xiuchuan, the charismatic leader of this great rebellion, was a failed degree candidate who, after reading some Protestant missionary tracts, believed that he was Jesus Christ's brother. Nevertheless, even the Taiping, which at one point controlled much of central and eastern China below the Yangtze River, drew basically on indigenous driving forces.

These four rebellions wrought enormous destruction, together causing the deaths of perhaps as many as 100 million people. To combat them, the Manchu-controlled throne encouraged key Chinese provincial leaders to develop provincial armies. As one consequence of the rise of these local armies, China therefore suffered from the existence of personal military forces not fully loyal to an institutionalized central military establishment.[52] The four great rebellions also greatly weakened the fiscal base of the dynasty by taking much land out of imperial control at a time when the land tax provided the largest share of the government's revenue. The court's ideological prestige suffered, too, and was not helped by the subsequent large-scale sale of government offices and titles to bring in new revenues for reconstruction. Overall, the postrebellion efforts to restore the country's strength failed to address these difficulties adequately.[53]

The factors evident in these events marked the decline of most previous dynasties. Internal corruption, a breakdown of discipline within the government administration, spreading social unrest, the decline of ideological élan, a growing role for the family members of the supreme leader(s), the elevation of weaker individuals to the top position, and the increasing importance of military versus civilian officials all spelled serious trouble, and sooner or later challengers would link up with sufficient power to overthrow the ruling house. They would then set up their own dynasty, perhaps after an interregnum of years, or even decades, of domestic strife.

Against this background, the Western challenge had begun to affect the Qing by the 1840s, but it did not become central to the fate of the nation until the waning years of the century. The period between the initial recognition of a nettlesome problem (around the 1830s) and the near collapse of the imperial system (in the late 1890s) saw the development of some political and social pathologies that have proven so enduring that they continue in one form or another to plague contemporary China.

THE WESTERN CHALLENGE

Although China had dealt with the West intermittently for centuries prior to the 1800s, this limited contact posed no serious challenge to China's sense of itself as the Middle Kingdom—the center of the civilized world—as the Qianlong emperor's letter to King George III indicated. Those Westerners who journeyed to China tended instead to be awestruck by the vitality of its economy, the sophistication of its scholars and officials, and the might of its empire. What changed during the course of the 1800s, moreover, was only in part China. The larger change occurred in the West itself—and therefore in the nature of the challenge the West posed to Beijing.

During the nineteenth century, the leading nations of the West realized the benefits of the revolution in transportation that began in the fifteenth century and the Industrial Revolution that began in eighteenth-century England. These developments enhanced the military capabilities—and especially the ability to project power—of the newly industrializing countries. More advanced technologies in communications, transport, metallurgy, and so forth effectively shortened distances around the globe. The newly industrializing countries sought to conquer far-flung empires to feed raw materials into their growing industrial plants, to consume the products of their increasingly productive industry, to siphon off their excess populations, and to add to their own sense of superiority.[54]

This new industry-based power produced new perspectives on the international order. The "superior" Chinese culture gradually lost its luster. British and other traders sought to draw China into the expanding international trading system without, however, fitting themselves into the Confucian cosmology so central to the self-perception of Chinese officialdom.

The Chinese responded piecemeal to the growing pressure to open the country up to the West's traders and products.[55] In the typical pattern, Chinese officials perceived a concrete problem, adopted the minimum response deemed adequate to cope with it, and then encountered two difficulties: their measures produced unintended consequences that created new problems, and those measures fell short of addressing the original challenge. In this cumulative fashion, the overall problem moved from periphery to core, eventually undermining the dynasty and the dynastic system itself.[56]

There is little reason to believe that before the 1860s the Chinese saw the Western challenge as anything out of the ordinary. The court tried to prohibit the importation of opium in the 1830s, but in the notorious Opium War of 1839–42 the British successfully won new trading concessions.[57] During the 1840s and 1850s the Chinese tried to fit the pesky Westerners into their system of handling other "barbarians"—that is, to limit their access to China, cloak that access in rituals of the tribute system, and thereby make the necessary concessions in a fashion that affirmed the basic Confucian view of the world.[58] They did this while, in the 1850s, concentrating their attention on the four great domestic rebellions that erupted in that decade.

Western forces, spearheaded by the British and French, continued pressuring the Chinese for greater access to their market and, for foreign missionaries, to their souls. This led to military conflict from 1856 to 1860 and a humiliating Chinese defeat. The West, though, decided that its interests would be best served by a strong government in Beijing that could effectively implement the concessions wrung from it. Some Westerners, therefore, organized an "Ever-Victorious Army" to serve the court in Beijing against the Taiping rebels.[59] This Western approach of supporting Beijing while wringing concessions from it persisted through the latter half of the 1890s.

During the 1860s some Chinese began to understand how dangerous the Western challenge could become. They advocated both learning Western ideas about international relations so as to use the Western conventions to protect China, where possible, and mastering Western military technology in order to use it to ward off Western aggression.[60]

The effort to acquire Western technology, though, produced unforeseen ripple effects. For example, this policy required that intelligent Chinese go abroad for training in foreign languages and in the pertinent mathematics, physics, engineering, and other subjects. Such travel and intensive training affected the views of many of these individuals in ways that extended well beyond simple weapons manufacturing.[61] In addition, the Qing system could not adequately reward these individuals, whose new careers removed them from the intensive training in the Confucian classics that provided the only legitimate path, via the examination system, to upward political and social mobility. Over a period of decades it became obvious that mastering Western techniques would require changes in core elements of Chinese society itself.

The Chinese thus learned that technology does not develop in a vacuum. Its use also transmits values and assumes certain patterns of social behavior. It has wide-ranging, complex effects on those who seek to absorb and utilize it. China's former paramount leader Deng Xiaoping expressed this same observation in the 1980s, saying "When you open the window, inevitably some flies come in with the fresh air." How far to open the window has been a contentious issue in China since the 1860s.

Foreigners sought bases in China from which to engage the Chinese market. They therefore pressured the government to grant them foreign-ruled "concession areas" in or near major cities. These concessions became foreign outposts within China itself. Over time, they also became subversive elements in the Chinese system, as revolutionaries could in some cases find security from the Chinese authorities by living in the foreign concessions. Because Chinese law permitted torture of prisoners to obtain confessions, foreigners also sought protection from the Chinese judiciary. The resulting system, called extraterritoriality, allowed for foreign law administered by foreign courts to apply to foreigners in China.[62]

The late Qing attempts to ward off external pressure ultimately proved inadequate. Worse still, Japan worked more effectively to meet the Western challenge, systematically studying Western (especially European) forms of government and ingeniously using strengths in its own traditional system to make the extensive modifications necessary to bring about industrial development. By the 1890s Japan had become stronger in warfare than its "elder-brother" civilization, China.[63]

Japan's decisive victory in the Sino-Japanese war of 1894–95 shocked China far more than anything the West had done to that point. This war revealed that even little Japan had mastered the secrets of Western strength to the point where it could humiliate the Middle Kingdom. Chinese intellectuals and officials directed much of their resulting ire against the Manchu rulers of the Qing dynasty. But some also concluded that the roots of defeat were sunk deep into the traditional system itself. Revolutionary political elites now began to emerge to challenge the Manchus and the entire system. Both the revolutionaries and the Qing loyalists sought desperately to achieve the goal shared by all Chinese: to enable the country to enjoy wealth and power in an age of Western and emerging Japanese imperialism.

THE QING RESPONSE AND COLLAPSE

Three broad strategies to obtain prosperity and security emerged by the end of the 1890s. Remarkably, these three strands of thought have, in shifting balances, dominated Chinese political debate over all the decades since then. These approaches are not so much totally independent policy packages as points on a continuum that runs from isolationism on one side to all-out modernization on the other. They represent sufficiently distinctive clusters of thought on key issues, though, that they warrant brief individual explanation.[64]

The first approach might be labeled "nativist," although like so many terms used by Westerners to describe phenomena in China, this one has no precisely equivalent Chinese translation. Nativists argue, essentially, that China fares best when it isolates itself from the international arena and finds an ideological basis for binding its massive population together in militant unity. They assert that no country can seriously threaten to conquer and rule another country whose populace is united against the intruders. The key task, therefore, is to find and nurture the ideological basis for unity. Nativists regard influences from the West as divisive. They thus stress the importance of massive popular and elite education in a unifying ideology and active efforts to limit the country's exposure to other ideas and influences. The ideology espoused by different nativists has varied greatly in content from the far left (dogmatic Maoism during the Cultural Revolution of the late 1960s)[65] to the far right (the New Life movement of Chiang Kai-shek in the 1930s).[66] Since the 1910s, though, even the nativists have generally rejected the imperial system for failing to protect the country from foreign aggression in the 1800s.

The second approach, that of the "selective modernizers," can be summed up in the words of a slogan first used in the 1870s, "Take Chinese learning for the base and Western learning for practical use."[67] This notion seeks to preserve the distinctive, superior qualities of Chinese civilization (supporters of this view differ on what these are) while importing sufficient foreign technology to make China strong enough to ward off external pressure. This idea makes a politically attractive program—it argues that the country can obtain security and prosperity without making fundamental changes. As indicated above, the ripple effects of technology imports have time and again made this approach untenable in practice even as it has remained powerful as a political platform.

The third view, that of the "iconoclastic modernizers," argues that China must become the type of society that can *itself* produce technological innovation. Failure to do this consigns China to perpetual dependence on the decisions of foreigners, who will never permit China to obtain full security. This third platform is "iconoclastic" in that its adherents are in principle willing to change *anything* in order to develop a technologically vibrant society. Few of these individuals favor comprehensive westernization; rather they envision a distinctive Chinese approach to modernization, but one that is unencumbered by obligatory adherence to traditions or ideology.

China's defeat at the hands of the Japanese in 1895 convinced the major Western powers for the first time that the Middle Kingdom could be conquered in classical imperialist fashion. The late 1890s saw a "scramble for concessions" in which various foreign countries sought to, in a phrase from that era, "carve China up like a ripe melon." In response to this suddenly escalating threat to the country, the Guangxu emperor in 1898 launched a brief surge of reforms against the wishes of the empress dowager Ci Xi and her conservative supporters. After one hundred days the empress dowager successfully put down the reforms and placed the Guangxu emperor in confinement.[68] Reformist officials who had supported the emperor either fled the country or suffered severe reprisals. In the ensuing conservative backlash a rapidly spreading secret society called the Righteous and Harmonious Fists, with tacit backing from the empress dowager, launched a wave of terror in 1900, dubbed by Westerners the Boxer Rebellion, against foreigners and the Chinese who supported them. In response, a multinational foreign expeditionary force occupied and sacked Beijing and obtained the punishment of conservative court officials who had encouraged the Boxer rampage.[69]

These events convinced the empress dowager and many other officials that change would be necessary to strengthen the country and save the dynasty. In the ensuing years Ci Xi implemented a number of reforms, including abolition of the examination system in 1905. But these reform efforts ultimately hastened the decline of the dynasty. The abolition of the examination system, for example, in a single blow cut off access to advancement for the tens of thousands of politically ambitious men who had spent their lives studying for these crucial exams. A policy of sending young people abroad (especially in the early 1900s to Japan) to study modern learning also exposed them to revolutionary thinking and anti-Manchu agitation. Other reforms, such as providing greater latitude for local gentry to participate in politics, produced increased political agitation from below and weakened Beijing in relation to the localities. In these and myriad other ways, the reformist medicine finished off the already sick dynastic patient.[70]

The international challenge based on the expanding Industrial Revolution required the Chinese government to raise far more revenue, change the way it recruited officials, modify its ideology, and adapt its social policies in ways that proved to be beyond its institutional and political capabilities. Chinese failures encouraged additional foreign initiatives. Ultimately, China could not succeed without basic changes in a system that had served it well for two millennia. In this sense, the pressures from the industrializing West and Japan provided the catalyst that transformed a typical dynastic decline into a revolution.

The final months of the Qing dynasty highlighted the issues that had assumed a commanding role in shaping modern China—disputes over foreign funding of capital projects, decentralized authority and local resistance to imperial commands, modern military force at the personal command of an ambitious figure, and weak and confused decision making by the imperial leaders. Specifically, a dispute over funding for railroad development in southwest China, in which Beijing seemed to be preempting foreign loans for the project, led to a revolt by the project's local investors. The revolt quickly caught fire and spread to other provinces, which in rapid order declared their independence from Beijing. The Qing government called on Yuan Shikai, the official who had in the preceding decade built up the country's most modern military force, to suppress the provincial defections. But Yuan instead utilized his own military leverage to bring about the abdication of the emperor, the end of the Qing, and the establishment of a republic with himself as the central figure.[71] The Qing was not so much overthrown as undermined: it simply collapsed. The forces producing that collapse had gradually gathered momentum over the previous decades and would continue to influence Chinese politics throughout the remainder of the twentieth century.

Toward the end of the Qing, for the first time in two millennia, China faced outside forces that were unwilling to conform to the Confucian world order and too powerful to ward off. The Confucian order had provided the bases for social ranking, for career mobility, for conferring prestige, and for shaping attitudes toward authority, education, and history. The loss of faith in this worldview dissolved the glue that held together the polity itself. Western—and especially Japanese—strength eroded the major premises on which the old Chinese order rested.

2
The Republican Era

The search for a new set of moral principles on which to base the Chinese polity has to date proved unsuccessful. The breakdown of the Qing was so fundamental that it seemed to leave all of Chinese society topsy-turvy. As late as the 1890s, Confucianism still dominated the ideological scene, foreign ways were suspect, and a military career held little prestige. By the late 1910s, all of this had changed. The elites heatedly debated the best ideology to utilize, but all the contestants—anarchists, socialists, liberals, democrats, pragmatists, nationalists, and others—were proponents of foreign schools of thought. Those with foreign-language skills and foreign educations had great advantages over those who sought to preserve traditional wisdom. Those with military know-how exercised power over those who mastered calligraphy, poetry, philosophy, and the other types of knowledge that formerly had set the political elite apart from mere soldiers and commoners. Chinese elites constantly debated the core question: how best to make the country wealthy and strong?

But no single persuasive answer emerged. Ultimately, civil war rather than civil debate decided who would rule the quarter of humanity who called themselves Chinese.

The Early Republican Era

The demise of the Qing gave birth to the Republic of China in 1912. Sun Yat-sen, the best known of the anti-Manchu revolutionaries, had advocated a republican form of government. Sun, however, had conducted his revolutionary activities primarily from abroad—from such places as Honolulu, San Francisco, and Japan. He learned of the collapse of the Qing while reading the newspaper on a train heading out of Kansas City. After his return to China, he held office in the new regime for only six weeks before being ousted by Yuan Shikai. Yuan ruled briefly via a parliamentary government, but by November 1913, after what was termed the "second revolution," he rendered the National Assembly inoperative. In 1916, Yuan tried to establish a new dynasty. The dynastic idea had well and truly died, however, as did Yuan several months later.[1]

The country quickly dissolved into regionally based warlordism. Warlords ruled by virtue of their personal military forces, and they fought each other over lands that could earn them additional tax revenues, which they often collected many years in advance. Some warlords, such as Yan Xishan in Shanxi Province, tried to carry out reforms and promote industrial development.[2] But most were determined only to enrich themselves at tragic cost to the population.[3]

Rampant taxation impoverished the countryside and forced many peasant youths into warlord armies. Foreigners became involved as various warlords competed to obtain the most effective foreign weaponry. Affronts to China's sovereignty thus festered and grew.

Some warlord territories were more important than others. The most important by the late 1910s was Beijing. Whatever warlord controlled Beijing organized the "national" government. Often the government actually administered little more than the city and its immediate suburbs, but whoever ran Beijing also received all maritime customs receipts from throughout the country. This arrangement extended back to the late Qing, when foreigners had taken over management of customs, agreeing to collect duties on behalf of the national government and to pay the resulting funds only to that government. Shanghai, with its great concentration of wealth, was the second most important prize in the battle among the warlords.

The national collapse and constant indignities of the warlord period produced anguish among the intellectuals, who argued over the directions in which the country should move. These debates proved irrelevant to most Chinese, whose immediate fates were determined by the constantly shifting fortunes of the numerous warlord armies that ravaged the land. The debates nevertheless had important long-term consequences that warrant attention. Initially, some leading intellectuals advocated two features deemed central to the success of the West—science and democracy. In pursuit of the latter, Hu Shi (1891–1962), as a student at Columbia University in 1916, began to argue that Chinese intellectuals should write in the vernacular language of ordinary people rather than in the archaic classical form of Chinese. The latter had not changed over a period of more than a thousand years, yet it remained the language in which all serious tracts were written. Hu argued that adopting the vernacular would make the country's political debates accessible to the common people and could spawn a popular press. He continued to advocate use of the vernacular (*bai hua*) instead of classical Chinese (*wen yan*) on his return to Beijing in 1917, and the idea soon found sufficient acceptance to create the ground for mass politics. Hu's proposal was officially adopted in Beijing in 1922.

Several developments, nevertheless, discouraged the pursuit of what were termed "Mr. Science" and "Mr. Democracy." World War I produced such slaughter on the battlefields of Europe that it tarnished the allure of Western civilization. China had joined the Allies during the war—promising, among other things, to stop German shipping along its coast—expecting that an Allied victory would end German concessions in the country. Beijing hoped to reap great benefits from such principles as self-determination that President Woodrow Wilson articulated in his Fourteen Points.

The reality proved deeply disillusioning. From 1900 to 1911 Japan had become a haven for Chinese revolutionaries, as many Chinese students went to Tokyo to study and, while there, converted to revolutionary politics.[4] After the downfall of the Qing and while the West was fighting World War I, Japan took advantage of the power vacuum in East Asia to pressure China. In 1915, Tokyo produced the notorious Twenty-one Demands, which would have turned China into a Japanese semicolony had Beijing fully accepted them.[5] The Japanese also pressured each president of China to appoint pro-Japanese cabinet officers. By the late 1910s, resentment of Japan ran high among Chinese intellectuals.

Japan also joined the war effort on behalf of the Allies, signing secret agreements with France and Britain that would turn German concessions in China's Shandong Province over to Japan instead of returning them to China. The Versailles Peace Conference upheld these secret commitments. When word of this betrayal reached Beijing in early May 1919, it touched off an explosion led by students that so rocked the political scene that it is still regarded by many as the birth of modern Chinese politics. The 1919 upheaval, called the May Fourth Incident, gave its name ("May Fourth") to the entire movement of political debate and ferment that engaged China's intellectuals from 1916 to 1921.

THE MAY FOURTH MOVEMENT

While warlords contested for power, the intellectuals sought some new base to reintegrate society. But the leaders in this effort were not the older scholars whose role had been central to the intellectual life of the Qing. Rather, university-age students and young faculty moved to the fore. Many of these had been trained in missionary schools or had studied abroad, often on money provided by the Qing government as reparations after the defeat of the Boxer Rebellion at the turn of the century.[6]

Because the imperial Chinese state reflected fundamental ideas about the nature of civilization itself, the collapse of the imperial system required reconsideration not only of the form of government but also of the basic ethics and social organization of society. Younger scholars began to attack the ethical base of the strong family system. Emancipation of women became one of the political currents among urban youths.[7] The educational system received critical scrutiny, and many schools of "new learning" cropped up around the country.

A movement led by young intellectuals, called the New Culture Movement, advocated changes in the organization of Chinese society and politics. New journals began to propagate foreign ideas. Among these, one called *Xin Qingnian* (*New Youth*), published at Beijing University and edited by Chen Duxiu, who later became a founding member and leader of the Chinese Communist party, proved especially influential. By the late 1910s, it began publishing articles on socialism. Beijing University, under the influential leadership of President Cai Yuanpei, became a seat for debate among advocates of very different schools of thought.

In response to the Chinese capitulation at Versailles, on 4 May 1919, some three thousand students from various universities in Beijing marched around Tiananmen Square to demand that the government fire its pro-Japanese ministers and refuse to sign the peace treaty with Germany. The students burned down the residence of the pro-Japanese minister of communications and assaulted Japan's ambassador to Beijing. A government crackdown led to arrests and bloodshed. In response, a mass movement quickly developed and swept across coastal China.

Hundreds of publications began to appear as the students tried to turn anti-Japanese feelings into a true mass movement. A boycott of Japanese goods took hold. Demonstrations broke out around the country, and the movement toward embracing modern ideas, including rights for women, greatly accelerated. The government in Beijing soon found itself confronting a major crisis. It dismissed three of its pro-Japanese ministers and refused to sign the final peace treaty with Germany.

More important, though, the May Fourth movement signaled a sharp break with the past and an urgent search to consolidate a new sociopolitical agenda. It created a new form of politics for China—mass politics.[8]

From the bewildering array of contending interests and factions of the May Fourth movement, two broad political efforts emerged, one led by the Nationalist party or Guomindang (GMD) and the other led by the Chinese Communist party (CCP). These two parties came to dominate the Chinese stage from the mid-1920s on with similar social and political origins.[9] They joined in strategic alliances from 1924 to 1927 and from 1936 to the early 1940s, and yet fought one another in bitter, deadly struggles for control of the country's political destiny. The Guomindang moved to Taiwan in the late

1940s. After a half century of GMD rule, Taiwan has developed into a multiparty democracy.[10] The Chinese Communist party, in contrast, has since 1980 produced startling economic growth on the Chinese mainland but monopolizes political power. The Guomindang is limited to Taiwan, a small island one hundred miles off the east coast of mainland China, and a few small additional islands, with a total population of not many more than 20 million people. The Chinese Communist party rules a population of nearly 1.3 billion. Had observers in the 1920s and early 1930s made predictions, they would have bet that these parties' fortunes would be the reverse of what has in fact occurred.

Although in 1924 the GMD and the CCP formally allied and adopted similar Leninist approaches to internal party organization, their styles, experiences, and ultimate priorities differed greatly. Because the CCP won a smashing military victory over the Guomindang in 1949, this book primarily addresses the development of the Chinese communist movement and its impact on the country. The Guomindang, however, ruled China from the late 1920s to the 1940s and left some enduring legacies. We begin, therefore, with an analysis of the core characteristics of the GMD's approach to governing China.

THE GUOMINDANG

The Nationalist party formed under the leadership of Sun Yat-sen and was the successor to a series of revolutionary political movements he had guided since the 1890s. Driven out of power within a year of the collapse of the Qing, Sun had spent part of the 1910s in Japan and part trying to organize a political base on the Chinese mainland. During the early 1920s he found himself in his native province of Guangdong, where he sought alliances with warlords and sufficient aid from foreigners to permit him to extend his political influence.[11]

Sun's political philosophy was summed up in what he termed the "three principles of the people" (*sanminzhuyi*). He had articulated these principles in various forms during the decades of his revolutionary activities, first against the Manchus and then against the warlord-dominated governments after 1912. In 1923 he finally summed them up and clarified them, but each still remained broad and diffuse. The "three principles" became widely known, though, and indicated the three major directions in which Sun thought national policy should go.

The first principle was "nationalism." The term Sun chose for this, *minzuzhuyi,* connotes putting the country, defined as one nationality, first. Sun had used this term originally as a vehicle for rallying Chinese opposition to Manchu rule toward the close of the Qing. By the 1920s, it meant something close to "self-determination" for both the Chinese and the other nationalities in China. This principle captured the anti-imperialist sentiment so powerful during that era.

The second principle is usually translated as "democracy," but again the translation misses the essence of the Chinese term Sun used. "Democracy" is now translated as *minzhuzhuyi,* which literally means the "doctrine of rule by the people." But Sun actually used the term *minchuanzhuyi*, which means "doctrine of the rights of the people." His explanations of this term made clear that he foresaw a political system that provided for elections, the right of recall, referendums, and so forth. In sum, Sun felt the people should be able to control their own government through various devices. But he also thought that Chinese were not yet ready for the full implementation of this type of system, and thus he called for a long period of "tutelage" that would prepare the people to assume the duties required by full democracy. The tutelage period would, among other things, establish schools that would raise people's educational level to that required by democracy.

The third principle, "people's livelihood" (*minshengzhuyi*), also lacked specificity. The practical directions in which Sun seemed to move called for massive projects to build the country's infrastructure, along with efforts to equalize land holdings and develop a just system of taxation. Sun was not advocating a free-market approach to economic prosperity. He felt the state had a determining role to play in creating a just economy.

One reason it is difficult to pinpoint the content of Sun's revolutionary ideas is that he was almost always consumed with the practical tasks of finding allies and gaining support for his next attempt to overthrow the government and seize power. He frequently had to trim his sails in order to firm up support from the United States, Japan, revolutionary Russia, or other sources. Nevertheless, Sun was an excellent orator, and his name and basic ideas became widely known. As of the early 1920s, he probably had more of what in contemporary American politics would be termed "name recognition" than did any other Chinese politician.

During the early 1920s, the GMD consisted largely of personal factions organized in almost secret-society fashion. In 1923, Sun met with a man named Joffe, an agent sent from Moscow by the Communist International (Comintern), which had been formed to promote revolutions abroad without directly embroiling the new Russian state in the resulting problems. Joffe convinced Sun that he should accept Soviet aid, Soviet advice about how best to organize a revolutionary party, and an alliance, brokered by Comintern, with the fledgling Chinese Communist party. Another Comintern agent was Mikhail Borodin, a remarkable man whose revolutionary career had taken him at various times into the Chicago public school system, the European workers' movement, and Soviet politics. Borodin implemented the ensuing CCP / GMD alliance, which became effective in January 1924. The Guomindang at that time reorganized itself along the lines of the "democratic centralism" that Lenin had utilized so effectively in seizing and consolidating power in Russia seven years earlier.[12]

Sun, with Soviet aid, proceeded to develop his armed forces with the object of achieving control over the country through military conquest from the south to the north. His primary training facility, the Whampoa Military Academy near Guangzhou, provided both military training and political indoctrination. Chiang Kai-shek commanded this academy, while Communist party member Zhou Enlai headed up the academy's Soviet-type political-commissar system. The Whampoa Academy attracted a substantial group of relatively idealistic, strongly nationalistic young men, many of them from rural upper-class families.[13]

In March 1925, Sun died during a trip to Beijing, where he was seeking to broker a political deal with the northern warlords. He left a party that comprised many different types of groups—from communists to social reformers to right-wing nationalists. His successor was Chiang Kai-shek, a former stock broker in Shanghai who had spent years in Japan and had received military training. Chiang headed a very diverse party, however, and his real base of power resided in the bonds of loyalty he had developed with the military commanders he trained at Whampoa. From 1925 onward Chiang never felt secure and unchallenged in his control over the Guomindang party itself. His personal inclinations, moreover, tended toward nationalist antiimperialism but away from radical domestic social reform. His relations with the Chinese communists were, therefore, especially tenuous, but he recognized that he had to maintain this tie as long as he needed Soviet aid.

In 1926 Chiang launched a military campaign, dubbed the Northern Expedition, to reunite the country. In this effort, the GMD did not face a unified opposition but rather confronted numerous free-standing warlord armies. In a fateful set of decisions, Chiang set out to negotiate the absorption of these various forces into his own National Revolutionary Army (NRA) rather than risk the destruction of his own troops in pitched battles.

The Northern Expedition of 1926–27 took the NRA from its original base in Guangdong north to the Yangtze, then east and west to Shanghai and Wuhan, and finally north to Beijing. It consisted as much of mergers as of battles. Chiang would apply pressure on his warlord opponents and then offer them face-saving compromises, replete with commissions in the NRA and preservation of their forces intact as NRA units. In the early stages of this effort, Communist party agitators helped to soften up resistance through political agitation in advance of the NRA forces. This combination of outside military pressure and political agitation behind the lines proved effective in bringing nominal success to Chiang's forces. It also meant, though, that the NRA itself became a jerry-built concatenation of largely independent military units, and the GMD became home to the warlords and corrupt officials who had ruled northern China before the Northern Expedition.[14]

In the midst of the Northern Expedition, moreover, Chiang took the fateful step of breaking decisively with the Chinese communists. In the process, he slaughtered upward of 90 percent of the CCP's members. The initial attack occurred on 12 April 1927, when Chiang linked up with the "Green Gang" and "Red Gang" secret-society forces in Shanghai to ferret out and execute as many communists in the city as could be identified.[15] The second shoe dropped that July, when more leftist members of the GMD who had maintained ties with the communists in the middle-Yangtze city of Wuhan yielded to Chiang's blandishments and exterminated the remnants of the CCP there.

Chiang's break with the communists marked a strategic shift in his approach to the international arena, as well. By turning against the CCP, Chiang and the

GMD cut themselves off from future aid from Moscow. They could do this because, with CCP help, they had captured the city of Shanghai and the rich lower-Yangtze region, which held a large percentage of the entire country's modern industry and wealth. In addition, however, the GMD began to mute what had to date been its very strong anti-imperialist thrust and to blunt the social revolution that had been gaining momentum. Relations with the major Western powers would remain tense and uncertain for some years, but the beginnings of a modus vivendi were taking shape as of April 1927. Eventually, foreign aid for Chiang would follow.

In 1927, the GMD shifted the nation's capital to Nanjing (Nanking); their period of rule before the Japanese invasion of 1937 is often called the Nanjing decade. The lower Yangtze region where Nanjing is located is far more business oriented and has more natural resources than Beijing. The foreign presence in this region—especially that of the British—was also more extensive than in north China. Reflecting these differences, the political leadership of the Nanjing decade rested in the hands of the newly important forces in Chinese society: those educated abroad, those with ties to commerce and industry, and those with military and/or secret-society bases.[16]

Having ousted the communists and formally unified most of China by late 1928, Chiang sought to consolidate the flimsy structure that had emerged from the Northern Expedition. He relentlessly continued a purge of communist elements and in the process caught many of the country's most politically energetic and creative individuals.[17] Moreover, the absorption of the northern warlords into the GMD toward the end of the Northern Expedition further diluted the party's ideological commitment; the resulting organization became something very different from the disciplined Leninist party that Borodin had proposed to Sun Yat-sen in 1924.[18]

The Nanjing decade saw many substantial economic achievements, which were especially impressive in view of the global depression of the 1930s. In some parts of the country during this period, the national government bureaucracies reached more deeply into the grass roots than had previously been possible. At the same time, though, because of the overall weakness of the central government, significant experiments in social and economic reform occurred in various locales, especially in some rural counties. On a broader level, a huge array of "bottom-up" political and social organizations developed, such as local chambers of commerce and trade unions.[19] China's industrial production expanded significantly, and commerce grew apace. These accomplishments suggest that any government able to impose a modicum of order in China without suppressing all independent and local initiative would have benefited from significant economic growth—growth that had been stunted precisely by a combination of political instability, repression, and internal military strife. China attained its peak levels of output in industry, agriculture, and commerce in 1936—levels that would not again be achieved until well into the communists' first decade of rule in the 1950s.

But internal weakness, domestic opponents, and foreign adversaries limited the GMD's success during this period. All three challenges, moreover, were interrelated.

Damaged from within, the GMD had largely ceased to be an effective party. The absorption of northern warlords and the purge of left-leaning cadres stripped the organization of its ideological aplomb. Three of the worst features inherent in traditional Chinese political culture—nepotism, corruption, and an emphasis on correct speech versus effective action—surged to the fore under these conditions. By the early 1930s it had become common for new appointees to government office to fire virtually all of their subordinates and to replace them with friends, relatives, and politically loyal subordinates. Officials at the highest levels also used their power to have relatives appointed as county magistrates and to other positions that were sources of lucrative graft. The resulting widespread corruption and lack of party discipline gravely harmed the Nationalist movement.

In addition, the GMD embraced the notion that correct speech, not effective action, is of primary importance because it demonstrates correct thinking. This policy had pernicious consequences during these years. The GMD held numerous meetings and issued a multitude of proclamations and manifestos. Government organs drew up elaborate plans and high-sounding position papers for any number of projects and initiatives. Generally, however, these pronouncements and documents sought not to solve actual problems but rather to demonstrate loyalty via participation in the process and adherence to proper forms. As explained in Chapter 1, in Chinese culture the individual's identity is as part of a group. These rituals of policy making confirmed group identity and solidarity. They had the effect of divorcing the policy makers almost totally from the society they governed and from the actions of local officials that affected the lives of the populace.[20]

Moreover, Chiang Kai-shek had to spend a considerable portion of his time during the Nanjing decade engaged in civil wars to maintain his rule. The Northern Expedition left Chiang in relatively strong control of the military forces of central and southeast China, but the armies in the north, northeast, northwest, and southwest remained loyal to Chiang's nominal allies instead of directly to the central government. Throughout the Nanjing decade, therefore, Chiang could travel to most provinces outside of the lower Yangtze region only after an exchange of hostages.

With depressing regularity Chiang's GMD "allies" teamed up in various combinations to unseat the central government through military challenge. A partial list of the major warlords and their challenges to the central government from 1929 to 1931 illustrates the dimensions of this problem (see Table 2.1).

While Chiang waged almost constant warfare to keep at bay the various warlords who had nominally joined the Guomindang, he focused his primary attention on completing the job that he had begun in April 1927—that is, exterminating the communists. Given the treachery that surrounded Chiang on all sides, it is not clear why he harbored such implacable hatred for the communists in particular, but his perseverance in seeking their destruction is remarkable. He once referred to the CCP as a "disease of the heart," which, he said, must be cured before other, more superficial challenges to the body politic (in this case, he was referring to the Japanese!) could command the spotlight.

TABLE 2.1 *Civil Wars from 1929 to 1931*

DATE	CHALLENGER	LOCALE	NUMBER OF CASUALTIES
Mar. 1929	Li Zongren	Guangxi	Unknown
May 1929	Feng Yuxiang	Henan	Unknown
Oct.–Nov. 1929	Feng Yuxiang	Henan	Unknown
Dec. 1929	Tang Shengzhi	Henan	Unknown
May–Oct. 1930	Coalition forces Feng Yuxiang Li Zongren Tang Shengzhi Yan Xishan	Beijing and elsewhere	230,000
1931	Coalition forces Li Zongren Wang Jingwei	Guangzhou	Unknown

Chiang effectively destroyed the communists as an urban political force during the late 1920s, and the main body of the movement found refuge in various mountainous bases along provincial borders at that time.[21] Beginning in 1930 Chiang launched a series of "annihilation campaigns" against the communist base areas. Either civil war or Japanese aggression cut short each of the first four of these campaigns. The fifth, carried out with substantial assistance from German military officers, succeeded in routing the final communist base area in the southeast, at Ruijin, Jiangxi, in the fall of 1934. Chiang's army then chased the retreating communist forces across south and southwest China and up into the central region of north China, where the CCP eventually established a headquarters in the small town of Yan'an. During this major year-long retreat, dubbed by the communists the Long March, the CCP again lost nearly 90 percent of its strength but ended up in a part of north China far less vulnerable to Chiang's attack.

Chiang's concentration on the communist threat diverted his attention from the Japanese challenge that grew and became more ominous during the late 1920s. As noted above, Japan had tried to take advantage of Western preoccupation with World War I to force China to accept its Twenty-one Demands in 1915. With the renewal of a Western presence in China after the war, the Japanese focused their efforts more on China's northeast. In 1928 they assassinated Zhang Zuolin, the major warlord of that region. In 1931 they seized the entire northeast and split it off into a Japanese puppet state named Manchukuo. To head this state they installed Pu Yi, the child emperor whose abdication in February 1912 had marked the end of the imperial era.[22]

In 1932 Japanese militarists launched a brief, violent foray into Shanghai. By 1935 they effectively took over the two northern provinces (including Beijing) that bordered Manchukuo. Chinese intellectuals grew increasingly frustrated with Chiang Kai-shek's insistence on destroying the communists rather than on protecting the country against the Japanese. The Chinese communists lost no opportunity to encourage students and intellectuals to give priority to the growing Japanese encroachments.[23]

In late 1936 Chiang assigned Zhang Xueliang, the son of the assassinated northeast warlord Zhang Zuolin, to lead his Manchurian troops against the communists at Yan'an. Chiang personally went to Zhang Xueliang's nearby base camp at Xi'an to spur them on. But during his stay there Zhang and several of his colleagues kidnapped Chiang Kai-shek and held him captive to force a change in the GMD's policy toward the Japanese. Zhou Enlai, a top communist leader, traveled to Xi'an from Yan'an to participate in the discussions. In what must have been a wrenching assignment, given the massive casualties Chiang had inflicted on the communists over the previous decade, Zhou persuaded Zhang to spare Chiang's life in return for Chiang's promise to lead a national effort that would include the communists and that would give its highest priority to driving the Japanese out of China.[24] Thus began the second united front between the CCP and the GMD—a cooperative effort that began in late 1936 and lasted effectively until the early 1940s (although it did not end formally until after the conclusion of World War II).

The following year Japanese forces launched an all-out attack on China proper, driving the GMD from its base in the rich lower-Yangtze region deep into the country's impoverished interior. Eventually the GMD leadership settled in the southwest Chinese city of Chongqing (Chungking) behind the mountainous eastern boundary of Sichuan Province. From 1938 to 1945, Japan occupied the key cities and major communications links throughout eastern China, setting up puppet governments in the areas under its control.

Separated from its natural base in the rich, cosmopolitan lower-Yangtze region, the GMD military forces initially put up strong resistance to the Japanese, and sentiments regarding national unity and purpose ran strong.[25] But Sichuan and its surrounding areas were extraordinarily backward places (in neighboring Yunnan the wheel was not widely used before the 1930s!), and as the war dragged on spirits sagged, corruption grew, and factionalism deepened. At some point after the American entry into the war in 1941 Chiang decided that he would count on foreign forces to win the war. From that point on he held his own best troops back to cope with what he was convinced would be an inevitable postwar communist challenge.[26]

The resulting combination of phony war, feudal surroundings, effective isolation, and severe wartime shortages (due in part to America's failure fully to support the Guomindang's war effort) sapped the will and discipline of the Nationalist forces. Inflation became widespread, corruption became endemic, and esprit de corps disappeared. Intellectuals who had fled to Chongqing to fight alongside the GMD began to lose hope.[27]

Against this background, America's unexpectedly rapid defeat of Japan in 1945 with the atomic bombings of Hiroshima and Nagasaki suddenly thrust the GMD back into control of all of China's major cities. With American help, the Nationalists took the Japanese surrender throughout China (except in the northeast) but muffed their resulting chance in the late 1940s for national renewal. Instead of returning property confiscated by Japan to its Chinese owners, the GMD simply took over that property. After years of privation in the deep interior, Nationalist officers and politicians gorged themselves on the relatively wealthy eastern urban economy, producing levels of corruption that soon undermined popular support. Hyperinflation had become a serious problem in the Nationalist areas in the final years of the war, and gross mismanagement spread this disease to the entire economy in the late 1940s; by the winter of 1948–49 much of China still under Nationalist rule had been reduced to a barter economy.

With the war-weary populace ready to turn against any party suspected of starting a civil war in the wake of the Japanese retreat, the Nationalists and the communists initially engaged in half-hearted peace negotiations. General George C. Marshall was dispatched by President Harry Truman to mediate these negotiations, but ultimately they came to naught. Chiang Kai-shek decided to exterminate the communists through all-out civil war starting in the winter of 1946–47.

Strategic errors, military corruption, and factional infighting eroded the capabilities of the Nationalist forces, however, and despite their vastly superior numbers and firepower, they suffered catastrophic defeat.[28] The communists had entered northeast China in force in the wake of World War II. They won their first major battles south of the Great Wall only in January 1949, but they crossed the Yangtze that April, seized Guangdong on the southeast coast in September, and by the spring of 1950 had captured the entire country except the island province of Taiwan and a few small coastal islands. In the final stage of the war, the Nationalist collapse unfolded so rapidly that communist forces had difficulty keeping up with the retreating GMD forces.[29]

So many things went wrong in the final years of Nationalist rule on the mainland that it is difficult to sort out the fundamental from the more marginal causes of defeat. The GMD never successfully transformed itself into a disciplined political party. With its social bases in the urban Yangtze delta area, the GMD proved unable to adopt and implement policies that would effectively address the tremendous ills of rural China. Factionalism remained deeply ingrained in party practice, and by the early 1930s a major part of the party membership had lost any commitment it originally had to real public service. The prolonged privation of the war years worsened the tendency toward corruption and malfeasance in the party apparatus. When faced with the communist military threat and the multitude of socioeconomic problems confronting the country at the end of World War II, the GMD simply proved unable to rise to the challenges it faced.[30]

China's society, which in various parts of the country had sprung to life in the 1920s and early 1930s, had been brought to its knees by 1949. The brutal Japanese occupation, civil war, corruption, GMD and CCP terror tactics, and unbridled inflation weakened the social fabric and left the people disorganized and dispirited; many were eager for a strong state to impose order and provide the populace with a firm sense of direction. Whereas the 1920s and early 1930s had witnessed flourishing development of social, economic, cultural, and religious organizations and spirited debates among intellectuals, by

1949 little of this was left to counter the CCP's efforts at revolutionary social change.

The Communist Rise to Power

The Chinese Communist party arose from the ferment of the May Fourth movement. Radical young intellectuals were impressed by Russia's withdrawal from World War I in the wake of the Bolshevik Revolution and, especially, by Moscow's subsequent disavowal of all Russian concessions that the tsarist state had wrung from the Qing dynasty. Marxist writings had begun to find their way into China via Japanese translations and articles in *New Youth* and other May Fourth–era journals. They presented a "scientific, advanced" Western theory that predicted the collapse of the Western capitalist system in revolutionary upheaval. Some Chinese intellectuals thought a Marxist revolution could catapult the country into the vanguard of civilization as defined by this doctrine. Through its analysis of imperialism as the highest stage of capitalism, Leninism also seemed cogently relevant to the conditions in which Chinese found themselves. When Soviet agents of the Comintern added practical advice on revolutionary politics and financial and military aid to this heady mixture, the result was the formation of the Chinese Communist party, which held its first congress in Shanghai in July 1921.[31]

The CCP's victory over the Guomindang in 1949 has had enormous consequences for the subsequent fate of the country. It is, therefore, important to understand the forces that shaped the ideas of the party's leaders and the practices and capabilities of the movement they headed. The Chinese Communist party evolved differently from either its Soviet mentor or the various Marxist parties of Europe. Its distinctive character is in large measure a product of the particular rural, military path to power it pursued. In the process of expanding from the clandestine group of some fifty CCP members who met at the first congress in 1921 to the 5 million victorious party members at the establishment of the People's Republic of China in 1949, the party acquired outlooks, capabilities, and practices that deeply affected its exercise of power after 1949.

In part, the CCP's prolonged, rural-based revolution shaped its ideology, giving successful party leaders a distinctly un-Marxist faith in the ability of will and strategy to overcome objective obstacles. In addition, the communists' pre-1949 path to power left the party at the time of national victory with a membership that consisted overwhelmingly of poorly educated peasants, a cohort that continued to exert influence well into the 1980s. This peasant composition of the CCP explains many of the differences between Chinese and Soviet practices in the 1950s and later. The party's pre-1949 experience also produced means of stimulating change adapted to the poor education and the strong commitment of the peasant cadres, including mass mobilization in the form of political "campaigns." The Chinese term for this peculiar type of guided mass action is *yundong.*[32]

To succeed, any revolution must grow from weakness to strength. All revolutionary forces start out numerically small and on the margins of society. The revolutionary party is thus inevitably shaped not only by its initial energizing ideas but also, profoundly, by the particular strengths and weaknesses of the regime it is trying to overthrow.[33] Almost all revolutionary movements, moreover, fail. The few that succeed typically are influenced by their mistakes and by their defeats as much as by their successes. Mistakes not only curtail particular strategies but also often eliminate the leaders who espoused them and the cadres who most ardently supported them. They also leave memories of failure in the minds of the survivors. Therefore, it is important in understanding the molding of a revolutionary party to analyze both its energizing ideas and its various missteps and their consequences.

THE PATHS TO POWER

The CCP's path to power was characterized by uncertainty, experimentation, disappointment, and tenacity. In its early stages it had primarily an urban civilian cast and took its guidance from abroad. Later, it became solidly rooted in some of the poorest regions of this Third World country, and it developed a deeply indigenous, highly militarized identity. Along the way the Guomindang and its allies repeatedly decimated the ranks of the movement, and at two points (1927 and 1934–35) communist losses apparently reached 90 percent of party membership. These changes and the repeated revitalization of the movement toughened and gave confidence to the leaders who survived. Six basic strategies were adoped seriatim in this complex, wide-ranging struggle to achieve national power.

Labor Mobilization (1921–23)

The CCP began with what appeared to be a classic revolutionary strategy for a "communist" party: it sought to mobilize China's nascent proletariat, directing its efforts to arousing the workers to anti-imperialist and anticapitalist fervor. In a sense, these early efforts proved successful. The party formed a labor secretariat, through which it organized trade union activity in central-south and east China cities and along the major rail links.

The fundamental problem this strategy encountered was the extraordinarily small size of China's proletariat, which was well under 1 percent of the population. Even a militant proletarian organization, therefore, would prove a weak reed in an agrarian country dominated by warlords and their private armies. Events in 1923 drove this basic fact home to the communists in particularly brutal fashion.

Early that year, communist organizers precipitated a strike on the Beijing-Hankou railway to improve the lot of the workers. Unfortunately for the CCP, this strike interfered with the plans of one of the major warlord generals, Wu Peifu, to move troops to the north as part of his incessant game of military parry and thrust. Wu, who had previously shown considerable sympathy for the communists, broke the strike by calling in his troops and, in what became known as the February Massacre, slaughtering the railway workers.

Wu's previous support of the CCP made this defeat particularly startling to the young revolutionary leaders of the party. They then took to heart two essential truths about gaining power in China of the 1920s: that they would have to find a way to link up with a broader spectrum of the population than the workers alone; and that they would have to secure ties to supportive military forces in order to avoid being overrun by any warlord they angered.

Shortly after the massacre in 1923, the Comintern counseled the CCP to link up with the GMD, then based in the Guangzhou (Canton) area of Guangdong Province. Although it lacked substantial independent military forces at the time, the GMD did have two valuable assets: recognition in China as a party that theoretically represented a broad spectrum of the populace, and a party head, Sun Yat-sen, who conferred legitimacy in that he was widely regarded as the father of the Chinese republic.

As noted above, in January 1924 the CCP formally allied with the GMD. In joining the GMD the communists agreed to give up their independent existence (a pledge they did not honor) and carry out all future propaganda under the name of the GMD rather than their own. With Comintern assistance, the GMD then set up the Whampoa Military Academy. It also set up a Peasant Movement Training Institute in Guangzhou to foment change in the countryside.

United Front with the GMD (1924–27)

Through the united front with the GMD, the communists sought to gain access to a broader spectrum of the populace, help the GMD ride to national power, and then edge out the GMD leaders and take control. Within the united front, the CCP focused its efforts primarily on political organization in the urban areas, preaching a line of anti-imperialism, rather than of class struggle, to reach their constituency. The CCP also made a side effort in rural areas. Communist party members, including the future CCP leader Mao Zedong, dominated the Peasant Movement Training Institute. The noncommunist GMD concentrated more on training an officer corps capable of leading their anticipated expedition northward to reunify the country. The communists also became involved in political organization within the military, staffing a political commissar system on the model of a parallel apparatus recently developed by Leon Trotsky in Russia for the Red Army.

For a time, the united front proved beneficial to both sides. CCP activities benefited from the communists' identification with the GMD, which was recognized internationally and domestically as a force for Chinese nationalism. CCP membership grew rapidly whenever incidents occurred that whipped up antiforeign fervor. Given the large number of foreigners resident in China at the time—and their often high-handed attitudes toward the native Chinese—such incidents occurred with regularity. For its part, the GMD benefited both from Soviet aid and, especially, from the advice on revolutionary political and military organization provided by Borodin and his colleagues.

Nevertheless, tensions between the CCP and the GMD lay barely beneath the surface even in the best of times. The Guomindang was itself a loose alliance of individuals with a broad array of political inclinations. Some were virtually identical to the Chinese communists, but other views spanned the spectrum, including the far right. In the jockeying for power that followed Sun Yat-sen's death in March 1925, the distaste of many GMD party members for the CCP became quite clear. Nevertheless, over time Chiang Kai-shek gained primary power in the GMD, and the alliance with the CCP held together. Under these shaky conditions, in 1926 the Guomindang launched the Northern Expedition to unify the country, as described above.

Fundamentally, Chiang wanted to carry out an anti-imperialist revolution of national unification. Although the CCP sought the same objective, it also champed at the bit to move on to social revolution. Communist efforts at political mobilization to weaken the rear areas of warlords opposed to the Northern Expedition helped the GMD effort but also rang alarm bells. Often the communists used class-based appeals to whip up support, thereby threatening the social and economic bases of many NRA officers, who disproportionately came from the landed upper classes. They demanded that the communists be reined in, escalating tensions.

As we have seen, the situation came to a head in April and July 1927, when first in Shanghai and then in Wuhan the GMD forces and their allies in the secret societies slaughtered the communists and their supporters. This turnabout had profound effects on the future development of the communist movement in China.

By 1927 the CCP had developed two quite different thrusts. Most party leaders emphasized the urban revolution and regarded Russian advice from the Comintern as sacrosanct. It was precisely these cadres who were working in the major cities at the time of the GMD betrayal and repression. Relatively few of them survived.

The CCP had also developed a rural revolutionary movement, growing out of the Peasant Movement Training Institute and related efforts. These cadres tended to see the countryside as the real source of China's revolutionary potential. The revolutionary gurus in Moscow, by contrast, viewed political work among the peasants as important but still basically supplementary to the main revolutionary efforts in the cities.

Mao Zedong was by no means the only important Communist party figure to gravitate to the rural revolution, but his subsequent role as father of the Chinese communist revolution warrants special attention to his ideas and activities.[34] Mao had been raised a peasant in the central Chinese province of Hunan. As a teenager he left his village to go first to the provincial capital of Changsha, where he enrolled in one of the schools that taught "new learning," and then later to Beijing. There he worked as an assistant at the Beijing University library, where he gained his first exposure to Marxist thought. His political thinking went through various phases and ideas, as was true of almost all those who wound up in the communist movement in the early 1920s.[35] Once he (and others) founded the CCP, Mao focused primarily on organization work among the peasants.

In early 1927, while working in the Hunan countryside, Mao wrote a report on a violent uprising in the province that resulted in a brief term of political power for the local peasantry before it was put down by Hunanese military forces. Mao's report on that uprising reveals how impressed he was with what had occurred. On the basis of his findings, he declaimed that

[a] revolution is not a dinner party. . . . [I]t cannot be so refined, so leisurely and gentle, so temperate, kind, courteous, restrained, and magnanimous. A revolution is an insurrection. . . . In a very short time . . . several hundred million peasants will rise up like a mighty storm . . . and will send evil gentry into their graves. Every revolutionary party and every revolutionary comrade will be put to the test, to be accepted or rejected as they decide. There are three alternatives. To march at their head and lead them? To trail behind them, gesticulating and criticizing? Or to stand in their way and oppose them? Every Chinese is free to choose, but events will force you to make the choice quickly.[36]

Mao considered this report so important that when his official selected works appeared in 1960, it was the second selection in the first of the four volumes published before his death.

The GMD repression of 1927 killed off disproportionate numbers of communists whose urban priorities clashed with Mao's views. Those left after 1927 were far more inclined toward peasant mobilization. The repression also sowed seeds of doubt about the wisdom of Comintern advice. As signs of impending GMD betrayal had multiplied in early 1927, Stalin had insisted that the CCP firmly maintain its alliance with the GMD. Stalin's advice proved disastrous, although it is not clear that the CCP could have done anything to stave off the GMD's offensive.[37] Survivors like Mao began to question whether the revolutionary leaders in Moscow really understood the conditions the communists confronted in China.

The survivors learned two other lessons. They realized that although the GMD represented many different views, the CCP could not rely on any sector of the GMD to protect it from that party's right wing. The GMD as a whole, in short, could not be trusted. Along with this, the communists realized that they could not seek protection in the military force of an ally; rather, they would have to develop their own army totally loyal to the party. Anything shy of this would lead to disaster in China's violent warlord politics.

Not all members of the Chinese Communist party drew these lessons at the time.[38] Some, including Mao, did, however, and the events of the ensuing five years made the rest of the party follow suit. Mao's perspicacity did not, though, immediately ensure his leadership over the entire communist movement.

Adapting to the Countryside (1929–34)

The repression of 1927 left the CCP a shambles, with surviving groups only poorly coordinated and largely working on their own instincts. Late in the year Mao led some forces into the Jinggang Mountains (Jinggangshan) of Jiangxi Province, a remote area populated primarily by the Hakka, a minority that had formed the major base of support for the early stages of the Taiping Rebellion in the 1850s.[39] There Mao linked up with forces under a colorful, older communist commander, Zhu De. The two men and their troops together fought battles and suppressed attempts to unseat them. Within two years they had established the Jiangxi Soviet in Ruijin, in the western Jiangxi Mountains, where they began to develop the techniques to adapt the communist struggle to a rural base of operations.

The forces of Mao and Zhu were not the center of the communist movement at the time, but their activities warrant particular attention because other efforts by the CCP in various locations failed, bringing the center of gravity to the Ruijin experiment. The Jiangxi Soviet itself was one of a number of communist base areas scattered among the mountains of southeast China. In these remote provincial border areas, a power vacuum existed that permitted the communists to survive and establish local organs of authority. At the same time, the official central organs of the CCP remained in Shanghai and, despite ongoing repression, continued until 1930 to prepare for an urban uprising as the major thrust of the strategy for seizing power. GMD harassment eventually forced this urban remnant to abandon Shanghai during 1931–32 and move to Ruijin.[40] GMD military efforts closed down the other base areas one by one, until in 1934 only the Jiangxi Soviet remained as a major communist base in southeast China.

In Ruijin, Mao began to develop his understanding of four crucial issues: how to carry out land reform; how to develop and sustain political activity among peasants; how to govern territory under the CCP's control; and how to develop, train, and utilize military forces in the countryside. In all these spheres Mao's thinking took years to mature, and in each case the rest of the party did not quickly or easily accept the approaches he advocated. At its Jiangxi base during the early 1930s, the party underwent a crucial transition to a rural strategy, but the techniques for winning national power through a rural revolution did not fully develop until a later period, called the Yan'an era, discussed below.

Early in the development of the Jiangxi Soviet, Mao seized on land reform as a major vehicle for winning favor among the region's Hakka peasants. He was inclined at first to carry out a radical land-reform effort, taking land from all those who could earn a reasonable living from it and distributing it to the landless and the land-poor. This approach quickly established a base of support among the destitute of the region, but it also caused a sharp reduction in agricultural output. Mao's initial foray into the politics of land reform—the crucial socioeconomic issue in overwhelmingly agrarian China—had not gone well.[41]

Mao subsequently developed an analysis of social groups in the countryside that provided a useful guide to the likely effects of different land-reform strategies. Over the ensuing years he accordingly formulated a more flexible rural policy. Under Mao's aegis the party divided the countryside into five classes: "landlords," who could live primarily by land rents rather than cultivation of land with their own labor; "rich peasants," who both worked the land full time and hired extra labor or rented out land because they owned more than they themselves could cultivate; "middle peasants," who worked full time on the land they owned and whose production provided an adequate income to support their family; "poor peasants," who owned some land but still had to hire themselves out because their own land could not provide a subsistence income; and "landless laborers," who lived wholly by hiring out their labor.[42]

Experience taught the party over the years that removing the landlords did not necessarily decrease agricultural output, as the most productive farmers were the rich peasants. Indeed, eliminating the landlords enabled the party to strengthen its position in the countryside by replacing them as the major source of rural credit. Removing the rich peasants, though, did adversely affect the harvest. The effects of land reform, therefore, depended crucially on where one drew the line. Attacking rich peasants as well as landlords made more land available for redistribution, but this land came at a high price in terms of production. Seizing only the "excess" land of the rich peasants affected output far less than stripping them of all their holdings.

During the Jiangxi Soviet era, Mao and his colleagues also began to develop techniques for achieving sustained peasant political involvement. As Mao indicated in his February 1927 Hunan Report, quoted above, peasants are generally quiescent politically; they understand intuitively how much they risk if they challenge authority and lose. However, when aroused, their political activity tends to "rise up like a storm" that unleashes tremendous violence and passion but then quickly spends itself, leaving exhaustion and ennui in its wake. The explosive character of peasant protest activity was not well suited to a long-term strategy for gaining power through control of rural turf. The CCP had to develop the means to harness peasant political protest, direct it at specific targets, and then consolidate the gains.

To accomplish these goals, the party first sought to package its appeals in terms that were directly relevant to the concrete interests of local peasants, rather than in broad abstractions such as "exploitation" or "anti-imperialism." Second, it gained experience in peasant mobilization by launching specific "campaigns" based on fervent but targeted political participation. Third, it elaborated techniques for forming "mass organizations" that would generate some level of peasant activity between campaigns. All of these efforts were continually adjusted as increasingly peasants themselves led the effort to mobilize and sustain the fervor of still more peasants.[43]

In order to control base areas, the CCP had to form actual administrative units to govern territory. Indeed, the Chinese communists accumulated rich experience before their victory in 1949—very much unlike the Bolsheviks, who seized power in Russia in 1917 without having ever previously ruled any patch of ground. The CCP began experimenting with different ways of organizing the countryside, recruiting administrative personnel, and combating the natural tendency in China toward elitist, exploitative bureaucratic organizations. They began by drawing on the basic administrative divisions that had characterized the Qing and the republican governments. But later during the Yan'an era, they worked on adjusting these administrative arrangements to new tasks.[44]

Finally, the Jiangxi Soviet period witnessed the first systematic efforts by the communists to recruit and train their own revolutionary army and to develop pertinent military tactics. Since the party's military position throughout this period remained weak, the tactics adopted tended to be more appropriate to fighting an enemy with superior firepower. Mao seems to have drawn heavily from traditional Chinese military thought, especially from his understanding of the fourth-century B.C. writings of China's great strategist, Sun Zi. He adapted these writings into principles for fighting a guerrilla war against better-equipped forces. The resulting precepts included, eventually, such now-famous tactics as trading space for time; luring the enemy in deep; "when the enemy advances we retreat, when the enemy encamps, we harass, when the enemy withdraws, we attack"; concentrating superior force to wipe out an isolated enemy unit, but never engaging in battle where the enemy has superior strength on the spot; developing relations between the troops and the populace as close as those "between lips and teeth"; and using the countryside to surround the city.[45] Much of this can be summed up as giving priority to intelligence capabilities, good relations between officers and men, and tactical advantage in choosing fields of battle.

The impoverished Jiangxi mountain populace did not provide the CCP with recruits of high caliber. However, it may not have been too difficult for the party to establish an esprit de corps among the Hakka minority, who strongly sensed their distinctiveness from the non-Hakka Chinese of the Guomindang.[46] Furthermore, the party honed its techniques for absorbing bandit and secret-society forces, recruiting peasants as an offshoot of the land-reform effort, and using political indoctrination to develop military forces undaunted by the rigors of guerrilla warfare.

Although the Jiangxi Soviet period proved important for the development of techniques appropriate to rural-based revolution, this period was far less successful both for Mao personally and for the immediate fortunes of the party as a whole. Mao had initially developed the Jiangxi Soviet, but Russian-trained members of the CCP continued to hold the top positions in the party. When the party's top leadership moved to Ruijin from Shanghai in 1932, Mao was pushed aside, and he did not obtain a leading position in the party again until over two years later at the Zunyi conference on the Long March.

The displacement of Mao also led to the communists' abandonment of his guerrilla strategy to engage the enemy in favor of more conventional, positional warfare under the direction of a Comintern military advisor named Otto Braun and the Soviet-trained Chinese communist leaders. When Chiang Kai-shek's fifth annihilation campaign of 1934 succeeded in routing the communist forces, Mao subsequently persuaded his colleagues that the major fault lay with the new defensive tactics applied by the Soviet-oriented Chinese leaders.

The fifth annihilation campaign forced the communists to abandon their final base area in southeast China and undertake an extraordinary strategic retreat. The few years of the Jiangxi Soviet's existence had, however, left their mark on the CCP. During these years the party became fully separated from its urban base and increasingly composed of peasant recruits. It had begun to develop its own military arm and had started to learn how to survive and grow in the rural areas. In addition, Mao skillfully used the final defeat of the Jiangxi Soviet to demonstrate that his own brand of Chinese Marxism—what later became known as Mao Zedong Thought, defined by the CCP as "the application of the universal truth of Marxism-Leninism to the concrete conditions of the Chinese revolution"—could provide success, whereas the advice coming from Moscow led only to disaster.

Strategic Retreat: The Long March (1934–35)

Party legend to the contrary, the Long March was actually a costly strategic retreat. It took the main body of communist forces from Jiangxi in southeast China across to Sichuan in the southwest, and then deep into the interior of north China to Baoan and finally to a new base area centered on the dusty town of Yan'an.[47] It was a searing experience in the lives of the survivors, so difficult that many of them suffered stomach ailments and insomnia for the rest of their lives. Ever after, the CCP differentiated between those who participated in the march and those who did not. The former, called "Long March cadres," enjoyed a prestige and camaraderie that set them apart even within the ranks of the party itself.[48] It is not an exaggeration to say that Long Marchers led the Chinese communist movement from the time of the march to the mid-1990s.

An American journalist, Edgar Snow, captured the spirit of the Long March best in his classic *Red Star over China*, published shortly after the conclusion of the march and based on interviews with communist leaders, including Mao. As Snow wrote,

The Long March had an average of one halt for every 114 miles of marching. The mean daily stage covered was 71 *li*, or nearly 24 miles, a phenomenal pace for a great army and its transport to average over some of the most hazardous terrain on earth. Altogether the Reds crossed 18 mountain ranges, five of which were perennially snow capped, and they crossed 24 rivers. They passed through 12 different provinces, occupied 62 cities, and broke through enveloping armies of 10 different provincial warlords, besides defeating, eluding, or outmaneuvering the various forces of Central Government troops sent against them. They entered and successfully crossed six different aboriginal districts, and penetrated areas through which no Chinese army had gone for scores of years. However one may feel about the Reds and what they represent politically (and there is plenty of room for argument!), it is impossible to deny recognition of their Long March—the *Ch'ang Cheng*, as they call it—as one of the great exploits of military history. In Asia only the Mongols have surpassed it.[49]

The Long March took a devastating toll on the ranks of the CCP. Various sources provide different figures, but it appears that 80 to 90 percent of those who began it did not survive to settle in Yan'an. The severe privations of the march sparked sharp disputes among the leaders as to the best route to follow, the appropriate destination, and the composition of the leadership.

The Long March left two legacies for the subsequent development of the movement. Most important, early in the march, Mao Zedong achieved leadership of the march itself at a meeting convened in January 1935 at the village of

Zunyi in Guizhou Province. The meeting lasted for three days and witnessed bitter polemics. A major issue concerned the route that the communist forces should take and where they should aim to go. This issue became intricately bound up with the question of who should lead the main body of forces on the march.

At the Zunyi meeting, Mao launched a blistering critique of those who had followed the military advice of Comintern representative Braun during the latter part of the Jiangxi period.[50] Mao achieved greater primacy in the party at this meeting, but for the next seven years he had to fight to consolidate his victory over Wang Ming. Wang had spent the 1930s in Moscow as the leading Chinese representative at Comintern headquarters. He returned to China after the Long March, and it is an indication of Moscow's continued importance to the CCP that Wang immediately became the major rival to Mao's leadership.[51] Mao finally achieved absolute leadership only in the years from 1942 to 1945 in Yan'an. He then retained that supreme position until his death in 1976. During his long reign Mao showed time and again that he never fully forgave many of the individuals who had argued against his taking initial control of the party and the Long March at Zunyi.

Second, the march became the basis for a heroic myth about the CCP that greatly bolstered the party's unity and prestige in subsequent years. The unity of the march veterans did not shatter until about three decades later, when Mao initiated the Cultural Revolution in the 1960s.

The Long March changed the strategic location of the Chinese communist movement. After much debate, the main forces in the march finally decided to head for Yan'an, where a small communist base area had existed for some time under the leadership of Liu Zhidan. This shift took the communists largely beyond the range of the GMD's military capabilities. It also, as it turns out, positioned the CCP well to expand its bases in rural north China once the Japanese drove the GMD out of the main cities of that area.

The Yan'an Era (1935–47)

The Yan'an era had a profound effect on the Chinese Communist party and its fortunes. When the communists completed the Long March, the CCP consisted of a relatively small band (10,000 to 25,000) of bedraggled southern troops displaced to a desolate and desperately poor area in the north China hinterland. The GMD, for all its shortcomings, represented in the popular mind the hope for Chinese nationalism.

By the end of the Yan'an era, the CCP's forces had grown to nearly 2.8 million members, and the party governed some nineteen base areas that contained a population of nearly 100 million people. Many, especially in north China, felt that the CCP had acquitted itself better than the GMD during the prolonged war against Japan. During World War II the GMD was driven from its base, degenerated as a resilient political force, and lost considerable credibility with the populace. During this same period, the Chinese Communist party vastly expanded its base, greatly developed its techniques of governance, and significantly enhanced its political prestige.[52] The Japanese invasion thus saved the CCP—although it did so because the communists proved so much better than the Nationalists at learning how to adapt to the new circumstances and gaining through adversity.

When the CCP negotiated Chiang Kai-shek's release during the Xi'an incident in December 1936, the united front against the Japanese on which they insisted contained terms that reflect the lessons the CCP leaders had learned from their earlier bitter experience with the GMD. The communists agreed to incorporate their military forces into the GMD but would do so only on the condition that these forces remained separate units under direct communist command. The CCP also agreed to stop calling for the overthrow of the GMD and for class warfare, but they demanded that they be allowed to govern their own base areas. On the sensitive issue of land reform, the communists agreed to a mild reform consisting primarily of the limitations on land rents that the GMD itself had adopted in national legislation but had never effectively implemented. Communist propaganda focused on Chinese nationalism and on the need to combat the Japanese. All landlords who supported this cause and agreed to the specified rent reductions would be tolerated in the communist base areas. In return for these concessions the GMD made three major commitments: to cease attacking the CCP, to provide the communist base areas with aid, and to fight the Japanese.[53]

In reality, neither the communists nor the GMD faithfully carried out the letter of their agreement, which was hardly surprising given the deep bitterness between them. But each side adhered enough to the spirit of the agreement during the first few years that their cooperation proved reasonably successful. By 1940, however, the spirit of mutual help had become frayed on both sides. Within another year the GMD had cut off aid to the communists and was blockading the CCP base areas. The united front had ended in fact if not in name.[54]

The legacies of the Yan'an era proved fundamental to the subsequent history of the Chinese Communist party. Enormous success crowned this period as the party overcame seemingly insuperable odds to grow and develop. As a consequence, the methods employed in Yan'an acquired a kind of halo. In future times of need, Mao showed a strong tendency to revert to the core elements in the heady mixture of success of the Yan'an era.

Party membership was strongly shaped by the devastation of the final battles for the Jiangxi Soviet, the Long March, and the numerous clashes with the Japanese during the Yan'an era. With only very few early members of the CCP surviving to the end of the Yan'an period, by the mid-1940s the party consisted overwhelmingly of peasants recruited from the base areas of north China. Its leadership, however, reflected the CCP's origins south of the Yangtze, supplemented by intellectuals who trekked out to Yan'an to join the party during the war against Japan.

Many of the policies in Yan'an were a maturing and fleshing out of approaches that had first been tried in Ruijin. The tentative initiatives of the early 1930s now became complete systems of operation along with supporting theoretical rationales. During the early 1940s the CCP paid particular attention, for example, to reducing bureaucratism among its administrative personnel and developing a united-front system of governance that gave non-communists a sense of participation in the communist-dominated base areas. During these years the communists also enhanced their confidence and improved their proficiency in waging guerrilla warfare.[55]

Several major developments during the Yan'an era had particularly important long-term consequences. The consolidation, especially from 1942 to 1944, of Mao Zedong's personal rule within the party was one of these. Another was the 1945 adoption of a party constitution that stipulated Marxism-Leninism Mao Zedong Thought as the guiding ideology of the CCP. This move recognized the importance of Mao's major adaptations of the Moscow party line to the specific conditions of China.

To consolidate his position of preeminence in the CCP, Mao undertook a "thought-reform campaign" from 1942 to 1944. This effort reflected Mao's desire to eliminate any remnant influence of Soviet-oriented communists and his understanding that under conditions of separate base areas and incessant warfare, he could not rely on discipline alone to ensure obedience in the CCP ranks. The techniques developed to implement thought reform, "washing the brain," as the Chinese also called it, included isolating individuals in "study groups." Under the guidance of a group leader, they studied specified documents to understand key principles. They then had to relate those principles to their own lives in a critical, concrete, and thoroughgoing way. Other members of the group put the individual under extraordinary pressure to examine fully his/her most deeply held views, and to do so in the presence of the group. The individual then had to write a full, self-revealing "confession." Other group members isolated the individual during this process. Only when the confession was accepted would the person be drawn back into an accepted position in the group and in the larger society.

These techniques of pressure, ostracism, and reintegration can be effective in any society. They were particularly powerful in China, where the culture assigns great value to saving face, protecting one's innermost thinking, and above all, identifying with a group. Individuals put through thought reform later described it as excruciating. The resulting changes in views were not permanent, but the experience overall seriously affected the lives of those who went through it. In a milder form, the CCP used these same types of techniques on millions of Chinese after 1949.[56]

Like thought reform, many of the other techniques the communists developed during the Yan'an period reflected the evolving political conditions in which they found themselves. During these years, the CCP followed a strategy of infiltrating behind Japanese lines throughout north China, and by 1945 the communists had established nineteen base areas there. Japanese areas of control, however, divided the CCP base areas from each other, and communications both between and within the base areas were extremely tenuous and primitive.[57] At all times, moreover, many of the base areas were threatened with Japanese military attack, causing the CCP to follow a military strategy of prolonged guerrilla warfare. The Japanese menace on one side and the post-1940 Guomindang blockade on the other severely limited the resources available to the communists in these very poor areas. The demands of guerrilla war placed a premium on developing strong, mutually supportive bonds between the troops and the local populace.

By the end of the Yan'an period, the CCP had developed an operational set of principles and practices that differed markedly from the centralized, functionally specialized, hierarchical, command-oriented approach imposed by Stalin in the USSR. In what some authors have labeled the "Yan'an complex," the CCP stressed a combination of qualities that can be summed up as:

☐ decentralized rule, with considerable operational flexibility allowed to local leaders;

☐ the importance of ideology in keeping cadres loyal to the goals of the leaders and reasonably consistent in their approaches to problems;

☐ a strong preference for officials who could provide leadership in a range of areas—politics, administration, and military affairs—instead of only in a particular, specialized area;

☐ an emphasis on developing and maintaining close ties with the local population rather than relying on impersonal commands issued from government offices;

☐ a related focus on egalitarianism and simple living among officials as highly preferred ways of keeping in touch with the population.

Although the communist movement fell short of realizing these principles in practice, they nevertheless became deeply held party values.[58] In later years they would become integral parts of the CCP mythology about the success of the Yan'an era.

Another, darker, set of methods also became an integral part of CCP practice during the Rectification campaign in Yan'an. This was the use of false accusations, torture, and "special case groups" to elicit confessions from real and imagined foes within the communist movement. Kang Sheng, working with Mao's support, was the central figure in this effort. Kang had played a key role in the CCP intelligence apparatus in Shanghai in the late 1920s. He then went to the Soviet Union, where he learned techniques of mass terror and secret police work from Stalin's henchmen. While in the USSR he had strongly supported Wang Ming, and he returned to China with Wang in 1937. Once in Yan'an, however, Kang soon switched his loyalty to Mao Zedong, and Mao brought Kang to the center of power. Kang was a complex man—well educated and a connoisseur of art, yet possessing a sadistic capacity to inflict pain and a tendency to see enemies everywhere.

With Mao Zedong's backing, Kang conducted a reign of terror that paralleled the early 1940s Rectification campaign. His actions were so violent that he aroused strong criticism from other CCP leaders, and after 1945 he was removed from intelligence and police work. But his legacy of Stalinist-type methods lived on alongside the better-known Maoist penchant for thought reform. In Mao's later years he brought Kang back to the center of power, and all of China paid the price during the Cultural Revolution that began in 1966 and continued for a decade.[59]

During the Yan'an period, the social composition of the CCP became even more thoroughly peasant. In the context of ongoing guerrilla war, moreover, the party and the military became so intertwined that the distinctions between them were largely artificial. And finally, the leaders of various base areas and military groups became powerful figures with deep personal bonds of loyalty to their immediate comrades. While impressive obedience to central command continued to characterize the movement, decentralization and local initiative became core operating principles.

Fighting a Civil War (1947–49)

After the sudden capitulation of Japan in the wake of the atomic bombings of Hiroshima and Nagasaki, the United States army airlifted Guomindang troops to China's major cities to take the Japanese surrender. At the same time, during the final weeks of World War II the Soviet Union attacked Japanese forces in northeast China and proceeded to occupy the area that had previously been Manchukuo.[60] Because the Chinese people were by this time thoroughly sick of warfare, neither the communists nor the Nationalists wanted to be seen as the instigators of additional fighting. During much of 1946 an American mediation effort attempted to find a way for the two sides to cooperate. Relations, however, deteriorated, and in early 1947 the Guomindang launched an all-out attack to wipe the Chinese communists out of north and northeast China, beginning with the capture of Yan'an itself.

While maintaining control over much of the north China hinterland, the CCP concentrated its efforts on recruiting new supporters among the peasants of the northeast, where it sent many of its forces directly after the Japanese surrender. The communists did their recruiting through a radical land-reform campaign that employed violence in targeting landlords, rich peasants, and a portion of the middle peasants. This campaign produced a flood of new recruits but wreaked havoc with agricultural production in the northeast.[61]

The communists' basic civil war strategy was to surround the major cities and cut them off from the hinterland. They also sought to interdict interurban transportation wherever possible. This general approach became famous as the hallmark of the guerrilla, rural-based strategy for revolution. By the end of 1948 the Nationalist garrisons in the northeast had become thoroughly demoralized and could no longer be sustained by the GMD resupply effort. They were withdrawn in the final months of that year.

The year 1949 began with a major communist victory—the largest of the entire civil war—called the Huai-Hai campaign. In this single effort, communist forces wiped out half a million Guomindang troops, dealing a fatal blow to the GMD's hopes for maintaining its position in north China. Tianjin, China's second largest commercial and industrial center, fell in mid-January after two days of fighting, and Beijing surrendered peacefully to the surrounding communist forces at the end of the month.[62]

From February 1949 until their ultimate victory, the communist forces used conventional positional warfare rather than guerrilla tactics to uproot the Guomindang. Like the Qing dynasty in the final days of its rule, the GMD after the Huai-Hai campaign proved a hollow shell, and it collapsed more rapidly than either it or the communists had thought possible. Communist armies swept across China in two major thrusts, one down the eastern provinces to Guangdong (captured in September–October 1949) and then to the southwest, and the other cutting straight across central China to the southwest. These efforts routed the GMD forces from the major southwest province of Sichuan in the winter of 1949–1950 and secured the surrender of Tibet to Beijing's sovereignty in the spring of 1950.

The shift in late 1948 from a guerrilla war to a conventional war strategy reflected the communists' realization that the fighting would not continue as long as they had initially anticipated. In 1947, Mao Zedong had commented that he expected to achieve nationwide victory in five years. The party simultaneously began to worry about rehabilitating the devastated national economy and about preventing the flight of urban talent and capital abroad in advance of the communist armies.

In 1948, therefore, the communists shifted their political line. They sharply criticized the radical nature of the land reform that had been implemented in the previous two years and adopted, instead, a far milder version of this effort that would preserve a rich-peasant economy. They also began to cultivate the capitalists and intellectuals in China's major cities in an effort to win them over to the communist cause. In so doing, they promised a long period of "new democracy" before the country would be ready for an eventual transition to socialism.[63]

The rapid collapse of the Guomindang on the Chinese mainland and the organization of the CCP's military forces into different "field armies" meant that various parts of the country came under the rule of particular communist armies and their leaders. These military establishments became the basis for the subsequent civilian administrations that were formed to govern these areas. In most cases, the military commanders who had captured the areas switched hats to become key local government and party officials.

LEGACIES OF THE CCP'S PATH TO POWER

The CCP enjoyed remarkable success in all its various approaches to mobilizing the Chinese population against the existing system. The communists were successful regardless of the type of appeal they made (class struggle in the early 1920s, anti-imperialism in the mid-1920s, and so on), the groups to which the appeals were directed (workers, various classes of peasants, déclassé elements, intellectuals), or the geographical area in which the political activity took place (southeastern cities and countryside, northern hinterland, northeast countryside). All this demonstrates that from the 1920s to 1940s China's malaise made it an eminently "mobilizable" society. Regardless of issue, target, and locale in this widely diverse and socially stratified country, the feelings of dislocation and discontent ran deep, and revolutionary forces could rapidly gain support.

Irrespective of its success in mobilizing support, however, the party typically failed to translate that support into sustainable political strength. The party eventually found that the key to survival lay in seeking out and occupying the interstices of power in the mountainous regions between provinces where no other forces held sway, in desolate parts of north China, or where foreign occupation of cities and transport lines (the Japanese in north China during World War II and the Russians in northeast China from 1945 to 1946) created a vacuum of power in the countryside. From the 1920s to the late 1940s, virtually wherever the CCP faced the GMD head on, the CCP suffered defeat.

This observation raises questions about the many conventional analyses of the CCP's rise to power.[64] According to these standard views, the CCP forced the GMD defeat by astute use of political mobilization to support guerrilla and then mobile conventional warfare. Without doubt, the communists posed problems for the GMD that diverted the Nationalists' attention and resources from other pressing issues. But the major forces behind the defeat of the Nationalists seem, on closer examination, to have been the Japanese invasion, which separated the Nationalists from their natural bases of political power in the lower Yangtze and along the southeast coast, and the related corruption and factionalization of the Nationalist movement, which brought such disaster to China of the late 1940s.

By this reckoning, the CCP's key accomplishment was to find the means to sustain itself as the only viable alternative to GMD rule.[65] But in the final analysis, the GMD collapsed on the mainland primarily of its own dead weight. Indeed, starting in mid-1949 one of the CCP's main problems became the speed of the retreat of the GMD forces. Those forces in south China often fled so rapidly that the CCP military had difficulty keeping up, and the bandit gangs that took over in the interregnum proved nettlesome for the communist forces when they arrived.[66]

The significance of the strategies the CCP employed in attaining power lies, therefore, in their effect on the dynamics of the communist movement. Regardless of the CCP's repeated disappointments and failures, key elements in their tortuous path to power became integral to the party mystique. The myths concerning the Long March and especially the Yan'an period played powerful roles in shaping Mao's views about how to overcome crises when the CCP encountered them after the conclusion of the First Five-Year Plan in 1957. The years in the wilderness, in short, had stamped the CCP with a distinctive character. The following were some of the most important dimensions of that persona.

Mao Zedong attained a stature in the party that was unchallengeable. Mao had brought the party from the devastation of the failure at Ruijin in 1934 to nationwide victory in 1949. As leading communist officials have subsequently commented, "We felt Mao could see farther than we could see and could understand more than we could understand. Therefore, when we did not understand Mao, we assumed that he was right and we were wrong."[67] The result was what could be termed a bandwagon type of political leadership, in which virtually all top officials tried to sense the direction in which Mao was beginning to move so that they could quickly follow in that direction.[68] There were no institutional constraints on Mao's power, and he psychologically and politically dominated most other leading CCP officials.

The consultative leadership style Mao practiced in the late 1940s produced fairly benign informal rules of competition among China's communist leaders. But the Rectification movement of 1942–1944 had seen Mao support selective use of another style of rule—a Stalinist approach that centered on witch hunts, false accusations, confessions under torture, and executions. That Mao had shifted his approach after 1945 should not obscure the fact that his more benign late-1940s style—and therefore the system itself—could change at his whim. This core flaw proved highly consequential for the subsequent history of the PRC.[69]

The party membership was overwhelmingly rural in composition, and many in the movement were functionally illiterate. These people tended to be instinctively antiurban and anti-intellectual. They could not handle the paper flows characteristic of large-scale bureaucratic organizations. Yet they had earned the right to hold positions of importance in the political organs being established to run China. Consequently, many of the characteristics of the PRC's governance through the 1970s—decentralization, mass political campaigns, extensive use of face-to-face meetings, repeated vicious attacks on intellectuals, and so forth—reflect in major part the adaptations of the post-1949 political system to the distribution of capabilities and the attitudes of the peasant cadres who took over the country.

The peasant-based military path to power left a party and army so deeply intertwined as to be virtually indistinguishable by the late 1940s. The party leadership, moreover, viewed the army as a resource that could serve political as well as security functions. Virtually all party cadres had extensive experience in the military. None viewed the military as a force that should be kept separate from domestic politics. Indeed, as noted above, the pattern of military conquest from 1948 to 1950 determined which clusters of military/civilian cohorts would hold power over each of the major regions of China during the ensuing decades. Thus, in sharp contrast to, for example, the Russian communists when they seized national power, the Chinese communists generally distrusted the cities, regarded the countryside as more revolutionary, and viewed the military as a core force for the revolution. The organization that conquered China in 1949 was more a party army than a political party in the normal sense of the term.

Myths about the governance of the communist base areas during the Yan'an era, which like all myths had a substantial basis in reality but also glossed over much, had already developed and been enshrined in the party's consciousness by 1949. These myths highlighted the party's close relations with the masses, encouragement of spontaneity based on confidence in shared underlying values, utilization of mass mobilization techniques to achieve goals, avoidance of bureaucratic airs that limit contact with—and understanding of—mass sentiment, and cultivation of officials who are expert at political matters, government administration, and military affairs (that is, who can effectively guide all spheres of work). Elevated to myth, these approaches took on a sanctity that made them powerful tools in Mao Zedong's hands in the post-1949 politics of China.

Perhaps most important, their pre-1949 experiences convinced the Chinese communist leadership that the proper combination of will and strategy could overcome seemingly insuperable objective difficulties. Time and again the communists faced overwhelming odds and were advised to seek compromise. Time and again they instead shifted to a new strategy and continued their pursuit of ultimate power. Their final success made those who had stayed the course confident that the types of "objective" matters that dominate the thinking of intellectuals and experts could yield to the superior insights and tenacity of the CCP's top leaders and their followers. By 1949, nobody believed this more firmly than Mao Zedong.

Finally, the Chinese communist leaders had learned to cast a critical eye on Soviet advice, which at virtually every turn had proven inappropriate to the best interests of the CCP. It is this final element that makes so startling the party's virtually total acceptance of Soviet guidance for the first phases of the revolution after 1949. Moscow encouraged the Chinese to establish a system that in almost every major dimension ran counter to the essential qualities of the Yan'an myth, and the CCP responded with remarkable enthusiasm for, and fidelity to, almost all Soviet prescriptions.

The complex legacies of the paths to power, however, eventually weakened the Sino-Soviet relationship, just as these same legacies affected nearly every facet of the PRC's domestic politics from the substance of policy decisions to the means of reaching these decisions and the processes for implementing them.

Part Two
POLITICS
AND POLICIES
SINCE 1949

3

The Maoist System: Ideas and Governance

By the time Mao Zedong stood with his colleagues atop the gate at Tiananmen Square on 1 October 1949 and proclaimed the founding of the People's Republic of China, he had already engaged in revolutionary politics for almost thirty years and had headed the Chinese Communist party for nearly fifteen. He had proved that he was a man of tremendous will, tenacity, and skill who was deeply read in China's traditions of statecraft and fully schooled in the realities of power politics and warfare.

Mao, in short, was a strong leader who would not shrink from bloodshed and sacrifice to reach his goals. And his goals were extraordinarily ambitious. He wanted not only to govern China but to change the very nature of Chinese society and culture to eliminate the country's weaknesses and earn it respect in the modern world.

Governance and revolutionary change are, however, mutually antagonistic. Government administration works best in an environment that permits development of long-term programs, staffed by competent individuals who agree on the basic goals they wish to nurture. For a continent-sized country with a population in 1949 of about half a billion people, effective government would require the formation of large bureaucracies, with their complex problems of management.

Revolutionary change, in contrast, is by its very nature unsettling. Its adherents must maintain a level of frenetic intensity and passion that rarely is compatible with smooth administration. Revolutionaries tend to view complex administration as an obstacle to their goals, whereas civil servants often want to temper the enthusiasm and lack of technical expertise that accompany the policy thrusts of revolutionaries.

Mao Zedong and his colleagues were no anarchists.[1] They recognized the importance of developing powerful bureaucracies to govern China. One of their major concerns was to develop—for the first time since the downfall of the Qing dynasty—strong national organizations that would permit the leaders in Beijing to govern the entire country. They also believed that China, too, had to undergo an industrial revolution to gain the economic power that alone would give it both prestige and security in the international arena.

The Chinese Communist party that came out of the poverty-stricken interior ran the administrative apparatus, with the result that crucial officeholders throughout the system tended to be poorly educated former peasants and soldiers committed to the communist cause. Over the years many better-educated individuals, usually from urban backgrounds, did staff these offices and make them work; while Mao accepted the necessity of tolerating this bureaucratic apparatus, he fought repeatedly against its natural tendency to frustrate the types of revolutionary changes he was determined to make.

Understanding Maoist China thus requires understanding the interplay of the two key elements in the system: Mao's own revolutionary ideas, and the formal administrative system he and his colleagues set up to run the country. That administrative system became so complex that its details are elaborated in Chapters 6 and 7, which are specifically devoted to governing organizations and processes in the PRC. Only a brief introduction to the administrative apparatus is provided in this chapter to provide background for the overview of post-1949 politics in Chapters 4 and 5.

The Features of Mao Zedong Thought

Mao Zedong was a voracious reader and a prolific writer. He was also a practical politician who exercised enormous day-to-day influence on the conduct of party, government, and military affairs. As a consequence, he left behind a prodigious and complex record of writings, speeches, and decisions. This record reveals a person who was often inconsistent, who wrestled with ideas, changed his mind, and played practical power politics to the hilt.[2] Mao did not think in terms of Aristotelian logic, and it is hard to find examples of logical reasoning in his writings. He reveled in contradictions and delighted in discerning underlying frictions and countercurrents. For almost any generalization about Mao's ideas, therefore, one can find specific discordant examples or exceptions. Mao's concrete actions, moreover, often cut against the grain of his core principles. Although he promoted a puritanical society, for example, Mao himself was a prodigious womanizer. He stressed the importance of simple living but unlike such colleagues as Liu Shaoqi, Mao's putative successor until he was purged early in the Cultural Revolution, Mao made extensive use of lavish residences built for his exclusive pleasure around the country.

For all these contradictions, certain fundamental concerns and basic long-term thrusts to Mao's political life stand out. To weigh down the discussion of these ideas with numerous specific qualifications and exceptions is to miss the tremendous impact they had overall in shaping both the history of the PRC under Mao and the legacies of that period for China's subsequent efforts.

Mao's thinking naturally reflected a mixture of influences, including his central China rural background and his subsequent failure to become more than a marginal member of the Beijing intelligentsia in the late 1910s. He regarded himself as well versed in China's history and culture, but chose a life full of risk and violence. In the most personal terms, for example, he flouted convention and abandoned his first wife, to whom he had been matched in a traditional, arranged marriage. He evidently loved Yang Kaihui, his second wife, but the Guomindang captured her and beheaded her in the late 1920s. His third wife suffered a breakdown on the Long March, and Mao deserted her to marry Jiang Qing, an attractive Shanghai actress who journeyed to Yan'an to join the fight against the Japanese. Mao's brother, Mao Zemin, was killed while on political assignment in northwest China in the 1940s, and Mao's only mentally and physically capable son was killed by American forces during the Korean War. Some say Mao left two daughters with peasant families while on the Long March. If so, neither was ever subsequently located. His remaining son had, by the late 1950s, developed mental problems and proved incapable of handling official responsibilities. Mao's political career therefore directly cost the health and lives of many of his closest relatives. In the tradition of China's literati, Mao himself wrote poetry and critiqued the essays of his colleagues; he also had nothing but disdain for armchair politicians and specialists who had never put their lives on the line to achieve their goals.

Mao Zedong believed that China's malaise had been caused first of all by exploitative imperialist forces, and his reading in Marxism and Leninism provided him with a systematic explanation of this phenomenon. But he also was keenly sensitive to the internal weaknesses that made the country vulnerable to external aggression. These internal problems, Mao believed, were substantially cultural. The Confucian notions of civil identity based on networks of relationships precluded the broader class identity and ardent nationalism that Mao believed were necessary to galvanize the people of the country into effective action. Mao also felt that Chinese in general were too fatalistic and too passive. He attributed this in part to the elitist elements of Confucianism and the sense of dependency that the resulting hierarchical society nurtured.

Mao—like most great leaders—was as much a product of his society as a rebel against it. His attacks on traditional culture and polity, therefore, incorporated some very traditional elements. During the Cultural Revolution of the late 1960s, for instance, he demanded the unthinkable in Confucianism: that youths rebel against their elders. At the same time, however, he promoted his own writings as the revolutionary catechism, which resonated deeply with the tradition of memorizing the Confucian classics as a key to political advancement and social virtue in traditional China. To be sure, Mao stressed activism and rejection of the old (one of his favorite slogans was, "Smash the old, establish the new"), hardly the spirit of Confucian ideology. But in this as in many instances, Mao was shaped by tradition even as he launched frontal assaults on the legacies of imperial China.

Overall, Mao sought to move China, to wield its people as a powerful tool to shape the country's destiny. Virtually throughout his life he found himself in an objectively inferior power position, and he thus had to appeal to others to act in concert with him. Before 1949, he continuously confronted enemy forces that had far more firepower than he could command. After 1949, he sought to make a place for China in a world dominated by the United States and the Soviet Union. Almost his entire box of political tools, therefore, concentrated on turning weakness into strength in order to overcome the challenges he faced.

China's domestic politics after 1949 formed the one exception, the one arena in which Mao became the center of power. In his dominant position, Mao became so arrogant that he eventually seemed to lose touch with reality. By the mid-1960s he accepted no other authority, not even that of his doctors regarding his own health.[3] Furthermore, he continued to frame issues and devise solutions in terms he had developed before 1949. These included such approaches as political campaigns, the mass line, the united front, and advocacy of egalitarianism and self-reliance, all of which are described below. But beneath this facade of continuity lay the pathologies of megalomania and, it seems, growing paranoia, which transformed these familiar techniques, devised to change and empower the people and to temper the party, into devices to bend the populace and the party to Mao's personal will. This transition occurred over a period of years. By the mid-1960s, with his launching of the Cultural Revolution, it was complete.

PROMINENCE OF IDEOLOGY

In good Confucian fashion, Mao Zedong believed that right thinking was integral to right conduct. He therefore gave enormous emphasis to matters of ideology and to the importance of ideological education of the people. To put it differently, Mao did not use ideology as window dressing to brighten his practical actions with a theoretical gloss; rather, he saw the development and propagation of ideology as central to the success of the movement he led. One of Mao's key sources of power, moreover, was his monopoly on determining what would constitute correct ideology for China.

The extent to which Mao lost faith in his own revolutionary ideas and cynically used his ideology as a weapon to deal with his enemies is uncertain.

Probably, the reality is more subtle and more tragic than any simple notion of Mao as a tyrant conveys. Mao more likely succumbed to hubris, believing that only he could understand the dangers the country faced and what measures were needed to pull "victory" out of looming defeat. By the end of the 1950s, everyone else was too afraid to tell him the truth. Mao, his colleagues had good reason to think, always asked for the truth but dealt ruthlessly with those who told it. In his increasingly unreal inner sanctum, he resorted time and again to the techniques he had developed before 1949, but as time wore on, the resulting efforts created more bloodletting and tragedy than progress.

No single canon of works was ever designated as the sum and substance of Mao Zedong Thought. The closest Beijing ever came to this was the "little red book" of selections from Mao's works grouped under topical headings that the political wing of the military put out in the early 1960s. It became required reading throughout the country during the Cultural Revolution in the late 1960s. Overall, though, Mao Zedong Thought incorporated the pieces contained in Mao's four-volume *Selected Works* (to 1949) along with many post-1949 texts and political statements by the leader. This was, thus, a living and evolving canon of doctrine. Its very range and lack of precise definition enabled Mao to draw from it to support virtually any direction he wanted to lead the country at a particular time.

Despite this inherent flexibility, the ideology should be taken seriously. Mao believed that it would be impossible to lead the world's most populous country solely on the basis of formal government administration. He would have to instill in the people certain principles and a commitment to certain types of authority that would enable him not only to remain in power but also to remold the country over which he ruled. In a political system whose technical and human limitations greatly restricted the information available to the leaders and their ability to analyze the consequences of their own policy options, moreover, ideology would be a key tool for ensuring compliance among lower-level officials.

VOLUNTARISM

Marxism propagates a philosophical theory of change called materialism, which holds that the underlying development of the material world—in the case of Marxism, especially of the economic structure of the society—determines human consciousness and therefore the boundaries of major human activity. Lenin modified this materialist doctrine to exploit more fully the potential effectiveness of political agitation and revolutionary efforts to accelerate history. Mao went a large step further. Although he always proclaimed himself a materialist, his lifelong activities were based on the conviction that properly motivated people could overcome virtually any material odds to accomplish their goals. On this basis, for example, during the 1950s he developed advanced socialist forms for governing China even though the country labored under a backward, agriculturally based economy. Also, as we shall see, for a time after 1957 Mao believed that China could "leap" into economic development by the concentrated efforts of its people.

Mao ascribed tremendous power to people's volition and believed that the ability to mobilize people to attack problems in a concerted way virtually equaled the ability to solve those problems, a philosophical position called voluntarism. He became convinced of this wisdom through the remarkable survival, growth, and victory of the CCP.

Much of Mao Zedong Thought, therefore, consists of various approaches to molding the will of the people and bringing that will to bear in support of Mao's goals. These approaches include the mass line; campaigns; struggle; and egalitarianism, or plain living.

Mass Line

Mao Zedong abhorred the Confucian notion that rulers know what to do because of their mastery of the classical doctrine and that therefore the poorly educated masses must simply obey their superiors. This idea produced a passive population and a backward-looking leadership, just the opposite of the activist society and dynamic leadership that Mao believed were critical to the success of the revolution. Mao portrayed himself as more of a populist who believed in the inherent wisdom and power of the people. He also permitted no one to question his belief that he better than anyone understood the hearts of the Chinese peasantry, which represented more than 80 percent of the population.

Especially during the Yan'an era, the CCP developed a leadership doctrine, dubbed the mass line, that incorporated both the vanguard role of the party and a strong participatory role for the populace. The basic idea was that officials in direct contact with the masses should always remain close enough to the people to understand their fundamental desires and concerns. These officials would report their understanding up the hierarchy to provide the leaders a good sense of what people would welcome and implement and what they would not. The top leaders, with their superior understanding of the laws of history and of China's overall conditions, would then reach appropriate decisions that would push forward the revolution in a strong but realistic fashion acceptable to the masses. As the resulting orders for new initiatives were issued, the local officials would try to involve the people in implementing these directives in order to win popular commitment through popular participation. Mao summed up this whole process in the pithy saying, "From the masses, to the masses."

The mass line was a means to alleviate two problematic tendencies of dictatorships: losing touch with popular sentiment and generating political apathy among the people, who come to believe they cannot influence their own leaders. This technique did not compromise the party's dictatorial rule, because it eschewed any notion that the masses could act against the rule of higher-level authorities. But it did call for popular political activity, and it demanded that government bureaucrats keep their ears to the ground and regularly get out among the people.

In practice, the political system that developed after 1949 seriously corroded the mass line. Local officials often shied away from accurately reporting the views of the populace for fear of exposing discontent with their own work. People grew hesitant to voice their real opinions to officials who could wreck their lives with virtually a wave of the hand. The lack of informational resources such as a truly independent press meant that the incentives for skewed reporting at each level of the national bureaucratic hierarchy (work unit, township/commune, county, city, prefecture, province, and national ministry) further degraded the information available to those at the very top. At its worst, such pressures led to utter tragedy, as when the top leaders in 1960–61 overestimated the harvest. They consequently collected far too much grain in taxes—so much, in fact, that nearly 30 million peasants starved to death before the leadership fully realized what was occurring.[4]

Despite these failures of the mass line, the party took the concept seriously as a technique of rule. Chinese bureaucrats were under constant pressure to "go down to the masses" and to "learn from the masses." These efforts sometimes took the form of actual requirements, such as the regulation adopted in 1958 that military officers work one month each year in the ranks as common soldiers. Top leaders, moreover, adopted a practice of making personal inspections of particular locales to hear directly the views of the people.

Each of the highest leaders tended to develop a few places where he regularly tested the waters on policy directions and results. Liu Shaoqi typically went to Tianjin. In 1949, for instance, he met with a wide range of businessmen in that city to examine the party's united-front approach to winning over business confidence. Liu chose Tianjin both because he had fought in the party underground there and because his wife, Wang Guangmei, came from a prominent Tianjin business family.[5] Chen Yun went to his birthplace, Qingpu County near Shanghai. There he sounded out the peasants at the height of the Great Leap Forward to ascertain their real views of this massive effort.[6] The mass line thus helped convince the top leaders that they remained in close touch with the Chinese people, and few accusations against an official in the political hierarchy were as damning as the declaration that she or he had "lost touch with the masses."

By combining dictatorial leadership with mass participation via the mass line, Mao felt he could mobilize the Chinese people to change the country. The mass line, in short, was critical to Mao's voluntaristic notion that through "people power" (in Maoist jargon, the "power of the masses") the huge Chinese population could overcome the daunting obstacles that kept the country poor and weak. The mass-line approach, in turn, utilized specific techniques and issues to whip up a mixture of enthusiasm, commitment, and hysteria among the populace. Here the techniques of campaigns and struggle, and the issue of egalitarianism, became lodged in the PRC's political system.

Campaigns

Campaigns, or *yundong*, were concentrated attacks on specific issues through mass mobilization of the populace. Their broad goals were sociopolitical transformation and economic development. Campaigns of the first sort aimed to change the ways people thought about key issues and social relationships; for example, some mass campaigns, such as the Cultural Revolution of 1966–1976, sought to arouse real feelings of hatred toward those the regime designated as class enemies. The second type of campaign was utilized to change the basic forms of production—for example, to collectivize agriculture or to socialize industry and commerce—and to convince people to make superhuman efforts to improve their economic performance. Often, especially during the 1950s, these two types of effort merged into a single campaign to change the organization of production in an economic sector, inspire hatred toward the former elites in that sector, and generate enthusiasm for the new system and a willingness to work hard to make it succeed. Such was the case, for example, with the Land Reform campaign of 1950–1952, the Agricultural Cooperativization campaign that began in the summer of 1955, and with the Great Leap Forward, which began in 1958. By the 1960s, Mao's campaigns, most notably the Cultural Revolution but also including the Four Cleanups and others, increasingly focused on sociopolitical change and devoted less attention to achieving major increases in production (see Table 3.1).

Over the years, most campaigns conformed to a basic pattern regardless of their goal.[7] This regularity emerged even though the campaign approach was meant to break down normal bureaucratic control over issues so as to attack them head on. Campaigns typically began with mobilization around some broad themes—fighting corruption, promoting agricultural collectivization, ferreting out those with "rightist" thoughts, and so on. At this early stage, people were given documents to study and were organized to undertake this study in a concentrated, high-pressure fashion. Often the newspapers, radio, journals, and officials at every level of the political system whipped up popular fervor, warning darkly (but vaguely) of the enormous dangers to the country's well-being that lurked in society's midst. During this early mobilization phase, people often neglected their jobs and concentrated all their energy on the campaign. In campaigns of sociopolitical change and structural transformation, the economy therefore typically suffered dislocations.

At some point, the national authorities would signal the start of the second stage of a campaign. In their second stage, campaigns became more concrete, zeroing in on specific individuals and groups as targets of the wrath of the campaign. The targets would suffer severely, undergoing "struggle" sessions in which they would be subjected to overwhelming psychological and physical abuse. They were expected to "confess" their transgressions and to beg humbly for the forgiveness of the masses. During this period of fervor, campaigns for organizational changes, such as collectivization of agriculture, would begin to implement them on a trial basis.

In the third stage, campaigns became more clearly coercive, as the targets that emerged during the course of the campaign received formal punishment. In many cases, this punishment took the form of long years in prison at hard labor, although it could also range from public execution to simple admonitions to improve one's thought.

Regardless of their specific objectives—and these varied widely—campaigns

TABLE 3.1 *Major Nationwide Campaigns during the Maoist Era*

YEAR	CAMPAIGN
1950–52	Land Reform
1951	Suppression of Counterrevolutionaries
1951–52	Three Anti Five Anti; Thought Reform of Intellectuals
1955–56	Agricultural Cooperativization Socialist Transformation of Industry and Commerce Anti–Hu Feng Su-Fan (against counterrevolutionaries)
1957	Hundred Flowers Antirightist
1958–61	Great Leap Forward
1963–65	Four Cleanups Second Three Anti
1966–76	Cultural Revolution
1968–69	Shang shan xia xiang (rustication of urban youths)
1973–74	Anti–Lin Biao and Anti-Confucius
1976	Criticize Deng Xiaoping

tended to emphasize an interrelated, distinctive set of priorities. In the "high tide" of almost any campaign, anti-intellectualism, egalitarianism, and voluntarism surged to the fore, as did those cadres who were less well educated but were skillful in political mobilization. Although between campaigns China tended to value technical skills, to utilize material incentives, and to stress the need to plan and address objective problems, during campaigns the country turned sharply in the other direction on each of these issues. These huge policy swings were important. Those individuals who tended to stand out during the consolidation phases between campaigns, for example, often fared very badly during campaign periods; similarly, the less educated who became prominent at the height of a political campaign tended to recede during periods of normal politics. The influence of the campaign cycle on career mobility tended, over time, to create strong vested interests among some cadres in initiating the next campaign and equally strong interests among others in moving the polity away from utilizing political campaigns as a governing technique.

In Mao's thinking, campaigns served several purposes. By periodically taking issues outside the normal bureaucratic routines, they prevented the bureaucracy from becoming too great an obstacle to Mao's more radical goals. Some campaigns, such as the Three Anti in 1951–52 and the Cultural Revolution starting in 1966, specifically targeted party and government cadres. Their use of intense study and of specific social targets helped to "educate" the populace in Maoist values. From his experience in Yan'an, Mao believed passionately that tension and struggle were necessary to motivate people and to defeat his enemies. He launched these disruptive, frightening campaigns as a necessary adjunct to the more regularized party propaganda and coercion. This style of addressing major problems also fitted well with the political capabilities of the peasant cadres who had joined the party during the days of struggle before 1949. They were, like most peasants, uncomfortable with bureaucratic routines and more at home with politics "outdoors."

Mao made the campaign style a prominent feature of Chinese politics— the country experienced at least one major campaign almost every year until his death in 1976. Many of these campaigns proved so traumatic for participants that Chinese interviewed at the time and later tended to date events more by their relation to the major political campaigns ("just after Three Anti Five Anti," "just before the Four Cleanups," and so on) than by calendar years. A question about what someone was doing in mid-1957 might well draw a blank, but asking about the time of the Antirightist campaign (which began in June 1957) would elicit a clear and precise response. Bureaucrats, too, lived in constant fear that another political campaign would begin soon. Mao's extensive use of the campaign technique, developed during the Yan'an era, thus severely affected on the pace, style, and substance of the post-1949 polity. The campaign form epitomized Mao Zedong's core belief that he could motivate people sufficiently to accomplish almost any goal he set for them.

Struggle

Mao scorned the Confucian ideal of harmony as an absolute social value. Confucius, writing at a time of social and political turbulence, taught that a hierarchical society could maintain stability if every person knew and accepted the rights and obligations attached to his or her place in society. To Mao, this notion ensured that China would be dominated by backward-looking elites whose misguided rule would keep the country from surging to the forefront of the world stage in the twentieth century.

Mao did not totally eschew harmony and the gentle persuasion and mediation necessary to achieve it. He did, however, also believe in the absolute value of tension and of a qualitatively more severe phenomenon, struggle— that is, of direct confrontation that broke previous rules through outrages and violence. Struggle, he felt, built courage and character in a people who, Mao believed, were by inclination and culture too passive and accepting. Through struggle, the Chinese could realize their potential to seize control over their fate. Time and again Mao created situations in which his subjects would have to engage in personal struggle, perhaps even at the risk of their lives. Whereas most political leaders around the globe have tried to ensure their people peaceful lives, Mao constantly stirred up the social pot as a calculated part of his rule. Struggle became the linchpin of Mao's voluntarism.

Struggle (*douzheng*) consisted broadly of a politically motivated, direct act against another person in massive violation of social conventions. It often entailed bringing down someone who formerly had high prestige and authority. Struggle was not an impersonal administrative process; it was highly personal, direct, violent, and public. Students, for example, who "struggled" against their teachers would face the teachers in front of a school assembly and denounce them, accuse them of specific "crimes," declare that they were no longer hoodwinked by their former mentors, and "draw a clear line" between themselves and their teachers by calling for harsh punishment for the latter. They might also physically slap or beat their teachers, humiliate them by hanging disparaging signs around their necks, torture them by locking them in dank closets for months at a time, and so forth.

The whole object of struggle was to smash prevailing social inhibitions in such a dramatic and traumatic way that the participants (both the activists and the targets) could never again reestablish their prestruggle relationship. Mao made struggle part of a permanent system in which some people became recurring victims, hauled out for new abuse every time the regime wanted to stir up the masses again. Such hapless individuals typically were those given "bad class labels," that is, those designated as members of a pariah class such as capitalists, landlords, or rich peasants.

Mao utilized struggle in part to give Chinese a sense of empowerment so that they could be mobilized to scale the ramparts of revolutionary change and economic development. But he also made this tool a key weapon in combatting the deeply embedded Confucian notion that social identity should be based on an individual's web of social relationships. Mao spent his life fighting to change the type of society that the Confucian legacy had produced, a society in which individuals in different networks found it virtually impossible to work together. This required, Mao felt, welding together large numbers of individuals into broad social groups with which they could identify, groups such as workers, poor peasants, and so forth.

Struggle contributed to this change of social identity. The purpose of struggle was to create major social and political fault lines between people who typically belonged to the same web of social relationships. Thus, for example, during the land reform of 1950–52 many peasants found themselves struggling against landlords who were also their relatives. The struggle itself, through violence and through violation of other social taboos, weakened the old social network and, Mao hoped, began to create a new social identity in the minds of the participants.

Struggle sessions usually were violent. Over the twenty-seven years that Mao ruled the PRC millions of people died as a direct result of political struggle. Tens of millions of other citizens were tortured, incarcerated, and deeply wounded. Very often, moreover, the close relatives of a "struggle target" would also come under fire unless they "drew a clear line" between themselves and the victim: wives, for example, were expected to divorce their "reactionary" husbands and children to denounce and beat their "backward" parents. Mao did not regard violence and death as experiences to avoid; rather, his own revolutionary experience had taught him that he could vanquish his enemies and that China could move forward only on the basis of violence, that the revolution needed a vanguard and a hard leading edge. People learned about life through risk and violence, Mao believed, and he did not hesitate to whip up storms of intolerance to destroy those he opposed and to instill in his subjects the priorities he held dear.

Egalitarianism

One of the most enduring substantive themes of Mao's political program was the virtue of egalitarianism, which to Mao meant primarily frugal living. In a desperately poor country such as China, where there was no practical way to raise most people's standard of living, this meant leveling average incomes down to those of the poorer strata. Mao often extolled the virtues of poverty and simplicity. He believed the poor were inherently more willing to build a new society because they had so few vested interests in the old. He constantly exhorted his fellow communists to live simply, both because that would reduce the distance between them and the masses and because he felt that poverty itself created a more virtuous person.

In a country of China's size and variety, there is no way to equalize the standard of living in different areas; soil quality, amount of rainfall, state of the infrastructure, access to transport, educational levels, and so forth varied so widely that major differentials in living standards were unavoidable. In this situation, Mao aimed to develop a society in which such regional inequalities would be offset by powerful measures to spread egalitarianism within the immediate social environment of each individual. Thus, measures to promote income leveling and prohibit conspicuous consumption kept economic stratification minimal within given villages or work units. Measures associated with the mass line, such as encouraging workunit leaders to discuss some issues extensively with employees, were aimed at decreasing the psychological distance between leaders and led throughout the country, even in the context of highly stratified political power.

Although Mao himself enjoyed the perquisites of rule, he nevertheless reacted at the gut level against others' extravagance and attachment to physical comfort. Egalitarianism was, Mao felt, essential to the effective implementation of the mass line—and therefore to his entire vision for changing China. Without egalitarianism he could not fully mobilize the populace, and without mobilization Mao's voluntaristic approach to political change and economic development would fail. Even though Mao lived well himself, therefore, his commitment to egalitarianism greatly affected the lives of his officials and subjects alike.

ANTI-INTELLECTUALISM

Mao Zedong was only marginally an intellectual in the China of the 1910s and 1920s. He had obtained a solid education in both classical and "modern" learning, but he had not achieved high intellectual standing. He worked for a while in the library of Beijing University, where he gained access to the leading currents of political thought in the country, but he was not on the level of a student or a professor at this renowned institution. Throughout his life, Mao would engage in some of the practices of traditional intellectuals: he wrote poetry, published his calligraphy, and criticized the writing of his colleagues.

He constantly cited ancient history and philosophy as well as more contemporary domestic and foreign thinking in his speeches and texts. Yet throughout his life he detested the Chinese intelligentsia, which included doctors, scientists, engineers, and journalists, as well as scholars and creative writers.[8]

To Mao, intellectuals embodied the traditional ways of China. Their knowledge linked them to past values and practices. More fundamentally, though, Mao disdained intellectuals as people who studied books and then put on airs about their supposedly superior knowledge. They thus violated three of the cardinal sins in Mao's political universe: they did not dirty their hands by going out among the people to learn about real conditions; they were nay-sayers who constantly pointed to technical constraints on actions that Mao innately felt the masses could accomplish if properly motivated; and they reinforced social inequality by their air of superiority.

Mao also was well aware of the intellectuals' role in imperial China of protecting the moral code of society against the vagaries of powerful emperors even as they served those emperors. Mao would not tolerate even this small deviation from loyalty in his polity.[9]

Mao's dislike of intellectuals deeply affected the Chinese polity. Intellectuals early on became key targets of struggle sessions. During mass campaigns, they were forced to engage in manual labor and suffered myriad other humiliations. Their ideas often were disparaged. As early as May 1958, Mao boasted that he had far outdone the first emperor of the Qin dynasty in his policy against intellectuals: "He buried only 460 scholars alive; we have buried forty-six thousand scholars alive. . . . You [intellectuals] revile us for being Qin Shi Huangs. You are wrong. We have surpassed Qin Shi Huang a hundredfold."[10]

Mao's anti-intellectualism clashed directly with the Soviet model the Chinese imported. That model stressed full utilization of technical expertise while maintaining tight reins on the artistic and creative intelligentsia. During the First Five-Year Plan (1953–57), which was developed and implemented with substantial Soviet support, the Chinese stressed technical expertise in very much the Soviet manner. But in the wake of the Antirightist campaign at the end of that plan period, the virulent anti-intellectualism of the Great Leap Forward (1958–61), and the murderous repression of intellectuals at the time of the Cultural Revolution (1966–76) virtually eliminated highly trained specialists from most significant decision making outside of key military projects.

Mao's anti-intellectualism extended to his views on science. He often insisted on "scientific" inquiry, and typically proclaimed that party pronouncements had a "scientific" soundness to them, but there is little indication that he understood the critical inquiry that is central to the scientific method. Mao viewed science as selective empiricism; that is, he believed strongly in trying an idea out in one or a few cases and in summing up the results of those efforts. He regarded that summation and the lessons drawn as "scientific" because they had been "tested" in "practice." This, Mao thought, was preferable to the science espoused by intellectuals, which he believed derived from intellectual gymnastics. Constant use of the scientific method to question the validity of earlier findings was totally alien to Mao's idea of science. To him, "science" confirmed rather than questioned; he felt most intellectuals used methods that failed to establish "scientific" validity, and he allowed no one to challenge this notion.

In his anti-intellectualism Mao found himself in tune with the party's large peasant cadre. To many of these peasants, intellectuals represented the elitist, urban-based culture against which they had fought the revolution. They were not about to allow these same urban elites to steal the fruits of victory by claiming that the country could develop rapidly only with intellectuals in positions of power and prominence. United-front rhetoric often proclaimed the communists' commitment to good relations with the intellectuals under the slogan, first articulated in 1956 and made the basis for a 1957 political campaign, of "letting a hundred flowers bloom and a hundred schools of thought contend." Nevertheless, intellectuals were despised by both Mao and the peasant ranks of the CCP, and were made to suffer a great deal of hardship as a result.

Repression of intellectuals cost the country dearly in developmental progress. All governments make mistakes in public policy, but few suffer missteps of the magnitude that afflicted China due to its repression of intellectuals. The consequent economic losses and human tragedies assumed a scale that is difficult to comprehend. These disasters stemmed directly from the influence of Mao Zedong Thought.

CONTRADICTIONS AND THE UNITED FRONT

Mao viewed the world as a complex of forces in tension and conflict, with some conflicts being more important than others. An effective leader understood the conflicts underlying events—"contradictions" in Maoist terminology—and adopted a strategy to play off these conflicts. Identifying and addressing the essential conflict at hand was critical to development of an effective strategy.

Mao repeatedly asserted that all efforts should be devoted to identifying and resolving the major contradiction of an existing situation on terms favorable to the communist cause. As soon as that contradiction had been resolved, attention should be turned to identifying the new conflict at the core of the new alignment of forces. Addressing each major contradiction, Mao mobilized all the forces he could muster. Secondary contradictions, he felt, deserve analysis and some attention, but the key always lies in understanding and dealing effectively with the major contradiction.

It was this viewpoint, along with Soviet advice, that led Mao at the time of the Xi'an incident in 1936 to adopt the surprising policy of sparing Chiang Kai-shek's life and allying with the Guomindang to fight the Japanese. The GMD had been responsible for untold suffering to the communist cause as a whole, and Mao had lost his second wife to a Guomindang executioner. He certainly had more than ample reason to distrust Chiang personally. Yet, at the end of 1936 both he and Moscow saw the contradiction between Japanese imperialism and China's interests as more important than that between the CCP and the GMD. He therefore subordinated the latter to the former. With the defeat of Japan in 1945, the underlying CCP/GMD contradiction again became primary, and Mao shifted tactics accordingly, this time against Moscow's desires.

Viewing politics and life as a perpetual series of struggles, Mao always focused on what divided people and groups from each other so that he could play off those divisions to achieve his ends. He saw the world as endlessly changing; he could never rest on his laurels. Mao's notion of conflict and struggle, fundamentally at odds with China's Confucian heritage, in fact pervaded every aspect of his political and social thinking. Mao could never be satisfied with the status quo—in this sense, he was a true revolutionary.

The theory of contradictions led Mao to develop a mature set of strategies for marshaling forces to prevail in key conflicts. These strategies were collectively known as united-front work, and in post-1949 China the CCP actually set up a United Front Work Department under the party's Central Committee. The basic idea was a simple one: the communists, themselves always a minority of the population, would have to gain support of many noncommunists to achieve their goals. Having analyzed the key contradiction and the secondary contradictions, therefore, the communists would have to devise a program that the vast majority of people could support to move things toward the desired outcome. This required understanding the attitudes of broad target groups, which in turn depended on the mass line. It also required the CCP to cloak its real objectives behind rhetoric designed to win the active support of people outside the movement.[11]

For example, when the Japanese threat posed the key challenge, the CCP, as noted previously, adopted united-front policies that stressed anti-Japanese nationalism and provided for inclusion even of landlords so long as they acted in a patriotic fashion.[12] After the Japanese surrender and the emergence of the GMD/CCP conflict as the key contradiction, the communists launched a land-reform campaign that targeted all landlords as class enemies and dealt brutally with them.[13] Though Westerners might view this change as inconsistent and cynical, Mao and his colleagues would view it as natural and necessary. Policy and political commitments were always contingent on the identity of the key contradiction the movement faced.

At all times, therefore, the CCP has pursued a united-front strategy, though the partners in that cooperation and the issues that sustain it have changed greatly over the years. There was a strong philosophical basis in Mao Zedong Thought for this flexibility, but over decades of CCP rule it produced bitterness and cynicism among many in China who found themselves at some point suddenly outside the united front and a target of its often brutal tactics.

CLASSES AND CLASS STRUGGLE

Mao Zedong drew his notion of contradictions partly from Marxist dialectics but also from traditional Chinese philosophy. His ideas concerning classes seem to have originated more clearly in his exposure to Marxism-Leninism, although here too he gave the concept a distinctive Chinese twist.

Marx wrote that society could be analyzed according to the way various groups, or "classes," fit into the production process, given the dominant mode of production (such as feudalism or capitalism) of the period. The motive forces for historical development were the clashes among the major classes brought on by contradictions in the production process. Lenin added a practical political dimension to the Marxist doctrine of class conflict primarily by developing the proletarian party into a disciplined tool for revolutionary struggle.

It is hard to imagine a society less subject to class analysis than was China of the 1910s and 1920s. Capitalism had barely penetrated the country, and feudalism in its traditional European form had long since ceased to exist. Among the key players were regional warlords who had no place in the Marxist analytical scheme. Even Chiang Kai-shek seems to have acted primarily for himself and the GMD rather than in the interests of any of the classes in China at the time.[14] Members of China's urban proletariat were, in most cases, the first generation off the farm and retained strong personal ties to the countryside. In the rural villages, strong ties of kinship cut across supposed class divisions, and clan associations managed the village rituals. With the Chinese understanding of social relationships stressing hierarchical webs of personal ties, class definitions based on relations to the means of production must have struck many Chinese as extraordinarily artificial.

But Marxism-Leninism did make sense to some intellectuals because it provided an explanation for imperialist aggression, and it also explained in "scientific" fashion how China could weaken the imperialist system and become a leading country in the international arena. The prescribed means of making this happen was struggle, which fitted well with Mao's predispositions based on a class analysis of history and China's predicament.

Mao initially embraced class analysis based on people's relations to the means of production; in the countryside the basic productive resource was land. In the urban areas, he not only made a traditional class analysis (identifying, for example, the proletarians and the bourgeoisie), but he also divided the bourgeoisie into those whose interests were harmed by imperialism (the national bourgeoisie) and those whose relationship to imperialism was either more ambivalent (the petit bourgeoisie) or totally supportive (the comprador bourgeoisie).

Some less orthodox aspects of Mao's class analysis in this early period may have been affected by a peculiarity of the Chinese translation for the term "proletariat." Whereas Marx's original use of that term had a distinctly urban meaning, the Chinese translation, *wuchan jieji,* means "the class without property." This difference may have made it easier for Mao to consider himself an orthodox communist in the 1920s while still touting the superior revolutionary virtue of poor peasants—that is, of the rural "class without property."

Although translation problems conceivably facilitated Mao's unorthodox interpretations of Marxist class concepts in his early years, by the late 1950s he was using the notion of class analysis in ways that bore little resemblance to the initial Marxist conceptions. The results left a deep imprint on the politics and society of the PRC.

From 1950 to 1952, the period immediately after their victory over the GMD, the communists undertook a series of mass political campaigns (Land Reform, Suppression of Counterrevolutionaries, Thought Reform of Intellectuals, Three Anti Five Anti) in which they determined the class status of each urban and rural inhabitant. These campaigns were the prelude to the collectivization of agriculture and state takeover of the urban economy, both of which were complete by 1956. With private property eliminated, the issue of class identity became potentially murky and confused.

Mao addressed this problem in an un-Marxist fashion. He decided that political attitude (rather than relations to the means of production) could determine class status. For example, during the Antirightist campaign in 1957 he labeled hundreds of thousands of intellectuals as "rightists" based on their behavior during the Hundred Flowers campaign, a label that they retained in most cases until 1979. Mao also held that if political attitude did not change it, class status would be hereditary. Most Chinese who were too young to have received a class status in the early 1950s would inherit their status from their parents, and it would be passed from generation to generation, regardless of wealth or position. This approach created permanent pariah groups—those people who had received a bad class status (landlord, rich peasant, capitalist, and so on) in the early 1950s, and their descendants.

In addition, the targets of major political campaigns received negative political labels that acquired the quality and hereditary nature of class status. Those targeted during the campaign to suppress counterrevolutionaries in 1951, for example, were thereafter labeled as counterrevolutionaries, which damned both them and their offspring from that point on.

Even though "class" almost completely lost its Marxist meaning in CCP usage, the ideas of class and class struggle remained central to Mao Zedong Thought and the politics of the PRC. In his unique fashion, Mao always viewed enemies and friends in class terms, and he saw society as the battleground for unceasing class struggle. At times when that underlying conflict was not terribly obvious to his colleagues, Mao admonished them, "Never forget class struggle."

Class analysis formed the basis of Mao's theory of struggle, contradictions, the united front, and even mass political campaigns. One result of Mao's ideas on class was the emergence in the PRC of a society based on castes—that is, social orders with permanent, hereditary status that sharply contoured one's life experiences and prospects. Few Chinese considered allowing their children to marry someone of bad class background, since that person was always vulnerable to political attack and personal destruction. The bad classes became permanent enemies in a society that defined progress as requiring unremitting struggle against adversaries. A large portion of the country's creative intellectuals, capable business people, and efficient farmers, moreover, fell under this miasma of permanent class oppression. Eventually, class struggle even consumed the political elite, as Mao during the Cultural Revolution turned on many of his party colleagues and branded them "representatives of the capitalist class."

SELF-RELIANCE

Self-reliance (*zili gengsheng*), another major theme in Mao Zedong Thought, did not mean that the CCP or the PRC should rely only on their own efforts. Rather, the basic thrust of self-reliance is more accurately captured in another of Mao's admonitions—that one should "keep the initiative in one's own hands."

Mao applied the concept of self-reliance to China as a whole except for the period of maximum Chinese dependence on the USSR, from 1949 until the Great Leap Forward beginning in 1958. China gained enormous benefits from its close relationship with the Soviet Union before 1958. But the increasingly bitter Sino-Soviet estrangement after that year led to a sudden withdrawal of Soviet aid in the summer of 1960. This Soviet turnabout contributed significantly to the dire economic consequences of the Great Leap Forward.

In reaction against what he considered Soviet perfidy and the costs it imposed on China, Mao insisted that in the future China follow a strategy of national self-reliance. In its subsequent foreign-policy dealings, the PRC under Mao went to significant trouble to minimize its dependence on any single foreign country. The PRC, for example, obtained supplies of a given commodity from multiple sources whenever possible, even when this raised prices and greatly complicated internal logistics.

In the domestic economy, Mao also viewed self-reliance as a virtue outside the core economic sectors, such as mining, metallurgy, and railways, where the state exercised tight administrative control through national planning. Especially after 1958, Mao encouraged each section of the country to become self-reliant, and in subsequent years he strengthened government policies in support of this goal. This not only required that each part of the country develop an appropriate array of small-scale industries; it also demanded that every part of China try to grow enough grain to be self-supporting. Given China's varied topography and climatic conditions, this latter policy imposed enormous costs by requiring grain production in areas totally unsuited for it.

Mao's commitment to self-reliance was in part ideological, growing out of his success with this policy during the Yan'an era. In his mind, self-reliance was bound together with such other desirable goals as simple and frugal living, struggling to overcome objective difficulties, gaining confidence through determined efforts, and group effort through common commitment.

Practical and strategic considerations also played into Mao's concern with self-reliance. He felt, for example, that China could best withstand an attack from either the United States or the Soviet Union by retreating into the interior and then wearing down the enemy by launching attacks from secure base areas. This would require that interior areas be able to support both themselves and a war effort without close ties to the coast or to foreign trade. In addition, China's continental size, combined with its poor transportation facilities, weighed against extensive trade among macroregions, making some effort to promote the self-reliance of various areas a necessity.

The notion of self-reliance, therefore, had both normative and practical components. Some analysts have mistakenly construed this term to mean "total independence." The real test of self-reliance, however, was whether a community could sustain itself even in adverse circumstances. The ability to "keep the initiative in your own hands" proved to be a major force in Mao's thinking, and over the years many policies in both domestic and foreign affairs bore the imprint of the high value he attached to *zili gengsheng*.

The Governing System

Mao's ideas took effect by means of a massive political administrative apparatus set up after 1949 to govern the country. Here we will merely introduce the names and basic organization of this administrative system. Chapters 6 and 7 provide far greater detail on these structures and their development over time.[15]

The formal Maoist administrative system borrowed heavily from that of the Soviet Union, although it also drew inspiration from China's imperial past, the GMD, and the base-area experiences. China's formal alliance with the Soviet Union was forced by the Cold War tensions of 1949, which allowed no room for a neutral stance between the two postwar superpowers; in addition, China's ideological perspective was naturally more sympathetic to that of the Soviets. The Soviet Union had devised the means to use state controls to produce an industrial base rapidly, and the Chinese were anxious to learn how to do this themselves. Stalin, for his part, strongly urged his allies to follow the Soviet model of rule as closely as possible.

Like the Soviets, the Chinese set up parallel national party and government (or state) administrative apparatuses. Thus, at each level of the political system in China—the Center (Beijing), the province, the prefecture, the city, the county, and the locale (township or commune)—there is a full array of party and state organs, with the party in addition having committees, branches, and cells embedded within the state organs. In principle, the party is to make policy and the state is to administer it, but, as we shall see, reality has not been that neat.

With their deep attachments to the military, in which they had all spent decades of their lives before 1949, the CCP leaders set up the military as a third nationwide bureaucracy. On the eve of their victory in 1949, the CCP had pulled all its scattered military forces together and organized them into the People's Liberation Army (PLA), encompassing the army, navy, and air force. The military hierarchy does not completely parallel its civilian counterparts, although the three intersect at key points: most military districts, for example, are coterminous with provinces. To China's top leaders, the PLA has been a major instrument for achieving both international security and domestic policy goals.

The PLA is thus a core component of the Chinese communist system. It has been, moreover, purposely kept beyond the government's jurisdiction. The PLA is assigned a bureaucratic rank equal to that of the State Council, the government's highest level of authority. This means that the government cannot issue binding orders to the military. Rather, the military answers directly to a party body called the Military Affairs Commission, which Mao Zedong personally chaired until his death in 1976 (though it is the vice chairman of the commission who is in charge on a day-to-day basis). This unusual arrangement reflects the fact that the military's first job is to protect the party rather than the government. The party can utilize the military just as for other purposes it might utilize the government apparatus.

China's military operates as a state within the state. At all times in Maoist China, a large percentage of the party's central leadership was military officers. There were complex and subtle connections among the government, party, and military at various levels of the system. Strong personal and career ties bound the military leaders to civilian officials who had previously served with them in communist army units before 1949. In many cases, groups of individuals had fought side by side for one or two decades, and these bonds became an important thread in the tapestry of post-1949 politics. At the end of the civil war these groups controlled various parts of the country, which added a territorial dimension to the situation.

The Chinese communists designed their system with several major goals: to be centralized enough to give the top leaders in Beijing leverage to determine the national domestic agenda; to promote and manage rapid industrial development, in part by obtaining resources from the rural sector; and to bring about guided social change.

At each administrative level (Center, province, and so on) a small party committee exercises ultimate power. At the Center, this body, typically having fourteen to twenty-four members, is called the Politburo, and it has a staff under it called the Secretariat. Mao Zedong served as chairman of the Chinese Communist party, and by virtue of this position he headed the Politburo. The Standing Committee of the Politburo, usually consisting of five or six people, contains the most powerful leaders in the country.[16] Generally, each person in the Politburo also holds at least one other substantive position and has special responsibility in one or another field, such as propaganda and education or finance and economics.

The Communist party also established a Central Committee, which had nearly one hundred members until 1966, closer to two hundred members through the 1970s, and nearly three hundred members since the 1980s. During the Maoist era, this body held little real power. Membership included those holding some other position of great importance—the head of a province, for example—and those serving some representative function, such as being a model peasant or model worker. Full meetings of the Central Committee are called plenums and are numbered sequentially following each Party Congress, the party organ charged with, among other things, formally electing the Central Committee membership. (In reality, these elections are ratifications of decisions already made by the Politburo.) The Party Congress, which has had as many as fifteen hundred delegates, convenes infrequently; in the Maoist era there were congresses in 1956, 1969, and 1973 (respectively, the Eighth, Ninth, and Tenth Congresses in the history of the CCP). A Central Committee plenum might, therefore, be called the "tenth plenum of the Eighth Central Committee," meaning the tenth time the Central Committee selected by the Eighth Party Congress convened (see Table 3.2).

Although the Central Committee as a body has no real power, party departments, called Central Committee departments, exercise a great deal of power. These have various responsibilities, and have included the Rural Work Department, the Propaganda Department, and the Organization Department (in charge of staff appointments), among others.

The top government body is the State Council, established in 1954 to replace the transitional Government Administrative Council, which had existed since 1949. The State Council is headed by the premier (in the Maoist era, this was Zhou Enlai); a number of vice premiers have specific fields of responsibility. The State Council includes commissions and ministries. Commissions generally take charge of major issues that concern a number of ministries. These commissions have included, for example, the State Planning Commission, in charge of long-term and annual plans; and the State Economic Commission, in charge of resolving interministerial problems that cropped up in plan implementation.

Until the late 1990s a large portion of the ministries worked primarily on developing and running the urban economy, while the rural sector was run more directly by the party bureaucracy. For example, until 1998 separate ministries had charge of the metallurgical industry, the electronics industry, the transportation industry, and water resources (primarily, flood-control and irrigation projects). Over the years, the ministries have been merged and split apart by dozens of organizational changes meant to improve effectiveness as the economy and problems of administration changed, and the total number of ministries has ranged from several dozen to more than sixty.

This basic organizational structure, on both the party and the government sides, is largely duplicated at every level of the national administrative system. The terminology changes somewhat as one goes down the administrative hierarchy, but the overall organizational charts of all the territorial layers remain quite similar. The leading party bodies below the Center are called committees—the Politburo at the Center becomes the Provincial Party Committee in the province, followed by the Municipal Party Committee, and so forth. The government bodies are called, simply, governments (provincial government, municipal government, and so on). The party penetrates the government at every level through a variety of means, including having party bodies (committees, branches, and/or cells) in every government organ.

In addition, virtually every ministry, commission, and Central Committee department heads its own national bureaucratic hierarchy that extends from Beijing down through the provinces, cities, counties, and so forth. In some instances, these individual bureaucratic empires have been highly centralized, while in other cases the lower level units are made answerable primarily to the local territorial party and government leadership. The distribution of lines of authority has changed often, and each has produced its own peculiar prob-

TABLE 3.2 *Chinese Communist Party Congresses and Central Committee Plenums, 1949–2003*

DATE	EVENT
5–13 Mar. 1949	2nd plenum of 7th CC CCP
6–10 June 1950	3rd (enlarged) plenum of 7th CC CCP
6–10 Feb. 1954	4th (enlarged) plenum of 7th CC CCP
4 Apr. 1955	5th plenum of 7th CC CCP
4–11 Oct. 1955	6th (enlarged) plenum of 7th CC CCP
22 Aug., 8 and 13 Sept. 1956	7th plenum of 7th CC CCP
15–27 Sept. 1956	*8th Nat'l. Congress of the CCP*
28 Sept. 1956	1st plenum of 8th CC CCP
10–15 Nov. 1956	2nd plenum of 8th CC CCP
20 Sept.–9 Oct. 1957	3rd (enlarged) plenum of 8th CC CCP
3 May 1958	4th plenum of 8th CC CCP
5–23 May 1958	*2nd session, 8th Nat'l. Congress of the CCP*
25 May 1958	5th plenum of 8th CC CCP
28 Nov.–10 Dec. 1958	6th (enlarged) plenum of 8th CC CCP
2–5 Apr. 1959	7th (enlarged) plenum of 8th CC CCP
2–16 Aug. 1959	8th (enlarged) plenum of 8th CC CCP
14–18 Jan. 1961	9th (enlarged) plenum of 8th CC CCP
24–27 Sept. 1962	10th (enlarged) plenum of 8th CC CCP
1–12 Aug. 1966	11th (enlarged) plenum of 8th CC CCP
13–31 Oct. 1968	12th (enlarged) plenum of 8th CC CCP
1–24 Apr. 1969	*9th Nat'l. Congress of the CCP*
28 Apr. 1969	1st plenum of 9th CC CCP
23 Aug.–6 Sept. 1970	2nd plenum of 9th CC CCP
1972	3rd plenum of 9th CC CCP
24–28 Aug. 1973	*10th Nat'l. Congress of the CCP*
30 Aug. 1973	1st plenum of 10th CC CCP
8–10 Jan. 1975	2nd plenum of 10th CC CCP
16–21 July 1977	3rd plenum of 10th CC CCP
12–18 Aug. 1977	*11th Nat'l. Congress of the CCP*
19 Aug. 1977	1st plenum of 11th CC CCP
18–23 Feb. 1978	2nd plenum of 11th CC CCP
18–22 Dec. 1978	3rd plenum of 11th CC CCP
25–28 Sept. 1979	4th plenum of 11th CC CCP
23–29 Feb. 1980	5th plenum of 11th CC CCP
27–29 June 1981	6th plenum of 11th CC CCP
6 Aug. 1982	7th plenum of 11th CC CCP
1–11 Sept. 1982	*12th Nat'l. Congress of the CCP*
12–13 Sept. 1982	1st plenum of 12th CC CCP

TABLE 3.2 *(continued)*

DATE	EVENT
11–12 Oct. 1983	2nd plenum of 12th CC CCP
20 Oct. 1984	3rd plenum of 12th CC CCP
16 Sept. 1985	4th plenum of 12th CC CCP
24 Sept. 1985	5th plenum of 12th CC CCP
29 Sept. 1986	6th plenum of 12th CC CCP
25 Oct.–1 Nov. 1987	*13th Nat'l. Congress of the CCP*
2 Nov. 1987	1st plenum of 13th CC CCP
15–19 Mar. 1988	2nd plenum of 13th CC CCP
26–30 Sept. 1988	3rd plenum of 13th CC CCP
23–24 June 1989	4th plenum of 13th CC CCP
6–9 Nov. 1989	5th plenum of 13th CC CCP
9–12 Mar. 1990	6th plenum of 13th CC CCP
25–30 Dec. 1990	7th plenum of 13th CC CCP
25–29 Nov. 1991	8th plenum of 13th CC CCP
5–9 Oct. 1992	9th plenum of 13th CC CCP
12–18 Oct. 1992	*14th Nat'l. Congress of the CCP*
19 Oct. 1992	1st plenum of 14th CC CCP
5–7 Mar. 1993	2nd plenum of 14th CC CCP
11–14 Nov. 1993	3rd plenum of 14th CC CCP
25–28 Sept. 1994	4th plenum of 14th CC CCP
25–28 Sept.1995	5th plenum of 14th CC CCP
7–10 Oct.1996	6th plenum of 14th CC CCP
6–9 Sept. 1997	7th plenum of 14th CC CCP
12–18 Sept. 1997	*15th Nat'l. Congress of the CCP*
19 Sept. 1997	1st plenum of 15th CC CCP
25–26 Feb. 1998	2nd plenum of 15th CC CCP
12–14 Oct. 1998	3rd plenum of 15th CC CCP
19–22 Sept. 1999	4th plenum of 15th CC CCP
9–11 Oct. 2000	5th plenum of 15th CC CCP
24–26 Sept. 2001	6th plenum of 15th CC CCP
3–5 Nov. 2002	7th plenum of 15th CC CCP
8–14 Nov. 2002	*16th Nat'l. Congress of the CCP*
5 Nov. 2002	1st plenum of 16th CC CCP
24–26 Feb. 2003	2nd Plenum of 16th CC CCP

lems. The trend under the post-Mao reforms has been overwhelmingly in the direction of increasing the power of territorial party and government leaders and moving power away from Beijing.

This complex structure reflected the communists' determination during the 1950s to control all developments in the country from above—party and government units were created to take charge of every type of activity imaginable. Copied from the Soviet system, the governing structure was designed to enable the state to channel resources directly and overwhelmingly to heavy industrial development. The State Planning Commission, along with other bodies, developed plans to be implemented by administrative means rather than influenced by the play of economic forces. This involved direct government management of the economy in all its main features and determined government actions to force resources into heavy industrial development.

This system increasingly employed both ideological indoctrination and naked force to whip the population into line. Indeed, Maoist techniques such as political campaigns and mass struggle often obscured the distinction between indoctrination and terror. Mao excelled at creating a system in which he was able to set Chinese against Chinese to assure the security and promote the goals of the party leadership. An extensive system of forced-labor camps awaited millions who fell afoul of the official line.[17]

Although this overall approach to political organization was established during the 1950s, the same structures endured into the the decades after Mao's death, albeit with many changes in the dynamics of their operations designed to encourage significant initiative in various localities. This system has afforded the political leadership unchallenged control over the society and economy, but it has also produced numerous problems of governance.

First, the structure of the system itself has proved complex and unwieldy. By the mid-1950s, the governing apparatus of the PRC was probably the largest vertically integrated set of bureaucracies in the history of the world. The details of the reporting lines, moreover, gives the system the characteristics of a fragmented authoritarianism: authoritarian in the discipline demanded from subordinates and the lack of real protections for the people or opportunity for them to articulate their interests; and fragmented in that territorial and functional lines of command intersected in hopelessly complex ways.

Mao Zedong regarded this system as endlessly frustrating. In part, Mao simply found abhorrent the tendency he saw in Chinese bureaucrats to put on airs, to concern themselves with privilege, and to become petty tyrants. In part, too, he chafed at the ability of the governing bureaucracies to frustrate his policies.

To overcome the natural reluctance of bureaucrats to implement revolutionary programs and to reduce the tendency toward fragmented authority, Mao made major efforts to indoctrinate officials to his own way of thinking. To him, ideology was a major means to bind this system together. In addition, although Mao refused to set up a highly centralized, bureaucratically independent terror apparatus like the one that Stalin had created in the mid-1930s, he nevertheless used powerful weapons such as "struggle" and "special case groups" reminiscent of the Yan'an-era Rectification to assure that officials would comply with his wishes.

Ultimately, though, Mao Zedong never fully resolved the tensions between his impulses toward revolutionary change and the economic need for predictability and reasonably stable administration. His frustrations over this conflict led him in his later years to take initiatives, such as launching the

Great Proletarian Cultural Revolution in 1966, that severely damaged the country. Only in the post-Mao era, under Deng Xiaoping, did China finally move fully from revolutionary upheaval to straightforward governance. But even during the Deng and post-Deng eras the tensions involved in reforming an authoritarian bureaucratic state have persisted.

4

The Maoist Era

Mao personally and Mao Zedong Thought as an ideology had such a huge impact on China after the revolution that it is appropriate to consider the period from 1949 until Mao's death on 9 September 1976 as the era of Mao Zedong. Mao's unique role in the Chinese political system meant, effectively, that his own ideas profoundly shaped the politics of the PRC.

Mao's stature by the time of victory in 1949 was without equal or challenge. He had led the party from the miserable days of the Long March retreat to victory over both Japan and the Guomindang in a period of fourteen years. Time and again, the broad strategic assessments he made had proved accurate, and his basic tactics had turned out to be effective. He had become the source of ultimate wisdom at the vortex of the greatest revolution in human history. His judgments in the years after 1949 could be discussed to the extent he permitted, but even his most powerful ministers could not oppose them successfully.

Mao's prestige within the movement was such in the early 1950s that one foreign scholar has conceptualized the policy making of the period as an example of the bandwagon effect.[1] That is, other leaders would always try to sense the direction in which Mao was leaning on a particular issue so as to jump on the Maoist bandwagon at the earliest moment possible. The few instances of serious policy disagreements and purges resulted, it appears, from one or another player either misreading Mao's intentions or being purposely misled by the Chairman.[2]

Even Mao's key political position—chairman of the CCP—was unique. No other ruling communist party had a chairman above the general secretary (i.e., the chief administrative officer) of the party. In China, the chairman's role was not defined. He was the person to keep the party on the right track and to make broad strategic judgments. As with the emperor in the imperial state, no legal or administrative boundaries limited the power and responsibility of this position. In addition to holding this crucial post, Mao also assumed the leadership of the military (by heading the CCP's Military Affairs Commission) and the symbolic leadership of the state (as president of the PRC until he resigned from this government post in 1959).

Mao used his power to find a path to rapid industrial development, but did so in a fashion that produced massive human tragedies and diminishing returns on the investment he squeezed from the Chinese populace. He modeled the Chinese system on Soviet practice because Stalin had achieved rapid growth of heavy industry in a poor, basically rural country. He then launched the country into first the Great Leap Forward, starting in 1958, and then the Great Proletarian Cultural Revolution, beginning in 1966. These frenzied, indeed utopian, efforts at economic, social, and political transformation were entirely delusional and left millions of dead in their wakes.

Mao could stray so far from reality in part because his power drew deeply from the widely accepted tradition of relying on a good leader to produce results, rather than monitoring performance, restricting prerogatives, and limiting tenure. Revolutions in any case tend to put forward charismatic leaders whose power cannot be reined in. Mao Zedong had built his success before 1949 on his ability to investigate possibilities, consult widely, understand the real prospects that confronted the communists, and act accordingly. Ironically and tragically, he changed fundamentally on all these counts during his twenty-seven years as China's supreme leader. While still espousing the idea that "without investigation, one has no right to speak," he in fact increasingly succumbed to hubris, which allowed him to act in almost total disregard of actual conditions in the country.

In practical terms, Mao used many techniques to assure his dominance of policy making at the Center. For example, at the major annual communist conclaves called central work conferences, which lasted weeks or even months at a time, Mao reserved the right to sum up the discussions at the end of each meeting.[3] His summation—which at times departed significantly from the thrust of the sessions themselves—became the formal set of conclusions drawn from the conclave. In similar fashion, he issued a directive in March 1953 to the effect that no document issued in the name of the Central Committee of the Communist party could be valid unless he personally had read and approved it first.[4] And in the 1960s he encouraged the development of a cult of personality that made him into a godlike figure.

Naturally, no single individual could monitor closely and make, rather than ratify, decisions on all issues confronting China. Mao did intervene virtually across the board at one time or another in China's national agenda. But he felt himself particularly qualified to make judgments in three issue areas, in each of which his impact was constant and decisive. These were relations with the United States and the Soviet Union, policies to promote the revolution in China (which in turn, of course, connected to many issue areas from culture to economics), and agricultural policy. The arena in which Mao felt least comfortable and that he understood the least was urban economics, and this policy arena would frustrate him throughout his career.

Wielding Power, 1949–76

China's development under Mao Zedong's leadership was spasmodic, a pattern of lurching from politically induced crisis to crisis. This was not, in short, an ordinary political system seeking to nurture steady development and gradual improvement in the lives of its citizens. It was an extraordinary system of both tremendous strength and startling instability whose leaders were determined to bring about rapid industrial development and equally committed to fundamental social change.

The political leadership from 1949 to 1976 made major changes in its strategies every five to ten years, with often staggering consequences for the Chinese population. Each strategy, in turn, utilized substantially new tactics to deal with the problems engendered by the previous strategy. Each, therefore, retarded China's progress toward developing stable political processes and governing institutions. This section provides a brief overview of each of the major strategies adopted, the concerns that prompted their adoption, and the results produced.

Any periodization of a span of years is inevitably artificial. Key developments in the economy or in the military, for example, may not coincide with those in elite politics or other spheres. But during China's Maoist years, sharp changes in strategy were sufficiently wide ranging—affecting, for example, economics, military policy, foreign affairs, cultural matters, and social affairs simultaneously—that periodization of this era is remarkably straightforward. The following basic divisions emerge: 1949–56, economic and political recovery and basic socialist transformation; 1956–57, contradictions and rethinking the Soviet model; 1958–61, Great Leap Forward; 1962–65, recovery and growing elite divisions; 1966–69, Red Guard phase of the Cultural Revolution; 1970–76, final phases of the Cultural Revolution and the struggle for succession.

FROM VICTORY, THROUGH RECOVERY, TO SOCIALIST TRANSFORMATION: 1949–56

Mao Zedong declared in March 1949 at the second plenum of the Seventh Central Committee that, looking at the prospect of nationwide victory, "We have taken only the first step in a march of ten thousand *li*."[5] This was a remarkable statement from the leader of the revolutionary movement, who had already fought for almost three decades across the length and breadth of the country. But it was also a prescient one.

Mao recognized that the CCP had garnered extraordinary experience and skills in rural revolution but that the party's and the revolution's future would be determined by its ability to govern urban China. The cities, though, posed enormous new challenges to the revolutionary movement, which was supported for the most part by peasants, generally illiterate and unfamiliar with urban ways and amenities. They viewed the cities as seats of reaction, the bases of Western imperialism, the Guomindang, and the Japanese.

Thus, China could be captured from the countryside but it could be governed only from the cities, which meant that the experience garnered in previous decades would no longer suffice. The highly decentralized, militarized nature of the communist movement was inappropriate to the task of running the major urban centers and the national economy.

For the CCP as for all revolutionary movements, therefore, victory brought a crisis. It shifted the party's tasks from familiar ones to alien ones. The communists had to switch from a strategy of attacking those in power to one of exercising power itself. As the CCP became the "establishment," it faced a host of new and difficult issues.

The Setting

On 1 October 1949, Mao Zedong stood atop the Tiananmen, "Gate of Heavenly Peace," at the entry to the centuries-old Forbidden City and proclaimed the formation of the People's Republic of China. Joining with Mao on top of the Tiananmen rostrum were the other top leaders of the Chinese Communist party, such as Zhu De, Zhou Enlai, and Liu Shaoqi, along with many prominent noncommunist personages lending their support and prestige to the new national government.

After more than a century of humiliation following the Opium War, and some thirty-seven years after the collapse of the imperial system, the Chinese people were ready to embrace a movement that could bring strong government, national unity, and real independence. Many worried about the communists' programs, and far larger numbers were simply ignorant of them. But most were willing to see whether the CCP could fulfill the promise implicit in Mao's confident assertion that "The Chinese people have stood up." They would sacrifice greatly to make this promise come true, and they would forgive a great deal in the name of creating a strong nation. In the hope all Chinese held for their future, the Chinese communists enjoyed an enormous reservoir of support. The strong governing apparatus they established, in short, faced a pliant society.

But the situation they confronted was grim. Urban China's economy was in a shambles. World War II and the civil war had destroyed large parts of the industrial plant and had severely disrupted normal domestic trade patterns. The hyperinflation of the late 1940s had demoralized the population and rendered business virtually impossible. The cities were cut off from their rural markets, and much interurban transportation had been disrupted.[6] The situation was so bad in many cities that, according to a *New York Times* report from Tianjin, local capitalists looked forward to the communist takeover as likely to be good for business.

The urban and rural populations alike were war weary. After decades of warlordism, resistance to the Japanese occupation, and finally civil war, the populace craved peace and stability. The civil war had, in addition, left millions of men under arms in the GMD and CCP armies, and most longed to return to their farms to begin having families and enjoying the fruits of economic recovery.

Indeed, China's modern history had been so tortured that the CCP inherited a society deeply torn in several directions. The Japanese occupation had produced many collaborators who now feared retribution. The rampant corruption of the late 1940s had ruined the lives of many while enriching others. Decades of military conflict on Chinese soil had at one time or another pitted millions of Chinese against each other in deadly combat. Various regions of the country had lived under different political and social systems for much of the previous twenty years. It would take great skill and a very strong hand to pull together this fractious situation and start the country on a clear path to recovery.

The CCP thus faced serious challenges during the initial years after 1949. It had to create political institutions, bring about economic recovery and growth, initiate revolutionary social changes, and establish a secure position in the international arena. Among these, economic recovery assumed initial priority. Nothing could buy the communists the support of the urban populace more rapidly than taming inflation and getting the economy going again. The situation placed so many demands on the leaders that the early years brought a whirlwind of activity in many spheres. The new regime responded to its many challenges with a remarkably strong start.

Gaining Momentum

The Communist leadership moved quickly to organize the population and mobilize especially China's youth to create a sense of a positive new era. In the early years the leaders had four broad substantive priorities: to cement the terms of their relationship with the USSR; to establish a governing apparatus that could rule urban China and unite the country; to restore the urban economy; and to consolidate control over the countryside while paying off a historical debt to the peasantry by instituting land reform on a nationwide basis. Given the pressures from all sides, they had to move simultaneously in all these areas.

The linkup with the USSR was of fundamental importance. China in 1949 faced a bipolar world in which the cold war had already taken shape. Neither the United States nor the Soviet Union recognized the possibility of neutrality in this international system. Forced to choose sides, China allied itself with the Soviet Union, and within two months of founding the PRC Mao left China for the first time. His destination was Moscow, where he stayed for nearly three months to hammer out the Sino-Soviet relationship.[7]

The historical record hints that at least some CCP leaders toyed with the possibility of an American option as late as the spring of 1949. But these hints, although tantalizing, are thin, and the political situation in the United States, which was then moving into the anticommunist excesses of the McCarthy era, was not conducive to the type of subtle, flexible diplomacy required to develop a healthy relationship with the deeply suspicious leaders in Beijing. In Washington, in any case, the political realities of 1949 demanded continued support for Chiang Kai-shek's forces, which had retreated to Taiwan, until such time, presumably in 1950, when the People's Liberation Army overran Taiwan and brought the Chinese civil war to its conclusion.[8]

The Soviets negotiated hard with the Chinese. They promised a modest amount of financial aid. More important, they dispatched many advisors and, ultimately, numerous blueprints and documents that permitted China to benefit from engineering and technological advances the Soviets had made. They also advised China on governing structures and on techniques the state could use to industrialize rapidly under a planned economy. And Moscow formally entered into an alliance with Beijing that would lend military support should China suffer an attack. But the Soviets also demanded special access to several territories and ports in China, and the right to establish several companies with the Chinese to exploit mineral resources in the PRC. China, in addition, had to toe the Soviet line in all important international matters.

All indications suggest that Mao sincerely wanted all the Soviet advice he could obtain and that he took this advice seriously. Mao had largely made his career in the CCP before 1949 by arguing successfully for a distinctive Chinese road to power. But once he had won nationwide victory, he saw Stalin and his colleagues as the only people who understood how to build a socialist system that worked.

While the Soviet tie put the Chinese communists at odds with the United States, the outbreak of the Korean War with the surprise North Korean attack on the South on 25 June 1950 led to events that made Washington and Beijing implacable enemies.[9] America responded to the North Korean aggression by, among other things, assigning the U.S. Navy's Seventh Fleet to prevent the PLA from crossing the ninety-mile-wide Taiwan Strait to finish off the Nationalist remnants on Taiwan. This action signaled Washington's view that the North Korean incursion was part of a Soviet-coordinated series of thrusts to expand communist power. But the result was to place the United States in the middle of the Chinese civil war, a position from which it has never fully extricated itself.

The Chinese early on became worried about a U.S. threat to the security of the northeast, and these fears worsened as the United Nations forces, largely composed of American troops sent to aid South Korea, proved very effective in rolling back North Korean forces in the fall of 1950. The American commander General Douglas MacArthur heightened Beijing's anxieties with unauthorized remarks suggesting that UN forces might keep on moving into China to undo the results of the Chinese revolution. As a consequence, Mao Zedong overcame the deep-seated reluctance of almost all other Chinese leaders and dispatched troops into Korea in October, calling them Chinese People's Volunteers to make them seem less official.[10]

From late 1950 until an armistice in mid-1953, Chinese and American forces confronted each other on the Korean peninsula in a bloody conflict that left extremely bitter feelings on both sides. One American reaction to this was to tighten an economic noose around China, cutting off the PRC to the maximum extent possible from trade with the West. This not only set back Chinese economic development but also forced the PRC to lean even more strongly in the direction of the Soviet bloc. In addition, the United States formally recognized the Nationalist government on Taiwan as the sole legal government of all of China, thus blocking the PRC's entry into all noncommunist international organizations including the United Nations and the World Bank. These American policies remained unchanged until the early 1970s.

The CCP acted very quickly in the cities it captured in 1949–50 to bring down inflation and get the urban economy moving forward. The new governing authorities confiscated the enterprises that had been run by the Guomindang and worked to put them back on sound footing. They also generally promoted a probusiness climate to rehabilitate the urban economy and used their influence on the workers to assure labor discipline. They used strong-arm tactics to force hoarders to yield up their hidden stocks of goods, and then dumped these goods on the market when necessary to bring down prices. They held meetings with leading businessmen to assure them of the CCP's understanding and support. And they converted the GMD's virtually worthless dollars into the new "people's currency" (*renminbi*) and then in 1950 used stringent budget and tax measures to withdraw large amounts of currency from circulation.[11]

The net result of these measures was that by the end of 1950 the CCP had broken the back of the inflationary spiral that had left urban dwellers disoriented and demoralized. The economy would have picked up somewhat in any case simply due to the cessation of the civil war and the reestablishment of traditional urban-rural and interurban trade routes. But these concerted measures, developed primarily by Chen Yun and Zhou Enlai, proved a boon to the economy and earned the CCP a reputation as an effective, activist leadership with strong reformist policies. The related sharp decline in corruption as the GMD officials fled and the PLA soldiers took over enhanced the initial favorable impression.

Against this background, the ability of the Chinese People's Volunteers to fight the U.S.-backed United Nations troops to a standstill in Korea added enormously to the CCP's prestige. This marked the first time in more than a century that Chinese troops faced those of Western countries and did not suffer a humiliating defeat. Even though many Chinese were uneasy about the

CCP's long-term goals and about the Sino-Soviet alliance, feelings of pride and hope—sentiments long absent from the Chinese scene—by all accounts surged through substantial portions of the urban population by 1951.

Mao and his colleagues had, of course, more than reform on their minds. In mid-1950 they started a drumbeat of mass political campaigns, each targeting a segment of the population, that shortly would change substantially the social, economic, and political lives of China's peasants and urban residents. These campaigns included Land Reform (starting in June 1950); Suppression of Counterrevolutionaries (spring 1951); Three Anti Five Anti (winter 1951–52); Thought Reform of Intellectuals (winter and spring of 1951–52); Agricultural Cooperativization (late 1955–56); and Socialist Transformation of Industry and Commerce (late 1955–56). The first of these paid off the peasants and established a communist power structure in the countryside; the next three softened up urban society; and the final two established a socialist urban and rural economy.

As discussed in Chapter 2, the CCP had experimented with land reform at various times since the Jiangxi Soviet period. Indeed, by the time of the communist victory in 1949 large areas of north and northeast China had already gone through this process. In June 1950 Liu Shaoqi announced adoption of a land-reform law for the rest of the country. This new law aimed to classify all peasants into one or another class and to knock the landlords out of the system. In this way the party would simultaneously replace the old rural elites with a communist power structure in the countryside and settle a profound debt incurred to the peasants during the years of rural-based guerrilla warfare.

The Land Reform campaign of 1950–52 involved some of China's city dwellers as well as its peasants. The CCP formed land-reform teams of urban youths to go to the countryside to carry out the transformation there, which was often violent. Although figures vary, it appears that at least eight hundred thousand landlords were killed during this period.[12] This outright violence against leading members of village society changed the nature of village social relationships.[13] Even decades later, in interviews many peasants recalled vividly the deep impression this violence had made on them. The resulting land redistribution sought to preserve a rich peasant economy so that agricultural production would not drop (see Table 4.1). Removing the landlords as a class vastly enhanced the CCP's own access to the villages. The related process of classifying the peasants as rich, middle, or poor peasants or agricultural laborers also laid the groundwork for later campaigns to collectivize agriculture.[14]

With land reform remaking rural China, in early spring 1951 the CCP turned its attention to the cities. It launched a Suppression of Counterrevolutionaries campaign that targeted two urban groups: some civil-servant holdovers from the GMD regime (the CCP had kept on many of the former civil servants, especially those in the police forces), and the secret societies that operated in many urban areas. These secret societies were gangs that had for years controlled much of the urban transport and intercity transport systems. The Suppression of Counterrevolutionaries campaign used brass-

TABLE 4.1 Regional Land Holdings before and after Land Reform

	BEFORE LAND REFORM			AFTER LAND REFORM				
	CENTRAL-SOUTH	SOUTHWEST	OTHER	CENTRAL-SOUTH	SOUTHWEST	EAST	NORTHWEST	NORTH
Landlords								
Population*	4.20	7.40	7.40	4.30	4.60	4.20	7.40	0.20
Land†	41.40	38.40	29.30	4.30	4.40	3.40	5.60	0.20
Index‡	9.81	5.19	3.96	0.99	0.97	0.82	0.75	1.15
Rich peasants								
Population*	5.00	7.30	3.00	4.80	6.90	4.80	6.60	1.30
Land†	12.10	14.30	6.40	7.00	8.10	8.00	10.10	1.00
Index‡	2.42	1.96	2.13	1.47	1.17	1.67	1.53	0.79
Middle peasants								
Population*	26.30	44.30	38.60	22.90	30.90	40.50	50.70	90.00
Land†	24.80	30.80	42.30	26.10	31.80	44.30	59.00	90.80
Index‡	0.94	0.70	1.10	1.04	1.03	1.09	1.16	1.01
Poor peasants								
Population*	55.60	38.50	n.a.	55.00	50.60	44.60	32.80	8.50
Land†	14.00	8.60	n.a.	52.40	48.10	37.70	24.70	7.40
Index‡	0.25	0.22	n.a.	0.95	0.95	0.84	0.75	0.87
Agricultural laborers								
Population*	0.90	0.60	n.a.	5.20	5.80	3.70	4.20	none
Land†	0.00	0.10	n.a.	4.80	5.80	3.30	3.10	none
Index‡			0.35§	0.92	0.98	0.90	0.74	none

Source: Before land reform: Edwin E. Moise, *Land Reform in China and North Vietnam* (Chapel Hill: University of North Carolina Press, 1983), pp. 28–29; after land reform: *ibid.*, pp. 138–39. The data are based on the averages of several surveys and thus do not add up to 100 percent.

*Percentage of total population.

†Percentage of total land.

‡Index: Per capita holdings of each class relative to the average per capita holdings of the rural population as a whole.

§Index includes landholdings of poor peasants and laborers.

knuckle tactics to root out and destroy its targets. Numerous public executions marked this brief, violent initiative.

For all its drama, though, the Suppression of Counterrevolutionaries campaign seems, on the basis of later interviews, to have passed largely unnoticed outside the specific groups targeted by the effort. This campaign did not involve mass mobilization of the urban populace, and its targets were relatively small, distinct groups.[15] The same cannot be said of the Three Anti Five Anti campaign, which convulsed urban society in the winter of 1951–52 and marked a fundamental turning point in the communists' relationship with the urban populace.[16]

Three Anti Five Anti seems to have had two motives: the CCP needed additional funds to fight the Korean War, and party leaders became worried about corruption seeping into party ranks in the cities. The latter was a natural phenomenon. Mao had warned the party to watch out for the "sugar-coated bullets of the bourgeoisie" in his March 1949 speech to the second plenum of the Seventh Central Committee. He knew that urban China worked primarily through the cultivation of personal relationships, and that exchanges of gifts and favors were of central importance to this process. He also knew that most of the peasant revolutionaries as of 1949 had never been in a city or seen running water or indoor plumbing, and would be dazzled by the material wealth available to them in urban China.

By late 1951 evidence of corruption was sufficient to cause alarm. The CCP therefore launched the Three Anti campaign (against waste, corruption, and bureaucratism) against the cadres at the basic levels of its own urban organization and the Five Anti campaign (against corruption, tax evasion, stealing state property, cheating on state contracts, and stealing state economic secrets) against urban businessmen. Corruption was the issue that tied these two efforts together. The campaign utilized all the techniques developed in the Yan'an era: mass mobilization, study groups and thought reform involving criticism and self-criticism, social ostracism, vague promises of rewards to those who confessed and denounced others and punishment to those who refused to confess, and so forth.

One businessman in Tianjin described this campaign as the most traumatic experience of his life. Before this, he had welcomed the CCP as a positive reformist leadership. By 1951 he had begun to develop ties to the local revenue authorities to avoid tax payments, and had continued to keep two sets of books, as all businesses did. He also had bought and sold gold, a common practice in those days of currency uncertainty. By the end of three months of isolation in a study group during the campaign, he had become a heavy smoker (he had never previously smoked), never subsequently able to break the habit. He became, he said, a pliant tool in the hands of the communists, recognizing that they were determined revolutionaries and that his life would never again be the same.

During the period the businessman was in the study group, CCP officials had organized his workers into a trade union and recruited one young unskilled worker to become a party activist. After that, the businessman never again enjoyed easy relations with his workers, and everyone feared the young party activist. When the campaign ended, the businessman had to pay a substantial fine for past misbehavior, a sum he had to borrow from the government to pay to the government. His "transgressions" had previously been considered normal business practice, but during the Three Anti Five Anti campaign the CCP declared them to be crimes and applied retroactive penalties.

For the next few years he formally remained manager of this business, but he in fact took his cues from the party activist and never again sought to exercise real authority. When he was given the opportunity to sell the enterprise at a fire-sale price to the government in late 1955, he quickly seized the chance. His experiences were typical of those of China's business class.[17]

During September 1951 through the late spring of 1952, the CCP also implemented the Thought Reform of Intellectuals campaign. This effort mobilized students in universities to criticize their teachers and forced changes in university curricula away from American and European models to the Soviet system and texts. This campaign also used thought-reform techniques, and it traumatized many on the teaching staffs.[18]

The mass campaign approach then eased off for a while after mid-1952. All sectors of society—peasants, urban cadres, business people, workers, students, and intellectuals—had experienced the traumas of mobilization techniques that deliberately violated all the norms of traditional social relationships. Each campaign had forced people to challenge and denounce those to whom they owed deference according to traditional standards: peasants confronted the leading figures in their villages, students confronted their teachers, and workers confronted their firms' owners and managers. Indeed, one hallmark of the campaigns was that they pressured victims to provide information on those with whom they had the closest *guanxi* ("connection"), thereby transforming the traditional social tie from a secure bond to a source of potential danger. The techniques employed had been honed during the years before 1949, especially in the 1942–44 Rectification campaign in Yan'an. From personal experience, by late 1952 virtually everyone in Chinese society could clearly distinguish between reform and revolution.

The next great effort for the party was the socialist transformation of the economy. In 1952, under Soviet tutelage, the Chinese had established a State Planning Commission, and they were fleshing out the organization of major economic ministries. The Russian advisors then worked closely with Beijing to develop the First Five-Year Plan, which would formally run from 1953 to 1957. A total of almost 150 Soviet-assisted new enterprises constituted the core of this plan. The new state structure would seek to capture resources from throughout the economy and funnel them into investment in these key enterprises.[19]

Agricultural reform presented a difficult problem. Chinese agricultural production remained poor, and land reform had not provided the basis for major long-term improvements in productivity. In addition, the state did not have adequate means for capturing the agricultural surplus to invest in industrial development.[20] According to Soviet experience, the answer was collectivization of agriculture.

China moved toward this goal in several stages. Beginning in 1953, peasants were encouraged to form Mutual Aid Teams. These generally amounted to pooling labor for agricultural tasks such as plowing, planting, seeding, weeding, and harvesting; in many cases these teams simply formalized what had long been standard rural practice. Beginning in 1954, peasants were strongly encouraged to enter lower-level Agricultural Producers Cooperatives (APCs). These required a contribution of animals, tools, and land to the cooperative, with people paid from the profits of the cooperative. Half the payment would be based on work done for the co-op, and the other half would be based on the land, equipment, and animals contributed. Not surprisingly, rich peasants tended not to participate, and even many middle peasants proved reluctant to give up clear title to the land the revolution had given them.

In early 1955 the CCP allowed those who wanted to withdraw from the cooperatives to do so. Beijing was surprised by the number that took advantage of this opportunity. This sparked a debate over agricultural collectivization at the highest levels of the party. Soviet practice endorsed collectivization as the best way to create large enough agricultural units for the state to be able to take the surplus effectively out of agriculture. Given China's far lower levels of per capita agricultural production, however, Beijing needed to both create a larger surplus and capture a portion of that for urban economic development.[21]

In the ensuing debate, Mao argued that agricultural cooperative organizations would expand the size of fields and the scale of activity so that peasants themselves would want to introduce more mechanized farming to meet their new needs. With that mechanization, Mao argued, production itself would go up. More orthodox Marxists, such as Mao's putative successor Liu Shaoqi, suggested that instead the Chinese should introduce more mechanization first. The changes mechanization would produce in farming practices would make the peasants realize the importance of consolidating fields and pooling their labor, and they would then voluntarily enter collective farms. This debate reflected a more fundamental issue of broad importance: Mao felt that political efforts could create the conditions for rapid economic growth, whereas Liu felt that political efforts should be constrained by the existing types and level of economic production. Mao won the argument.

The issue came to a head in mid-1955. The second session of the First National People's Congress, the nominal legislature, met from 5 to 30 July and adopted a report on the First Five-Year Plan presented by Li Fuchun, the head of the State Planning Commission. This report anticipated gradual collectivization of agriculture. On 31 July, Mao Zedong convened a meeting of provincial, municipal, and lower-level CCP leaders and called for far more ambitious targets. This began the so-called high tide of agricultural cooperativization, a surge which put 92 percent of peasant households into collectives by the following spring (see Table 4.2). Within another year, Mao brought about a transformation of lower- to higher-level APCs. The difference between the two was crucial: in the higher-level APCs, members were paid only according to the work they did, not according to the capital they had put in. This took away the advantages of the remaining richer strata of the peasantry.[22]

Mao subsequently met often with provincial and lower-level party figures

TABLE 4.2 *APCs and Communes* (Percent of Peasant Households)*

YEAR	LOWER-LEVEL APCs	HIGHER-LEVEL APCs	COMMUNES
1952	0.1		
1953	0.2		
1954	2		
June 1955	14	0.03	
Dec. 1955	59	4	
Feb. 1956	36	51	
June 1956	29	63	
Dec. 1956	9	88	
Apr. 1958		100	
Aug. 1958		70	30
Sept. 1958			98

Source: Mark Selden, *The Political Economy of Chinese Socialism* (Armonk, N.Y.: M. E. Sharpe, 1988), p. 71.

*Communes were very large rural organizations introduced in 1958.

to garner support for ambitious schemes that had generated little enthusiasm among his colleagues in Beijing. He referred to these meetings as his way of getting in touch with those who were close to the front line, and who therefore understood true conditions in the country. But in meeting with these officials, Mao always had his way. The functionaries stood in awe of the Chairman, and most worked very hard to cultivate their relations with him. By the late 1950s, for example, many provincial party leaders had established palatial estates for Mao's exclusive use. Some reportedly even formed special provincial "cultural troupes" of attractive young women for the Chairman's personal pleasure.[23]

The provincial party leaders were mostly individuals of peasant stock who distrusted the more urbanized and technically proficient specialists at the Center and had a natural inclination toward decentralization and mass mobilization. Mao thus found an eager audience on his frequent trips to the provinces.

At the same time that agriculture was being collectivized, the Socialist Transformation of Industry and Commerce campaign gave urban capitalists the opportunity to sell their enterprises to the state at bargain prices. After their traumas of the previous few years, most quickly did so. In Shanghai, the owners of the local textile factories actually formed a parade along the Huangpu River waterfront to the municipal Communist party headquarters in the old British Shanghai Bank Building to request that the municipal government take over their businesses. As they marched, they held up banners and heard celebratory gongs and firecrackers along the sidewalks. Many were kept on as managers in their former firms while the communists learned how to run them, but after a few more years, not many remained in positions of authority.

By mid-1956 the Chinese communists had fought the UN forces in Korea to a standstill, rehabilitated the urban and rural economies, embarked on the ambitious First Five-Year Plan, and created socialist-type organizations for both peasants and city dwellers. No substantial private sector remained in the urban or rural economies. The country had been galvanized, organized, and directed toward a socialist future.[24]

Takeover Politics

The years from 1949 to 1954 also witnessed the transformation of the guerrilla communist army and party into a ruling elite. This involved decisions about appointments to various posts, how to organize the bureaucratic apparatus given differing conditions in various parts of the country, and what to do with the enormous armed forces left over from the civil war.

The CCP's basic approach to organizing political power was to establish a moderately decentralized arrangement for a transitional period, with the intention of centralizing this when conditions permitted. The party divided the country into six major regions—northeast, north, east, central-south, southwest, and northwest. It created sets of party, government, and military organs to take charge of each region. Each region initially was put under martial law; as conditions permitted they shifted to civilian rule.[25]

With this organization, the party acknowledged that the timing of policy initiatives would have to vary by region. The Three Anti, for example, began in the northeast in the early fall of 1951, then spread to north and east China early that winter, and then moved to the other parts of the country. Most policies followed roughly this same geographical phasing during these early years.

This system reflected the guerrilla-war and base-area experience of the CCP. Each of the major regions fell under the sway of one of the "field armies" into which the communists had organized their forces during the guerrilla war. Each was led by one or two of the major CCP figures, who typically held a series of posts giving them effective control over all activities in the region. In the important northeast region, for example, Gao Gang, a poorly educated peasant who had risen to the top communist ranks by the late 1940s, simultaneously became the head of the regional party committee, head of the regional government, and head of the regional military organization. Essentially, Gao was the regent for the northeast.

From 1952 to 1954 the CCP gradually shifted people out of the regional political structures, assigning them either to provinces or to the Center. This created jealousies and tensions regarding which individuals would receive high posts in Beijing, and thereby fueled the first major falling out at the top of the party.

Gao Gang was shifted to the Center in 1952 to take charge of the newly formed State Planning Commission, probably because of his close personal ties with the Russians. Gao, however, regarded this commission with some disdain. He felt he should aspire to the premiership, and he believed, mistakenly as it turned out, that Mao Zedong felt the same way. Gao thus began to try to line up the other key players, among them Deng Xiaoping in the southwest and Chen Yi in Shanghai, to support him. He argued that they and he were not being treated well by the clique of those, like Zhou Enlai and Liu Shaoqi, who had been in charge of dealing with the areas outside of communist control, called the "white" areas, during the Yan'an era. The base-area leaders were not faring well in the scramble for positions, and Gao assured the others that they would receive excellent jobs in a Gao administration.

The effort failed. Deng and others informed Mao, and Mao refused to back Gao. Zhou Enlai, Liu Shaoqi, and others then purged Gao and his closest collaborator Rao Shushi, who had been one of the top two leaders in Shanghai, for factionalism. Gao subsequently committed suicide; Rao was imprisoned. The incident was significant primarily for the spotlight it threw on the desire for jobs and the factional identities that grew out of the long pre-1949 experiences of the top CCP cadres.[26]

In broad terms, the political strategy in the early years generally favored the PLA troops and cadres that had captured various regions at the end of the civil war over the local guerrilla forces that had fought in those areas on the communist side for many years. It was felt that the latter had too many close ties in the localities, and Mao was keenly concerned with the need to create a political apparatus that would be loyal to the Center. Much as under the Qing dynasty, a kind of "law of avoidance," in which officials were not allowed to serve in their native locales, came into play. In the vast majority of cases, people were put in charge of areas far from their native places. For decades afterward civilian apparatuses were clearly identified with the various field armies that had swept across China from 1948 to 1950[27] (see Table 4.3).

Also, the CCP as a general rule sought in the initial years to recruit leading noncommunist personages to the new government. These individuals brought both prestige and skills to party efforts. The communists promised them that the CCP would delay China's socialist transformation to first rehabilitate the country and put it on its feet. Rarely did such noncommunists acquire real power. The well-known GMD general Fu Zuoyi, for example, had surrendered Beijing to the PLA in January 1949 without a pitched battle. Fu was rewarded with honors and the portfolio for flood control in the new government, but even in his own ministry he served only as a figurehead. The promises of gradual changes, in any event, proved hollow. The united front soon narrowed significantly.

In October 1954, just five years after the founding of the People's Republic of China, the First National People's Congress convened in Beijing. This meeting formally declared the government transition period to be over and established the permanent ruling organs for the new state, to be headed by the State Council. It kept in place the figures who had held the top transitional state positions during the previous years. It also formally abolished the regional government/party/military bodies that had been established in 1949. The Center would henceforth deal directly with the provinces. China had been unified swiftly and successfully, albeit with a great deal of blood spilled in the process. Now the communist leaders would have to determine the long-term path of development to take.

TABLE 4.3 *Field Armies and Localities at the End of the Civil War*

FIELD ARMY	REGION
First	Northwest
Second	Central and Southwest
Third	East
Fourth	Northeast and Guangdong
Fifth	North

FROM SUCCESS TO CRISIS: 1956–57

The period from 1949 to early 1956 had witnessed missteps and problems along with concentrated violence against target groups. At the end of this period, moreover, material hardship still consigned most of the country's population to severe poverty. It was not until 1956, for example, that every county headquarters in the country had a telephone.[28] But the spiritual malaise that had deepened for a century had visibly lessened in less than seven years.

The new Beijing elite may have broken a lot of eggs to make their socialist omelet, but numerous Chinese found this dish far more palatable than the bitterness they had been forced to eat for many years. In Mao Zedong's own words, China had "stood up" internationally and had recaptured a sense of unity under an ideologically strong government at home.

Political leaders do not change a winning formula without strong reasons for doing so. Yet, by mid-1958, the communist leadership made major alterations in their approach to governing China. This radical turnabout stemmed from four important tensions lying beneath the surface as of early 1956 that, together, propelled Mao Zedong and his colleagues into an ultimately calamitous course called the Great Leap Forward.

One of these tensions concerned the role of Mao himself in the system. Mao occupied a position effectively unconstrained by law or regulation. He felt most comfortable when dealing with ideology and politics, great power relations, agriculture, and social transformation. He chafed at bureaucratic routine and had little understanding of, or patience for, the details of urban industry and finance. After agricultural collectivization and socialist transformation, though, the focus of government activity shifted to the details of urban economic planning and administration, a forte of the state but not of the party or army. To put it differently, the successes of 1949–55 had produced a system that did not *need* Mao, but the Chairman could not find a way to exit from day-to-day leadership—in his terminology, to "retreat to the second line"—and still feel confident about his control of the party and the country.

Another tension involved the social and political results of Soviet-style economic development, which Mao found distressing. The centralized planning system favored top-down command control, regularization of procedures, and specialization of jobs, as well as inequalities in prestige, income, reward structures, and power across economic sectors and geographical areas.

In good Stalinist fashion, the system also sought to exploit the "backward" countryside to serve the morally and politically superior urban population. These values, priorities, and work styles contrasted sharply with those developed during the Yan'an era, and they discomfited Mao. He might have kept his unease in check had it not been for the third underlying tension, regarding sources of capital for industrial development.

The Soviet aid program had been crucial to China's economic development. The financial portion of this assistance, however, took the form of low-interest loans rather than outright grants. In 1956, Chinese repayments of these loans began to exceed the value of new Soviet monetary aid. Whereas China previously had been able to rely on the USSR to provide a substantial portion of its net investment capital, after 1956, China would have to rely primarily on itself to generate such capital. This would require new techniques to mobilize domestic capital formation. Eventually, Mao saw this as a looming crisis that demanded radically new approaches to the development process itself.

The fourth tension was between peasant cadres and the urban intelligentsia. Despite intensive political indoctrination, the intelligentsia continued to regard most cadres from the countryside as bumpkins. The peasants, in turn, regarded intellectuals as elitist and "bourgeois."[29] Yet the Soviet model placed a high premium on the administrative and other skills of the urban intelligentsia. This tension between peasants and intellectuals inevitably bound up the fate of the Soviet model with the social cleavages that had fed—and been exacerbated by—the Chinese communist revolution.[30]

With agricultural cooperativization and urban socialist transformation at a high point, Mao decided to resolve the tensions between the intellectuals and the communist cadres. Premier Zhou Enlai, the best educated of the top CCP leaders, made the initial speech in this effort at a conference on the working conditions of the intellectuals held in January 1956. Zhou's speech called for better treatment and higher regard for the country's technical and creative intelligentsia.

Developments in the Soviet Union also encouraged party efforts to improve ties with the Chinese intelligentsia. Both the 1955–56 thaw toward Soviet literature and Khrushchev's dramatic de-Stalinization speech at the Twentieth Party Congress of the Communist party of the Soviet Union in February 1956 created ripple effects in China. The former simply made it appropriate for the Chinese to follow the Soviet lead in relaxing pressures on intellectuals. The latter, however, had more profound repercussions.

Khrushchev's blistering attack on Stalin caught the Chinese by surprise and severely embarrassed Mao. Mao had spoken of Stalin with high praise and had published a fawning eulogy to the Soviet dictator on his death in March 1953.[31] In addition, Khrushchev's address essentially warned against a willful leader's having his way, just after Mao had personally launched the socialist transformation of the Chinese economy.[32] Finally, Khrushchev's speech led to unrest in Eastern Europe and, reportedly, to greater tensions in China itself later in 1956. Mao began to have doubts about Khrushchev's wisdom and leadership qualities.

During March and April 1956, therefore, Mao initiated a searching reevaluation of governing methods and priorities, holding thirty-four special briefings from many departments and State Council ministries and commissions. The result was a framework document entitled "On the Ten Major Relationships." This called, overall, for reduced military spending, much greater decentralization in Chinese administration of the economy, and other changes. In it, one sees Mao beginning to modify the Soviet model to make it more palatable to his own values and priorities.

In September 1956 the CCP convened the first session of its Eighth Party Congress, the first Party Congress since the 1945 Seventh Party Congress had enshrined Mao Zedong Thought as part of the party's official ideology.[33] The Congress adopted new Party Rules, the party equivalent of a new constitution. Almost certainly in reaction to the Soviet de-Stalinization initiative, these rules stated that the CCP took only Marxism-Leninism as its guiding ideology. Mao Zedong Thought was dropped from the formula.

Of greater long-term consequence, Mao sought to address tensions in the party's relations with the intellectuals. The Chairman had always believed in manipulating tension as a way to promote his goals. But Soviet socialist theory had played down the idea that frictions between the party and the "people" could persist once socialism had been achieved. The 1956 uprisings in Poland and Hungary, though, made clear that explosive conflict could erupt in societies ruled by Communist parties.

In late February 1957 Mao gave a talk entitled "On the Correct Handling of Contradictions among the People," in which he addressed the issue of conflicts of interest in socialist China.[34] He divided them into two categories: "antagonistic contradictions" and "contradictions among the people." Mao asserted that "contradictions among the people" can be resolved through discussion. He suggested that only a small number of contradictions under socialism are "antagonistic," meaning they cannot be resolved by reasonable discourse. These "antagonistic" contradictions would inevitably be handled through violent struggle, in which the "enemy" would be vanquished.

Mao's speech was intended to energize the intellectuals to address and reduce the "contradictions among the people," but after experiencing the many political campaigns of the previous years, they remained cautious. In the spring Mao strongly encouraged intellectuals to speak their minds, to point out the errors of party officials, and to "let a hundred flowers bloom and a hundred schools of thought contend." By this Mao meant that the communists would not require everyone to accept one orthodoxy in all intellectual matters.

The dam finally broke in May 1957, as the intellectuals unleashed an outpouring of grievances against arrogant and ignorant functionaries. At the same time they raised basic questions about whether China should continue to draw so close to the Soviets, and whether the CCP should maintain a monopoly on political power. In essence, China's intellectuals in May 1957 tried to reclaim a position as loyal guardians of the proper moral framework for the political system. Once started, the momentum of criticism gathered steam, and local party officials found themselves under increasingly severe attack. Workers, too, began to press economic grievances through strike actions and other organized activities.

Mao did not let this stirring last for long. On 8 June 1957, the major party newspaper *People's Daily* ran an editorial that marked the end of the Hundred Flowers campaign. The editorial said that "rightists" had taken advantage of the new freedom in order to attack the party and undermine the revolution. This, according to the editorial, amounted to an antagonistic struggle "between the enemy and the people"—a struggle that could only be resolved through dictatorial force. The Antirightist campaign, under the administrative direction of the party's General Secretary Deng Xiaoping, quickly got underway. It had major, long-term consequences for the PRC.[35]

The Antirightist campaign initially targeted all those who had voiced criticisms during the Hundred Flowers period. It was conducted in such indiscriminate fashion, however, that numerous "rightists" were branded on the basis of anonymous denunciations. Indeed, local officials throughout the country received quotas on the number of "rightists" they were to uncover and denounce in their own units.[36] During the course of the summer and early fall of 1957 roughly four hundred thousand urban residents, including many of the intelligentsia, were branded as rightists and thrown into penal camps or sent to the countryside to do forced labor.[37] Beginning in late summer the brunt of the campaign shifted to the countryside itself, where it targeted those who had voiced any opposition to rapid agricultural collectivization.

The Antirightist campaign had two important results. First, by late 1957 it would have taken a very brave person to object to a shift toward radical political and economic policies in Beijing. More important, the revolution lost the skills of a significant portion of the engineers, professors, economists, and scientists who arguably were crucial to the successful implementation of a Soviet-type development model. These people disproportionately came from government organs, state enterprises, and universities, not from the Communist party bureaucracy itself. Mao had turned decisively in favor of the peasant cadres instead of their intellectual critics. Without the latter, the highly centralized, government-administered (as opposed to party-administered) approach to rapid economic development would be hard to sustain.

The effects became obvious almost immediately. At the July 1957 meeting of Communist party leaders at Qingdao, Shandong Province, trends emerged toward greater administrative decentralization and increased party involvement with the economy. A Central Committee meeting that convened in October significantly accelerated these tendencies.

All this took place as China's leaders debated the targets and methods for the Second Five-Year Plan, to run from 1958 to 1962. Mao and his colleagues were determined to continue the rapid expansion of the country's industrial base, with increasing steel production a top priority. But new sources of capital would have to be found, and the level of potential Soviet aid and support would have to be ascertained.

During the latter half of 1957 the increasingly radical political atmosphere created a sense of excitement and held out the possibility of major change. At the same time, the relative ease with which the major socialist transformations had been carried out the previous winter convinced Mao that the general populace strongly supported the party and could become a major resource for accelerated economic development. The problem lay in identifying the key to unlock that energy. The disastrous results of the Hundred Flowers campaign, moreover, had convinced Mao that the intelligentsia were antisocialist and effectively the allies of the now-defunct bourgeoisie. He determined to sharpen the people's vigilance so that they would wage class struggle against these antisocialist elements.

The winter of 1957–58 was a time of experimentation with methods to resolve these new issues on the Chinese agenda. Mao and other leaders traveled to Moscow in November to ascertain, among other things, whether the Soviets would commit themselves to major new infusions of aid to China. At the same time, Beijing adopted new administrative regulations that called for major decentralization in management of the economy.[38] Regarding the countryside, a debate raged over how to expand irrigation facilities without large new expenditures of capital. The solution was an enormous mobilization of corvée labor, which in turn created pressures to enlarge and greatly strengthen the APC.

As of November–December 1957, it was not clear where all of this would lead. But the mood among the top party leadership was one of radical renewal, sparked both by the alarming problems growing out of the previous Soviet-led approach and by an increasingly ebullient sense that tapping the latent potential of China's huge population could produce a miracle. During 1958 this spurred Mao and the party to launch the Great Leap Forward, a radically new approach to economic and social development. In the final analysis, it amounted to a tremendous, willful leap away from reality, with tragic consequences that included, ultimately, the deaths of tens of millions of Chinese.

LEAPS FORWARD AND BACKWARD: 1958–61

The Great Leap Forward developed during the spring and summer of 1958 as a set of policy initiatives. This extraordinary approach to economic development grew out of the trends noted above: the purge of intellectuals; the surge of less-educated radicals; the need to find new ways to generate domestic capital; rising enthusiasm about the potential results mass mobilization might produce; and reaction against the sociopolitical results of the Soviet development strategy.

The Great Leap did not emerge as a full-blown strategy at any specific time. Rather, it was formed out of many initiatives, and it had different effects on various sectors of society. It is most accurately viewed not as an integrated strategy but as a broad spirit and basic set of priorities.

The fundamental idea behind the Great Leap was that China could leap over the normal stages of economic development through the expenditure of extraordinary effort by the entire society for a concentrated period of several years. This idea rested on the notion that the masses possess great dormant productive power and can, by dint of effort and organization, transform their labor into capital.

The Great Leap strategy depended on the mobilization of peasants to provide for themselves without drawing resources from the urban economy. In addition, they were to provide food, industrial crops, and even steel for the urban economy. Thus, the peasants were called upon to increase irrigation, produce farm machinery, develop education, participate in militia activities, and feed themselves without new investment from the national budget. Originally, Mao and his colleagues expected Moscow to provide substantial new assistance that they would use solely to speed urban industrial growth. Although Soviet aid did rise in 1958, increasing Sino-Soviet frictions—in part because of Chinese deviation from the Soviet model—soon made clear that the Chinese could not rely on their Russian neighbors for much additional help. This further increased the burden placed on China's peasants to fund industrial growth.

A strategy that required very extensive mass mobilization was by its very nature more suited to the capabilities of the Communist party apparatus than to those of the government bureaucracy. The Great Leap approach therefore greatly expanded the role of the CCP at the expense of the government—and greatly decentralized policy implementation in the process.[39] China's leaders had assigned the State Council primary responsibility for economic development during the First Five-Year Plan, but they shifted to greater reliance on the CCP itself when they adopted the Great Leap approach to rapid industrial growth.

In January 1958, Mao Zedong criticized Premier Zhou Enlai at a meeting of the top party figures, called the Nanning Conference because it convened in Nanning, Guangxi Province. Mao's comments highlighted his frustration with the old system. He complained that the State Council experts worked up policy proposals so thoroughly that by the time they got to Mao he confronted two problems: the proposals generally allowed little room for new ideas, and they were so technically complex that he could not understand them. He noted that he had responded in recent years by simply approving the proposals without even trying to understand them fully.[40] With a shift to the Great Leap strategy, Mao brushed aside this specialized State Council system and put himself back at the helm in all major substantive matters.

The Great Leap in many ways harked back to the Yan'an spirit. It stressed egalitarianism, experimentation, ideological fervor, mass mobilization, and the application of organization and will to the accomplishment of technically "impossible" goals. The Great Leap disparaged technical constraints and the experts who warned about them. Its spirit was summed up well in one of its key slogans: "Strive to go all out to achieve more, faster, better, and more economical results." In the final analysis, as later Chinese authors admitted, "better and more economical results" were sacrificed to the goals of "more and faster."

Mao correctly gauged the tremendous response the CCP could generate across the country. The CCP had so effectively cowed all opposition and developed such a strong can-do reputation among the Chinese people that China in 1958 took off into a nationwide frenzy of activity. Previous work habits and even existing bases of social organization changed dramatically, at least for a time.

In August 1958 the Chairman called for the organization of all rural inhabitants into "people's communes" (*renmin gongshe*). These were large, centralized organizations in the countryside meant to facilitate meshing the government administration with economic production in the rural areas. Mao wanted to devise a unit in the countryside that could directly manage the various major tasks there: agricultural and small industrial production and marketing; corvée labor for infrastructure development; health-care delivery; education; and security. People's communes initially provided the key for this. The whole countryside was communized in a matter of months in late 1958. Although actual conditions varied, the average commune had about twenty thousand members as of 1959. The commune formed the lowest level of state administration in rural areas.

In the communes, huge numbers of people worked incredibly long hours at arduous tasks for months at a time. Indeed, so many new manufacturing efforts such as "backyard steel furnaces" were undertaken that in the fall of 1958 the country actually experienced an acute agricultural labor shortage. Even the most fundamental aspects of peasant daily life changed at the peak of the Great Leap frenzy. People contributed their cooking utensils to be smelted as part of the drive to create backyard steel furnaces, and they ate in communal dining rooms. Some communes debated whether to give up using money altogether. The Great Leap amounted in many ways to the regimentation and militarization of life in the countryside.

The Great Leap's effects were not limited to the agricultural sector. In the military, the Chinese decided to abandon Soviet manuals and develop their own; they also sought greater egalitarianism by making all military officers serve as common soldiers for one month per year. The military also became deeply involved in domestic economic construction and in developing extensive militia organizations. In all these ways, the Great Leap moved the PLA away from the trend toward professionalism it had been following since the Korean War in favor of recapturing some of its guerrilla-war traditions.[41]

In industry, the Great Leap strategy pushed technicians aside, with workers running machinery for long periods of time with no maintenance. Income differentials among workers and managers diminished, and nonemployed urban residents were organized into small production and commercial groups. The educational system admitted large numbers of new students by organizing part-work, part-study programs at the expense of quality.[42] Even government officials became subject to *xia fang*, the policy of sending people in authoritative urban positions "down" to the production front, often in the countryside, to labor among the masses.

Measured by levels of mobilization, the Great Leap succeeded. In one example, millions of sparrows—scourges of agriculture—were killed in the summer 1958 by people standing on rooftops and making loud noises every time one landed; the sparrows were thus kept airborne until they literally died of exhaustion! In addition, the Chinese made seemingly extraordinary gains in production that year. There were large increases in steel output, one of the core goals of the Great Leap strategy, and substantial growth in other targeted industries. Only later did it become clear that a significant portion of this growth took place because many key Soviet-aided plants, which began to be built from 1953 to 1955, finally came on line in 1958. Unusually favorable weather also helped produce bumper crops.

The successes of 1958 induced euphoria in the national leaders. They decided, for example, that in 1959 they would leave roughly one-third of the country's arable land fallow, as otherwise they would have trouble handling all the food produced. The top leaders also began to talk confidently of having invented a new strategy for socialist economic development—a strategy that could work far more successfully than that of the Soviet Union.

In late 1958 the leaders did acknowledge that the Great Leap had produced some disorganization and problems; but they remained blind to the magnitude and nature of the difficulties that were developing. By ignoring economic and social laws on a phenomenal scale, the Great Leap eventually created a disaster of gargantuan proportions.

One major problem concerned the people's communes. The communes had the advantage of being able to allocate massive amounts of labor in a planned fashion. However, these organizations were too large to link rewards closely with labor, and they fitted poorly with the natural bases of identity among peasants. Peasant life traditionally had revolved around the clan, the village, and the standard marketing area (SMA). The SMA consisted of the various villages (usually more than a dozen) whose people marketed their goods together at the same town every few days. More than economic transactions occurred in these market towns. People from different villages got to know each other, exchanged gossip, arranged marriages, and so on. Over many years, SMAs thus became identifiable by the social as well as the economic connections that people made. The footpaths and cart tracks among villages were visible evidence of the need to funnel the goods of a village into one market town.

The initial communes were so large that each drew together, on average, the people of three SMAs. This created a political, social, and economic unit different from any the participants had previously experienced. The party officials in charge of these huge units did not understand the complexities of meshing different SMAs, and soon fundamental problems of administration and morale cropped up.[43]

One reason the leaders in Beijing missed the seriousness of the emerging difficulties was that at the height of the mobilization phase for the mass campaigns, lower-level officials had no incentives to report the truth to their superiors. Rather, they were expected to provide evidence that the masses had responded enthusiastically to the calls of the leaders and that great results were pouring in. Consequently, officials at every level of the national bureaucratic hierarchy conspired to inflate production figures as they went up the line, with the result that the central officials lived in substantial ignorance of actual conditions in the countryside in the fall of 1958. Hearing about nothing but success—and wanting to believe that they were indeed charting a new, quick path to industrial power and a communist society—they time and again added new demands and new initiatives to the burgeoning Great Leap Forward.

During the fall and winter of 1958 the costs of disorganization began to become apparent. Too many people had been yanked from the fields to permit successful harvest of the fall crop. Steel produced in backyard smelters was of such low quality that it could not be used for much. The transportation system became clogged and disrupted to the point where major urban steel producers could not obtain the coking coal they needed. Poor maintenance practices began to diminish the performance capacity of many machines.

In the early spring of 1959 Mao Zedong began to appreciate the existence of these problems, and he attempted to rein in the excesses of the Great Leap without abandoning its basic strategy. He argued against overcentralization of commune administration, which had produced irrational work assignments and had destroyed peasant incentives to do their work well. He therefore called for the creation of three levels of administration within each commune—team, rising to brigade, and then commune level—with individuals' incomes and work assignments being decided at the team or brigade level rather than at the commune level. In this and other respects, he sought to tame the tiger he had unleashed in the system. He found it very difficult, though, to convince lower-level officials at provincial, municipal, county, and commune levels, whose power and resources had grown enormously under the Great Leap decentralization, to heed his suggestions to redistribute power yet again.

This situation came to a head, with a bizarre and fateful twist, at the Lushan conference and Lushan plenum in July and August 1959. These two meetings, held at one of the favorite resorts of the party leadership atop Mount Lu ("Lushan") in Jiangxi Province, convened originally to review the overall situation and to make plans once the spring planting had been completed and the leaders had some idea of the likely size of the fall crop.[44]

At the Lushan conference, Peng Duhuai, who was minister of defense and vice chairman of the Military Affairs Commission, and some others sharply criticized the excesses of the Great Leap strategy and argued that they had resulted from an abandonment of the consultative decision-making process that the leadership had previously used. Peng and his supporters also indicated that they felt the country was rapidly slipping into crisis because of the terrible conditions being created by the Great Leap.

Although most of these criticisms echoed those Mao himself had made earlier in the spring, the Chairman nevertheless smelled a rat. He interpreted the actions of Peng and his colleagues as an orchestrated attack on his own position, perhaps quietly inspired by the Russians, who were very unhappy at China's abandonment of the Soviet model. Mao let his critics speak and then, late in the conference, he electrified his audience with a blistering attack on those who had spoken up. He questioned their wisdom and their motives, and he demanded that all top officials attending the conference make a clear choice between Peng and his colleagues or Mao. Never one to miss an opportunity to add extra tension to a situation, Mao proclaimed that if the meeting sided against him he would take to the hills, raise another army, and overthrow the CCP!

Under this pressure, the party leadership sided overwhelmingly with Mao and branded Peng and some others an "antiparty" group. These individuals were purged. By the end of the summer, Peng was no longer minister of defense or vice chairman of the Military Affairs Commission, having been sent to do gardening in a village in the suburbs of Beijing instead. The conference and the succeeding plenum then produced two sets of decisions. One denounced the crimes of the "rightists" who had revealed themselves at the highest level of the party and called for new vigilance against other rightists at all levels of the system. The other highlighted again the excesses of the Great Leap and called for the same types of consolidation measures that Mao had been espousing all spring.[45]

The clash at Lushan prompted several fateful results. First, Mao's vicious response to Peng's criticism seemed to change the unwritten ground rules of policy debate among the leaders. Before Lushan the leadership at the top conclaves had felt it proper to voice their opinions, within some self-imposed constraints, before a decision was made. The denunciation and purge of Peng suggested this would no longer be possible. Second, Mao chose Lin Biao to replace Peng as minister of defense and vice chairman of the Military Affairs Commission. Lin had long been a favorite of Mao's; Peng had not. Lin then tried to position himself to succeed Mao, and in the process he became a major contributor to tensions and infighting among the top party leadership.

Finally and most important, the decisions emanating from the plenum proved contradictory in spirit if not in substance. The attack on "rightists" undermined the leadership's attempt to rein in the excesses of the Great Leap. Indeed, the opposite occurred: with everyone eager to demonstrate that they leaned to the "left" instead of to the "right," radicalism surged anew in late 1959 and 1960. Communes now appeared in many cities, and radical excesses and misreporting of production figures became even more widespread. The system spun out of control in an orgy of mobilization and of "reporting" that proved little better than utopian fantasy. The result was a national tragedy.

The core of the tragedy was the leaders' demand for sufficient food to feed the cities even as agricultural production plummeted due to bad policies, mismanagement, confusion, and unfavorable weather. Local officials collected the food because their jobs depended on pleasing those above them, not those whom they governed. As a consequence, China's countryside slipped into famine. The full extent of the famine did not become widely known because officials sought to cover it up, and not all areas of the country crossed from hardship into crisis. But demographic figures that became available in the 1980s detail the horrors of 1960–61: roughly 30 million people, primarily the very young and the old, starved to death. Nearly another 30 million who would have been born in this period were either stillborn or not conceived. All the horrors of famine such as cannibalism of children occurred, and in some parts of the country primary schools did not reopen—because no children survived—for years afterward.[46]

The Chinese economy as a whole spun into deep depression. In part, this reflected the economy's substantial reliance on inputs from the agricultural sector, inputs that in 1961 simply dried up. In addition, Moscow had become so unhappy with both Mao's policies and his claims about a new road to socialism that in July 1960 the Soviets abruptly withdrew all their technicians from China and canceled their aid program. This severely affected many of the country's heavy industrial plants. The double blow of agricultural collapse and loss of aid produced a far more pronounced decline in economic output than the United States experienced at the nadir of the Great Depression in 1932.

The Great Leap Forward, born of a sense of growing crisis and harnessed to a fundamental faith in ideology, organization, and the masses, was an extremely radical, wildly unrealistic approach to economic development and the transformation of social values. It reflected both Mao Zedong's utopian ideas and his virtually boundless political power. The greatest part of the tragedy occurred, moreover, during the Second Leap, the new upsurge following the Lushan plenum of August 1959. A direct response to Peng Dehuai's supposed challenge to the Chairman's power, the Second Leap resulted from Mao's attempt to wipe out "rightism" throughout the party. He waged this political battle at the expense of consolidation efforts that he knew were necessary. From 1960 to 1962, Mao's political hubris, combined with the incentives lower-level officials had to lie to their superiors, resulted in ten thousand times as many deaths as the United States suffered in the terrorist attacks of September 11, 2001.[47]

The Great Leap thus failed because of flaws in its basic policies and in the inherent dynamics of China's political system, including the incentives for falsifying information from the grass roots. The withdrawal of Soviet aid and three years (1959–61) of particularly inclement weather deepened the failure. As a result, the Communist party, which had previously proved itself to be rough, violent, but above all successful, had now demonstrated that it could err catastrophically. Mao Zedong himself, moreover, bore a large part of the responsibility for the disaster.[48]

INCREASING TENSION AMID RECOVERY: 1962–65

As Beijing's leaders became aware of the extent of the Great Leap disaster, they adopted emergency measures. When urban food shortages became severe, the leaders decided in June 1961 to shift the major part of the burden back onto the peasants. They did this by forcing more than 20 million people who had entered the cities during the Great Leap back to the countryside from 1961 to 1962. This was achieved in large part by the rationing of nearly all urban food and consumer goods. Urban residents received coupons that were valid only for the purchase of specific items, in specific locales, and for specific periods. Peasants, who were not similarly given ration coupons, were thus unable to support themselves in the city.

In the wake of this mammoth resettlement effort, the CCP adopted a series of policies that had the effect of freezing people into their current work units.[49] Workers and staff in state enterprises from then on would be entitled to lifetime employment with benefits, but they lost their right to change places of work without the permission of the management. Enterprises then became all-encompassing units for their employees, providing housing, health care, recreational activities, rationed goods, pensions, and so forth. Political education and other government policies affected employees through their enterprises, and thus the place of work (called by Chinese the "unit," or *danwei*) became the key interface between urban employees and the political system. The units became so self-enclosed that most employees retained few contacts with, and had little knowledge about, those outside of their work unit.

The urban unit system combined with strict residence registration requirements in the countryside to prevent further rural-to-urban migration after the early 1960s. This had the effect of formally dividing China into a two-tier system, with a privileged urban society supported by substantial state subsidies and a highly exploited rural society whose members were denied access to jobs in the urban economy.

The ameliorative policies in the countryside included dividing communes into smaller units that closely approximated the former standard marketing areas and establishing the three-level system (team, brigade, and commune) that Mao had first advocated in March 1959. Related initiatives in other sectors included relaxing policies toward literature and art, inviting many specialists back into positions of authority, and generally undoing the radical excesses of the Great Leap. These new policies began in 1960–61. By 1962 many officials felt that the next appropriate step would be further decollectivization of agriculture, which had, in any case, occurred spontaneously in various localities that had been particularly devastated by the famine. Mao personally took a back seat as these policies were developed and implemented, but in the summer of 1962, as the peak of the crisis passed and the economy began to recover, he again stepped to the fore.

Mao's summer 1962 resurgence highlighted the disparate lessons that China's leaders had drawn from the devastation of the Great Leap. For many of the top figures—including Mao's putative successor Liu Shaoqi and Chen Yun, one of the leading economic officials—the Great Leap demonstrated once and for all that the country should no longer utilize massive political campaigns to accomplish national goals. Society had become too complex for this "primitive" means of policy implementation developed during the party's days in the wilderness.

For Mao the lessons were different. He gave up on the idea of using mass campaigns to achieve major advances in economic development, but he still felt these campaigns had a crucial role to play in bringing about changes in values. Mao's faith in the beneficent effects of struggle persisted despite the bitter experiences of the Great Leap.

From 1962 to 1965, therefore, two quite different agendas emerged on the national scene. Most leaders concerned themselves with cleaning up the mess left over from the Great Leap, a job that required pragmatic economic policies and related efforts. Mao and some of his supporters, in contrast, became obsessed with the fear that economic rehabilitation policies would steer the country away from revolution, and they demanded continuing mobilization to attack internal political enemies.

Mao's belief evidently stemmed in part from developments in the Soviet Union under Khrushchev. As the Soviet leader tried to move his system away from its Stalinist heritage, he took measures that Mao regarded as an abandonment of socialism. Khrushchev's decision in 1960 to withdraw aid from

China lent further credence, in Mao's view, to the thesis that the USSR under Khrushchev was no longer a socialist society. Mao found this thought deeply alarming; he had never before contemplated the possibility that a socialist revolution could be undone and could degenerate into what Mao regarded as a class-based, exploitative system. He now focused on the possibility that China could follow the same path after his death.

With the Soviet Union's experience very much in mind, Mao took two initiatives between 1962 and 1965. He began to educate the Chinese on the dangers of "Soviet revisionism" under Khrushchev.[50] He also began to look for signs of agreement with Soviet methods among his colleagues. Others, including the defense chief, Lin Biao, and Mao's wife, Jiang Qing—who might benefit from Mao's distrust of many of his colleagues—egged him on and fed his darker suspicions.

The resulting mix of policies was schizophrenic. Substantive economic policies stressed material incentives, coordinated development, clear hierarchies of authority, realistic planning, and use of technically skilled personnel. Yet along with these conventional policies the country experienced a steady drumbeat of political agitation advocating ideological commitment, denouncing internal enemies linked to the external threats from the United States and increasingly from the Soviet Union, and promoting egalitarianism and class struggle. Polemics against "Khrushchev revisionism" poured forth. In 1964 Mao also dictated the start of a huge new program of economic investment deep in the interior of southwest China, the "third line" or "third front," to prepare the country for the possibility of war with the United States should the hostilities in Vietnam continue to escalate.[51] In addition, various intense political campaigns took place: among others a second urban Three Anti and a rural Four Cleanups.[52]

As Mao became concerned with combating "revisionism" he increasingly relied on the People's Liberation Army, headed by Lin Biao, to achieve his domestic political goals. The government bureaucracies under the State Council had implemented the First Five-Year Plan; the CCP had run the Great Leap Forward. With Mao doubtful about each of these two nationwide political hierarchies, he turned toward the third pillar of the PRC, the army. Lin's political ambitions led him to pursue a dual strategy within the army based on mass indoctrination in Mao Zedong Thought, which Lin had excerpted and compiled into the "little red book," and development of the atomic bomb. China tested its first nuclear weapon in October 1964.[53]

Lin's skillful handling of politics and high technology in the army seemed to Mao to resolve what the CCP termed the "red versus expert" problem—that is, the problem of combining political commitment and technical expertise.[54] The PLA seemed to blend technical expertise, organizational discipline, and ideological fervor. Mao thus began to expand the administrative and political roles of the PLA into society. In 1964 Mao called for the population to learn from the PLA, implicitly instead of from the party, a remarkable step in a communist society. He also established political organs staffed by PLA officers in many government offices.[55]

Mao's political apprehensions may have reflected his more general worries about his own mortality. His speeches in 1964 make frequent mention of the inevitability of death. Increasingly conscious that his time was limited, Mao likely felt it urgent to ensure the continuing vitality of the revolution after his death.

The economic policies of 1962–65 brought about a remarkably rapid recovery: the economy regained average 1957 levels of output by 1965. But the political atmosphere remained relatively tense, with ambitious people such as Lin Biao and Jiang Qing trying to secure their power at the top by undermining Mao's relations with other colleagues. This was an unstable mix, and it did not last.

THE GREAT PROLETARIAN CULTURAL REVOLUTION—
THE RED GUARD PHASE: 1966–69

Mao Zedong was a political leader of extraordinary daring. In the Great Proletarian Cultural Revolution, he again demonstrated his commitment to revolution, his skill in mobilizing the Chinese against each other, and his readiness to sacrifice the lives of huge numbers of people to achieve his goals. Mao's own character was central to the Cultural Revolution, because without his actions it would not have occurred. Put differently, nothing inherent in the PRC system of governance would have led to the Cultural Revolution had not Mao guided the system in this direction.

Mao Zedong seems to have had four broad goals in the Cultural Revolution.[56] First, he sought to change the succession. As of 1965 his likely successor was Liu Shaoqi, but Mao had come to distrust Liu and the level of his commitment to revolution. Mao wanted both to dislodge Liu and to put another successor in his place, probably Lin Biao. But to remove a figure as deeply entrenched as Liu, who had been Mao's putative successor since the Seventh Party Congress in 1945, would require a major effort to blacken his name.

Second, Mao wanted to discipline the huge bureaucracies governing the country. Always deeply concerned about the inherent tendency of officials to put on airs, to take advantage of their offices for private gain, and to lose contact with the populace, he determined to force them to stand up to the test of mass criticism and potential humiliation. In this way, they would have to prove their leadership mettle again or they would fall. To make sure that officials could not shield themselves, Mao conspired with Lin Biao to have the army stand aside when the mass attacks occurred in the latter half of 1966. He probably also had Kang Sheng, head of the public security (police) system, have the civilian security forces do the same.[57]

Third, Mao wanted to expose China's youth to a revolutionary experience to, in his words, "raise a whole generation of revolutionary successors." Acting out of his faith in the ordeal of struggle as a force in shaping character, he created a situation in which this postrevolutionary generation of youth would have to live by their wits to come out whole. A period of testing and radical uncertainty, Mao felt, would make China's youth develop strength of character and commitment to the revolutionary cause.

Finally, Mao wanted to make substantive changes in various policy areas. Seeking to reduce income inequalities and material incentives, he eliminated wage increases and bonus payments for urban employees.[58] He sought to reduce urban-rural differences by, for example, spreading China's limited health-care resources more evenly around the country rather than permitting them to be concentrated in major cities, where health professionals preferred to work. In the countryside, he also sponsored the training of peasant medics, called "barefoot doctors."[59] In education, he sought to eliminate practices such as university admissions that favored those who scored best on exams. In China as elsewhere, examinations inherently favored those from intellectual and elite backgrounds. He also wanted the educational system to stress ideology and practical knowledge rather than scholarship. In the military, he tried to reduce status differentials by, among other things, eliminating the system of military ranks. Officers subsequently were addressed by their substantive position, such as Brigade Leader Zhang or Division Commander Li.[60] Overall, he sought to minimize the scope of any kind of private activity and to commit the Chinese to a fully collective, materially frugal existence.

At some point between 1965 and 1966—the details are still debated among scholars—Mao decided to take drastic action. The goals outlined above informed the specific efforts he made. Yet the Cultural Revolution was so base and violent in its focus that one has to ask about the dark emotional elements that may have contributed to Mao's decisions. Within four years of pursuing policies that had produced 30 million deaths and had thrown the country into a deep economic depression, Mao now launched Chinese society on a trajectory toward civil war. He instigated youths to beat and kill their elders.[61] He had many close colleagues with whom he had worked for more than three decades beaten, tortured, and left to die without medical treatment.[62]

The national response to Mao's call to launch a Cultural Revolution amounted to wild adulation of the leader who had caused such enormous suffering. The school-age generation of China in the mid-1960s had been taught to demonize and dehumanize whole classes of people and to tolerate and celebrate gross violence, even sadism, against them. The system was also characterized by a pervasive Maoist personality cult and bureaucratic repression of anyone stepping out of line. The numerous mass political campaigns over the previous fifteen years had left many personal grievances. These factors combined to produce a massive popular response to Mao's calls for political violence.[63]

Tactically, Mao used his strong ties to Lin Biao to secure the basic agreement of the military to his demand in 1966 that they step back from the fray. He also secured the support of Premier Zhou Enlai, who may have felt that it was useless to oppose Mao but possible to influence his policies and their implementation by aligning with him. A less flattering interpretation has Zhou seeing the Cultural Revolution as a vehicle for ousting Liu Shaoqi, with whom he was never close.

Mao used his wife, Jiang Qing, and her followers as surrogate leaders of the important propaganda bureaucracy once he ousted the officials there. In short, from late 1965 through first half of 1966 Mao put together a coalition of key players that enabled him to launch a frontal assault on the party bureaucracy and on the leadership of many state organs.

Having quietly secured the allegiance of the military, Mao then used the propaganda apparatus to bolster his own prestige among the masses and to demonize his targets. In this, he was helped by the stream of official propaganda that from 1961 to 1965 had consistently portrayed Mao as virtually infallible and had shifted blame for the Great Leap Forward disaster onto hapless lower-level officials. This effort to maintain the legitimacy of the system now came back to haunt those leaders whom Mao wanted to unseat.

In August 1966, having lined up his Cultural Revolution coalition at the apex of the political system, Mao unleashed the Red Guards to attack the party. Most Red Guards were urban high school and college students. Mao ordered the schools closed but did not let the students return home. He encouraged the students to form Red Guard groups and, quoting some of the exhortations of the time, to "make revolution," "do battle with revisionism," "yank out the small handful of capitalist roaders in the party," "overthrow China's Khrushchev [i.e., Liu Shaoqi]," "knock down the number two person in authority taking the capitalist road [i.e., Deng Xiaoping]," "destroy the old and establish the new," and "bombard the headquarters [i.e., the Communist party]." At the same time, he instructed all top leaders not to suppress the Red Guards but rather to face them and answer to them.[64]

Red Guard groups quickly launched a reign of terror in most big cities. They waved the little red book of Mao quotations and engaged in contests to see who could recite the quotations most rapidly from memory. Millions of Red Guards traveled to Beijing to march in parades past Mao, who stood atop the Tiananmen Gate to review them in the late summer and early fall of 1966. The Red Guards also took to the street, in the slogan of the day, "to destroy the four olds." This translated into destroying old culture by raiding houses, burning books and antiques, beating and humiliating people who seemed not to be in the spirit of things, and killing those who tried to resist. In all these instances, the police stood aside and let the youths wreak havoc. In addition to causing general mayhem, the Red Guards also attacked officials at all levels of the political system. Through the end of 1966, the military and police permitted this violence to unfold virtually without interference.[65]

Mao fairly easily overcame opposition at the top of the party to the Cultural Revolution, which, after all, broke almost every inner-party norm about how to address party problems. The Chairman "packed" the eleventh plenum of the Eighth Central Committee in August 1966, and he obtained from this plenum a "sixteen point declaration" on launching the Cultural Revolution "with fanfare."[66] In October 1966 the top leadership convened for a major review of the situation (such conclaves, called "central work conferences," occurred several times a year except from 1967 to 1976, during which only a few were held).[67] At this meeting Mao heard bitter complaints about Red Guard behavior throughout the country; he himself stated that he had been surprised at the power of the movement he had unleashed. He nevertheless decided to let it continue for a while so as to "further test" his colleagues.

Beginning in January 1967 in Shanghai, Red Guard groups and their counterparts among urban workers, generally called "revolutionary rebels," actually seized power from the local party and government. "Seizing power" literally meant that they stole the seals of office so that neither the party nor the government could officially receive or send out documents. In reality, the municipal party and government officials were swept aside, and a committee of Red Guard and revolutionary rebel leaders took over and briefly formed what they called a Shanghai commune. This power seizure quickly received the blessing of the Cultural Revolution leaders in Beijing. It marked the start of a process over the coming two years of power seizures in various provinces and cities and the formation of new "revolutionary committees" to exercise authority.[68]

In February 1967 many of the old marshals, the top leaders of the military, teamed up with a few others (excluding Lin Biao, of course) to challenge the thrust of the Cultural Revolution. They held a series of meetings with the leading radicals who were guiding the Cultural Revolution under Mao's aegis. Zhou Enlai chaired these tense, hostile sessions, and he reported the proceedings to Mao. Mao decided against those who challenged the Cultural Revolution, and this series of meetings then became known as the "February adverse current." The Cultural Revolution continued, becoming more violent and anarchic.

From 1967 to 1968, shocking episodes of increased Red Guard radicalism and violence alternated with more settled times. Mao instructed the military to "support the left" early in 1967 but did not indicate what that meant in any given situation. During this period, moreover, China shut itself off from the outside world to a remarkable degree. At one point in 1968 the PRC had only one ambassador actually posted abroad, in Egypt. Beijing's relations with virtually all its neighbors except Vietnam also deteriorated, and ties with the Soviet Union became extremely tense.

The spring of 1968 was perhaps the most violent time, although no firm statistics exist to confirm this impressionistic statement. During those months China slipped into virtual civil war as Red Guard factions turned against each other to do battle for power. Many had obtained guns and explosives, and the skirmishes ranged from melodramatic conflicts between opposing loudspeakers to extremely cruel, bloody assaults with automatic weapons and other deadly force. Taking prisoners, widespread use of torture, and other human rights abuses became common practice. The outside world obtained a glimpse of the violence when trussed-up corpses, many without heads, began floating down the Pearl River into Hong Kong. Nobody in Beijing exercised close control over this orgy of political violence.

Confronted with this fragmentation of the movement, Mao became frustrated with what he viewed as the self-centeredness of the Red Guards, who seemed incapable of uniting together to cooperate in building a new China. He therefore ordered the army to reestablish order in the cities and to send the Red Guards out to remote rural areas in order to "make revolution" there. Military forces in many cases carried out these orders with relish, suppressing radical Red Guard groups and "convincing" these radicals to resettle in harsh interior and border regions. About 18 million Red Guards were sent to the countryside in this effort.[69]

When radical Red Guard leaders in Beijing questioned whether Mao supported this military activity, the Chairman convened a meeting with them and announced, "I am the 'black hand' [who has been ordering your suppression]. If you leave this meeting and try to say something different, I warn you that I am making a tape recording of the meeting and will make it public." The PLA thereupon virtually took over the administration of China, placing military representatives in all major schools, factories, offices, hospitals, theaters, and other urban work units.

Mao's move toward suppression of the Red Guards may have been inspired in part by the Soviet-led Warsaw Pact invasion of Czechoslovakia in August 1968. In the wake of that invasion the Soviet leader Leonid Brezhnev had said that the USSR and its allies were obliged to put back onto the socialist path any country that had strayed from it. Beijing felt threatened by this new Brezhnev doctrine—and for good reason, given the rapid buildup of Soviet offensive military forces along the PRC's northern border. The nonstop buildup had begun at the start of the Cultural Revolution. Mao needed to restore order and prepare the country for possible war.[70]

The Red Guard phase of the Cultural Revolution ended in 1969. In April of that year the CCP convened its Ninth Party Congress, which declared the "victory" of the Cultural Revolution, restored Mao Zedong Thought to the Party Constitution along with Marxism-Leninism as the CCP's guiding ideology, and inscribed in the same constitution the explicit mandate that "Lin Biao is Mao Zedong's closest comrade in arms and successor."[71] Mao then abolished the special committee, called the Cultural Revolution Small Group, that he had established to run the Cultural Revolution.

SETTLING THE SUCCESSION: 1969–76

Between 1966 and 1969, the Cultural Revolution had destroyed a great deal and produced little of long-term value. It had inflicted enormous violence on the population, especially in the cities, and had left deep scars and social fissures. Although no reliable figures are available, those who suffered incarceration, serious injury, or death certainly reached into the millions. The CCP itself and much of the state apparatus had been paralyzed, with a large percentage of leading figures at all levels humiliated, stripped of power, and forced to do manual labor or to suffer a worse fate. The economy largely stagnated because of disruptions in transportation, decline in worker discipline, and the virtual destruction of the central economic statistical apparatus. Worse yet, as nativist impulses in the country surged to the fore, technological innovation stagnated almost completely.[72] The PLA assumed control over administration of economic, governmental, police, and social units, but this in turn raised tensions and political conflicts at all levels of the military.[73]

The late-1960s phase of the Cultural Revolution shaped a generation of China's youth. These were high school and college students whose institutions shut down in the early summer of 1966 and either remained closed or reopened only in a grossly altered form during the ensuing three years. These millions of students thus spent an important part of their teenage years on the streets, treating social and economic issues as political concerns and resolving political conflict through brutality, intolerance, and fanaticism.[74] This would become a "marked" generation of China, one that would remain a social and political problem for the country in the decades ahead. In 1969 and 1970, however, they were being shipped out to the countryside—often to the most isolated and desolate parts of the border regions and the interior—by the millions.[75]

With so much disruption and flux, the political succession remained undecided. Lin Biao was the putative successor, but he worried, with good reason, that Mao would abandon him. His close association with Cultural Revolution violence caused many to dislike him. In addition, Lin was in poor health and therefore vested much authority within the military in his wife, Ye Qun, and his son, Lin Liguo. Ye became a member of the ruling Politburo in the wake of the Ninth Party Congress.

The attacks on institutions from 1966 to 1969 threw the top leaders back on their personal resources and networks in the increasingly deadly game of Chinese power politics. To put it in imperial terms, the intrigues of the "inner court"—the personal relations of top leaders—became so important to politics that the functioning of the "outer court," the bureaucratic machinery of the state, faded considerably in determining political outcomes. The new Politburo membership ratified by the Ninth Party Congress in April 1969 reflected the growing importance of inner-court politics. Mao placed his wife, Jiang Qing, on this Politburo. Lin Biao's wife, Ye Qun, also joined, as did Zhou Enlai's wife, Deng Yingchao.

Within the military, Lin increasingly relied on two very loyal groups. The first was the officer corps of the Fourth Field Army, the group with which Lin had fought for years before 1949.[76] The second was the air force, which was headed by a close associate and, less formally, by his son Lin Liguo. From 1969 to 1971 Lin tried to secure his own power base, but Mao Zedong and Zhou Enlai gradually undermined him. Mao chastised key Lin supporters and removed them one by one in 1970 and 1971. Zhou sponsored domestic priorities that focused on economic development rather than the more radical policies with which Lin had become associated.[77] It appears that in these strange times even Jiang Qing, the very symbol of radicalism, bided her time and quietly cooperated with Zhou in order to unseat Lin Biao.

These complex machinations came to a head in September 1971 when, allegedly, Lin in desperation tried to assassinate Mao and claim the mantle of leadership for himself. Mao, it is said, learned about the plot in advance and avoided the danger. Lin and his family, except his daughter, then supposedly tried to flee to the Soviet Union, but their plane crashed in Mongolia with the loss of all aboard. All the bodies were burned beyond recognition. Lin's demise discredited the military itself, since Lin had supposedly orchestrated a military-based coup.[78] Taking advantage of the PLA's disgrace, Zhou Enlai then acted quickly to begin removing the army from civilian administration, a job that took years to accomplish.

More important, Lin's death discredited the Cultural Revolution itself and the national leadership in the eyes of many Chinese. When the story of Lin's alleged plot and his fate was relayed to the population in late 1971, many felt that the enormous suffering and bloodshed of the Cultural Revolution had been imposed on them as a consequence of the game of power politics in Beijing. The people had been mobilized, after all, to fight to the death to defend "Mao Zedong and Mao Zedong Thought," which represented the purity and perfect knowledge of the revolution itself. Mao had fully backed Lin as his chosen successor, the one who best understood and applied Mao Zedong Thought. Suddenly, though, the propaganda organs put out the story that Lin had been a scoundrel all along and that Mao had always understood this. Mao had only *seemed* to back Lin in order to flush him out and expose his true colors, at which point Mao foiled Lin's plot and rid the system of this usurper.

Even people who had been persuaded to regard Mao as virtually a god—and by 1971, Chinese citizens typically bowed three times before Mao's picture each morning and evening, "reporting" the day's events and their thoughts to the Chairman at each evening ablution—did not believe this new story. Lin's treachery, whatever it might actually have been, made cynics of many believers and greatly eroded the credibility of the entire leadership and its policies.

With Lin gone, the tacit alliance between Zhou and Jiang Qing soon frayed, as each maneuvered to gain the succession. In 1972 Mao suffered a heart attack and other severe health problems.[79] Although hidden from the general public, these setbacks must have sharpened intrigue over the succession in China's equivalent of the White House, the Zhongnanhai. The same year Zhou learned he had terminal cancer, adding still more intensity to the succession issue. During 1973 the battle lines over the succession shaped up, and the issue dominated Chinese politics for the ensuing five years.

The remaining three years until Mao's death witnessed a seesaw battle between the "moderates" headed by Zhou Enlai and the "radicals" led by Jiang Qing.[80] Zhou pulled together many former officials whom he managed to rehabilitate from their Cultural Revolution purgatory. In addition, Deng Xiaoping, who had been the number-two target of the Cultural Revolution after Liu Shaoqi, came back into Mao's good graces during 1973. By 1974 Zhou pulled Deng into his own camp. Jiang Qing solidified a radical group that, at the top, was headed by herself, the former Shanghai cultural-affairs official Zhang Chunqiao, the former editor Yao Wenyuan, and the former factory security official and then leading labor organizer early in the Cultural Revolution Wang Hongwen. All had spent important parts of their careers in Shanghai, and all by the early 1970s held important positions in Beijing. After their ouster in October 1976, they were dubbed the Gang of Four.

Like selective modernizers before him throughout the twentieth century, Mao had late in his career turned toward a nativist position out of frustration over the contradictions inherent in the selective modernizer approach. He, like earlier leaders in the twentieth century, had found that modern technology and the needs of industrial-production affect the structure and values of the society in ways he could not abide. During the 1970s, though, Mao sought again to achieve a balance in which economic development could proceed without doing fundamental damage to his radical social and autocratic political ideas. In this context, the personal tragedy of Mao Zedong in his later years was that he could not find a successor who sought both to spur economic development and to limit the sociopolitical repercussions of that process. Mao therefore intervened periodically in the conflict between Zhou's moderates and Jiang's radicals to tip the scale in one direction or the other, but he never permitted either side to gain decisive advantage.

From 1973 to 1976 the moderates generally controlled the executive organs of the political system, while the radicals had the upper hand in the propaganda and cultural apparatus. The military was not clearly committed and remained an object of concern for both sides. The moderate political platform edged somewhat toward that of the iconoclastic modernizers throughout the century, those who felt China should make whatever changes were necessary to develop modern technology and a modern economy. The radicals, by contrast, typified the nativist belief that China fared best when it isolated itself from the international arena and found an ideological basis for binding its massive population together in militant unity.[81]

In broad terms, the radicals gained the upper hand from late 1973 through the summer of 1974 and again from late 1975 to the summer of 1976. The moderates, increasingly led by Deng Xiaoping as Zhou Enlai weakened from cancer, held the initiative from mid-1974 to the fall of 1975. When Zhou Enlai died on 6 January 1976, the radicals soon succeeded in removing Deng from power again. But by the time of Mao Zedong's own death from natural causes on 9 September 1976, several developments had shown that the radicals were widely disliked, although they retained a core of supporters. Most notably, on 5 April 1976, large-scale popular demonstrations ostensibly in honor of Zhou Enlai at Tiananmen Square quickly assumed an antiradical thrust. The radicals successfully suppressed the demonstrations, arresting and beating many people in the process. But popular knowledge of these events weakened the radicals' legitimacy and their chances of surviving Mao's death.

As the succession battle raged, the radicals repeatedly used their control over propaganda to stir up mass campaigns to put pressure on the moderates. The rapid changes in policy lines that these campaigns produced exhausted and embittered the population.[82] Politics had more than ever taken a deadly turn, and most individuals tried to find ways to weather the storm by disguising their real emotions and thoughts even more than usual. The Chinese polity had entered a bizarre period that was brought to a conclusion only by the death of Mao and the arrest, a month later, of the leading radicals.

SUMMARY: THE MAOIST SYSTEM

The Maoist era was a remarkable time for China. Mao led a movement that provided strong central authority in a country that had experienced profound social and political malaise over many decades. He proved his assertion that the people of China had "stood up" in the international arena. One of his last major foreign-policy moves was to agree to a limited rapprochement with the United States, inviting President Richard Nixon to Beijing in February 1972. From that moment on, China had a key role to play in what became known as the "strategic triangle" (China, the USSR, and the United States).[83]

Under Mao and with help from the USSR in the 1950s, China began to develop a heavy industrial base and imported a great deal of fairly modern technology. It also copied a system of government that produced state ownership of the major means of production, collective ownership under state management of agricultural production, and a Leninist-type political structure that suppressed any truly autonomous social or economic organizations. To be sure, the Chinese system developed a style that differed from that of the Soviet Union. But the fundamental system was Communist party–dominated and Leninist, and this preempted the establishment of vibrant independent organizations as part of the Chinese development model.

Although committed to the rapid development of heavy industry, Mao remained sensitive to the inherent tendency of policies based on the Soviet model to increase inequalities, create a bureaucratic class, and widen the urban-rural gap. He therefore repeatedly intervened in the workings of this system to change its social and political results, primarily toward egalitarianism among those who live and work together, anti-intellectualism, antiurbanism, and antibureaucratism. In this sense, Mao periodically went into battle against his own creation, and in the end the tumult exhausted both Mao and "the system" without producing a clear winner. Both the battles and their outcomes left major footprints on the Chinese body politic.

One of the most notable features of the Maoist system is how powerful Mao himself remained. In a country of such enormous size, with national and provincial leaders who had climbed the rungs of power by dint of courage, skill, and ruthlessness, it is remarkable to note the extent to which Mao was able to overwhelm his colleagues and set the broad agenda. Mao's stature in part be seen as a product of China's long tradition of imperial rule.

Mao also combined his control over the prevailing ideology with great tactical political skill, ruthlessness in dealing with enemies, and the power that derived from his personality cult.[84] The bureaucracies and the people of China did not always respond as Mao wished.[85] However, his unique role in the system at virtually all times enabled him to define the terms of battle. That a committed revolutionary remained in a position of exceptional power for twenty-seven years after the CCP's victory in 1949 explains a great deal about the history of the PRC during that period.

If we sum up Mao's legacies as of 1976 in the political arena, the balance sheet may read as follows. Mao created massive institutional structures—party, government, army—to run China but severely undermined the integrity and legitimacy of those same structures with the Great Leap Forward and the Cultural Revolution. The structures were too massive to disappear, but they were in such disarray by the time of Mao's death that making them "whole" would consume years and in some ways be impossible. Mao brought to power a very strong group of experienced revolutionaries, but in his later years set them against each other. The scars would prove lasting. Mao's expansion of the educational system during the 1950s had been undercut by his later attacks on intellectuals, and by 1976 China suffered an acute shortage of intellectual capital. Having established a strong, legitimate political system after years of turmoil in China, Mao spent his final decades destroying the effectiveness of that very system.

As a revolutionary who spent over twenty-five years fighting for national power, Mao devoted great attention to raw power as a crucial dimension of Chinese politics. In 1949 he inherited a weak, deeply fragmented society, a country desperate to regain unity and the belief in some central, energizing idea, and to recapture lost pride and stature. Throughout the remainder of his career, Mao used the goal of unity to goad the populace and his colleagues. Time and again he proved most adept at finding the fault lines in the Chinese body politic and then manipulating and exacerbating them to maintain his control. He thus never fully developed a centralized KGB apparatus like that in the Soviet Union. He relied instead on keeping people divided and off balance and ultimately dependent on him to provide the right way to escape from the country's predicaments. Considering his fondness for division and struggle, it is little wonder that Mao left a country exhausted by social conflict and a bureaucratic system in which mistrust and factionalism had become endemic.

The system Mao created sought to isolate social groups as part of its strategy for limiting potential challenges from below. Numerous policies worked toward this end: peasants could not link up with urban groups; a system of residence registration prevented peasants from moving into cities. Moreover, the state forced peasants to deal with the urban economy only through the mediation of state-run "supply and marketing cooperatives," effectively cutting off almost all nongovernmental urban-rural contact.[86] Within cities, most residents after the Great Leap disaster were locked into their units, the places of employment or study assigned them by the party. These units generally became economic, social, and political cocoons, and contact between units became structurally more and more difficult—to the point where major units maintained "foreign affairs offices" to manage their contacts with other Chinese units. Typically, urban residents spent their entire careers in the unit assigned them when they first found employment in the state sector of the economy.[87]

The intelligentsia, normally a bridge between various social groups (disaffected intellectuals, for example, had played key roles in many major peasant revolts throughout Chinese history), became especially isolated. The 1957 Antirightist campaign and the virulent anti-intellectualism of the Cultural Revolution made members of the intelligentsia a despised, outcast group with no social standing. They were by the late 1960s referred to as the "stinking ninth category."[88] In a political system that sought to deny recognition and independence to social groups in general, the intellectuals became a target of especially acute violence intended to grind them down and destroy their cohesion.

Even within the governing bureaucracies, Mao utilized rectification campaigns and other methods to prevent power centers from developing. In the system he sought to create, administration would be decentralized and flexible while power would be highly centralized under his personal control.

Finally, Mao's strong belief in the inherent value of struggle led to policies that subjected the citizenry to extraordinary levels of violence. The overthrow of the initial targets of the revolution—landlords, capitalists, and others—did not end the violence. Intellectuals and other "rightists" came under the gun in the second half of the 1950s, to be followed in the late 1960s by all those who seemed committed to traditional culture, to represent bureaucratic authority, or to be "disloyal" to Mao and Mao Thought.

Perhaps the greatest weakness of the Maoist system was precisely that the Chairman loomed so large in it. In one fashion or another, Chinese politics from 1959 through 1976 centered on the issue of the succession to Mao. Mao's futile attempt to guide his own succession brought suffering to tens of millions. The deterioration of the system in Mao's later years undid some of the major political accomplishments of his first decade: it reinfested the system with acute personal factionalism; it reduced the extent to which military forces answered to national unified commands; and it left the country uncertain of the correct ideology to follow to achieve wealth, strength, and international stature.

Mao Zedong was thus an extraordinarily powerful man who left legacies for China of enormous importance. Had he died in 1956, he would be remembered as a remarkable leader. But by his death in 1976 his impact on the PRC had become disastrous, and Mao's successors faced an enormous task in grappling with his mistakes.

5
The Reform Era

The quarter century and more since Mao Zedong's death has witnessed changes in China nearly as fundamental as those Mao imposed between 1949 and 1976. Mao left a system that could not continue without him. But it took decades to reshape this system, and as of 2003 this project is still a work in progress. The remainder of this book explains first the politics of this "second revolution," then its institutional dimensions, major challenges, and potential futures. Before providing these details, it is important to appreciate the overall scope and ambition of the post-Mao reforms.

At the end of the Mao era China had an extremely low information system. All independent sources of opinion had been suppressed: people had learned as early as the political campaigns of the 1950s not to voice their real views. Within the party and the government, repeated purges had cowed officials at all levels, afraid to tell those above them the truth or to take any independent initiative. The residence (*hukou*) system and the work unit system drastically restricted the horizontal flow of information, as well as the physical mobility of the population. All news from outside China was censored, and few foreigners gained unsupervised access to the country. This was also a highly egalitarian society in terms of distribution of physical wealth. All signs of ostentation were banned to the point that even clothing and recreation seemed to the untrained eye not to vary much by station in life. It was also a highly coercive society. Even party officials held their tongues for fear of purge and punishment.

The government administered the economy almost completely. Market forces and personal incentives played virtually no role in the system. The highest priority was developing heavy industry for defense (and prestige reasons) and maximizing urban employment, with no noticeable attention to issues of efficiency or to effective use of capital. The result was lackluster economic growth, with nearly all real gain stemming from bringing more resources to bear rather than from improvements in productivity based on better technology and systems. There were no private property rights and virtually no private property at all (with the exception of peasant housing). There was almost no international trade, as Mao had pursued a policy of autarky. Foreign borrowing and foreign direct investment were prohibited.

The contrast with the China of today could not be more startling. Now, China's political system sets high educational requirements for officials, and there is enormous debate over policies both inside and outside the governing institutions. Economic growth has become the major goal of the political system. Market economics and the integration of China into the global economy are seen as key methods. For some of the years since 1992 China has been second only to the United States in terms of attracting foreign direct investment (FDI). FDI into China in 2002 exceeded that into the United States. The PRC has since the late 1970s maintained the highest rate of real growth of any major economy in the world. China has developed a substantial middle class. Its plunge into the electronic revolution has moved it to the front ranks of the wireless communications society. In rich cities such as Beijing and Shanghai, even most peddlers today carry cell phones.

China has also become rapidly more unequal. Especially since the early 1990s the rate of growth of inequality has been among the fastest ever observed globally. Part of this is geographical. The eastern coastal provinces have substantial per capita GDPs that are growing in multiples of those in the interior. But part of this inequality is also within individual localities. Officials who control economic decisions at all levels have become so corrupt that many of them enjoy standards of wealth far above those of other officials and citizens. China has also developed a rapidly growing cohort of very wealthy private entrepreneurs who drive luxury Western cars, belong to extremely high-priced private clubs, and generally value conspicuous consumption.

Personal mobility has grown very substantially. Over 100 million peasants have moved to the cities since the 1980s, and another 100 million are expected to do so before 2012. State-owned enterprises (SOEs) no longer provide lifetime employment, and large numbers of workers have been laid off or are unemployed. Those with skills often job hop to improve their incomes, but those without skills often have no permanent place of employment as they do what they can to make ends meet.

All of these changes, moreover, are accelerating as of 2003. China has committed to make massive shifts in the way it runs its economy as a condition of its having joined the World Trade Organization (WTO). New leadership at the apex of the system opens the possibility of increasingly significant political change. And massive problems are forcing China's leaders to take major new initiatives to cope with the wide-ranging results of the decisions they have made in the reform effort.

The story of China's reforms is one of taking bold initiatives and then scrambling to adjust to the consequences and keep the effort moving forward. At the start of the post-Mao reforms, nobody anticipated the situation that now exists. Political management of this process has required enormous skill and has occasionally faltered. The story is dramatic and still unfolding. Its consequences have the potential to reshape the political economy of Asia and the well-being of the more than 50 percent of the world's population that inhabits the region.

Setting the Stage

Mao Zedong's death on 9 September 1976 and the coup against Jiang Qing and her key supporters the following month left the Chinese political system in crisis. Mao's last years were especially pernicious for the long-term viability of the CCP's rule. In the mid-1970s, for example, he advanced the thesis that the "capitalist roaders" who wanted to lead the country to "revisionism" were located "right in the Communist party itself," thus dealing a body blow to the CCP's remaining institutional legitimacy. The vicious political infighting of that period totally undermined the normal paths for making policies and settling disagreements, causing the whole system to suffer a serious decline in capabilities. And the population itself seems to have been exhausted and disillusioned.

Mao elevated his own role to the point where he personally, rather than the Communist party as an institution, defined the prevailing line. Mao became the sole deity in what amounted to a political theocracy, and he left no successor or authoritative high priest in his wake. He purged Deng Xiaoping a second time in April 1976 and had him stigmatized for making a "right deviationist attempt to reverse correct verdicts," referring to verdicts on the Cultural Revolution and its victims. Mao's own wife was arrested in October 1976 amid charges that Mao for years had not trusted her and had warned her against scheming. Since 1973 Lin Biao, who had died in 1971, had been castigated as "leftist in form but rightist in essence." In short, Mao's death left a power vacuum and a degraded state system in which those who were politically sainted one day could, the next, be overthrown and dragged through the mud, with often horrendous consequences for their families and major supporters.

In some desperation during his last years, Mao had turned to Hua

Guofeng as a potential successor. Hua had joined the revolution in the 1940s and found himself in charge of Mao's home town after 1949. He met Mao in the early 1950s and thereafter gradually rose through the communist hierarchy, first in Mao's native Hunan province and then, starting in 1971, in Beijing. Jiang Qing's leftists waged open warfare with the moderates, led first by Zhou Enlai and then by Deng Xiaoping from 1974 to 1976. Mao positioned Hua as a compromise candidate who might lead the country when the Chairman passed away.[1] Hua, however, lacked the stature and the power base in Beijing to consolidate power after Mao's death.

By late October 1976 China's leaders had to figure out how to repair the political system and how to explain to the population what had gone wrong. Initially, they took the easiest path: they rallied behind Hua Guofeng as a "wise leader," blamed all problems of recent years on the underhanded maneuvering of the Gang of Four, and attempted to resume the regular central work conferences and other activities that had characterized the CCP's style of governance before the Cultural Revolution.[2] However, the core issues on the immediate political agenda remained: whether to rehabilitate Deng Xiaoping; how to resolve the grievances of the tens of millions who had been wronged during the Cultural Revolution; and how to regard both Mao Zedong and the Cultural Revolution itself.

Deng Xiaoping's potential rehabilitation faced opposition from Hua Guofeng, who was trying to establish his own legitimacy as China's leader after Mao. Hua's political allies, like Hua himself, had been helped in their careers by the Cultural Revolution, or at least had not suffered grievously because of it. These allies included Wang Dongxing, a former personal bodyguard to Mao whom the Chairman had made head of the 8341 Division of the PLA (China's equivalent to the American secret service, which provided personal security for the CCP's top leaders); Wu De, the mayor and first party secretary of Beijing, who had given the orders to clear Tiananmen Square on 5 April 1976, during popular demonstrations there against the Maoist leadership; Ji Dengkui, a poorly educated man who had risen primarily through the industrial bureaucracies; and Chen Xilian, Military Affairs Commission vice chairman, whose political base was in the southern part of northeast China.[3] These three and others like them sat on the Politburo. All shared a strong interest in maintaining Mao's good name and in affirming the value of the Cultural Revolution.

Of all the top leaders, Hua had the greatest stake in protecting the reputation of Chairman Mao. In 1976, in the wake of Deng's second purge, the deathly ill Mao supposedly told Hua, "With you in charge, I am at ease." This quotation alone provided the basis for Hua's initial assumption of the top military, party, and government posts on Mao's death. Hua had these posts confirmed at the Eleventh Party Congress in August 1977.[4] If Mao were to become less than infallible, Hua's base of legitimacy would quickly erode.

Not surprisingly, Hua sought to maintain his power in part by sanctifying Mao's name and decisions. At a Central Committee work conference in March 1977, he favored a position that became known as the "two whatevers"— whatever Mao had decided would remain valid, and whatever instruction Mao had issued should not be contravened. At that meeting he also argued against rehabilitating Deng Xiaoping, a move being advocated by older leaders such as Chen Yun and Wang Zhen.

Deng's rehabilitation was an issue of central importance. Deng had been a major target of the Cultural Revolution during the late 1960s. Rehabilitated in 1973, Deng aggressively and effectively moved the country away from Cultural Revolution radicalism until his second purge in 1976. Hua knew that he could not compete with Deng's competence and political stature. Hua had risen as a product of the Cultural Revolution, whereas Deng would almost certainly steer China on a very different course. Hua therefore argued that one of Mao's last acts had been to purge Deng, in April 1976.[5]

The effort to maintain his own position allowed Hua little room for change in the face of deep popular disenchantment with the conditions the country faced. He quickly began to give way. In April 1977 Deng wrote a letter to the Central Committee that accepted Hua's leadership, and that summer Hua agreed to Deng's reassuming all the party and military posts he had held as of his purge in 1976: vice chairman of the CCP; member of the Standing Committee of the Politburo; vice chairman of the CCP's Military Affairs Committee; and chief of staff of the PLA.[6] At the Eleventh Party Congress in August 1977 Hua declared an official end to the Cultural Revolution but warned that such political movements would continue to be periodically necessary.[7]

Surveying the crisis-ridden Chinese system in 1977 and 1978, Deng decided that only major reform would permit the CCP to remain in power. The party, Deng felt, would have to improve the standard of living of the populace, and to do this it would have to eschew Maoist egalitarianism and collectivism. Deng, like most other twentieth-century Chinese leaders, sought to make the country prosperous and strong. Unlike Mao in his later years, though, Deng felt this required opening up to—rather than shutting off—the rest of the world.

Deng Xiaoping's Reform Impulse

Under Deng Xiaoping's aegis in the late 1970s, China began the farthest-reaching, most systematic reform effort that any socialist country had attempted to date. This chapter focuses on the reforms at the apex of the political system, reforms that ultimately decentralized political power, energized and changed the ways the economy and society functioned, and made it necessary to follow far more than politics in Beijing to understand the direction in which China was moving.

Political considerations in Beijing dictated the pace and thrusts of the reform effort throughout the 1980s. As China entered the 1990s, the need to cope with the unintended consequences of reform increasingly drove policy forward. The two key players into the early 1990s were Deng Xiaoping and Chen Yun, both members of the CCP since the 1920s. Each had allies within their own generation of political leaders, and each had a following among those ten to twenty years younger than they. Deng's most prominent protégés were Zhao Ziyang and Hu Yaobang, and Chen's were Li Peng and Deng Liqun;

in the mid- to late 1980s all held dominant positions within the system. Deng's protégés themselves took some initiatives by the mid-1980s, and each finally ran afoul of their patron. The protégés also contended among themselves. Ultimately, though, the key political cleavage developed between the patrons, Deng Xiaoping and Chen Yun. Deng at all times remained the more prominent of the two—a result in part of his greater political ambitions and energy. But neither Deng nor Chen ever tried to remove the other, and the political story of the first decade of reform thus revolves in a fundamental way around their evolving contention over policy initiatives, political power, and official positions for their followers.

It was Deng Xiaoping's commitment to move China in the directions explained below that created the opportunity for major change to take place without mass upheaval. It was Chen Yun's initial support for and then ultimate concerns about the directions of the reforms that substantially explain the major swings in Beijing's policies from 1978 through the early 1990s.

In many instances, local-level officials and even major segments of China's population took advantage of political initiatives coming from Beijing as well as political disagreements among the leadership to push reforms forward "on the ground," creating new situations that became national policy when leading reformers subsequently endorsed them.[8] In each instance, though, the developments at the apex of the political system—in the form of either policy initiatives or political struggles—created "space" for flexibility and initiative at lower levels. This chapter seeks to explain the ideas and politics at the Center since 1978. The remainder of this volume then considers the linkages between the Center, the lower levels of the political system, society, and the major issues that confront the system.

There was no single blueprint for reform. In many instances the initial reform policies recalled approaches taken during the 1950s and during the recovery period in the early 1960s. In the 1980s the difference was that Deng understood the inadequacies of previous policies and encouraged more significant change as required. The results raised difficult political issues and challenged deeply entrenched interests. Among Deng's greatest accomplishments was his ability in the late 1970s and much of the 1980s to sustain, on balance, proreform momentum in a badly divided political system.

Although the reforms followed a sometimes tortuous course, their outcomes were remarkably successful in some key areas, even as they created grave problems with which the system must yet grapple. In the economy, China's real gross domestic product (GDP) per capita more than doubled during the first decade of reform, an astonishing feat even from a low initial base (see Table 5.1). At the same time, the political system changed in significant ways, with substantial improvements in information flows, policy process, and flexibility in adapting to local conditions. China's relations with the international economy and with various foreign groups and institutions grew rapidly. But these changes came at the cost of any consensus on national values. And major elements of the political system changed little or not at all, thus becoming more out of touch with an evolving social and economic milieu. Bursts of inflation and endemic corruption became serious problems.

TABLE 5.1 *Gross Domestic Product*

Year	Per Capita GDP (Yuan)(1978 Price)	Per Capita GDP (%)(1978 = 100)
1978	379	100.00
1979	402	106.10
1980	428	113.00
1981	445	117.50
1982	478	126.20
1983	523	137.90
1984	594	156.80
1985	665	175.50
1986	713	188.20
1987	783	206.60
1988	858	226.30
1989	879	231.90
1990	899	237.30
1991	969	255.60
1992	1093	288.40
1993	1226	323.60
1994	1366	360.40
1995	1493	394.00
1996	1619	427.10
1997	1745	460.30
1998	1863	491.49
1999	1978	521.70
2000	2120	559.24
2001	2259	596.10

China Statistical Yearbook (Beijing: China Statistics Press, 2002).

At the start of the reforms in late 1978 Deng lacked an overall plan, but he had decided that it was necessary to create an economically efficient society with a capacity for technological change if the PRC were to become prosperous and strong. He also recognized the need to impart legitimacy to CCP rule after the disasters of the late Mao years.

In broad terms, four major conclusions informed Deng Xiaoping's specific reform efforts. These conclusions derived from Deng's own experiences and concerned developments both in China and abroad.

First, Deng held that on a global scale, the basis for rapid economic growth had shifted from extensive to intensive development. That is, by the late 1970s growth stemmed more from new production technologies than from added production capacity. Deng recognized, however, that China's Soviet-type system performed very poorly both in generating new technology and in bridging the gap between research and development and actual production. The influx of capital, technology, and managerial know-how necessary to overcome these problems was available to those who would participate in the global economy, as the recent experiences of South Korea, Taiwan, Hong Kong, and Singapore had demonstrated; but Deng knew also that the Chinese system was poorly structured to enter the global economy. Moreover, Deng regarded the necessity of keeping pace with the worldwide trends toward technological dynamism and economic efficiency as a matter of China's long-term national security. This conclusion edged Deng toward the iconoclastic modernizers' position on the century-old continuum of views on how China should attain wealth and power.

Deng was convinced that excessive bureaucratic control stifles change and efficiency. To develop efficiency, it was necessary, therefore, to decentralize power within the state and to permit at least part of the Chinese economy to develop outside the noncompetitive state sector. Competition, in Deng's view, would force the state sector itself to become more efficient and dynamic. It would also require far-reaching changes in employment practices, the legal system, property rights, social policy, the incentive system, and so forth. In addition, Deng recognized the importance of rehabilitating intellectuals and allowing them to develop their professional expertise if China wanted to be able to become technologically proficient.

Second, Deng concluded that after the disillusionment of Mao's last years, ideological exhortations rang hollow, and that the Chinese people sought a higher standard of living. Events during the 1970s had so eroded the legitimacy of the Chinese Communist party that a new source of confidence in the party's right to rule would have to be found. Deng decided that source must be more and better resources for the populace, and argued that the party's only hope was the utilitarian principle that it could consistently "deliver the goods."

Third, Deng felt that even with economic reform and a wealthier society, China would have to be ruled solely by the CCP. Deng had always held deeply authoritarian views concerning China, and believed that anything less than total control by the CCP would produce chaos and violence. The tumultuous years of the Cultural Revolution reminded everyone of the dark potential of social forces in China when they were set free. Many feared that a reduction in party strength would produce an avalanche of efforts by individuals and groups to settle scores from the Cultural Revolution, with the prospect of widespread attendant chaos.

Finally, in the international arena, in the early 1980s Deng concluded that China could obtain a period of peace if it astutely utilized diplomacy to do so. It could then use this temporary respite from military preparation to build up its industrial capabilities to the point where over the longer term the Chinese economy could support a modern, powerful military force. Achieving this goal would of course require that China actively play the game of U.S.–USSR–PRC trilateral diplomacy to its own security advantage.

Although he had a general notion of the directions he wanted to move the country, Deng did not have a real plan in mind. His unfolding reforms required a great deal of adaptation to the cross-pressures created by earlier initiatives. Deng's genius, in fact, lay not so much in his ability to foresee the measures that would be necessary as in his extraordinary skill in establishing and maintaining the political viability of a wide-ranging reform effort through the twists and turns of Chinese politics starting in the late 1970s.

Managing the Politics of Reform

Once rehabilitated, Deng first had to remove Hua Guofeng and lay the groundwork for major change. He quickly undermined Hua's power. Power in China derives as much from personal resources, such as relationships developed over the years, as it does from formal office. This was especially true in the wake of the institutional havoc wrought by the Cultural Revolution. Deng was rich in personal relationships. He began his career in the CCP while working in France in the early 1920s. Back in China, he became a staunch early supporter of Mao Zedong in the hinterland, took part in the Long March, and served for years as a political commissar in one of the major communist guerrilla armies that eventually swept across China in the late 1940s. He ended the civil war in his native Sichuan Province in the southwest, but within three years was posted to Beijing. In the capital he spent most of the time until 1966 serving as general secretary of the CCP, a post that kept him in close contact with a large number of party officials throughout the country.[9]

Deng's career gave him rich experience in both military affairs and civilian administration before his final purge in 1976. He also had been purged twice (in 1966 and 1976) but never turned against colleagues, which stood him in good stead with the populace and many of the cadres. Deng thus came into office in 1977 with tremendous political resources to work his will.

Deng recognized the widespread desire to move decisively away from Cultural Revolution–type politics, and he acted accordingly. In 1977–78, even initiatives to restore the pre–Cultural Revolution system seemed bold and reformist, given the decade-long attacks on this system that had torn the country apart. Deng thus was able to unite two groups of officials: those who longed for the days before the prolonged streak of leftist radicalism that had begun with the Great Leap Forward; and those who had decided that more fundamental changes were needed to create a more humane political system and market-driven economy.

Both these groups in Deng's proreform coalition were composed of pre–Cultural Revolution officials: some of them had become targets of the Cultural Revolution and had spent many years in difficult political and personal circumstances; others had survived relatively intact but had not been key supporters of the upheaval. The issue that divided Deng's coalition in its early years, though, was fundamental: whether reform should return China to what many felt were the halcyon days of the mid-1950s, or change the way the PRC had been governed at any point since 1949.

Those who adhered to the former position had relatively clear ideas about what they wanted to accomplish. During the late 1970s, those in the latter camp generally had only a vague sense that past methods would not work. At the outset, they lacked the knowledge and skills to develop a picture of the specific alternatives they sought. Nevertheless, they argued for greater experimentation and increased willingness to take risks to find effective policy proposals. During the early and mid-1980s, these more radical reformers gradually moved far enough beyond their more moderate counterparts that eventually serious, open tensions developed.

It was important that from 1978 to 1984 Deng managed to keep these two approaches to reform contained within one coalition. The Cultural Revolution had so thoroughly damaged the political system that all agreed that basic steps toward rehabilitation of former institutions and methods of governance would have to come first. Specifically, it was not difficult for Deng to achieve wide agreement among his supporters in favor of:

☐ rehabilitating cadres who had been persecuted without good cause during the Cultural Revolution witch hunts;

☐ giving priority to economic development, which would require rapid restoration of the country's pertinent institutions to run the economy and abolition of the commune system in agriculture;

☐ providing significant resources and incentives to bail out the agricultural sector, which had become a serious drain on the entire economy;

☐ moving away from class struggle and mass movements (that is, mass political terror) as methods of policy implementation;

☐ breaking out of the rigidities imposed by the dogma of Mao Zedong Thought; and

☐ opening to the outside world, meaning the rest of East Asia and the West.

Only in 1984, once major progress had been made on all of the above, did the tensions in the coalition rise to the point where they dominated subsequent policy making. Before 1984, though, even key figures such as Chen Yun, Wang Zhen, Hu Qiaomu, and Deng Liqun, all moderates in 1978 who in later years came to be regarded as archconservatives, provided crucial support for Deng's agenda.

Deng initially pursued his efforts along two major lines: loosening the ideological straitjacket and creating a general sense of new opportunities to generate excitement and support.[10] Among the top leaders, he engaged in intricate ideological gymnastics to demystify the system after the excesses of the Maoist personality cult. He needed to clear away the psychological barriers to wide-ranging changes in the polity, as his emerging program amounted to a fundamental reversal of many of the ideologically derived priorities for which the blood of millions had been spilled during the Cultural Revolution.

Deng began almost at once to tackle the ideological question.[11] His message from the start was that Hua did not really understand the essence of the theology for which he was claiming the position of high priest. Through 1978 Deng pursued more flexibility in the interpretation of Mao. During that year a discussion began on Mao's notion of "seeking truth from facts." Deng did not initiate this effort, but a key protégé of his, Hu Yaobang, played a major role in promoting it once it began.[12] Hu had become vice president of the Central Party School in October 1977, and he used his position there to promote publication of this proposal. Deng used the notion of "truth from facts" adroitly to undermine Hua's "two whatevers." This was the centerpiece of an important speech he gave to a political work conference of the military on 2 June. By the end of that year, Deng had garnered widespread support for the idea that the essence of Mao Zedong Thought was that one should always "seek truth from facts, *and make practice the sole criterion of truth.*" Deng added the italic clause to the well-known Maoist dictum, thereby creating an ideological basis for making reality, rather than Mao Zedong Thought, the test for determining the correctness of policy.

This pragmatic guide to action permitted the leadership to delve into the country's actual conditions and to suggest innovative solutions to the problems they uncovered. Although this may seem an unremarkable situation, in fact it is quite startling that this shift from ideology toward pragmatism had come about within two years of the death of the godlike Mao Zedong.

Deng also quickly signaled his willingness to move policy along rapidly to create new possibilities for major groups in the population. The resulting broad policy initiatives of mid-1977 through the end of 1978 marked dramatic departures from Cultural Revolution orthodoxy. They cascaded from the top echelons of the party with a speed and scope that outraced China's capacity to keep up.

The evolution of policy toward the use of foreign loans and capital offers one example. It went from a strict ban on accepting any loans or investment in early 1977, to a willingness to accept credit in the form of long-term deferred payments for imports as of the spring of 1977, to accepting outright loans from private foreign sources in that summer, to accepting foreign government concessionary loans (that is, foreign aid) in the fall of 1978, to writing a law to permit foreign direct investment (that is, formation of joint ventures between Chinese and foreign firms) during that winter. By the end of 1978, Beijing indicated that it sought to bring in U.S. $40 billion in foreign investment—an amount that the country had absolutely no ability to absorb and utilize.[13]

Cultural Revolution priorities and restrictions were quickly abandoned in many other fields. In education, for example, the Maoists had abolished examinations for university entrance or graduation, substituting a system of "recommendation" of applicants by work units, which favored those with good political connections and those from disadvantaged backgrounds. This system sharply discriminated against those from "bad" classes. The predictable results included the admission of unqualified students and the erosion of academic standards in the universities. But in the summer of 1977 entrance examinations were reinstated, thus radically shifting the social base of students who would gain admission. By the spring of 1978, the government had introduced tracking systems and key schools that would receive the best students, teachers, and resources. That summer, Beijing decided to start sending students and teachers abroad for advanced training.[14]

This almost bewildering succession of plans and initiatives was too hurried to make much economic or administrative sense. To some extent, it reflected a system lurching toward reform without the information and procedures necessary to fine-tune the efforts. More fundamentally, though, it also reflected a political calculus. Having decided to challenge Hua Guofeng and set the country on a different course, Deng sought to mobilize as much excitement as he could from various quarters.

The slogan that guided this effort was that China must achieve the "four modernizations"—that is, the modernization of agriculture, industry, science and technology, and national defense. Zhou Enlai had first used this slogan in late 1964, but it had quickly disappeared. Zhou again raised it in his last official address in January 1975, at a meeting of the National People's Congress. Again, politics aborted the effort to make this a national priority. By 1978, though, the four modernizations had become the touchstone of national policy. There was disagreement, however, about how to achieve them.

At a meeting of the National People's Congress in February–March 1978, Hua Guofeng announced an ambitious "ten-year draft program" formally covering the years from 1976 to 1985. It called for the completion by 1985 of 120 large-scale projects, including the construction of fourteen integrated industrial bases, development of ten new oil fields, and doubling steel and coal output.[15] Hua based his ambitious plan on the idea that Maoist types of political mobilization remained an effective tool to achieve rapid economic development. Although Deng supported Hua's plan when it was announced, during the winter of 1978–79 he moved adroitly to distance himself from it.

In 1978 the gross output data of the economy indicated such rapid growth that in July of that year Hua and the national press began to talk about a "new Leap Forward." But the enormous growth actually stemmed from the return of production factors that had been left idle or were vastly underutilized during the Cultural Revolution and its immediate aftermath. Evidence mounted that this type of crash development program would quickly run into critical bottlenecks and could not be sustained.

In 1978 the United States and Japan stepped into the fray in a fashion that provided support to Deng Xiaoping. In May of that year President Jimmy Carter's national security advisor Zbigniew Brzezinski traveled to Beijing and, in essence, informed the Chinese leaders of the great benefits China could reap if Beijing were fully to normalize its diplomatic relationship with Washington. Many of these benefits would stem from American support of foreign investment in China and of China's greater access to the international economy. Shortly thereafter, the Chinese signed a long-term trade agreement with Tokyo that provided for substantial development assistance in exchange for Chinese energy exports.

As U.S.–Chinese and Sino-Japanese diplomatic and economic contacts intensified, and as signals multiplied in Beijing of departures from Maoist orthodoxy, foreign firms and banking institutions began to flood Beijing with offers of capital and specific projects. This was a time of substantial liquidity in the international economy, which enhanced the attractiveness to the West of the virtually untapped Chinese economy.

In December 1977 Deng Xiaoping placed Hu Yaobang in charge of the CCP's Organization Department, the organ most directly concerned with implementing party control over personnel appointments. In this position, Hu attacked head on the explosive issue of rehabilitating those who had suffered during the Cultural Revolution. Controversy ensued, some arguing that those who were rehabilitated would inevitably feel deeply aggrieved for their families' suffering and might seek revenge. China's peculiar personnel system, moreover, would typically put these individuals back to work in the very positions from which they had been ousted, thus forcing them to work alongside their accusers and tormentors. Hu nevertheless insisted that the party correct as many wrongs as possible. He led these efforts energetically throughout 1978. Hu's initiative mobilized important additional support for Deng even as it stiffened the resistance of those who had benefited from the Cultural Revolution.[16]

Deng, in short, pursued a multipronged policy to box in Hua Guofeng and undermine resistance to change. His policy overall included the following elements:

☐ Creating flexibility within Maoist dogma. By making "seek truth from facts . . ." the core idea in Maoist ideology, Deng successfully utilized the Chairman's prestige to release China from the shackles of Mao's political dogmas.

☐ Providing quick payoffs to supporters. Deng sought both to generate enthusiasm and to create constituencies with vested interests in his success. He therefore reinstated bonuses for urban workers, supported higher procurement prices to peasants for their goods, rehabilitated millions of people who had been attacked, and so forth.

☐ Creating vociferous domestic advocates of modernization. Deng in the late 1970s systematically sent central and province-level leaders on trips abroad to see how far behind China had fallen; many came back shocked. He also sent students abroad, promoted the rapid distribution of televisions, and used television to present images of the outside world to China's populace.

☐ Disciplining the bureaucracy. Deng supported removal of Cultural Revolution radicals from positions of power, rehabilitation of former officials, development of a "discipline inspection" bureaucracy to enforce orders from Beijing, and other related measures to counteract the results of years of radical Maoist advocacy of rebellion from below.

Whenever the leaders create political "space," China's citizens take advantage of the opportunity to voice their opinions. Given the PRC's grossly underdeveloped institutional means for the populace to convey its views to the leaders, such expressions typically take the form of mass demonstrations and other forms of direct actions such as putting up wall posters and writing petitions. Deng's wide-ranging efforts thus soon produced stirrings on the streets of Beijing. By the late fall of 1978, posters written by workers appeared calling for more rapid reforms. A wall leading to the intersection of Chang'an and

Xidan streets in the western part of the city center became a gathering place for dissidents, who posted their proclamations and sold political broad sheets there. Quickly dubbed Democracy Wall, this area immediately attracted the attention of Western journalists and the Chinese leadership. Posters on Democracy Wall dealt with many issues and conveyed increasingly fundamental critiques of the situation in China. Most called for further reforms. Initially many denounced Stalin as a way of indirectly criticizing Mao Zedong; some became bold enough to attack Mao Zedong directly.[17] Generally, these posters and proclamations strongly supported the directions in which Deng was moving the system.

Chinese party leaders convened a month-long central work conference in November–December 1978, followed immediately by the third plenum of the Eleventh Central Committee, which met 18–22 December. At the work conference, Deng and his allies seized the initiative from Hua Guofeng. They pointed to both economic studies and the voices of people at Democracy Wall to argue that serious changes must be made, and finally won the argument that it was no longer tenable to assert that Mao Zedong had always been correct. How would it be possible to rehabilitate many of the people who had been purged while the party maintained that Mao had never erred? Declaring Mao's infallibility and placing all blame for Cultural Revolution excesses on the dead Lin Biao and the purged Gang of Four simply would no longer suffice.

The central work conference and the ensuing third plenum turned the tide and set the stage for further changes. Subsequent party histories proclaim that at these meetings the long-term "leftist deviation" in the party, which had started with the Great Leap Forward in 1958, finally ended. These meetings were so consequential that it is worthwhile to review the major issues on which they made important decisions.[18]

The plenum declared that henceforth the top priority goal would be to achieve the four modernizations—in agriculture, industry, science and technology, and national defense—and that the correctness of all policies would be judged in terms of whether they facilitated or hindered achieving that goal rather than in terms of their fidelity to Mao Zedong Thought. The plenum also announced that the campaign to criticize Lin Biao and the Gang of Four had been successfully concluded. Now the goal could shift from carrying out this campaign to nurturing economic development. The plenum also described the "two whatevers" as incorrect and endorsed instead the discussion on "seeking truth from facts. . . ."

Additionally, the plenum mandated significant increases in crop payments to peasants, the protection of peasants' private plots, and the provision of production incentives. It specifically criticized the ideal of achieving egalitarianism. It established a Discipline Inspection Committee to enforce discipline in the party, which was directed against the leftists who had dominated party affairs throughout the Cultural Revolution. It also called for management reforms in state enterprises and for some decentralization of urban economic administration.

In personnel affairs, the third plenum ousted the head of Mao's personal security force, Wang Dongxing, from his major posts, reportedly because he refused to accept the above decisions during the debates at the central work conference. It placed Chen Yun, Wang Zhen, and Hu Yaobang, among others, in the Politburo. In addition, it announced the political rehabilitations of Defense Chief Peng Dehuai, who was purged in 1959 and died in 1974, and the former Guangdong party boss Tao Zhu, the economic administrator Bo Yibo, and the head of the Central Committee General Office Yang Shangkun, all ousted in the Cultural Revolution.[19]

The third plenum acted on one additional matter: on 16 December, two days before the plenum convened, Beijing and Washington announced the normalization of diplomatic relations between China and the United States. Deng Xiaoping had personally negotiated the key elements in this agreement during the preceding weeks. With the announcement, Hua Guofeng held a press conference in Beijing in which he signaled clearly his skepticism about the deal that had been struck. The third plenum, however, appraised the foreign policy of the time as "correct and successful."

The third plenum thus marked a major defeat for Hua Guofeng in his effort to hold back the tide of movement away from the Cultural Revolution. By the end of the plenum, Deng Xiaoping had the initiative in his hands, and he pushed the country toward greater political consolidation, openness, and economic development. Deng had not yet thought through the limits of the reforms, but he had gotten things moving in a big way. Difficulties, however, would soon rein him in.

Deng's wide-ranging assault on the Cultural Revolution's legacies in China opened a Pandora's box, and in early 1979 trouble began to appear in various spheres. China's relations with Vietnam had deteriorated sharply in 1978, especially over China's support for the increasingly anti-Vietnamese Khmer Rouge in Cambodia. In late 1978, Vietnam had swept across Cambodia, driving the Chinese-supported Pol Pot regime from power and installing a puppet government loyal to Vietnam. In February 1979 Deng ordered an attack against Vietnam along the Sino-Vietnamese border to "teach Hanoi a lesson." By March, Democracy Wall had become more of a hindrance than a help to Deng's plans. The focus of criticism increasingly shifted from the specific despotism of Mao to the more general issue of dictatorship in China. A courageous dissident named Wei Jingsheng called for China to adopt the "fifth modernization"—that is, democracy—as a necessary step for achieving the better-known original four modernizations.[20] Deng, who had never favored democracy, ordered Democracy Wall shut down. Wei was arrested and sentenced to fifteen years in prison for allegedly revealing state secrets during the Chinese attack on Vietnam.[21] Arrests of other Democracy Wall activists ensued.

During the winter of 1978–79 the evidence quickly mounted that China's plans to absorb huge amounts of foreign investment were simply unrealistic. Lower-level Chinese economic officials, perhaps sensing that their opportunity to acquire direct foreign investment might be short lived, rushed to sign numerous deals without much attention to their feasibility. The top leaders soon recognized that the current binge of deal signing might obligate the PRC to take on a far larger hard currency debt than it could manage. Within China, moreover, new studies pointed to severe investment imbalances and other problems symptomatic of an overheated economy, and fears of inflation grew.

In March 1979 a central work conference brought out admonitions from Chen Yun and other moderate reformers that China would need a period of "readjustment" to damp down inflationary fires and solidify the leaders' control over the changes occurring in the country. At other times—in early 1959 and again in 1961–62, for example—Chen had played a key role in putting the country back on an even keel.[22] Deng now went along with Chen's cautious call for reducing overall investment levels, shifting the investment mix more toward light industry and agriculture, and imposing stronger centralized monetary controls and limitations on the import of foreign capital. Having achieved political victory at the third plenum, Deng did not oppose some loss of momentum after that victory was sealed.[23]

In the spring of 1979, Deng also responded to increasing concerns about the system's spinning out of control by articulating the "four cardinal principles." These stressed that all future policies must be in conformity with (1) Marxism-Leninism Mao Zedong Thought, (2) the socialist road, (3) continuation of the people's democratic dictatorship, and (4) absolute political dominance by the Chinese Communist party. It subsequently became clear that there was little agreement on the concrete, operational meaning of the first three of these policy tests. But the fourth amounted to a firm commitment that, as political and economic changes reshaped Chinese society, the CCP would suppress any independent political forces that sought to represent new social interests.

Although Deng still had not forced Hua Guofeng's removal, by the summer of 1979 he, along with a broad coalition of older cadres, had gravely weakened Hua and his many supporters who had benefited in career terms from the Cultural Revolution. Most of Deng's key backers at this stage were people who wanted to exorcise the Cultural Revolution from the system but did not wish to change fundamentally the nature of the system itself. Chen Yun typified those who placed priority on economic growth and avoiding the excesses produced by Mao Zedong's revolutionary initiatives.

Chen believed firmly in a planned economy but also felt the state should recognize the limits of the plan. He believed that people are motivated by material incentives and not solely by ideological exhortation, and he therefore supported growth of consumer industries and abandonment of the previous policy of radical egalitarianism. Chen had always felt that obtaining adequate food supplies for the cities was one of the most crucial issues confronting China, and he supported reforms in the agricultural sector designed to boost rural production, especially of grain. Chen also advocated ties with the international economy, but he was concerned with limiting those connections so that China would not lose control over its own fate.

Chen also felt that the state should occupy a dominant role in the economy to bring about rapid industrial development. Fearing runaway inflation and the social upheaval it might cause, he sought to create an economic policy that would produce managed growth. Chen thus wanted to improve the efficiency of the state sector, strengthen the agricultural sector's ability to supply foodstuffs and industrial crops such as cotton for the urban economy, and utilize market forces to supplement the state economy. This was a far cry from blind belief in the magic of the market, but it nevertheless brought Chen on board for many reforms of the late 1970s and early 1980s.

In addition to people such as Chen Yun, Deng's coalition also brought together reformers who, as noted above, were groping toward more radical approaches. Generally, these individuals were more than a decade younger than Deng and his generation of leaders. Zhao Ziyang and Hu Yaobang typified this more adventurous group.

Hu had been a close associate of Deng's for almost his entire career, rising and falling over the years with Deng's own political fortunes. He had headed the Communist Youth League in the years before the Cultural Revolution. As noted above, Hu became head of the CCP's Organization Department in December 1977. A year later he moved laterally to take over the party's Propaganda Department, where during 1978 he played a critical role in promoting the discussion of "seeking truth from facts. . . ." Then in February 1980 Hu became general secretary of the CCP, and in July 1981 he replaced Hua Guofeng as chairman of the Chinese Communist party. He retained the general secretary post when the chairmanship was abolished a short time later.[24]

Zhao Ziyang's pre–Cultural Revolution career had kept him outside Beijing, and there is no evidence to link him with Deng Xiaoping before the Cultural Revolution. Zhao had served in Guangdong Province, which borders Hong Kong, from the beginning of the 1950s until his purge early in the Cultural Revolution. In October 1975, he had been appointed both governor and first party secretary of Sichuan Province. This landlocked southwest Chinese province, which included Deng Xiaoping's birthplace, had a population at the end of the 1970s of about 100 million people. Sichuan had suffered grievously from civil strife during the Cultural Revolution.[25] Its economy was in poor shape when Zhao took it over.

Once the winds of change began to blow in Beijing in 1977, Zhao was bold and adept at rehabilitating Sichuan's economy. He loosened the collective agricultural system and increased peasant incentives, and quickly the province reverted to its traditional role as a net food exporter. His experiments with new incentive systems in industry also seemed to work. Deng and other leaders at the Center took note of these developments and began to groom Zhao for responsibilities in Beijing. Zhao worked in Sichuan through 1979, but during that winter he moved to Beijing. He became a member of the Politburo of the CCP in February 1980, vice premier of the State Council two months later, and premier that September. During 1980 Zhao also became head of a commission with substantial authority to develop economic reform proposals.[26]

Between 1977 and 1984 Hu Yaobang and Zhao Ziyang became convinced that China would benefit from relatively bold actions to change the system. Hu focused especially on policies toward intellectuals, while Zhao targeted the economy. Both became deeply involved in expanding China's relations with the outside world, especially with Japan and the West. Increasingly, they came into conflict with the supporters of moderate reform, such as Chen Yun, who wanted to apply the brakes once the system had been cured of its most harmful maladies. Hu, Zhao, and their followers wanted to press forward.

With Hua and his supporters defeated between 1978 and 1981, the 1980s witnessed a seesaw battle between different sides of the increasingly divided reformist coalition. It pitted advocates of only modest reform led by Chen Yun against those who wanted to move decisively to a market system, led by Deng Xiaoping with Hu Yaobang and Zhao Ziyang as his chief lieutenants. There were tensions within each camp, and from time to time other issues not directly pertaining to economic policy intruded, but essentially the conflict was about the extent of reform in the management of the economy.

The ensuing politics of the 1980s and early 1990s demonstrate the system's failure to institutionalize consensus building and compromise at the top even after Mao's death. By the mid-1980s both Deng and Chen had developed very different policy packages. Deng stressed marketization and diversification of the economy, the depoliticization of society, opening to the international arena, and higher rates of growth. Chen sought planned growth, greater attention to political ideology, a more limited opening to the outside world, and more modest rates of growth. Because no rules or institutions could limit the activities of these two leaders, no mechanism existed to integrate their programs or balance their powers. Policy, therefore, tended to lurch from one policy package to another. Neither leader sought to knock out the other one; perhaps the bitter memories of Cultural Revolution political battles were too fresh. But this contention imparted instability to politics and policy throughout the 1980s and into the 1990s.[27]

A policy cycle developed that favored first Deng's priorities and then Chen's. Radical reformers loosened up the controls Beijing exercised over the economy. Lower-level officials then quickly took advantage of their new opportunities to bring prosperity to their own localities. This produced soaring budget deficits, rapidly rising inflation, worsening corruption, and rampant materialism among the population. As a consequence, Chen Yun–type reformers, who by the late 1980s had become true conservatives, argued for consolidation, retrenchment, and readjustment. This would entail the reimposition of some administrative controls, a clampdown on increases in the money supply, new drives against corruption, and greater attention to ideological education. This seesaw dynamic produced, in the terminology used by Chinese, alternate periods of "loosening" (*fang*) and "tightening" (*shou*).

The first such cycle took place in 1980. During that year the Chinese economy began to overheat as the early stages of reform took effect. Localities took full advantage of looser controls to increase their rate of investment, and paid out too much money to workers in bonuses. As a consequence, inflation set in, too much currency was issued by the Bank of China, and the central government confronted looming budget deficits. A meeting of provincial party secretaries in September 1980 could not agree on how to respond to this situation, but at a CCP work conference that November Deng yielded to Chen Yun's proposal to initiate a period of retrenchment. The agricultural reforms, nevertheless, continued apace.

In 1981 think tanks established by Deng's protégé Zhao Ziyang in Beijing worked on developing new reform initiatives. The most fundamental reform begun to date had been the initiation of a process that was leading to full decommunization of agriculture and a return to family farming. No other reform so significantly affected the lives and livelihoods of so many people. The exceptionally good harvests, which seemed to stem from the rapid return to family farming, provided support for those who argued in favor of more radical reforms. Agricultural results would continue to provide a major boost to the radical reformers through the bumper harvest of 1984. In the urban economy, the retrenchment continued through 1982.[28] At the end of 1982, however, the Twelfth Party Congress provided a springboard for major new reform efforts.

The Twelfth Party Congress and the first plenum of the Twelfth Central Committee directly following it called for far-reaching rectification of the party apparatus. The more radical reformers hoped to utilize this rectification to weed out opposition to their policy proposals. Hu Yaobang almost immediately began to encourage further loosening up in the ideological realm. He articulated more explicitly than ever before the notion that the CCP continued to have the right to rule China because it could produce improvements in the general standard of living. This rationale played very much to the strengths of the radical reformers, with their concerns for providing individual incentives and for raising incomes.

Zhao Ziyang had spent his pre-1980 career in provincial positions. During 1983, Zhao began forming a reform coalition with coastal provincial leaders and with leaders of the "special economic zones"—coastal areas designated by Beijing in 1980 to provide special incentives for foreign investment. He did so by arguing for decentralization of budgetary authority, which would leave far greater resources in the hands of the leaders of China's wealthier provinces. This fit in with Deng's economic rationale of boosting the national economy by encouraging local initiative. The related political calculus was to build alliances with key provincial and local players in the Chinese system, most of whom were members of the Central Committee of the Chinese Communist party.[29]

The radical reformers' coalition strategy naturally produced opposition from those left out. They included a wide range of important players: leaders of interior provinces; members of such bureaucracies as propaganda, personnel, and security, whose tasks were complicated further and whose prestige was lowered by the reforms; and Chen Yun's group, which feared both the economic and the sociopolitical consequences of the more radical program. Chen's coalition struck back. At the top, his supporters included Song Ping, Li Xiannian, Yao Yilin, Hu Qiaomu, and Deng Liqun, all of whom had strongly encouraged the initial reform efforts in the late 1970s. Hu Qiaomu had served at times as Mao Zedong's secretary and was one of the few well-educated members of the CCP elite; Deng Liqun was in 1983 in charge of the CCP's propaganda bureaucracies. During the latter part of 1983 Hu Qiaomu and Deng Liqun deftly turned the proreform rectification, an effort to tighten discipline and weed out leftists, into an antireform campaign against "spiritual pollution." At an elite level, they minced few words in blaming Hu Yaobang for what they perceived as a sharp decline in the ethics of the Chinese system.

Hu Yaobang and Zhao Ziyang responded to this challenge by eliciting Deng Xiaoping's support for a major effort to vault China into the ranks of advanced nations through a Chinese technological revolution. Using, among other things, the writings of Alvin Toffler on the "third wave," they persuaded Deng that the key to China's development lay in rapid expansion of the country's scientific base.[30] This would, in turn, demand greater freedom of education and thinking. Deng came out in support of this initiative in February 1984, and as a consequence the radical reformers were soon able to beat back the "antispiritual pollution" campaign. A Hu Yaobang protégé, Hu Qili, replaced Deng Liqun as the man in charge of CCP propaganda, and Zhao Ziyang increased his control over urban economic policy and over science policy. Political offices are part of the spoils of Chinese politics, and each time a faction surges in power it quickly takes advantage of the opportunity to reward its members with new appointments.

At the third plenum of the Twelfth Central Committee in October 1984, Hu Yaobang and Zhao Ziyang promoted far-reaching urban economic reform. This plenum was symbolically important, given the pivotal role of the third plenum of the Eleventh Central Committee in December 1978. In 1984, the third plenum adopted a document of principles on urban economic reform that pointed the way toward Deng Xiaoping's preference for radical reorganization of the urban economy along market lines. This document maintained some role for the planned economy, but it strongly favored market forces to guide most economic outcomes. The constantly improving harvests of 1979 to 1984 lent great credibility to the Deng group's arguments. In the countryside, the reformers had successfully brought about fundamental changes in rural production, shifting from people's communes to family farming between 1979 and 1984. The results were better than anyone could have anticipated. The radical reformers now asked, essentially, for similar freedom to reconfigure the urban economy.

Deng Xiaoping also mulled over the prospects for long-term peace along China's borders during 1984. By the end of the year he began to call for reductions in the size of the military establishment and for major reforms within the military system, both of which he pursued in earnest during 1985.

The year 1985 began with a new surge of reform initiatives, starting yet another cycle of expansion and retrenchment. This cycle entered a retrenchment phase in 1986, and those opposed to the radical reformers managed in January 1987 to convince Deng to oust Hu Yaobang from power. As Deng had looked to a Hu Yaobang–Zhao Ziyang team to take over for him once he stepped aside, this purge signaled major trouble for the political system. It raised the possibility that Deng would, like Mao, be unable to designate successors and then assure a smooth transition of power.

Yet another cycle began in early 1987, as Zhao Ziyang articulated new reform initiatives that were embodied in the decisions of the Thirteenth Party Congress, which convened that fall. But these, too, quickly ran into trouble, and by the summer of 1988 the opposition led by Chen Yun counterattacked. Party decisions late that summer called for retrenchment, but by then the party was so divided that the effort proved half-hearted. This retrenchment really took effect only after the Tiananmen massacre in June 1989, and it lasted for two years. In early 1992 Deng Xiaoping personally intervened to start a new expansionary cycle.[31]

Overall, the radical reformers never won a full political victory, and the relations between moderate reformers and their radical colleagues became increasingly embittered as time wore on. Because both sides were led by octogenarian Long March party elders, moreover, both contended over the eventual political succession to this older generation. The unresolved succession thus remained an important ingredient that further limited the ability of the various groups to reach a stable consensus.

Against this background of recurrent cycles, intraelite and state-society tensions associated with the reforms surged most dramatically in the spring of 1989. The first months of that year witnessed conflicting dynamics. Zhao Ziyang and his radical reform colleagues sought to keep the reform effort moving ahead, with encouragement from an increasingly articulate and bold collection of intellectuals and scientists. Nevertheless, the general thrust of policy at that time was toward retrenchment, and some efforts were made to tighten up, especially in the financial realm. In the midst of this tense political situation, Hu Yaobang died of a heart attack in mid-April. Hu had been purged in 1987, and his death touched off student demonstrations calling for the leadership to recognize his full merits as a reformer. Hu had been an advocate of greater political and intellectual freedom; he thus provided frustrated students and intellectuals a vehicle for their criticisms of the more conservative leadership.

The demonstrations over Hu Yaobang during the ensuing six weeks turned into a fundamental challenge to the regime itself.[32] This was partly, it can be argued, because the leaders treated it as such. The top leaders responded ineptly when the demonstrations began, perhaps because they initially assumed the guise of mourning rituals for the departed leader. Official missteps enraged the students of Beijing, who expanded their efforts and eventually turned the demonstrations into explicit challenges to the way China was being led.[33] Official corruption and soaring inflation, both closely associated with the reforms, became two of the key targets of the demonstrators. They argued that these and other problems could be resolved if the leaders would permit a freer press and greater democracy. The student movement hence became known in the world's press as a pro-democracy movement. It focused its activities on the huge urban space that is the physical and political center of Beijing—Tiananmen Square.

The size and dynamics of the Tiananmen movement epitomize the tremendous changes that the first decade of reforms had wrought in society. The reforms had among other things reduced political repression, encouraged greater freedom of thought, exposed many Chinese to foreign ideas and images, and focused people on improving their material standard of living. These changes produced demands by urban Chinese to be treated as citizens and not simply as members of the "masses." Student protest has a prominent history in modern China (recall the student-led May Fourth demonstrations in 1919), and with reforms reshaping society without producing major changes in the political system, tension was bound to erupt into social protest.

The Tiananmen demonstrations began as student actions in Beijing, and they subsequently spread to many other cities. Perhaps even more worrisome to China's autocratic leaders, the protests quickly involved not only intellectuals but also workers, entrepreneurs, and even many communist officials. For example, on 4 May the huge crowds cheered when a contingent from the CCP Central Committee Propaganda Department marched into the square holding aloft a banner proclaiming that henceforth they would publish only the truth. Similar contingents came to the square from the major party news organizations, from the Academy of Social Sciences, and from other nonstudent units.

By the end of May many students, workers, and others had formed self-proclaimed "autonomous" organizations to represent their interests.[34] This marked a further challenge to the state. Until that moment, the communists had denied all citizens the right to participate in organizations other than those officially sanctioned by the authorities. Agreeing now to the legality of autonomous organizations would change the very nature of the communist system.

The student demonstrations played into elite politics in Beijing. In the spring of 1989, Zhao Ziyang feared he was close to being removed by Deng as a scapegoat for the country's economic difficulties. The reformist Soviet leader Mikhail Gorbachev, however, was scheduled to visit Beijing in mid-May for a summit meeting that would formally end the long Sino-Soviet split, and the Chinese did not want to carry out top leadership changes just before the Gorbachev visit. As May arrived with the massive student challenge to the leaders continuing, Zhao knew he was in serious political trouble, but that he would remain in office until at least a decent interval after the Gorbachev visit. In a related development, virtually all the major international media had decided that the Gorbachev visit to Beijing was so important that it demanded priority coverage. A very large number of TV anchors, reporters, and cameramen descended on the city from abroad in late April and early May, just as the student demonstrations were gathering steam.

Facing this mix of forces, Zhao decided in early May that he would signal to the students his sympathy for their demands. This marked a considerable turnabout for Zhao. He had associated himself with ideas of greater political democratization in 1987, but more recently his followers had begun to support the idea that the best path to successful reform would be to have a strong, autocratic leader use his power to implement change.[35] This view, called "neo-authoritarianism," was intended to lay the groundwork for Zhao to become an autocratic leader in Deng's wake. Because of this and because Zhao's sons allegedly had become corrupt businessmen in Guangdong Province, Zhao had originally been as much a target of the demonstrators as were the other top leaders.

Zhao Ziyang's sympathetic response to the students was broadcast on the national evening news on 3 May. His remarks made him an instant hero among the demonstrators, and this intensified the sense of crisis at the top of the system. The top leaders felt they could not act decisively to regain control over the situation until after the mid-May Gorbachev visit; in the meantime, the students and their supporters gained center stage and enormous global publicity.

President Gorbachev's visit proved acutely embarrassing. Students staged a hunger strike in Tiananmen Square that garnered widespread popular sympathy. The Chinese government therefore could not hold the usual arrival and departure formalities for visiting heads of state in the square. Directly after Gorbachev's departure there was a showdown among the leaders of China in which the octogenarians, who had formally retired from their executive posts—especially Deng Xiaoping, Chen Yun, Yang Shangkun, Wang Zhen, and Li Xiannian—banded together to make all the key decisions.[36] On 19 May Zhao Ziyang was removed from power, and martial law was declared in Beijing. When troops then tried to move into the city, however, they found that virtually the entire urban population turned out to block their paths; they were stymied and eventually had to retreat. The situation then simmered for several weeks in a virtual standoff until, on 3 June, troops reentered the city in force, this time with orders to seize their objectives utilizing "all necessary means." In the early hours of 4 June widespread shooting began, producing a bloodbath seen live on television around the world. During the following few days the PLA troops continued to consolidate their control over the city, with much violence and numerous arrests. Beijing subsequently announced a death toll of 331. Outside observers place the toll between nine hundred and three thousand, but no fully reliable figures are available.

The situation throughout the country quickly quieted down once the top leaders demonstrated their willingness to draw blood to impose order. But though the use of force provided a tactical victory, it also produced a strategic disaster. Global public opinion turned sharply against Deng and his colleagues, who overnight changed in the public perception from reform leaders to retrograde autocrats and killers. Many countries imposed economic and other sanctions on the PRC in the wake of the Tiananmen massacre. Within China, moreover, the party's use of troops against the population of Beijing produced tremendous revulsion and cost all the top leaders a precious amount of public support. Within the governing bodies themselves, moreover, the Tiananmen incident left a legacy of great bitterness, as many key officials had strongly opposed the use of force and found the students' demands reasonable.

On a popular level, the Tiananmen movement provided China's citizens with a rare opportunity to learn how many people shared their own criticisms of China's leaders. The unit system that Mao had imposed on China had reduced tremendously the amount of "horizontal" communication among people in different units. Thus, citizens had little opportunity to find out whether their own views were unique or widely shared. During the demonstrations, people learned that not only other ordinary citizens but also many ranking officials shared their sense of alienation. In the early evening of 3 June just hours before the bloodbath, for instance, the normally reserved Beijingers hailed strangers on the street to exchange gossip and views, typically concluding each brief encounter with some sarcastic remarks about the political leadership. In the aftermath of the 4 June massacre, the authorities reimposed the unit system, but the events of April–June made clear how much society had changed and revealed to everyone the extent of popular alienation.

On 9 June, in the wake of the massacre, Deng Xiaoping called for a period of several years of stability.[37] Deng also demanded that the party produce results to rebuild support among the population. With Deng's first two anointed successors, Hu Yaobang and Zhao Ziyang, having fallen, the new people to move to the fore were Chen Yun's protégé Li Peng as premier; Jiang Zemin, the former head of Shanghai Municipality, as general secretary of the party; and Deng's ally Yang Shangkun, an octogenarian, as vice chairman of the Military Affairs Commission. During 1989–94, Li and Jiang ostensibly shared civilian power. In reality, however, the dynamics of Tiananmen demonstrated to all that the octogenarians were still a decisive force in the political system. Li Peng positioned himself with Chen Yun, while Jiang Zemin took his cues more from Deng Xiaoping. On the whole, the Tiananmen tragedy left the top level of the Chinese political system gravely weakened and in disarray. On balance, the Chen Yun forces had the upper hand in the wake of the purge of Zhao Ziyang and the bloodletting in Beijing.

The Tiananmen repression did not, however, resolve the fundamental debates about the best economic path to pursue, which continued virtually unabated. Within the group of elders the important divisions over the reform effort between Deng Xiaoping and Chen Yun remained. A new political challenge arose with the unexpected downfall of Communist régimes throughout Eastern Europe and the Soviet Union from 1989 to 1991, which produced strong concerns among conservative leaders in the PRC. They reacted by heightening propaganda against what was termed "bourgeois liberalism" and taking new measures to try to limit the "corruption" entering China from the outside world.

The reform decade finally reached a crisis, therefore, in 1989, when the problems created by the reforms and the forces set loose by them combined to create a fundamental challenge to the system. The leaders beat back this challenge with brute force, but the system itself had changed enough to make any effort to turn back the clock impossible. By mid-1989 China had opened to the outside world and had let loose dynamic forces for domestic change. Yet in the wake of the Tiananmen massacre the country faced such major challenges that many observers doubted whether the system itself could survive for long.

Deng Xiaoping, who had initiated China's transformation, for the most part skillfully kept it moving forward. In January and February 1992, at age eighty-eight, he made another bold move to generate momentum for renewed reform. Deng traveled to the Shenzhen Special Economic Zone bordering Hong Kong and then to other parts of Guangdong Province and Shanghai. In each place he called for the whole country to push ahead with rapid market-oriented changes, emulating the economic development of Shenzhen. He also insisted China open still wider to the international arena.[38]

Deng's "southern journey"—the expression *nan xun*, used in the Chinese press, is reminiscent of the terminology formerly used for tours by the emperor—was part of a strategy to seal the succession and solidify the reforms. The Fourteenth Party Congress was scheduled to convene in the fall of 1992, to be followed by a new National People's Congress the following spring. Deng wanted to see reform-oriented officials secure the top party and government slots at these two meetings, and the Fourteenth Congress to give a firm imprimatur to market reform for the 1990s. Deng seemed keenly aware that this would be the last Party Congress he and the other octogenarians would live to see. He was right.

The spring and summer of 1992 brought numerous indications of a see-saw battle, as reformers and conservatives tried to hammer out a deal that would permit the Congress to convene. Finally the Fourteenth Congress met on 12–18 October, and proved to be only partially successful. Its substantive economic program gave an unrestrained endorsement to market-oriented reform. In political terms, however, the Congress produced a far more mixed victory for reformers. This disjuncture between the economic and political outcomes of the Congress was repeated at the National People's Congress in March 1993.

Deng's journey through the south touched off an explosion of economic activity throughout China. Local officials seized the opportunity to increase investment and sign deals. Individuals at all levels of the system sought ways to make additional money through entrepreneurial activity. A new expression soon developed for plunging into the market—*xia hai,* literally, "to go down into the sea." The government allowed foreign firms to take the first steps toward entering major new sectors of the economy, such as insurance, retail sales, and legal work. Foreign direct investment in the PRC soared to roughly U.S. $20 billion in 1993 alone.

This expansionary cycle produced remarkable results that highlighted pent-up frustrations with the conservatives' failures. China's economy began to expand at a rate of more than 13 percent per year, and both foreign trade and foreign direct investment soared. Supported by huge investments from Beijing, Shanghai began a breathtakingly rapid economic transformation into a modern commercial and financial center.

Like all previous expansions, though, this one also led to high inflation, growing corruption, and bottlenecks in key goods. Zhu Rongji, a former Shanghai leader, assumed responsibility for reining in the double-digit inflation while not disrupting economic growth. He worked wonders in accomplishing this high-wire act. By 1997 China enjoyed both strong growth and low inflation, and it managed to avoid slipping into crisis during the Asian financial crisis that started later that year. Indeed, Beijing undertook a new set of radical reform initiatives in 1998.

The stabilization effort during 1989–91, followed by rapid growth in 1992–97, bought breathing space for the regime to put Tiananmen behind it. The old leaders' dominance of the system faded, moreover, as Deng Xiaoping became largely incapacitated by illness in December 1994 and Chen Yun died in April 1995. Deng died in February 1997.

Jiang Zemin moved adroitly to become the first among equals in the collective leadership that formed in the mid-1990s. Jiang, Li Peng, Zhu Rongji, and Qiao Shi worked reasonably well together, and largely without higher-level interference, from late 1994 to 1997. Qiao Shi, the oldest of this collective leadership group, was forced to retire in a reshuffle in early 1998, as the Jiang-Li-Zhu team embarked on a major new stage in the reform effort. This stage grappled primarily with acute problems created by the dynamics of the reforms themselves. These included reforming state-owned enterprises, cleaning up the banking system, stabilizing rural incomes, clearing the way for rapid growth of the private sector, and gaining China's accession to the World Trade Organization (WTO). Chapter 9 details these efforts and their results, which, with the exception of the WTO effort, generally proved only moderately successful at best.

The magnitude and complexity of the ongoing reform effort has, since the mid-1990s, meant that there are no longer two competing sets of views about reform among the very top party leaders, with an observable cycle shifting the balance back and forth. Rather, the Politburo Standing Committee has undertaken a process of grappling with very difficult issues under a system of an agreed division of labor. All involved in the Politburo are committed to sustaining overall rapid economic growth, and all recognize the basic necessity of increasing the use of market forces and of leading China to further integration with the international economy. To be sure, political conflict did not disappear in the mid-1990s, but it has not revolved around broad, competing domestic-policy packages. Indeed, the politics of this period are better understood in terms of the dynamics of succession than in terms of the repercussions of the politics of reform.

The Succession Issue

One of the most acute flaws of Leninist party systems is that power is concentrated at the apex of the system without any means to assure a smooth political succession at that level. China has paid dearly for this flaw. The succession to Mao Zedong arguably began to unsettle Beijing as early as 1956, and succession politics contributed enormously to the chaos the country endured during Mao's final decade. The reformers recognized, therefore, that finding a less disruptive path to leadership change at the top, and indeed at all levels of the system, must be a key objective of their efforts. The magnitude of this goal is highlighted by the fact that violence, purges, and disruption had characterized most leadership transitions in China, not only since 1949 but stretching all the back to the 1880s.

Both systemic and elite succession processes have thus loomed large on the reform agenda since the 1980s. Since 1980, China has witnessed the complete replacement of the original revolutionary generation and massive changes in the norms of recruitment, promotion, and retirement throughout the system. Over the past decade, moreover, the succession processes at the top have become more regularized, even if they remain largely nontransparent and potentially destabilizing.

SUCCESSION AT THE TOP

Despite decentralization, stability in the PRC still depends on effective leadership at the Center. But the PRC, like imperial China and all Leninist systems, has found it impossible to institutionalize succession fully. As Chapter 7 explains, China's political institutions impose few real constraints on the top leaders—and this is especially true regarding the position of "core leader." Formal succession arrangements cannot be regarded as immutable constraints on the quest for power at the highest level of the Chinese political system.

For its first four decades, the Chinese system suffered from a fundamental succession conundrum. Every core leader sought to choose his successor. Because the successor-designate had at all times to reassure the core leader of his continuing fidelity, it was difficult for him to build up an independent base of support to see him through the political struggles once the core leader passed from the scene. To the extent that the designated successor tried to develop his own base, he risked losing the support of the core leader. Autocrats are notorious for suspecting that their protégés wish to unseat them, and China's autocrats have been no exception. Because power at the top in this system is not institutionalized, when the core leader died his power died with him; a successor therefore needed his own base of support to compete successfully for the top position.

The net result over the first four decades was generally predictable: either the core leader purged his protégé because of suspicions about the protégé's power and plans to assume power too soon (Liu Shaoqi, Lin Biao, Hu Yaobang, Zhao Ziyang), or the protégé assumed power after the death of the core leader, but was unable to consolidate his position and was soon nudged aside by other contenders (Hua Guofeng). Given the extraordinary importance of the core leader during these years to the way the Chinese system operated, this structural uncertainty regarding the transfer of this power constituted a major flaw that proved highly damaging to the system.

Things began to change significantly in the 1990s. Jiang Zemin was able to build up his base during the mid-1990s, when Deng Xiaoping was incapacitated but still alive. Jiang, in turn, in 2002 had to confront the fact that Deng had designated Hu Jintao as Jiang's ultimate successor, and Hu by then had served on the Politburo for about a decade. In addition, the role of the core leader diminished with the passing of the revolutionary generation itself. Jiang clearly became the first among equals, but he failed to dominate the leadership to the extent that either Mao or Deng had managed.

In November 2002 the PRC achieved its first timely and peaceful party leadership succession. Hu Jintao became General Secretary of the CCP in November 2002 and President of China in March 2003. It wll take time for him to consolidate his power, but he and his colleague, Premier Wen Jiabao, made effective use of their handling of the SARS epidemic in the spring of 2003 to move this process forward.

SUCCESSION STRATEGY

After years of vicious succession politics, in the wake of Mao Zedong's death Hua Guofeng assumed all the top offices in the land: party chairman, premier, and chairman of the party's Military Affairs Commission. Since he owed his position solely to Mao's patronage, he insisted that China remain loyal to every word that Mao had uttered. But, as noted above, Hua proved unable to consolidate his power, Deng Xiaoping effectively became the core leader in 1978, easing Hua out of his major positions over the following three years. This demonstrated once again that power in the CCP resides in informal connections, prestige and command, not in formal positions.

Deng, himself twice purged by Mao, understood well the potential tragedy that struggles to succeed an all-powerful core leader can produce. He therefore almost immediately set out to put into place the building blocks of a stable, predictable succession. This produced several related initiatives: (1) he tried to keep within some bounds his own importance to the system so that his eventual retirement or death would not prove overly disruptive; (2) he chose two successors early on, built up their reputations, and gave them opportunities to construct their own political bases; (3) he tried to encourage his colleagues in his own generation to retire so that they would not interfere in the succession arrangements; and (4) he sought to enhance the importance of institutions and of regularized procedures to the politics of the top power elite so as to make the transfer of power more predictable.[39]

Deng circumscribed his own role primarily by refusing to assume two of the top three positions: those of premier and head of the party (as chairman or general secretary). He served for a number of years as a vice premier and as a member of the Standing Committee of the Politburo, but he left the top posts for his chosen successors, exercising his personal influence outside the formal channels of authority. The one key position that Deng did assume was that of chairman of the Military Affairs Commission of the CCP. He felt that the direct control over the military was too important to entrust to others. To some extent, moreover, the military itself probably sought this arrangement, which enabled it to enjoy direct access to the party core leader.

Deng's chosen successors were Zhao Ziyang and Hu Yaobang. Zhao was a provincial official who made his early career in Guangdong province. He fell from power during the Cultural Revolution. When he returned to office, he became party secretary in Inner Mongolia (May 1971–April 1972) and in Guangdong (until 1975) before taking charge of Deng's native Sichuan Province. In Sichuan, Zhao was enormously effective in restoring the province's economy from the ravages of the Cultural Revolution through relatively bold reforms, first in agriculture and then in management of state industries. These reforms caught Deng's attention. He moved Zhao to Beijing and made him premier of the government in 1980. Deng counted on Zhao to implement a nationwide economic reform effort.

Even before 1949, Hu Yaobang had been a close friend and associate of Deng's, serving with Deng in Sichuan Province from 1949 to 1952. From then until the Cultural Revolution, Hu headed the Communist Youth League while Deng ran the party Secretariat. Both were purged early in the Cultural Revolution and rehabilitated in the early 1970s. Hu reappeared in April 1972, nearly a year before Deng's rehabilitation, then was purged again when the Gang of Four attacked Deng in early 1976. Both came back into office for a second time in 1977. Deng successively placed Hu in charge of two of the most sensitive areas of national policy, personnel (for 1978) and propaganda (for 1979). He then had Hu appointed general secretary of the CCP (February

1980) and party chairman (June 1981—until the abolition of that office in September 1982).

Deng gave both Zhao and Hu considerable leeway to propose and implement programs and to cultivate followers. Hu Yaobang focused his attention primarily on the traditional areas of party apparatus concern: propaganda, personnel, and rural policy. A remarkably impulsive and lively figure, Hu toured the countryside in the mid-1980s, encouraging local officials to double economic output in the coming few years. He popularized the slogan calling for rural families to become "ten thousand–*yuan* households"—that is, to raise their earnings to ten thousand Chinese dollars per year, far above the national average at that time. Politically, Hu sought to "emancipate minds" and to bring younger, more intellectually open people into office. In terms of personal political strategy, he made a concerted effort to place people who had worked closely with him during his Communist Youth League days into key positions at both the provincial and central levels.

Zhao Ziyang took charge of the Finance and Economics sector and focused primarily on the urban industrial economy. He strongly advocated rapid economic reform and became a champion of a coastal development strategy closely linked to the international economy. Zhao pioneered in the development, noted above, of a group of think tanks in the State Council. These focused respectively on political reform, foreign affairs, and the intersection of economics, technology, and social change. They became impressive organizations for investigating problems and generating policy options.[40] On the whole, Zhao moved aggressively to bring up younger people who had shown some initiative and talent in the late 1970s. Many of them had been sent to the countryside during the later stages of the Cultural Revolution and thus had some feel for the realities of rural China as well as for the politics of the cities.

Thus, both Hu Yaobang and Zhao Ziyang sought to make their marks and to create strong political bases. Neither was simply a toady to Deng, their patron, but neither would have dared to oppose Deng when he made his position on a matter clear. Deng went some distance toward permitting them to build up the political resources necessary to see them through the succession, but both served at Deng's sufferance. Deng protected each at various times from attacks by more conservative members of the older generation associated with Chen Yun. In addition, Deng gradually withdrew himself from day-to-day operations—in China's terminology, he "stepped back to the second line"—during the mid- and late 1980s.

Beyond setting an example for officials in general, Deng also urged the older members of the Politburo to step down voluntarily. He spoke of this as their last major contribution to the revolution, but his elderly colleagues on the Politburo resisted. Finally, Deng adopted a strategy of creating posts that permitted partial retirement. The most important of these was the Central Advisory Commission (CAC) by the Twelfth Party Congress in September 1982. Deng personally headed this commission until late 1987, even while he retained his posts on the Politburo. In November 1987, he stepped down from both the Politburo and the CAC, evidently as part of a deal he struck with Chen Yun for the latter to move from the Politburo to be the CAC's chairman.

The CAC had no direct executive powers. It did, however, provide its members with a number of conveniences and with the right to carry out investigations and make reports to the authorities. Members of the Standing Committee of the CAC also had the right to sit in on Politburo meetings but not to cast formal votes at those meetings.

In short, the CAC provided a vehicle for old leaders to step out of their executive positions but still meddle in politics. It thus was an intermediate zone between full power and real retirement. CAC membership did not carry the potential opprobrium of retirement, but it did permit the assignment of younger officials to the top positions of formal authority in the party, government, and military. Deng conceived of the CAC as a temporary device to suit the peculiar situation in which the older revolutionaries were yielding power. He anticipated that this commission would be abolished once that generation fully retired or passed from the scene. The Fourteenth Party Congress in fact abolished it in late 1992.

Deng also encouraged strengthening regular institutional routines throughout the party and government, including at the upper echelons of power. Whereas in Mao's last decade nearly all institutions experienced enormous disruption, under Deng regularized meetings and procedures became more the norm. Thus, for example, the Party Congress has met as scheduled every five years since 1977. Central Committee plenums began by the early 1980s to meet on a fairly regular basis each fall. The National People's Congress is supposed to be elected anew every four years and to hold a plenum once each year. Under Deng and since his death, these criteria have been met. The spring plenum of the NPC has become a key event on the annual political calendar, as has a regular summer central work conference at the seaside resort of Beidaihe. It appears that the Politburo, the Secretariat, and the State Council also began to meet on a more regular basis in the 1980s, although the evidence here is thinner.

The above initiatives demonstrate that Deng Xiaoping seriously tried to reduce the chances of a destabilizing struggle for political succession. He recognized from the start that the lack of institutionalized succession is a dangerous flaw in the Chinese political system, and he gave considerable priority to remedying the problem. Ultimately, though, Deng failed.

THE COLLAPSE OF DENG'S SUCCESSION STRATEGY AND JIANG'S RISE

Both the nature of the Chinese system and Deng Xiaoping's personal failings unraveled his attempt to lay the groundwork for a smooth, predictable political succession. Although no single event undermined this effort, his handling of the Tiananmen pro-democracy movement proved especially damaging.[41] But substantial problems were evident even before Tiananmen brought them dramatically to the fore.

Deng's strategy itself proved fundamentally flawed. By denying himself the top formal positions other than in the military, from which he stepped down in 1989, yet at the same time exercising supreme power, Deng demon-strated on a daily basis that his vaunted institution building was a front and a sham. His designated successors, Zhao and Hu, held the highest positions, but those positions did not convey supreme power. As the 1980s wore on and the older generation (Deng, Chen Yun, Li Xiannian, Bo Yibo, Wang Zhen, and so forth) retired from the Politburo at the Thirteenth Party Congress in 1987, the difference between formal position and real power became even more acute. The Politburo became a committee of protégés who answered to the real pow-ers behind the scenes, the elderly patrons whose deals among themselves determined who would serve on the party's top bodies. Even though Deng retired from his last formal post in 1990, for example, by his bold initiatives to rekindle reform in 1992 he fully demonstrated his continuing ability at age eighty-eight to affect the agenda of Chinese politics despite his near total deaf-ness and declining health.

Deng might have rectified this situation to some degree had he person-ally given up power in the mid-1980s, once Zhao and Hu were firmly in place. But he refused to do so, evidently regarding himself as indispensable to pro-tecting the reform program both from the more conservative elders and from potential excesses by his successors. But Deng ultimately proved unable to convince the other elders to retire completely while he personally remained actively involved in politics. The inevitable result was the ongoing corruption of the leading institutions by the activities of a powerful, meddling group of aged revolutionaries.

To make matters worse, Deng, like Mao, purged his own designated suc-cessors when they displeased him. By 1986, Hu Yaobang felt that it was time for the successors to take over the system fully. He personally coveted the chairmanship of the Military Affairs Commission. Reportedly, at a meeting late that year where Deng proposed his own retirement, all those attending except Hu Yaobang urged Deng to stay on "in order to protect the reforms." Deng regarded Hu's position as an indication that his younger successor (Hu was seventy-one years old at the time), with whom he had worked for nearly half a century, had become too anxious to seize power. When Hu ran afoul of military leaders and of other elders later that year, therefore, Deng did not protect him. Hu's ouster itself was decided on in January 1987 outside of the boundaries of the Politburo, the only body that had the formal right to make such a decision.

Later in 1987 Deng further damaged the institutional arrangements he himself had created. The new Party Constitution—formally known as the Party Rules—adopted in 1982, had specified that the head of the Military Affairs Commission must be a member of the Standing Committee of the Politburo. But in November 1987 Deng dropped off of the Politburo in part, as mentioned above, to bring about Chen Yun's retirement from the same body. Deng, however, retained the chairmanship of the Military Affairs Com-mission, thus demonstrating yet again that among the power elite the PRC remained a system of men rather than a system of law.

The Tiananmen events thus dealt a body blow to an already severely weakened succession structure. But the body blow was nevertheless of enormous importance. Several aspects of the response to this challenge had major repercussions for the succession, as follows:

☐ From April to June 1989, all important decisions were made by the elders rather than by the formal leaders of the party and government. Deng and /or his elderly colleagues, sometimes after heated debate, decided on the initial reaction to the April student demonstrations in the wake of Hu Yaobang's death, mapped out the strategy at each succeeding stage, decided to impose martial law and to remove Zhao Ziyang from office, and made the fateful decision to order troops to take back the streets and Tiananmen Square itself at any cost on the night of 3–4 June. Throughout this entire period, the normal organizations of the leadership either did not convene or met only to hear and approve the decisions made elsewhere. Almost all political systems strain institutional boundaries at times of crisis. But the Chinese during these crucial weeks effectively set aside their institutional structure and revealed to all the locus of real power at the top—the semi-"retired" octogenarians—ten years after the reforms began.[42]

☐ The struggles of April–May produced the purge of Zhao Ziyang, the second of Deng's two designated successors. This totally undermined Deng's 1980s effort to pick successors and to put them into position to inherit and consolidate power after he left the system. All subsequent designees would understand that they could not escape the quandary of having to retain the support of their patron even as they sought to create their own political base. People in Beijing were heard to comment in late May 1989, "The old men in their eighties are meeting to decide who in their sixties should now retire from politics."

☐ Tiananmen strengthened the harder-line leaders who opposed Deng's more radical reform activities and thus ensured a more embittered, faction-ridden political environment for the early 1990s.

☐ Tiananmen produced the appointment of Jiang Zemin as general secretary and his subsequent designation by Deng as the "core leader" of the new generation. But Jiang did not have Zhao Ziyang's stature or political base of support. He had to tread very carefully and follow a complex strategy to build the support ultimately necessary to carry the day after Deng's incapacitation in the mid-1990s and his death in 1997.

The events of 1989, in short, severely complicated the succession and highlighted the very limited extent to which Deng had put this critical issue on track. When he was promoted and moved to Beijing in mid-1989, Jiang Zemin was allowed to bring only one supporter, Zeng Qinghong, from Shanghai with him. Jiang had to move very cautiously to maintain Deng's good graces while gradually building his base in the capital.

Jiang took not threatening Deng and Chen Yun as his first priority. During the early years after he moved to Beijing, foreigners and others who met with Jiang came away almost without exception with the idea that they were dealing with a lightweight. Jiang orchestrated conversations to demonstrate that he was a pretty innocuous fellow. He also held back from taking strong policy stances that might have alienated either Li Peng and the conservatives or Deng Xiaoping himself.

Jiang came out more forcefully on one side of the ongoing policy debate over future directions only after Deng Xiaoping made his famous "journey to the South" in 1992 and called for an acceleration of reform. Deng essentially drew a line that forced Jiang to take a position, and Jiang opted to side with Deng. During that same year Deng, pushing for rejuvenation of the party ranks, indicated that Hu Jintao should eventually succeed to Jiang as the core of the "fourth generation" of leaders.[43]

Deng's effective incapacitation several years before his death in 1997 gave Jiang an opportunity usually denied to designated successors of authoritarian leaders. Jiang was able to use this period more assertively to establish his own base and undercut his rivals. At the same time, he enjoyed both Deng's protection and protection from Deng—the former because Deng was still alive and venerated and the latter because Deng was too feeble to orchestrate an effort to replace Jiang. In addition, Jiang was fortunate that Chen Yun died before Deng, thereby further ensuring the succession that Deng had stipulated. This stood in marked contrast to Deng's own fate in 1976, when Zhou Enlai predeceased Mao Zedong.

Jiang maneuvered deftly to become the first among equals in the Politburo Standing Committee of the mid- and late 1990s. Zeng Qinghong provided important tactical advice on how to outmaneuver Jiang's key rivals, the Politburo Standing Committee members Chen Xitong (head of the Beijing municipal party committee) and Qiao Shi (head of the NPC). Jiang caught Chen in a corruption scandal and established a Politburo Standing Committee retirement norm of age seventy to remove Qiao.[44]

Hu Jintao followed a very patient strategy to ascend to the top party post. During his pre-1992 career he had demonstrated an ability to work effectively with both conservatives (such as Song Ping) and reformers (such as Hu Yaobang). He built up a reputation for being very smart (with, it is said, a photographic memory), effective, disciplined, modest, and loyal.[45] As noted above, Deng personally identified Hu as the designated core of the "fourth generation," reportedly at Song Ping's suggestion.[46]

Hu jumped to the Politburo Standing Committee on Deng's recommendation in 1992, and he became head of the Central Party School in 1993. On the Politburo Standing Committee, he took on politically sensitive tasks, such as the responsibility for preparations for a party congress. But he apparently handled issues in a way that avoided creating resentments and enemies, evidently counting on Deng's having designated him as Jiang's successor to see him through if he made no mistakes. Hu thus over time built up a reputation as a capable, hard-working, consensus builder. He also developed a wide-ranging network, including the powerful cohort of fellow graduates of Qinghua University.[47]

Nevertheless, during the summer of 2002 Jiang Zemin reportedly tried to convince his colleagues to allow him to stay on as General Secretary, even though he had promised in the run-up to the Fifteenth Party Congress that he would step down after one more term. Failing in this effort, Jiang then succeeded in October of 2002 to obtain agreement to a Politburo Standing Committee list that expanded that body from seven to nine members and filled it with a majority of Jiang's protégés. Jiang also had himself reelected to a new five-year term as the chairman of the powerful Military Affairs Commission directly after the Sixteenth Party Congress.

In the wake of the Sixteenth Congress, Hu quickly took the initiative to identify himself with a distinct political agenda, focused on improving the lot of China's peasants, providing greater protection to migrant workers, developing a social safety net, increasing transparency of government operations, enlivening the media, and improving the quality of operations in the party and government. Wen Jiabao visibly identified himself with these concerns.

Hu also took care in the first months of his leadership to pay respect to Jiang Zemin and to appear frequently together with Zeng Qinghong. He may have calculated that establishing good working relations with Zeng might wean him away from rigid support for Jiang Zemin. But the SARS (severe acute respiratory syndrome) epidemic that became public in March–April 2003 created a major new issue with substantial political repercussions.

Jiang Zemin and his protégés adopted the traditional approach of taking measures against the epidemic while downplaying publicly its real scope and threat. Military hospitals under Jiang's overall command, for example, refused to release data on their SARS patients, even to the civilian party leadership.

In late April Hu and Wen, in contrast, committed the government to full transparency and implemented severe measures to bring the epidemic under control. They used this opportunity to empower officials who were not part of Jiang Zemin's coterie and to reinforce their distinctive major themes of greater government transparency, concern for the poor, improved media quality, and so forth. In the process, they also vastly increased their name recognition and deeply affected popular views of their energy and determination.

SARS thus quickly became an element in the succession mix, straining the ability of various groups to work together. As of mid-2003 it is too early to tell how the political repercussions of SARS will play out. If the epidemic reemerges and inflicts prolonged damage, Jiang's followers may try to point the finger at Hu and Wen for mishandling the challenge. But success in bringing the epidemic under control might instead strengthen Hu's and Wen's positions and enable them to assume real command more quickly than observers had thought possible.

The November 2002 Sixteenth Party Congress thus marked a major step in the gradual institutionalization of elite succession in China by ushering in a change to a younger group without attendant purges and major battles. But it remains to be seen whether Jiang's last-minute changes to the succession and the unexpected shock of the SARS epidemic have created a situation that includes long-term leadership friction and conflict.

THE PROSPECTS FOR ELITE SUCCESSION

Regardless of the specific allocation of top posts, several broad observations are very likely to hold true regarding politics at the top over the coming half decade.

A more or less collective leadership will continue. This is a distribution of power that tends to give major vested interests increased influence over elite decisions. The "outside" interests may be *tiao* or *kuai* organizations or some combination of the two. (As explained in Chapter 6, *tiao* are institutional sectors, such as the military, and *kuai* are geographical locales.) However, these interests almost certainly will not include independent groups or nongovernmental organizations of citizens, as their support cannot translate into political power at the top. The basic dynamics of this type of situation make it likely, on balance, that the Center will play a weaker role in the overall political system, more a regulator, adjudicator of interests, and supplicant for support than a mobilizer of energies and resources. This type of political leadership may find it more difficult to discipline the bureaucracies, to call for national sacrifice, or to focus efforts on major national problems.

The lack of clarity about the dynamics surrounding Jiang Zemin's future role in the system means there is continuing risk of an open, paralyzing split among the top leaders and their supporters. This could be especially true as the leadership confronts new crises, as reactions to a crisis may be influenced by various leaders' desires concerning the overall level of influence that Jiang should maintain. During the early stages of the 2003 SARS epidemic, for example, crisis management intertwined with Jiang's role in several ways. At the start of the epidemic, Jiang partisans held the top position in both Guandong province, where SARS initially appeared, and in the Ministry of Health. In both places, they systematically underplayed the seriousness of the SARS issue. Jiang also controlled the military, and military hospitals even in the capital refused to provide the information on their SARS patients that the civilian and international health authorities required. The first purge of top officials for their performance regarding SARS removed Jiang's protégé Zhang Wenkang as minister of health. But to strike a factional balance, the purge did not then remove either the pro-Jiang Guangdong provincial leader or Jia Qinglin, a former Beijing party boss and close Jiang supporter elevated to the Politburo Standing Committee at the Sixteenth Party Congress. Rather, the new mayor of Beijing, a Hu Jintao supporter, was fired. Nevertheless, Hu and Wen quickly seized on the SARS epidemic to place key people who were protégés of former premier Zhu Rongji rather than of Jiang Zemin in charge of antiepidemic efforts and to nudge Jiang supporters more broadly into the background.

The political jockeying growing out of the succession, therefore, affected the dynamics of crisis response to SARS, and how the epidemic ultimately plays out may affect the evolution of the succession itself. Should ongoing disagreements within the leadership escalate, the possibility of rapidly escalating social disorder can grow exponentially. This danger arises from three factors.

First, open divisions at the top create mixed signals for officials and security personnel at all levels and thus risk paralyzing these forces. This occurred during April and May of 1989 until the imposition of martial law on 20 May of that year.

Second, in Chinese political culture the line between order and chaos is relatively thin, a thinner line than in Western political culture. Unlike Westerners, Chinese tend to see order and chaos as nestling up against each other, with a situation fairly easily slipping back and forth across that line. Westerners, in contrast, tend to assume that society is always in a state of moderate disorder. The transition from order to chaos in China can occur with astonishing speed—as can the subsequent return to social order. Open, paralyzing divisions at the top of the system signal that the old order is no longer certain, and the result can be large-scale social dislocation and unrest.

Third, many citizens and officials are discontented with the political system. Relatively few can envision in concrete terms any viable substitute for the current system, but many would be delighted to vent their anger and frustrations through demonstrations if they thought they could do so with impunity. This is especially true of the many millions of laid-off and unemployed workers, of some portion of the tens of millions of migrants, and of many peasants who feel exploited by rapacious local officials.

The above factors combine to create a possibility of large-scale social breakdown even in the context of a rapidly growing economy. If major unrest should occur, moreover, it is likely to differ from the protests of 1989 in that workers and migrants, rather than students and intellectuals, will take the lead. This could pose far greater dangers to the system than in 1989. Clearer succession arrangements by the Sixteenth Congress would have diminished this prospect by ensuring the continuation of a relatively clear hierarchy of authority.

Elite succession has overall improved greatly and become considerably more institutionalized, even as the role of the Center in the system has diminished over time. But the system at the apex remains top-down, personalized, and largely opaque. It is thus too early to state that elite succession has become sufficiently institutionalized to remove it as a potential vulnerability in the system. The succession that occurred at the end of 2002 may still produce destabilizing outcomes.

Systemic Succession

Succession below the Center has seen two major developments. First, a major turnover of elites in the early 1980s, brought in younger, better-educated officials throughout the system. The new officials in many cases replaced individuals who had joined the revolution before 1949 and had held their posts for decades. Then, during the 1990s a concerted effort was made to identify and rapidly promote much younger leaders as the generation of older revolutionaries completely left the scene. The result has been a rise in education levels throughout the political apparatus, with a college education almost always required for advancement to the highest levels of the system. Those who now staff the CCP and government did not personally participate in the revolution.

The transition from a revolutionary to a postrevolutionary system is complete in terms of personnel, and the key efforts are now devoted to making a postrevolutionary system more effective in handling the major challenges that confront the PRC.

CHANGES TO DATE

Hu Yaobang's late-1970s rehabilitation of millions of cadres led, ironically, to a determined effort in the early 1980s to retire many of these same individuals. These included nearly 2.5 million cadres who had joined the revolution before 1949, along with an additional 2,353,000 cadres who had been recruited from 1950 to 1952. The rehabilitations were an acknowledgment of the moral and political imperative to rectify the gross injustices of the Cultural Revolution. The retirement initiatives implied that these individuals were, on the whole, not capable of implementing a program of market-oriented economic reform.

Disagreements among the leadership over actual retirement policy produced vague and conflicting instructions to lower levels, which resulted in massive rehabilitations but few retirements from 1978 to 1981. In February 1982, however, a clearer set of guidelines forced action, and throughout the 1980s large numbers of veteran cadres made way for their younger counterparts. Careful research on this process by Professor Melanie Manion highlights the reluctance of the older cadres to retire and the many side deals that they were able to cut.[48] But the overall results—in both the civilian and military sectors—have been impressive. In the course of implementing this policy, moreover, a new norm—that being an official is a job from which one retires rather than the lifetime commitment of a revolutionary—began to take hold.

A number of studies of leadership changes during the 1980s suggests that the degree of turnover was large and that the changes reached down to every level of the administrative system.[49] In broad terms, concentrated personnel reforms from 1982 to 1984 sought four major objectives: to instill the new norm of retirement for officials; to reduce the number of officials overall, and especially of leading cadres; to recruit younger, better-educated cadres; and to identify yet another batch of individuals who should be cultivated to take over key positions after an additional few years. Later in the decade, particularly between 1984 and 1987, Zhao Ziyang promoted an effort to develop a civil service system for China that would govern the recruitment and promotion of individuals who hold technical staff—versus political—positions. China previously had not clearly differentiated these two groups.[50]

The results of the 1982–84 reforms at the upper levels of the system received much publicity. Summary results are presented in Tables 5.2 and 5.3.

In terms of gross statistics at a leadership level, therefore, the system moved toward a smaller number of younger, better-educated leading officials. A broader sample survey of changes among cadres of more than sixty-two hundred county-, city-, and prefecture-level units provides important additional information on the real depth of the changes of 1982–84.[51]

TABLE 5.2 *Age and Education before and after the 1982–84 Reforms*

	AVERAGE AGE		% COLLEGE EDUCATED	
	BEFORE	**AFTER**	**BEFORE**	**AFTER**
Ministers and vice ministers	64	58	38	59
Directors and deputy directors of State Council	59	54	35	52
Directors and deputy directors of central CCP organs	66	62	43	53
Heads and deputy heads of bureaus of central CCP organs	60	54	50	56
Provincial CCP secretaries, governors, and vice governors	62	55	20	44

Source: Hong Yung Lee, *From Revolutionary Cadres to Technocrats in Socialist China* (Berkeley and Los Angeles: University of California Press, 1991), p. 256.

TABLE 5.3 *Reduction of Bureaucracy via the 1982–84 Reforms*

	NUMBER BEFORE	NUMBER AFTER	PERCENT REDUCTION
State Council			
Offices	98	52	47
Ministers and vice ministers	1,000	300	70
Directors and deputy directors	5,000	2,500	50
Persons in the state council	49,000	32,000	35
All cadres at the central level	600,000	400,000	33
Central party organs			
Offices			17
Directors and deputy directors			40
Heads and deputy heads of offices			14
Provincial level			
Secretaries, members of standing committee, and governors, vice governors	698	463	34
Heads of bureaus	16,658	10,604	36
Municipal-level leaders			36
District-level leaders			29
County-level leaders			25

Source: Cui Wunian and Wang Junxian, *Zhongguo ganbu jiegou di bianqian* (Changes in the structure of China's cadres) (N.p., n.d.).

TABLE 5.4 *Promotions, 1979–84*

Cadres in 6,262 Leading Bodies at County, City, and Prefecture Levels
Number of cadres as of 1984: 20,732
Number of promotions, 1979–84: 20,309

Source: Cui Wunian and Wang Junxian, *Zhongguo ganbu jiegou di bianqian* (Changes in the structure of China's cadres) (N.p., n.d.).

Table 5.4 indicates that roughly 98 percent of the cadres in these leading bodies as of 1984 had been promoted since 1979. That almost certainly somewhat overstates the case. It is probable that in at least some instances one position on a leading body went through two or more new incumbents during this five-year period, while other positions may have been occupied continuously by one individual. Overall, however, the figures suggest strongly that the vast majority of the positions on leading bodies at these lower levels of the Chinese leadership experienced turnover from 1979 to 1984. Other evidence supports this general picture.

Indeed, data on the average age of leaders at the lower administrative levels of the political system highlight both the timing of changes and a critical transition in officeholders between 1982 and 1984 from those who joined the revolution before victory to those who joined the new regime after 1949 (see Table 5.5).

Table 5.5 shows the enormous continuity in generation of leadership at the subprovincial levels of the political system nationwide before the reforms. It also indicates that as of 1975 the party secretaries and deputy secretaries at the prefecture and subprovincial city levels averaged 25 to 29 years of age when the communists came to power. Most had probably participated in the revolution itself, many joining during the civil-war phase of the late 1940s. Their nationwide counterparts in 1984 had been, on average, only fifteen to eighteen years old in 1949. These latter were very likely individuals who did not join the revolution until after it had become the "establishment."

For county-level units, including cities with the bureaucratic rank of a county, CCP secretaries and deputy secretaries throughout the country in 1976 were on average seventeen to twenty-one years old in 1949; for their 1984 counterparts, the equivalent average ages were ten to thirteen years old, very likely too young to have participated in the revolution. Thus, party leadership at the prefecture, county, and municipal levels passed to a predominantly postrevolution generation between 1979 and 1984.[52]

Looking at the heart of the bureaucracy at the Center, the Cui and Wang study investigated the bureau (*ju*) and department (*chu*) cadres in eighteen of the State Council ministries and commissions. It found that from 1982 to 1984 nearly three-quarters of the cadres were newly promoted to these positions. The study concludes that at the bureau and department levels, at the end of 1984 "the cadres already are those who began their work after the founding of the PRC."[53]

TABLE 5.5 *Birth Dates of Leading Cadres at Prefectural and County Levels Nationwide, 1975–84*

	1975	1976	1977	1978	1979	1983	1984
Prefectural level							
CCP secretary	1921	1921	1922	1922	1923	1930	1931
Deputy secretary	1924	1925	1925	1925	1925	1934	1934
Subprovincial cities*							
CCP secretary	1921	1921	1922	1921	1921	1928	1930
Deputy secretary	1924	1925	1925	1924	1924	1933	1934
Standing committee	1926	1927	1927	1926	1925	1934	1935
Counties / cities†							
CCP secretary	n.a.	1928	1929	1929	1929	1932	1936
Deputy secretary	n.a.	1931	1931	n.a.	1930	1934	1940
Standing committee	n.a.	1932	1932	n.a.	1930	1934	1941

Source: Cui Wunian and Wang Junxian, *Zhongguo ganbu jiegou di bianqian* (Changes in the structure of China's cadres) (N.p., n.d.).
*Cities of a bureaucratic rank below a province and above a county.
†Counties and cities with the bureaucratic rank of a county.

As noted above, these changes in leadership sought to raise the educational level of cadres throughout the system. The results at the central and provincial levels are provided in Table 5.2 above. The numbers for the city and prefecture level in nine locales from very different parts of China are presented in Table 5.6. This table brings in locales from every major part of China, and it includes both wealthy and poor areas. Several facets of Table 5.6 warrant particular attention:

□ As of 1979, in every locale the percentage of cadres with a higher education was lower for the leading groups than for the entire group of cadres in that locale. This reflects the low educational level of the revolutionaries who seized power in 1949 and stayed in those positions in subsequent decades. Indeed, on average roughly 85 percent of the cadres in each locale's leading bodies had only a junior high school level of education or less. Only 1.5 percent, on average, had at least some higher education. Subordinate administrative personnel, in contrast, had a higher level of educational attainment.

□ In 1984, in every locale the percentage of cadres with a higher education in the leading body had grown significantly larger than the comparable percentage for the cadre group as a whole. Clearly, higher education provided a major boost for admission to the readjusted leading bodies. Overall educational levels also rose for the cadre group as a whole in each locale, but there simply were not enough people with a higher education available to match the composition of the leading bodies in terms of educational structure.

□ In every locale but one, the number of cadres in the leading bodies declined significantly from 1979 to 1984, very much in line with the figures

TABLE 5.6 *City and Prefecture Cadre Educational Levels, 1979 and 1984*

CITY OR PREFECTURE	NUMBER OF CADRES	HIGHER (%)	HIGH SCHOOL OR POLYTECHNIC (%)	JR. HIGH OR LOWER (%)	YEAR
Dezhou					
	242	0.00	13.22	90.08	1979
	184	45.70	21.70	32.60	1984
	53640	9.48	33.09	57.43	1979
	72048	12.70	48.00	39.90	1984
Weifang					
	257	3.5	8.17	88.33	1979
	188	53.7	23.90	22.30	1984
	78426	10.3	32.20	57.50	1979
	96658	13.4	47.70	38.90	1984
Anyang					
	186	2.69	6.45	90.86	1979
	120	51.70	30.00	18.30	1984
	32747	11.3	24.5	64.02	1979
	50943	13.7	37.2	49.00	1984
Zhumadian					
	255	1.18	6.27	92.55	1979
	139	52.50	23.70	23.70	1984
	48951	9.4	27.22	63.43	1979
	67417	12.0	44.00	44.00	1984
Baotou					
	126	2.38	15.87	81.75	1979
	104	58.70	26.90	13.50	1984
	39579	6.2	22.6	71.2	1979
	48716	44.0	38.0	18.0	1984
Wulumuqi					
	82	1.22	28.05	70.73	1979
	88	28.40	29.70	41.50	1984
	21308	13.6	35.0	51.4	1979
	27898	15.2	43.8	41.0	1984
Foshan					
	141	0.71	7.8	91.40	1979
	107	28.80	29.7	41.50	1984
	46372	11.39	24.5	64.0	1979
	64729	17.00	37.0	47.0	1984

(*continues*)

TABLE 5.6 *(continued)*

CITY OR PREFECTURE	NUMBER OF CADRES	LEVEL OF EDUCATION			
		HIGHER (%)	HIGH SCHOOL OR POLYTECHNIC (%)	JR. HIGH OR LOWER (%)	YEAR
Sanming					
	199	1.5	14.57	83.92	1979
	160	60.0	30.00	10.00	1984
	35613	15.11	39.75	45.14	1979
	48731	20.20	49.60	30.20	1984
Ningbo					
	159	0.63	8.18	91.40	1979
	124	57.30	20.20	22.60	1984
	46987	13.16	35.0	51.4	1979
	69022	20.90	42.7	36.4	1984

Source: Cui Wunian and Wang Junxian, *Zhongguo ganbu jiegou di bianqian* (Changes in the structure of China's cadres) (N.p., n.d.).

For each locale, the first two lines of figures represent cadres in the "leading bodies" of the locale. The second two lines represent all the party and government cadres at the municipal and prefecture levels within the given locale. Weifang, Anyang, Baotou, Wulumuqi (Urumqi), Foshan, Sanming, and Ningbo are cities; Dezhou and Zhumadian are prefectures.

for higher levels presented in Table 5.3. This reflected the overall effort to cut back on the number of cadres in the bureaucracy. However, contrary to the desires of the leaders, the number of cadres *overall* shot up substantially—by an average of 35 percent—in every single locale. Reports from elsewhere, moreover, confirm that this was a general phenomenon. For example, according to the figures in one article, the number of personnel in party and state institutions grew by an annual average of about 3 percent between 1966 and 1979, by about 7.7 percent between 1979 and 1989, and, within that period, by nearly 9 percent between 1984 and 1989.[54] Administrative and management expenditures increased from 4.1 percent of the state budget in 1978 to 7.8 percent in 1985 and to 8.3 percent in 1988. Bureaucratic streamlining thus failed below the top leadership at all levels of the political system.

☐ The overall numbers of city and prefecture level cadres at just these nine locations are also worthy of note. The figure totaled 403,623 cadres in 1979 and 546,162 cadres in 1984. The governing apparatus of China confronts huge problems of cadre management.

The above figures are unusual in that they include detailed information on the middle and lower levels of the bureaucratic system. In broad terms, though, the picture they portray is largely consistent with the generalizations often found in the Chinese media about changes in the political administration staffing since the start of the reforms.

A final condition for promotion—that the candidate be committed to economic development and reform while retaining loyalty to the CCP—is not possible to measure directly with objective numbers. Interviews by scholars have tended to support the notion that, especially at local levels in the political system, the new cadres are highly oriented toward rapid economic growth but that their level of enthusiasm for a revolutionary party is uncertain.

Hong Yung Lee's analysis of the prior work experience of those who held leading positions in 1982 (before the cadre reforms) and in 1987 (after the first wave of these reforms) lends indirect support to these observations. Lee looked at the previous work experience of ministers, provincial CCP secretaries, governors, and Central Committee members. In most categories—economics and management, functional bureau, Youth League, military, and mass organizations—the numbers involved were small and little change occurred. But in two categories, engineering and "CCP secretary and political fields," the numbers and the amount of change were telling (see Table 5.7).

In other words, before the reforms most of the incumbents (except for Central Committee members) came from backgrounds in political work. After the reform wave, the balance tipped toward backgrounds in engineering—that is, practical problem solving.

A Chinese analyst writing for the *Guangming ribao* (*Brightness Daily*) in 1991 summed up these changes and the issues they pose. He observed that

It should be . . . noted that with the replacement of old cadres by new ones, the main bulk of the cadres' ranks has now shifted from cadres who began working before the birth of the PRC and who were tested in the blood and fires of revolutionary struggles to those who started working after the birth of the PRC and who grew up in an environment of peace. A considerable number of them are university and technical school graduates of the 1980s. These young cadres possess a higher level of scientific and cultural knowledge as well as active minds and can accept new things more easily. However, most of them . . . still have some weaknesses and shortcomings in terms of ideology and politics.[55]

In short, once the party leaders convinced old officials to retire, they faced the problem of recruiting younger individuals who had better training and a more open mind toward reform—and who also were loyal to the party. In the ensuing years and especially in the 1990s, new recruitment remained very active and technical skills clearly increased, but identification with a revolutionary or even Maoist ideology clearly faded as China entered its second and then its third decade of concentration on economic reform and development.

Three major shifts have occurred since the mid-1980s in the overall composition of China's officialdom.[56] First, the east coast provinces have largely replaced Guangdong and the provinces of the interior (Sichuan, Hunan, Shanxi), which provided the bulk of the cadres before the 1980s. Reform policies have given great advantage to the east coast, and the very success of those provinces has in turn naturally enhanced their role as spawning grounds for officialdom. The generally higher educational levels and greater sophistication of those provinces has served them well, given the overall directions of change of the PRC.

TABLE 5.7 *Leaders' Work Experience, 1982 and 1987*

	YEAR	MINISTERS NO.	%	SECRETARIES NO.	%	GOVERNORS NO.	%	CENTRAL COMM. MEMBERS NO.	%
Engineering	1982	1	2	0	0	0	0	4	2
	1987	17	45	7	25	8	33	34	26
Security and police work	1982	26	60	24	83	23	84	91	48
	1987	2	5	10	36	7	30	38	29

Source: Hong Yung Lee, *From Revolutionary Cadres to Technocrats in Socialist China* (Berkeley and Los Angeles: University of California Press, 1991), p. 268.

Second, provincial political apparatuses have become increasingly indigenized. Largely due to changes made in the nomenklatura system that are explained in Chapter 7, larger percentages of officials in each province are serving in the provinces in which they have long resided. This both increases local knowledge and commitment and creates stronger challenges to the Center in achieving disciplined implementation of policy preferences that disadvantage particular provinces.

Third, the generation that came into major positions of power in the early 1990s not only is better educated than their predecessors but also includes an increasing admixture of specialists trained in the social sciences, especially lawyers and economists, as well as financial specialists. Their predecessors had obtained mostly technical education in engineering. Again, this change reflects ongoing directions of the reforms and the needs for expertise generated by China's changing system.

In addition, family ties have played a significant role in the advancement of a significant number of current powerful officials. Some are the sons and daughters of top leaders; others married into powerful families. Such ties do not determine who will rise to the top in the Chinese system—when this appeared to be a potential future for China it met significant opposition in the late 1980s. But in many instances, talented offspring of top leaders have had a significant advantage in pursuing careers in officialdom, the military, and business.[57]

THE POLITICAL IMPLICATIONS

China has evolved from roughly three decades of rule by revolutionaries through two decades of transition to the current system, in which officials see the political system largely as a crucially important force in bringing about rapid economic development and improvement in living standards. Those promoted to leadership under this new regime tend to be people with good educations who are strongly committed to rapid economic growth. The political apparatus is no longer ideologically oriented. Rather, leaders are problem solvers who give the impression of seeing economic development as the best way to handle the most important problems they confront.

Westerners have a natural tendency to assume that individuals with technical and social science educations who profess little commitment to ideology must be democrats and nascent capitalists. But in fact these individuals' education and background do not necessarily strongly predispose them toward any particular set of values and preferences. Those who grew up in the Maoist system generally became thoroughly disillusioned with the excesses of radical socialism; others grew up under the materialistic ethos of Deng's reform era. Most have not had sustained exposure, however, to Western democratic values, as opposed to Western standards of production and consumption.

This is, indeed, on the whole a nonphilosophical group. If given choices of bureaucratic interference versus market forces, personal corruption versus selfless service, government authority versus individual rights, and economic growth versus environmental protection, most would not likely systematically choose the latter option in each pair. The choices, rather, would probably depend more on the specific pressing problems these officials confront and the options available for dealing with them quickly. In this most basic sense, the Chinese revolution has ended, and a more technocratic successor generation has taken over at all levels of the system.[58]

This chapter has set up a basis for understanding the Chinese system by explaining the ideas that energized reform, the politics of the reform effort at the Center since 1978, and the changes in the system brought about by political succession at elite and lower levels. But China's system consists of far more than raw politics and national policies. The country still boasts by far the world's largest governing organizations, bureaucracies that themselves have grown considerably during the reform era. These bureaucracies, on the whole, generate the information on which the leaders depend, and they strongly influence both the development and implementation of national policy. In addition, many bureaucrats now also operate as entrepreneurs in the Chinese marketplace. Any analysis of China requires, therefore, detailed examination not only of leadership politics but also of the ways in which politics, administrative structure, and bureaucratic practice interact.

Both the governing bureaucracies and Chinese society itself have evolved greatly under the reforms to the point where the nature and dynamics of basic linkages—between the Center and the provinces, the provinces and the basic levels, and basic levels and the populace—are matters of heated debate among those who follow developments in China. The following chapters focus first on the political apparatus itself from its apex to its foundations to explain both the formal organizational arrangements and the real topography of power. The remainder of the volume examines the complex dynamics of this state system as it wrestles with the core issues that confront it: managing the economy, limiting environmental damage, coping with a changing society, and dealing with the global arena at the beginning of the twenty-first century.

Part Three

THE
POLITICAL
SYSTEM

6

The Organization of Political Power and Its Consequences: The View from the Outside

As the victorious Mao Zedong approached Beijing from the Fragrant Hills in the western suburbs in March 1949, he carried with him two works of traditional Chinese governance, the *Shi Ji* (Records of the Historian) and the *Cu Zhi Tang Qian* (the General Mirror for the Aid of Government).[1] He intended to draw deeply from the wisdom of his predecessors in developing his techniques of rule. He also sought advice from a quite different source: Stalin's socialist system in the USSR. Mao would wed imperial China to Soviet experience to build his regime in the PRC.

The imperial Chinese and the Soviet systems in fact had a number of points in common. Both stressed centralized control and bureaucratic administration. Both utilized ideology to buttress the legitimacy of the system and held that the leaders embodied the correct ideology, leaving no room for private, individual interests or for organized opposition to the state. Both consciously fostered competition among various bureaucracies in order to maximize control by the top leaders.[2] Naturally, the overlap was very far from complete: the substance of the respective ideologies differed enormously, for example, and the imperial Chinese system did not seek to maximize economic growth as did the Stalinist system.

Since its Soviet-style beginnings in the mid-1950s, the PRC's political system has experienced significant upheaval, including the Great Leap Forward, the Cultural Revolution, and the reforms after 1978. Nevertheless, some of the decisions made in the regime's early years about the formal structure of the system have endured, even though substantive issues, policies, and the allocation of power have changed greatly over time. Individuals who joined the Communist party in the 1920s maintained control in China into the 1990s. It was only in the late 1990s that some of the fundamental building blocks of the system began changing.

This chapter introduces the political system as it appears to outsiders and is portrayed on the PRC's official organizational charts. As Chapter 3 notes, the Chinese system is divided into three nationwide bureaucratic hierarchies—the party, the government, and the military. Each civilian hierarchy includes four major territorial entities: the Center (*zhongyang*), the provinces (*sheng*), the cities (*shi*), and the counties (*xian*). In the party and government hierarchies these entities are organized in roughly the same way, although the party structure always exercises ultimate authority over its government counterpart. This chapter first examines their operation in detail, then presents some of the inherent matrix problems the structure creates, and finally explains the solutions adopted at various times to these and related problems.

Political organization below the level of the county has been complex and variable as the party has experimented with how best to link up the government with the economy. Beijing has enmeshed natural villages in different types of administrative hierarchies at various periods. The key current administrative unit between the county and the village is called a "township," of which as of 2000 China boasted over 45,000.[3] The townships have grown rapidly since the mid-1980s, when Beijing began to encourage local governments to develop township enterprises.

The place where Chinese work, called the "unit," has until recently formed a key part of the political structure in the cities. In one of the major political changes under way since the late 1990s, the urban work unit is losing its political role for many city residents, and the CCP and government are moving toward a residential basis of urban political power. But the work unit's past history and present legacies remain sufficiently important to warrant consideration in any analysis of the Chinese political system (see Chart 6.1), along with an explanation of the new "community" centered approaches to urban governance.[4]

As with all major political systems, the real topography of authority and methods of governance in China differ considerably from the image created by formal organization charts and published rules of procedure. Chapter 7, therefore, explains the hidden parts of the Chinese political system, and how the system looks to the inside participants. The picture given in Chapter 7 is not totally separate from that presented in the current chapter. Organic rela-

CHART 6.1 *Territorial Layers of State Administration*

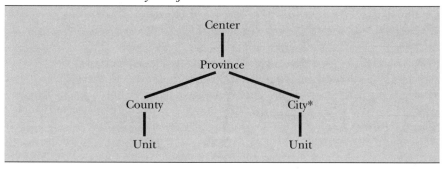

*Cities have various ranks, depending on their size and importance. Four cities—Beijing, Tianjin, Chongqing, and Shanghai—have ranks equivalent to that of the province. These and other large cities have suburban counties under their jurisdictions.

tionships connect the two. Neither suffices without the other to explain the PRC's past and future.

Formal Organizational Structure

THE ORGANIZATIONAL CHART AT THE CENTER

Because the Chinese political system largely duplicates itself at each of the territorial levels, this section outlines the structure at the Center in some detail. The province, city, county, township, unit, and urban community levels are dealt with more briefly directly following this discussion.

Each territorial level of the Chinese system, on both the party and the government sides, has a basic organizational flow. Each has a large congress that meets infrequently but is in theory the most powerful body; a smaller committee that brings together important people and meets somewhat more frequently; and a still smaller committee that brings together the top few people. In theory, the larger the body, the more powerful it is. In reality, the opposite is true—the smallest committee is the most important structure. Under these committees, administrative departments actually run day to day the various party and government organs.

At the Center, the major party organs are, in ascending order of importance, the Party Congress, the Central Committee, the Politburo, and the Politburo Standing Committee. There is a Secretariat for administration and specific departments nominally under the Central Committee (see Chart 6.2). The *National Party Congress* has the largest membership—recent Congresses have had over fifteen hundred delegates—and it meets infrequently.[5] Meetings of the Party Congress are major events; policy debates among the leaders are often affected by the need to reach a consensus in time to convene an upcoming Congress. Each Congress solidifies the central political tasks for the

CHART 6.2 *Party Organization at the Center*

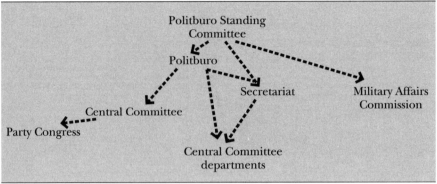

Arrows indicate general direction of authority in practice.

party. The Twelfth Congress in 1982, for example, anointed the post-Mao reform effort; the Thirteenth Congress in 1987 legitimized nonstate ownership; the Fourteenth Congress in 1993 gave a major political boost to market-oriented changes; the Fifteenth Congress in 1997 called for restructuring the system of state owned enterprises; and the Sixteenth Congress in 2002 formally permitted private sector entrepreneurs to join the CCP and become officials. Party Congresses also provide the occasion for appointments (or reappointments) to top party posts and to the Central Committee.

But people do not work for the Party Congress—rather, much like an American political party convention, it convenes, hears many speeches, passes resolutions, adopts rules of procedure, and disbands. In theory, the Party Congress is the highest organ of authority, but in fact its large size and infrequent meetings make it a vehicle for announcing and legitimating some major decisions rather than for initiating and deciding important policies.

The *Central Committee* is a smaller body but still, in recent decades, has had several hundred members. Like the Party Congress, the Central Committee convenes infrequently (recently, once or twice a year), and its members all hold other substantive positions. Indeed, many official positions, such as heading the party in the important metropolis of Shanghai, bring with them almost automatic membership in the party's Central Committee. Central Committee members receive a number of special privileges and have access to inside information on party affairs. But with few exceptions the Central Committee meetings (called plenums) discuss and announce policies rather than decide them. Each Central Committee is formally chosen by a Party Congress. In reality, the Politburo in consultation with others determines the list of nominees to the Central Committee. Only at Thirteenth Party Congress in 1987 did that list consist of more people than the number of slots to be filled on the Central Committee (the 1987 list had five more people than positions). Meetings of the Central Committee, as explained in Chapter 3, are numbered sequentially until the next Party Congress convenes to choose a new Central Committee.

The *Politburo* also functions as a committee, albeit a small and powerful one. This is considered the command headquarters of the party, and it typically has fourteen to twenty-four members (and sometimes a small number of "candidate" members). Nearly all members of the Politburo are among the twenty-five to thirty-five people (described further at the beginning of Chapter 7) who form the top power elite. As with the other bodies just discussed, membership on the Politburo is not itself a full-time job. Indeed, usually some members head distant provinces such as Guangdong and, presumably, miss most Politburo meetings.

The truly powerful inner circle is the *Standing Committee of the Politburo,* a small body with four to nine members that seems to meet weekly. (Before late 2002, these meetings were not announced publicly.) Until 1982, the chairman of the Chinese Communist party headed the Standing Committee, with typically one to six vice chairmen. When these posts were abolished at the end of 1982 to prevent anyone from rising above the party as Mao Zedong had done, the general secretary became the top bureaucratic official in the party. This individual has the right to convene and to preside over meetings of the Politburo and its Standing Committee. Deng Xiaoping had served as general secretary from April 1954 to 1966, and the wide-ranging contacts with the party bureaucracy that this post required provided a major base of support for him when he sought to begin the reforms in the late 1970s (see Table 6.1).

The general secretary is the formal head of the *Secretariat.* For most of its existence, this body has functioned as the staff support for the Politburo and the Central Committee. Its members oversee the preparation of documents for Politburo consideration and turn Politburo decisions into operational instructions for the subordinate bureaucracies. The Secretariat's functions have changed quite a bit over time, being very broad and activist during some periods, such as the early Great Leap Forward, and much less so at other times, as in the early 1990s.

The *Military Affairs Commission* is in charge of the People's Liberation Army.[6] This commission has existed in one guise or another in the CCP since the 1930s. Until 1989 only two individuals—Mao Zedong and Deng Xiaoping —had headed this body (with a brief transitional leadership by Hua Guofeng directly following Mao's death). Lower levels of the party have no equivalent of the Military Affairs Commission. Jiang Zemin has headed this body since November 1989.

Central Committee departments at the national level assume responsibility for various issue areas. Those that have existed continuously since 1949 (with some exceptions during the Cultural Revolution) are Organization (personnel appointments); Propaganda (media, education, political study, and public health)[7]; United Front (relations with noncommunists); and International Liaison (foreign affairs and relations with other communist parties). In addition, the General Office coordinates many of the administrative details of the central party bureaucracy.[8] A Subordinate Organs Committee does party work in the organs directly under the Central Committee. A State Organs Committee makes sure the party bodies in the central government organs receive appropriate documents and carry on party activities (such as holding discus-

TABLE 6.1 *Top Leaders of the CCP (post-1949)*

Chairmen of the CCP

Mao Zedong	Oct. 1949–Sept. 1976
Hua Guofeng	Sept. 1976–June 1981
Hu Yaobang	June 1981–Dec. 1982

General Secretaries of the Secretariat*

Deng Xiaoping	April 1954–1966†
Hu Yaobang	Dec. 1978–Jan. 1987
Zhao Ziyang	Jan. 1987–May 1989‡
Jiang Zemin	June 1989–Nov. 2002
Hu Jintao	Nov. 2002–

*The General Secretary was called Chief Secretary from April 1954 to September 1956 and from December 1978 to September 1982.

†De facto, as the Secretariat ceased to function during the Cultural Revolution, which began in 1966.

‡Zhao was Acting General Secretary for January–October 1987.

sion meetings). There has also been at times a powerful Policy Research Office.

On the government side, the basic current structure was adopted in 1954, although many changes in specific structures and allocations of responsibility have occurred since then. A new *National People's Congress* (NPC), the putative legislature and government equivalent of the Party Congress, is chosen every four years. Since the reforms began, the NPC has convened in plenary session annually, and each meeting in recent years has brought together roughly three thousand delegates. The NPC has a Standing Committee that meets more frequently. More important, during the 1980s it developed permanent committees that hired their own staffs and began to function on a regular basis.

Evidence suggests strengthening of the NPC's role in policy deliberation, as this body is significant in drafting and revising major laws and has stalled some initiatives desired by leading party officials.[9] Indeed, over the past two decades the NPC has developed a remarkable corpus of formal law, bringing the PRC from a state in which virtually no law existed as of Mao Zedong's death to a country that in many areas has relatively comprehensive legal underpinnings. Part of this effort reflects necessary initiatives in order to attract foreign investment, but much of it has centered on providing greater regularity and predictability to the Chinese polity. The NPC is still far from a fully independent legislature. But under Mao Zedong it had been virtually supine, and that is clearly no longer the case.

Both the NPC's institutional capacities and its roles have developed considerably under the reforms. With the substantial body of law adopted by the NPC, China has also sought to develop a viable system of courts and related organs. The country's movement toward a market economy has provided a major spur to this effort, as contracts, property rights, white-collar crime, and related issues require legal structures to manage the myriad related challenges. Many such issues require the kind of detailed expertise that political officials are unlikely to possess, and national leaders have therefore supported development of legal institutions. This development also reflects their recognition that many of the problems that arise are not inherently political in nature and thus are best resolved by more "neutral" bodies. But there is ample evidence to conclude that the court system remains short of necessary expertise and resources; it is also subject to political pressures where officials want to achieve a particular outcome. The Chinese legal system is no longer an empty glass, but it is a glass half full, at best.[10]

The *State Council* is in theory chosen by the NPC (see Chart 6.3). It is headed by the premier (Zhou Enlai to January 1976; Hua Guofeng to September 1980; Zhao Ziyang to April 1988; Li Peng to March 1998; Zhu Rongji to March 2003; Wen Tiabao since March 2003), and it serves as the cabinet in the Chinese political system. As explained in Chapter 3, a number of commissions and ministries are subordinate to the State Council. Most ministries and commissions head their own nationwide vertical bureaucratic hierarchies, with offices at each subordinate territorial level of administration. The State Council membership itself consists of the premier, vice premiers, state councilors (equivalent in rank to vice premiers), and virtually all heads of commissions and ministries.

The actual organization of the central party and state apparatus is, of course, vastly more complex than this basic outline conveys. On both the party and government sides numerous additional bodies have been established for particular purposes. A long-term party body at the Center, for example, is the Central Discipline Inspection Commission, which has the task of ferreting out violations of rules in the party. This commission has existed in various guises since 1949, except during the Cultural Revolution.[11] Other central party bodies, such as the Central Advisory Commission (which existed only from 1982 to 1992 and was used as a kind of way station to full retirement for leaders), have been the products of specific political needs at particular historical periods.

To a far greater extent than the party, the government has changed its organization over the years. Relatively few government organs below the level of the premier have avoided mergers, divisions, or other major organizational changes since 1954. The number of ministries, for example, has varied from two dozen or so to over sixty, and reorganizations at this level are common. These amalgamations and divisions of ministries reflect two contrasting tendencies: the desire of specialized bureaucracies to achieve ministerial status; and the desire of the State Council to limit the demands made on it to coordinate lower-level units and resolve disputes among them.

The ministries in charge of petroleum, coal, electric power, and water resources, for instance, have at one time or another stood independently or been combined in every mathematically feasible way since 1949. One high official commented in the late 1980s that the water resources ministry had been forced in the early 1980s to amalgamate with the electric power ministry to form the Ministry of Water Resources and Electric Power because the State

CHART 6.3 *Organization of the Government at the Center*

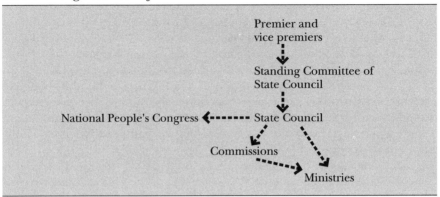

Arrows indicate general direction of authority in practice.

Council was tired of having to resolve the constant battles between these two units. The electric power ministry wanted China's water resources used for hydroelectric generation, while the water resources ministry saw irrigation and flood control as its primary missions. The political rules in China require that the minister present a unified "ministerial" position to the State Council. By amalgamating the two units, therefore, the State Council essentially required that they resolve their differences "in house." This amalgamation did not change much: all but a few of the bureaus of the ministries remained as they were, and the offices even remained in distinct buildings. The forced unification, moreover, did not last long.[12]

In March 1998 the NPC instituted a government streamlining program aimed at qualitatively redefining the core functions of the state and shedding its noncore institutional activities. This effort reduced the number of ministries from forty to twenty-nine, in many cases making former economic ministries into bureaus in the new ministries and then in 2001 turning those bureaus into corporations. State Council ministries and commissions previously directly ran the economy. Under the planned economy before the reforms the SOEs were in reality the lowest level of the national economic ministerial bureaucratic hierarchies. Under the reforms until the late 1990s, the various ministries still typically both regulated and operated the enterprises under them. The March 1998 NPC announced a fundamental restructuring of this system designed to limit ministries to a regulatory function so as to let the market work more fully. This restructuring also sought to achieve budgetary savings in the cost of government operations. It produced a 50 percent reduction—from thirty-two thousand to sixteen thousand slots—in the rosters of the State Council ministries and commissions by the end of 2000.[13] In order to meet the goal of sharply reducing the government's administrative management of economic activity, this streamlining effort fell with particular severity on the government bodies concerned with China's economy. The same reform effort included other measures to classify every ministry according to the type of function it performed so as to reduce the previous tendency for each ministry to branch out from its core function (say, management of the iron and steel sector) into ancillary activities (related transportation, education, provision of health care, and so forth). The goal was to create a more efficient government that would regulate rather than administer an increasingly market-driven economy. In addition, most ministries now no longer directly lead their equivalent bodies at the province and lower bureaucratic levels. The governments at those levels exercise direct leadership, and the State Council ministries have assumed more advisory and supervisory roles.

PROVINCES

The Center reaches out to deal with the country through thirty-one province-level bodies. Provinces vary so much in their size, wealth, topography, dialect, culture, and even purpose that a view of China that recognizes national uniformity at the cost of appreciating provincial diversity is deeply flawed. A fundamental thrust of the reforms has been to encourage provinces to become entrepreneurial so as to accelerate the country's economic growth. But in almost every dimension this basic strategy has produced startling differentiation in provincial challenges and accomplishments.

Many provinces have larger populations than do all but a few countries in the United Nations. Guangdong, for example, has over 86 million people, Jiangsu has nearly 75 million, Zhejiang has about 47 million, and Jiangxi has over 40 million. Sichuan in the southwest touches no foreign borders and had a population of well over 100 million until 1997, when China placed most of the area of eastern Sichuan province under the administrative control of Chongqing municipality and raised Chongqing to provincial rank (Beijing, Shanghai, and Tianjin are the other municipalities with provincial rank). This change in boundaries and rank made Chongqing nominally by far the most populous city in the world and reduced the population of Sichuan province to below 100 million.[14]

Some provinces are sparsely populated. Xinjiang in the northwest has a vast expanse of land, but its population is 1.9 million. The western provinces of Tibet and Qinghai have populations, respectively, of 2.6 million and 5.2 million.[15] Indeed, dividing China on a diagonal from southwest to northeast, putting half of the country's land area on each side of the line, finds roughly 90 percent of the population on the southeast side of this division, reflecting the fact that China's fertile land is in the east and that deserts, mountains, and high plateaus dominate the west.

Economic structures also vary very widely. Shanghai is famous for both heavy industry and high technology, whereas Guangdong's urban economy focuses more on light industry. Although both have large amounts of foreign investment, Shanghai has more state-owned industry, whereas Guangdong has a larger private sector. One key goal of the reforms has been to attract foreign direct investment, and China has established an extraordinarily successful record overall in this effort. But different provinces have had vastly different levels of success. After two decades of reform, some are deeply integrated into the international economy, but others are barely touched by external economic developments. As of 1999, for example, Guangdong province had attracted a total of U.S. $12 billion in foreign investment, but Guangxi province just to its west had received only $635 million, and the poor northwest province of Qinghai had less than $5 million of foreign investment.

Cultural characteristics also vary greatly. Guangdong people are considered highly entrepreneurial, and most Chinese who have emigrated to other Asian countries and to the United States hail from Guangdong Province. People from Hunan are considered hot tempered: many early leaders of the CCP—including Mao Zedong—hailed from Hunan. A traditional saying avers that Sichuan was typically the first to rebel and the last to be pacified in times of trouble. Beijing, in comparison, is relatively staid and bureaucratic; people from Hebei are considered frank and solid. Some provinces have very large non-Han populations, including Tibet, Yunnan, Guangxi, and Inner Mongolia. Xinjiang, a huge province in the far northwest dominated by mountain ranges and vast deserts, is populated largely with non-Han minorities, the majority of whom are Muslim.

Many provinces are separated by natural topographical barriers, and most have names that reflect geographical features. Shandong, for example, means "east [*dong*] of the mountains [*shan*]," Shanxi is "west of the mountains," Hunan is "south of the lake," Hubei is "north of the lake," Shanghai is "on the sea," Sichuan is "the four rivers," and Heilongjiang is "black dragon river." Beijing means "northern capital."

Provincial borders, moreover, only occasionally coincide with the boundaries of the macroregions analyzed by G. William Skinner. In other words, provincial boundaries do not necessarily lie along natural economic fault lines; densities of population, transportation links, and commercial activities, with their influences on social identification, dialect, and so forth, do not closely match provincial divisions.

Provinces are a very important component of the political system. *Province* itself refers to a rank in the national political administrative hierarchy that is fully equal to the rank of a ministry in the central government. Twenty-two units at provincial rank are actually called "province" (e.g., Guangdong Province, Hunan Province); four are named "metropolises" (Beijing City, Shanghai City, Chongqing City, and Tianjin City); and five are named autonomous regions (Tibet, Xinjiang Uighur, Ningxia Hui, Guangxi Zhuang, and Inner Mongolia). Because all territorial units with the rank of province are formally equal in rank to each other and to central government ministries, none of these units can issue binding orders to any others. Some provinces, especially those such as Shanghai that contribute a great deal of money to central government coffers, are actually more important than others, and their leaders generally are accorded more respect in Beijing than are most government ministers. Provincial rank is, therefore, a powerful one in the political hierarchy.

Unlike states in the American system, provinces do not have powers that inherently belong to them by law. Rather, in China's unitary system the powers exercised by the province-level units are all delegated to them from the Center. Nevertheless, the provinces are crucial actors in the political system, especially recently. They constantly lobby the Center for resources and greater leeway and exploit the growing flexibility allowed them by the Center. In this effort, they derive leverage from several sources:

☐ All major "central" construction projects and enterprises require active provincial cooperation in mobilizing and organizing resources and support services. While the Center knows that provinces cannot simply reject central commands, both sides recognize that provinces can largely scuttle the Center's initiatives through delays and "mishaps." The Center can in theory override this provincial power through harsh penalties (such as purges) for inadequate support, and under Mao this sometimes happened.[16] But over the long run, active cooperation works better for both sides than does the Center's use of coercion. The post-Mao reform efforts depend heavily on a cooperative relationship with the provinces—indeed, on stimulating provinces to take major initiatives to improve their own economies and to experiment with new approaches to challenges thrown up by the reforms.[17]

☐ The richer provinces are a major source of funds for the Center, but at least until implementation of the 1994 restructuring of the tax system, local units collected all taxes. The Center then bargained with the provinces over the division of funds. Because the reforms have sought to encourage provincial enthusiasm, the provinces enjoyed considerable strength in these negotiations.[18] Since 1994 that leverage has decreased but not disappeared.

☐ Many provinces are themselves the size of European countries. Their enormous populations require the provincial political leaders to have considerable authority to coordinate the development of goods and services in their territories. Beijing cannot manage a country the size of China without important tasks being performed at lower levels of the political system.

☐ The loss of ideological discipline, the officially sanctioned scramble for wealth, and resulting corruption have significantly eroded the leverage of the Center over activities of the provinces. Although Beijing retains important resources to bring provinces to heel, provincial leaders often evade orders that are not quite specific or are not given high priority by the national leaders.

☐ Fundamentally, the reform has shifted power toward territorial units and away from national bureaucracies in Beijing. This fundamental policy approach is designed to encourage every territorial political body to do its utmost to develop its local economy fast enough to maintain social and political stability. This national strategy in turn requires that provinces and lower level territorial units enjoy very considerable room for initiative and be able to enjoy the fruits of their success.[19] This strategy has greatly strengthened the provincial and lower territorial levels.

☐ Certain core features of the political system (detailed in Chapter 7) give the provinces leverage. Since 1984, for example, each province has largely controlled the appointment of all but the highest provincial officials.

The structure of reporting lines for most civilian bodies other than the party committees themselves is quite decentralized, with a powerful role for the territorial party committee at each level. The provincial territorial party committee is thus an extremely important actor in the Chinese system.

Although provinces vary enormously, clearly the east-coast provinces have as a whole benefited far more from the reforms than have their northeastern and inland counterparts. These provinces have generally grown wealthy by reaping the benefits both of preferential national policies and of access to foreign markets and foreign capital. Today, for example, it is said that more than three hundred thousand businesspeople from Taiwan reside in Shanghai, where they have set up operations. Shanghai has been China's most rapidly growing provincial-level unit in the past decade and has also been a pathway to national-level political power. Not surprisingly, the enormous rural-to-urban migration that has accompanied the reforms has basically consisted of migrants who cross provincial boundaries from the interior to the east. Of the seven provinces that saw the highest number of their people leave for jobs in other provinces in 1999, six are interior provinces.[20] Nearly half of all 1999 transprovincial migrants went to Guangdong. The other major recipients of migrants are all east-coast provinces: Jiangsu, Fujian, Shanghai, Beijing, and Zhejiang.[21]

As noted above, the political structure at the provincial level largely mirrors that at the Center. This similarity has developed because most provincial organs must deal with their counterparts at the Center, and the Center has therefore essentially replicated itself in each province. When the Center split off Hainan Island from Guangdong province and elevated Hainan to provincial status, for example, it initially sought to create a simplified government structure in the new province. But over time, the Hainan provincial government added organs to match its counterparts in Beijing and in other provinces, because Hainan otherwise found it too difficult to manage its responsibilities.[22] Typically, provincial-level governments have between 5,300 and 7,500 authorized slots. Only the sparsely populated western provinces have smaller governments.

CITIES

Cities can plug into the national political administrative hierarchy at any bureaucratic rank, depending on their size and importance. As noted above, for example, four major metropolises—Beijing, Tianjin, Chongqing, and Shanghai—have the rank of province. According to a 2001 handbook, China has over 660 cities at the rank of county or higher.[23] Each city has a full set of party and government organs that basically parallels that of the Center, province, and county. Headed by mayors, city governments are typically organized into departments and bureaus.

The reforms have increasingly made cities the key level of organization for the economy. National-level regulations on many important urban issues such as health insurance and pensions, for example, are implemented in a different way in each major metropolis, with the city making the key decisions on how to take the national principles and turn them into actual programs within its jurisdiction. To foster rational use of the cities as economic centers, the reformers have brought large rural areas around major cities under the administrative control of the municipal authorities to integrate rural development more closely with the urban economy. Many cities, therefore, include suburban counties in their municipal boundaries; there are a total of 787 such counties under municipal jurisdiction throughout China. Beijing, for instance, encompasses nine suburban counties; Shanghai has ten. As at the provincial level, a party committee is in charge of each city, and that committee is the most powerful political body in each metropolis.

COUNTIES

Although myriad adjustments are made to the boundaries of counties each year, the overall number of counties has remained between 1,400 and 2,500 for millennia. As of 2000, China had 2,461 counties, some of which trace their continuous histories back two thousand years or more![24]

Counties play a strong role in the political administration of China. Typically, orders from above call for implementation of policies that take into account local peculiarities, and thus counties often exercise considerable discretion within the territories they administer. Increasingly, moreover, counties have been given leeway to pursue their own strategies of economic development, and many dynamic county leaders have seized the initiative to transform their localities. Counties derive political power from many of the same factors that bolster the positions of provinces and cities vis-à-vis the Center.

Like provinces, counties contain almost the full array of party and government organs so that they can deal effectively with their counterpart bodies at the level of the municipality or province. The bureaucratic system generally replicates itself yet again at the county level.

TOWNSHIPS

Townships were submerged into the people's communes during the Great Leap Forward, reemerging as separate units only after the advent of the reforms. They became key localities for establishing local enterprises staffed by peasants, especially during the 1980s and early 1990s, and they have continued to serve as a very important source of nonfarm income for many peasant families. Indeed, during the late 1990s roughly 50 percent of peasant migrants to cities went no farther than their own or a neighboring township to find work.[25] Changes in residence rules have allowed peasants to move to townships without obtaining special permission to do so, although the situation on the ground varies by locality.

Villages began to carry out elections for leaders in the late 1980s, but township governments still are not elected. Good relations with township leaders are often crucial for successful exercise of village leadership. Today, many townships actually operate largely as company towns, with the township leaders playing a major role in the various enterprises in their jurisdiction. Future plans call for a vast expansion of townships to absorb an expected new surge of migration off the farms during the coming decade.

Given their small size, township governments are structurally simpler than are their county and higher-level counterparts. But they still retain the basic major structures on both party and government sides found in higher level territorial bodies. In 2000, China had some 44,867 townships, of which 1,356 were specially designated as having large minority populations.

UNITS

During the Maoist era the "unit" (*danwei*) became the key vehicle for the interaction of the state and society. For most Chinese, the unit refers to the place of work—factory, research institute, ministry, and so forth. While agriculture was communized, the peasant's unit was the commune. Units in the state and collective sectors are the lowest level of the political system, not wholly independent organizations. During the famine of the early 1960s, the PRC completed the development of the *danwei* as a major vehicle for controlling citizens' behavior and channeling their efforts. At that time, virtually every citizen belonged to a unit. Many retired urbanites continued to be included in their former place of work; for others the neighborhood Residents Committee became their "unit" for purposes of state access to them.[26]

Urban units became multipurpose bodies that isolated people from those who worked in other units. A major urban enterprise would, for example, be the source of many things for its employees: housing, recreational activities, schooling for the children, health-care facilities, and so forth. The *danwei* also provided ration coupons for food, clothing, and furniture; administered the birth-control program; mediated marriage disputes; and provided pensions and burial funds. The *danwei*'s permission was required to get married, obtain a divorce, or change jobs.

The *danwei* also engaged in purely political tasks: political campaigns generally were carried out *danwei* by *danwei*. This created lasting cleavages, as campaigns first targeted one group and then another. Mao Zedong utilized these cleavages when he set the Chinese against each other. Through this technique of manipulating tensions and creating mutual antagonisms within *danwei*s, Mao largely obviated the need for a separate, centralized police apparatus such as the Soviet KGB. The *danwei* also organized compulsory political study, enforced "surveillance" on individuals who had committed "mistakes," and spied for the police via *danwei*-based "order maintenance committees." The rural *danwei* carried out a roughly parallel set of tasks.

Key to the *danwei*'s importance was the fact that very few individuals ever obtained permission to transfer from one *danwei* to another. For peasants, this meant that they could not freely move about the countryside or migrate to the cities. For workers, this tied guaranteed lifetime employment to loss of labor mobility. Each *danwei*, therefore, became a relatively isolated social and political entity, with little communication between members of different units. The quality of life of a citizen depended crucially on the resources and leadership of his or her *danwei*.[27]

Each of the pertinent higher-level political units had tentacles that reached directly into the *danwei*. A large urban enterprise would, for example, have a cultural/educational office directly subordinate to the CCP propaganda apparatus, a party committee subordinate to the municipal party committee, and a security section subordinate to the local police apparatus. The head of the *danwei*, therefore, did not fully control the activities in it.[28]

The reforms have significantly affected the *danwei* system. They have permitted increasing mobility in the countryside and have eliminated the commune. The ration system that previously buttressed geographical immobility has been discarded. The reforms have also permitted development of joint-venture, collective, and privately owned enterprises in the cities that are not merely extensions of the government apparatus. Changes endorsed at the NPC in March 1998 are producing a basic restructuring even of the state-owned enterprises themselves, which are becoming somewhat more like modern corporations and less like the basic-level government bodies they were in the past. Many SOEs are being privatized completely. Lifetime urban employment in one *danwei* has given way to considerable job insecurity, unemployment, and mobility. The reforms have also created an urban "floating" population.[29] Over 100 million people are not attached to any urban *danwei*.[30] In sum, the *danwei* level of the Chinese system is changing fundamentally, and in the future will cease to be an integral part of the political structure.[31] Few Chinese still work in a *danwei* that functions as the work unit did before the reforms.

The reforms are thus eroding the fundamental link the Maoist system created to handle the relationship between the state and society. One of the important tasks of the coming years will be to create alternatives to the *danwei* system, which emerged full blown about four decades ago. In the cities a shift is being made under the Ministry of Civil Affairs to a more residence-based unit of organization, dubbed the "Community Committee" (*shequ juweihui*). This new urban form is now moving from an experimental effort in a few large municipalities to nationwide application.

One model Community Committee in Beijing highlights the basic character this new organization seeks to attain. This Community Committee is more professional than was the former Residents Committee that it replaced. It has a full-time staff of five to six people and also employs migrant workers in some of its activities. The director is elected, but there was only one candidate (the CCP secretary of the local party branch organization), and the CCP branch controls this committee. The staff consists of recent university graduates and laid-off workers. All full-time staff but the director are female, live in the locality, and receive about 500 yuan per month, plus health-care coverage, from the state payroll. The Community Committee is responsible for day care, teenage community activities, security, elderly care, birth control, a clinic (primary health care), intervention services where there is drug or alcohol abuse or family violence, legal aid, newspaper delivery, trash removal, barber services, mail delivery (the post office provides the mail to the Community Committee, which then delivers it to the households), laundry, weekend entertainment, and a small shopping center. Many of these are moneymaking businesses to support the activities of the Community Committee.

In sum, the Community Committee system is more professional and wide ranging than was the former Residents Committee. A comparable community-level party-building effort is designed to assure that the CCP retains control over this new approach to urban organization. These developments reflect the reality that a combination of the shrinkage of the scope of public ownership and the increase in personal mobility means that state services must increasingly be delivered on the basis of residence rather than work unit.[32] Because these committees lack the formal ties to various ministries that their *danwei* predecessors maintained, though, far more social services must be delivered through citywide programs (such as pension plans and health insurance), and the overall ability of the state to focus political messages to the populace has diminished considerably. In addition, there is no rural equivalent to the urban Community Committee, and even in the cities they are at an experimental stage. They reflect the fundamental reality that China's governing reforms have produced changes in the economy and society that in turn require major adjustments in the structure and functions of the political system itself.

One of the key characteristics of the Chinese system that has not changed with the reforms is the *duplication of both party and government structures* on all levels of the national bureaucracy. This creates an extraordinarily complex matrix of vertical and horizontal authority that results in serious problems of governance.

The Matrix Muddle: *Tiao/Kuai Guanxi*

In an integrated, multilevel nationwide bureaucratic system, China must mesh both vertical (coordination from center to locality) and horizontal (coordination within a given geographic area) requirements. For example, it must be concerned both with environmental issues nationwide—that is, vertically (under an environmental ministry, with environmental departments at each level of the political system) and locally—that is, horizontally (through coordination of environmental efforts with economic and other issues within each political jurisdiction). The leaders' determination that the Communist party dominate the system adds further complexity to the bureaucratic web.

Western scholars of organizational dynamics term this cross-hatching of horizontal and vertical lines of authority a "matrix" problem. All large-scale organizations must deal with matrix issues. Since China has developed the largest bureaucracy in the history of the world, its matrix complexity is on an unprecedented scale.

The Chinese use vivid terminology to describe their crisscrossing jurisdictions: the vertical bureaucracies are called lines (*tiao*), while the horizontal coordinating bodies at various levels are called pieces (*kuai*). The relationships between the vertical and horizontal bodies are called *tiao/kuai guanxi*. And Chinese officials often talk about whether, in a particular instance, the "horizontal serves the vertical" or the "vertical serves the horizontal." What do they mean?

Despite the highly authoritarian nature of China's political system, actual authority is in most instances fragmented. There are numerous reporting lines throughout the system—through the party, through the government, to the territorial organs, and so forth. As Chart 6.4 illustrates, a hypothetical energy department under the Zhongshan county government would be subordinate to *both* the Zhongshan county government *and* the energy bureau under the Guangdong provincial government. At the same time, the Zhongshan county government must answer to both the Zhongshan county Communist party committee and the Guangdong provincial government. In addition, the organization department of the Zhongshan county Communist party committee will strongly affect the career opportunities of the leaders of the Zhongshan county energy department, who must also obey party discipline as members of the party committee of the energy department (see Chapter 7 for more information).

The simple point is that the officials of any given office have a number of bosses in different places. In this sense the Chinese polity can be considered one of "fragmented authoritarianism."[33] It becomes important in these circumstances to determine which of these bosses has priority over others. Typically, the Chinese cope with this in a minimal way by indicating that the primary leadership over a particular department resides either on the vertical line (*tiao*) (that is, with the Guangdong provincial energy bureau in the above example) or with the horizontal piece (*kuai*) (that is, with the Zhongshan county government itself, in the above example). The one with priority has what is termed a "leadership relationship" (*lingdao guanxi*) with the department in question, while the other one has a nonbinding "professional relationship" (*yewu guanxi*) with it.

But the distinction between leadership and professional relations does not come close to resolving all the problems. In reality, many organs can get access to issues that pass through the various departments. And if, as is often the case, a problem is large enough that its solution requires action by not just one department, but also by other departments (such as Construction and Finance, or the energy department of another county), then the lines of crisscrossing authority become exceedingly complex and cumbersome. It may be well-nigh impossible to find one official who has leadership authority

CHART 6.4 *Lines of Authority to the Hypothetical Zhongshan County Energy Department in Guangdong Province*

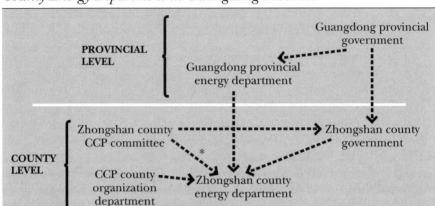

Arrows indicate general direction of authority in practice.
*Party discipline over party members in the energy department.

over all the pertinent units at any level below that of the Politburo in Beijing. This fragmentation of authority in the Chinese political administrative hierarchy makes it relatively easy for one actor to frustrate the adoption or successful implementation of important policies, especially since units (and officials) of the same bureaucratic rank cannot issue binding orders to each other.[34] The system is a muddle in that it can easily bog down in its own bureaucratic complexity.

Techniques for Making the System Work

With nationwide hierarchical bureaucratic empires under ministries and Central Committee departments defined by the functions they perform, and with powerful territorial party and government coordinating bodies at multiple levels of the system, the Chinese political system faces potentially severe problems: *overload* at the top, as lower-level officials avoid responsibility by pushing decisions "up" the system; *gridlock* from the fragmentation of power into different functional bureaucracies and territorial fiefdoms; *lack of accurate information* because of the distortions created by multiple layers of bureaucracy and because the CCP has not allowed any completely independent sources of information, such as a free press, to develop; and *indiscipline, corruption* and petty *dictatorship* as officials at each level have the opportunities and incentives to violate rules and cover up their transgressions.

To manage this complex party-state, the CCP has developed various basic operational techniques and principles specifically designed to mitigate some of these problems; virtually all these techniques have evolved significantly during the reform era. None of these remedies has fully resolved the problems, but all have affected the way the system has worked.

IDEOLOGY, DECENTRALIZATION, AND NEGOTIATIONS

As indicated above, one consequence of the structure of the Chinese political administration is that important issues require the cooperation of officials who are in different bureaucratic domains and who therefore lack jurisdiction over each other. Construction of a major new steel plant, for example, may demand the active support of individuals in the Ministry of Commerce, the Finance Ministry, the State Development and Reform Commission, and the local government and party authorities (for road building, housing construction, sanitation, removing peasants from their land, and so on). If foreign capital is involved, the People's Bank and others will also have to come on board.

For many such issues, the only level of the political system where one body has authority over everyone involved in the project is the Center. There is thus a natural tendency for the conflicts among the various bureaucracies to be pushed "up" to the Center for resolution. The Center tries to control the types of issues that land on its docket in part by proclaiming that in principle the "importance" of an issue should determine the level of political administration at which it is to be taken up. But there are no hard and fast rules to decide how important an issue is, and importance varies in part according to the priorities of key individuals at the Center at any given time. During one of the periodic drives against corruption, for example, the case against an important county official may be referred all the way to the Center for a decision on publicity and punishment. During more normal times, county and, possibly, municipal or provincial authorities would deal with a county corruption problem. Even without hard criteria to determine importance, though, time and again Chinese officials stress that it is the importance of an issue that determines how it is handled.

In practice, the importance principle works primarily to make sure that certain types of issues *are* decided at a high level. It does little to mitigate the problem of too many issues being pushed up the national political hierarchy.

A second widely applied operational principle is, therefore, that a problem should be handled at the lowest level in the system at which consensus can be reached to resolve it.[35] To put it differently, in most cases the Center prefers that lower levels manage problems without taking the time and attention of the Center in the process. On the whole, a large proportion of the decisions that affect day-to-day operations of almost every sort are taken at local or middle levels of the political system. Naturally, the Center wants to guide lower levels with its broad policy statements that articulate policy lines and goals. The pervasive role of ideology during the Maoist era contributed greatly toward achieving this coordination. At that time, officials at all levels were taught to view the Center as the fount of wisdom and themselves as local extensions of the will of the Center. Rigorous programs of ideological indoctrination for officials maintained a relatively high degree of sensitivity to themes and priorities articulated by the Center. The ready recourse to an iron fist for those who deviated reinforced the tendency of officials at all levels to strive to understand and implement priorities directed from Beijing.

The Cultural Revolution and its aftermath did fundamental damage to the use of ideology as a resource of the Center. Officials at all levels lost their innocent belief in the automatic validity of Center-mandated policies when they witnessed the enormous destruction and waste produced by the ill-conceived policies of Mao and his radical supporters. Deng Xiaoping recognized this sea change in the Chinese political climate when he began to articulate his reform programs.

The reforms have further contributed to the loss of ideology as a resource available to the Center to coordinate and enforce its priorities. This developed naturally from several circumstances. The reforms required a reevaluation of Maoism, thus removing the cloak of official infallibility from the Chairman and tarnishing the CCP, which had so stridently and ruthlessly proclaimed that infallibility for decades.[36] The reforms encouraged people to exercise initiative and make money, all of which made them less receptive to communist ideology.[37] The reforms opened China not only to foreign investment but also to foreign ideas, and these made people recognize that the party had grossly misled them for decades about conditions in the industrialized countries of the world.[38] And the reforms created strong incentives for localities to make money for themselves, which encouraged local officials to differentiate their own interests from those of the Center.[39]

No longer operating as the legitimate source of ideology has been a major blow to the power of the Center. Among other consequences, it has produced a situation in which the normative (that is, value-based) incentives for officials to obey Beijing have diminished considerably. Moreover, these developments have occurred during a period when Beijing has purposely diminished its control over two other potential resources—material and coercive incentives—to encourage local coordination and compliance.

As noted in Chapter 5, Deng Xiaoping recognized the importance of reducing Beijing's direct administrative role in the economy to spur rapid economic growth. The reform leadership thus increased the discretionary budgetary and extrabudgetary funds of provincial and lower-level units. Deng also recognized that the system would have to become less coercive if the leadership wanted lower-level officials to utilize fully their talents and initiative. The results have been diminished use of the security forces to enforce discipline at lower levels and, to a very limited extent, greater recourse to law instead of political command.

Although the Center's ability to utilize ideology as a vehicle to enhance policy coordination has diminished drastically, Beijing still does make use of broad policy pronouncements to set a general tone and direction that it asks lower levels to support. This tone is usually summed up in several slogans or formulations (*tifa*) that officials at all levels of the system utilize habitually.

Although these *tifa* do not in themselves provide much concrete assistance to policy coordination, they do create an atmosphere that affects behavior at all levels of the system. Also, the Center always gives top priority to some very particular matters for which it seeks direct control.

Because of the general fragmentation of authority in the system, resolving a matter below the Center often requires building a consensus among an array of pertinent officials. This need to construct a consensus generally predisposes officials to negotiate with other relevant officials from an early point. Chinese policy making is, consequently, characterized by an enormous amount of discussion and bargaining among officials to bring the right people on board.

The resulting bargains are often wide ranging, complex, and fragile. They may involve personnel assignments, funds, access to goods and markets, or substantive issues concerning a project or policy itself. And officials assume that others will try to "trade up" on their deals as soon as conditions warrant their doing so.

The proposal to build a mammoth dam at the Three Gorges section of the Yangtze River illustrates the bureaucratic deals that must be struck. The dam will provide badly needed electric power to the downstream provinces, especially Hunan and Hubei (see Map 6.1). It will also increase the flood protection afforded these provinces, which would suffer greatly if weather conditions produced simultaneous flood surges on the Yangtze and the Han rivers. But the Three Gorges Dam is displacing more than a million people who live above the dam site (primarily in Chongqing municipality), and the residents of this municipality and of Sichuan province will receive little of the electric power and none of the flood-control benefits.[40] The dam might also disrupt river traffic along the vital Yangtze artery. But because Sichuan, Chongqing, Hubei, Hunan, and the central ministries involved are all of the same bureaucratic rank, none has operational authority over the others.

Among the tradeoffs dam proponents accepted in order to build a consensus on the dam are the following: most important, the dam height is being held to 175 meters instead of the more than two hundred meters originally proposed. This lower height won over Chongqing municipality. At 175 meters, the reservoir behind the dam will end at Chongqing Harbor and thus will make that city the major trading center between Sichuan Province and the rich provinces of central China. A greater height would have flooded Chongqing; a lesser height would have left the smaller and less politically powerful city of Wanxian as the key trading port. The dam is being constructed with an elaborate and expensive ship lift to satisfy the concerns of the former Ministry of Communications. Chongqing itself is receiving special investment funds from the government to offset costs of relocation of people displaced by the dam reservoir. The former Ministry of Water Resources (whose primary task is flood control) was the key promoter of this dam project, and it negotiated these and additional concessions to other parties in order to win their support, or at least reduce their opposition.[41] Such deals are the basis of much of Chinese political decision making.

Despite its unitary nature and the general lack of real legal constraints

MAP 6.1 *Three Gorges Dam Project*

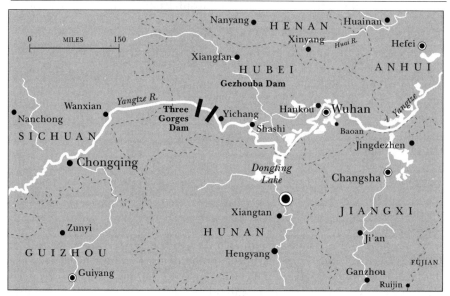

on the activities of the Center, therefore, the Chinese political system is characterized by an enormous amount of negotiations among officials, and many decisions are taken at relatively low levels in the national bureaucratic hierarchy. Given the deflation of the ideological power of the Center, little else would make the system work effectively.

IMPROVING AND CHANNELING INFORMATION

One of the most serious problems of a vertically integrated system such as China's is the difficulty leaders have in obtaining accurate information. Most data are reported level by level up the national administration, and typically officials at each level have incentives to introduce biases and distortions. For example, a county official interviewed for a scholarly research project in 1990 protested that the county did not have data on the county finances at issue. When the Western scholar noted that the province published provincewide data that must have been aggregated from the county reports, the county official responded, "Oh, you want *those* data! I had thought this was a scientific project that required accurate numbers." In another instance, shortly after the Sino-American rapprochement of the early 1970s the Chinese government asked Washington to provide it with American satellite information on the area under cultivation in China. America did so—and in this way Beijing found out that local officials were not reporting roughly 20 percent of its cultivated land. This did not, however, resolve the problem of underreporting. As late as 1997, Chinese official figures indicated that the PRC had in the neighborhood of 90 million hectares under cultivation. A U.S. government study of the time demonstrated that the true figure was more than 145 million hectares. More recently, the State Statistical Bureau reported national GDP growth of 8 percent for 2002, but every single provincial level unit separately reported its own GDP growth to be higher than this national "average."

Leaders have used many methods to circumvent their own officials in order to obtain reliable information. Mao Zedong usually traveled around by train, and he was known to order unscheduled stops so that he could pop in at a nearby village and pump the local officials with questions. (Mao's guards reportedly often beat him to the village, however, and it is unlikely that local people would in any case tell the august Chairman the real story on local conditions.) Mao also selected at least one member of the 8341 Division of the PLA (China's guard regiment for the top leaders) from each county, and he personally debriefed many of them when they returned from home leave. But it was well known among his officials that though Mao always sought the truth he rarely liked to hear it, and thus few dared to present him with unvarnished reality.[42] As we have seen, one who did—Peng Dehuai at the Lushan conference in July 1959—paid for it immediately with his career and later with his life during the Cultural Revolution.

Many top Chinese officials cultivated one or more locales where for particular reasons they knew the people well enough to get a straight story from them. For Chen Yun, this was Qingpu County near his native place of Shanghai; for Liu Shaoqi, it was his wife's hometown of Tianjin (where Liu had also worked in the CCP underground). They often used their contacts in these places to obtain feedback on policy implementation or to initiate small experiments that, if successful, might provide the basis for policy advocacy later on. It appears, though, that the post-Mao generation of leaders has not continued this stratagem to the same extent.

China's leaders have traditionally used two major devices to improve the quality of the information they receive, and in recent years they have added a third. The first longstanding device is the mode of operations called "democratic centralism," which Beijing learned from the Soviets. The "democracy" element has nothing to do with votes or multiparty systems. Rather, "democracy" here means consultation. The idea is that before an issue is decided, consultations should occur with all pertinent people. During that period, individuals may express their views freely on the issue so that necessary information is made available to the decision makers. Nobody should suffer for the views expressed in this phase of the decision-making process. Once a decision is reached, however, centralism prevails, which means that people must implement the decision regardless of whether or not they agree with it.

Democratic centralism is an attempt to enjoy the advantages of disciplined dictatorship without sacrificing free discussion and the airing of views. It is at best an uncertain technique, as only rarely is there a clear distinction between making one decision and modifying a previous one. More fundamentally, though, during the Maoist era experience soon showed that people were vulnerable for the opinions they had expressed during the consultative, "democratic" phase of this process, and thereafter the quality of information available to the central leaders fell off dramatically. The huge famine of 1961–62 was greatly exacerbated, for example, by the imposition from above of absurdly high quotas for grain procurement. As noted in Chapter 4, the quotas, in turn, were based on gross misinformation about the true state of affairs in the countryside.[43] This set of errors resulted in roughly 30 million deaths.

Starting in the late 1970s, Deng Xiaoping and the reformers made considerable efforts to rein in the terror and to nurture greater freedom of discussion, especially within the policy-making process. Numerous comments by Chinese officials indicate that these efforts achieved some success and that the system became more effective in gathering and transmitting information during the 1980s.

A second long-standing approach to information gathering drew on the meeting system and the document system. The Chinese communists believe in using face-to-face meetings extensively. In the initial years, this may have been encouraged in part by the low levels of literacy among many peasant guerrilla fighters who assumed high office after 1949. Barely able to read documents, they functioned best when they could go over things orally.[44] This style of operation has continued in somewhat attenuated form even as educational levels among officials have risen dramatically.

Virtually the entire top political elite gathers at least once a year—since the 1980s, during the summer at the seaside resort of Beidaihe—for an extended meeting that reviews the state of the country and decides on basic priorities for the coming months. These meetings—called central work conferences—typically involve all members of the Politburo, heads of major Central Committee departments and State Council ministries and commissions, all provincial party and government heads, and others, depending on the major topics of the meetings. Such meetings may last for a month or more. They involve some plenary sessions, but for the most part participants are divided into smaller groups that meet daily. A fairly elaborate system of reports and bulletins from these groups lays the groundwork for the top leaders at the end of the meeting to pull things together and reach a series of conclusions. The meeting chairman has the formal right to sum up the conclave—a power that Mao Zedong often used to political advantage.[45]

These long meetings also provide ample opportunity for delegates and their spouses to mix informally. Gossip circulates, news is revealed, and as at Lushan in July 1959, these meetings have been the occasion for many of the political sparks that have flown since 1949. In similar but less elaborate fashion, work conferences are held at all territorial levels of the political system and in the various functional systems (*xitongs*) discussed in Chapter 7.

The meeting system is so elaborate that the Chinese have even put out handbooks on key meeting types and on preparation for various kinds of meetings. Almost any bureaucratic body can convene a meeting, and an official can bring in the people he or she wants to participate in the discussion simply by declaring that the meeting is "enlarged" (that is, attended by people who do not normally belong to the group that is meeting). This arrangement gives many officials a legitimate vehicle for testing out ideas with a hand-picked group without being accused of under-the-table scheming.

Although the meeting system is important to the overall political system, firm rules are hard to come by. In some instances of important decisions by central work conferences (for example, the Lushan conference decisions to purge Peng Dehuai, launch a related Antirightist campaign, and scale back the targets for the Great Leap Forward), a Central Committee plenum convenes immediately afterward to give these decisions formal endorsement. Another instance was the August 1958 conference at Beidaihe that decided, among other things, to adopt people's communes as the form of organization for agriculture.[46] Here Mao Zedong used an enlarged Politburo meeting very much in the way a central work conference would normally be utilized. No Central Committee plenum convened to lend added legitimacy to the resulting decisions. It thus is not clear what the boundaries are on the types of actions these meetings can take. But central work conferences in recent years have generally produced strategies and decisions that are then embodied in formal acts by statutory bodies and conclaves.

The current Chinese political system also maintains an extensive document system that in many ways reflects the imperial Chinese bureaucratic system that came before it.[47] Every ministry has its own in-house document series, as does the Central Committee, the central CCP Secretariat, every territorial government and party committee, and other major bureaucratic bodies. Typically, these documents are numbered sequentially from the first one of each calendar year.

The document system determines the ways various documents are handled. Each document has a label that specifies its type. Specialized personnel sort the documents, and handbooks have been published to guide the document handlers in their work. Document types include the following: an order (*mingling*) that must be carried out precisely by the recipient, with no deviation; an instruction (*zhishi*) that should be modified to suit local conditions, with approval of the modifications by the next highest territorial level; a circular (*tongzhi*) that provides information for reference, with the implication that it would be a good idea to utilize whatever might be appropriate; and an opinion (*yijian*) that simply expresses the current views of an official. Many more gradations of literalness fill the gaps between the strict *mingling* and the nonbinding *yijian*.

The Chinese system has been hindered in its ability to collect accurate information by many factors, some of them matters of deliberate choice. Until the 1980s, poorly educated people had a tight hold on the system. Many of these revolutionary cadres discriminated against people who were highly literate. As the administrative system became more complex, this anti-intellectualism imposed increasing burdens on the functioning of the bureaucracy.[48] This was especially true during the Cultural Revolution, with its wholesale attacks on intellectuals and the virtual destruction of, among other things, the state statistical system by know-nothing radicals.[49] Reformers during the 1980s worked hard to bring younger, better-educated individuals into office.

Attacks on individuals for remarks they had made during various meetings in previous years had the effect of producing a bureaucratic apparatus of yes-men, a high price to pay in a system deficient in independent sources of facts. The very degree of domination of the party over society increased its problems in understanding popular moods and tolerances. The Mao Zedong cult, which grew to gargantuan proportions by the mid-1960s, added another major obstacle to accurate reporting up the national hierarchy.

In addition, the Chinese system developed an extraordinary degree of secrecy. Virtually all documents were classified, and individuals generally saw information strictly on a need-to-know basis. Normally, office workers did not discuss their work with colleagues, as a presumption of secrecy prevailed. Information was thus strictly channeled. Even Politburo members below the very highest level were not allowed access to information freely in spheres outside their designated areas of responsibility. With information scarce, control over information naturally became a type of power in itself. Ministries and other bodies therefore zealously guarded their data, which in turn inhibited consideration of what effect the decisions of one unit would have on the activities and interests of others.[50]

The result was a system forced to work with little reliable information. The system was strongly geared toward transmission of orders downward, with much less sensitivity to the need for a good flow of data upward. Time and again, the Center tried to move an issue along without the data needed for a finely tuned analysis and decision. China paid dearly for this situation.

The reformers took many measures to mitigate the problems in the information system. As previously noted, for example, they greatly reduced the incidence of political persecution of officials for having made suggestions that were not ultimately accepted. They also reduced substantially the degree of secrecy in the system, in part at the urging of the World Bank and other foreign and international financial institutions, and they encouraged the publication of more data and the discussion of more issues in widely circulated journals and other forums.[51]

The reformers also tried a new method to deal with the paucity of data. In his years as premier, Zhao Ziyang developed a group of State Council think tanks outside the normal bureaucratic system. These think tanks derived their power primarily from the direct access they enjoyed to the premier. Those who wanted to influence policy, therefore, were well advised to be responsive to requests from the new think tanks. The people who staffed these new bodies were generally young reformers who recognized the problems in the extant bureaucratic system. They worked hard to cultivate direct ties with units at all levels of the national administration and to bring the resulting data to bear on policy matters.

The think tanks made considerable progress in improving the information flows to the top, and in some instances lower-level bodies in the provinces and cities made similar improvements.[52] But in the final analysis this structural innovation was weakened when Zhao became party general secretary, which soon took him away from direct responsibility for the economy, and then was purged in the wake of the Tiananmen massacre of 4 June 1989. Ultimately, the think tanks had been Zhao's personal creations and grew out of his personal networking. Some were either dismantled or substantially gutted with Zhao's fall from power. But Zhao's innovation has been sustained; an array of think tanks still plays a role in contemporary policy making.[53]

Broader trends under the reforms have continued to improve the quality and quantity of information available to the top leaders. The installation of computer systems throughout the government has vastly improved the flow of information and data, along with increasing officials' ability to analyze the data they receive. Strenuous efforts were made during the 1990s to improve the quality of personnel and of the system in the state statistical apparatus and the sampling frames and models they employed. These changes account for the fact, noted above, that the State Statistical Bureau produced a 2002 national GDP growth rate lower than that reported by any provincial level unit. The SSB used its own sampling frame to generate its conclusions.

The Chinese media, while still under broad political controls, nevertheless also became a more important and unfiltered source of information. Since even before 1949, the New China News Agency has provided leaders with secret reports that reflect information its reporters gathered. But the reforms have increasingly required that China's media develop sources of funds for their programming, and this in turn has encouraged in some cases more hard hitting investigative reporting. Thus, for example, CCTV in 1994 began broadcasting what became an extremely popular investigative reporting show, *Focus* (*jiaodian fangtan*). Among other things, in 1998 *Focus* alerted Premier Zhu Rongji that he been duped when he visited a state-owned grain facility that had been praised in the official media. As *Focus* revealed in its nationwide broadcast, many of the sacks of grain that had so impressed Premier Zhu had been borrowed from other facilities for the occasion.[54]

Overall, therefore, the Chinese have used a variety of means—including advocacy of democratic centralism, formal meeting systems, elaborate document systems, experimentation with think tanks, and increasingly aggressive media reporting—to enhance the quantity and quality of information available to policy makers. The reformers have in many ways improved the situation, which in Mao Zedong's later years had seriously deteriorated. Nevertheless, all autocratic political systems have major difficulties in generating good-quality information about themselves, and China's geographical size, poverty, and enormous population combine with its authoritarian system to limit the national leaders' understanding about what is happening throughout the PRC.

Petty Dictatorship and Corruption

China, like the former USSR, set up a system in which every official is highly vulnerable to those above but is able to act like a petty dictator toward those below. Each official must be sure that his or her own bailiwick works effectively, and typically each has considerable ability to skew in favorable directions the information that goes to higher levels. Usually, upper levels do not enquire very closely into how things are done—so long as the key priorities seem to be met.[55]

Under the *danwei* (unit) system, officials in China had an extraordinary degree of leverage over their subordinates. For the most part, they could strongly influence careers, even to holding a subordinate virtually hostage in a meaningless position for years at a time. They also controlled available housing, a crucial matter in a country with a severe urban housing shortage. Permission to have a child, permission to marry, permission to divorce, and access to many goods and services could be influenced or determined by the boss at the office or factory. Before the reforms, commune, brigade, and team officials held similar power over peasants. Many of these sources of personal leverage are declining sharply with the decline of the *danwei* system, the increase in personal mobility, and the shift of allocation of many goods (such as housing) to the market, but some remnants of this system remain in place for many urban Chinese.

Such power often breeds despotism and corruption. Ironically, the reforms have encouraged the latter in several ways. Most important, they have occasioned a drastic decline in any sense of ideological élan that might have restrained people from turning their political power to personal advantage. The reforms have also increased the legitimacy of amassing money and material goods—and thus of demanding these things in return for favorable decisions. And the reforms have created many gray areas in terms of what constitutes entrepreneurial activity as versus illicit moneymaking through abuse of power.

China's leaders have always recognized the potential for corruption among officials at all levels of the political system, but they have not done well in curbing abuses. The issue badly divided the leadership during Mao Zedong's reign. For example, in the Hundred Flowers campaign and in the Cultural Revolution, the Chairman proved willing to bring in nonparty people as part of his effort to curb officiousness by cadres. Other leaders, such as Liu Shaoqi, opposed "rectifying" the party by going outside of its ranks.[56]

The Chairman's attacks on the political apparatus during the Cultural Revolution left the party a shambles. Fully half its membership by 1978 had been recruited during the Cultural Revolution, and most of these individuals had joined because of their dislike of the older party cadres. But in the late 1970s, as explained in Chapter 5, virtually the entire older generation was rehabilitated. The changing policy lines, the rapid coming to grips with the reality of Mao's damaging policies, internal rifts within the party, and other factors made the party itself a very poorly disciplined and uncertain instrument of rule as of the early 1980s.

At several points during the 1980s the top leadership focused on the growing corruption and other problems in the party and tried to correct them. They set up Discipline Inspection Commissions, but these proved wholly inadequate. Indeed, the lines of authority even now have each Discipline Inspection Commission reporting to the territorial party committee that it is supposed to supervise![57]

The net result of these half-hearted efforts is that corruption and lack of discipline within the party appear to have grown considerably since the early 1980s. Periodically, some officials are arrested and given exemplary punishment—including, sometimes, execution—with attendant publicity intended to have a deterrent effect. But comparatively few high-ranking officials have been arrested for corruption since the reforms began, and many lower-level officials complain privately that the upper levels corrupt the entire system—both by their example and by the payoffs they demand from below. Thus, corruption has spread to the point where colleagues view an official who refuses side payments with some suspicion, and cynicism over corruption is pervasive. At the high end, estimates suggest the corruption involves sums that total nearly 15 percent of China's GDP.[58]

State Dominance over Society

The above sections outline the formal organization of the Chinese political system, highlight the resulting matrix muddle, and explain basic attempts to mitigate some of the most severe problems the system confronts. The overall picture presented is of a fragmented authoritarianism that is extremely complex, increasingly decentralized, and suffering from ideological deflation, growing corruption and, to some extent, petty despotism. Relations between this political system and Chinese society have changed enormously under the reforms, especially since the early 1990s.

Until the early 1990s, almost all CCP leaders agreed with both their Confucian predecessors and their former communist counterparts in other countries that the leadership knows best what is in the overall interests of the society. This basic idea did not absolve the leaders from trying to find out the real state of things, including the attitudes of citizens. But it did make the leaders feel that citizens have no right to demand that the leaders adopt policies the citizens prefer. Rather, the leaders believed that citizens cannot understand what is best for society and therefore do not have the right to promote their own inevitably flawed views on policy.

This attitude encouraged China's leaders to try to gather information about the objective issues they confronted but to suppress any attempts by individuals or groups to promote their own views. Mao Zedong's approach was the mass line, which sought to gather information from the populace but reserved to the leaders the right to make decisions. He believed that actively involving the population in implementation of his decisions increased popular support for those policies.

The Chinese system has been, thus, in principle, one in which the state dominates the society. Neither in theory nor in practice was individual advocacy or interest-group activity regarded as legitimate. The political leaders expended enormous resources—in ideological indoctrination, political coercion, and manipulation through material incentives—to bolster the top-down nature of this system.

In the minds of the CCP leaders, the best way to address issues was through the creation of official organizations. For example, many peasants have an immediate interest in flood control. The leaders created a specialized bureaucracy (the name changed over the years, but generally it has been known as the water-resources bureaucracy), one of whose major tasks is to further develop the system of flood control. That bureaucracy is expected to fight hard to protect and expand the regime's work in the flood-control area, and in this sense, the peasants' interest in flood control is "represented" in the system. But if peasants organized to demand greater attention to flood control from the authorities, this was regarded as an insurgency and would be suppressed, violently if necessary. Only the leaders had the right to determine what was in the "real" interests of the peasants and of other groups and to create appropriate official organs and assign appropriate tasks to them.[59]

The regime utilized an extraordinary array of controls to assert its dominance over society. All nonofficial organizations existed only at the sufferance of the party, and the CCP permitted relatively very few of these to form. Even today, religious and public-health organizations typically require party approval of their leadership, and when the party senses any domestic political threat, it usually quickly restricts the activities of any independent bodies.

Relations between the Chinese state and society are, however, changing very rapidly—to the extent that few hard and fast rules now apply. Formally, all citizens are obligated to register with the government any organizations they form, and the government retains the right to suppress groups its finds threatening. Tens of thousands of organizations have formed to bring together citizens around shared interests, though the nature of the relationship between these organizations and the political system is contested and in a state of flux. In theory, this relationship is uniformly "top down." But the realities are far less uniform than the theory and are part of the dynamic changes unleashed by the reforms in the way China is governed. Signs of serious change are everywhere. For example:

☐ Although religious organizations are obligated to register with the government, local authorities in some areas tolerate underground churches. Underground Christian churches apparently have a membership larger than that of the official churches.

☐ Environmental and other advocacy groups have sprung up. Some of these fail to register. Others shop around for sympathetic officials who use their own units to register the group and provide it with protection.[60]

☐ The media are full of articles that push the government to pay more attention to problems that it has failed to address effectively.

☐ Tens of thousands of voluntary groups—professional societies, hobbyists' clubs, affinity organizations, school alumni groups, and so forth—have formed throughout China, typically with little or no real government supervision or interference.

☐ Citizens have gained some access to the public media. Shanghai municipality, for example, has a call-in radio show with a reputed audience of ten million. Many callers complain about problems with the local government.

□ Chinese citizens have been given the right to sue officials for abuse of power. The incidence both of such suits and of judgments against the government has grown rapidly in the late 1990s.

These signs of change coincide with structural developments that reduce the points of leverage the state formerly exercised over society. The restrictive *hukou* and *danwei* systems are eroding; satellite television and the Internet have seriously breached the state's monopoly on information; students no longer are subject to state-dictated job assignments on graduation; the private and foreign invested enterprises—which generally contain few if any party members—are employing more people; and so forth.

In sum, although still authoritarian, the Chinese government is no longer totalitarian in either its views or its practices. The government can repress major challenges to its authority but generally seeks to entice, rather than order, the population to do its bidding. This requires that the authorities seek to understand popular desires. Many government units now sponsor social surveys to learn popular attitudes, and government officials expect to hear from disgruntled citizens. The government has also accepted the notion that large areas of social existence lie outside of the realm of politics and thus should be left for individuals to shape for themselves.[61]

Therefore, whereas under Mao the political system dominated—and decimated—society, the Deng-era and subsequent reforms have brought a conscious reduction in the state's tight control of social and economic activity. The decline of ideology; the reality of the revolution in telecommunications; the development of nonstate sectors of the economy; the conversion to family farming in the countryside; the greater dependence on market forces rather than official orders to determine the allocation of goods, services, and opportunities; the emergence of relatively well-off people; the increased exposure to the international arena; and the purposeful policies of political relaxation have created a situation vastly different from that of the prereform or early reform period. China's leaders now assume that their citizens have individual interests and will act on them. They readily think in terms of interest-driven politics instead of the Maoist (and Confucian) notion of an organically unified society.

Transitions

The formal political system, as indicated above, has remained basically constant in its structure but has changed very significantly since the start of the reforms in the way it works and the roles it seeks to play. This is, moreover, still very much a work in progress, with additional major changes in the offing.

In many ways China has developed a more efficient, transparent, and dynamic political system. As compared with the period in the early stage of the reforms, problems are more thoroughly researched and receive fuller vetting internally before decisions are reached. Information is more widely available, opinions are more freely offered, and the statistical tools and models employed are more sophisticated. International technical advice is now available on everything from banking regulations to development of the legal system to slowing the spread of HIV/AIDS and of SARS and is accorded significant attention. In addition, the government has sharply reduced the array of outcomes it seeks to control, ceding many issues to individual choice, market forces, or other determinants. By narrowing the scope of its ambition, moreover, the political apparatus has inherently increased its ability to do well in the narrower scope of things it attempts.

China's leaders now fundamentally accept that people act primarily according to their interests and that it is therefore necessary both to understand those interests and to structure incentives accordingly. One unintended result of this acceptance has been a poverty of thinking about values and a major retreat in the efforts to nurture and shape the principles that guide behavior. In lieu of serious attention to values, the political system has instead come to rely overwhelmingly on a combination of appealing to people's material interests or to their fear of punishment.

At every level–province, city, county, township, and unit–leaders have been given strong incentives to act creatively to bring about rapid growth in their locality while maintaining overall political stability. This fundamental approach has unleashed enormous energy and creativity that in turn has sustained rapid economic growth for more than two decades. But serious structural problems confront China's formal political system as it moves forward. China's leaders are well aware of the following issues, but in each case they still need to take controversial and politically very difficult measures to address the concern satisfactorily.

□ *Tenuous basis of legitimacy.* From the start of the reforms through the mid-1990s most sectors of the population experienced net gains almost every year from the reform effort. Since the mid-1990s this has been less and less the case. Increasingly, the reforms are inflicting severe pain on some groups—such as grain-producing peasants in central China or middle-aged workers laid off from SOEs in northeast China—while providing enormous benefits to others, such as successful private real estate developers and other entrepreneurs, as well as many officials. The pain has both a geographical dimension and a generational component. The people along the east coast are overall faring well, but those in northeast, central, and western China are doing more poorly. Younger members of the labor force are finding vast new opportunities, but middle-aged and older people are losing security and seeing their prospects narrow. The implicit decision made in the 1980s to gain support for the political system by making the economy grow is thus now at risk as increasing portions of the population are seeing more losses than gains. This problem is exacerbated by widespread dismay at the extent to which officials at all political levels have become corrupt. As a result, although many of the "winners" from the reforms appreciate the progress that the political system has generated, few even among those winners extol the virtues of the system itself. When support is largely utilitarian, the potential for shortfalls in performance to generate systemic crises grows.

☐ *Structural corruption.* Corruption has become deeply rooted in the political system within both the party and the state. It is now so ingrained that many officials have few real compunctions about engaging in corrupt behavior. Approvals and licenses are often granted only on payment of illicit fees. Regulations of all sorts are set aside on receipt of bribes. Officials siphon budgetary funds to invest in speculative projects and hope to pocket the resulting gains. Too often, of course, such projects fail, and as a result agencies lack the money allocated to them for their work. Some officials simply embezzle funds and put them in private bank accounts or send them abroad. Despite strict regulations on official appointments, some positions are actually bought with bribes. Such corruption has systemic consequences. The lure of personal wealth often causes officials to bend or ignore policies and laws and to report false information to higher levels. It also causes many officials to act with astonishing disregard for the well-being of the constituencies they govern, engendering bitter feelings about the local political system among many in the populace. And corruption breeds cynicism among officials themselves, draining from the political system of a sense of esprit.

☐ *Coercive deficiencies.* The political system has retained not only its authoritarian posture but also its substantial coercive apparatus. It has large bureaucracies and uniformed forces to suppress dissent and maintain order. But on balance China is not a well-policed society. This problem stems in part from the realities of government corruption and of the continuing weakness of the country's legal system. But it also reflects the fact that much of China has a severe shortage of well-trained police forces. This fundamental shortfall in effective agents of official coercion has allowed criminal activity to mushroom. In many cases, citizens have legitimate grievances about police abuse that is not sanctioned by higher-level policy. Anecdotal accounts suggest that torture is widespread in police interrogations and that many police are so corrupt that they sometimes amount to little more than official thugs for hire.[62] By failing to provide adequate protection to citizens and engendering grievances from its own misbehavior, China's government coercive apparatus further saps support for the political system among many of its constituents, especially those in smaller cities and towns and in parts of the countryside that do not receive priority in the allocation of effective police forces.

☐ *Representation.* China's leaders have in the past taken it as an article of faith that they understand the needs of the population better than the citizens themselves. This view derived from the belief that communist ideology gave them superior insight into how society ought to function, and their investigative efforts enabled them to appreciate the practical difficulties they confronted. But Chinese society under the reforms has become enormously dynamic and complex, and Chinese citizens now have access to more information and options than ever before. As detailed above, moreover, increasing numbers of citizens no longer work in units that fit effectively into the governmental structure. In the process of adapting to the results of the reforms, the political system is consciously changing its bases of recruitment to its own ranks. Educational requirements now sharply restrict political career mobility for those from rural or poor backgrounds. Even the CCP, with the adoption of the "Three Represents" as official doctrine at the Sixteenth Party Congress in 2002, is blessing the recruitment of successful private-sector entrepreneurs into its ranks. A result of these developments is that a growing portion of the population sees the political system as no longer responsive to its own needs and interests. And the political apparatus itself, increasingly staffed by those who have fared well, has refused to adopt structural means that could build into the system representation for many peasants, the floating population, unemployed workers, and others on the margin. Although some efforts, such as village elections and public-opinion polling, help to mitigate this problem to a limited extent, the system as a whole is running an increasingly serious risk of failing to understand or respond adequately the minimum needs and interests of large portions of the populace. Yet even the thinking about future reforms appears to be limited to extending elections to the township and eventually to the county level. Allowing the formation of new political parties and extending elections to the provincial and national levels appears to be beyond the realm of consideration of even the more reformist officials in the upper ranks of the system. China requires a political system that retains strong executive authority to deal with the problems detailed in the remaining chapters of this volume. But failure of the system to build in more effective means of eliciting and representing interests of major population groups is an increasingly serious problem, given the dynamic economic and social changes the reforms are continuing to generate.

□ *Funding.* The reforms produced a shift from acquiring the income of SOEs to relying on taxes, levies, and debt to fund the political system itself. After experimenting with many different tax systems in various provinces, in 1994 China adopted a unified system for collecting taxes nationwide that established separate tax bureaucracies to collect central and local levies.[63] The early years of shifting to a tax based system had left the Center with too few funds to cover its obligations. Now the Center is again in reasonable financial shape, as are most provincial-level bodies.[64] The problem now is that county and township governments are carrying a burden of unfunded mandates that have left these local governments wallowing in debt with no clear path other than rapid local economic development to reduce their debt burdens. Responding to obvious signs of increasing peasant discontent, the national government in December 2001 prohibited local governments from imposing miscellaneous fees and levies on their constituents. It also required that peasants travel to the tax bureau to pay their taxes owed so that tax collectors could not go into the field and fleece the locals out of sight of supervisory authorities. And, completing the implementation of the 1998 government streamlining effort, it mandated that local governments reduce the number of their employees by 20 percent. The problem is that the elimination of fees and levies has not been matched by a reduction in requirements for local government services. And government employees who have been let go are still receiving their base salaries for an indefinite time into the future.[65] Thus, the government fiscal crisis in the current system is focused on local levels of government—the very levels that deliver most services to the population. This compounds the fiscal problems addressed in Chapters 8 and 9.

The formal political system and its trends and problems as described in this chapter are very important, but we must also understand both organizations and rules behind the scenes to see how this system actually functions. The following chapter introduces the "insider's view" of the Chinese body politic.

7

The Organization of Political Power and Its Consequences: The View from the Inside

Chapter 6 described the formal organization of the PRC's political system and its consequences. The present chapter focuses on the real configurations of political power and on the behavior of the key individuals within the system, the several million party cadres who govern China. In shifting focus to the actual exercise of power in the PRC, we must draw a distinction between "organizations" and "institutions," for the Chinese political system is strewn with organizations that have not become institutions. "Organizations" are coherent, internally interdependent administrative or functional structures. "Institutions," in contrast, are practices, relationships, and organizations *that have developed sufficient regularity and perceived importance to shape significantly the behaviors of their members.*

Organizations—committees, offices, and their rules—exist in abundance, even at the highest levels of the Chinese system. But in reality the top power elite, the twenty-five to thirty-five individuals who at any given time oversee virtually all sectors of work and politics, personally redefine the real rules of the game on an ongoing basis. The presence of organizations more than institutions is not limited to the upper echelons; at all levels of the political system the PRC is a highly personalized system embedded in a complex organizational matrix.

Although such things are hard to measure, it appears that the PRC has been far less institutionalized as a political system than was the imperial Chinese government.[1] Even the Republic of China developed more formal civil-service requirements in its first decade than the PRC produced in its first fifty years in power. The PRC's revolutionary origins as a peasant-based party, its ambitious goals to revamp China's society, and its being ruled into the early 1990s by the original party revolutionaries who seized power in 1949 have proven major obstacles to the development of enduring political institutions.

This chapter presents a view from the inside. It first analyzes the way power is actually allocated behind the formal organizational facade among the top power elite as presented in Chapter 6. It then branches out to consider how this small group deals with the country's massive bureaucratic apparatus and the configurations of authority within the apparatus itself. It concludes with a consideration of the strategies used by the PRC's political cadres. Chinese officialdom generally tries to keep these key dimensions of the political system—its physiology rather than its simple anatomy—carefully hidden from view.

The Top Twenty-five to Thirty-five

Right from the start the CCP established a basic approach to organizing power at the apex that in its essentials has endured into the twenty-first century. The key group has been the top twenty-five to thirty-five leaders headed by a core leader who together determine the direction of policy in all important spheres.[2]

Naturally, a great deal has changed in the composition and dynamics of relations among the top power elite since 1949. In the early years they consisted wholly of hardened revolutionaries who had fought for decades to achieve national political power, a diverse group of accomplished individuals. In a country where geographical distinctions are sharp, the members hailed from widely differing areas: Mao Zedong, Liu Shaoqi, and Peng Dehuai from the central China province of Hunan; Zhou Enlai from the eastern province of Zhejiang; Deng Xiaoping and Zhu De from the huge southwest province of Sichuan; Chen Yun from the metropolis of Shanghai; Peng Zhen from the north China province of Shanxi; Lin Biao from Hubei; and so forth. They also came from different social classes. Zhu De and Peng Zhen, for example, were from very poor peasant stock, Mao and Deng hailed from relatively well-off households in the countryside, and Zhou came from an elite family. They also had very diverse educational backgrounds. Among the group, only Zhou Enlai acquired an elite formal education. Most had either led or shared the leadership of entire armies or of major underground networks for years before 1949. This was not a homogeneous group of toadies around a single strong leader.

Nevertheless, the extent to which all these individuals paid homage to Mao Zedong is extraordinary. During the revolution, Mao acquired enormous stature among his colleagues as someone who consistently made the right strategic choices in life-and-death situations. After 1949, he bolstered his power through both his ruthlessness and his astute manipulation of the political resources at his command. For example, he had his central guards unit provide him with intelligence on the personal habits and activities of his colleagues, then used this information to embarrass a colleague when he wanted to weaken him or throw him off balance politically.[3] At times he took advantage of his control over military appointments to change the garrison commander in the locality where a contentious central meeting was convening, thereby assuring himself of the personal loyalty of the local troop commander. And he made other leaders dependent on him simply by virtue of the importance of his personality cult to the legitimacy of the entire political system.

Undoubtedly, traditional ideas about the strength and power of the first emperor of each new dynasty also contributed to this deference. In the late 1960s, for example, Lin Biao is reported to have declared, "We may not always understand what Chairman Mao means, but we must always do as he says. The first emperor of each new dynasty is always very strong."

Mao often absented himself from Beijing and allowed many issues to go forward without his active intervention. He would indicate the broad directions in which policy should move but then sit back to see how his colleagues handled the issue. But Mao adopted many measures to make sure that he remained apprised of all important developments. As noted above, in 1953 he decreed that no document could be issued in the name of the Central Committee until he personally had reviewed and approved it.[4] And, to repeat, he brooked no opposition when he felt strongly about an issue. There are virtually no instances of other leaders directly opposing Mao when he had made his position and feelings clear.

Though Mao insisted on having the last word where he had a policy preference, he nevertheless abhorred bureaucratic routine and the details of daily office work.[5] Western scholars have debated whether the best way to think about the Mao era is in terms of "Mao in command" or in terms of Mao as "first among equals." In retrospect, this division seems to have missed the mark, and the Chinese may have found the best terminology in defining the key position simply as that of a "core leader."

Mao's personal style became increasingly despotic during and after the Great Leap Forward. He trusted primarily those in his inner circle—his administrative secretaries, called *mishu* (a group discussed below); personal guards under Wang Dongxing; his physician; a few close associates, relatives, and mistresses—and minimized face-to-face contact with other leading officials. Even those closest to him found themselves constantly vulnerable to his whims, including his penchant for dispatching others to remote rural areas for long periods of time to toughen them. He set his entourage to spying on each other, and he had the last word even on the diagnoses and treatment of medical problems that other leading officials developed. Mao dictated, for example, the timing of operations on Zhou Enlai's cancer in the early 1970s.[6]

Mao's despotism came fully to the fore during the Cultural Revolution, when he first placed under house arrest and then permitted the public humiliation and torture of the majority of leaders who had been in the top power elite of the 1950s. One author who interviewed many of Mao's surviving colleagues states that Mao seemed to enjoy toying with his beleaguered comrades before having them done in. For example, he called Liu Shaoqi in from house arrest and told him that he was pleased with Liu's self-criticism. Liu immediately reported to his family that their troubles were about to end. Instead, Mao almost immediately afterward permitted Liu's public beating and torture, which went on for more than a year and from which he died in 1969. Mao also ordered Liu's wife, Wang Guangmei, thrown into prison, where she languished in harsh conditions of solitary confinement for more than a decade. Liu's children were beaten and scattered around the country.[7]

In similar fashion, Luo Ruiqing, the former head of the public security apparatus and deputy defense minister, was crippled and in 1978 died from the complications stemming from torture.[8] Peng Dehuai also died from torture. Deng Xiaoping fared slightly better, but one of his sons, Deng Pufang, became a paraplegic when Red Guards reportedly threw him out of an upper-story window. Mao's power was such that even during his final months in 1976, when he lay almost immobile on his bed, virtually unable to communicate and largely unaware of his surroundings, every intelligible word he uttered still had the force of law.[9]

When Deng Xiaoping gained the political initiative in 1978, he tried to establish a new set of norms to govern relations among the top power elite. He attempted to give some substance and credibility to the top organizations of the party and government, all of which Mao had changed at will during his last decade in power. Deng therefore encouraged regular meetings of key bodies, nurtured more extensive consultation, and stopped Mao's practice of throwing purged leaders into prison or subjecting them to beatings and torture.

The obviously disastrous consequences of Mao's personal rule helped Deng initiate these changes—all of his colleagues could readily see the dangers of granting one leader unbridled power. In addition, Deng personally had not gained his legitimacy so much through revolutionary struggle as had Mao, and therefore he stood on a somewhat more equal footing with the surviving generation of increasingly elderly revolutionary leaders. Yet Deng also faced a dilemma: in wanting to bring about change, he had to maximize his own power to effect reforms at the same time that he circumscribed his power in order to make the leading political organizations more like real institutions.

Far more than Mao, Deng ultimately had to play a game of coalition politics. He was first among equals, at least among the party elders; this was not a "Deng in command" system. Deng made a virtue of necessity by specifically rejecting the trappings of Mao's power: he not only refused to become party chairman, he abolished that post altogether in 1982; he never moved into the Zhongnanhai, the old imperial abode where Mao had made his home in Beijing; and he attempted to build up the prestige of his protégés in the party and the government. In all of this, he had to negotiate with powerful elderly colleagues, most notably Chen Yun, but also Li Xiannian, Bo Yibo, Peng Zhen, and Wang Zhen, each of whom had large support bases in the party, the government, or the military.[10]

Nevertheless, Deng retained some of Mao's important powers. His high domestic and international prestige as a symbol of China's reforms bolstered his position in the Zhongnanhai, where the top party and government bodies are located. Like Mao, Deng had the critically important right to determine who would belong to the top power elite itself.[11] Leaders of Chinese factions strengthen their positions in substantial measure by providing appointments for their followers.[12] Chen Yun, for example, gave Li Peng a critical boost to his career in 1983, and Li subsequently remained loyal to Chen's policy preferences. Deng took care to consult with his colleagues about these decisions— and he allocated positions with an eye to maintaining coalition support. For example, he left the State Planning Commission in the hands of Song Ping, a supporter of Chen Yun, even when Deng's appointee Zhao Ziyang held responsibility for overall economic policy.[13] But the ultimate power stayed in Deng's hands, not by any statute but simply because of his prestige and connections in the system.

Deng also injected himself into the policy process to set national priorities. He did this in a detailed fashion in the late 1970s and early to mid-1980s. After that, his involvement became more selective and sporadic as age slowed him down. As befits the core leader in the Chinese system, Deng's major policy decisions concerned everything from economic priorities to personnel appointments to foreign policy initiatives to ideological pronouncements to restructuring the military system.

The generation immediately following Deng and Chen Yun has differed significantly from its predecessors. Its members did not participate in revolutionary struggles. They spent most of their careers working their way up various bureaucratic hierarchies. They are far better educated and more urban oriented than their predecessors, and they hail primarily from coastal rather than inland China. Most are far more knowledgeable about the international arena. They, in sum, mark the transition to a nonrevolutionary leadership. They and their successors favor stability, sustained economic growth, effective management, and professionalism.

In these regards, Jiang Zemin is typical. Jiang hails from Jiangsu province and was educated in Shanghai. He did a stint in the USSR in the 1950s and subsequently held posts in the automotive, machine-building, and electronics sectors before becoming mayor of Shanghai in 1986 and head of the Communist Party in Shanghai in 1987. Deng Xiaoping moved Jiang to Beijing during the Tiananmen Square democracy movement crisis in 1989 and designated him the future "core leader" of the CCP. Jiang quickly acquired a panoply of top posts, including secretary general of the CCP (1989), head of the Military Affairs Commission of the CCP (1989), and president of the PRC (1993). From 1989 to 1994 Jiang conducted himself with a keen eye to the desires of both Deng Xiaoping and Chen Yun. But as noted in Chapter 5, with Deng's physical incapacitation in December 1994 and Chen's death in 1995, Jiang began to take real charge of politics in Beijing.

Jiang proved himself to be tough and astute—nobody can rise to his position in the Chinese system without such qualities. He orchestrated the purge of the former head of Beijing municipality, a key opponent at the top, and he brought important supporters from Shanghai into the central leadership group. But Jiang also played coalition politics, taking care to nurture the support of important colleagues.

From 1994 to 1997 Jiang governed in a coalition with Li Peng (as premier) and Qiao Shi (as head of the National People's Congress). Both, of course, held membership on the Standing Committee of the Politburo. The Ninth NPC in 1998 accepted Qiao Shi's retirement (this had actually been mandated by the Fifteenth Party Congress the previous fall), promoted Zhu Rongji to premier and confirmed Li Peng as the new head of the NPC. Li had to step down as premier because he had served in that position for two terms, the maximum period allowed by the constitution. Reflecting changes in the Chinese system as a whole, Li's job change in 1998—forty-nine years after the founding of the PRC—was the first by a top leader in response to constitutional requirements.

In the wake of the November 2002 Sixteenth Party Congress, China is still led by a self-selected elite whose major constraints are imposed by the views and activities of others in the top group, rather than by formal institutional requirements. But several important changes have occurred since the early 1990s:

□ The core leader has less power over his colleagues than was the case for either Mao or Deng. This was true for Jiang Zemin in the late 1990s and is even more the case for Hu Jintao, as Hu is surrounded on the Politburo Standing Committee by men who have had closer ties to Jiang Zemin than to him.

□ Formal requirements laid down in various rules and regulations are taken more seriously, even within the top group. Yet at this level of the system, politics is still informed more by small-group dynamics than by formal rules and institutional boundaries.

□ The top group is less cohesive in that, unlike its predecessors, its key members have not worked together for more than half a century.

□ The top group is less powerful than its predecessors in relation to the rest of the political system.

□ Retired revolutionary elders are no longer making the key decisions behind the scenes.

The members of the top power elite are themselves differentiated in two ways: by *functional area of work* and by *degree of specialization*. The Chinese assign the top executive members of the power elite responsibility for distinct fields of work. Intermingled with this division of responsibility is a distribution of members into three layers, based on degree of specialization.

The *key generalists* are those at the very top of the system who may be considered the equivalent of the chief executive officer or president of a major corporation. These individuals, including the general secretary of the Communist party and the premier of the government, become involved in many operational issues on a day-to-day basis, and they carry heavy work loads and responsibilities.

The *bridge leaders* are more narrowly specialized than are the key generalists. Each is responsible for helping to develop policy within a certain sphere, coordinating the activities of the bureaucracies relevant to executing that policy, and resolving the differences that crop up between them. Each of these bridging leaders heads a "leadership small group" that coordinates between the relevant bureaucracies and the top leadership. Typically, these bridge leaders are themselves members of the Standing Committee or the Politburo. To continue our metaphor of "PRC, Inc.," these bridge leaders are vice presidents in charge of major functions.

Specialized leaders have control over individual important bureaucracies. They include the heads of the State Development Planning Commission (renamed in 2003 as the State Development Reform Commission), the CCP Organization Department, the Ministry of Foreign Affairs, and so forth. The heads of a few key province-level bodies are also at this level in the system. These leaders run the most important bodies in the system. In corporate terms, they are in charge of top-level departments (strategic planning, finance, and so on) and the heads of the most important operating divisions of the firm.

The division into functions and layers demonstrates to an important extent how relations among these leaders are structured. To reiterate, though, no rules limit the way the top leaders organize themselves or constrain what they are able to do. For example, as top generalists both Jiang Zemin and Zhu Rongji also assumed control over certain key coordinating bodies that are normally the bailiwick of what are termed "bridging" leaders above. The only effective intra-elite check on each of these leaders is the attitudes and actions of the other leaders. Despite two decades of reforms, in this realm of Chinese politics organizational boundaries, tasks, memberships, and identities change often and easily, and they do so at the command of the very top leaders. Actual power depends nearly as much on personal ties with other leaders as on the formal office held.

Surrounding the top leaders are *personal assistants,* of which the two most important types are the personal secretaries and the personal guards. Regardless of the formal office, each of the top leaders has a personal office and personal bodyguards. The personal office consists of a group of "secretaries" (*mishu*), the number varying by leader.[14] Mao Zedong usually had at least five *mishu* for his daily needs, to read to him when he wanted to relax, and for his substantive policy work. Zhou Enlai had more than ten *mishu* at a time. Indeed, since Zhou's death some of his *mishu* have published books on their experiences.

The *mishu* are close to the top leaders but are not a part of the open bureaucratic system. They can derive great power from their proximity to key leaders—indeed, over time they may become substantial officials in their own right. For example, Chen Boda headed Mao's personal office before 1966; Mao then spun him off into the Cultural Revolution Small Group, the campaign headquarters for the Cultural Revolution, through which Chen wielded enormous power. Other *mishu* of Mao included Lu Dingyi, who then became head of the propaganda apparatus, and Hu Qiaomu, who later became a Politburo member in his own right. Zhou Xiaozhou, a provincial leader purged with Peng Dehuai at the Lushan conference in 1959, had been a *mishu* of Mao's in the 1940s. Indeed, the cases of Chen Boda and Zhou Xiaozhou suggest that Mao both promoted his *mishu* into major positions after they left his office and then reacted with a strong sense of betrayal if they subsequently disagreed with any of his policy preferences. This underside of Chinese politics has played a very important—and little-known—role in the PRC.

Leaders choose their own *mishu,* who typically have not worked their way "up" the bureaucratic ladder. But since a *mishu* may have to represent his boss at official meetings and in other official capacities, he is assigned a bureaucratic rank as if he were a part of the formal bureaucracy. Once the *mishu* leaves the office of his patron, he is then often assigned a formal position equivalent to his rank. Most *mishu* of the top leaders receive at least the bureaucratic rank of deputy governor of a province or vice minister of the State Council. When they leave the personal office of their patron—and if their patron is still in good standing and they themselves have not made an error—they assume very important positions.

The *mishu* system thus provides a vehicle for factional politics. Top leaders use their ability to recruit *mishu,* assign them formal bureaucratic ranks, and then after a period of time "seed" them in various official posts as a means of enhancing the leaders' own political bases at the Center and in the provinces. For example, at times the Policy Research Office of the CCP has been a very important body. Mao Zedong tended either to recruit the head of that body to be one of his *mishu,* or to make one of his former *mishu* the head of that body. Zhao Ziyang made Bao Tong, his former *mishu,* both secretary to the Politburo and the head of the major institute charged with developing reforms of the political system. Bao was purged and arrested when Zhao fell from power in 1989. More recently, Jiang Zemin's *mishu* Wang Huning became head of the Central Committee Policy Research Office when Jiang stepped down from the Politburo in November 2002.

Mishu influence can be extraordinary. For example, one of Lin Biao's *mishu,* Zhang Yunsheng, wrote a memoir in which he revealed that during the critical early years of the Cultural Revolution Lin relied on his *mishu* to provide a summary of the documents that came into his office each day, rather than reading the documents himself. Since Lin almost never left his office compound, this *mishu* provided a major part of Lin's links with the outside world when Lin's actions were of critical importance to the development of the Cultural Revolution.

Indeed, Mao Zedong, according to the testimony of his political colleagues, would after the 1950s accept frank criticism only from his *mishu.* Thus, his key secretaries, such as Tian Jiaying and Hu Qiaomu, became vital conduits for objective views to reach the Chairman, to some extent compensating for his increasing intolerance of the other top leaders in the system.[15]

Much of what we know about the *mishu* system comes from the memoirs of former *mishu* of the Maoist era. Far less detail is known about the current use of *mishu*, although this clearly remains an important, if hidden, part of the Chinese political system.

The *mishu* system exists at all levels of the Chinese hierarchy, and it works in largely the same fashion at each level. It provides key assistance to top leaders who are not well versed in some of the matters they must deal with. The *mishu* are often well educated and quite capable of looking up needed information or obtaining it from the *mishu* of other leaders whom they get to know.

Only the top leaders at the Center are able to pick their *mishu* without effective interference from the CCP Organization Department, which is normally responsible for vetting personnel appointments. At lower levels, *mishu* must pass muster with the Organization Department before they can start work. Although *mishu* typically develop good personal networks with the *mishu* who serve other leaders at the same level of the system, they do not deal with *mishu* at different territorial levels.

In addition to *mishu*, each top leader has personal guards. For at least the older generation of revolutionary leaders, these guards were truly personal: although the central guard unit under Mao's personal aegis provided overall security, each leader chose at least some guards of his own. Though most of these guards have come from the PLA, the PLA has not retained operational control over them. In fact, although all the personal guards nominally belong to a single guard unit, interviews indicate that even the head of that unit has no authority over them.[16]

Personal guards render a range of services to their bosses, including advance security work for them when they travel in China. For example, if a top leader is going to a province, the provincial security forces in consultation with the Center will make numerous preparations. (Zhou Enlai had overall responsibility for these arrangements under Mao.) Nevertheless, the leader will not travel to the province until one of his personal guards goes to the province himself to check the preparations and make any adjustments he sees fit.

This brief introduction to the top levels of the power elite highlights several important facets of the Chinese system since 1949: it has been intensely personal, with individual relationships extremely important in determining career mobility and political decisions; power at the top has been highly concentrated in a very small number of individuals, roughly twenty-five to thirty-five, who have wielded ultimate authority in the executive, legislative, and judicial spheres; the core leader has had extraordinary authority to determine who else will be in the upper echelons of the power elite; and some aspects of the system do not appear on organizational charts (for example, the use of *mishu* and the division of labor) but are in fact extremely important to the politics and the ordinary functioning of the system. These characteristics to some extent are evident in the Chinese political system at each level of the national political hierarchy. And at all levels, this intensely personal system among the elite exists in a dynamic tension with the very large, complex system of bureaucratic organization described in Chapter 6. Recent years have witnessed some attenuation of all of these features, resulting in less hierarchy, greater regularity, more meaningful division of responsibility along institutional lines, and a less dominant role for the core leader. But the Chinese system, although in transition, is far from having fully shed the features left over from its revolutionary origins and authoritarian mode.

Configurations of Political Power

We can best understand the actual configurations of political power by leaving behind the organization charts and instead thinking in the terms Chinese officials use when they talk among themselves about their system. In their vocabulary, the key concepts concerning the organization of power are the *xitong* (led by leadership small groups) and the tensions of *tiao/kuai* relationships.[17] These organizational arrangements and tensions transcend the party-government divisions in the system.

THE LEADERSHIP SMALL GROUP

As noted above, in broad terms the Chinese organize the top executive members of the power elite into major functional areas. Historically, the four broadest of these have been party affairs, government work, state security, and foreign affairs. Each of the first three has a nationwide network of bureaucracies under it. Because the full assignment of leadership small group responsibilities among the leaders who assumed their posts in the wake of the Sixteenth Party Congress is not yet clear as this book goes to press, this discussion uses the division of labor among the leaders before the Sixteenth Congress to illustrate the system.

Typically, the preeminent leader—Mao Zedong, then Hua Guofeng, followed by Hu Yaobang, Zhao Ziyang, Jiang Zemin, and since November 2002 Hu Jintao—heads party affairs. Government work is focused primarily on economic development, and the number-two and/or -three people in the executive power elite are typically in charge. Zhou Enlai first led this group. In the mid-1980s Zhao Ziyang took over with Yao Yilin. By 1989, Li Peng and Yao Yilin shared leadership of this area. Li Peng and Zhu Rongji led next, and in 1998 Zhu Rongji alone assumed top responsibility for government affairs. Wen Jinbao assumed this role in March 2003.

State security encompasses both public security (that is, the police) and state security (counterespionage). It may also carry some responsibility for the People's Armed Police and the military. In the mid-1980s, Yang Shangkun and Wan Li reportedly headed state security. Qiao Shi then took over, followed by Wei Jianxing.

Foreign affairs is rather unique in that this functional system does not control major nationwide domestic bureaucracies. Zhou Enlai led this group until his death. Li Peng was in charge for most of the 1990s, and Jiang Zemin took over this portfolio in 1998. Hu Jintao now holds this responsibility.

A somewhat narrower set of functional portfolios—all also headed by the top executive officials—is nestled beneath the four broad portfolios just described. Typically, a "leadership small group," consists of a Politburo Standing Committee member and several others in and outside of the Politburo.[18] Leadership small groups form a bridge between the top leaders of the political system and the major bureaucracies that generate information and implement policy. Each of the major leadership small groups, which are the apex of their related functional portfolios, leads an array of related party, government, and/or military bureaucracies (see Chart 7.1). In a fundamental sense, the leadership small groups define the way political power in both the party and the government is organized.

On the eve of the November 2002 Sixteenth Party Congress, the key leadership small groups and their leaders were:

☐ Finance and economic affairs (urban economic policy): head, Jiang Zemin; deputy head, Zhu Rongji

☐ Taiwan work (cross-strait relations): head, Jiang Zemin; deputy head, Qian Qichen

☐ Foreign affairs: head, Jiang Zemin; deputy head, Qian Qichen

☐ Agricultural affairs: head, Wen Jiabao

☐ Party-building work (CCP membership and organizational development): head, Jiang Zemin; deputy heads, Hu Jintao, Wen Jiabao, Zeng Qinghong

☐ Propaganda and ideological work: head, Hu Jintao; deputy head, Ding Guangen (also head of the CCP Propaganda Department)

☐ Commission for public sector reform (in charge of the 1998 government streamlining program):* head, Hu Jintao; deputy head, Luo Gan[19]

☐ Financial work commission (appoints all high-level officials in the banking system):* head, Wen Jiabao

☐ Large-scale-enterprise work commission (in charge of appointments of all heads of and of all reforms in the largest SOEs):* head, Wu Bangguo

☐ United Front Department (policy toward non-CCP people):* head, Wang Zhaoguo

☐ Political and Legal Affairs Commission (civilian law and order):* head, Luo Gan

In early November 2002, all of the above individuals were members of the Politburo or its Standing Committee. The only exception was Zeng Qinghong, a very close associate of Jiang Zemin's who was an alternate member of the Politburo until his elevation to the Politburo Standing Committee in the wake of the Sixteenth Party Congress. Jiang Zemin headed economic affairs, foreign affairs (including cross-strait relations), and party building (that is, member-

* Not called "leadership small groups" but serve the same function.

CHART 7.1 *Organization of Power*

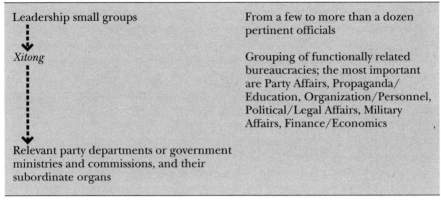

Leadership small groups — From a few to more than a dozen pertinent officials

Xitong — Grouping of functionally related bureaucracies; the most important are Party Affairs, Propaganda/Education, Organization/Personnel, Political/Legal Affairs, Military Affairs, Finance/Economics

Relevant party departments or government ministries and commissions, and their subordinate organs

Arrows indicate direction of control.

ship and organizational development). Jiang also was (and still is) in charge of the Military Commission of the CCP and was the president of the country. Zhu Rongji was the premier of the State Council. Qian Qichen was a vice premier and former foreign minister who coordinated foreign-affairs work under Jiang. Wen Jiabao held the dual portfolios of finance and agriculture, two very difficult and problem-laden areas. He was also a vice premier. Luo Gan, also with vice premier rank, took charge of the civilian law and order portfolio, with a related role in organizational streamlining.[20] Hu Jintao was in operational charge of party construction (under Jiang) and in overall charge of propaganda work. Hu was also vice president of the country and head of the Central Party School. The latter placed him in a key position to structure the training curriculum that all top CCP cadres must take. Ding Guangen was operationally in charge of propaganda. And Wu Bangguo, another vice premier, headed up policy toward state-owned enterprises (SOEs).

The remaining Politburo Standing Committee members hold the top "outside" posts: Li Peng chaired the National People's Congress (head of the legislature); Li Ruihuan headed the Chinese People's Political Consultative Congress (formal body of notables); and Wei Jianxing headed the CCP Discipline Inspection Commission (in charge of party discipline and ferreting out corruption). Among Politburo Standing Committee members on the eve of the Sixteenth Party Congress, only Vice Premier Li Lanqing lacked a top executive post.

Although the "leadership small group" system is largely hidden from public view, it is very important. For example, as noted above Li Peng headed the Foreign Affairs Leadership Small Group during the early and mid-1990s. Many foreign governments paid Li little attention, focusing instead on President Jiang Zemin; Qian Qichen, the vice premier with foreign affairs responsibility; or the foreign minister and other officials. Li generally avoided diplomatic activities during these years, reflecting in part foreign negative views of the very public, hardline role Li played in suppressing the 1989 student movement. But foreign governments were well advised to consider Li's views carefully and to recognize his very important behind-the-scenes role in China's foreign affairs policy-making process.

THE *XITONG*

Xitong, meaning "system," is the name used to indicate a group of bureaucracies that together deal with a broad task the top political leaders want performed.[21] A *xitong* generally is led by the leadership small group usually headed by the member of the Standing Committee of the Politburo in charge of that *functional portfolio*. Different *xitong* cover various spheres (foreign affairs, finance and economics, and so on). The boundaries of various *xitong* have changed over the years. Six *xitong* have been particularly important for concrete management of the country: Party Affairs, Organization and Personnel, Propaganda and Education, Political and Legal Affairs, Finance and Economics, and the Military. Both Organization/Personnel and Propaganda/Education are under the aegis of the party affairs *portfolio*; Political/Legal and the Military (to an extent) are under the aegis of the state security *portfolio*; and Finance/Economics falls under government affairs. Each includes executive agencies from the top to the bottom of the system, and each encompasses a major sphere of domestic governance.

The party/government distinction erodes in this dimension of the system, and most public sector *danwei* contain personnel who represent two or more of these *xitong*. But current reforms are seeking to remove the administrative links between the bureaucratic *xitong* and the enterprises and social organizations around China. A state enterprise, for example, traditionally had a party committee, a personnel department, a propaganda office, a security administration, and an enterprise manager. Though specific names of these organs could vary, each in fact was part of a different hierarchical nationwide bureaucratic *xitong*. Therefore, neither the party head nor the enterprise manager had absolute control over all the activities that took place in the enterprise.

The present reform effort seeks to restructure this set of relationships so that the government and the party no longer directly administer most enterprises and social organizations (such as research institutes). The government is slated to focus on providing a regulatory and broad policy framework, rather than detailed administrative control. Over the coming years this set of reforms may significantly change the dynamics of the Chinese government's relations with enterprises and social organizations. The communist party is retaining the right, however, to appoint the leaders of these units, even after they are no longer subject to government administrative management. Even under the reforms, understanding *xitong* will still be important to understanding how the governing bureaucracies are organized and interact with each other.

Xitong may over time have somewhat variable boundaries: specific organizations may shift from one *xitong* to another in their reporting lines if the leadership wants this to occur. As the leadership began to reconstruct the bureaucratic system after the Red Guard phase of the Cultural Revolution, the Organization/Personnel and the Propaganda/Education *xitong* were temporarily combined under one extraordinarily powerful leadership small group. As this example suggests, political battles among top leaders have often been reflected in the changing scope of authority of the various *xitong*, as each leader tries to expand the scope of his *xitong* and those of his allies. During the early stages of the Cultural Revolution, for example, Mao Zedong worked with Lin Biao and Jiang Qing first to take over and then substantially expand the scope of the Military *xitong* and the Propaganda/Education *xitong* in order to weaken Mao's adversaries, who headed the Party Affairs (Liu Shaoqi) and various other *xitong*. This flexibility returns us to our core theme: China's political system is awash in organizations but generally has weak institutions. Key appointments in the elite power game, moreover, are those to the hidden leadership organizations that manage the various *xitong*.

The six major *xitong* and their core tasks are as follows.

Party Affairs *Xitong*

The Party Affairs (*dangwu*) *xitong* is headed by the general secretary of the party, Hu Jintao. Its most important personnel are the first secretaries of every territorial party committee, down the hierarchy through the level of the township. These individuals are the key personnel that make the Chinese system "work" on a territorial basis. They oversee implementation of political priorities sent down from above, play a crucially important role in all leadership appointments within their bailiwicks, shape major decisions, adjudicate disputes, coordinate efforts, and lobby higher levels on behalf of their localities. They head the territorial party committees that in turn bring together the most powerful officials in each region. The first secretaries are, in short, the most important generalists at all levels of the Chinese political system.

The Party Affairs *xitong* has major participants that number in the thousands. These include the party's general secretary, the leading secretaries of the thirty-one provincial-level party committees, the leading secretaries of more than 2,400 county-level party committees, and the heads of the roughly 660 municipal and 44,867 township (*xiang* and *zhen*) party committees.[22] Ultimately, the people in the Party Affairs *xitong* become involved in a vast array of issues and activities. Just as the party itself tries to be the ultimate decision maker in all matters, the leaders of the various territorial party committees are key to the governance of the localities under their aegis. They do not have absolute power—each of the other *xitong* slices into virtually every locality in China. But the reforms have privileged territorial committees over the vertical functional lines of control, and the top party secretaries of the territorial party committees and the party committees themselves bear a special responsibility for making sure that things in their area work well. Without strong territorial party committee leaders, it would be virtually impossible to coordinate adequately the work of various other *xitong* within any given locality.

Importantly, the Party Affairs *xitong* is unusual in that the vertical relationship among different levels of the political system in this *xitong* are characterized by what the Chinese term "leadership ties" (*lingdao guanxi*). That is, each territorial party committee is directly subordinate to the equivalent party committee on the next highest level. A suburban county party committee, for example, is subordinate to the party committee of the city within which the county is located. Leadership relations mean that the upper level can dictate to the lower level, and the lower level is obligated to obey. In addition, the *government* in any territory must obey the party leadership of that territory when the latter decides to take action on an issue or appointment.

The Party Affairs *xitong* is thus potentially very centralized, if the Center chooses to issue detailed orders and insist on close compliance. Past heads of the Party Affairs *xitong* have been Liu Shaoqi, Hua Guofeng, Hu Yaobang, Zhao Ziyang, and Jiang Zemin.[23] Except during and immediately after the Cultural Revolution, the Party Secretariat has typically been used to manage the Party Affairs *xitong*.

The CCP decides all major issues and controls access to and advancement in the political system. In short, the party dominates and monopolizes political power in China, and therefore China is often called a party-state. The Chinese formally treat party affairs as internal matters and feel little obligation to make party organization, structure, processes, and decisions transparent, especially to foreigners. Even basic information about the average ages, educational backgrounds, and other characteristics of the membership of the party as a whole are only released in conjunction with a National Party Congress every five years. But many of the decisions ostensibly taken and publicly announced by state or other public bodies in fact reflect prior determinations reached by the pertinent bodies in the party itself. And despite the many decisions that have effectively reduced the scope of political activity under the reforms, the party prohibits any autonomous political organization that might challenge its power and prerogatives.

Organization Affairs *Xitong*

The major task of the Organization Affairs (*zuzhi*) *xitong* is to determine who should be appointed to positions of authority throughout the political system and in related bodies such as schools and hospitals. This *xitong* thus does the staff work for the party's nomenklatura (described on pp. 234–39). To a large extent, it influences who will get ahead in China and thus the types of individuals that will run the system. It does so, in the language used by pertinent books in China, so as to "organizationally guarantee implementation of the party's political line." Organization departments investigate the backgrounds of officials, and they also do studies of the PRC's personnel system itself. The Party-Building Work Leadership Small Group leads this *xitong*.

This *xitong* consists primarily of the organization and personnel departments at all levels of the party and government bureaucracies. At the provincial level alone, each such department typically had from 100 to 150 officials working in it before the 1998 streamlining program was implemented. Current figures are probably roughly 80 percent of the earlier number.[24] At the Center, this *xitong* encompasses both the Central Committee's Organization

Department and the government's Ministry of Personnel. The organs of the Organization *xitong* exist not only in the various territorial party committees, but also in all functional government bodies and all other state-owned enterprises and organs. The tentacles of this *xitong*, in short, reach into almost every important nook and cranny in the public sector of the Chinese system.

The specific management of personnel in the PRC has evolved a great deal over the years. Indeed, as noted below, the original idea of dividing the system into broad *xitong* itself appears to have grown out of the system for personnel assignments adopted in the early 1950s. What eventually emerged is a system of organization departments at all levels in the party that maintains personnel dossiers and does the staff work on which personnel assignments and promotions are determined. Their specific relations with related party, government, and other organs are too complex to warrant detailed examination here.

The dossiers kept by the Organization *xitong* are extremely powerful factors in the lives of Chinese.[25] They contain not only information on the individual's birth, ethnicity, education, and work history, but also the results of annual assessments and the contents of any political charges ever made against the person or other negative factors from the person's background. An individual never has the right to review his or her own dossier, yet a negative entry in the dossier can destroy the chances that a person will ever advance in a career unless he or she finds employment outside the public sector. For example, very likely all students who were identified on Tiananmen Square in 1989 had this unfavorable information entered into their dossiers, and this will generally keep them from holding positions of responsibility in state organizations unless the personnel system itself should change. Not surprisingly, personnel dossiers cause great anxiety and pain in China. An individual's dossier stays with him or her, even if the person changes place of residence or jobs.

All organization departments in the party (and the personnel departments in other organs) are supposed to operate according to instructions peculiar to the Organization *xitong*. In this sense, this *xitong* is a power unto itself. The author, for example, once received permission from the deputy head of a large state-owned department store to examine a selection of personnel dossiers for individuals in that enterprise. But the head of the store's personnel department then refused to obey his "superior," citing regulations that were internal to the national Organization *xitong*.

Although this *xitong* is extremely important and powerful, it in fact operates in a quite decentralized way. The units in this *xitong*—for example, the organization department of a municipality and that of the province in which the city is located—are linked by "professional relations" (*yewu guanxi*), rather than by leadership relations. Professional relations require consultation on professional issues and "guidance" from above, but they do *not* give the higher-level body direct command authority over its subordinate. In fact, the organization department's territorial party committee—or, in a functional organ, the party committee of that organ—directly commands the organization department.

The party committee and its organization department in each territorial or functional unit in the system therefore form a very powerful combination. Interviews indicate that new incumbents to the position of top secretary of a party committee typically regard as their highest priority placing "their" person in charge of the organization department under that committee. Once that is accomplished, the party committee leader adds control over appointments and careers to the arsenal of resources to use to obtain obedience from subordinates. Western scholars call the list of positions subject to party appointment the "nomenklatura," a term that derives from Soviet usage.[26] It is discussed in detail below, in a section devoted to the tools used by the party to control other bodies.

Propaganda and Education *Xitong*

The Propaganda and Education (*xuanjiao*) *xitong* is, like its organizational counterpart, quite decentralized. Relations between territorial administrative levels in this *xitong* are characterized by "professional" (not "leadership") ties. This has, nevertheless, at times been a very powerful *xitong* in the Chinese system. At its apex is a Propaganda and Education Leadership Small Group. The Central Committee has an information (until 1998 called "propaganda") department, too.

If the task of the Party Affairs system is to lead and coordinate on a territorial basis and the task of the Organization system is to affect career patterns, the central task of the Propaganda and Education system is to shape the values and perspectives of the entire population. Numerous units fall under the sway of this *xitong*. They include all print and broadcast media, all schools and colleges (except the specialized institutes directly run by various ministries and the party schools themselves) and virtually all research institutes (again, other than those directly under the various ministries), and cultural units such as museums and performing art troupes. For peculiar historical reasons, the state-run public health system also comes under the Propaganda and Education *xitong*.

The Propaganda and Education *xitong* formerly played an enormous role in mass political campaigns: the initial stage of such campaigns witnessed an upsurge in the state's propaganda effort, with the media and other resources propagating the key themes of the political mobilization effort. This role has become sharply attenuated under the reforms, as the system has evolved in directions that rely far less on political mobilization, permit much greater freedom of thought, and require most media outlets to secure funding from advertising and other sources rather than from state budget appropriations.[27] Most urban Chinese no longer participate in the political study groups that were a major feature of the system through the 1980s.[28] Although the Propaganda and Education *xitong* encompasses education, professional educators have played a weak role in it. The major task of this bureaucratic system has been to create people who think along socialist lines as interpreted by the top party leaders. But professional educators have tended to favor the development of knowledge that implicitly adheres to standards other than simply those of political rectitude. In addition, officials have generally seen schools as institutions that eat up a lot of investment, provide no immediate profit to the state, and often are sources of trouble because of dissident activities by students and teachers. As a consequence, the professional side of the educational system has generally been under the thumb of the propaganda side of the Propaganda and Education *xitong*. This arrangement proved most damaging during the Cultural Revolution, when in 1966 Mao Zedong closed all the country's schools for several years and virtually wiped the higher-education system clean of all serious scholarship for a full decade.

Although Mao's Cultural Revolution extremism created a national tragedy in terms of lost educational opportunities, the bureaucratic weakness of education in China has continued to be evident even under the reforms.[29] These reforms demand a more educated populace to master the economic and scientific tasks necessary to be competitive in the international arena. But China's education budgets on a per capita basis remain in 2003 among the lowest in the world, and the country is suffering from a shortage of well-educated individuals. Primary and secondary teachers' salaries remain very low, and growing school fees in recent years have meant that many rural and poor children are missing basic educational opportunities.

Mao Zedong's death and the ensuing reforms have thrown the propaganda side of the Propaganda and Education *xitong* into malaise. The problem confronting this bureaucratic system is fundamental: in an era of repudiation of Maoist values and of opening up to the international arena, what is the substance of the values that should be conveyed to the populace?

With the official dominant political slogan of the early 1980s being "seek truth from facts," many in the Propaganda and Education *xitong* could not figure out what they should in fact be doing. The explicit repudiation of political campaigns as a technique of rule furthered this sense of uncertainty for those in the Propaganda and Education *xitong*.

The Tiananmen pro-democracy movement of April–June 1989 revealed just how far the malaise in the Propaganda and Education *xitong* had advanced. As noted in Chapter 5, among the groups marching on Tiananmen Square on the historic day of 4 May 1989, one held up a banner declaring that it represented the Central Committee Propaganda Department and that its goal now was to tell the unvarnished truth. Another represented the *People's Daily*, the Communist party's most authoritative newspaper. The Propaganda and Education *xitong* had cracked apart right up to the top. In the wake of the repression of the pro-democracy movement, the hard-line political leaders carried out their most thorough purges of dissidents in this *xitong*.

The tumultuous political and economic changes China has made since Mao's death have rendered the fundamental tasks of the Propaganda and Education *xitong* virtually impossible. The Chinese population now appears to have no consensus regarding the values that all should embrace. In reality the primary values conveyed to the population concern seeking a higher standard of living and standing up for the country. For example, even the state-run television broadcasts soap operas and other shows that portray high living as an ideal in order to attract advertisers and viewers. Materialism is rampant, and few value-based constraints operate to soften the edge of individuals' efforts to maximize their incomes. Corruption is very widespread. Also, the reach of this *xitong* into society has diminished with the extensive development of nonstate enterprises, some with foreign capital, in which the presence of the propaganda apparatus is limited. Many nonstate schools are also opening. Finally, increasing access to the Internet and the growing availability of telephones and cell phones has drastically reduced the virtual monopoly that the propaganda and education apparatus previously exercised over citizens' access to information. As of early 2003, over 200 million households have telephones and over 200 million Chinese own cell phones.[30]

Political and Legal Affairs *Xitong*

The *xitong* in charge of the civilian coercive apparatus is called the Political and Legal Affairs (*zhengfa*) *xitong*. It is headed by the Political and Legal Affairs Commission in Beijing. The highly authoritarian PRC political system has constructed an appropriately elaborate system of repression to maintain the rule of the Communist party. Part of this repressive system consists of the People's Liberation Army, which has historically played a major domestic garrison role. This military component of the system is discussed below.

The Chinese decided not to duplicate the KGB when they adopted major components of the Soviet political system under Stalin. That is, they decided that they would not develop a secret police apparatus that penetrated the party and government, that operated in highly centralized fashion, and that became a state within a state, answerable ultimately only to the supreme leader at the top.[31] Perhaps reflecting the lessons and operational styles developed during their long guerrilla war before 1949, the Chinese communist leaders opted for a somewhat more decentralized repressive apparatus with greater emphasis on political controls embedded in the *danwei* and with a taboo, broken only during the Cultural Revolution, on having the police apparatus penetrate the party itself. Thus the largest bureaucratic hierarchy within this *xitong*—the nationwide public-security apparatus—utilizes a system of "dual leadership." Public-security organs are under the control both of their territorial party committee and of the public security organ one level higher in the national administrative hierarchy.

The Political and Legal *xitong* that was established in the 1950s was, nevertheless, large, wide ranging, and powerful. At one time or another it has run the court system, the prosecutors, the labor camps, the prisons, the fire departments, the border guards, the uniformed police, the secret police, and the issuance of passports, among other things. This system also provided the leadership with reports on the political attitudes of the populace, essentially substituting to an extent for the public-opinion polls and free press common to Western democracies. Reportedly, the public security system employed four hundred thousand police in 1978 and twice that number by 1994. In addition, by 1994 the armed component of the civilian security forces, the People's Armed Police, numbered some six hundred thousand troops.[32]

Various parts of this repressive empire had different histories. During the early and mid-1950s, for example, the PRC made significant efforts to develop a set of legal codes to replace the Guomindang law that had been abolished with the revolution. The court system also expanded considerably during these years. But with the Antirightist campaign of 1957 and the Great Leap Forward of 1958, this entire policy thrust disappeared.[33] Until 1977, the PRC still lacked any formal criminal, civil, or other legal codes. As noted in Chapters 5 and 6, one component of the reform effort has been to develop such codes, especially to provide a firmer legal basis for the economy.

The party has always maintained its own internal bureaucratic organs, usually called Discipline Inspection Commissions, to investigate problems and enforce party discipline.[34] When a party member has committed a serious crime, often that individual is first expelled from the party and only then turned over to the Political and Legal Affairs *xitong* organs for judgment and punishment. Powerful party figures, however, typically but not always escape punishment by the judicial organs.

The major government ministry under the Political and Legal Affairs *xitong* is the Ministry of Public Security. For most of the period of the PRC, this ministry and its subordinate organs have been able to investigate, arrest, prosecute, and imprison Chinese citizens without allowing them any recourse. Mao Zedong's frequent calls to intensify "class struggle" often meant specifically calling for the Political and Legal Affairs *xitong* to "ferret out" and persecute additional "class enemies." Each major political campaign of the Maoist years brought additional people into the Chinese gulag run by the public-security system.[35]

Indeed, the Ministry of Public Security was the major bureaucratic unit that enforced the class system that developed in Maoist China. People categorized as landlords during the Land Reform campaign of the early 1950s, for example, subsequently had to report as frequently as once a week to the local organ of the public-security apparatus. Many were made to maintain diaries that would be turned over at these meetings for inspection by the authorities.

The Maoist leadership often expressed the principle that the Chinese should "cure the illness to save the patient" in its approach to handling those who fell out of favor. To some extent, it practiced this approach—at least more than the Soviets did under Stalin. Nevertheless, the public-security system made ready use of execution, and many were put to death in public rituals designed to "educate" the rest of the population. Nobody knows the numbers of individuals executed over the years by China's public-security authorities. Some estimate that currently China carries out far more than half the total number of executions globally each year.

The public-security system runs both prisons and "reform through labor" camps. In both instances, prisoners are forced to engage in manual labor, except those held in solitary confinement or who are for other reasons restricted from working. Figures are not available on the total number of people in the Chinese gulag. The fullest study to date on the system estimates 15 to 20 million, but there is no way to determine whether this is accurate.[36] The value of goods produced and the types of labor that prisoners perform are also uncertain. Anecdotal evidence suggests that prisoners have played major roles in construction, in translation of works into foreign languages (many intellectuals have been put into Chinese prisons), and in production of various goods for the market.[37] Under Stalin, the Soviet Union utilized prison labor on a massive scale in mining, construction, and other areas, making slave labor a significant portion of the overall Soviet economy. Chinese prison labor very likely has played more than a trivial role in the country's economic performance, but it appears that it has never approached the significance of such labor in the Soviet system under Stalin.

The public-security system ran into deep trouble in the early stages of the reforms in the late 1970s. During the Cultural Revolution, public security for the first time penetrated directly into intraparty political battles, and many of the officials who were overthrown were given over to the public-security apparatus.[38] Kang Sheng, who as noted in Chapter 2 was trained by the Soviet KGB in the 1930s, gained great power in this *xitong* in the late 1960s and used it, along with extrabureaucratic "special-case groups" he formed, against Mao's purported political enemies.[39]

When Deng Xiaoping and his reform-minded colleagues came into power, they took measures alarming to the public-security authorities. They decreed that the public-security people could no longer penetrate the party itself. They also promoted the development of laws intended to improve the treatment of citizens. Most fundamentally, the reformers brought back into power those who had been purged during the Cultural Revolution, and they also declared in 1979 the end of large-scale class struggle. These two moves were profoundly disheartening to members of the public-security apparatus.

Suddenly, top party leaders in power included those who had suffered grievously at the hands of the public-security organs over the previous decade. Those who had carried out the repression were frightened at the possibilities of retaliation. The issue came to a head in the celebrated—and tangled—case of Zhang Zhixin. This woman was arrested early in the Cultural Revolution for the "crime" of indicating that Liu Shaoqi, Mao's chief personal target in the Cultural Revolution, had not been wrong and disloyal in everything he said. She was kept in harsh conditions in prison, with an inmate overseer who was promised a sentence reduction if she could make Zhang repent. Zhang, however, remained steadfast.

Finally, Zhang's stubborn support for Liu produced a decision to execute her. The provincial party leadership approved the execution (it is not clear why this case reached so high a level). The day before the execution, Zhang Zhixin's vocal chords were cut out without anesthesia "to make sure she would not shout reactionary slogans" at her public execution. She was shot the following day.

The question hotly debated in 1981 was whether those involved in this horrendous case should themselves be punished. After national attention to the issue, the reformers decided not to go after the executioners because it would only prolong the country's agony and turmoil. But such stories—and there were many of them—diminished the prestige and shattered the confidence of many in the public-security apparatus.

The 1979 decision to declare that most former members of the exploiting classes had now become members of the proletariat and peasantry—and the virtually concurrent decision to release the "rightists" from the prisons and labor camps—reduced the role of the public-security apparatus. No longer would this bureaucracy intrude regularly into the lives of the dozens of millions of people who had "bad" class labels. The labor camps themselves lost inmates numbering in the millions during the rehabilitations after Mao Zedong's death.

The rise of the post-Mao reformers and the implementation of their programs not only directly hurt the bureaucratic interests of the public-security apparatus, it also created a more complex situation for these people to confront. The civilian repressive apparatus is in charge of counterespionage via the State Security Ministry and of regular maintenance of public order, as well as enforcing political order. But the reforms vastly increased the contacts between Chinese and foreigners, created markets and increased the circulation of money in a fashion that nurtured sophisticated economic crimes, and encouraged the development of greater independence and resistance on the part of large sectors of the population. They also loosened residence controls and brought some 100 million people off the land. Rooting out crime, dealing with foreign espionage, and even maintaining control over corruption within the public security system itself became far more difficult in the more open, complex, dynamic society that the reforms produced.

Even under the reforms, however, the public-security apparatus remains very large, extensive, and powerful. In 1989 China published a volume that for the first time specified the number of positions in the organs of province-level units in the government.[40] This volume's data revealed that even after a decade of reforms designed to make the economic system grow, the total number of provincial-level cadres in the civilian repressive apparatus under the Political and Legal Affairs *xitong* remained massive. According to this volume, most provinces as of 1988 had between 1,000 and 1,500 officials in this *xitong at provincial level alone.* For four localities with special security needs, the numbers at provincial level were far higher: Beijing (11,516); Shanghai (7,111); Tianjin (7,629); and Guangdong (3,953). These figures omit the far larger numbers of officials in the public-security apparatus below the provincial level, in addition to uniformed police on the street, security personnel within *danwei*, prison administrators, and the presumably huge networks of informers.

But still, as indicated in Chapter 6, China suffers both from poor training of a significant part of its public-security forces and from very uneven distribution of these forces around the country. The tremendous concentration of attention on key cities and provinces noted above has left much of the country underserved in terms of quality systems of law and order. Consequently, one of the most persistent demands raised by delegates to each National People's Congress has been for strengthening the political and legal *xitong* and implementing more effective policing of the country.

Finance and Economics *Xitong*

The Finance and Economics (*caijing*) *xitong* is charged with making the urban economy grow. Given the centrality of economic growth to the tasks of the state, each premier has taken management of the economy—especially of the urban economy—as a major area of responsibility. Concerns about the rural economy have focused more on extraction of resources than on producing new growth.

At times the Finance and Economics *xitong* has been headed by a Finance and Economics Leadership Small Group or a Finance and Economics Commission. This is a complex, multifaceted bureaucratic *xitong*. Even under Mao Zedong, different constituent parts of this *xitong* often were at loggerheads with each other. The Ministry of Finance, for example, often argued (typically unsuccessfully) with then extant State Planning Commission. The latter always pushed for major new projects and faster economic growth, whereas the former worried about the financial consequences of overly ambitious investment plans. Such tensions between finance officials and the production and construction people are typical of most political systems.

The economic reforms have been both a blessing and a bane to this *xitong*. To an extent, the priority given to economic growth under the reforms has redounded to the benefit of officials in the Finance and Economics *xitong*. Since the late 1970s, for example, this *xitong* has suffered far less interference from the interventions of the Political and Legal Affairs *xitong* or the Propaganda and Education *xitong*, both of which had previously increased their role in economic units—typically at the cost of economic growth—during political campaigns.

In addition, more resources in general have flowed to the economic sector under the reforms, and opportunities for improvements in personal living standards for officials in this sector have grown, sometimes a great deal. Some such officials, for example, have been well positioned to take advantage of the need for numerous approvals for business projects in order to engage in large-scale corruption. Others have enjoyed many chances to have contact with foreigners and to go abroad—both of which produce increased opportunities to acquire scarce goods, foreign exchange, and new skills. And many government departments in this *xitong* have seized opportunities to run very profitable businesses.

The economic reforms have also, however, sharpened contradictions within this *xitong* and have created problems for it as a whole. Insofar as the reforms progress toward a market system, the state planning officials within the Finance and Economics *xitong* lose power, and that transformation is accelerating as China implements its WTO accession agreement. The government personnel streamlining program initiated in 1998 fell with particular force on the organs in this *xitong*. Almost all ministries governing specific economic sectors were either abolished or reduced to bureau-level bodies under the former State Economic and Trade Commission.[41] New regulations are reducing the number of approvals required for business projects.

The actual boundaries of the Finance and Economics *xitong* are somewhat vague. It includes the State Development Reform Commission, the Ministry of Commerce, the finance ministry, the banking system, the subordinate organs of these bodies, the few remaining economic sector ministries (such as, as information) and the state-owned enterprises. This encompasses a huge array of bureaucratic organs and personnel. The level of centralization of decision making varies in the different subsectors within the Finance and Economics *xitong*, but overall the reforms have encouraged greater decentralization and more of a regulatory than a command role for the government. Although the Finance and Economics bureaucratic system does not wholly encompass the nonstate urban sector or the agricultural sector, the decisions made in this *xitong* nevertheless have a profound impact that reverberates throughout the economy.

Military *Xitong*

The final system that warrants individual treatment is that of the Military (*jun-shi*) *xitong*. The communists' armed struggle for power lasted more than twenty years and created an almost unique, symbiotic relationship between the party and the military. The party leaders of the older generation virtually without exception had extensive pre-1949 military experience. Mao Zedong was a military strategist of the first rank. Deng Xiaoping had so much experience in warfare before 1949 that when in 1955 the PRC conferred the highest military rank (marshal) on ten individuals, it also offered this honor to Deng. He declined. To the communist leaders in China, the military has had both national-security and domestic political roles.[42]

After 1949, therefore, the military retained a very special place in the new political system. As noted in Chapter 3, shortly before nationwide victory the army, air force, navy, and other military arms were combined into the People's Liberation Army (PLA). The PLA does not answer to the government, though there is a Ministry of Defense and a government Military Affairs Commission. The Ministry of Defense in reality has little real power over the military and is primarily a convenient vehicle for dealing with foreign military organizations and visitors. Likewise, the government Military Affairs Commission is a hollow shell whose membership totally overlaps with that of its party counterpart.

The real leadership of the Chinese military is exercised through the Military Affairs Commission of the CCP, and it is a measure of party dominance of the system that the PLA is sworn to defend the Communist party. The Military Affairs Commission has the same bureaucratic rank as the State Council and is thus not under government control. Rather, this commission has been headed at all times, other than during the brief Mao/Deng interregnum and during 1989–94, by the most powerful individual in the Chinese Communist party: Mao Zedong until September 1976 and then Deng Xiaoping from June 1981. In 1989, Deng had Party General Secretary Jiang Zemin, who had no prior military experience, appointed to chair the Military Affairs Commission in order to help build up Jiang's political base for the succession, but in reality Deng retained supreme military command authority until physical incapacity ended his role. Jiang, in somewhat similar fashion, made his likely successor Hu Jintao the vice chair of the Military Affairs Commission in 1999, although Jiang chose to retain his chairmanship of the Military Affairs Commission even after he stepped down from the Politburo in November 2002.

Unlike the other *xitong* discussed above, the Military *xitong* constitutes virtually a state within the state.[43] Party control is exercised at the very top via the Military Affairs Commission. Below this is a General Political Department that has subordinate organs at lower levels of the military hierarchy. The General Political Department is largely in charge of running party activities in the PLA. It also plays a major role in military personnel decisions and in security and counterespionage work in the PLA. In other words, civilian party committees, the Organization *xitong*, and the public security apparatus are not allowed to penetrate the PLA itself.

The PLA also has a General Logistics Department that runs a vast network of military industries and transportation links. There are no accurate figures to indicate the size of this military sector within the country's economy, but it almost certainly has been very large. In the transportation sector, not only were many airfields dedicated to exclusive military use, a substantial portion of the nation's rail system also was reserved for the PLA. During the 1980s reform policies were adopted to convert some military industries to civilian or to dual-use production, and in at least some instances military transportation facilities were opened to limited civilian traffic. But the notion of a significant system of production and transportation facilities dedicated to almost exclusive military use remains accurate as of 2003. The Finance and Economics *xitong* does not penetrate the portion of the economy under military aegis.

The PLA has a General Staff that includes the heads of its military service arms, the army, navy, and air force. Fittingly for a continent-sized country, the army is the most important of the three. Until the mid-1980s it had manpower levels of over 4 million, making it the largest force in the world.

For most of the years since 1949 the army retained a deep imprint of its pre-1949 existence. In the late 1940s the PLA grouped its forces into five "field armies" that swept over different parts of China. As noted previously, each field army in 1949 and 1950 "settled" into a different section of the country, depending on where the civil war had left it. (Lin Biao's Fourth Field Army actually ended the war in two places: northeast China and Guangdong Province.) In each instance, during the early 1950s many of the officers of the field army were assigned to civilian responsibilities, and to a large extent these civilian officials governed their regions into the 1980s. Notwithstanding the "state-within-the-state" characterization of the military system above, therefore, the personal ties between field army officers and the party and government officials of the locality often were long standing and close. Western scholarly research strongly indicates, moreover, that field army affiliations continued to play an important role in military promotions and career patterns through the 1970s.[44]

The decade of the 1980s brought some important changes in this situation, though. Deng and the reformers sought to upgrade the quality and reduce the average age of both military officers and civilian leaders in the localities. During the mid-1980s, therefore, there was massive turnover of military officers, with very large-scale retirements of older leaders and their replacement by generally better-educated younger people. At the same time, new military regulations required formal officer training school for promotion into the commissioned officer corps. Other measures taken to improve the quality of the officer pool further weakened field army ties.[45]

China generally divides its army in two ways. First, it separates strategic reserve forces from garrison forces.[46] The former are well equipped, relatively highly mobile units under the direct control of the Center. They are used for national security purposes and have generally been kept out of domestic political and economic activities. The garrison forces are less well equipped and have been deployed in military regions around the country.[47] These forces play more important roles in domestic politics and economics than in protecting the country from external attack. They can be deployed to assist in emergencies such as floods and fires, to provide manpower for major construction projects and for agricultural work, to back up party and government directions with force and quell civil unrest, and to perform other duties. These were the forces called on to take over management of society in 1968, when Red Guard battles plunged the country into virtual anarchy. Their extensive involvement in civilian activities further enhanced the ties between the military officers and officials in various localities, although competition over resources and other matters also produced tensions in many of these relationships.

More than in any other communist country, therefore, the military has been important in domestic governance in China. As further evidence of this, at all times through the early 1980s the Politburo included both individuals currently serving in the PLA and many "civilians" who had spent one to three decades in military service. Only in the late 1980s did this situation begin to change significantly. As a part of his reforms, Deng Xiaoping sought to modernize the military establishment, professionalize it, and focus its efforts more on national security than on domestic matters. These efforts were set back somewhat by the dramatic and costly use of the PLA to suppress the Tiananmen demonstrations in 1989. But the longer-term trend is in the direction Deng sought, and the continuing turnover of lower-level officers and officials due to the reforms has produced real changes in the dynamics of the military's involvement in local affairs. The passing of the elder party leaders during the 1990s marked a very important step in the further disengagement of the military from the domestic political system. Now none of the top party leaders has extensive military experience.

During the 1990s the PLA, partly on the basis of lessons it learned from watching the United States evict Iraqi forces from Kuwait in Desert Storm, increasingly focused on developing the capacity to fight a local war under high-tech conditions. Political developments in Taiwan in the mid- and late 1990s led to an additional task: to develop the capacity to force a political solution to the cross-strait issue.

These new emphases have led to increased attention to the navy, air force, and rocket forces and to developing force-projection capability in general. The PLA has increasingly emphasized combined arms training exercises and such nontraditional pursuits as electronic warfare. In the 1990s, China also began purchasing significant advanced weapons systems—including fighter aircraft, destroyers, and antiship missiles—from Russia. The new requirements demand higher-quality, better-trained forces, along with the development of a noncommissioned officer corps. In all these areas, procedures, budgets, and attention have shifted substantially since the early 1990s.[48]

The PLA is thus becoming a more professional military force, reducing the imprint of its revolutionary origins, and it has become less involved in domestic politics throughout the country. This marks a fundamental change from the era of Mao Zedong, when regional military commanders had close political ties with their civilian counterparts. As this occurs, the military's role in maintenance of domestic order is diminishing, with responsibility here shifting to the People's Armed Police (which would revert to PLA command in a time of major domestic disorder).

But the PLA is now a very powerful interest group that is able to secure significant budgetary increases and perquisites. It may be playing an increasingly influential role in China's foreign policy, especially in Asia. After shrinking dramatically in the mid and late 1980s, PLA budgets began to grow very substantially in the late 1990s, reflecting the higher cost of new PLA tasking and the related more high-tech, more effective set of forces.

In political terms, the CCP retains control at the top of the military system through the Military Affairs Commission. In addition, as noted above, the party plays a crucial role in military promotions through the General Political Department's bureaucratic system. A fundamental principle of the Chinese system remains that the party controls the gun, and the military protects party rule.

Summing Up

Overall, the Chinese political system is not divided up as neatly as the above overview of the six most important *xitong* might suggest. Matters that seem as though they should fall completely within the boundary of one *xitong*, such as vehicle assembly under the Finance and Economics system, may in fact pop up in some instances under another, such as Propaganda and Education. This reflects the natural tendency toward empire building—and reluctance to be dependent on others—that takes place throughout the Chinese polity.

In broad terms, though, several major observations about these *xitong* are in order:

☐ All of the *xitong* aim to shape the behavior of China's people. The Finance and Economics system uses primarily economic incentives; the Propaganda and Education system employs moral incentives; and the Political/Legal, military, and Organization/Personnel systems utilize coercive punishments and/or career rewards. The Party Affairs system makes use of all three types (remunerative, normative, and coercive) of incentives.

☐ Generally, the Finance and Economics *xitong* played the most important role during the First Five-Year Plan (1953–57). The Party Affairs system took command of the Great Leap Forward. The PLA surged to the fore during the Cultural Revolution. Under Deng Xiaoping's reforms, the Finance and

Economics *xitong* has in relative terms done best, but its role is changing fundamentally with the transition to a market economy. The military has also fared well since the mid-1990s, although before then the reforms had produced sharp reductions in military prestige, budgets, and roles. The interests of the other four *xitong* have been hurt badly by the reforms, and this highlights the truly remarkable successes of the reformers in sustaining this effort, despite major setbacks.

☐ The *xitong* as such, as noted previously, are virtually invisible on China's organization charts. Yet Chinese officials very much think in terms of these broad functional systems, and the vocabulary they use reflects this way of looking at the political system. In addition, studies of career mobility suggest that most officials tend to spend their entire careers within the bureaucratic organs of a single *xitong*.[49]

☐ Most of the organs in *xitong* other than the military report to the territorial party committees rather than up the line within their *xitong*. With limited exceptions in the state security apparatus and to a still lesser extent in the public security apparatus, Propaganda, Organization and Personnel, and Political and Legal Affairs, are all characterized by only professional (*yewu*) relations up the bureaucratic hierarchy. The same is true for many, but not all, of the organs within the Finance and Economics *xitong*. The key bureaucracy that integrates the various levels of the national political system is, therefore, the *party* bureaucracy, working through its hierarchy of territorial party secretaries.

Party Control of the Government

The Communist party has a dual identity. It consists in part of the people who hold offices in the formal party apparatus—that is, who have executive positions in the party bureaucracy. Only roughly five hundred thousand members fall into this category, but most discussions of "the party" are actually concerned with precisely this minority.[50] The larger portion of the party consists of people who are members of the party but who do not have jobs in the party bureaucracy itself. Most officials in the government and officers in the military, for example, are party members, as are numerous workers in state enterprises, peasants, administrators in universities, and others. Party membership in 2003 totals over 66 million people. Although the party thus defines the political elite of the country, therefore, many party members are at best very marginal members of that elite.

Concerted efforts to assure party control over the various organs of rule (the state, the military, and myriad mass organizations) date back to 1942, when the party leadership in Yan'an first confronted this issue as the base areas grew in size and complexity.[51] The party's approaches to assuring its continuing control have evolved since 1949. In the mid-1950s, the decisions of the top party leaders in the Politburo were actually implemented through three bodies: Deng Xiaoping's Secretariat for party and mass work; the CCP's Military Affairs Commission for military affairs; and the State Council for economic and foreign affairs. In October 1955, the party's Central Committee established departments that paralleled similar bodies, called "staff offices," that had been set up under the State Council to run the economy. These new bodies originally focused on personnel assignment work, but eventually their responsibilities broadened and they became key organs—the leadership small groups discussed above—in the party's exercise of power over the state bureaucracy.

Further evolution occurred during the Great Leap Forward, when expansion of the overall role of the party meant that the Party Secretariat assumed tremendous power at the Center and the party committees throughout the political system usurped the work of their government counterparts. The party then retreated somewhat with the collapse of the Great Leap in the early 1960s, and during the Cultural Revolution Red Guard attacks on the party rendered independent party work virtually impossible. In the late 1960s the new official organs of power, called "revolutionary committees," actually fused party and government bodies into a single unit. The party gradually was resurrected during the 1970s, and the revolutionary committees themselves were turned back into government organs in the wake of Mao Zedong's death. Officials made a concerted effort to differentiate the party and government more clearly and to increase the independence of government organs in the late 1980s, but this effort largely disappeared in the wake of the Tiananmen movement's suppression and the purge of Zhao Ziyang.[52]

The Chinese Communist party retains the power to decide all major political, social and economic policy issues and to appoint the leaders to all public sector bodies (including government offices, public institutions, and SOEs). The CCP employs four basic methods to achieve continuing control over the other bureaucracies: nomenklatura appointments and interlocking directorates, leadership small groups, party "core groups," and "party life." All four of these date back to the 1950s or before. These four practices in their totality lock government officials into such a powerful web of party interference and controls that one of the major issues confronting the Chinese political system today is how to establish a meaningful separation of party and government functions.

NOMENKLATURA APPOINTMENTS AND INTERLOCKING DIRECTORATES

The nomenklatura (as noted above, the term comes from usage in the former USSR) consists of lists of leading positions over which party units exercise the power of appointment and dismissal, lists of reserve candidates for those positions, and rules governing the actual processes of appointments and dismissals. Through its nomenklatura system, the CCP exercises control over who attains leading positions not only in the party, but also in the government, judicial system, schools and universities, enterprises, research establishments, religious organizations, museums, libraries, hospitals, and so forth. *All* positions of real importance in China fall under the CCP's nomenklatura—even many of those, such as the head of the National People's Congress, that are stipulated in the State Constitution as "elected" offices. Through this vehicle the party monopolizes the power to determine who will join—and who will be forced out of—the country's elite in all spheres.

Professor John P. Burns has written the most thorough analyses of China's nomenklatura system to date.[53] As Burns indicates, nomenklatura authority is actually distributed among a number of different party organs, each of which controls the appointment power of a specific array of positions. One significant measure of any organ's importance to the party leadership is the number of its positions on the nomenklatura of the highest levels of the CCP. For example, as of 1990 the Chinese Academy of Sciences had the following positions on the Central Committee's nomenklatura list: president, vice presidents, all the members of the party core group, and the head of the discipline inspection group. The same was true for the Chinese Academy of Social Sciences. For "key point" institutions of higher learning, in contrast, the Central Committee's nomenklatura required only reporting (presumably, for approval) of appointments of the president, vice presidents, party secretaries, and deputy secretaries. In late 1990, the central party leadership felt it was more important to control tightly leadership appointments in the Chinese Academies of Sciences and of Social Sciences than those in the most important universities.

The actual rules governing the nomenklatura have varied over time, and little information is available in the public domain about its scope and operations. Before the Cultural Revolution, the Central Committee departments that took responsibility for various economic sectors evidently exercised nomenklatura power within their domains. These specialized departments ceased to function during the Cultural Revolution and were not revived by the reformers after Mao Zedong's death. In their stead, the Organization Department of the Central Committee has assumed some of the burden and has farmed part out to other units, as explained below.

An additional consideration in China's multilayered bureaucracy is how far "down" appointment power should reach. China is such an extraordinarily bureaucratic society that virtually all public organizations, whether formally part of the state or not, are assigned particular bureaucratic ranks. Table 7.1 presents the rank equivalents among government organs in somewhat simplified form.

Nonstate public organs fit into this same system. The China International Trust and Investment Corporation and the Chinese Academy of Social Sciences, for example, have the rank of State Council ministries, even though the former is a state-owned investment bank and the latter is a research organization. Enterprises, hospitals, and so forth also have assigned bureaucratic ranks that determine many aspects of their relationship to the political system.

As a general rule, from the mid-1950s until 1984 the nomenklatura allowed appointments two ranks "down" in the system. The Central Committee, therefore, had on its direct nomenklatura list the leaders not only of ministries and provinces, but also of ministerial bureaus and provincial

TABLE 7.1 *Rank Equivalents among Government Organs*

CENTER	PROVINCE	COUNTY
State Council		
Ministry	Province	
General bureau	Commission	
Bureau	Provincial department	
	Prefecture	
Division		County
Section		County department

Source: Kenneth Lieberthal and Michel Oksenberg, *Policy Making in China: Leaders, Structures, and Processes* (Princeton, N. J.: Princeton University Press, 1988), p. 143.

departments—a number of posts that extends well up into the thousands. Since the "two-ranks-down" system in numerous cases put the same post on two different nomenklatura lists (for example, of the Central Committee and of the province), it appears that both levels participated in the final choice but that the upper level had the final say in case of disagreement.

In August 1984, however, this system was modified in several ways to make it more effective and more flexible, without giving up party control. The first of the two key changes was a shift from a two-ranks-down system of appointment to a one-rank-down nomenklatura system. This considerably reduced the number of positions listed on, for example, the Central Committee's nomenklatura, dropping the total figure at the time to about five thousand. This change enabled the central authorities to exercise their nomenklatura powers in a more serious fashion. The huge numbers of positions on the previous nomenklatura lists had too often resulted in pro forma consideration and de facto approvals of whomever the lower territorial unit nominated. At the same time, the shift to a one-rank-down system meant that leaders in provincial and lower territorial units gained almost complete control over appointments and dismissals of officials within their territorial jurisdiction. Only the very highest officials at each territorial level—the top party secretaries and the governor and vice governors at the provincial level, for example—would still be appointed by the next highest level, and except in extraordinary cases even these appointments were subject to substantial consultation with the unit affected.

The second change shifted many nomenklatura slots at the central level from the direct control of the Central Committee to the authority of the party core group within each ministry. As detailed below, the party core group typically consists of the top party members who are officials in the ministry, and it almost always includes at least the minister and several vice ministers, along with possibly one or two others. This group often will caucus separately to decide the major issues confronting the ministry. All members of the party core group are on the nomenklatura list of the Central Committee. The party core group, in turn, may control the nomenklatura list for those at a level below them in the ministry. These second-level appointments must then be reported to the Central Committee for the record.

These 1984 changes create the possibility that provinces and ministries will increasingly become ingrown, since appointments to all but the top-level positions are controlled from within. Adequate data are lacking to judge whether this trend has in fact appeared in the staffing of ministries where, in any case, promotions from "in house" had been the rule for many years. Evidence shows, however, a general increase in the percentage of provincial appointments below the top level in which the appointee's previous position was in that same province.

In addition, the 1989 student movement elicited such broad support from key party and government units that after putting down this movement on June 4, the top leaders took measures to strengthen their control over key appointments.[54] This included, in part, extending the list of appointments that must be reported to the Central Committee and possibly exercising veto power over these positions. Because the nomenklatura system is constantly being adjusted and the most recent list available is that for 1990, details of the system as this book goes to press are not clear. But the fundamental structure—an institutionalized vehicle for party influence or absolute control over leadership appointments in many types of nonparty bodies—remains very much in place as a key source of ongoing CCP power.

Actual leadership over nomenklatura appointments may vary. The Politburo Standing Committee decides on the CCP secretary and governor of each province. In some instances, leadership small groups play a critical role in appointments within their bailiwicks. For example, all of the top banking positions, at least through 2002, were formally on the Central Committee's nomenklatura list but in fact were controlled by the Financial Work Commission, which until the November 2002 Sixteenth Party Congress was headed by Wen Jiabao, a Politburo member, a member of the Central Secretariat, and a vice premier.

The major staff organ in the nomenklatura effort at every territorial level of the political system is the organization department under the party territorial committee. At the national level, this is the Organization Department of the Central Committee. As noted above, the organization departments keep extensive personnel files and lists of individuals whom they regard as good potential appointees as posts become vacant. The organization departments make the key recommendations for appointments for all positions on the nomenklatura of their parent party committee. The party committee has the final power of approval, but the organization department's dossiers and recommendations typically narrowly constrain the options of the parent committees.

Since the mid-1990s the party has sought to improve the ranks of the leadership bodies and increase transparency in the appointment process without giving up control over the outcomes. This effort suffuses the regulations on the promotion and employment of leadership cadres in the party and government published on July 23, 2002. The regulations posit requirements in terms of educational level, training, and prior work experience for various types of positions and endorse the idea that officials should move up the system one step at a time. They encourage nomination of more candidates than slots available and provide for extensive consultations and even balloting among those in the unit for which leaders are being chosen. But exceptions are allowed for virtually every rule: for example, Article 17 stipulates, "Democratic nominations should be considered one of the important bases for deciding whom to select for closer examination, but simply relying on ballots to select people should be prevented."

The 2002 regulations apply to the selection of leaders and subordinate units of the CCP Center, the NPC, the State Council, the Chinese People's Political Consultative Conference, and the Discipline Inspection Commission, and the leadership of the Supreme People's Court and the Supreme Procuracy and their internal organs, as well as the local counterparts of the above organs above the county level. They are also supposed to serve as the reference for selection of leaders of trade unions, the women's federation, youth league, and other public social organizations, for the selection of nonparty leading cadres, and for the selection of nonleading officials above the division (*chu*) level.

The 2002 regulations cover virtually the entire leadership stratum. They stipulate that the first guiding principle is, "[T]he party controls [the selection of] cadres." The concrete provisions place all final decisions firmly in the hands of the pertinent party committees, with much of the staff work done by the pertinent party organization system organs. This public document leaves no doubt about the party's continuing control of appointments to all significant leadership posts.

Every state enterprise, school, and other public body also has a personnel department within it. For a unit of any size or significance, moreover, the same unit also has a party committee, under which is an organization section. Typically, all members of the nonparty personnel department are party members, most of whom are also part of the organization section. Through this device, the party controls a huge number of positions that extend well beyond the nomenklatura for leadership positions just discussed.

In sum, the Communist party controls career mobility for all elites outside the private sector in China, and it exercises this control tightly. With the reforms since the late 1970s, the party has made efforts to pull back from detailed involvement in many activities, but at all times it has retained total control over the appointment and dismissal of the elites.[55] As of the late 1980s, it appears that the party's nomenklatura lists included more than 8 million posts. (No concrete number has been published, and this figure is Professor Burns's well-grounded extrapolation.) Even outside this "top 8 million," moreover, the party intervenes massively in decisions on appointments and career opportunities. It is virtually impossible, therefore, to alienate the relevant party officials and still enjoy career success other than in a foreign-invested joint-venture enterprise or a private firm. In this sense, the decentralization of personnel decisions under the reforms has increased the chances of local despotism over those who do not find exit into the nonpublic sector.

Beyond using appointment and dismissal power to assure control over leaders of state organs, the party has also exerted its leverage via "interlocking directorates," that is, having key party officials themselves directly take charge of state bodies. In the 1950s this practice reflected in part the scarcity of skilled individuals whom the top party leaders felt they could fully trust. It was often the case, therefore, that one individual acted as both the top party secretary and as the head of government in a territory. In 1951, for example, Huang Jing was both party secretary and mayor of Tianjin City; Peng Zhen held both positions in Beijing; Chen Yi did the same in Shanghai; Lin Ruoyu was party secretary and governor of Shandong Province; and Tan Zhenlin held both positions in Jiangsu Province, as did Ye Jianying in Guangdong. In addition, the same person often held an important post in the local military organization—typically, as political commissar of the provincial military district.

The reforms of the 1980s sought, among other things, to reduce the instances of this multiple hat-wearing. Since the early 1990s there have been virtually no instances in which the top party secretary of a province or city simultaneously serves as governor or mayor. Yet interlocking directorates continue to be important, because the top officials in the government in each territorial jurisdiction typically also hold positions on the party committee that governs that jurisdiction. For example, the CCP Politburo includes the government premier (Wen Jiabao), the head of the legislature (Wu Bangguo), the president (Hu Jintao), the head of the Chinese People's Political Consultative Conference (Jia Qinglin), all three vice premiers (Wu Yi, Zeng Peiyan, Huang Ju), and the top figures in the military (Guo Boxiong, Cao Gangchuan).

The party's nomenklatura system gives the CCP the powerful political weapon of being able to determine who will join—and who will remain in—the elite at all levels of the system. Interlocking directorates further consolidate party control by placing many individuals who hold key government positions onto the party committee in charge of that territory as a whole. But even these devices understate considerably the real power of the party over the state apparatus. The core organization of this power is hidden from view because it is sculpted around a series of secret bodies—the leadership small groups and the party core groups—that do not appear on organization charts.

PARTY CORE GROUPS AND PARTY LIFE

The party has formally constituted "party core groups" in the various government ministries. This form of organization evidently is not used in government bodies below the level of a ministry. In those lower-level government units, the party members are formed into party committees with branches and other subordinate divisions, depending on the number of party members in the unit. The ministerial-level government bodies, however, have both a party core group and a party committee. The former is by far the more powerful body.[56]

Party core groups date back to the early days of the PRC. The initial idea was to have a separate forum for the top party members to utilize, given that in those days the CCP had visions of bringing a moderate number of nonparty individuals into positions of some authority. After the political campaigns of the 1950s, this original rationale no longer held, as virtually no individuals other than CCP members retained high positions in the ministries. The practice, nevertheless, continued.

The party core group includes the top few party members in each government ministry and commission. These individuals caucus as party members to decide issues confronting the ministry and to review appropriate directions from above. They then don their government hats as ministers and vice ministers to issue directives and carry them out. The actual membership of party core groups is secret.[57]

In the late 1980s, the reformers sought to phase out party core groups, arguing both that they no longer served a distinctive purpose and that nonparty individuals of talent should be allowed to hold a few top positions. This idea actually was adopted as policy in 1987, but its implementation remained incomplete and was aborted in the wake of the Tiananmen Square repression in June 1989.

In addition to the party core groups, each government body organizes its CCP members into a party committee or into smaller bodies, depending on the number of party members. Where there is no party core group, the party committee performs all the functions that the core group would undertake (including making key personnel and policy decisions). In addition, the party committee runs "party life." This is a series of activities intended to familiarize CCP members with the policies of the party and to maintain a sense of discipline and esprit de corps among party members. Party life typically includes regular meetings of the membership, at which documents are read and issues discussed. Through these channels, party members are supposed to learn about new policies or problems before their nonparty colleagues do.[58]

Party life was very important in the years before 1966, but it declined in vigor during and immediately after the Cultural Revolution and has suffered further erosion under the reforms. Still, party membership includes the obligation to participate in these activities, and it also entails willingness to bend to party discipline on issues on which the CCP leadership demands compliance. Party life thus forms another brick—albeit a chipped and flaking one—in the edifice of Chinese Communist party controls over the government and other bodies.

The Party's Roles and Challenges

The CCP no longer enjoys the sense of discipline and commitment among its members that typified its earlier days. Today many Chinese regard party membership primarily as a ticket to career advancement and a higher living standard. Large doses of ideological education and tough political demands no longer confront aspiring members. Changes formally adopted at the Sixteenth Party Congress in 2002, which allow capitalists to join the CCP, place an official stamp on the party as the organization of the elite that has emerged from the reforms.

The party's continuing relevance stems from its ongoing monopoly on the exercise of political power. As explained above, party bodies make the decisions on the major substantive issues that confront not only the government but all public institutions. Party decisions also determine who will join the elite and what positions they will hold in public bodies. Such decisions are typically made on the basis of extensive consultation with nonparty bodies, but the power of final determination still resides in the CCP. The legislative and legal systems increasingly influence outcomes, but nothing effectively stops the party from acting when the relevant CCP leaders decide to take a decisive stance on an issue. Most importantly, the party also decides China's foreign and security policies.

The leadership relations that govern ties between higher and lower level party committees provide for nationwide discipline in policy implementation. Various factors—self-interest, corruption, manipulation of information, and so forth—erode this discipline, but on balance, because of the CCP China retains a remarkably strong executive capability for a developing country of its size and diversity. By integrating all political activity into one overarching organization, moreover, the CCP constrains what otherwise might become paralyzing fissiparous tendencies among various provinces and interests.

But the CCP's monopoly of political power also means that problems in the CCP become problems for China's overall political system. These problems are very substantial and include the following:

☐ Corruption and lack of commitment to real public service within the party are by no means universal but are widespread. Given the party's ability to override legal and regulatory constraints, these problems can have very severe consequences both for the quality of governance and for popular sentiment.

☐ Changes to China's society and economy are occurring faster than are comparable adjustments in party organization and function. As noted in Chapter 6, for example, urban governance is shifting from delivery of services via the *danwei* to utilization of community-based organizations. The party is also shifting to construct basic-level party organs on a community basis, but this effort may be lagging behind the changes in the government.

☐ The private sector, which is the most rapidly growing and dynamic sector of the Chinese economy, has relatively little participation in the CCP. New efforts to recruit private entrepreneurs to the party will address this problem to a limited degree, but workers in private-sector firms are unlikely to feel that the CCP is becoming more responsive simply because the owners are joining it. The same concerns about responsiveness are even truer for unemployed workers, migrant peasants, and others who fall largely outside the ken of the current party structure.

☐ Many in China's increasingly well-informed and sophisticated population question why a country of this wealth and complexity should be governed by a corrupt political party that depends largely on its ability to deliver rapid economic growth to stay in power. This is especially true among those who feel that economic growth since the late 1990s has not provided them with concrete benefits. The CCP has proven adept at steering China's growth effort but has not developed the capacity to amalgamate, articulate, and adjudicate the various interests in Chinese society in a way that inspires confidence among broad segments of the population.

In sum, China is changing in ways that disadvantage the CCP. The most dynamic sectors of society are those in which the CCP is relatively poorly represented. An increasingly well-informed population seeks political vehicles that are responsive to their critical needs. China is evolving away from its revolutionary century, and the CCP must cope with an increasingly self-aware, mobile, modern, and differentiated population.

The party is actively wrestling with how best to improve the quality of its ties with the population. Many of the issues under consideration involve increasing "democracy" within the CCP itself by, for example, actually allowing each party congress to elect the leadership of the party at its own territorial level, rather than having the congress simply ratify nomenklatura appointments decided by the next highest level. The issues the party confronts as it seeks to adjust its posture are complex and wide ranging. In the words of a knowledgeable insider in the summer of 2002:

The issue of reflecting the interests of various sectors of society in the CCP is recognized by everyone [in the CCP] as a key issue. Clearly, people now feel that they do not influence the CCP at the local levels. The higher levels of the Party feel that changes are necessary, but there is a lot of disagreement at higher levels over what to do on this. Some advocate expanding elections upward to the *Xiang* and *Zhen* [that is, township] level for both the CCP and the government. Some say we should promote this first outside the CCP and should push elections up to as high as the county level, then have progress in the CCP follow these developments in the government. Others say that the CCP itself must lead in the process of democratization—that this should start with the village committee and then move up. But there is still no agreement on how to pursue this. . . . [Some feel that] at each level progress should be made simultaneously both inside and outside the CCP at all levels, including the Party center. We should pursue this step by step. For example we can have the county CCP secretary really elected by the county CCP congress, but we need to get there in steps. An early step would be to announce the candidates who are being appointed for a period of public comment before the appointments actually take effect. Another step is to have more candidates than offices. And so forth. We have a concern that if you allow democracy outside of the CCP before you allow it inside of the Party, then you run an increased risk of having the CCP suffer the fate of the CPSU [the Communist Party of the Soviet Union].

These issues of party reform are being considered against the background of very pressing economic, social, environmental, security, and other concerns with which the CCP must grapple over the coming years. The following chapters explore the details of these key issues within the context of the political system that has evolved from nearly a quarter century of post-Mao reforms.

Part Four

THE

CHALLENGES

AHEAD

8

Economic Development

Developing a more efficient economy that can produce technological change, raise living standards, and bolster international security has been at the core of China's reforms. The reforms have in fact improved the standard of living of the vast majority of Chinese at a remarkable rate since 1979. But these very successes inevitably have produced related changes—in popular attitudes, social stratification, population mobility, and so forth—that during the early years of the twenty-first century potentially threaten the political system itself.

History since the start of the Industrial Revolution shows that rapid industrial development entails enormous domestic and international consequences. This process literally alters the way people live, think, and produce. It changes the internal distribution of wealth as well as a country's ability to project power beyond its borders. At best, this is an unsettling process, producing enormous social strain and requiring substantial political accommodation. When an industrial revolution takes place simultaneously with the electronics revolution, including sudden participation in international telecommunications, the repercussions are all the more unsettling.

Although quick economic growth may help to satisfy escalating popular demands, it can also contribute to tension and instability. Extremely rapid economic development in most cases means that people's lives in the aggregate are changing faster than are the normative systems that sustain a society and give it meaning. The dislocations always associated with urbanization and the shift to factory labor are, therefore, exacerbated by confusion in values and sharp generational conflicts.

Since the early 1980s, China has been the world's fastest growing major industrial economy. Overall per capita gross domestic product (GDP) in constant *yuan* roughly quadrupled between 1978 and the turn of the twenty-first century. In 1978 about 11 million Chinese had direct access to television.[1] Today such access either at home or nearby is virtually universal, and the content of television itself has changed from dull state-sponsored programming to, in many cases, uncensored international satellite broadcasts.[2] As a result, despite its enormous economic successes—indeed, in part *because* of these successes—China in the early years of the twenty-first century confronts potentially destabilizing challenges to its political order. The incentives to maintain extremely rapid growth are, moreover, unrelenting.

Incentives for High Growth

As explained in Chapter 5, Deng Xiaoping started China's economic reforms at the end of the 1970s largely because he recognized the dangers to China of falling so dramatically behind the growth rates being achieved elsewhere in East Asia. He saw that Mao Zedong's highly collectivist approach to development could not produce adequate results, and he realized that China had to find a way to generate productivity growth, a goal that had eluded all of the socialist economies of the era. Deng also saw the need to deliver material rewards to a population that had become bitterly disillusioned with ideological hyperbole by the end of the Maoist era.

In the most fundamental sense, therefore, China's economic reform strategy has been guided by a strategic vision at the top of the political system. This vision links China's security, global influence, and domestic stability to the state of its economy. While this vision recognizes that in the short-term China's fastest growth can only come from utilizing its relatively cheap labor force in the international division of labor, it also views productivity growth as an integral part of maintaining rapid economic expansion over the long run. It is also premised on the notion that a centrally administered, planned economy is inimical to the technological dynamism that contributes to productivity growth.

This grand strategic vision has provided incentives for economic reform and rapid growth. However, now that China has developed a large economy, the effect at the grassroots level of economic decentralization, market transformation, and demographic pressures provides the greatest structural imperative to *sustain* a

TABLE 8.1 *Population Size, 1970–2001 (in Millions)*

YEAR	POPULATION
1978	962.59
1980	987.05
1985	1,058.51
1990	1,143.33
1991	1,158.80
1992	1,172.50
1993	1,185.50
1994	1,198.50
1995	1,211.21
1996	1,223.89
1997	1,236.26
1998	1,248.10
1999	1,259.09
2000	1,265.83
2001	1,276.27

Source: China Statistical Yearbook 2002 (Beijing: China Statistics Press, 2002), Table 4.1.

growth-oriented economic strategy into the future. In other words, political leaders now feel they must create new jobs rapidly to maintain social stability as many millions of people either enter the urban labor force for the first time or seek to shift from farm to nonfarm jobs. China, the leaders believe, is threatened with social and political upheaval if it seriously slows economic growth.

Much that occurs in China reflects the underlying need of the political system to accommodate the largest population in the world (see Table 8.1). China's population of nearly 1.3 billion people is greater than the *combined* populations of the United States, Canada, Western Europe, and the fifteen countries that formerly made up the Soviet Union. Even with a highly effective birth-control program in place, the PRC's net population increase (that is, births minus deaths) in the early twenty-first century is about 11 million people per year (twenty-one people *per minute*). China thus adds the equivalent of the population of Australia to its demographic base every twenty-one months, and it adds a population nearly equal to Taiwan's every two years.

China has, moreover, a double danger in its population configuration: improvements in public health threaten the country with substantial increases in the number of older people whom society must support. By 2025 China will have more than 200 million people age sixty-five and over, with that number rising to more than 300 million by 2050. In addition, the working-age population in China is growing at an average of over 8 million people per year between 1995 and 2020. Given the massive ongoing migration from the countryside to the cities, moreover, urban job creation will have to expand at a very fast clip to keep up with the labor supply. Chinese officials expect an additional 100 million rural dwellers to shift to urban residence from 2002 to 2012. Urban employment problems potentially affect stability far more than do employment difficulties in the countryside. Interviews with county and municipal leaders reveal that their actions are strongly motivated by the resulting pressures for job creation. "On the ground," therefore, when given a choice, local political leaders use their power to accelerate growth. The basic reform strategy has vastly increased the power of precisely those individuals at the front line of the system.

The fact that the profits of local industries provide the major source of income for the local levels of the state also fuels growth pressures by linking the self-interest of local officials with a rapid expansion of the township and city economies. Because industry and commerce are taxed at a higher rate than is agriculture, local officials often favor development of the urban over the agricultural economies.[3] In sum, the combination of enormous demographic pressure, exacerbated by some of the market-oriented reform measures and the devolution of considerable decision making to the basic levels, has created tremendous momentum behind policies aimed at rapid short-term growth throughout most of China. The Center is equally committed to longer-term fast growth to maintain political stability and to address major challenges that will require large capital commitments in the coming decade. It struggles to put in place the physical infrastructure, laws, and institutions that will make such growth possible.

Reform Trends

The Maoist system gave national leaders great control over resource allocations in terms of sector, geography, and society. At the same time, it prevented the free flow of information and factors of production, market-determined prices, and the competition necessary to gain economic efficiency and technological dynamism. It also prevented China from fully exercising its comparative advantage of cheap labor in the international economy. The reforms have now significantly affected every dimension of the Maoist economic system.

The major focus of the reforms in the economy shifted over time. From 1979 to 1984, the reformers made marked changes in policies toward agriculture and, more timidly, toward international borrowing, trade, and foreign direct investment. In 1984 the emphasis turned to reforming the urban economy, a far more complex task. Initial efforts concentrated especially on increasing incentives for territorial leaders to take the initiative in producing rapid local growth and in motivating SOE managers to increase output and improve efficiency. In 1993 the leadership officially declared the goal of creating a market system, and in 1994 China revamped its tax structure. In 1997, the leaders decided to privatize many SOEs, and in 1998 they gave official sanction to development of the private sector. In 2001 China assumed far-reaching obligations for domestic economic change when it joined the World Trade Organization (WTO). As noted in Chapter 7, in 2002 the CCP decided to reverse its 1989 decision prohibiting private entrepreneurs from be party members.

These decisions were not clearly in view at the start of the reforms. They reflect a basic step-by-step approach, and in many instances they became necessary because of the unanticipated consequences of previous decisions. But overall policy has consistently moved toward material incentives, broader application of market forces, more efficient utilization of labor and capital, broader and deeper integration into the international economy, and retreat from economic administration to economic regulation as the core economic function of the government.

The reforms have not reached their end point. Today the Chinese government and the CCP still play an enormous role in the economy beyond simple regulation. Many obstacles block the play of market forces. Capital is still allocated in grossly inefficient ways. And at most a handful of Chinese firms have become competitive at an international level. The following overview of the reforms concentrates first on the evolution of policies in key areas, then on the impressive accomplishments to this point, and finally on the equally impressive challenges facing China's economy in the years to come.

Reform Policy Sequences

From the start, the reforms increased the importance of market forces and material incentives and reduced the government's administrative controls over the economy. But in 1979 even the most ardent reformers would have been aghast at the thought that China should develop a fully marketized economy. The role of the market initially expanded as a set of incremental steps to improve incentives and efficiencies. Only in the 1990s did the creation of a market economy become a conscious national strategic goal.

China's reform efforts follow a consistent pattern in each issue area. Initial steps begin to address underlying issues. Those steps produce benefits and also disruptions, which invite a broadening and deepening of the initiatives. China's reformers never simply leaped from a planned to a market system. Rather, they adopted policies that unsettled the previous status quo and then built on the newly created situation to amplify the changes as the political situation allowed. This discussion highlights the major steps in the most important issue areas.

AGRICULTURE

In the late 1970s the reformers took various measures to ease peasant burdens and increase rural incomes. Government investigations made in 1976–77 produced the shocking revelation that peasants were no better off than they had been in the mid-1950s; an additional twenty years of rule by the victors of a revolution made in the countryside had not produced real benefit for the vast rural population. A series of ameliorative measures quickly followed. Procurement prices for agricultural products were raised, thus directly putting more money into the hands of farmers. Some restrictions on the types of crops that could be grown were eased so that farmers could make more sensible choices in crop selection. The reintroduction of the right to sell products into rural markets gave peasants the incentives and information to make better crop-selection decisions. Fertilizer became more widely available. Most important, from 1979 to 1984 the commune system was dismantled, and peasant families gained the right to lease land from the collective.[4]

As a result of these and other measures, the country's agricultural output surged from 1980 to 1984, growing from 320 million tons of grain equivalent in 1980 to 407 million tons in 1984. During that period the reforms as a whole became very closely associated with the enormous successes taking place in the agricultural sector. Urban dwellers generally readily accepted rapid increases in rural incomes as appropriate, given the terrible poverty of the countryside.

Additional changes followed. Because experience in the early 1980s showed that short-term contracts created incentives to use the land but not to maintain it, many of these land contracts are now written to last up to fifty years. To encourage further maximum output from the land, since the mid-1980s the peasants can, within limits, buy and sell land contracts. People with larger holdings can hire others to help them work the land. More efficient farmers are now able to expand their land holdings, while others can sell their land contracts and seek other employment. The overall trend has thus been from communes to the family responsibility system to limited commercialization of land.

The payoffs from giving the peasants more capital, establishing better incentive systems, allowing greater freedom of crop selection, and other related changes in the structure of the administration of agriculture were, however, primarily realized during the initial years. After 1984, additional increases in farm production required substantial new investment. But the government instead turned its attention to the urban economy and relied increasingly on complex policies in areas such as agricultural price supports to influence rural output. Official government investment in agriculture fell off dramatically. Basically, Beijing counted on the peasants to spend much of their new income on making the investments necessary to keep output growing rapidly.

The government guessed wrong. Peasants instead put their money into new housing and the purchase of consumer goods to improve their quality of life. In addition, the new housing they built and the physical expansion of cities, townships, roads and other nonagricultural infrastructure took significant acreage out of agricultural production. As urban reforms opened up opportunities for peasants to leave the land, over 100 million moved to townships and cities. Overwhelmingly, young males, who are the most productive farmers, made this change.

With the national-level leaders paying little attention to agriculture, moreover, a price scissors began to open up to the disadvantage of the farmers—that is, the prices farmers had to pay for inputs such as fertilizer and farm machinery went up faster than the increases in prices for the farmers' crops. Perhaps more important, the interests of township and county officials became intricately tied up with expanding production of local urban collective and private enterprises. They therefore increasingly resorted to such tactics as diverting money allocated by the Center for crop procurement to investment in new township enterprises, giving the peasants IOUs instead of cash for their produce. They also levied a dismaying variety of local taxes and fees on the countryside to support rapid township development.[5] The political system effectively placed few obstacles in the path of local officials who wished to exploit the rural areas under their control.

The authorities tried to increase peasant satisfaction by encouraging elections in the villages so that peasants could choose their immediate leaders.[6] But township officials play a major role in determining the goods and services available to the surrounding villages and in linking the villages to higher levels of the political system. Elections have not been permitted to extend to the township level, and the fiscal system systematically starves townships of the funds they require to meet their responsibilities.[7] Consequently, many township governments, despite higher-level admonitions to the contrary, resort to heavy-handed measures to impose illegal exactions on the peasants in their jurisdictions, and rural services have not kept up with demands.

These policies and practices have by now produced a deeply disgruntled countryside. Many east coast peasants have moved into labor-intensive, high-value farming, producing fruits, vegetables, cut flowers, and other profitable products for domestic consumption and export. Many additional peasants benefit from living near lucrative major urban markets. But vast numbers of peasants, especially in central and northeast China, have seen their agricultural incomes decline in recent years. Peasant revolts have occasionally been reported in locations as diverse as Sichuan in the southwest and Jilin in the northeast. National production of basic grains, including rice, has not kept up with the rate of increase in the population. Not until 1989 did the grain output again reach that of 1984. In per capita terms, the 2001 grain harvest is below that of 1984 (see Table 8.2), although diversification of China's diet away from grains (a reflection of increasing wealth) renders the slow growth of grains an increasingly inadequate reflection of total domestic food production.

THE FISCAL SYSTEM

China's fiscal system has been weak since the latter years of the Qing dynasty. Under the Maoist system, revenues came primarily from manipulating prices to ensure large profits for the SOE sector and then appropriating those profits for state use.[8] The financial system itself was highly attenuated.

The reforms sought in part to create incentives for the SOE sector to perform more efficiently by allowing enterprises to develop real profits and to keep part of their profits as a reward for their success. This fundamental decision required myriad adjustments in order to move toward real prices, substitute market forces for state procurement, recast the role of banks so they

TABLE 8.2 *Agricultural Harvests, 1978–2001*

YEAR	FOOD GRAIN OUTPUT (Millions of tons)
1978	304.77
1980	320.56
1984	407.31
1989	407.55
1990	446.24
1991	435.29
1992	442.66
1993	456.49
1994	445.10
1995	466.62
1996	504.54
1997	494.17
1998	512.30
1999	508.39
2000	462.51
2001	452.62

Source: *China Statistical Yearbook 2002* (Beijing: China Statistics Press, 2002), Table 12.2.

could become active decision makers in the allocation of credit, create capital markets, develop meaningful accounting systems, protect property rights, and allow greater decision-making authority at the SOE level. It also required substituting a tax on SOE profits for the former system of appropriating all SOE income. But despite these various initiatives, the profits of state enterprises that under the Maoist system provided the major source of revenue for the national authorities declined sharply under the reforms because the most rapid economic growth since the early 1980s has taken place in the local collective sector and more recently in the private sector in the townships and cities, outside the official state sector. The reforms also sought to create strong incentives for officials at every level of the national political hierarchy to promote economic growth in an entrepreneurial, flexible fashion.

The fiscal system has seen significant experimentation and has been shaped by the interaction of the above goals, bureaucratic capacities, and local initiatives.[9] Beijing has needed both to assure itself adequate fiscal revenues and to provide meaningful incentives for localities and firms to increase economic output. In broad terms, the fiscal system has evolved through three major stages:[10]

☐ *Replacement of appropriating profits with taxing profits.* This change was adopted in 1983–84 and sought to provide SOEs with incentives to earn and increase profits by leaving a portion of those profits in the hands of the firms. But given the enormous inequalities in factor endowments of different SOEs, the still blanket nature of state regulations that constrained what SOEs could do, and the highly artificial price system, the state in the name of equity essentially had to negotiate individual tax deals with many major SOEs to get this system off the ground. The result was a great deal of disgruntlement.

☐ *Fiscal contracting with the provinces.* Starting in the mid-1980s, Beijing negotiated distinctive tax deals with selected provinces. Each deal was based on a different approach designed to create incentives for provinces to expand their economies without starving the Center for funds. Provinces such as Guangdong, Jiangsu, and Sichuan played key roles in this experimental effort. For example, Guangdong Province agreed to pay 1 billion *yuan* to Beijing annually for five years, with the province keeping whatever revenues it collected above that figure. Toward the end of this period, Guangdong's effective tax rate was very low, as the province achieved annual growth rates during this period of roughly 20 percent.[11] In 1988–89, Beijing adopted on a national level an approach that had it negotiate a fiscal contract with each province. Many provinces negotiated tax deals that allowed them to retain substantial portions of any new economic growth they generated.[12] But this new approach proved unsatisfactory. For the provinces, it left too much uncertainty, because in reality the Center could change the negotiated deals at will. In addition, this system created incentives for massive tax evasion at each level and for local governments to direct their investments to locales that had been given especially light tax burdens (for example, special economic zones such as the Pudong area in Shanghai). Beijing's share of total tax revenue declined from well over half to 38.6 percent in 1992.[13]

☐ *Division of the tax-collection system.* In 1994 Beijing decided that, for the first time in China's history, the country should establish separate systems for collecting local taxes and national taxes. Prior to that time, all taxes were collected by local authorities, which then passed a portion of their collection up the ladder. This system created problems of leakage and misreporting at all levels.[14] After 1994 Beijing established a two-tier tax collection system: a state system specifically dedicated to collecting taxes for the Center, and a separate system in each province that collected all taxes that would be used solely within the province. At the same time, Beijing stipulated in law tax rates and which types of taxes would go to central coffers. A value-added tax of 17 percent, of which 75 percent goes to the Center, is a major component of the new system. To make these changes, Beijing negotiated with the provinces in late 1993 and promised to phase in the adjustments in a way that would not take any current income away from the provinces.[15] As a result of these reforms, the Center now again captures over 50 percent of all revenues. In 1994, Beijing also committed itself to a revised program of revenue sharing with the provinces. Thus, the Center's revenue intake has significantly increased, but local government expenditures have also grown as the Center has remitted substantial funds back to lower levels. This new system gives the Center a surer fiscal base and provides it a somewhat larger role in determining where public funds are allocated throughout the country. It also allows provinces very considerable flexibility on how to spend tax revenues in their own locales.

In broad terms, the reform era has seen detailed control over funds shift markedly from Beijing to provincial and lower levels as part of Beijing's overall strategy of shifting initiative for economic entrepreneurship to provinces, local governments, and enterprises. Local levels, especially in the wealthy coastal provinces, are now far less dependent on Beijing's financial largesse. Even in the poorer provinces in the northern and western parts of the country, which still need net transfers of funds from Central coffers, Beijing has decentralized control by giving the lower levels far more leeway than before regarding how to spend their money.[16]

Today China has a far more regularized tax system than before the reforms, and the tax system has become increasingly effective. By 2001 fiscal revenues were 90 percent greater than in 1997 and 120 percent greater than in 1996. The revenue-to-GDP ratio has risen by more than 1 percent per year since the 1994 reforms were introduced. Tax rates are fixed in law, as are revenue-sharing percentages. Separate national and provincial tax systems remove some of the distortions that a single integrated system formerly produced. And improvements in accounting systems, information infrastructure, auditing capabilities, and related areas have moved China in the direction of a real tax system instead of a system either of outright appropriation or of political deals over resources.

But problems are still abundant. Tax evasion remains widespread among individuals, enterprises, and governments. Corruption further reduces tax effectiveness. In ways too complex to warrant analysis here, collections of additional funds, some of which are "extrabudgetary" and others of which are "off budget," by government agencies reduce the clarity of the underlying fiscal situation. And the lowest levels of the government system, counties and townships, are now starved for funds and unable to meet obligations mandated by higher levels. In this area as in most, therefore, progress has been both substantial and incomplete.

FOREIGN TRADE AND INVESTMENT

From the beginning, the reforms moved China away from Mao's exaggerated notions of "going it alone," but the underlying thinking in dealing with the international economy has evolved a great deal since 1979. Initially, the reformers sought primarily to mobilize overseas Chinese, especially those living in Hong Kong, to contribute capital and know-how about both production and international markets to China's development effort. But residual deep distrust of the outside world from the Maoist period limited these initial steps.

In this as in other arenas, the reforms broadened and deepened over time. Gradually the reformers intensified their international quest for capital, managerial know-how, and technology, as well as for marketing expertise to expand exports that could take advantage of China's abundant supplies of cheap labor. With China's December 2001 accession to the WTO, the nature of the country's approach to the international system has again changed. Reformers in Beijing now see the changes required by China's WTO accession agreement as necessary in order to force domestic economic reforms that are, they feel, critical to China's long-term economic success.

In every sphere of China's complex interaction with the international economic arena, the story is one of very limited steps to test the waters turning into ever deeper, and wider-ranging reforms.

The approach to foreign direct investment (FDI) is typical. China's initial joint-venture law of 1979 legitimized foreign direct investment but confined it to minority shares in joint ventures with Chinese enterprises, where the ventures had a contractually limited life span. In addition, these ventures could be set up only in the four special economic zones created along the southeast coast, and they required stringent approvals on the Chinese side. The vast majority of FDI that came in under this system originated in Hong Kong and created simple assembly operations for export along the border in Guangdong Province.[17]

The FDI restrictions gradually eased considerably. During the 1980s Beijing allowed foreign investments in wider and wider areas of eastern China, then up the Yangtze River watershed, and eventually throughout the interior. Foreigners were allowed, step by step, to enter into a broader variety of types of joint ventures, including some in which the foreign firm held majority ownership. Additional sectors opened to foreign investment, and the size of investments that local authorities could approve grew. Various localities began competing ferociously to attract foreign firms to their areas and seeking the kinds of policy concessions from Beijing that would enable them to offer foreigners especially attractive deals.

Whereas originally all products of foreign joint ventures had to be produced for export, over time such ventures were permitted to sell most of their products on the domestic market, with the details varying by the sector and the type of venture. With China's joining the WTO, the domestic market is opening far more widely with former requirements for exports from foreign invested firms being terminated. Now, foreigners are allowed to establish wholly owned ventures in many sectors of China's economy; WTO implementation will substantially expand these opportunities by 2006.[18] In addition, the development of stock markets in both Shanghai and Shenzhen enables foreign firms to participate to a very limited extent in portfolio investment as well as direct investment.

As Tables 8.3 and 8.4 show, foreign direct investment has grown markedly in China, especially since 1992. Indeed, in the decade since 1992 China has consistently ranked as the largest developing country receiving foreign direct investment. This investment is, however, very unevenly spread around the country. Overwhelmingly, the major east coast locales of Guangdong, Jiangsu, Fujian, Shandong, Shanghai, Beijing, and Tianjin have attracted far larger foreign funds than have other parts of the country. Also, Japan, the United States, Hong Kong, and Taiwan have been by far the largest sources of such investment, with Hong Kong and Taiwan particularly active.[19] Hong Kong investment has been concentrated largely in Guangdong Province, and that from Taiwan has gone especially to Fujian and Shanghai.

TABLE 8.3 *Direct Foreign Investment by Region, 1988–2001 (in Millions of U.S. $)*

PROVINCE	1988	1989	1990	1991	1992	1993	1994	1995	1996	1997	1998	1999	2000	2001
Beijing	502.78	318.46	276.95	244.82	349.85	666.94	1371.57	1079.99	1552.90	1592.86	2168.00	1975.25	1683.68	1768.18
Tianjin	31.85	28.01	34.93	132.16	107.24	541.00	1014.99	1520.64	2006.37	2511.35	2113.61	1763.99	1166.01	2133.48
Hebei	16.73	26.86	39.35	44.37	110.19	396.54	509.48	541.75	825.87	1100.64	1428.68	1042.02	679.23	669.89
Shanxi	6.52	8.82	3.40	3.80	53.84	86.43	31.70	63.83	138.02	265.92	244.51	391.29	224.72	233.93
I. Mongolia	3.37	0.24	10.64	1.10	5.20	85.26	40.07	52.00	71.86	73.25	90.82	64.56	105.68	107.03
Liaoning	115.25	118.57	243.73	348.88	489.56	1262.69	1436.76	1421.75	1737.68	2204.70	2190.45	1061.73	2044.46	2516.12
Dalian	–	–	–	–	–	–	–	–	–	1319.44	–	–	–	–
Jilin	6.20	3.35	17.60	18.00	65.97	237.84	241.52	398.76	451.55	402.27	409.17	301.20	337.01	337.66
Heilongjiang	40.09	22.41	24.49	9.43	70.50	232.32	341.76	450.18	548.41	734.85	526.39	318.28	300.86	341.14
Shanghai	233.17	422.12	174.01	145.19	481.10	3160.25	2473.09	2892.61	3940.94	4225.36	3601.50	2836.65	3160.14	4291.59
Jiangsu	103.03	93.58	124.16	212.32	1460.00	2843.71	3763.15	5190.82	5210.09	5435.11	6631.79	6077.56	6425.50	6914.82
Zhejiang	29.57	51.81	48.43	91.62	232.38	1031.75	1144.41	1258.06	1520.50	1503.45	1318.02	1232.62	1612.66	2211.62
Ningbo	–	–	–	–	–	–	–	–	–	554.08	–	–	–	–
Anhui	11.51	4.78	9.61	9.54	50.02	257.64	370.00	482.56	506.61	434.43	276.73	261.31	318.47	336.72
Fujian	130.17	328.80	290.02	466.29	1416.34	2867.45	3712.00	4038.81	4084.51	4196.66	4212.11	4024.03	3431.91	3918.04
Xiamen	–	–	–	–	–	–	–	–	–	1378.67	–	–	–	–
Jiangxi	5.18	5.87	6.21	19.49	96.53	208.17	261.68	287.96	300.68	477.68	464.96	320.80	227.24	395.75
Shandong	43.09	131.32	150.84	179.50	973.35	1843.19	2531.53	2607.19	2590.41	2492.94	2202.74	2258.78	2971.19	3520.93
Qingdao	–	–	–	–	–	–	–	–	–	835.97	–	–	–	–
Henan	64.18	42.66	10.49	37.91	52.15	302.94	385.67	476.22	523.56	692.04	616.54	521.35	564.03	457.29
Hubei	22.31	22.95	29.00	46.43	203.08	537.70	601.83	624.74	680.04	790.19	972.94	914.88	943.68	1188.60
Hunan	7.71	6.43	11.16	22.76	128.53	432.67	325.11	488.02	703.44	917.02	818.16	653.74	678.33	810.11
Guangdong	957.86	1156.44	1460.00	1822.86	3551.50	7498.04	9397.08	10180.30	11623.62	11710.83	12019.94	11657.50	11280.91	11932.03
Shenzhen	–	–	–	–	–	–	–	–	–	1661.12	–	–	–	–

Guangxi	20.65	45.94	28.66	25.32	178.33	872.03	815.06	669.52	656.18	879.86	886.13	635.12	524.66	384.16
Hainan	114.21	94.97	103.02	176.16	452.55	707.10	918.09	1062.07	789.08	705.54	717.15	484.49	430.80	466.91
Sichuan	23.61	8.01	16.04	24.39	101.85	559.81	888.59	539.40	425.44	248.46	372.48	341.01	436.94	581.88
Chongqing	—	—	—	—	—	—	—	—	—	386.75	431.07	238.93	244.36	256.49
Guizhou	4.40	7.47	4.68	7.34	19.79	42.94	63.63	57.03	31.38	49.77	45.35	40.90	25.01	28.29
Yunnan	37.10	7.40	2.61	2.96	23.13	97.02	65.00	97.69	65.37	165.66	145.68	153.85	128.12	64.57
Tibet	0.03	NA	NA	NA	NA	NA	NA	NA	NA	NA	NA	NA	NA	NA
Shaanxi	111.73	97.19	41.91	31.59	45.53	234.30	238.80	324.07	325.09	628.16	300.10	241.97	288.42	351.74
Gansu	2.00	1.11	0.85	0.93	.035	11.95	87.76	63.92	90.02	41.44	38.64	41.04	62.35	74.39
Qinghai	2.70	NA	NA	NA	0.68	3.24	2.41	1.64	1.00	2.47	NA	4.59	NA	36.49
Ningxia	0.30	NA	0.25	0.18	3.52	11.90	7.27	3.90	5.55	6.71	18.56	51.34	17.41	16.80
Xinjiang	5.04	0.88	5.37	0.22	NA	53.00	48.30	54.90	63.90	24.72	21.67	24.04	19.11	20.35

Sources: Annual issues of *Almanac of China's Foreign Relations and Trade* (Hong Kong: China Resources Trade Consultancy Co., Ltd.): 1988, p. 594; 1989/90, p. 612; 1990/91, p. 554; 1991, p. 654; 1992: *Almanac of China's Foreign Economic Relations and Trade 1993/94*, pp. 723–24; 1993: *Almanac of China's Foreign Economic Relations and Trade 1994/95*, pp. 745–46; 1994: *Almanac of China's Foreign Economic Relations and Trade 1995/96*, pp. 763–64; 1995: *Almanac of China's Foreign Economic Relations and Trade 1996/97*, p. 780; 1996: *Zhongguo duiwai jingji maoyi nianjian 1997/98*, p. 609; 1997: *Zhongguo duiwai jingji maoyi nianjian 1998/99*, p. 630; 1998: *Almanac of China's Foreign Economic Relations and Trade 1999/2000*, pp. 701–02; 1999: *Zhongguo duiwai jingji maoyi nianjian 2000*, pp. 657–58; 2000–01: *China Statistical Yearbook* (Beijing: China Statistics Press, 2002).

Figures for 1985–92 are for utilized investment.

TABLE 8.4 *Direct Foreign Investment by Source, 1985–2001 (in Millions of U.S. $)*

YEAR	HONG KONG CONTRACTED	HONG KONG UTILIZED	JAPAN CONTRACTED	JAPAN UTILIZED	UNITED STATES CONTRACTED	UNITED STATES UTILIZED
1985	4,134.32	955.68	470.68	315.07	1152.02	357.19
1986	1,449.39	1,328.71	210.42	263.35	527.35	326.17
1987	1,946.61	1,598.21	301.36	219.70	342.19	262.80
1988	3,466.58	2,095.20	275.79	514.53	370.40	235.96
1989	3,159.66	2,077.59	438.61	356.34	640.52	284.27
1990	3,833.34	1,913.42	457.00	503.38	357.82	455.99
1991	7,215.10	2,486.87	812.20	532.50	548.08	323.20
1992	40,043.80	7,507.10	2,172.50	709.80	3,121.30	511.05
1993	73,938.52	17,274.75	2,960.47	1,324.10	6,812.75	2,063.12
1994	46,971.41	19,665.44	4,440.29	2,075.29	6,010.18	2,490.80
1995	40,995.55	20,060.37	7,592.36	3,108.46	7,471.13	3,083.01
1996	28,001.72	20,677.32	5,130.68	3,679.35	6,915.76	3,443.33
1997	18,222.29	20,632.00	3,401.24	4,326.47	4,936.55	3,239.15
1998	17,613.28	18,508.36	2,748.99	3,400.36	6,483.73	4,173.55
1999	13,328.92	16,363.05	2,591.28	2,973.08	6,016.11	4,215.86
2000	16,961.05	15,499.98	3,680.51	2,915.85	8,000.89	4,383.89
2001	20,685.86	16,717.30	5,419.73	4,348.42	7,514.87	4,433.22

Sources: *China Newsletter* 105 (July–August 1993), pp. 20–21; State Statistical Bureau of the People's Republic of China, *China Statistical Yearbook 1986* (Beijing: China Statistical Information and Consultancy Service), p. 500; *China Statistical Yearbook 1987*, p. 532; *China Statistical Yearbook 1988*, p. 734; *China Statistical Yearbook 1989*, p. 646; *China Statistical Yearbook 1991*, p. 568; *China Statistical Yearbook 1993*, p. 587; *Almanac of China's Foreign Relations and Trade 1993/94* (Hong Kong: China Resources Trade Consultancy Company, Ltd., 1994), p. 720; 1993, *Almanac of China's Foreign Economic Relations and Trade 1994/95*, pp. 742, 744, 747, 753; 1994, *Almanac of China's Foreign Economic Relations and Trade 1995/96*, pp. 758, 762, 765, 771; 1995, *Almanac of China's Foreign Economic Relations and Trade 1996/97*, pp. 771, 779, 781, 786; 1996: *Zhongguo duiwai jingji maoyi nianjian 1997/98*, pp. 606, 608, 610, 616; 1997: *Zhongguo duiwai jingji maoyi nianjian, 1998/99*, pp. 626, 629, 631, 634; 1998: *Almanac of China's Foreign Economic Relations and Trade 1999/2000*, pp. 705, 708, 709, 711; 1999: *Zhongguo duiwai jingji maoyi nianjian, 2000*, pp. 653, 654, 657, 659, 662; 2000–01: *China Statistical Data 2001/2002* (Beijing: All China Marketing Research Company, Ltd.).

In a process similar to that regarding FDI, China has over time fundamentally changed its views on foreign borrowing. All such borrowing was prohibited until the end of the Mao era. Early in the reforms, the PRC began to utilize buyers' credits. In 1981, it joined the World Bank and followed this with membership in the other major international financial institutions (IFIs), the most important of which were the IMF and the Asian Development Bank. It also began to seek and accept foreign aid, and by the late 1980s Japan had become its largest aid donor. Control over this foreign borrowing also gradually loosened. Initially, Beijing imposed tight controls on all such activities, and it has retained approval rights over all loans from IFIs and all foreign aid. But financial institutions and local governments in China gained the right to borrow funds from abroad directly, and many went on a borrowing binge in the 1990s. Foreign sources generally made such loans because they assumed Beijing would not allow these local institutions to default on their obligations. When the Guangdong Trust and Investment Corporation did default in the late 1990s and Beijing failed to come to its rescue, foreign lending sources began to make more careful assessments of lending risks in China. But Beijing's attitude is that the country is now basically open to accepting foreign credit.

Foreign-invested firms have played a significant role in expanding China's foreign trade. Many imports consist of intermediate products for such firms, and most such firms have exported at least a portion of their products. Partly as a consequence, China has shifted from having one of the lowest per capita foreign-trade volumes in the world to being one of the major trading countries in the world.

Other important measures also contributed to the expansion of foreign trade. China progressively reduced its tariffs so that by 2001 they were very low by developing-country standards. Over time, Beijing gradually expanded the array of Chinese firms that could engage in foreign trade and the channels they could use to do so. China also reduced nontariff trade barriers. WTO obligations will, moreover, further reduce tariffs, eliminate many nontariff trade barriers, and in other ways free up China's foreign-trade system considerably.[20]

China's foreign trade in constant dollars has increased at an average rate of nearly 15 percent per year since 1979, considerably faster than overall increases both in China's GDP and in world trade. It has, moreover, maintained a trade surplus since the 1980s (see Table 8.5). China's foreign trade is now a larger percentage of its GDP than is the case for other large continental countries such as India, Brazil, and the United States.

PLANNING

The system of national planning, with the planners directly administering the economy, has been gradually abandoned.[21] Initially, many items shifted from "mandatory" plans to "indicative" plans, and the number of items separately listed in the annual plan document fell dramatically over time. Indicative

TABLE 8.5 *GNP and Foreign Trade, 1978–2001 (in Billions of U.S. $)*

YEAR	GNP (Billions 1995 constant U.S. $)	EXPORTS	IMPORTS	TOTAL FOREIGN DEBT
1978	140.91	9.75	10.89	0.62
1980	163.44	18.12	20.02	4.50
1985	272.52	27.34	42.49	16.72
1990	398.41	62.09	53.35	52.55
1991	434.67	71.91	63.79	60.85
1992	495.96	84.94	80.59	69.32
1993	560.93	91.74	103.96	83.57
1994	631.60	121.01	115.62	92.81
1995	688.45	148.78	132.08	106.59
1996	755.91	151.05	138.83	116.28
1997	820.17	182.88	142.19	130.96
1998	884.14	183.59	140.31	146.04
1999	946.91	195.15	165.79	151.83
2000		249.21	225.10	145.73
2001		266.20	243.60	170.11

Sources: GNP, 1978–1999: World Bank, *World Development Indicators CD-ROM 2001.* Exports and imports, 1978–92: State Statistical Bureau of the People's Republic of China, *China Statistical Abstracts, 1993* (Beijing: Statistical Publishing House, 1993), p. 101; 1983–99, World Bank, *World Development Indicators CD-ROM 2001;* 2000, National Bureau of Statistics of China, *Statistical Communiqué of the P. R. China on the 2000 National Economic and Social Development (2000 guomin jingji he shehui fazhan tongji gongbao)*; 2001, National Bureau of Statistics of China, *Statistical Communiqué of the P. R. China on the 2001 National Economic and Social Development (2001 guomin jingji he shehui fazhan tongji gongbao).* Total foreign debts, 1978–92: Total foreign debt, 1978–84: World Bank, *World Tables 1994* (Baltimore: Johns Hopkins University Press, 1994), pp. 206–07. All figures save foreign debt for 1993: The Economist Intelligence Unit, *Country Report: China and North Korea* (London: second quarter, 1994), p. 4. 1993–99: *Finance Year Book of China, 2000* (Beijing: China Finance Publishing House, 2000), p. 511; 2000: *China: Facts & Figures 2001* (China Internet Information Center).

In 2001 the Chinese figure for their external debt for the first time includes short-term trade credits. Numbers for earlier years have not been revised.

plans meant that local authorities set specific targets; the Center would provide only broad-brush indications of the allocations it preferred. Through the mid-1980s the economy still operated overwhelmingly according to government-set plans, but the role of locales increased substantially in this process.[22]

Gradually, though, planners at all levels have reduced their direct administrative control over the economy. By the early 1990s, most small commodities for daily use were produced totally outside the planning system. Even many larger items were produced at the initiative of local authorities in order to satisfy local needs and larger markets.[23] In 1998 the State Planning Commission became the State Development Planning Commission, with a new role of doing studies for strategic economic efforts. In early 2003 this became the State Development Reform Commission. Today virtually no part of the Chinese economy, other than major state-initiated infra-structure projects, works according to a concrete national planning docu-ment. Indeed, in August 2002 China's NPC Standing Committee began considering the draft of a law that will, if adopted, clarify and substantially reduce the array of economic activities that requires government approval at all.[24]

PRICES

Under a planning system, prices are set administratively to suit the needs of the planners. Such prices do not necessarily bear any relationship to real sup-ply and demand, and thus they provide extremely poor guides to activities once a country has moved toward a market system. The pricing of coal, on which China depends for over 70 percent of its energy, illustrates the point.

During the 1950s, coal prices were set at levels that by the 1980s were well below the real costs of mining the coal. The more powerful metallurgical industry, for which coal is a key input, blocked all attempts by the coal indus-try to have the prices raised.

As China's reformers tried to shift toward greater reliance on market forces, they gradually moved away from state-fixed prices on coal in several ways. In the early 1980s, they permitted the rapid expansion of production by "local" coal mines—generally, poorly equipped mines operated by individuals or local authorities that produced low-quality coal for local consumption. Coal from these mines could sell at a higher price than the coal produced in the larger state mines that operated under the national plan.

Beijing then used its administrative power to raise the prices for some types of coal produced by the state mines. It also permitted provinces to sell a part of this coal on their own at higher prices. From the initial situation of hav-ing the vast majority of coal produced in state mines and sold at one fixed price, therefore, by the early 1990s a far more complex situation had devel-oped. About half of all coal output came from "local" mines and sold for market-driven prices. Provincial officials could sell part of the coal from state mines for a price that was influenced by market forces. The remainder of the coal from state mines, which was a shrinking proportion of overall produc-tion, sold at state-fixed prices.

But even for the portion of state coal that sold at a fixed price, further differences were introduced. Coal sold to state enterprises to support produc-tion of goods still on the national economic plan had to be sold at a quite low, state-determined price. Coal from the state mines sold to enterprises for pro-duction of items "off" the plan could sell at a considerably higher—albeit still state-determined—price.[25] By the mid-1990s, pricing for all coal production other than for coal used in power plants was liberalized, and government fix-ing of coal prices even for power plants ceased in 2001.

In broad terms, by the mid-1980s the state had set up a dual-price system for most major goods. That portion, if any, of an enterprise's output that was fixed on the economic plan would sell at a state-determined "plan" price, generally well below the market price for the item. The enterprise was rewarded by being guaranteed access to cheap inputs to produce its "planned" output. All production above the plan target could be sold at either a free-market price or within a price band set nearer a free-market level. This dual-system strategy sought to retain some controls while moving toward a free-market price system. Gradually, Beijing's leaders felt, the percentage of goods produced for the "above-plan" prices would grow, and thus the country would over time move to a market-based price system without suffering from the cataclysmic inflationary jolt that freeing up prices all at once would have produced.[26] This approach, however, left China with multiple prices for exactly the same items until state-fixed prices for the vast majority of commodities were abolished in 1992–93. The multiple-price situation created enticing opportunities for corruption for the better part of a decade.

As of 1992 the State Council's departments retained specific pricing authority over 141 goods and services. Changes in August of 2001 reduced this number to thirteen, primarily consisting of such sectors as water, electricity, and some aspects of transportation. In reality, the continuing existence of monopolies and other problems means that prices of many goods and services are still highly regulated—although not specifically fixed—by the state. But today roughly 90 percent of goods and services in China trade at other than state-mandated prices.[27]

BANKING

The reformers sought to change the banking system into a more flexible instrument of economic policy. Under the Maoist socialist system, the banks served merely as vehicles for economic transactions.[28] They did not impose real costs on capital, did not independently evaluate the economic prospects of potential borrowers, and often did not collect the loans they made. They simply provided a means of handling money and of keeping track of the flow of funds.

Changes in the banking system are intended to make the banks function more like their Western counterparts. Increasingly, for example, funds are supposed to be loaned out from banks on the basis of the economic returns that can be expected from the project borrowing the money. Banks try to attract funds through offering more realistic interest rates, although most interest rates are still heavily regulated by the Central Bank. Banks attempt to control investment, at least in part, by changing the interest rate structure. Since 1978, moreover, a number of specialized banks have been established to focus on the needs of particular economic sectors.

An important meeting of the CCP Central Committee in late 1993 called for basic restructuring of this system along the lines of slightly loosening the constraints on the People's Bank of China as the central bank; establishing three specialized "policy" banks (for policy loans, long-term investment, and rural development) that would direct funds to projects high on the leaders' priority list; and making all other banks function as real commercial banking enterprises responsible for their own profits and losses. Later on, Beijing restructured the regional branches of the banking system to reduce the influence of provincial leaders over bank decisions. And in the late 1990s the government formally stopped directing banks to allocate the major portion of their loans to SOEs, although other forces have in reality kept the proportion of loans to SOEs far higher than the economic fundamentals of China would warrant.

The overall real changes in the banking system, however, remain relatively modest. There is still no independent central bank. Rather, the People's Bank of China (nominally the central bank) is headed by a government minister and subject to the dictates of the national political leadership. Moreover, the structure of power at local levels has often made it very difficult for local banks to make loans only to projects and activities that promise a reasonable return on the money. Therefore, although the banking system moved in the direction of becoming a key vehicle for deciding how to allocate capital efficiently, it did not achieve the degree of independence from the political system necessary for it to play this role effectively.[29]

Results

The above selective overview indicates some of the ways in which the economy has changed since 1978. The commune system in agriculture gave way to the family-based "responsibility system," and land has increasingly become a commodity. China has shifted from its Mao-era economic isolationism to a desire to be involved in the international market and to combine its vast labor supply with foreign investment to sustain growth. The system of central planning gave way to indicative planning, which in turn has yielded increasingly to market allocation of goods and services. The practice of fixing prices administratively for all goods was replaced first by a dual-price system for many items and then by a market-based system for the vast majority of products. The fiscal system has been changed, strengthened, and institutionalized. The banking system, once a vehicle simply to reallocate funds according to policy and plan directives, is itself beginning to concentrate capital and make decisions on its allocation.

These interactive changes, taken together, have profoundly affected the way the Chinese economic system works. Generally, they have produced the types of results the leaders have desired. Most fundamental, China's overall economic growth averaged about 9 percent per year in real terms from 1978 through 2002, giving the PRC the fastest-growing major industrial economy in the world over this entire period. This overall economic growth has stayed far ahead of population increase and has produced real improvements in the standard of living for most citizens. This is an impressive record, especially because it was achieved during a period when the national leaders were forcing significant changes in the way the economic system operates.

Almost every year, China's foreign trade grew at an even faster rate than did its GNP, reflecting the steadily increasing extent to which the PRC's economy is effectively integrating itself into the global economy (see Table 8.5). The PRC maintained a healthy trade surplus and built up foreign exchange reserves that are among the largest in the world. Since 1992, moreover, China has led all developing countries as a target for foreign direct investment. Even though much of this comes from locales (Hong Kong and Taiwan) that the PRC formally considers to be part of the country, the record is still extremely impressive. China has transformed itself from near irrelevance to the world economy at the start of the reforms to being a major international economic player less than a quarter century later.

Beijing has also successfully energized both officials and ordinary citizens to seek maximum economic growth. The Maoist focus on egalitarianism and the virtues of poverty has been trampled under a rush to riches. Leading government officials at all political levels devote enormous energy to trying to develop additional ways to increase the size of the economy in their jurisdictions. Opinion surveys make clear that improvements in income and standard of living are among the very highest goals of most ordinary Chinese. The spirit of entrepreneurship, beaten down during the Mao years, is again very vibrant on the Chinese mainland.

In sum, Beijing has done a remarkably effective job of meeting the core goals of the reform effort: maintaining overall political stability while moving from a planned toward a market system, with all the related changes in institutions and regulations, and in the process greatly increasing economic output, foreign trade, and foreign direct investment. That this took place while the Soviet Union and the Soviet bloc collapsed is all the more impressive.

But not all is well. The strategies for pursuing economic reform have had notable effects that temper the major successes. Three fundamental elements in the reform strategy have proven particularly consequential: the determination of reform leaders to structure changes so that they would maintain the support of large numbers of officials; the adoption of an approach that included intrabureaucratic negotiations of special deals for different sectors and locales; and the strategic decision to implement decentralization in order to encourage entrepreneurship by provincial and lower-level officials. These strategies smoothed the way for reforms and helped to maintain political stability during the reform process, but also contributed greatly to some of the most pressing issues that China now confronts.

Despite the reforms to date, China is not yet close to having a fully market-driven economy. Special deals and the desire to keep officials on board have produced system in which leaders at all levels still retain enormous capacity to intervene in the economy and in the activities of individual enterprises. Although detailed mandatory planning is dead, official interference in economic activities remains pervasive. This is such a significant aspect of the current economic landscape that it is more accurate to think of China as having developed a "negotiated" economy than a market economy. A "negotiated" economy means that in many instances officials' decisions, more than the pure play of market forces, shape enterprises' outcomes.

The enormous power of officials over economic decisions has had serious consequences. It has, of course, provided fertile ground for corruption, as leaders make determinations that affect significant economic outcomes. Beijing has taken numerous steps to reduce corruption. It has eliminated the dual-price system that emerged in the 1980s that had encouraged corruption through price arbitrage. It has developed various types of auditing and other systems to reduce the opportunities for corruption.[30] And it has imposed very severe punishments, including execution, in selected cases of corrupt behavior. At times, these punishments have reached to near the very top of the political system.

But corruption remains pervasive, large scale, and systemic. In the cities of Xiamen and Shenyang, notably, criminal gangs effectively subverted whole segments of the municipal administration. Multiyear investigations involving hundreds of individuals produced wholesale changes in each city's power structure, along with attendant suicides and executions. In the case of Xiamen, the city administration was so thoroughly corrupt that a major part of the investigation had to be run from Beijing to prevent local police from tipping off officials as to what the investigators had learned.

Corruption stretches to the top of the system, although in the very few instances when a key central leader has fallen, corruption has served more as an excuse than as the precipitating cause. The highest-level purge for corruption, for example, caught the Beijing Party Secretary and Politburo Standing Committee member Chen Xitong. But the real impetus behind Chen's purge appears to have been a power struggle between Jiang Zemin and Chen, with the massive corruption in the Beijing municipal apparatus providing a convenient excuse to remove Chen from power. As noted above, officials at middle and lower levels of the system indicate that it will be impossible to clean up corruption there until such activities at the top are eliminated.

Officials also use their power to maximize growth of their own locales. One approach is to adopt protectionist measures in order to nurture local industry. Shanghai Municipality, for example, adopted technical standards for its taxis that eliminate all cars other than those produced in a joint venture by the Shanghai Automotive Industry Corporation. This type of protectionism has had the effect of creating major internal trade barriers in China. One result is that many Chinese firms cannot hope to achieve real economies of scale and become globally competitive. In addition to problems in the transportation infrastructure, companies also incur very high costs in paying tolls as goods cross administrative boundaries. It is, therefore, very difficult to develop regionwide or nationwide capacity. A related outcome is the duplication of production facilities in various part of the country. China has, for example, well over one hundred automotive assembly plants, most of which produce only a few thousand cars apiece per year. Local officials have successfully resisted all attempts by Beijing to consolidate this key industry into a few major assemblers.

The focus on maximizing growth within one's own locale also leads officials to seek special favors and exemptions from national regulations. Intrabureaucratic bargaining to obtain such dispensations has become a major element in the evolution of China's regulatory system.[31] As a result, specific policies gave certain east-coast locales a far greater boost than location and other qualities alone could provide. Especially during the 1980s, Guangdong, for example, enjoyed a very favorable tax environment, along with other unique concessions, in order to attract capital and expertise from Hong Kong. When Zhao Ziyang, who had deep career ties to Guangdong, fell in 1989 and was replaced by the Shanghai-based Jiang Zemin, the Center increasingly supported Shanghai's rapid development with funds and special policy concessions. Guangdong's annual GDP growth rate increased from 12.8 percent in the 1980s to 14.6 percent in the 1990s, while the comparable climb for Shanghai was all the way from 7.4 percent in the 1980s to 12.2 percent in the 1990s.[32] Those areas that have won permission to create special economic and development zones have fared better, on the whole, than did others.

The overall result is that the regulatory regime actually changes by locality and by product or service line to the point where the entire country is a complex puzzle of different regulatory pieces. Varying local interpretations of national rules add even more inconsistency, especially as local courts typically bend to the political will of local officials on cases that engage the latter's interests. China therefore has overall developed a large market, but in most cases that market is fragmented, and economies of scale are very difficult to achieve. Those who seek regional or national operations must often invest time and money to set up essentially duplicate facilities in each major locale in which they want to market their products and services. Efficiency and competitiveness are casualties of this on-the-ground reality.

The weak court system and ongoing official interference in the economy have also resulted in a very poor level of protection of physical and intellectual property rights. Producers often find that pirates steal their technologies and products. Officials in the locales where the pirates set up their production operations typically protect the pirates, who provide sources of additional employment and taxes (and, presumably, bribes). Despite strong laws to protect intellectual property, the local courts rarely have either the expertise or the political independence effectively to put a stop to these piracy operations.

Notwithstanding many measures to make SOEs perform more like real enterprises, moreover, the property rights of these firms are generally ill defined and easily compromised. SOEs that perform well are often required to absorb those that are in trouble. Various official units may claim control over different parts of an SOE, to the point where nobody clearly understands where ownership lies. This creates a situation in which both restructuring SOEs to achieve better outcomes and selling equity shares in SOEs to raise capital become problematic.

Political attention to SOEs distorts other major dimensions of the economy. For example, even though SOEs are less competitive than many firms in the private sector, typically only SOEs are approved for listing on the country's two stock exchanges, in Shanghai and Shenzhen. This directs the capital that flows through these exchanges to one of the least productive sectors of the economy. In addition, the government retains roughly two thirds of the shares of the SOEs. Through the Large Scale Enterprise Work Committee, the CCP (possibly now shifting to the new State Property Supervision and Management Commission) exercises its power to appoint the top leaders of major SOEs. As a consequence, stock-exchange listings provide no vehicle for investors to discipline SOEs and force improvements in their performance. The Shanghai and Shenzhen exchanges thus cannot give liquidity and discipline to newly emerging, dynamic sectors of the economy.

The political attention to SOEs also severely affects the banking system. Until recent years, banks were required to lend according to a credit plan that directed roughly 70 percent of lending to SOEs. This structure of lending meant that most SOEs could count on sufficient funds to keep operations going even if their personnel's business skills were very low and profits nonexistent. Not surprisingly, the banks ran up very large portfolios of nonperforming loans. Recently the credit plan has been dropped, and the state established Asset Management Companies to take roughly 25 percent of the banks' bad debt off their hands. But most lending by the state-owned major commercial banks still goes to SOEs. This seems to result from a combination of habit, ease, and the reality that bankers will encounter less political trouble for bad loans to SOEs than they will for such loans to the private sector.

This combination of circumstances has created a banking system that is effectively bankrupt. Citizens continue to pour large amounts of savings into the banking system because they lack other places to put their money and they believe that the central government will prevent any of the major banks from failing. But this is creating a vicious cycle: scarce capital is put into the banking system, which channels the bulk of it to the worst-performing sector of the economy while starving more dynamic sectors for credit. The large nonperforming loan portion of the banks' portfolios in turn makes them more cautious about lending overall, and this affects overall credit availability.

The banking and SOE problems are thus tightly linked, and both reflect continuing large-scale interference in the economy by government officials. Because of official interference, SOEs are not led by the most competent entrepreneurs, they lack clear title to their property, and they are not disciplined by the financial markets. Therefore, on the whole they perform poorly, despite many reform measures. The banks are afraid to lend primarily to the private sector, yet the SOEs are generally incapable of using bank loans effectively to expand the economy and pay their debts. It will take major infusions of funds to rectify the situation in both the banks and the SOEs, but such infusions are unlikely to produce the desired results unless fundamental changes occur in the degree and modalities of government intervention in the economy. Officials have in recent years sanctioned the sale of many medium-size and smaller SOEs, with attendant layoffs of a large portion of their labor forces. But this has simply removed many problematic firms from the SOE stable. It has not turned around the major firms in the state sector that absorb most investment capital and employ a major portion of the labor force. Today, China's one hundred largest firms are still all SOEs.

On a broader scale, political constraints prevent a market-driven distribution of China's overall work force. At the end of 2002, roughly half of China's laborers worked in agriculture, over 27 percent in services, and about 22 percent in industry. But agriculture contributes less than 11 percent to the total value of output, whereas services contribute roughly a third and industry contributes over 55 percent. There is thus a huge disjuncture in the value of output per worker. Surveys in China's major cities find, moreover, that there is significant pent-up demand for expansion of the service sector.

Given these parameters, we should expect very large-scale movement from rural to urban areas. This has, in fact, been taking place, with the urban population percentage growing from 31 percent to over 37 percent from 1999 to 2001. But the still-extant politically imposed *hukou* system of residence registration both restricts the flow of peasants into cities and constrains the types of activities they can engage in once they have made this move, creating major obstacles to achieving a better allocation of labor in China's population.[33]

Preparations are under way to abolish the *hukou* system by 2013, but this is a very complex task. For example, Jinan, the capital city of Shandong province, decided in the summer of 2002 to eliminate the *hukou* system as it applies to all residents of the rural counties under Jinan's administrative jurisdiction, hereafter treating all such individuals simply as "Jinan municipal residents." Jinan is also eliminating *hukou* distinctions among in-migrants to the city from other areas. But the *hukou* designation as a peasant will still be stamped in the documents of Jinan peasants with a land contract in one of Jinan's counties who go to some location outside Jinan's administrative purview. Otherwise, the new Jinan system could not mesh with the requirements governing other parts of the country.[34] Fully eliminating the *hukou* system will be a protracted, complex process that will play out in China's smaller and medium-size cities before it applies to most major metropolises. During this long transition, residence restrictions will continue to distort the nation's overall allocation of labor.

China's economy has undergone massive changes and achieved remarkable growth. But China remains very much in the midst of the transition from plan to market, having by now substituted a "negotiated" economy for the previous planned and administered economy. This intermediate phase involves wrenching difficulties, as unemployment due to shutting down small and medium SOEs soars, peasants increasingly cannot improve their lot through agricultural production, and both social and geographical inequality rapidly increase. During this time, by far the most rapidly growing sector in China has been the private sector, but it remains starved for funds and highly vulnerable to predatory behavior by local officials. The domestic market as a whole, moreover, has remained quite protected by a combination of nontariff barriers and requirements that most foreign-invested firms export a large percentage of their products.

The party is allowing people to carve out a nonpolitical sphere of life and to develop a consumer culture, but in the name of stability it insists on retaining the capacity to interfere in all aspects of economic activity. This interference in turn sets in motion many dynamics that prevent China from realizing the full benefits of a large internal market and the efficiency and competitiveness that market forces encourage. Despite massive imports of technology, capital, and management expertise, China thus has failed to develop manufacturing and service sector enterprises that have achieved international competitiveness on any basis other than cheap labor. Only a few completely indigenous Chinese firms have achieved the dynamic efficiency necessary to compete abroad.[35] Reformers recognize these drawbacks, and many have concluded that China will not be able to compete effectively in the international economy over the long run unless it makes major additional changes in order to create a more fully market-driven economy.

Looking Ahead

Dynamic economic growth will remain key to China's future. The government will need to commit massive funds to cope with the combined problems of dealing with domestic debt, rehabilitating the banking system, restructuring the SOEs, addressing critical environmental issues such as the water shortage in North China discussed in Chapter 9, establishing a social safety net, and making local governments whole financially. All of this will take place, moreover, during an ongoing migration of tens of millions of farmers off the land.

China's economy has experienced a steady decline in its rate of economic growth in recent years, from a high of over 13 percent in 1994 to a low of under 8 percent in 2001.[36] This slowing rate of economic growth reflects the ongoing failure to maximize efficiencies because China still must traverse considerable ground in the transition to a market-driven economy. Key reformers have been stymied by the political difficulties involved in further separating government and party officials from control over economic activities.

The largest overall effort to change the economy over the coming decade revolves around China's implementation of its World Trade Organization accession obligations. Beijing had negotiated for entry into the WTO for nearly fifteen years. In 2001, it finally agreed to an accession package that requires potentially very wide-ranging changes in the way the domestic economy functions.

The WTO is itself an *international trade* organization. However, its demands for China's entry require such significant changes that Beijing's leading reformers accepted this accession package partly as a vehicle for pushing through reforms that they otherwise lacked the political leverage to bring about. By being able to point to formal international obligations, the reformers seek to move the domestic economy in distinctly new directions. In the process, they believe China will be well positioned to take advantage of the opportunities potentially afforded by increasing global economic interdependence.

China's fundamental commitments under its WTO accession accord broadly require:

☐ Reductions in tariffs and in nontariff barriers

☐ National treatment, that is, dropping rules that discriminate against foreign enterprises

☐ Expanding the array of economic segments in which foreigners can invest and operate and also expanding the permissible geographical scope of foreign economic activities

☐ Creating transparency in the policy process and rules and regulations on issues that can affect foreign trade

☐ Increasing protection for trade-related intellectual property rights[37]

The WTO accession accord was negotiated by the top levels of the political system—specifically, by the leaders of the Ministry of Foreign Trade and Economic Cooperation, with the supervision and final approval of Zhu Rongji and Jiang Zemin. Yet this agreement has consequences for officials at all levels of the political system, potentially deeply affecting the distribution of winners and losers. When China formally entered the WTO in December 2001, no full Chinese translation of the entire accession accord had been completed. The key officials were briefed on the accord's obligations and its implications only over the course of the twelve months or so following accession.

China's leaders see several potential benefits from WTO implementation. It will, they believe, vastly increase the amount of foreign direct investment that pours into the country and solidify China's role as the manufacturing center of Asia. It will also, they hope, decrease the chances that China's growing exports will provoke protectionist measures elsewhere, such as those Japan encountered in the 1980s in the wake of a prolonged streak of rapid export growth. It will bring in financial services that should help China utilize its scarce capital more efficiently, and in the process it will make more funding available to the most dynamic part of the Chinese economy, the private sector. It should also help to expand jobs in the service sector, which is viewed as a major potential source of new employment at a time when unemployment is viewed as a potentially destabilizing issue.

Perhaps most fundamentally, the key reformers in Beijing at the time of WTO accession viewed the agreement as opening China's domestic economy up to significantly increased foreign competition. As of early 2003, despite the trade growth and FDI that had poured in over a number of years, the domestic economy as a whole remained substantially fragmented and protected. This is one key reason why, even after about a quarter century of reform efforts, almost no wholly Chinese firms in the manufacturing and service sectors had become internationally competitive on any basis other than cheap labor. But China's reformers believe that over the long term the country must begin to move up the ladder to higher value-added capabilities.

Today, the majority of Chinese manufacturing exports consists of products assembled in China largely from components made elsewhere. The value-added ratio in these processed exports has, however, increased significantly in recent years. It averaged less than 20 percent in 1993 and 1994 but exceeded 35 percent in 2001. This suggests the development of backward linkages from processing firms to other firms that are increasingly producing the parts and components that were previously imported.[38] The future challenge is to be able to produce internationally competitive products that are not made by foreign-invested firms or firms producing on foreign license.

Foreign competition in China's domestic market, along with WTO-mandated rules forbidding many types of subsidies, will force numerous Chinese firms to become more competitive or die. Foreign banking and insurance services will help create the financial wherewithal and know-how to promote development of efficient Chinese firms, especially in the private sector. Foreign access to China's agricultural markets should also force changes in crops grown so that China takes greater advantage of its comparative advantages in labor-intensive cultivation and puts less emphasis on land-intensive grains.

All of these changes should increase the efficiency with which China uses its resources, but they will also prove unsettling, with many major social tensions and transitions in the labor force. For example, people in their teens and twenties in the major east-coast cities should find an array of career opportunities open to them that is wider and more rewarding than any their predecessors enjoyed. But workers in their mid-forties and older are more likely to encounter an accelerated loss of job security without an adequate social safety net to catch them when they fail to find new employment at close to their previous levels of compensation. Overall, there will be enormous churning in the labor force, with much attendant tension.

In agriculture, many of the east-coast cultivators are moving into higher value-added areas, such as producing cut flowers or mushrooms for export. Those in China's far west are unlikely to feel major pressures because they largely consume their own agricultural production and are too poor to change their eating habits. They still live largely outside of the national agricultural market. But the vast numbers of peasants in central and northeast China may be negatively affected, as wheat, corn and soybeans from abroad compete with the crops they raise for China's markets. Grain producers are already suffering from low market prices, and foreign products will increase the downward pressures.

The net effect of the WTO in the agricultural sector should be not only more efficient use of China's scarce arable land but also more rapid movement of people off the land to nonagricultural jobs. But this in turn will increase job competition at the low end of the work force in the cities and will also exacerbate the problems of developing and funding an adequate urban social safety net. As in other sectors, the WTO impact in agriculture will increase long-run output and efficiencies but will very possibly produce unsettling shorter-run pain.

In sum, China is both basking in the glow of its rapid transition from a largely autarkic, low-income country to a serious participant in the world economy that delivers a vastly higher standard of living to the bulk of its own citizens. The fact that it has made this transition without political upheavals greater than those of 1989, moreover, is a remarkable achievement.

But enormous challenges face the PRC's economy in the immediate future. Some of these—such as restructuring the banking system to reduce the portfolio of nonperforming loans, developing an urban social safety net, developing new funding sources for county and township governments, and addressing major environmental constraints—essentially require Beijing to begin to allocate hundreds of billions of dollars and focus high-level attention on problems that had been put off since the late 1990s in order to maintain

TABLE 8.6 *National Budget Deficits, 1979–2001 (in Billions of Chinese* Yuan*)*

YEAR	DEFICIT
1979	−13.54
1980	−6.89
1985	0.06
1990	−14.65
1991	−23.71
1992	−25.88
1993	−29.34
1994	−57.45
1995	−58.15
1996	−52.96
1997	−58.25
1998	−92.22
1999	−174.36
2000	−229.9
2001	−247.3

Sources: 1979–90, State Statistical Bureau of the People's Republic of China, *China Statistical Yearbook, 1991* (Beijing: China Statistical Information and Consultancy Service, 1991), p. 183; 1991–92, International Monetary Fund, *International Financial Statistics* 46 (July–August 1993), p. 162; 1993–99, National Bureau of Statistics of China, *Statistical Yearbook of China 2000* (Beijing: China Statistics Press, 2000); 2000, National Bureau of Statistics of China, *Statistical Communiqué of the P. R. China on the 2000 National Economic and Social Development (2000 guomin jingji he shehui fazhan tongji gongbao)*; 2001, National Bureau of Statistics of China, *Statistical Communiqué of the P. R. China on the 2001 National Economic and Social Development (2001 guomin jingji he shehui fazhan tongji gongbao).*
Domestic and foreign debts are excluded from this table.

rapid growth. The required expenditures are of a magnitude great enough to have a negative effect on short-term economic growth, and they will be much more difficult to bear if substantial growth cannot be maintained. This set of challenges is especially stark in view of the country's rapidly rising annual budget deficits (see Table 8.6).

In this context, the added pressures created by measures to implement China's WTO agreement will increase the general level of social tension and, possibly, political infighting. Despite its seeming economic robustness and outward confidence, China's economy and politics face a potentially very difficult and dangerous period. The social dynamics, environmental constraints, and transnational issues that will shape Beijing's ability to navigate these underlying economic shoals successfully are the subjects of the following chapters.

9

The Environment

One of the major challenges China faces currently is the decline of its environment. Such factors as a large population, rapid economic growth, and limited natural resources combine to spell severe environmental trouble for the PRC. China now has more extensive environmental degradation, for example, than did today's industrialized countries at comparable stages in their economic development.[1] How the PRC manages the tensions between maximizing growth and protecting the environment in the long run to achieve what is termed "sustainable development" will have major consequences both for the citizens of China and, in some dimensions, for the global community. China has already become the second largest producer of greenhouse gases (the gases that contribute to global warming), after the United States, in the world.[2]

Gaining control over China's environmental problems will require Beijing's concentrated attention and the commitment of massive funds. Unfortunately, the science of environmental protection is not very precise. The interactions of the many processes that contribute to various environmental phenomena are extremely complex, and the effects of changing one or several of these processes are often impossible to determine. In China as elsewhere, it is difficult to persuade political leaders to commit resources where uncertainty clouds the scientific picture.

Concerns about human health might spur environmental initiatives, but the consequences of environmental degradation on human health have been the subject of much debate. For example, the rates of suspended particulate matter in China's air have been shown to be very high. The World Health Organization considers 60 to 90 micrograms per cubic meter (mcg/m^3) of suspended particulate matter an acceptable range. The average total of suspended particulate matter in China's large cities in 1995 was about 400 mcg/m^3, down from 700 a decade earlier but still far above safe levels.[3] These are among the highest readings in the world.[4] International environmental monitoring of Guangzhou and Shanghai from 1981 to 1989 never found a mean value per year as low as 90 mcg/m^3. The figure never dipped below 220 mcg/m^3 for Beijing, Shenyang, and Xi'an.[5] This almost certainly bears some relation to the incidence of pulmonary disease. Chronic obstructive respiratory disease is the leading cause of death in China and occurs at a rate more than twice the average for developing countries as a whole. Urban air pollution as of 1995 was conservatively estimated to cause 178,000 premature deaths a year, with indoor air pollution adding another 111,000 to this grisly annual toll.[6]

But though the increasing rates of death from chronic pulmonary disease do correspond with increasing levels of suspended particulate matter in the air, they probably also result to some extent from increased use of tobacco products over a longer period of time by a wealthier population that is growing older because of basic improvements in the health-delivery system and diet. The actual extent of each contribution to the outcome—and the interaction among the various causes—requires considerable additional study.

Not only does controversy rage about what ill effects may be attributed to environmental degradation, and how widespread those effects may be, but expensive measures to remedy environmental insults are often politically unattractive because they pay off only over the long term, at best. Few leaders in any country are willing to depress current standards of living to benefit their successors. This is especially true when popular attitudes do not consistently give highest priority to environmental issues. Such is the case in China.

Many environmental issues are, thus, politically difficult to manage. The underlying science contains large gray areas, remedies are uncertain and expensive, payoffs are long term, and—to add to the difficulties—the problems often do not fall neatly within existing political jurisdictions. Despite much rhetoric on the subject, on a worldwide level few governments, especially in developing countries, have acted preemptively to head off environmental insults or have developed rigorous, comprehensive programs to reverse environmental degradation.

Given these difficulties, why look at the PRC's environmental situation? Because conditions in China have in many regards reached a critical stage.

Vast populated areas are desperately short of water. Water is so scarce in north China that the government has decided to build what has been described as "the greatest feat of civil engineering since the Great Wall" at a cost budgeted at $24 billion to bring water from central China to the north.[7] Without such a project and related conservation measures, Beijing itself will become severely disrupted by water scarcity by 2010. Deserts are spreading, old-growth forest cover is being destroyed, cancer and lung disease are increasing, and significant parts of the country may deteriorate environmentally to the point where millions will be forced to go elsewhere to earn a living.

Water scarcities and pollution, loss of arable land, and other environmental challenges are imposing a significant direct cost on China's economic growth. Estimates of the damage vary. The World Bank concludes that environmental degradation in 1997 cost China over $60 billion annually, close to 8 percent of GDP. Professor Vaclav Smil concludes that the real 1997 figure was closer to 18 percent of GDP.[8] Even the lower World Bank estimate means environmental costs of roughly the same magnitude as China's enormous GDP growth. Given the PRC's political dependence on rapid economic growth to maintain social stability, these unsettling figures can have major consequences for the international community. Unfortunately, the structure and dynamics of China's political system pose serious obstacles to its dealing fully with these environmental problems.

Environmental Problems Originating before 1978

The PRC currently suffers from major environmental problems along two axes: the availability and distribution of natural resources, and effects of the political economy created after 1949. Each of these facets warrants brief consideration.

NATURAL RESOURCE ENDOWMENTS

Although the PRC is 2 percent larger in area than the United States, its per capita availability of productive land is modest by world standards. Fully 20 percent of the country consists of mountains, and huge deserts claim much of the rest. China is usefully seen as divided into three major topographical regions: the northwest, which is arid and suffers from wind erosion; the southwest, which is cold and contains high plateaus and some of the world's tallest peaks; and the east, with extensive rivers that have created valleys and alluvial plains.[9] About 95 percent of China's nearly 1.2 billion people live in this eastern region, which constitutes a little more than half of the land area of the entire country.

Given this topography, it is not surprising that China has relatively little useful terrain. With some 22 percent of the globe's population, the PRC contains only 7 percent of the world's arable land. Per capita, it has less than 30 percent of the worldwide average of croplands, less than half the average of grasslands, about 15 percent of the average of forest cover, and about 17 percent of the average of wilderness areas.[10]

The pressure exerted on these small areas by China's large population is great. Every available inch is cleared for cultivation, housing, and other human uses, as the country struggles to feed a population whose expectations about diet are rising with its average income and its exposure through the media to living standards elsewhere. The results of this population pressure are starkly evident in major areas of the country. For example:

☐ The loess region of north China's Shanxi Province has seen its population more than double since 1949, and intensive cultivation there has totally removed the ground cover and accelerated erosion to the point where 30 to 50 percent of the land, scarred by deep gullies and ravines, is unusable.

☐ The hills in the red-soil region of south China's Guangxi Province have been deforested and cultivated, resulting in siltation that has reduced the irrigation system to 30 percent of its capacity, and severely depleted the upland soils.

☐ The mountains of southwest China's Sichuan Province have been substantially deforested, releasing large quantities of silt into the Yangtze River, vastly increasing the danger of flooding in the densely populated central China region and greatly complicating efforts to harness the river for hydropower.

☐ The country's major lakes are being filled in to expand the availability of arable land, so that huge lakes such as Taihu in east China and Dongting in central China have lost about half their water surface area since 1949.

☐ Wetlands along the coast are being drained and planted to the extent that within a matter of years they may be totally eliminated, along with the pollution-control, fish-spawning, and biodiversity contributions they make.

China also suffers from maldistribution of its natural resources. The energy and water situations are emblematic in this regard. As mentioned earlier most of the country's population lives in the east, where most of its industry is also concentrated.

China has natural gas, but not in sufficient quantities to make it a major source of energy. In addition, the largest proven gas reserves are in Sichuan Province, far away from the centers of industry.

The fact that the country's topography generally slopes down from west to east, from the high Himalayas and Pamirs to the coast of the East China Sea, creates substantial hydropower potential. But the major changes in altitude occur before the topography flattens out in the eastern half of the country. The bulk of hydropower potential therefore is located in the mountainous regions of southwest China, far from the country's major consumers of electricity. Hydropower, in any case, requires dam construction that may severely damage the environment, as debates over the huge Three Gorges Dam on the Yangtze have shown.[11] In addition, deforestation in the southwest has increased the silt content of the major rivers and vastly complicated the prospect of hydropower development.

The country's weather and population distribution also diminish solar power potential. The sunny western desert areas are sparsely populated, whereas much of the eastern part of the country usually has many days of cloud cover. High concentrations of suspended particulate matter in the air of the eastern sections further diminish solar-power potential, especially near the major industrial cities where power needs are greatest.

Finally, China has modest oil reserves with its major East China fields well past their peak production. The PRC is rapidly increasing oil imports. Locational issues mean that for now and a long time into the future coal will provide the basic source of fuel for China.[12] Over 60 percent of the country's energy consumption comes from burning coal. Coal is used extensively for household cooking and heating, as well as for electricity and industrial power production. Burning coal is relatively harmful to the environment, and much of China's coal has a high sulfur content, which adds to the damage it does. Nevertheless, China's basic distribution of energy resources dictates that it will rely on coal as its major source of power.[13]

China overall has less than one third of the average global per capita water resources, a condition exacerbated by very uneven distribution within the country. Considering only the more densely populated eastern half of the country, northern China has only one fifth of the per capita water resources of southern China.[14]

Moreover, the water table in north China as a whole declines by about three feet per year, as river systems and aquifers are drained at an unsustainable rate. In Beijing Municipality itself the water table has for decades dropped by more than six feet per year. The overall result is that future growth and well-being throughout north China are severely constrained in the absence of major efforts to utilize water more efficiently and to provide additional water resources to the region.

MAOISM AND THE ENVIRONMENT

The nature of the political system established in 1949 has in some ways aggravated the country's environmental problems. On balance, the Maoist system contributed in several dimensions to the damage the Chinese environment has suffered.[15]

Maoist China placed primary stress on development of heavy industry as a means to achieve great-power status. Heavy industry in general consumes more resources per unit of output than does light industry. Mao invested state funds in heavy industrial development even more than did Stalin during the Soviet forced industrialization of the 1930s.[16] During the First Five-Year Plan of 1953–57, for example, 80 percent of state investment went into industry, and 80 percent of this industrial investment went into development of heavy industry.

In giving priority to heavy industry development, the PRC under Mao created a system of strong industrial ministries and central planning. Each of these powerful central organs stressed physical output targets. Environmental repercussions received no attention. (To be fair, the Western industrialized countries generally became environmentally conscious only in the 1960s.) In addition, each ministry looked to its own interests and paid little if any attention to the externalities—that is, the effects on other issues—of its decisions.[17] As a result, decisions that made sense strictly in terms of developing a particular industry often had very harmful environmental effects on major population centers.

For example, the industrial ministries and the State Planning Commission did not consider the environmental consequences of where they built new plants. As a consequence, heavily polluting steel and chemical industries were developed in Beijing's suburbs to the west and north—precisely the directions from which the Gobi Desert's winds wash over the most populated areas of the city. In Shanghai, the city's major effluent discharge pipe was placed right alongside the major intake pipe that provided the bulk of the city's water supply. This may have been the result of having different bureaucratic departments take charge of the supply of water to the city on the one hand and of disposal of waste water on the other hand. In any case, this situation went uncorrected until a foreign expert noticed the problem in the 1980s.[18]

The Maoist system of administered prices consistently undervalued basic natural-resource inputs such as coal and water, while overvaluing the industrial products produced. This fundamental approach encouraged factory managers and consumers to be profligate in their use of natural resources.

In addition, like those under all Stalinist-type systems, industrial enterprise managers under the Maoist system were motivated to meet the physical output targets specified in their production plans, but they had virtually no incentives to increase efficiency through technological upgrading, thereby producing more products with fewer inputs. Without the competition generated by market forces and without a national political leadership sensitive to environmental concerns, there was little consideration of preservation of resources at the level of the production enterprise. The resulting industrial system contained deep structural biases against environmental factors.

Development efforts in the countryside also wreaked environmental havoc. Perhaps the most devastating was the series of initiatives bound up with the Great Leap Forward. The water conservancy campaign during the winter of 1957–58, for example, mobilized peasants to dig new wells on a massive scale. This was done without thought for groundwater levels, potential capillary action, and future salinization of soils. Since this campaign, the water table on the north China plain has been dropping precipitously, and extensive salinization of soils has occurred. The resulting zones of ground depression now cover an area as large as Hungary. As noted above, the groundwater level in the Beijing area drops nearly six feet per year.[19]

Other campaigns forced the peasants to bring every possible inch of land under cultivation. Especially during the Cultural Revolution, this resulted in extensive terracing of marginal lands and reclamation of poor-quality spaces. The efforts during the 1960s and 1970s to make each region of the country self-sufficient in grains to better prepare for a prolonged war produced the conversion of many grasslands to cultivated fields. In many instances, these efforts damaged the land to the point where its productivity has declined, soil erosion has increased, and extensive work is now required simply to restore the previous situation.

Indirectly, the fact that Mao's economic strategy kept the countryside poor also contributed to environmental damage. Obtaining adequate fuel is one of the major problems Chinese peasants confront. Most peasants, where possible, resort to gleaning forest floors for twigs, leaves, and other combustibles for cooking and heating. Such activities reduce the quality of forests by preventing the cycles of decay and nourishment of the soil that would normally occur. Peasant incentives to cut down forests and overwork land to alleviate their poverty are also high.

Not all aspects of the Maoist system were inimical to the environment, however. Generally speaking, urban dwellers consume more resources and contribute more pollution to the environment than do rural residents. China's rigorous post-1961 efforts to curtail urbanization thus had the unintended side effect of saving the country from some environmental damage. Mao's policies of very low personal consumption also produced an ethos of conserving materials in a fashion that had even urban residents doing relatively little damage to the environment. The prohibition on private cars similarly reduced potential environmental insults. In addition, Maoist China devoted some efforts consciously to environmental rehabilitation, such as frequent afforestation campaigns. China had lost much of its forest cover during the half century before the communist revolution.[20]

On balance, though, the Maoist system sowed the seeds of tremendous environmental injury through its emphasis on heavy industry; its adoption of wasteful technologies for production; its pricing policies, which systematically encouraged waste of natural resources; and its conscious focus on maximizing industrial output without regard for environmental impact. Despite the famine of the early 1960s, Mao's pronatalist policies increased the country's population rapidly, further stressing the natural environment. These factors set the environmental stage on which Deng's reforms have played out.

Post-1978 Reforms and the Environment

The post-1978 reforms have had a mixed impact on the environment. Some have increased the incentives to utilize resources wisely, thus limiting environmental damage; others have sharply escalated environmental damage. On balance, China's environmental problems have worsened significantly since the start of the reforms. Evidence of this general phenomenon is everywhere. From 1982 to 1989, for example, the country lost one third of its mature forests. Arable land diminishes by 0.5 percent per year. China now reportedly has nine of the world's ten cities with the most polluted air. Only six of the country's twenty-seven largest cities have drinking water supplies that meet government standards. Roughly one third of China's arable land is affected by acid rain.[21]

Some basic reform thrusts should mitigate damage done to the environment by continuing economic growth. The reforms, for example, have specifically sought to alter the mix of investment to provide more funding for light industry at the expense of heavy industry. In addition, the most rapidly expanding sector of the economy in the coming decade should be the service sector. These changes in the sectoral balance of China's economy should have a basically beneficent effect on use of resources per unit of output.

China's move away from centralized planning should also prove environmentally helpful. Localities now play a far larger role in decisions on locations of new plants and are better able to take into account the environmental consequences of new approvals. Increased emphasis on profitability, with some movement of natural-resource prices in the direction of their true market values, should also increase incentives at the enterprise level to adopt resource-saving technologies.

Other changes, such as the gradual development in property rights, should have long-term beneficent effects. People and businesses have little incentive to make investments in environmental abatement if their rights to the property concerned are weak or nonexistent. China has developed certain property-rights laws under the reforms, and its likely 2003 adoption of a code of civil procedure should bolster its property-rights regime.

The reform era's steps toward greater intercourse in the international arena also contribute in various ways to environmental health in China.[22] Because environmental consciousness abroad in the 1980s exceeded that in the PRC, outside experts both sought to heighten Chinese awareness of these issues and to provide needed expertise to analyze the problems and provide solutions to specific issues.[23] The World Bank, for example, made both general and specific studies of the environmental problems China confronted, and began to insist on environmental-impact statements as part of the documentation for all projects in which it was involved. This insistence reflected an increasing environmental awareness within the World Bank itself. The international arena is also an important source of pertinent funds and technologies. Overall, China's Tenth Five-Year Plan (2001–05) anticipates that about 5 percent of environmental investment will come from abroad.[24]

Other aspects of the reform era have, however, accelerated the deterioration of the PRC's environment. The most fundamental short-term adverse force has been the reforms' very success in promoting China's overall economic growth. With the economy expanding at a real rate of about 9 percent per year from 1979 to 2001, even considerably greater efficiency in production is unlikely to prevent additional massive insults to the environment.

The breakup of people's communes and resulting movement of large numbers of farmers off the land has had various negative environmental consequences. Rural townships have expanded very rapidly, encroaching on the surrounding arable land. Approximately 100 million individuals have moved into urban environments, where they consume more resources and produce more waste than they previously did, and another 100 million are expected to make this transition by 2012.

Within cities, proconsumption policies are producing the consequences of a consumer society. The number of vehicles—motor scooters, cars, and trucks—is expanding rapidly, with related contributions to air and noise pollution.[25] The state's sustained effort since the early 1980s to expand grossly inadequate urban housing stocks is rapidly expanding urban areas, which are absorbing the generally fertile suburban agricultural lands. Even in the countryside, high-consumption policies have produced an enormous surge in home building. New transportation networks, including the construction of multilane highways across the country, are also taking up former agricultural areas, further depleting the pool of arable land.

Those remaining on the farm have reacted to these changes in part by seeking to bring more new land under the plow. They have not, in general, transformed marginal lands on hillsides and in remote, barren places, as the cost of doing so is too high and the rewards are too low. Rather, where possible they are instead encroaching on the rich soils around lakes and streams and in the coastal wetlands. These areas are being filled in and either cultivated or used for new housing at an alarming rate. The payoffs from increased agricultural production in highly populated areas are so great under the reforms that peasants are even planting areas that are in severe danger of flooding, such as the small flatlands inside the dikes along stretches in the lower reaches of the Yangtze River.[26]

In many ways, therefore, the reform era has brought with it behaviors and basic reallocation of people and resources that stress the environment, even as some changes in the system should provide the vehicles for more efficient, environmentally less damaging production. As in the Maoist era, the most fundamental policy affecting the environment is the underlying emphasis on maximizing growth of GNP. Still, it is hard to fault China's reform leaders for pursuing this goal.

The Political Economy of Environmental Management

China's leaders now accept the notion that the country will pay dearly in the future if it does not pay attention to the environment now.[27] Shortages of safe water are critical. Surveys show that virtually every major body of water in the country is severely polluted; just one in seven rural residents and only half of city dwellers have access to safe water; many water-storage areas and rivers in north China have dried up; and some 60 percent of all Chinese drink water with a higher fecal coliform count than World Health Organization guidelines recommend.[28] The PRC also suffers from soaring rates of pulmonary diseases such as asthma; heavy smog that descends regularly over many urban areas; and widespread damage due to acid rain, especially in southwest China. In the 1980s a fire burned for four days on a major river that runs through the center of Shanghai, and a later hepatitis outbreak there felled three hundred thousand people. These and other startling indicators of environmental degradation have brought home the fact that the country faces serious problems.

As a consequence, by the early 1990s China became an active participant in international environmental discussions. The country set up an Environmental Commission, a State Environmental Protection Administration, local administrative branches, and environmental bureaus in all ministries and many other units during the 1980s. It is building up a cadre of experts on environmental issues, and it has adopted numerous environmental laws and regulations. These laws establish rules, for example, for moving highly polluting industries away from major cities, for payment of fees for polluting water resources, and for prohibiting the adoption of certain highly polluting technologies in new plants. China has also established a system for monitoring air quality in major cities.[29]

Beijing is also giving environmental issues higher budgetary support. The Tenth Five-Year Plan stipulates spending approximately 1.3 percent of GDP annually on environmental projects, as compared with expenditures of 0.93 percent in the Ninth Five-Year Plan and 0.73 percent in the Eighth Five-Year Plan. The State Council allocated $7.85 billion to environmental efforts during 2002 alone.[30]

The structure and dynamics of China's semireformed system will determine the results of these environmental efforts. This is a highly complex issue, but in broad terms the basic structural issues are the following.

Despite reforms that seek to increase the role of market forces, administrative boundaries remain extremely important in determining economic outcomes. At the lower levels of the system, the major net gainers from the reforms have been the municipal, county, and township governments, which have greatly increased their decision-making power. These governments retain very substantial leverage over the firms in their jurisdiction: by their actions regarding taxes, investment funds, license approvals, application of regulatory rules, access to electricity and water, and so forth, they can make or break enterprises with which they deal. But these governments generally wish to maximize the growth of local industry and commerce, both to fill their own coffers and to expand the employment base for the growing working-age population. This presents several serious problems for environmental issues.

One complication is that very few environmental insults occur strictly within the administrative boundaries of one local political authority. Take, for example, China's fee system for contributing to water pollution.[31] Water is an ambient commodity and thus does not "belong" to any single place or authority. (The same, of course, is true of air.) China has developed a water-pollution fee system that makes an enterprise pay for polluting the water. The basic fee system itself has flaws. For instance, it requires charges only for the single pollutant the enterprise adds to the water that *most* exceeds official standards—all other water pollutants disgorged from the same enterprise are "free" and need not be controlled. In addition, the fee levied is often considerably less than would be the cost of reducing the offending discharge, and thus a rational enterprise manager in most instances simply builds the fee into the cost of production, rather than abating the environmental offense itself.

Appropriate changes in the fee regulations can resolve these flaws, at least in principle. Other difficulties with the fee system are more deeply grounded in China's current political economy and thus are less easily remedied. A fee system should in theory produce enterprise-level efforts to reduce pollution, for example, but its efficacy in the context of China's system is actually sharply reduced by two additional factors.

First, the local government often has an overriding interest in maintaining maximum production. In most countries, indeed, local governments are not the most effective units for remedying the environmental damage done by local industry, because at this level the industry is typically an extremely powerful political actor, due to its employment and financial contributions. Where the fee system threatens to impinge on the enterprise's operations, local governments in China have been known to find offsetting means—such as grants or tax abatements—to enable the industry to pay the fee without cutting back on production and employment.

Second, the fee system does not allow payments across administrative boundaries. Therefore, under the reforms counties and cities have tended to shift their most polluting enterprises near the downstream boundaries of their jurisdictions so that the effects of the pollution dumped into the water are imposed on the next government jurisdiction farther downstream. The local government that collects the pollution fees retains them—or funnels them back to the offending industry via the tax abatements and grants noted above. Thus, power to attack the problem must be in the hands of regional or national authorities. The reforms in China have fragmented power geographically to too great a degree in this regard. For day-to-day management of environmental issues such as the water pollution fee system, local level governments are the key units—but they are not the optimal units to use.

Even where higher-level administrative units exist, the system provides inadequate authority to environmental officials. The State Environmental Protection Administration, for example, originally had a lower bureaucratic rank than the various production ministries. It has subsequently been raised to ministerial rank but that is still not sufficient, as it cannot issue binding orders either to the ministries or to the provinces, which have the same rank. Thus the environmental ministry can raise issues and draft regulations, but it lacks the authority to force compliance.[32] In addition, many other ministries effectively control parts of the environmental agenda, resulting in competing priorities and lack of discipline and coordination. The Ministry of Water Resources, the Ministry of Agriculture, and urban construction bureaus, for example, all dominate parts of the environmental agenda.

In somewhat similar fashion, China has long had seven river-valley commissions to work on the integrated development of entire river basins. Such commissions exist for all the major rivers, such as the Yangtze, the Yellow, and the Hai rivers. But these commissions are only advisory to the Ministry of Water Resources, and they do not have the authority to issue orders to the provinces that fall within their jurisdiction. Since each province has the same rank as the Ministry of Water Resources, moreover, the commissions lack any direct route for exercising executive authority in their respective river basins.

As a result, it is virtually impossible to implement integrated plans for river-basin development, especially because most basins cross through parts of a number of counties, cities, prefectures, and provinces.[33]

The resulting problems for water policy are evident everywhere. Downstream locales are seeing their water become truly hazardous. Foreign scholars doing research in Zouping County in Shandong Province in the late 1980s found that the local water sources had been astonishingly defiled by wastes from the upstream capital city of Jinan. That county had, consequently, developed plans to tap directly into the Yellow River, which flows through a part of the county. But other investigators who queried county officials along a vast stretch of the middle and lower reaches of the Yellow River found that many counties had developed their own plans to tap the Yellow River's water. Consequently, in the late 1990s the Yellow River began running dry for months at a time before it even reached Zouping county.

Administrative jurisdictional boundaries are not the only source of problems in dealing with contemporary environmental issues in the PRC. The partial nature of price reform combines with the nature of a "negotiated" economy to reduce many of the benefits that a competitive market with good regulations would normally produce.

Water is short in many of China's major cities. A survey that covered 434 cities found that 188 are short of water and in 40 the water shortages are severe.[34] But enormous waste still occurs. Very few users pay directly for their water, and very few consumers have water meters. The incentives to install the necessary equipment have been minimized by the extraordinarily low prices charged for water use. In agriculture, nearly half the arable land is irrigated, and many of the types of irrigation systems used do not contribute to water conservation.[35] Again, underpricing produces waste of a scarce resource.

Even where price ratios should encourage conservation, the close ties between local industries and local governments often reduce the incentive effect to near zero. The reforms are aimed primarily at increasing output, and local governments typically have ample means within their jurisdictions to maintain incentives that favor production rather than conservation. Naturally, some individual local leaders have become environmentalists and strongly support sustainable development within their localities.[36] But they are more the exceptions than the norm. The natural-resource market does not yet work with sufficient rigor to make a serious difference in the areas where the local political leadership wants to see the economy grow at virtually all costs. A large portion of enterprises are still either state or collective bodies whose profits have to date depended more on negotiations with the state administration for favorable policies than on maximizing efficiency and improving technology in production.[37]

This dynamic has undercut the potential environmental benefits from the development of a large number of township enterprises. These firms are generally small and presumably should be more sensitive than large state enterprises to the cost structures they confront. Environmentalists had hoped that the proliferation of these enterprises would produce a somewhat less environmentally damaging way of increasing overall GNP growth, but they have been disappointed. Township and village enterprises in 1998 accounted for approximately 26 percent of China's GDP but produced about 50 percent of all pollutants nationally.[38] This is the case for three reasons. First, the nexus between the township enterprises and the local governments—these enterprises often account for up to 80 percent of the revenues of localities—has meant that real opportunity costs for the enterprises have typically not favored environmentally conscious decisions. Second, the small size and low capitalization of these enterprises means that they often adopt relatively low-technology production processes that are not particularly environmentally friendly. Third, the very large number of such enterprises means that it is very difficult for governments to monitor their performance in terms of air, water, and ground pollution.

To some extent, the resulting behavior conforms to what is termed a "free-rider problem." That is, although all counties, for example, have an interest in environmental protection throughout China, it is in the specific interest of each county for all *other* counties to sacrifice in order to achieve that collective interest. In this instance, the noncomplying county can hitch a "free ride" on the environmental cleanup efforts of others. The fact that under the current system no county can impose its will on any other county simply enhances the power of this logic. Why clean up the local water supply when one cannot affect the polluting actions of the offending counties upstream? Why do so when there is no way to receive reciprocal help from the counties that benefit downstream? The logical county in this situation adds pollution to the system in the process of maximizing its own employment and financial gains. This basically describes the behavior of a very large number of Chinese township, county, and city leaders.

Upper levels of the bureaucratic system are constrained in their ability to force local leaders to take account of the larger environmental costs of their actions. The most important constraint is simply the fact that a core thrust of the reforms is to accelerate GDP growth through decentralization. Administrative demands from the Center to slow down growth in favor of broad environmental goals are out of step with this basic reform impetus. Such higher-level interference is not impossible—and it does occasionally occur, typically in the form of actions such as ordering the closure of a group of highly polluting factories. But on balance the system is now geared in a different direction, and this limits the overall rigor with which national environmental regulations are implemented at the local level.

Even China's greater openness to the international arena under the reforms is not an unmixed blessing for the PRC's environment. Among the industrialized countries, some firms whose home governments have tightened their environmental regulations seek to invest in poorer countries where they are freer to pollute. Quite a few international environmentalists take a dim view of regional trade agreements that facilitate cross-border investments, precisely because they see these as cloaks to permit polluting industries to shift their damaging production processes elsewhere rather than clean up their acts.[39] Japan, South Korea, and Taiwan have adopted environmental policies that are making some of their more polluting firms look abroad, and investment in the PRC has become an attractive prospect for many of these enterprises. China welcomes investment from these places.

China's environmental difficulties cause problems outside of the PRC, too. Specifically, China's policies are increasing worldwide levels of greenhouse gases, and in the coming years China will replace the United States as the world's largest emitter of such gases.[40] China's carbon dioxide component of greenhouse-gas emissions originates primarily in coal burning. However, China also releases a great deal of methane, another greenhouse gas, into the atmosphere. This results from the country's extensive wet-paddy cultivation of rice, which releases methane as a by-product.

Besides greenhouse gases, China is also a source of acid rain, which is producing problems for the Korean peninsula and Japan. Somewhat ironically, many of the pollutants that cause acid rain do not create a problem in northeast China itself because the Gobi Desert dust that mixes with the air over that region is sufficiently alkaline to neutralize the acidity of that air. But the dust settles out, and the pollution that reaches the Korean peninsula and Japan produces acid rain there.

China's rising standard of living and greater urbanization under the reforms also contribute to transnational environmental problems in a broader sense. As noted above, arable land is being taken for urban development, and the land available for grain production has been shrinking rapidly. Since 1981, global land planted to grains has gone down almost every year, and developments in China are increasing the resulting stress on the remaining arable land. China's citizens, with their growing wealth, are becoming net importers of food, thus increasing overall pressures on global food stocks.

In other ways, China is actually and potentially a contributor to improved global environmental outcomes. Its very strict birth-control program, for example, has a significant impact on world population growth and thus on the level of stress on the environment. If Chinese reproductive behavior were instead at the levels of, for example, India or Indonesia, the global environment would be in more difficult shape.

China is also helping the international environment simply by becoming more energy efficient. Recognizing that the country lacks significant noncoal based energy resources and that coal consumption exacts very heavy related costs, since the 1980s Beijing has sought to improve energy efficiency; in 1998 the PRC adopted a National Energy Conservation Law. Energy efficiency efforts in many areas have produced results. GDP per unit of energy consumed has increased very markedly since 1980.[41]

Prognoses

Environmental issues are so complex that precise statements generally are not warranted. In broad terms, though, China's reform effort should, over a considerable period of time, lead to more environmentally friendly approaches to development. The changes being introduced hold out prospects of greater production efficiency, a smaller percentage of resources devoted to heavy industry, more rational pricing of raw materials and of pollution-control technologies, closer links with the international arena and its environmental resources, and so forth. As the reforms vastly increase China's wealth, they are creating an increasing number of people who demand more pleasant, less hazardous living conditions. China has reached the point where increasing environmental awareness is producing substantially greater investments in pollution prevention and abatement.

But the problems remain daunting. Continuing economic growth will add major strains to the environment. The country will have to depend primarily on coal for its energy sources for the long-term future. Total consumption of carbon-based fuels will continue to increase rapidly, even with substantial investments in pollution-abatement equipment. Urbanization and the creation of megalopolises will add to the problems of pollution control.

China also faces the immediate prospect of having to make major investments to mitigate the effects of the north China water shortage. In October 2000, Beijing adopted a plan to construct two major routes to move water from central China to north China. The eastern route will take water from the Yangtze River near Yangzhou City in Jiangsu province and move it through a route that takes advantage of the imperial-era Grand Canal to shift it north to where it eventually will reach Tianjin. This route requires relatively small-scale relocation of people, but the water along this route is some of the most polluted in the country. In addition to the investment required to construct the route, therefore, a great deal of money must be put into water-treatment plants along the way.

The central China route will, at least in its initial years, move water from the Danjiangkou Dam reservoir across north China to the Beijing area. This route must largely be built from scratch, and it requires heightening the Danjiangkou Dam, with the attendant displacement of over 370,000 people. This route will also require major investments in pumping stations and extensive tunneling to bring the water under the Yellow River.

These two projects formally began in December 2002 and will cost $24 billion, as noted above. When finished, they will constitute one of the most remarkable water transfer efforts in the world. They alone will not be sufficient to maintain adequate water supplies to the vital Beijing-Tianjin area. In addition, water prices must be raised and considerable investments in conservation and water treatment must be undertaken. Without this set of projects, north China cannot possibly continue its present record of economic expansion.[42] Indeed, China overall faces a rapidly rising environmental bill simply to sustain rapid economic growth.

China's growing wealth and technical sophistication should permit adoption of increasingly effective approaches to address its environmental challenges. But the political leadership is committed to continued high rates of growth of GDP as the key vehicle for maintaining popular satisfaction and overall social stability. Social disagreements over the priority that should be accorded to environmental concerns are likely, moreover, to grow as the country develops an increasingly sophisticated middle class while major portions of the population remain very poor and anxious over job opportunities.

Environmental problems may well become increasingly contentious issues, but China's evolving political system is likely to tilt the outcomes strongly in the direction of growth over environment for some years to come.

This prognosis might be somewhat mitigated if the Chinese increase public education on environmental issues and permit the formation of policy-oriented "green" movements among the populace. Precisely because environmental issues rarely coincide with existing political boundaries, green movements from below can be especially important in creating a constituency for targeted action by showing the true dimensions of specific environmental insults. These movements can pull together affected people from various political jurisdictions and create a unified front of information, opinion, and visibility. In both the Soviet Union and Eastern Europe, such movements became important to the political evolution of the regimes during the 1980s.

China is permitting the formation of social organizations on the condition that they become legal entities by registering with the government. An increasing number of these groups are engaging in environmental activities such as public education.[43] They generally do so in close cooperation with government agencies. But China's laws on such organizations permit only one organization to serve a particular constituency in any locality, and these organizations are not allowed to exist in more than one jurisdiction. It is, therefore, very difficult under current regulations for China to develop effective "green" NGOs that pull together the actual group of people affected by a particular environmental insult or issue. More broadly, officials' fears of any type of autonomous political organization make it very unlikely that real autonomous green movements will be tolerated any time soon.

In sum, the reforms to date have not changed the system to the extent that pressures from below will shape the environmental issues on the national agenda. The semireformed nature of the Chinese economy has unleashed vast initiatives at local levels for rapid economic growth, and it has also created a nexus of state-economic ties that still inhibit vigorously addressing environmental problems. Ongoing reforms should move the system over time in the directions necessary to address its environmental challenges more effectively. Ironically, the damage done in the interim may be of sufficient magnitude to constrain growth significantly and potentially to disrupt the social stability so coveted by the government.

10
The State and Society

We have focused to this point primarily on the state. Our analysis has portrayed the Chinese system as basically top-down, where the priorities and politics of the top political leadership and the bureaucratic maze through which the leadership deals with society are central to understanding the country. "Society," in this analysis, has been more the target of state action than a source of ideas and initiatives that affect the state. To be sure, this view notes the limits of the state's ability to reshape society and the disastrous consequences when the state oversteps these limits, such as the famine that resulted from the unrealistic policies of the Great Leap Forward. It recognizes as well that segments of society may resist the state; nevertheless the overall framework has been that society does not see itself apart from the state, or as having any means to make significant demands on it. But a quarter century of reforms has changed the parameters of state-society relations.

The reforms have produced profound changes in Chinese society. Many of these are obvious. The reforms have vastly expanded the information and communications capabilities of the bulk of the population. They have made available a standard of living far higher than that which previously existed, and they have significantly loosened the political straitjacket within which personal activities were confined earlier. The magnitude of the resulting physical, stylistic, and psychological changes is striking to any long-time visitor to the PRC.

More subtly, the reforms have enabled market forces to penetrate to a significant degree into urban and much of rural society. Few things are more revolutionary than the impact of such forces. They change the types of skills necessary in order to advance, the nature of relationships among units and individuals, the assumptions made about such fundamentals as education and opportunity, and the role of government in defining and assuring a just society.

The reforms have also created an extremely mobile and differentiated society. Mao Zedong rooted Chinese to their places of residence and employment. The *danwei* system virtually eliminated urban job mobility, and the *hukou* system did the same for geographical mobility. During the Cultural Revolution even wage raises were eliminated, as were most opportunities for career advancement. The reforms, in contrast, have opened up Chinese society. More than 100 million people have moved from rural to urban jobs, and the *hukou* system itself is slated for gradual elimination over the coming decade. Within cities the creation of private and joint-venture sectors and reductions in the size of the government and SOE sectors has vastly expanded job mobility, especially creating new opportunities for younger participants in the labor force. Whereas under Mao almost all Chinese had their life courses largely determined by their class origin and place of birth, people now have serious opportunities for personal choice that can dramatically affect future prospects. The results are vast differences of lifestyle, wealth, and perspectives.

On the whole, Chinese citizens have learned that they must take the initiative to define and pursue their interests. Chinese citizens have thus become better informed, more self aware, and more active. Officials now use public-opinion surveys and other methods to understand better the complex currents in popular thinking. They recognize the need to do this in order to govern effectively.

The Maoist State and Chinese Society

After an initial decade of promoting wholesale social, economic, and political change in the countryside, in the wake of the Great Leap famine the CCP shifted its priorities. While rhetorically continuing to tout the countryside as a seedbed of revolutionary fervor, in reality it sought to extract grain, limit state-financed rural investment, bottle up rural problems in the countryside, elicit protestations of peasant loyalty, and prevent rural-based rebellion. This amounted to a significant retreat from the original revolutionary agenda in the countryside. Even the Cultural Revolution intruded only superficially into most rural villages.

The major devices utilized to cut the countryside off from the cities and to isolate rural communities have already been discussed: the *hukou* residence-registration system that inhibited geographical mobility, especially from the villages to the cities; the Cultural Revolution–era stress on local self-sufficiency in agriculture; fiscal policies that largely restricted state subsidies for food, health care, education, housing, and welfare to the urban areas; indirect levies on the peasants through such measures as forcing cotton producers to sell all their output to the state at cheap prices, while forcing peasants to purchase all cotton goods from the state at high prices; and directing the major part of state investment funds into the urban economy.

There is little question that during the Maoist era the state succeeded in acting *on* the peasants and limiting peasant initiative. The structure of state control over the countryside after the Great Leap Forward created relatively isolated, inward-looking rural villages. One small group of people provided political, economic, and cultural leadership in each village. These local cadres thus had to balance the demands from higher levels—for grain and other resources such as corveé labor, for public order, and for professions of loyalty—against the need to develop local resources and protect the village from excessive exploitation by the state. The local cadres' income depended on the production of the villages they supervised, and they therefore had a self-interest in keeping resources from flowing out of the locality.

The resulting cadre behavior undoubtedly both protected the locality from state demands and functioned as a tool of the state to exploit local resources. Cadre behavior probably included understating local production, overstating the losses from natural disasters, and altering other information where possible to deceive the higher levels, though the actual balance between state and local interests struck by village-level cadres must have varied by the individual. It is possible, in addition, that grain-surplus areas witnessed more local protection than did localities that relied on subsidies from the state. A lively literature has begun to examine the extent of state penetration into the villages during the late Mao era.[1] More empirical work is needed for closure on this issue, though no author has asserted that the peasants actually sought to change state policy rather than to obtain exemptions from relevant policies for themselves.

The urban population under Mao also experienced major social, political, and economic change during the 1950s, but the pressures for urban change did not end with the failure of the Great Leap Forward. During the PRC's first decade, the CCP transformed the relations between the state and urban enterprises through the Three Anti Five Anti campaign in 1951–52, the Socialist Transformation of Industry and Commerce campaign in 1955–56, and the formation of a socialist system of economic planning that substituted for the forces of the market in shaping the nature of relations among the state, the managers, and thc workers. Virtually all urbanities, moreover, were encouraged to join state-sponsored mass organizations such as the women's federation, youth league, trade unions, residents' committees, sports federations, and patriotic associations. These state-supported organizations professed to represent the true interests of their members; therefore participation in politics had to be channeled through such state-controlled outlets.[2]

In the immediate aftermath of the Great Leap, the urban populace became, like their rural counterparts, fully locked into relatively isolated cells, the units (*danwei*) described in Chapter 6. The work units and residents' committees (for those without a work unit) brokered relations between the state and the citizenry. Again, there are debates about the posture assumed by the local cadres, whether they dominated their underlings on behalf of the state or protected their charges from excessive state demands. The former notion maintains that local cadres created cultures of dependence through clientelist networks, whereas the latter stresses the tension between the power of the state and the "immovable permanence of work unit membership."[3] It has also been suggested that the Maoist state did not wholly succeed in its attempts to restructure social cleavages along the lines dictated by Maoist politics.[4] Although the state was largely able to break up solidarity among, for example, workers as a class, incidents of popular protest nevertheless occurred when the state itself created space for such activities, such as during the Hundred Flowers campaign of 1957 or the early stages of the Cultural Revolution from 1966 to 1968.

The intellectuals warrant particular attention due to their strategic importance in traditional and modern China. In the traditional Chinese state, the scholar-officials were the high priests of the Confucian political-moral philosophy, combining moral authority with political power.[5] With the demise of the Qing dynasty, which marked the end not only of the imperial Chinese state but of basic ideas about civilization that had been sustained for millennia, Chinese intellectuals cast about furiously in search of a new moral foundation for state power. This search led to the patriotic fervor of the May Fourth movement and to numerous experiments with different forms of state building in various parts of China during the Republican era.

Mao Zedong built his communist movement after 1937 by utilizing both peasant power and the skills of intellectuals. In his Yan'an Talks on Literature and Art in 1942, Mao declared that the intellectuals must serve the communist cause and could not provide their own moral critique of the communist movement.[6] Wang Shiwei, an intellectual who joined the communist forces in Yan'an and then wrote critically about the growth of corruption and other problems there, was thrown in prison, where he was held until he was beheaded in 1947.

After 1949 intellectuals flocked to the communist cause. Although they accepted the legitimacy of party rule, many also sought to be guardians of the new political orthodoxy. This resonated with the position of intellectuals in imperial times and coexisted, sometimes uneasily, with their ardent patriotism and their desire to see a strong state succeed.

The Hundred Flowers and Antirightist campaigns in 1957 largely destroyed the role of intellectuals as guardians of orthodoxy. The party, still composed largely of peasant cadres, first invited constructive criticism and then harshly persecuted all who had accepted this invitation. The party sought to improve relations with intellectuals as the Great Leap Forward collapsed, but the Cultural Revolution crushed all semblance of intellectual input and prestige. Very few, if any, intellectuals survived the Cultural Revolution without suffering physical and psychological abuse.[7]

For the intellectuals especially, Antirightist and Cultural Revolution political violence resulted in prolonged separation of family members.[8] Many children watched their parents cowed by mobs and, literally, beaten and spat on. Quite a few had to join in these orgies of humiliation. Even in the 1950s spouses were pressured to divorce those who had run into political trouble.[9] Such pressures escalated to murderous proportions during the Cultural Revolution. It is difficult to know the emotional and intellectual residues such experiences left on the millions whose lives were touched by them.[10] Undoubtedly, they created a great deal of anguish about political authority, obligations to the state, social ends, and the goals of personal existence.

The Cultural Revolution had a wider-ranging effect on urban than rural society. For the middle-aged and older generations, it probably reconfirmed a long-standing belief that the young are not to be trusted with power and initiative. Many argue that Chinese more than most people fear chaos (*luan*).[11] The destructiveness of the Cultural Revolution probably reconfirmed the importance attached to order as well.

But the Cultural Revolution's impact was especially powerful on the urban youths who responded to Mao Zedong's call to spearhead this political movement. Primarily as a consequence of the Cultural Revolution, by 1976 China's younger people were in general profoundly ignorant of the outside world, as Mao cut off nearly all contact abroad. Even individual older Chinese who had spent time abroad or who had foreign contacts were isolated, attacked, and cowed into silence. The populace as a whole received no uncensored information about the international arena.

History became a handmaiden to politics during this period. From 1974 to 1976 major factional political battles were fought out partly through historical allegories in the media. Eyewitness accounts of party events written by foreign-educated Chinese scholars were considered to be of no historical value.[12] Chinese education during this period intentionally neglected the country's history and traditional culture, except as tools in the constant political battles of the period.[13] Very few students were even taught the classical Chinese in which most materials were written until the late 1910s.

Political participation consisted largely of acting on the latest "supreme instructions" that emanated from Beijing. The Cultural Revolution's destruction of much of the administrative apparatus led to bloodshed over the proper interpretation of these "instructions." Many younger people and workers gained experience in promoting their own interests through manipulation of ideological slogans and through street-level political and quasimilitary organization. Political issues were regarded in black and white, with "correct" and "incorrect" views and opinions but no gray areas or notions of contingency.

The true attitudes that resulted from such pressures are hard to judge, given the danger of expressing thoughts that were considered politically unacceptable.[14] It appears that widely accepted notions included the following:

☐ Intellectuals are unworthy. They are inherently elitist, of doubtful loyalty, and out of touch with China's real needs. They also fear political struggle. It is better to be a worker or a peasant than an intellectual.[15]

☐ Classes and class struggle are important. Members of pariah classes—those designated as capitalists, landlords, rich and upper-middle-class peasants, rightists, traitors, and others—should suffer greatly, as should those closely associated with them.

☐ Violence is a perfectly acceptable, even a necessary, form of political struggle. Without violence, enemies cannot be subdued and society cannot be purified. This was summed up in the popular slogan, "It is necessary to beat a mad dog in the water," meaning that an enemy should never be treated leniently, even when he has been knocked down.

☐ Plain living and basic egalitarianism are virtuous. Pursuit of personal whims and any form of ostentation reflect a "bourgeois" spirit that makes one suspect. It is right to struggle against those who seem to get ahead of the pack.

☐ The core leader guides the nation. Politics consists of implementing the spirit of directives from the Center, not of pressing for representation of individual or group interests in the political system. The objective is to obtain organic unity based on ideological purification as dictated by the leader.

☐ Political cadres other than the core leader are suspect. They may try to twist the infallible commands of the leader to suit the interests of their own factions. One should be prepared to attack even high-ranking cadres if the instructions of the core leader call for such actions. Few can be trusted to be correct.

☐ Foreigners are suspect. They seek to exploit the Chinese and possibly carve up the country.

It is impossible to know just how widespread the above attitudes were, but anecdotal evidence suggests that many urban dwellers—not only youths—accepted and acted on them. In 1976 Chinese society was unstable, prone to political upheaval, violent, anti-intellectual, poor, anticonsumer, and molded by castelike social divisions. Both peasants and especially urban dwellers had been taught to sever ties, to demonize those who ran afoul of political strictures, and to commit violence in the name of purification and as a form of self-identification with the correct political line.

In the final analysis, the Maoist state did not penetrate into every nook and cranny of its citizens' lives. Nevertheless, by the end of the Mao's life every social action was regarded as politically significant and thus could evoke a response from the political authorities. Despite the severe disruptions of the political apparatus caused by the Cultural Revolution, people continued to be *politically vulnerable*. The urban personnel system of individual dossiers meant that any recorded political transgression would never be shaken off.[16] Because no urban jobs existed except those assigned by the state personnel system, and peasants could not leave their collective without permission, those who ran afoul of a political judgment had no escape. The very comprehensiveness of this political blanket—ironically, even during periods of politically induced anarchy—was one of the most distinctive characteristics of state-society relations in the era of Mao Zedong.

State-Society Relations under the Reforms

Chapter 5 introduced the many sharp reversals the reforms produced in Maoist policy. The reformers sought to create and then enhance a nonpolitical sphere of activity for individuals, drop class labels, use inegalitarian distribution systems and conspicuous consumption as incentives for more work and creativity, rekindle interest in knowledge and technical skills, revive agriculture through a return to family-based farming, open the country to the international arena, and sharply reduce the overall level of political violence. These initiatives created the political space for Chinese society to bestir itself, and raise the question, How much has the state-society relationship changed since the reforms began?

On the surface, Chinese life has changed greatly since 1978. In Mao's last years even cities like Beijing, Shanghai, and Guangzhou presented images of dull conformity—millions of people dressed in similar blue "Mao jackets," uniform hair styles among women, no advertising, and no sense of liveliness or entrepreneurship. Now, varied clothing, huge traffic jams, vibrant consumer culture, karaoke bars and other entertainment centers, and the seemingly unending construction of modern buildings are the norm. The near-total isolationism of the late Maoist era has been cast aside; Chinese calling cards now typically boast telephone, fax, mobile telephone, and e-mail address information. Access to the Web is widespread. Large areas of China receive satellite TV with programming that includes Asian MTV and international sports, news, and films, all of which give the people of China vivid images of the outside world.

Visitors are constantly astonished at the get-rich-quick mood of the populace. Every unit and every person, it seems, is trying to find new ways to make money. In 1993 even the venerable Peking University emblematically tore down a wall bordering one end of the campus to put up a row of university-run shops. The number of schemes and scams is, it seems, almost unlimited. A county Communist party secretary in Jilin Province boasted to a foreign visitor that the Communist party secretary of Xiaoxing, a village that had done particularly well in developing local industry under the reforms, is "a big capitalist." The county secretary made the comment while giving the "thumbs up" sign in approval. The village secretary drives a new Cadillac.[17]

China has also developed a middle class, at least in its major cities.[18] Estimates of the size of this middle class vary widely, from about 20 million to more than 300 million. What is not in dispute is that the middle class now enjoys a distinctive lifestyle and that its numbers are growing very rapidly. Urban Chinese of means now have access to real choice and quality in restaurants, entertainment, communications, travel, clothing, housing, leisure activities, and so forth. Sixty to 70 percent of the housing stock in large east-coast cities is privately owned, for the first time providing the occupants with collateral that they are using to obtain bank loans for education, cars, and other purposes.[19] Some middle-class Beijingers have moved to the suburbs, using their personal or company cars to commute and stopping to pick up KFC or

McDonald's for the kids on the way home from work. A few Chinese have become rich enough to be included on *Fortune* magazine's list of the world's wealthiest individuals.

How has all this commercial ebullience and exposure to the outside world affected the nature of relations between the state and society? China's society has become so variegated, and career paths for many urban dwellers so numerous, that no single generalization can answer this. The data on issues such as attitudes and even behaviors, moreover, tend to be anecdotal rather than systematic. If we bear these caveats in mind, some broad observations are nevertheless possible.

The state no longer provides a moral compass for the population. Indeed, one of the striking features of contemporary Chinese society is the growth of nonstate sources of moral authority and spiritual well-being.[20] For example, Buddhism and Daoism have enjoyed resurgences. Almost all cities contain active temples as well as street vendors hawking spirit money, joss sticks, and the other accoutrements necessary to appease the gods and improve one's fortunes. Some traditional secret societies have reemerged, and many local sects of various kinds have sprung up in the countryside. Christian church attendance has rapidly expanded, and there are likely more Christians in China today than at any time before the revolution, though they still constitute only a small sliver of the population.

Some movements for spiritual renewal have developed nationwide reputations and mass followings. The Falun Gong is the most famous of these. It in the 1990s developed a mass following of many millions of adherents but then fell afoul of the CCP and was suppressed as an "evil cult."[21] But the broader quest for spiritual experience is widely in evidence. *Qigong*, an approach to health and spiritual renewal that involves restorative breathing, has many schools and is practiced far and wide. Even many state-run bookstores contain shelves of volumes that advocate and explain *qigong* and other such practices.[22]

Many affinity groups are forming, such as professional associations, sports clubs, and charitable organizations. Generally, these groups have not done much to create a social consciousness independent of the state. The vast majority are local in character, and all are obligated to register with the government in their locality. Authorities have not hesitated to disband such associations and groups if they become suspicious of them, and in many, such as the professional associations, the state typically plays a major role in determining who will hold the top offices.[23]

There have been some reports of local officials who have joined societal groups and then used their official position to protect the group's activities from higher-level scrutiny. Many such cases have involved rural cadres who joined secret societies or even underground Christian churches. When exposed, these officials generally claim that joining such organizations makes governing easier and ensures social order. These instances suggest the possibility that potentially threatening nonstate organizations exist in China that are concealed by local state officials.[24]

Many individuals, moreover, manage to skirt the state's authority to pursue their own personal agendas. The huge size of the floating population—

over 100 million and growing rapidly—demonstrates the gaps in the system's tight control over individual activities. Such problems as urban crime are increasingly blamed on these people who fend for themselves rather than belong to a unit. As of 2003, however, the floating population appears to be politically quiescent. They seek to find a place and earn a living in the cities, not to change the political system.[25] But the place with the greatest relative concentration of peasant migrants—Shenzhen in Guangdong province—has experienced increasing levels of worker protest among migrants, who in turn have begun to become aware of their rights under the existing labor laws. These migrants are not questioning the political system at this point, but that might change in the future. And this may be a harbinger of broader upcoming trends among migrants.[26]

LOCAL CADRES IN BETWEEN

Many local unit leaders remain firmly in command but are increasingly pursuing their own political and economic agendas rather than closely following orders from Beijing. Numerous basic-level cadres are not sympathetic to policies emanating from above. The summer of 1989 may have marked a turning point. The Center ordered cadres to conduct rigorous reviews of people's activities during the Tiananmen protest movement, and make appropriate notations in the personal dossiers of those who had defied the leaders. Throughout China, however, countless units subverted this policy by going through the motions without really seeking to determine how their members had acted. It appears that in the final analysis very few individuals had the dreaded notation on political unreliability put into their dossiers. In this instance, millions of citizens acting in a disaggregated way sent a quiet message to the top leadership that the Center could no longer set Chinese against Chinese at the unit level as a way to enhance Beijing's leverage. This tactic had been a hallmark of the Maoist era.

A meeting in Beijing of a major research institute, many of whose members had taken part in the demonstrations during May and early June 1989, typifies what took place. The party head in the institute called a "study meeting" to review materials on the Tiananmen massacre sent by the Central Committee propaganda department. The participants were supposed to discuss the materials in detail and then criticize each other's behavior and attitudes in accordance with the "spirit" of these documents. But in reality, the party head had everyone take a seat, passed out the documents, and asked if anyone wanted to say anything. Nobody responded. The party head then declared the meeting had served its purpose and asked that everyone give these materials full consideration on their own. Next, he adjourned the meeting and ostentatiously threw the propaganda department materials into the wastebasket as he left the room. Every participant in the meeting did the same. Higher levels were told that the meeting had a lively discussion but that no "serious problems" were uncovered.[27]

Some basic-level cadres take in political dissenters or those who have political black marks in their dossiers. For example, a private Dalian-based import-export company, spun off from a state trading corporation that wanted to slim down its ranks, actively recruited outcasts, including students who received damaging entries in their personal dossiers due to Tiananmen protest activities. Perhaps the firm believed that such individuals would work especially hard for the firm.[28] In another instance, the Stone Corporation, a high-technology collective enterprise in Beijing, became active in the Tiananmen movement. The Stone Corporation had also set up its own research firm whose activities promoted a democratic transition in China.[29]

 Local territorial leaders—especially those far from Beijing and not dependent on subsidies from the Center—have also begun to pursue their own interests, sometimes in open defiance of the top CCP leadership. During the austerity effort dictated by Beijing in July 1993, for example, Su Zhiming boasted to a reporter for the *Asian Wall Street Journal,* "A business talent like mine is worth more than one million *yuan* in Hong Kong. My brains are 100 percent occupied by ideas for making money." At the time, Su was both the Communist party boss and the mayor of Shiji, a town southeast of Guangzhou in China's booming Guangdong Province. That town already had more than one hundred imported cars when Beijing ordered a halt to new car imports. Nevertheless, Su ordered forty-two more, including a Rolls Royce. He had the money to do this because the incomes of the town's officials depended on the profits of the three dozen local companies operated by the town government. These companies engaged in property development, import-export trading, and light industry, including electronics and garments. With business going strong during 1993, local officials stood to receive bonuses amounting to six times their salary, which made Su's income considerably higher than that of the CCP general secretary Jiang Zemin.[30]

The reforms have stopped short of providing people with fully effective legal protections against despotic actions by local officials. One incident in Jilin Province in the summer of 1993 illustrates this. A village party chief confronted a peasant and demanded that he pay a tax for owning a bicycle. The peasant objected, and secretly wrote a letter to the head of the county party committee to complain of the village chief's exploitative activities. The county head admonished the village chief for dereliction because he had not intercepted the letter before it was sent, noting that they would all have been in trouble if the peasant had written to the provincial level. At the county head's suggestion, the village chief made an example of the peasant. He had the local police beat the peasant to death in front of a meeting of the entire village.[31]

In an attempt to deal with this and related problems, the National People's Congress in November 1987 adopted an Organic Law, which stipulates that village committees should be elected locally to run the villages. The law set up incentives both for responsiveness to the villagers' desires and for disciplined implementation of tasks handed down from the townships. The law sought to generate peasants' enthusiasm and curb local despotism via real elections at the village level while simultaneously making village cadres responsible for implementing tasks, such as tax collection and implementation of the birth-control program, assigned from above. The results of the

Organic Law have been mixed, however, and the current situation varies greatly from village to village.[32]

Local-cadre corruption and brutality have created a situation in which, somewhat ironically, many citizens look to the Center as the source of good laws and policies, which are being undermined by the cupidity of local officials. Citizen efforts are often directed at bringing local abuses to the attention of provincial and national leaders for remedy. Despite very widespread anger at local corruption and illegality, therefore, it appears that in most cases Chinese have continued to view the overall system itself as legitimate.[33] The Center, in turn, periodically takes well-publicized initiatives to bring local wrongdoers to account—and thus to burnish its own image.

Higher-level authorities do still maintain considerable leverage over local officials under certain conditions. Specifically, higher-level effectiveness is maximized when the top leaders fully agree on an issue, give the issue priority, and propose initiatives whose results can be measured concretely. Under these three conditions, few local leaders are willing to cross their superiors, and the state is able to function in a very determined, forceful fashion. But because the entire reform strategy seeks to elicit local initiative and promote local flexibility, the national leaders rarely issue directives that require disciplined implementation. In addition, the contending groups that make up the national leadership, as explained in Chapter 5, find it difficult to show complete unity on major issues.

On balance, the Center's ambition and authority to guide society have eroded significantly under the impact of the reforms. Many individuals seek to realize their own goals, vigorously when the opportunity permits and surreptitiously when the "wind" blowing out of Beijing is against them. The semireformed political and economic systems provide substantial space for such activities to occur in the normal course of events, and that space is growing as the state sector and state activities shrink. And of course, not all local cadres are despotic. There is great variation in their activities and attitudes. As noted, some have linked up with local social forces, whose activities they have shielded from view of the higher ranks.

THE STATE AND SOCIETY

The reforms have purposely drastically reduced the scope of state intervention in society. On the whole, the state is now satisfied politically if citizens do not engage in *organized* activity to oppose the authorities. What people actually think, how they choose to spend their leisure time, whom they marry, what careers they pursue, and related issues are no longer considered to be politically significant. Most Chinese now find it relatively easy to avoid all but the most pro forma types of political activity and do not live in fear of close political monitoring by the state. This change in the extent of state interference in people's lives is one of the most important repercussions of the past quarter century of reforms.

Scholarly literature on China has given substantial attention to the possibility that nonstate social forces are acquiring a sufficient sense of identity and critical mass to challenge the state, as such forces did in the Eastern bloc and the Soviet Union in their final years. Much of this literature focuses on the issue of civil society to ask whether a "public" sphere is developing that is not essentially a part of the state. The literature traces back some of the origins of such a nonstate "public" to the development and growth in the West of a market economy.[34]

The state's rules on such nonstate organizations are clear.[35] Each must register with a government body and receive approval as a legal entity. Only one organization is allowed to represent a particular issue or group in any locale. And no nongovernmental organization can branch out across different locales. In short, each self-identified group is allowed to be "represented" by only one body, and that body must reach an appropriate accommodation with the governing authorities. By not permitting any such organization to branch out into multiple locales, the government confines potential trouble to manageable proportions. This approach comes closest to a form of engagement dubbed "corporatism" in the Western literature.

The level of actual government control of various nongovernmental organizations (NGOs) varies a great deal. For many, the government plays an active role in designating their leadership and checking on their activities. Indeed, the term GONGO (government organized nongovernmental organization) is actually used to describe many of the Chinese NGOs because they are set up at the initiative of authorities and are highly responsive to government direction. Others, though, are self-initiated and legally register with a government unit whose officials may be sympathetic to the group and more inclined to shield the group than to interfere with it. There are also, to some unknown extent, underground organizations such as banned churches and groups of democracy activists. These, though, do not play the type of role assumed in notions of a liberal society, as the state actively seeks to suppress them. Only intensive interviewing provides a good picture of the situation with respect to any particular nonstate organization.[36]

Evidence overall thus suggests that the Western civil-society model does not apply to China's situation to date, which rather seems to be characterized by two major developments. First, the basic levels of the state are increasingly seizing the initiative, in many cases limiting the ability of the higher levels to penetrate the locale and extract support and resources from it. Individuals outside of the state administration, though, must develop complex, wide-ranging ties with local state officials as a condition for their exercising much initiative.[37] Second, the state is sharing management of many activities with the nonstate groups it has allowed to form. This duplicates a pattern seen in imperial and Republican China, before the Maoists destroyed all such groups and extended the direct power of the state.[38] Although these developments do not suggest the formation of a civil society in the classic sense, they do seriously qualify the idea, accurate in Mao's day, that China's state apparatus completely dominates its society (a situation characterized in the literature as a "strong state, weak society").[39] The national state administration is no longer tightly disciplined. Local officials negotiate their relations with the higher authorities and, at times, with the citizenry as well.

As stressed repeatedly throughout this volume, after the completion of the revolutionary changes wrought during the 1950s, the state adopted an approach that made state units—rural communes, state enterprises and social organizations, and state offices—the key vehicles to engage society. The unit both funneled state services to the population and performed a wide array of political and security functions. Appropriately, most of the *xitong* described in Chapter 7 penetrated each such unit.

But the reforms are fundamentally altering this model by casting very large numbers of people adrift from the state units. Communes are gone from the countryside, and more than 100 million peasants have become members of the floating population in the cities. Self-employment, private enterprises, and joint and wholly foreign-owned ventures provide employment opportunities for most of the urban population. This fundamental shift in places where people work and in the extent of labor mobility has substantially eroded the former system of brokering state-society relations.

This set of pressures has led the state to shift services from units to city-wide or countywide bases of delivery. The state is trying to develop social security, insurance, public health, housing, welfare, relief, unemployment and other resources that will be distributed by means other than the work units.[40]

The government is constrained, however, by its own difficulties in understanding the new dynamics of the society it is seeking to serve. In developing a pension system, for example, the officials need to have reasonably accurate mathematical models that predict the likely demands on such a system in the coming decades. But there is little reliable data on which to base such a model. In addition, limitations in institutional capacity also create serious obstacles to rapid forward movement. The Chinese government wants to develop an urban pension scheme that includes individual retirement accounts as part of the package. But this requires development of the financial system to the point where money can be invested relatively safely over long periods of time. The PRC does not yet have such a system. Finally, finding the funds to meet these social needs is a potentially very large challenge, especially as the deepening of market forces creates larger-scale unemployment and early retirements.[41]

Detaching such programs and resources from the work unit is profoundly changing the patterns of social activity and social dependence that have characterized China until recently. Increasingly, the state must replace lifelong subordination to the management of a *danwei* with other frameworks of state-society interaction, including development of a legal system that can regulate social behavior and adjudicate disputes over resource allocation.

HUMAN RIGHTS

The above trends provide a framework for discussing human rights in China. Few issues are more complex or more emotional. Complicating matters, the term *human rights* has different meanings to different people. To some, it means above all the freedom to express one's political views without being persecuted for doing so. This view typically also holds that no state has the right to torture its citizens or to subject them to inhumane conditions. For others, "human rights" acquires a broader meaning that includes protections afforded by due process in political, civil, and criminal matters; it means, in other words, the "rule of law." And for still others, "human rights" encompass what might be termed "social rights"—for example, access to health care, decent housing, job opportunities, and education.

Conceptions of human rights also reflect deep cultural values concerning social obligations and the proper role of the government in society. In America, "human rights" typically bundles the notion of rule of law—with a strong focus on procedural justice—with values and assumptions that presume a democratic, free-market system. These other assumptions place great store on individual autonomy, providing for a system that, broadly speaking, seeks to maximize individual choice so long as the choices made do not deprive others of the effective exercise of their own rights. This approach reflects America's unique history and society.

China has very different starting premises. Its culture stresses the interconnections between an individual and the social network within which he or she is embedded. The government traditionally sustains stability, prosperity, and security in part by promoting values that contribute to these outcomes. Confucianism and socialism have very different substantive answers to the questions of how best to promote stability, prosperity, and security, but both assume a large role for the government in molding society according to the dictates of the underlying theory.[42]

China is now in transition, neither Confucian nor socialist. Not surprisingly, the underlying value structure is muddled and actually varies greatly across the country and across age groups. As the country opens to the outside world and as the economy becomes increasingly integrated into the international market economy, one of the most crucial questions concerning the future is the nature of the value system that will emerge from the current decades of uncertainty.

There is little reason to believe that in future years China's system of values will closely resemble that of the United States. Almost certainly, it will remain more deeply authoritarian and communitarian. But America is at one end of the continuum of countries around the world on such issues—few other countries anywhere approximate the extent to which Americans value individualism.[43] China will far more likely find its balance closer to present value systems in countries such as Japan, the Republic of Korea, or Singapore. The nature of relations between the state and society in the area of human rights will inevitably reflect this underlying value structure.

China is, nevertheless, gradually increasing the role of the formal legal system in structuring state-society relations.[44] Regardless of underlying values, establishing a legal system that protects basic rights and limits the depredations a government can inflict on its own population is a globally recognized requirement for a reasonable human-rights regime.

Under Mao Zedong, China in reality had no law. Political decisions, policy lines, and party and government regulations defined the law, and China's citizens had no recourse against these often unpredictable lightning bolts from above. The major impetus for developing a serious legal regime under the reforms sprang from the pressure of foreign forces to develop a legal framework to allow foreign trade and investment to occur at reasonable risk. Over time, to an increasing extent popular attitudes have embraced a desire for legal protections from government arbitrariness, and this has also influenced the Chinese government's behavior. In the 1990s the NPC adopted a law that permits Chinese citizens to sue the government for abuse of authority by officials. Every year the number of such cases has increased, with a reported success rate of roughly 40 percent.[45]

Indeed, since the 1980s Beijing has explicitly recognized the importance of utilizing law to improve the quality of governance. At a minimum, all top leaders agree that issues should be decided by law when there is no major political interest at stake. This view is termed *rule by law*, as opposed to the term *rule of law*, widely used in the West. "Rule of law" makes the law supreme over the desires of individual officials, whereas "rule by law" makes officials supreme and the law an instrument of their governance. In reality, no country makes the law totally supreme over political power, but the differences are real and fundamentally important to a human-rights regime.

China is moving in the direction of "rule of law," and many official statements suggest that the leaders view this concept with increasing importance. No serious observer, though, would argue that China has already gone from "rule by law" to "rule of law." In fact specialists disagree considerably as to both how far along this process has gone and what will shape the end state. These disagreements reflect the very complicated situation in the country today.[46]

For example, it is common, at least in the major cities, to hear individuals complain about the Communist party leaders and such issues as corruption. Many do so in public, without fear of arrest or punishment. But China maintains large labor-camp and prison systems, and reports of mistreatment and torture are common. Pressures on penal officials to elicit confessions before cases come to trial open the door to abuse of suspects, who have no way to protect themselves from their interrogators. In addition, China retains a form of punishment called "reform through education," which permits the state to incarcerate any citizen for up to three years without trial or formal accusation, merely on administratively determined grounds that the citizen requires "reeducation." Reports indicate little difference between the "reform through labor" camps for those convicted of crimes and the "reform through education" camps for those incarcerated by administrative order.[47]

Thus, in the sense of protection against arbitrary action by the state, "human rights" in China are in evidence but are far from solidly grounded. China's leaders argue that to guarantee citizens' rights to agitate and organize against the state would risk throwing the country into social chaos and civil war, which twentieth-century China suffered enough from already. They point, instead, to the rapidly rising per capita GDP as a more significant indicator by which to judge human rights in the country. Popular views on this issue have been deeply informed by China's long history of authoritarian government and its related notions of society as an organic whole.[48] But the country is changing in unprecedented ways and is more exposed to alternative views and images through telecommunications from the international arena than ever before in its history. It is difficult, therefore, to measure with confidence how ideas about human rights are changing in the PRC or how the actual situation with respect to those rights will evolve. It is without question that in a country as large, complex, and poor as China, major violations of human rights will form at least a part of the political landscape for many years to come. And this will be the case despite the increasing importance of developing a viable legal system to permit China to reach its economic goals in a globalizing economy.[49]

POLITICAL EQUALITY

Clearly related to human rights is the issue of *political* equality. That is because the Maoist system rested so fundamentally on permanent discrimination against people who received "bad" class labels. They became outcasts, subjected always to the violence inherent in political campaigns, denied career and educational opportunities, required to report regularly to local police officials, and unable to free their spouses and children from the opprobrium of class discrimination. Class enemies also had no right to equal treatment in the courts, because law was itself assumed to have a class nature.[50]

Nobody knows the number of individuals who suffered from these types of discrimination. Mao Zedong preached the importance of uniting 95 percent of the people to struggle against 5 percent at any given time. This 95:5 ratio probably provides a very inexact measure of the actual numbers involved. And it very likely omits consideration of the family members of the victims, who also suffered. But in 1976, 5 percent of the Chinese population amounted to nearly 50 million people. Regardless of the precise numbers, class discrimination was a significant, large-scale source of social inequality in the PRC on the eve of the reforms.[51]

The reform era has dramatically reduced this political source of inequality. Class labels were removed for almost all those designated as class enemies at the start of the reforms. No such labels have subsequently been pinned on people. The legal system no longer recognizes class as a pertinent consideration in determining guilt and imposing sentences. This does not mean that people are no longer imprisoned for political offenses. Vaguely defined laws provide the government with ample "legal" flexibility to incarcerate those who cause political trouble. But no class of people is *automatically* presumed guilty and subject to harsher treatment simply by virtue of their political position. This is one of the most important social changes of the reform era, in part because it permits individuals of talent, regardless of their parentage, a chance to do well in the contemporary PRC.

One glaring exception to the blurring of class lines, as noted in Chapter 6, involves the offspring and relatives of the top officials who were rehabilitated after the Cultural Revolution. These individuals have on the whole been able to utilize their political connections to build economic empires and to insulate themselves from the normal risks of economic failure. Although the hard data necessary to make a firm determination are not available, the families of the communist elite from the prereform era have generally adapted well to the reform environment, and the members of this group tend to intermarry.[52] An elite class appears to have sustained itself across the Maoist and Deng eras.

The increasing differentiation of Chinese by wealth raises the possibility that moneyed interests are receiving better political protections than are poorer people. Given the broader developments in China, it would be surprising if this were not the case. Widespread corruption, including in the legal system, inherently provides more opportunities to those who have more resources. The rapid growth of China's legal profession also inevitably makes greater talent available to those who can afford to hire the best lawyers, despite the development of legal services for the poor in various parts of the country. The reforms have erased the politically driven Maoist forms of inequality that discriminated systematically against those from "bad" class backgrounds but are substituting the types of inequality more typically characteristic of countries with considerable corruption and inequality of wealth.

The CCP itself provides one additional form of political inequality. Party members, especially high-ranking party officials, manage to avoid most legal penalties when they break the law, despite repeated assertions that party status should not shield officials from the consequences of wrongdoing. This form of political inequality is hardly unique to China. In almost every country, political power makes it easier to avoid the full consequences of being caught in illegal activities. But in China as in many developing countries, the protections afforded by high party status appear to be greater than in comparable situations in industrialized societies.

CHANGES IN SOCIAL RELATIONSHIPS AND CLEAVAGES

The above sections focus on the changes that the reforms have wrought in the ties between the state and society. What changes, though, have occurred within Chinese society itself? Specifically, how have the reform policies altered the contours of socioeconomic inequality, and how have they affected the types of cleavages that characterize Chinese society?

Urban-Rural Incomes

The largest single cleavage in Maoist China divided urban from rural residents. The former had higher real incomes and many nonmonetary benefits. They also lived at lower risk of suffering the full brunt of economic catastrophe when Mao's policies went awry. The peasants, in contrast, bore the burdens imposed by the economic system and were less protected than their urban counterparts when national economic difficulties became severe.

Studies of urban and rural incomes in China must account adequately for urban subsidies and the value of rural housing. These elements play a large role in the Chinese scheme of compensation. Most studies have failed to account for these items and thus have tended to present false statistical pictures. Two surveys of household income, in 1988 and 1995 respectively, took pains to develop accurate estimates of these missing components and to factor them into the overall analysis.[53]

Three findings stand out: that the net effect of the reforms in the rural areas has been to increase rural inequality in general and to exacerbate gender differences in rural income; that urban-rural inequality even in 1995 remained very great; and that from 1988 to 1995, urban poverty became more widespread, with a major contributor being rising levels of urban unemployment. The surveys provide less clear results concerning changes in regional distribution of household income.

The reforms have aggravated rural income inequality in several dimensions. Most fundamentally, rural income from farming is quite equal, given the very high level of equality of rural access to land. But nonfarming sources of income—including wages, entrepreneurship, and property—are far higher than farm income, are far less equally distributed, and are growing as a percentage of total rural household income. Therefore, those engaged in rural nonfarming occupations have significantly increased their incomes compared with those who rely on farming.

This difference shows up in rural income distribution figures. In 1995, the richest 20 percent of rural individuals earned 78 percent of the income from wages. The poorest 20 percent of the rural population, in contrast, brought home only minuscule wage income. Poor residents received the overwhelming portion of their income from family production of farm and nonfarm products, a very high proportion of which they retained for their own consumption. But nearly all farm income is taxed, whereas the higher income of the richer rural residents includes substantial portions of nonfarm income from wages and business that escape taxation. Overall, the richest quintile in the countryside in 1995 had a total income roughly ten times that of the poorest quintile, a marked increase in inequality from that found in 1988.[54]

The ability to move into nonfarm work thus has a marked effect on income potential, and this opportunity expanded tremendously under the reforms. The data make clear, moreover, that men more than women have been able to take advantage of the chance to earn nonfarm income. Where women do participate in nonfarm work, they earn less at it than do their male counterparts.[55]

Specifically, women in 1988 constituted only 15 percent of rural technical workers, 26 percent of leading officials of state and collective enterprises, 6 percent of township or town cadres, 9 percent of township or village enterprise cadres, 15 percent of ordinary cadres in party and government institutions, 25 percent of ordinary workers, 32 percent of contract workers, and 21 percent of owners of private enterprises. Women were, however, 51 percent of all farmers. For those women who do earn a wage income, their mean regular monthly wage was only 81 percent of men's wages.[56]

As implied above, the state pursues a highly regressive taxation policy in rural areas. The portion of rural income that is most consistently taxed (that from farm production) is also the portion that is largest among poorer farmers. State policy toward urban residents effectively subsidizes their incomes, although the level of subsidies has declined under the reforms. The net result is an extraordinarily high level of rural-urban income differential by the standards of other developing countries in Asia.[57] From 1984 to 1995, growth in urban-rural inequality accounted for 74 percent of the growth in overall inequality in China.

The level of income inequality in China's cities increased very sharply from 1988 to 1995, more so than the growth in rural inequality over the same years. A great deal of this change resulted from the effects of the subsidized but limited privatization of housing.[58] Since the 1995 survey, many urban developments suggest that urban inequality has continued to grow. These changes include greater unemployment, rapid relative growth of the private sector and reductions in the more egalitarian SOE sector, and massive extension of the private housing market. The actual distribution of various kinds of welfare benefits to mitigate poverty varies greatly by city and thus is difficult to generalize.

A final issue concerns changes in regional income distribution. Across regions, inequalities, both urban and rural, are very substantial. For technical reasons, the 1995 survey does not permit comment on regional inequality. As of 1988, rural per capita incomes in Shanghai were about 2.95 times as large of those of the mountainous southwest province of Guizhou. Urban per capita incomes in Guangdong were nearly 2.2 times as large as those of Shanxi. These data, though, are not sufficiently precise to be very useful. For example, they are presented by province, but many provinces contain very large differences in income distribution. Some individual provinces are, after all, as large and populous as some European countries. Overall provincial averages of per capita income would also be skewed by the level of urbanization of the province, since urbanites generally make far more money than do their rural counterparts.[59] The available data, moreover, do not provide a good baseline from which to measure the changes in distribution of real per capita incomes on a regional basis since the start of the reforms. In broad terms, however, the southeast coastal provinces have fared best under the reforms, with other areas lagging seriously behind.

The overall effects of the reforms on income distribution as of 1995 were complex. Income distribution in the countryside had become less equal, as new opportunities to earn nonfarm income were unevenly distributed. Men received the larger share of this rapidly expanding part of the pie, and thus rural men seem to have benefited more from the reforms than have rural women in terms of per capita income.[60] In addition, as under Mao, the state has continued to intervene in favor of enhancing rural-urban inequalities in per capita income, although it now does so less than it did under the Maoist system. As of 1988 the state took 2 percent of per capita income in the form of taxes in the countryside, but it provided subsidies that on average enhanced urban earned per capita income by 64 percent, producing a net subsidy component of total urban per capita income of 39 percent.

The situation since 1995 has continued to change. As *hukou* restrictions are progressively relaxed, rural residents have increasing opportunities to raise their incomes by moving to the urban economy. Rapid growth of a private sector is producing distinctive middle and wealthy urban classes, but reliable data are difficult to find. Although overall urban subsidies are declining, opportunities to earn substantial urban incomes have increased. The rural-urban income gap thus probably remains the greatest single source of inequality in China, and the government's pertinent policies still on balance exacerbate rather than reduce this differential. The greatest contributions the government can make to reduce this inequality are to lift the *hukou* restrictions on peasant mobility and to create the infrastructure necessary to allow peasants to take advantage of the resulting opportunities to move into the urban economy.

Gender

Women had been one of the most oppressed groups in traditional Confucian society. After 1949, the PRC quickly adopted a new marriage law that made divorce easier to obtain, as well as other measures, such as generous maternity leaves, to meet women's needs. More fundamentally, the collective structures created by the Maoist system significantly weakened extended families, which had been bastions of male domination. In addition, employment practices that brought women into the labor force—where their wages were paid directly to them rather than to the male head of the household—tended to increase the leverage women had in the family.

These changes did not mean full equality for women. Male chauvinism remained deeply embedded in the Chinese psyche. An American leftist delegation that visited China in 1971 was astonished, for example, to find that when they had dinner at the home of Chen Yonggui, the former leader of Dazhai Brigade and a model peasant member of the Politburo, Chen's wife stayed in a corner, not daring to sit at the table.[61] When several female members of the delegation urged her to join them, she demurred, obviously discomfited by the suggestion. Even during the Cultural Revolution, a time of extreme egalitarianism, all female Politburo members had husbands (Mao Zedong, Zhou Enlai, Lin Biao) who were the real leaders of China. Only Wu Yi, who moved from being an alternate to being a full member of the Politburo in 2002, has held the latter status without having a husband who was also a Politburo member.

Generally, women received lower compensation than men. Sometimes they were shunted into lower-paying jobs; at other times, especially in the countryside, it was assumed they could not do the quantity and quality of work that their male counterparts could accomplish. More often than not, female peasants are left behind to till the fields while their husbands and brothers seek higher-paying urban jobs. Women also were generally expected to take care of the household chores, in addition to holding a job.[62]

It appears that urban women as well as rural women are not faring as well as men under the reforms. In urban areas, the Maoist system accorded women a number of benefits, including earlier retirement with pension rights, extended maternity leave with pay (with options for longer leaves without pay), and crèches and nurseries at the workplace. Because managers did not particularly focus on making profits, they did not begrudge female employees these benefits.

The reforms have changed the calculus, especially for the increasing number of urban firms that are not protected from market competition by state subsidies. Stories abound in the Chinese press about the reluctance of managers to hire female employees because of the financial burdens of these mandated benefits. Female university graduates have trouble finding work, whereas their male counterparts are snapped up by firms in the export sector and elsewhere.[63] A 1995 survey shows that urban women generally receive lower wages for the same jobs and are systematically underrepresented in upper-level management positions.[64]

In the countryside, the restoration of family farming has probably strengthened the role of male heads of households. Studies show that, as was the case before collectivization of agriculture, the head of the family generally allocates rural household incomes from farming among members. Often, this is the head of an extended, rather than a nuclear, family. Women typically do not fare well under such conditions. As noted above, moreover, females have been less able to take advantage of the higher-paying opportunities outside of farm labor that the reforms have opened up.[65]

Women especially bear the brunt of the birth-control effort, which has been enforced vigorously under the reforms. The PRC's extraordinarily strict and successful birth-control program places the responsibility for limiting births overwhelmingly on women.[66] Policy since the 1980s has limited each urban couple to only one child. Many rural couples are allowed to have a second child if the first is a girl. With the dissolution of the collectives, the financial advantage of a male child in the countryside—who will remain with his parents and will bring in a spouse to the household rather than moving to another family on marriage—has grown.

Experience in other countries such as India demonstrates that such pressures may lead to tragic consequences for wives who bear female offspring. They often assume "blame" for the sex of the child, and may suffer terrible abuse at the hands of the husband's family as a consequence.

Female infanticide is another expected result occurring in rural China.[67] Indeed, current statistics show that poor and minority localities, where the government's birth-control program is not rigorously implemented, have relatively low ratios of male to female births. Tibet is 1.02; Xinjiang is 1.06; Guizhou is 1.07; IMAR (Inner Mongolian Autonomous Region) and Ningxia are 1.08. But in wealthier areas where the birth-control program is more rigorously carried out, sex ratios of live births are much higher (Hainan is 1.36; Guangdong is 1.30), reflecting the determination to have male children if state policy precludes having second child.[68]

In addition, reports from China indicate that the old practice of kidnapping women and selling them to men who want a spouse has revived and is spreading. Gangs operate across provincial boundaries and deal in tens of thousands of victims. Some of these are urban women, but most are from rural households. Because this trade in human traffic is illegal, it is impossible to know its scale.[69] For similar reasons, there are no accurate statistics on the ubiquitous sex trade throughout China today.

In sum, it appears that on balance women's positions in society have suffered under the reforms. Like men, of course, women enjoy an improved overall standard of living as the economy grows; nevertheless, their position *relative* to men has in some important ways deteriorated. Tellingly and startlingly, the rate of female suicide in China is the highest in the world, with young rural women being most likely to take their own lives.[70]

Generations

Despite enormous economic growth, contemporary Chinese society is under great stress, with social tensions pervasive in both urban and rural life. Generational fractiousness adds to the strain. People generally form their basic political ideas and identity when they are in their teens and twenties. The turbulence of twentieth-century Chinese history has afforded different generations with very different socialization experiences, producing a society that is now deeply marked by strong generational cleavages.

One man, for example, became a prominent banker in pre-1949 China. Initially embraced by the communists in the early 1950s, he fell victim to the Antirightist campaign in 1957 and then suffered tremendously during the Cultural Revolution. Nevertheless, during the 1990s he became deeply chagrined that Mao Zedong was not accorded greater respect. Even though Mao destroyed his life, he still regarded the late Chairman as a true hero of the Chinese nation. Why? Because Mao led a political movement that united China after decades of warlordism and foreign invasion. In the words of this man in the mid-1990s, "That was not easy, and it took a hero to accomplish this. I will always respect Chairman Mao. No contemporary leader is his equal."

Many of those who joined the urban work force during the early and mid-1950s believe deeply in the kind of system that accorded them serious job opportunities, on-the-job training, and financial security. Recent studies show that these early job entrants after 1949 generally experienced substantial upward mobility. Many, now in retirement or nearing that age, find the new economics of the reform era, which has cast them aside, profoundly immoral. The socialist system served many in this generation well, and they see its virtues as well as—or more than—its faults.[71]

The Cultural Revolution generation is China's lost generation: people whose education was cut short when they were told to take to the streets to "make revolution" then found, when it was all over, that real opportunities would go to those with better educations. Those who were encouraged to attack the power elite in the party saw these same officials come back with a vengeance and their offspring also do well. Those who in the political heat of the times killed fellow students, tortured teachers, beat elderly people, and in some cases denounced their own family members must now live with the haunting memories of their deeds. And for the most part, these people lack the skills to succeed in the new society. These are disproportionately the workers and managers being laid off from SOEs. Many are finding ways to cope and accept their difficulties as necessary for China to reform its economy, but the rate of finding new employment for such individuals has dropped precipitously since 1999.[72]

Those growing up since the early 1980s are having very different experiences. Where the previous generation was raised on a diet of political struggle and personal sacrifice, the present generation includes many pampered offspring of single-child households. Raised during the consumer revolution, they have seen television and more recently mobile phones and computers become natural parts of their environment. They are taught to worship money rather than politics and not to cause political trouble, lest it become more difficult for them to get ahead. This generation is, overall, individually ambitious, materialistic, pampered, and politically agnostic. It is a postrevolutionary generation.

Each generation is more complex than indicated here, and this layering is also imprecise. Still, it may be said that in China few fundamental political and social values are widely accepted across generations. Generations differ sharply over the role government should play in shaping the economy and society, whether people should seek broad social engagement, and what types of careers and behaviors are respectable. Even views of China's past vary by generation. The present urban generation, moreover, has little understanding of—or respect for—the majority of the population that toils in the countryside.

Conclusion

Chinese society has been undergoing massive change, as are relations between the society and the state. So much is in motion that it is impossible to capture it all in summary fashion. Parts of China remain deeply traditional and largely separate even from the market, while major cities such as Shanghai are becoming integral parts of the global society culturally and economically. Anecdotal data about all of this abound, but the reality is that the social landscape is too variegated and dynamic to permit analysts to generalize with confidence.

Three broad questions—concerning state-society relations, the internal structure of society, and the ethical underpinnings of the system—are of fundamental importance for the future.

First, how will relations between the state and society evolve? The picture painted above is that of a retreating state seeking to form ties to society through corporatist-type structures, each of which embodies a social interest and has an approved relationship with the government. This approach, if it works, will allow both for social differentiation and recognition of varying interests and for the virtual elimination of competition to represent those interests in the polity. It therefore retains overall power in the hands of the state, which in turn engages through its various parts with social groups and sectors in orderly negotiated relations.

There is no cultural reason why this corporatist approach should fail. But corporatism requires that citizens generally find the state's actions to be reasonably fair and equitable. This approach therefore assumes that social tensions will be kept within manageable boundaries through sufficient state responsiveness to popular sentiments. Current changes in China do not assure this outcome.

The success of the corporatist approach will likely be shaped by the degree to which Chinese officials successfully address three related issues that are now very much on the policy agenda: developing more effective means to constrain predatory official corruption; developing the means to move increasingly toward rule of law so that citizens feel they are adequately protected from administrative abuse; and developing the integuments of a social safety net that keeps the losers in the reforms from losing all hope in the system.

If instead corruption becomes more widespread and deeply rooted, if local despotism becomes harsher, and if those who do not fare well under the reforms see the state abandoning them, then social movements in opposition to the state are likely to undermine the controlled evolution of state-society relations that corporatism seeks. Peasant discontent can form a major part of this problem. In the countryside, stagnant incomes, official exactions, and expropriations of land by rapacious local leaders are combining to produce rising levels of protest activity.[73] Should trends move in this direction, other developments, such as the vastly improved ability of Chinese citizens to communicate with each other and to move about the country, will become important ingredients in the mix of forces that will shape the ability of socially mobilized groups to resist and undermine state authority.

The second and related question is, What kind of class structure and class consciousness will emerge in society itself? China now has millionaires who enjoy very close ties with key government and part officials. Will these individuals be able to solidify alliances to protect their wealth and hold down competition? The Sixteenth Party Congress in November 2002 adopted the "three represents" as a new guiding principle for the party. One of the congress's key consequences is that wealthy Chinese who have made fortunes under the reforms will now be able to seek positions of political power. This raises the possibility that in a matter of decades the Chinese political system could evolve into a form of oligarchy.

An urban middle class has been forming very rapidly. In the West, this class played an especially crucial role in seeking protections for its property and activities from the feudal states from which it emerged. In China, privatization of housing, development of private enterprises, and the emergence of a consumer culture may move the new middle class in broadly similar directions, and foreign pressure for improved property rights (along with foreign models of individual rights) can add to this tendency. But to date the middle class in China has developed in close interaction with the state rather than in partial opposition to it. Many interviews indicate that members of the middle class generally view the state as a source of new opportunities and seek more effective ways to develop their ties with it. The type of approach the middle class will take to the state is therefore still very unclear, but this issue will potentially play a crucial role in defining state-society relations in the coming decades.[74]

The working class is another question mark. The privileged urban workers of the SOEs under Mao no longer hold sway. The influx of peasants into the cities, combined with the erosion of traditional employment structures and related understandings of social obligation, have together created conditions that allow for massive exploitation of many workers.[75] Worker discontent is thus high in numerous places, but there are very strong structural obstacles to the development of working class consciousness and organization. The workers in Shenzhen near Hong Kong, for example, are mostly young peasant migrants from the interior provinces of Hunan and Sichuan, who have no knowledge of the previous state socialist system and its mindset. Workers in the rust belt of the northeast, by contrast, generally have grown up in state-owned enterprises and bring a very different reference frame to bear. It is very hard for one of these groups to relate to the other. In addition, the party has outlawed independent labor unions. Each worker in an enterprise of twenty-five or more employees can join only one union, and that union typically works closely with management to undermine labor activism. Where labor unrest does occur—and it occurs almost daily—the authorities have developed generally effective means to cool things down and to prevent workers from different units from linking up. Should some spark produce major unrest, the potential for worker activism and violence in China now is much greater than in 1989. But the future is far from certain, and the growing influx of peasants to the cities will maintain pressure on workers to keep their grievances in check so as to keep to their jobs lest they be replaced by others only too eager to step in.

A final major question mark concerns the nature—and importance—of the value structure that will undergird China as it continues its rush to become a wealthy society. Massive movements of people off the land, changes in the terms and structure of urban employment, exposure to international capital and media, and rapidly changing income structures have exacerbated already existing generational cleavages to produce fundamental confusion over such basic social issues as status and rules of behavior. The only idea that seems to be widely accepted among Chinese now is that making money and improving one's standard of living are important. Attitudes toward culture, posterity, marriage, sex, and other core issues are in great flux.

Scholars of traditional China and of the Maoist era have typically felt that Chinese society was almost unique in the extent to which the political leadership was expected to provide and nurture a compelling moral framework, which in turn was an absolute prerequisite to social and economic well-being. A core issue confronting students of China is, therefore, whether this major facet of the conventional wisdom is still valid. If it is, one must now judge Chinese society—including the cadres at the basic level of the Chinese state—to be a potential source of major instability. Few even among basic-level officials now view the political leadership as providing moral authority. Thus, the ability of that leadership to buy social peace with economic success must be questioned.

The November 2002 Sixteenth Party Congress formally established the goal of making China a "well-off society" and quadrupling its GDP by the year 2020. It, however, left two questions unanswered. Can China achieve that level of success without in the process developing a meaningful value consensus to help hold the society together? And if it succeeds economically but without underlying ethical principles to guide behavior, what impact will that vastly more powerful China have on its neighbors and the world?

11
China Faces the Future

Even though China for the past quarter century has enjoyed enormous success, it faces an uncertain future. Knowledgeable observers have predicted everything from system collapse,[1] to the development of a federal system,[2] to a fundamental renegotiation of the country's dominant cultural ethos from a northern, inward-looking, anti-imperialist world view to a southern, outward-looking, cosmopolitan world view.[3]

These uncertainties emerge from the inconsistencies in China's current situation. China retains an authoritarian system; its political system has more officials than many countries have citizens. But numerous party cadres themselves no longer take communism seriously. The country does not have even an outward appearance of the regimentation and mechanical obedience associated with Leninist party systems.

China's sheer complexity magnifies the uncertainties. The fastest-growing parts of the country along the coastal regions in the south are being spurred ahead by private business and creative tie-ins with foreign capital, especially with overseas Chinese businesses. But China must also deal with both the world's largest rural population—much of it living in poor conditions—and a process of urbanization that involves more people leaving the land in a shorter period than at any previous time in human history. Because so many facets—the political system, the economy, and society—are changing significantly and simultaneously, it is little wonder that observers cannot agree on China's future path. Evidence can support seemingly any scenario; modesty in predicting the future is warranted.

This concluding chapter begins by reviewing the dynamics of the Chinese political system from the apex to the relations between leaders and society. On this basis, it assesses the key internal forces now shaping the future evolution of the domestic system. It then turns to China's interaction with the international arena. International developments have affected China's domestic agenda from the late Qing dynasty to the present. This chapter therefore concludes with an analysis of how the international arena and domestic developments might interact to shape China's future during the coming years, both internally and in foreign policy.

Understanding Domestic Developments

The Chinese state is now driven by the need to provide higher living standards for its huge, growing population. The structures of state control imposed by Mao Zedong froze people into place, distorted information, wasted technical talent, and forced economic enterprises to assume responsibilities for nonproductive tasks. These factors eventually made creating enough new jobs and satisfying material wants impossible. It was not so much enlightened beneficence as calculated fear that drove the leaders of China in the late 1970s to restructure the system. The reforms have altered not only the Chinese economy but the political system as well, making it less ideological, less coercive, less enveloping for the average citizen, and more inclined to utilize laws and regulations to govern. It is also, notably, far less centralized. But fear of unrest continues to be a major driving force of ongoing reform.

DECENTRALIZATION AND STABILITY

One of the most important, most confusing aspects of political change during the reforms has been the decentralization of decision making. Introduction of market-based economic development required shifting the locus of economic decision making to lower levels of the state. For economic growth and rising living standards to provide the key to stability, localities needed the flexibility to tap their resources for local economic success. Localities have therefore gained the ability to initiate policies and adopt strategies that differ significantly from those being articulated in Beijing. In return, Beijing demands that local officials maintain political stability.

Thus officials have struck an implicit national political bargain to achieve political stability based on rapid economic growth. In the words of the major report to the November 2002 Sixteenth Party Congress, "It is essential for the Party to give top priority to development," but "stability is a prerequisite for reform and development."[4] Rapid growth requires greater flexibility at all levels of the political system. The Center allows this flexibility, as long as growth and stability are the outcomes. Localities raise the specter of instability whenever Beijing tells them to rein in economic expansion.

This national political compact has made economic success an important part of the performance evaluation of local party and government officials. Party cadres no longer must enforce such former political priorities as egalitarianism; they now join fully in the effort to maximize local economic growth, as illustrated by the example of Su Zhiming in Chapter 10. This gives both party and government cadres strong incentives to circumvent those policies adopted in Beijing that might constrain local growth.

This local orientation of cadres marks a significant change from the Maoist era, when the incentives pointed up to higher levels more than down to the locality. The reform strategy has strengthened the new local focus by permitting greater localization in cadre appointments and encouraging rapid development of collective and private enterprises. Their profits fund much of the local state budget.

Real decentralization has thus occurred in China under the reforms. The territorial governing bodies at provincial, municipal, county, and township levels have gained enormous initiative at the expense of the vertical functional bureaucracies that reach to Beijing—the *kuai* has gained at the expense of the *tiao,* in Chinese bureaucratic parlance. The spirit of state activity has also changed. The state no longer promotes either revolution or ideological orthodoxy. Rather, it promotes economic growth by any means that do not produce massive social and political instability.

Measured against the criteria of the Maoist system, these changes appear to weaken China's state system. If we expect conformity to central directives and uniformity in outlook and behavior, then contemporary developments provide massive evidence testifying to the failures of the Center and to the potential for regime collapse. But the reforms have made this a misleading test of system resilience. The Center has come to rely on local initiative and flexibility to strengthen the regime as a whole.[5] To a certain extent, therefore, diversity now indicates adaptability, dynamism, and strength.

But where does power lie in this more decentralized system? Empirical studies create the impression that it lies almost wherever we look. Professors Jean Oi and Susan Whiting, for example, find that township- and county-level officials have become key political and economic actors. Many are highly entrepreneurial in promoting their local interests.[6] Yongnian Zheng finds that much the same is true on the provincial level.[7] How can these observations be reconciled?

Perhaps the most useful way to think about the overall Chinese system at this point is to see it as a nested system of territorial administrations, with substantial policy initiative at each territorial level: the township, county, city, province, and Center. Officials at each level give much attention to garnering resources and striking deals that will benefit the locality governed by that level of state administration. Each is willing to allow lower levels to do what they wish so long as this does not upset their own plans. In the absence of formal institutional mechanisms and a legitimate constitutional framework to give this system regularity and predictability, much is sorted out in practice through consensus building and negotiation.

The result is a dynamic, variegated set of relationships that combine bargaining, organizational routines, laws, and regulations in determining how officials actually behave. The particulars of this mix vary greatly across issues, locations, levels of the political system, and time periods.

THE CENTER

Despite substantial decentralization, the Center retains important powers. Even today, China's leaders still enjoy the powerful organizational resources they developed to govern a communist system: control over official appointments, and military and civilian coercive forces that are not constrained by the law when issues of political power are at stake. The new leadership lineup in the wake of the Sixteenth Party Congress, significantly, assigns a larger cadre of top leaders than previously to assume specific responsibility for overseeing domestic security.

But Beijing does not rely on force alone. Despite reform, the Center retains major leverage over the country's economy, setting national economic priorities and determining the allocation of a very substantial amount of centrally directed spending. It stipulates pertinent regulations on a very wide array of economic-related issues, apportions the tax burden, controls the money supply, and chooses the directors of the major SOEs. It also stipulates the regulatory environment and within some limits sets import tariffs, exchange-rate rules, and rules governing foreign direct investment.

In addition to disbursing funds, the Center also is a source of expertise on economic development issues.[8] Localities have plunged into expansion of their service sectors and light industries, which provide the most rapid returns on investment. But pressures are mounting for many locations to develop higher-technology industries in the face of international and domestic competition. The Center still has a significant edge in areas of advanced research, and thus many local authorities seek technical and other assistance from the Center as they try to march up the technology ladder.

In extremis, the Center dispatches special work teams to particular places to investigate problems and rectify local actions. These teams may conduct investigations that result in the imposition of fines, dismissal of officials, and the prosecution of offenders, as happened in the 1990s on a major scale in both Xiamen and Shenyang and on a lesser scale in other cities. Localities conduct their business with an eye to avoiding actions that might trigger a work-team investigation.[9]

Outside of the economic sphere, the degree of central authority varies by issue area.[10] Despite enormous opening up of the media, the Center is still able to have all domestic print and broadcast media carry its own version of stories and to block coverage of events and topics that it finds sensitive.[11] Where the Center chooses to take a strong stand, as in limiting population growth, it can produce impressive results. Enforcing a stringent policy of birth control in the face of the desire of almost all peasants to have male children requires local officials to intervene in the most private activities of spouses throughout the countryside. Since the 1970s, the Center has time and again demonstrated its seriousness in punishing officials whose jurisdictions run afoul of birth-control quotas.

Moreover, the weight of Chinese history significantly enhances the Center's role in the system. China's culture continues to instill habits of obedience and the desire for a strong, virtuous state, values that differ from the political attitudes and actions of those socialized in Western liberal societies. The political "line" emanating from the Center thus has force, not in dictating every detail of behavior but in creating a policy atmosphere that affects popular attitudes and actions. Deng Xiaoping's early 1992 "southern tour" in which he advocated faster growth, more openness, and more rapid movement toward markets, for example, had a marked effect on the activities of many officials throughout the political apparatus. In like fashion, since late 2001 the Center's implementation of China's WTO accession agreement obligations is markedly changing the way the country's economy is working, and having the Sixteenth Congress set the goals of developing China into a "well-off society" and quadrupling its GDP by 2020 should have a palpable effect on attitudes of officials at all levels.[12]

These elements combine to accord the Center strong leverage in the system. Provincial and lower-level leaders devote great time and energy to dealing with the Center, in cultivating relationships, seeking new resources, and asking for exemptions from various centrally dictated obligations. Every provincial leader tries to balance the demands of the Center with the needs of the province, and none can afford to let the balance tip too far in either direction without paying dearly for this error.

At the Center, both the trends and the limits of change are noteworthy. The trends are in hopeful directions. The average level of education of central level officials has rapidly climbed. Twenty-two of the twenty-five Politburo members elected at the Sixteenth Party Congress have university educations. That compares favorably with the seventeen out of twenty-four on the Fifteenth Politburo, and it marks a fundamental change from the Politburo elected in 1982, in which no member had a university education. Throughout the Center, levels of competence and sophistication are generally high. Differentiation is increasing between activities of the party and government and within the government between the executive and legislative bodies. On the government side, transparency has increased markedly. Ideological battles no longer drive outcomes or produce major policy swings; the range of political debate more nearly approximates that in noncommunist countries. Factionalism certainly exists, but the political game has become increasingly civilized in both its rewards and its consequences for the losers. And no single leader can rule by whim. Indeed, the distinctive powers of the "core leader" appear to be declining over time.

Overall, within the confines of a one-party authoritarian system, the operations of the Center have thus become increasingly competent, regularized, and transparent. The most recent succession provides evidence that even leadership change is becoming more predictable. In the Sixteenth Politburo, the members of the Fifteenth Politburo who had not resigned at the Sixteenth Party Congress filled all but two of the Politburo Standing Committee slots.[13] This suggests an informal system in which the next generation of Politburo Standing Committee members first becomes fully familiar with Politburo responsibilities and norms through service as a non–Standing Committee member of the Politburo. We would not expect this type of norm in a dictatorial system in which factional battles shape the outcomes.

But these trends, though palpable, are easily overstated. At the highest levels the communist party still pulls together all the key players. Party bodies are the locus of decision making for major choices on everything from the succession to economic, social, administrative, and security policy. The party side of the system remains highly nontransparent and is not subject to external checks and balances by the government, judiciary, media, or citizenry. Although the trend is toward greater specification of and adherence to rules within the party itself, the CCP remains on balance a highly undemocratic part of the political system. And factionalism has not disappeared.

The more fruitful questions to ask presently about the Center, therefore, concern not its leverage but its organizational capacity. Under the reforms, these capacities on balance have grown. Beijing's leaders have lost the control over subordinate levels that ideological commitment formerly gave them. But the changes they have made in the political system have enhanced their ability to gather information and to analyze it through better-trained professional staffs. Because political battle at the Center is no longer a matter of life and death, the views of most participants are now more freely aired, at least within party councils. This improves the quality of decision making at the Center.

In short, the array of activities the Maoist system seemed to control from the top was illusory. Too few people with too little information and too many ideological constraints meant that, very often, broad pronouncements from the Center left considerable room for local adaptation, even as the verbal affirmations of ideological loyalty created the impression of disciplined conformity. Now the mask is off, producing a superficial impression of less cohesion, but actually strengthening the capacities of the Center for realistic decision making.

It is also significant that one of the most important sets of decisions the Center has made has been to reduce its role in the system and to reduce, overall, the scope of activities by government and party bodies in the system as a whole. The fundamental concept is to free up the energies of lower bureaucratic levels and of individual citizens to produce new ideas and wealth. This set of decisions has not gone so far as to establish effective statutory or procedural limits on what the party and/or government can do if they choose to act, but the changes have produced a vast reduction in the overall level of ongoing, detailed interference in lower levels by the Center, as well as in the extent to which officials seek to shape the thoughts and actions of China's nearly 1.3 billion citizens.

BELOW THE CENTER

With the exception of control over the PLA, almost all the above types of resources available to the Center are also available to each lower territorial level of the system as it deals with its subordinates. Each territorial level retains control over nomenklatura appointments, certain police and security functions, aspects of the local regulatory environment, and so forth. Generally, all want their constituent localities to prosper and to maintain stability. But this system remains characterized by what the Chinese call powerful, interfering "mothers-in-law."

Systemic analytical capacities and information flows have improved greatly in many provinces and lower-level administrative bodies of the state. The increased flexibility resulting from the decentralization has made the system more adaptive to local peculiarities and responsive to local strengths and weaknesses. In sum, the system capacities of the state have in many ways grown overall since the reforms began, even as the state itself has become less disciplined internally.

But society has also become more vibrant and less responsive to state direction since 1978. The Maoist state prevented people from either expressing their ideas or changing their places of work or residence. The systems of unit-based study groups, activists, informers, and party members made people careful in their remarks, and the encapsulated nature of units prevented ideas from spreading through other than official channels.[14] The erosion of the unit system, therefore, carries with it a major consequence: the state no longer tightly combines control over political thought with control over the work environment and access to social welfare. Ideas can now spread horizontally among the populace to a greater extent than ever before. And ideology has thus basically disappeared as a tool to encourage social conformity.

Local governments have, moreover, become avid seekers of foreign direct investment, economic competitors with each other, collaborators with successful business people and, in some instances, accomplices with criminal organizations. They have also become centers of experimentation in testing out different types of political reforms.

This set of developments has increased the dynamism, diversity, and corruption in China's multilayered political system.

The Future

China has developed enormous momentum toward transforming itself into a modern country that will, in a matter of two decades or so, potentially be second only to the United States in international importance. This would symbolically represent the country's coming full circle from its peak during the Qing Dynasty, through a century and a half of troubles, back to a place of almost unique power and stature. The repercussions of the Industrial Revolution, resulting in a surge in the power projection capabilities and aspirations of newly industrializing countries, brought China low. China's leaders now believe that China's ability to leverage strategic participation in the process of growing global interdependence holds out the prospect of boosting the country to new heights.

There are many reasons to feel that China can sustain its current momentum and take advantage of future opportunities to continue its upward trajectory. Socialist ideological constraints no longer seriously bind the thinking of the elites. Market forces have increasingly been introduced into the economy without provoking a systemic crisis or collapse. The political system itself has adapted in profound ways to the new situation, recruiting talented people, adopting incentives that promote continued economic development, and changing everything from policy process to tax systems to the nature of basic level political organization in order to meet the new demands the reforms have created.

China is in fact accelerating its integration into the international economy through massive measures to implement its accession obligations under the World Trade Organization. If this process continues in reasonably steady fashion, China will become considerably more open to foreign investment, more transparent to its own citizens and foreigners alike, and more economically interdependent.[15] All of these processes, like those of the previous quarter century of reform, will further change the country's social structure, psychology, and political dynamics.

But as earlier chapters have indicated, this process will have to address successfully very daunting challenges. How the leadership deals with these challenges will determine the actual future of the PRC, as opposed to the rosy prospective future that current trends imply. The Sixteenth Party Congress stipulated that China should double its GDP by 2020 and indicated that the time from now until then will be crucial for determining the nature of China for the remainder of this century.[16] Additional issues currently obscure may loom up to play a crucial role, but the key, already evident issues that the country and its leaders will confront between now and 2020 are imposing and include the following.

THE MAJOR DOMESTIC CHALLENGES

Political transformation is of crucial importance. China's leaders now see their society as increasingly dynamic and differentiated. Their basic response is to make adjustments to the structure and political processes in the party in order to understand social and economic needs and respond effectively to them. They want the party to continue to hold the country together and guide it through a period of rapid economic and social change, even as they seek ways to enhance governmental efficiency by limiting party interference in nonessential issues.

But the party itself is an organization without esprit. No energizing ideology motivates its members to excel at public service and suffer personal sacrifice. Corruption has seeped deeply into the party's organization. With the party reserving to itself the right to make all major decisions, including those with potentially enormous economic consequences, a continuing party monopoly on power runs a serious risk that corruption will grow to the point where it imperils the moral authority and discipline of the party and actually undermines economic growth and social stability. Those at the top of the system fully recognize the danger, and the new administration under Hu Jintao is acutely aware of the need to address this issue seriously.

The future evolution of the party is, though, an issue fraught with peril. Some reformers advocate resolving the tensions between an authoritarian party and an increasingly pluralistic society by adopting the model of Japan's Liberal Democratic Party or of Mexico's Partido Revolucionario Institucional (before 1990)—that is, to have the party allow the development of various factions that compete for power within the framework of the party itself. In that way, political competition can be legitimized without the risk that the party itself will be swept from power. Various social interests could potentially feel that they have achieved a sort of "representation" in an ongoing one-party system.

The danger of such a development is that factionalism could overwhelm the cohesion of the party, leaving it unable to promote the changes necessary for China to continue to meet its economic development objectives. China's current financial problems, for example, may be on a scale comparable to those of contemporary Japan. Many analysts who are very pessimistic about Japan's ability to address these issues adequately are more optimistic about China's prospects precisely because the party is more able to take strong measures when necessary to address critical issues. Should the CCP become more like the LDP, that Chinese advantage may be lost.

Another approach to making the political system more responsive to an evolving society is to permit a gradual spread in the system of elections. Today, elections are held for leaders of villages and for members of the People's Congresses of townships. There is also some experimentation with elections for leaders of urban community committees. Some reformers now advocate that over the coming decade elections should gradually be permitted for the top executive leadership positions at the township, county, and city levels. In the contemporary Chinese system, the vast majority of decisions that directly affect most citizens are made at the city level and below. Allowing elections to that level would, therefore, potentially permit meaningful political participation along with tight control of national strategic issues by the CCP.

Allowing elections to positions at higher political levels involves nomination and campaign processes among ever larger communities. This would raise serious issues about the permissible nature of political organization. Would the party have to permit the development of other political parties to contest for local office? Would instead the CCP seek to maintain a monopoly on political organization but establish rules that allow nonparty people to run for office? The latter occurred in Taiwan in the 1980s, but the nonparty forces soon identified themselves as *dang wai* (literally, "outside the party"). Over a period of less than a decade, *dang wai* itself evolved into a quasi-party and then into various actual electoral parties. Beijing's leaders are well aware of this history.

China's political elite fears that a multiparty system may sweep the CCP aside but fail to substitute other political organizations capable of holding the country together and guiding determined economic development. They therefore are concentrating primarily on changes to make the party function internally in a more democratic fashion and to delineate more clearly the spheres of influence of the party, the government bureaucracies, and the legislatures. But this effort runs the risk that demands for more meaningful reform will outstrip the party's ability to change itself. Although there is ample reason for debate and uncertainty over the best path to follow, there is no question that determined efforts at political reform are necessary if China is to remain stable and on the upward economic trajectory that it seeks. This issue of political evolution is one of the most significant for anticipating how China will fare in the coming decades.

Broader changes in institutional capacity have also become pressing agenda items if China is to continue its present successful route. Essentially, in the late 1990s China's leaders allowed some problems to slide along without focused attention as they pursued policies to assure continued high rates of growth during and after the 1997–98 Asian financial crisis. The leaders must address those issues in the coming years if the dynamic stability of the Chinese system is to be sustained.

Development of a social safety net outside the work unit must be high on this agenda. As of early 2003, only about a third of the urban permanent residents work in public work units. Most work in the private, collective, and foreign-invested sectors. In addition, tens of millions are unemployed. As WTO obligations are implemented and as peasant migration continues and accelerates, these non-*danwei* segments of the urban population are certain to increase rapidly. The needs of all of these groups must be addressed via a new social safety net that exists outside of the public work units.

The solution is to accumulate funds at the municipal level and allocate those funds to various groups to meet vital needs in welfare, unemployment compensation, health care, pensions, and so forth. But all of this requires the development of institutional capacities to understand the evolution of urban society and to collect, manage, and allocate funds accordingly. At present, Chinese officials lack good statistical models of their own urban populations and therefore face daunting challenges in developing systems that embody long-term obligations for which citizens will hold the government to account.

In addition, marketization efforts since the late 1970s have unintentionally produced sharp deterioration in many of the public goods the government formerly provided. This erosion in state services is seen clearly in the rural public health system. Peasants formerly received basic health care services virtually free. Now, however, rural health infrastructure is very poor and, for the average peasant, very expensive. Rates of infectious diseases and of infant mortality have crept up under the weight of these changes. The 2003 SARS epidemic highlighted the importance of rebuilding the rural public health system infrastructure, especially since peasant mobility now establishes potentially dangerous linkages between rural health problems and urban well-being.

China faces severe domestic government debt problems. The government's official debt levels are rising very rapidly though still manageable, but additional obligations are daunting. Most notably, the four major state-owned commercial banks are technically bankrupt. Citizens continue to trust their very substantial savings to these institutions both because the Chinese have almost no alternative places to invest their funds and because of a universal expectation that the government budget and tax authority in reality stand behind these major banks. But the lack of alternatives for Chinese citizens is drawing to a close with China's WTO accession agreement, which requires that by 2006 the country allow foreign banks to conduct the same array of business activities as Chinese domestic banks do.

The Chinese banks will fare satisfactorily only if by 2006 they have brought their bad-debt levels down to the point where they can attract foreign investors and retain the confidence of Chinese depositors. This is likely to mean that the Chinese government must inject upward of $300 billion into the banking system, along with forcing through major institutional reforms. It will also require curtailing nonproductive loans to SOEs, thus running substantial risks of increasing unemployment (and therefore social safety-net) burdens. With those changes, foreign banks may prove willing to invest in Chinese banks at a level sufficient to provide the basis for healthy evolution of the Chinese banking system. Fixing China's financial mess is both necessary and burdensome as the leaders set their priorities for the coming years. Indeed, a potential financial crisis looms as one of the greatest potential threats to the country's economic health and stability over the next five years.

The financial problem is exacerbated by the already very high level of debt of county and township governments around the country, which has become so worrisome that drastic measures to address it are being considered. These include some proposals to abolish the township level of government completely, replacing it by some coordinating bodies belonging to the counties.[17] This would enable townships to shed many of the official positions that now increase their costs. But it would also create numerous new problems. For example, many township governments and officials now both hold substantial debt and are major investors in local industries. Abolishing this level of government would create very nettlesome problems of trying to straighten out the resulting equities. In addition, it is not at all clear where dismissed officials would find new employment. The effort to reduce the *bianzhi* at all levels that began in 1998 resulted in 50 percent reductions at the Center but only 20 percent reductions at the county and township because the higher levels could find alternative sources of income for those let go, but the local levels do not have this flexibility.

Straightening out townships is thus likely to be a complex and expensive proposition. This effort entails serious potential political complications, as it would replace a level of government currently considered ripe for moving to direct elections with an administrative organ even more divorced from the local population. This could prove a costly setback to the broader demand for the CCP to find ways to increase the sense of representation among the Chinese people. In addition, this set of changes would vastly complicate the administrative burdens on already stretched county governments.

Environmental issues further cloud the future. As explained in Chapter 10, only a combination of institutional changes to increase efficiency and expensive, socially disruptive projects to make more water available will prevent major water-based constraints on the future economic growth of the densely populated North China plain. Other environmental problems are producing rapid declines in the quality of arable land, escalating public health costs, and increasing worries about quality-of-life issues among the urban population. The economic, social, and political costs are rising constantly.[18]

Beijing has been increasing its commitment of funds for environmental efforts and has adopted sustainable development as, at least rhetorically, a major guiding philosophy. But the realities of the distribution of power and interests in the current Chinese political system, along with fundamental constraints such as China's ongoing reliance on coal as its major energy source, leave the adequacy of Beijing's efforts in doubt. Mitigating these problems will require a combination of political will and massive funds. It will also require institutional changes that shift more power into the hands of those regulators who give priority to environmental concerns.

THE MAJOR TRANSNATIONAL CHALLENGES

The huge domestic challenges add to the normal difficulties of managing a society as large and complex as the PRC. These challenges will consume the major part of the attention of China's post–Sixteenth Party Congress leaders, a group whose members in any case are notable for their career-long focus on domestic affairs. But in very significant ways the international arena will also intrude on these leaders' agenda, affecting their capacities to stay on top of their domestic concerns. Moreover, three major territorial political issues—Xinjiang, Tibet, and Taiwan—have not only domestic but also serious transnational political components.

China has grave concerns about some of its western territories. Over 90 percent of the country's population lives in the southeast half of its territory. The northwest half is populated primarily with minorities, some of whom are only poorly integrated into the national culture.[19]

In this context, the recent growth of Islamic fundamentalism and related terrorism in western Asia worries Beijing. The Soviet Union's collapse opened up central Asia to religious politics, and other developments during the 1990s strengthened fundamentalist and terrorist movements in Pakistan, Afghanistan, and elsewhere in the region. China responded starting in the mid-1990s by working with other countries in the region to form the "Shanghai Five" (later known as the Shanghai Cooperation Organization), which by 1998 had turned its attention to fighting terrorism. Beijing also brutally suppressed all activities that it regarded as either terrorist related or separatist in the Xinjiang-Uighur Autonomous Region. Xinjiang's Muslims inhabit a vast, sparsely populated area that contains large deposits of oil, natural gas, and minerals. China is determined to prevent this region from becoming unsettled by ethnic strife and violence, and it fears international developments that could potentially increase the terrorist threat emanating from this area. If Pakistan were to fall under fundamentalist Islamic control, for example, the security implications for China in its northwest would be palpable. Since the September 11, 2001 terrorist attacks on the World Trade Center and the Pentagon, these concerns have contributed to Beijing's willingness to work with the United States in its counterterrorism initiatives in Afghanistan and elsewhere. But China is anxious to see American activities throughout the region conducted in a fashion that does not inadvertently increase the ability of terrorists to recruit from local Muslim populations in and outside of China. Beijing also remains concerned about an ongoing American military presence in Central Asia.[20]

Tibet is also located in this sparsely populated northwest half of the PRC. High in the Himalayas, the Tibet Autonomous Region is far from Han Chinese areas both geographically and culturally. Beijing took control of this area in 1951 through an agreement that the Dalai Lama, Tibet's spiritual leader, signed under pressure. In 1959 a Tibetan revolt against Chinese rule failed, and the Dalai Lama fled into India, where he has ever since maintained a government in exile.

The Dalai Lama has traveled the world in search of support for efforts to maintain Tibet's indigenous Buddhist culture and distinct identity. Since the early 1990s he has achieved some measure of success: both Presidents George H. W. and George W. Bush and President Clinton spoke with him in the White House compound, although these gatherings were not designated as "official" meetings. He has been welcomed by governments in several countries in Western Europe, and he has received the Nobel Peace Prize.

Within Tibet, support is virtually universal among native inhabitants for the return of the Dalai Lama as leader of a highly autonomous region or fully independent nation, but no foreign country now recognizes Tibet as an independent entity. Beijing's fear is that the Dalai Lama's quasi-diplomatic successes may cause the Tibetan people to increase their pro-independence activities and possibly to gain greater political and material support from abroad.

Beijing has tried various approaches to bringing peace and stability to its control of Tibet. At times harsh repression has been the norm. During the Cultural Revolution, marauding Red Guards destroyed most of the region's temples and human religious infrastructure of monks and schools. In the 1980s Beijing began an effort to win over Tibetans through increasing investments to improve the local economy. Although real improvements in the standard of living of some Tibetans have resulted, the net outcome has been that many Han Chinese from Sichuan and other nearby provinces have migrated to Tibet to take the jobs being created in the more modern sector of the economy. Ethnic tensions, therefore, have remained high, and Beijing has been at a loss as to how to handle the issue more effectively. Beijing will not relinquish its control over Tibet peacefully, but the costs of maintaining that control may grow significantly.[21]

Taiwan presents a distinctive set of issues to Beijing, albeit issues that in various ways are loosely connected to the concerns generated by the situations in Xinjiang and Tibet. When the communists won the civil war in 1949, the GMD under Chiang Kai-shek fled to Taiwan and nearby islands, where they suspended the constitution and imposed a martial-law regime.[22] Beijing's plans to capture Taiwan in 1950 failed because the Korean War led the United States to extend a protective blanket over the Guomindang government on Taiwan. Given its lack of naval forces, Beijing was helpless against the U.S. Seventh Fleet across the Taiwan Strait.

Until the early 1990s, Beijing and Taipei agreed that Taiwan is properly seen as a constituent part of China. They disagreed only over what government legitimately rules both territories. Beijing's position, which it maintains today, is that the government of the PRC is the sole legal government of China and that Taiwan is a part of China. Taipei's position until the early 1990s was that the Republic of China established on the mainland in 1912 continues to exist and is the sole legal government of all of China, including the mainland, which, it said, was "temporarily under the control of communist bandits." In the wake of the Korean War, the United States and its allies continued to recognize the ROC government on Taiwan and refused to grant recognition to the PRC government in Beijing. The Soviet bloc took the opposite tack.

This situation broke down, however, even before the end of the cold war. Washington began a strategic rapprochement with the PRC in 1971 in an effort to gain leverage against the Soviet Union (and to help extricate itself with honor from the Vietnam war). In January of 1979 America formally switched recognition from the ROC to the PRC as the sole legal government of all of China. In the process, America retained a "one China" policy, continuing its long-standing recognition of Taiwan as a part of China. But it made very clear to Beijing that the expected absorption of Taiwan into the PRC would have to occur by peaceful means.[23]

Taiwan nevertheless to this day remains separate from the PRC, but very significant developments have occurred in the intervening years. First, after four decades of GMD rule through martial law, since the late 1980s Taiwan has evolved into a full-fledged democracy. This very likely could not have occurred had not a large percentage of the political elite received their graduate education in the United States, where to some extent they absorbed American values. Rapid economic development in Taiwan during the 1970s and 1980s also laid the groundwork for democratization through the development of a sizeable urban middle class and extensive international contacts. The GMD first lifted martial law and then allowed the gradual expansion of elections from the local level to, in 1996, election of the president of the ROC.[24] In the second presidential election, in March 2000, for the first time since the early twentieth century a party other than the GMD won the presidency of the ROC. That party, the Democratic Progressive Party, has a party constitution that calls for Taiwan to achieve legal independent status in the international arena.

The DPP is composed overwhelmingly of Taiwanese, individuals whose ancestors generally migrated from Fujian Province on the mainland more than four hundred years ago. Although of Chinese origin and for periods of time under mainland rule, over these centuries they developed a distinctive Taiwanese culture. Japan's rule of Taiwan as a colony from 1895 until the conclusion of World War II further enhanced that sense of distinctiveness from the Chinese mainland for many.[25] Taiwan's democratic evolution has thus vastly increased the role of Taiwanese—as opposed to the mainlanders who fled to Taiwan as they lost the civil war to the communists in the late 1940s—in the politics of the island.

This increasing political Taiwanization has called into question the previous agreement among all concerned that Taiwan is a part of China. This issue has progressed in stages since the early 1990s and has by now reached a rather advanced level. The GMD government's mandatory school textbooks, for example, portrayed Taiwan's history as a small part of China's history, but the DPP government has changed these books to stress the history of Taiwan as a central theme. Many other measures are being taken to increase Taiwan's citizens' sense of their historical identity as distinct from the histories of both China and Japan. The DPP president elected in 2000, Chen Shui-bian, often states that the ROC on Taiwan is an independent country with its own sovereign status and that it is not and never will be a part of the PRC. And in late 2002 Taiwan's government changed its treatment of both Inner Mongolia and Tibet in potentially provocative ways. It adopted measures that imply that it no longer sees these two regions as part of the ROC, but rather views them as territories with their own independent political authority. Taiwan has in recent years also dropped all ambition to regain political control over the Chinese mainland.

In response to these trends, in the mid-1990s Beijing began to build up military forces capable of inflicting tremendous damage on the island to deter Taiwan from declaring formal independence. Beijing's clear and oft-stated goal is to deter Taiwan from taking such a fateful move toward complete independence that it would force Beijing to respond militarily. This military buildup has produced resentment on Taiwan and has likely strengthened people's independent sense of Taiwanese identity. But it has also induced a note of caution on the island. Even Chen Shui-bian has assured the international community that he will not change the name Republic of China, which by its very history affirms a link to the mainland, to a name such as Republic of Taiwan, which would convey clearly that Taiwan no longer has a government that is organically tied in any fashion to a Chinese past. In addition, public-opinion polls on Taiwan repeatedly show that its citizens are not willing to risk provoking Beijing to military action. When given a choice of independence or the status quo, a large majority consistently opts for the status quo, which in reality provides for Taiwan's total domestic political independence.

In addition, the economic reforms on the mainland have made Taiwanese investment in the PRC crucial for Taiwan's own economic future. Taiwan now lies a short distance from the world's fastest growing major economy, and business people on Taiwan enjoy the advantages of being able to speak Chinese and to navigate effectively through Chinese culture. They recognize that in an increasingly globally interdependent world, they cannot survive without taking advantage of developments in China to enhance their own ability to compete internationally. Taiwan's government has been understandably uneasy about removing the restraints on trade and investment across the strait. The concerns include worries about the security implications and well as anxieties over potentially hollowing out Taiwan's own economy. Nevertheless, the underlying logic of increasing economic integration with the mainland has proved compelling. As of early 2003 Taiwan businesses have invested tens of billions of dollars on the mainland, and some three hundred to five hundred thousand Taiwan businesspeople reside there at any given time. These numbers, moreover, are increasing rapidly, bringing growing pressure on the government to further relax constraints on investment, transportation, and trade across the strait. Beijing, viewing these developments as helping to bind Taiwan to the mainland as well as contributing to the PRC's economic growth, is taking measures to further this process of cross-strait economic integration.

The Taiwan situation is thus complex and difficult to resolve. Beijing recognizes this fact and has since 1995 in bits and pieces laid out a series of offers concerning the modalities for reunification with Taiwan. These amount, in essence, to commitments to assure Taiwan total domestic autonomy and certain international prerogatives if Taiwan will agree that it is a part of China. Specifics include promises not to change Taiwan's domestic system, send any military forces to the island, take any taxes from it, or dispatch any mainland officials to serve there. Beijing has garnished these basic points with promises to allow some Taiwan officials to hold major posts in the mainland government and to drop the name PRC and the PRC flag in favor of a more generic national name, such as simply "China." It has wrapped these offers in the slogan "One country, two systems," and has offered to negotiate these and any other issues Taiwan chooses to raise as long as Taiwan accepts a "one China" principle as a basis for the negotiations.

The DPP government on Taiwan so distrusts Beijing's intentions that it has refused to accept any version of a "one China" principle as a basis for cross-strait talks and has not taken up any of the PRC's proffers as serious negotiating points. Therefore, Taiwan's dependence on access to the mainland economy and its fixed investments there are growing extremely rapidly, even as Taiwanization has advanced and a cross-strait arms race has developed. This is a potentially unsteady mix, and the potential for miscalculation and tragedy is evident as Taiwan seeks to affirm its identity and Beijing seeks to prevent Taiwan independence.

The United States plays a central role in this imbroglio. Although in January 1979 Washington shifted formal diplomatic recognition to Beijing and used the opt-out clause to end its military alliance with the ROC, it nevertheless continued to maintain a robust economic and security relationship with

Taiwan. The Taiwan Relations Act, passed by the Congress and signed into law by President Jimmy Carter in 1979, formally mandated that the United States treat any adverse changes in Taiwan's security as matters of "grave concern" to the United States. This and subsequent American actions committed the United States to enabling Taiwan to purchase on an ongoing basis sufficient defensive weapons to prevent it from becoming an easy target for the PLA. Taiwan also maintained very strong support in the U.S. Congress, especially as the ROC underwent a process of democratization just when the aftermath of the 1989 Tiananmen massacre, and the collapse of all other major communist governments, produced a sour taste in American mouths over the lack of steady liberalization in the PRC.

Today, therefore, America remains Taiwan's strongest security supporter. To be sure that it can effectively provide security to Taiwan if necessary, moreover, the George W. Bush administration is significantly increasing contacts between American and ROC military forces. Should the cross-strait relationship deteriorate to the point of armed conflict, therefore, this situation would entail a very large risk of bringing U.S. and Chinese military forces face to face in a shooting war. Because America bases key relevant military assets in Japan, the odds of those assets being called into play under such circumstances are very high. The result could easily rise to the level of major tragedy, especially given the heavy historical commitment of American credibility to Taiwan's security from unprovoked attack from the mainland. Consequences of such conflict could be long term, regionwide, and severe. But it is accepted wisdom in Beijing that, although this scenario is to be avoided at almost all costs, no Chinese government could long survive a successful—that is, internationally recognized—declaration of Taiwan independence. It is a fundamental national historical imperative that China not settle for anything less than the unification of all the major territories that were stripped from it through foreign incursion after the middle of the nineteenth century.[26]

China's thinking about how to reunify with Taiwan, along with the earlier arrangements it made to bring Hong Kong and Macao back under Chinese control in the 1990s, may be laying the groundwork for the construction of a quasi- or fully federalist approach to managing at least the areas of China that lie outside the core Han regions of China proper. This approach potentially could open the door to creative thinking about new arrangements for Xinjiang, Tibet, and even the Inner Mongolian Autonomous Region. It would require major steps beyond current thinking in Beijing. The issue of how best to secure good economic and political outcomes in the half of China outside the core Han areas and in Taiwan is a question that may prove critical to China's future.

Beyond the Xinjiang, Tibet, and Taiwan issues, elemental developments in the international arena are affecting China's domestic as well as foreign policies. Specifically, China's leaders have watched the march of technology enhance the prospects of higher levels of global economic interdependence. In the late 1990s they reached a fundamental conclusion that the PRC could reap huge benefits from full participation in this global transformation. Since then, the standard Chinese rhetoric about the importance of "self-reliance" has been replaced by calls to recognize global trends and to compete effectively in the global marketplace. To further its ability to pursue this basic agenda, China joined the World Trade Organization in late 2001, accepting entry requirements so stringent that they are reshaping not only on the country's international trade rules but also its domestic arrangements.[27]

China seeks in the coming years to become the manufacturing hub of Asia and beyond. It counts on its combination of almost unlimited labor resources, its central location in Asia, effective government measures to provide human and physical infrastructure, and a foreign policy designed to maximize its international economic opportunities to increase the size of its domestic economy and achieve an increasingly important global economic role. To a great extent China will seize on its natural comparative advantage in cheap labor to manufacture goods for export at very competitive prices. But as noted in Chapter 9, Beijing also wants the country to move up the skill and technology ladders to be able to reap the profits from higher value-added activities and, in some sectors, to become a global technology leader. In all of this, Beijing hopes to see China progress from its current situation, in which foreign firms take advantage of inexpensive production opportunities to manufacture goods for the international market, to a situation in which Chinese firms themselves become major international players.

This enormously ambitious effort can potentially make China second only to the United States in regional and global importance by 2020, if it can manage the extremely unsettling transitions it must make between now and then in the face of the daunting challenges noted above. SARS, though, has made this model more difficult. It highlighted abroad the potential dangers of expanding intercourse with an authoritarian country that too easily conceals its domestic ills. And it increased Chinese citizens' resistance to the costs of an economic model that places too great a priority on rapid growth to the neglect of such nonproduction infrastructure as the public health system. The political leaders must, therefore, convince China's citizens that the approach they adopt is best for China's long-term well-being and that the inevitable dislocations and sacrifices are thus acceptable for the good of the country.[28]

In historical terms, the current leadership is moving yet another step in the one-hundred-fifty-year transition toward an iconoclastic modernizer concept of the country. As Chapter 1 explains, China has seen gradual but very uneven movement over time along the nativist–eclectic modernizer–iconoclastic modernizer continuum. A nativist view says that foreign forces try to divide China, whereas an internally united China that preserves its own essential qualities is too strong for foreigners to defeat. This view emphasizes domestic ideological unity and seeks to keep foreign influence to a bare minimum. It has held sway periodically, most recently during the peak of the Cultural Revolution in the late 1960s. The selective modernizer perspective argues that China should preserve a distinctive essence while utilizing foreign learning and technology to ward off foreign threats. It therefore opens up to foreign influence but also stresses the importance of social, economic, and political distinctiveness. This position has been fraught with internal contradictions but also politically highly attractive for most of the twentieth century.

The iconoclastic modernizer position is the most radical of the three, arguing that China should make any changes required to itself generate and successfully apply the technology necessary to ensure its security and stature in the international arena. It therefore posits a goal of making China a very dynamic, internationally competitive country and derives key domestic policies from an analysis of what is necessary to reach this goal. No Chinese leadership before the late 1990s has come this close to adopting an iconoclastic modernizer position. This position has never proven sustainable, given the enormous weight of China's sense of its past, the great diversity within the country, and the huge difficulty of making the resulting benefits available to everyone at a reasonably equal pace. China is no Singapore, and its very size, complexity, and historical resonances have made an iconoclastic modernizer position impossible to apply rigorously for any sustained period of time.

In reality, even the most reformist elements of the present modernizing leadership will take into account "Chinese characteristics" as they pursue their agenda of making China a well-off society. But this should not obscure the extent to which the current national agenda is radical and far reaching, demanding major readjustments to the nature of the society, economy, and intercourse with foreign actors whether they are individuals, corporations, or states. The most important question confronting the country is whether China has reached the point where an agenda of radical domestic changes to take advantage of global integration is politically and socially sustainable. As in past times, policies have ripple effects that are hard to anticipate and often difficult to manage.

Alternative Prospects

Given the above domestic and transnational variables, it makes more sense to elaborate an array of reasonable prospects for China than to attempt to predict the path the country will actually take. It is sobering to confront the reality that the array of realistic possibilities concerning the basic characteristics of China's system even until 2020 remains startlingly broad.[29] The largest country in the world still has not settled into a predictable development path. Six distinct outcomes are quite feasible, depending on specific developments and choices over the coming two decades.[30] In brief outline, the prospects and the key issues associated with each are as follows.

Success. A successful China will be a country that has managed to maintain overall political and social stability while maintaining high rates of economic growth. It will play a major role in the international economy, with some indigenous firms becoming regionally and globally competitive. Given its position in the global political economy, it is likely to be a basically constructive force in multilateral institutions such as the World Trade Organization. It will also be the strongest Asian country economically and militarily.

Politically, a successful China is likely to have implemented limited competitive elections by 2020, but it will probably remain a one-party-dominant system at the national level. CCP variants might increasingly resemble the

Mexican Partido Revolucionario Institucional before the 1990s, the Guomindang on Taiwan at the end of the 1980s, or the Japanese Liberal Democratic
Party since the 1950s. The result would be a more liberal, quasi-democratic
political system that would still seek to concentrate political authority and use
that authority to support economic and security development. The dominant
party would not ban all competing political activity, nor would it reserve the
right to interfere decisively in all spheres of activity, as the CCP does at present.

This China should boast vibrant markets, a strong state economic role,
impressive qualities of government administration, a more effective legal system, improved provision of public services, and progress in government programs to reduce regional and social inequalities. It will be a key manufacturing
center for the global economy. It will still face major problems of environmental deterioration, public health, and poverty, but in most ways it will look in
broad terms like a successful East Asia–style modern state.

China will achieve these goals only if it takes determined government
action to resolve its financial problems, privatize many current SOEs, adopt
progressive political reforms, and nurture a viable model for citizen-based
organizations that provide major groups of people with a greater sense of
meaningful participation in political and social affairs. In addition, a "successful China" scenario will come to pass only if Beijing achieves three security
objectives over the next two decades: it must avoid a major war; it must reach
a peaceful resolution (even if in the form of a long-term modus vivendi) with
Taiwan; and it must manage its relations with the United States in a way that
allows it to avoid pouring funds into outsized defense budgets. These three
objectives are related, and failure in any one would arguably increase the
chances of failure in one or both of the others. China, in short, must avoid
major international conflict if it is to realize its ambitious economic and social
objectives over the coming two decades.

Such success over the coming years is by no means certain. Managing
foreseeable problems will require astute and forward-looking decision making, along with some luck. Additional debilitating challenges, such as the
potential spread of HIV/AIDS to several tens of millions of citizens, would
reduce the margin for success. And currently unpredictable obstacles are
bound to arise and add to the difficulties.

With the characteristics of a "successful China" as a baseline, the array of
alternative prospects as of 2020 include the following.

Elite authoritarian nationalist system. By 2020, China may become an
authoritarian, one-party system that is closely linked to domestic business
elites and attempts to keep the lower classes quiescent by promoting ardent
nationalism. The party is already actively recruiting top business leaders from
the private sector, and it has long embraced all corporate leaders from the
state sector. Many party officials have, moreover, become wealthy through taking advantage of their official powers for economic gain. It is thus quite possible that rather than moving toward real liberalization and democratization,
the party will ally with the elites who have emerged through the reforms to
consolidate an authoritarian and elitist system. The most likely way to maintain social peace in a system that basically serves the interests of a wealthy

political and economic elite is to encourage nationalism. Critics in China already refer to this as the potential "Latin American model" for the future.

An elite authoritarian nationalist system will most likely develop if China fails in the security challenges just noted and experiences limited war, Taiwan independence, and/or the need to maintain very large defense budgets to protect itself from the United States. Indeed, the combination of successful economic development and alarm over international security threats would tilt the odds in favor of this variant of the future Chinese system.

A soft and corrupt authoritarian system. A relatively undisciplined and corrupt authoritarian system is most likely to develop if corruption becomes so severe that government predation holds down the rate of growth, diminishing China's international stature and power. Failure to address effectively the current sources of corruption and to develop a strong legal system is a precondition for this outcome. Without a major national security threat, this system would almost certainly lack ideological élan and would be unable to mobilize the population around major national efforts. Low levels of popular unrest would continue, with strong police and military forces to maintain control.

The soft and corrupt authoritarian system would be devoted largely to keeping itself in power and serving the material desires of officials and their business cronies. This variant of a prospective Chinese regime would likely seek to muddle through international relations, not playing an effective leadership role either in Asia or in multilateral organizations.

A weak democratic system. The chances of China's developing a strong, nationwide multiparty democratic system of government by 2020 are very small. This book has argued that increasing levels of popular representation and democratic process are very important for achieving the "successful China" prospect described above. But China's political history, culture, and enormous challenges make it likely that evolution to a system with strong nationwide multiparty democratic institutions will at best require far longer than the period between now and 2020.

Indeed, should a fully democratic system emerge in China by 2020, it is most likely to be the result of unmanageable popular demands having produced a breakdown of the political system at some point before that date. Given the vast complexity of the country and its political history, any democratic system growing out of this trauma is likely in 2020 to be institutionally weak and highly corrupt, with strong local forces testing the territorial integrity of the country around its margins. Political parties would more likely represent localities than national social groups.

Such a system might eventually evolve into a vibrant democracy, but the process would take additional decades rather than a few years. A weak democratic system might prove institutionally unable to direct scarce resources to sustain economic growth, enhance environmental protection, maintain social stability, and protect the country's security. Should this crisis and transition occur during the 2010s, China in 2020 might have many of the political characteristics of the Indonesian polity of 2003.

Prolonged fundamental instability. This nightmare scenario posits fundamental breakdown of the political system, perhaps as a result of severe leadership splits over how to handle a major financial or other crisis that mush-rooms up and spirals completely out of control. The breakdown itself unleashes centripetal forces that cannot be contained, and it proves impossi-ble to reestablish meaningful national order. "China" may continue to exist as a nominal state, but for some considerable period of time the reality will be subnational governments and other forces contending for resources and power. Given China's century-long history of domestic political violence and the enormous complexities of the society, this scenario unfortunately cannot be wholly discounted.

This grim possibility would make the China of 2020 look in basic ways like Russia of the mid-1990s, with far-reaching, destabilizing consequences for the region and beyond. Problems might include a combination of the loss of out-lying territories, a contracting economy, reduced life expectancy and ability to control disease, environmental degradation and crisis, and unmanageable ethnic divisions and conflict. In this environment, transnational criminal gangs will be able to take advantage of China's territory and resources. The repercussions could vastly enhance the dangers of terrorism, proliferation of weapons of mass destruction and their means of delivery, epidemics, and ille-gal migration on a scale never seen before. Given China's size, location, and importance, this prospect would have the greatest adverse consequences for the international arena, even though it would vastly deflate China's national capabilities.

Conclusion

Twenty-five years ago Deng Xiaoping set the PRC on a course of major change in order to accelerate economic growth while maintaining political stability. In so doing, he and his colleagues, in the Chinese phrase, "mounted a tiger." Over the ten years since the first edition of this book was published, China's accomplishments have vastly increased its importance in global politics and the international economy. Its future is an issue of major concern throughout not only Asia but the international arena as a whole.

As China faces the future, the forces Deng unleashed continue to propel the country forward, but with great uncertainties and dangers and toward an outcome still too unclear to predict with confidence. Bright prospects can enable China to play a very important and constructive role, consolidating its stature and bringing to a close the long agony of recovery from its nineteenth-century fall from grace. But a variety of potentially far less favorable outcomes are also possible. The tiger, in short, has not yet been tamed.

Glossary of Selected Individuals Cited in the Text

Bo Yibo (1908–): Born in Shanxi Province, Bo joined the Communist party in the 1920s and after 1949 was a long-time member of the Politburo. He played a major role in economic decision making, rising to the rank of vice premier in the government. For most of the 1990s, Bo was one of the octogenarians who retained influence even though he held no formal office. At age ninety, Bo was instrumental in forcing seventy-three-year-old Qiao Shi to give up his Central Committee membership because of Qiao's advanced age (he was past the cut-off age of seventy) during the Ninth NPC in February–March, 1998.

Mikhail Borodin (?–?): A Russian Jew (his real name was Mikhail Gruzenberg) who was raised in Latvia and began secretly working for Lenin in 1903, Borodin spent most of 1905–17 in exile in the United States, teaching in Chicago. He returned to Russia after the Bolshevik Revolution and thereafter took on revolutionary assignments in Europe, Central America, and in 1923, China.

Chen Xilian (1913–1999): Born in Hubei Province, Chen became an important military figure in post-1949 China. He commanded the PLA artillery forces from 1952 to 1959 and belonged to the Politburo from 1969 to 1980. From a base in Liaoning Province in northeast China, Chen played an active role in national politics during the Cultural Revolution.

Chen Yi (1901–1972): Born in Sichuan Province, Chen commanded the forces of the Third Field Army just prior to 1949 and served as mayor of Shanghai and the leading CCP figure in the city in the early 1950s. He then moved to Beijing, where in 1958 he became the minister of foreign affairs. A colorful figure and a strong personality, Chen was cruelly persecuted during the Cultural Revolution.

Chen Yun (1905–1995): Born near Shanghai Municipality, Chen was unique among the surviving leaders of the Long March in having been a member of the urban proletariat. Chen at various times played key roles in organization/personnel work and, especially, in economic decision making. Mao typically turned to Chen to bail out the urban economy when it ran into trouble in the 1950s. Chen strongly supported Deng Xiaoping's reforms initially but by the late 1980s led the conservative critics of Deng's efforts. During the 1980s and early 1990s he was the most influential octogenarian other than Deng himself.

Chi Haotian (1928–2003): Born in Shandong Province, Chi pursued a military career. In November 2002 and March 2003 respectively, Chi stepped down from his posts as minister of defense, vice chairman of the Central Military Commission, State Councilor, and member of the Politburo.

Chiang Ching-kuo (Jiang Jingguo) (1909–1988): Born in Zhejiang Province, Chiang was the eldest son of Chiang Kai-shek. He took power on Taiwan after the death of his father in 1975 and played a key role in laying the basis for democratic reform there during the ensuing years.

Chiang Kai-shek (Jiang Jieshi) (1887–1975): Born in Zhejiang Province, Chiang was the dominant political figure of the Republic of China after 1926. He headed the Guomindang, with only brief and insignificant interruptions, from the mid-1920s until his death. As such, he was China's national leader from 1927 to 1949. A graduate of the Whampoa Military Academy, Chiang found his strongest political base in the military. He was an authoritarian ruler.

Ci Xi (Yehe Nara)(1835–1908): The empress dowager in the last decades of the Qing dynasty. A highly capable and ruthless leader, she exercised power through control over the last few Qing emperors. She sided with conservatives during the 1898 Hundred Days of Reform and during the Boxer Rebellion two years later. In her final years, she began grudgingly to introduce some reforms into China, but not enough to save the dynasty.

Deng Xiaoping (1904–1997): Born in Sichuan Province, Deng throughout his career demonstrated extraordinary leadership capabilities. He was a leading figure in the Second Field Army before 1949, and by the mid-1950s had become one of the top six leaders in the CCP. He headed the party Secretariat from the mid-1950s to the Cultural Revolution. Purged in 1966 and again in 1976, Deng surged back after Mao Zedong's death to become the architect of China's post-Mao reforms. Until his death in 1997, he was the most powerful of the party elders and was referred to as the "core leader," although declining health largely incapacitated him after 1994.

Deng Yingchao (1904–1992): Born in Henan Province, Deng early on joined the communist revolution. She married Zhou Enlai. After 1949, she worked primarily in the Women's Federation and achieved independent political influence only after Zhou's death in 1976.

Deng Zihui (1896–1972): Born in Fujian Province, Deng joined the CCP in the mid-1920s. After 1949 he served as the key figure in the central-south administrative region. He transferred to Beijing in 1954 and thereafter played an important role in economic policy, especially regarding agriculture. He clashed with Mao Zedong several times in the 1950s over the cooperativization of agriculture.

Feng Yuxiang (1882–1948): Born in Hebei Province, Feng was a major north China warlord.

Fu Zuoyi (1895–1974): Born in Shanxi Province, Fu was a key Guomindang general who effected the peaceful surrender of Beijing to the communists in January 1949. He thereafter became a figurehead minister of water conservancy in the PRC.

Gao Gang (1905–1954): Born in Shaanxi Province, Gao was the leader in northeast China from 1949 to 1952, when he moved to Beijing. He was accused of maneuvering to replace Liu Shaoqi in 1953, as a consequence of which he was purged. He committed suicide in prison in 1954.

Guangxu emperor (1871–1908): The Guangxu emperor nominally reigned from 1875 to 1908. In reality, he assumed the throne as a minor at the age of four. His mother, the empress dowager Ci Xi, exercised real power. When he reached maturity he determined that the Qing dynasty needed to reform, and in 1898 he launched the wideranging Hundred Days of Reform. The empress dowager allied with court conservatives to cut short this effort and effectively held the emperor under house arrest from then until his death in 1908. Many believe the emperor was poisoned on the orders of his mother, who knew her own death was imminent.

Heshen (1750–1799): An imperial bodyguard, Heshen caught the eye of the aging Qianlong emperor, who elevated Heshen to the post of grand councilor. He remained a confidant of the Qianlong emperor for the rest of his reign. But Heshen became enormously corrupt and was forced to commit suicide in 1799, shortly after the death of the Qianlong emperor.

Hu Jintao (1942–): Born in December 1942 in Jixi County, Anhui Province, Hu rose rapidly and in the course of his career became closely associated with both conservative (Song Ping) and liberal (Hu Yaobang) leaders. He pursued tough policies as head of Tibet in 1988–92 but followed more reform-oriented approaches as head of the Central Party School from 1993 to 2002. In 1992 Hu was catapulted onto the Standing Committee of the Politburo and designated Jiang Zemin's successor. Hu became vice president of China in 1998, general secretary of the CCP in November 1992, and president of the PRC in March 2003.

Hu Qiaomu (1912–1993): Born in Jiangsu Province, Hu caught Mao Zedong's attention through articles he wrote while in Yan'an in the early 1940s. After 1949 Hu at various times was a leading figure in the propaganda sphere, an assistant to Mao, and a member of the CCP Politburo. He became a conservative critic of Deng Xiaoping by the mid-1980s.

Hu Shi (1891–1962): Born in Shanghai Municipality, Hu Shi was a prominent advocate of Western ideas in Republican China. He played a major role in promoting use of the vernacular in the written language, thereby facilitating the development of mass political propaganda. Hu went to Taiwan when the Guomindang took control there.

Hu Yaobang (1915–1989): Born in Hunan Province, Hu joined the revolution as a teenager. Until the Cultural Revolution he spent his career focused on youth work and developed close ties with Deng Xiaoping. Hu served as official head of the CCP from 1981 to 1987 and, along with Zhao Ziyang, was a major architect of the reforms and prospective successor to Deng. A lively individual, Hu was purged in January 1987. His death from a heart attack in April 1989 provided the initial momentum for what became the Tiananmen student movement, leading to the Tiananmen massacre on 4 June 1989.

Hua Guofeng (1921–): Born in Shanxi Province, Hua made his pre–Cultural Revolution career in Mao Zedong's native Hunan Province. Hua moved to Beijing early in the 1970s and served as a transitional leader between Mao's death in 1976 and Deng Xiaoping's consolidation of power in late 1978. Loyal to Mao, Hua lost his last political posts in 1981.

Huang Jing (1911–1958): Born in Zhejiang Province, Huang is reported to have been married to Jiang Qing in the 1930s, before Jiang met and married Mao Zedong. From 1949 to 1953, Huang was the top political figure in Tianjin municipality. He subsequently led the State Technology Commission until his death from illness in 1958.

Ji Dengkui (1923–1988): Born in Shanxi Province, Ji saw his political career soar during the Cultural Revolution, when he jumped from the Henan provincial apparatus to become an alternate, and then later a full, member of the Politburo. Loyal to Mao Zedong's ideas, Ji lost power in 1980 as Deng Xiaoping consolidated his own position.

Jia Chunwang (1938–): Born in Beijing Municipality, Jia served as Minister of Public Security from March 1998 to March 2003. He is the son-in-law of Bo Yibo.

Jiaqing emperor (1760–1820): The Jiaqing emperor ruled from 1796 to 1820, taking over from the great Qianlong emperor, who abdicated in 1796 after a reign of sixty years. The Jiaqing emperor inherited a system that had begun to decline from corruption and rebellion in peripheral areas.

Jiang Qing (1913–1991): Born in Shandong Province, Jiang Qing had been an actress in Shanghai in the 1930s before moving to Yan'an, where she met and married Mao Zedong. She played a leading radical role in the Cultural Revolution. She particularly focused on policy toward culture, over which she assumed ultimate control in the late 1960s. Jiang chafed for many years under restrictions on her activities imposed by the CCP leaders, who had opposed her marriage to Mao. She used the Cultural Revolution, in part, to settle these numerous scores. She was imprisoned in 1976 as a member of the Gang of Four, which also included Wang Hongwen, Yao Wenyuan, and Zhang Chunqiao. She reportedly committed suicide while still incarcerated.

Jiang Zemin (1926–): Born in Jiangsu Province, Jiang held posts in the automotive, machine-building, and electronics industries from the 1950s to the mid-1980s. He became mayor of Shanghai in 1986 and secretary of the Shanghai Municipal party committee in 1987. In 1989 he moved to Beijing, where during the 1990s he gradually became the core leader. His top posts included general secretary of the Communist party, chairman of the CCP Military Affairs Commission, and president of the PRC. He stepped down as general secretary in November 2002 and as president in March 2003 but retained his leadership of the party's powerful Military Affairs Commission.

Kang Sheng (1898–1975): Born in Shandong Province, Kang sponsored Jiang Qing's membership in the CCP in 1931 and remained close to her thereafter. Kang trained in Moscow in the 1930s and became a key figure both before and after 1949 in using brutal tactics to purge suspected enemies in the CCP. He played a prominent role in the Cultural Revolution. Kang was known both for his fine artistic sensibilities and for his sadism in torturing his victims.

Kangxi emperor (1654–1722): The first of the two great Qing dynasty emperors (the other was the Qianlong emperor), the Kangxi emperor reigned from 1661 to 1722. He stabilized the northern and western borders of the new dynasty and in 1689 signed the Treaty of Nerchinsk with Russia.

Lee Teng-hui (Li Denghui) (1929–): Born in Taiwan, Lee assumed the presidency of the Republic of China on Taiwan upon the death of Chiang Ching-kuo. Lee continued Chiang's efforts to Taiwanize the Guomindang and to democratize Taiwan. During the 1990s Lee increasingly moved toward a pro-independence stance for Taiwan. He stepped down as president in May 2000 but has remained an influential political figure on Taiwan.

Li Fuchun (1900–1975): Born in Hunan Province, Li by the mid-1950s had become a vice premier of the State Council and head of the State Planning Commission, positions that he held until the 1970s. He was a key economic decision maker in Beijing.

Li Lanqing (1932–): Born in Jiangsu Province, Li stepped down from the Politburo Standing Committee in November 2002 and from his position as vice premier in March 2003.

Li Peng (1928–): An adopted son of Zhou Enlai and Deng Yingchao, Li received part of his education in Moscow in the late 1940s and early 1950s. He spent his subsequent career in the power industry until the 1980s, when he began to assume broader political responsibilities. Li served as premier from 1988 to 1998. He was the head of the

National People's Congress from 1998 until March 2003. A Standing Committee member of the Politburo until November 2002, he is widely regarded as a conservative. He took a hard-line public stance against the pro-democracy demonstrators in 1989 and in support of the June 1989 Tiananmen massacre.

Li Ruihuan (1934–): Born in Tianjin Municipality, Li first achieved fame as a key leader in the construction of the Great Hall of the People in 1958–59. He had a highly successful tenure as head of Tianjin from 1983 through the end of the decade. He became a member of the Politburo and its Standing Committee, from which he stepped down in November 2002. A carpenter by training, Li rose by dint of his great organizational and problem-solving skills and keen political sensibilities. From 1998 to 2003 Li served as Chairman of the Chinese People's Political Consultative Conference.

Li Ssu (?–208 B.C.): Born in the Ch'u state, Li was a ruthless minister under the first emperor of the Qin dynasty. Li advocated use of vicious punishments, including torture and mutilation, to maintain order among the populace. Accused of treason after Qin Shi Huang Di's death, Li was sawed in two in the marketplace, a punishment in keeping with his own approach to discipline.

Li Xiannian (1909–1992): Born in Hubei Province, Li was a political leader in his native province until 1954. He then spent more than two decades as vice premier of the State Council and minister of finance. Li served on the CCP Politburo from 1956 to 1987 and held the largely honorific post of president of the PRC from 1983 to 1988. He was a key economic decision maker from the 1950s to the 1980s. From 1981 to 1988, Li also headed the Leading Group for Foreign Affairs.

Li Zongren (1890–?): Born in Guangxi Province, Li served in the National Revolutionary Army before 1949 and briefly became the president of the Republic of China in 1949.

Lin Biao (1907–1971): Born in Hubei Province, Lin was one of the Chinese communists' greatest military strategists during the years before 1949. After 1949, he suffered from real or imagined illnesses that kept him inactive for years at a time. He nevertheless became a leading Politburo member in 1958 and the operational head of the military in 1959. Lin fostered the Mao Zedong personality cult and played a key role in the Cultural Revolution, becoming Mao's designated successor in 1969. Lin died in a plane crash in Outer Mongolia in 1971, purportedly while fleeing after a botched attempt to assassinate Mao.

Liu Bocheng (1892–1986): Born in Sichuan Province, Liu had a distinguished military career, working closely with Deng Xiaoping, before 1949. He became a marshal (the highest military rank) in the PLA, one of only ten individuals to be accorded this honor when the PLA established ranks in 1955. Liu's post-1949 career focused on military training and policy; he was a leading member of the Military Affairs Commission. Although a member of the Politburo from 1956 to 1982, Liu in fact was largely inactive in his later years due to illness.

Liu Huaqing (1916–): Born in Hubei Province, General Liu was a career military man who fought in many of the key battles during the 1930s and 1940s. He attended the Voroshilov Naval Academy in the USSR in the mid-1950s and thereafter played a central role in developing the naval arm of the PLA. Deng Xiaoping brought Liu out of retirement to serve on the Politburo in the 1992 to help secure control over the PLA in the wake of the removal of Yang Baibing and Yang Shangkun. Liu stepped down from the Politburo at the Fifteenth Party Congress in 1997.

Liu Shaoqi (1898–1969): Born in Hunan Province, Liu became a strong supporter of Mao Zedong in the early 1940s. He was widely regarded as Mao's likely successor but was purged and vilified during the Cultural Revolution. Liu concentrated on running the CCP organization and he believed strongly in organizational discipline. Starting in 1959 he served in the honorific post of president of the PRC. Liu died of the severe treatment he received during the Cultural Revolution, when he was branded as the "number one person in authority taking the capitalist road" and as "China's Khrushchev."

Liu Zhidan (1903–1936): Born in Shaanxi Province, Liu was one of the founders of the north China guerrilla base that later became the final destination of the Long March.

Mao Zedong (1893–1976): Born in Hunan Province, Mao was one of the founders of the CCP and led the party from 1935 until his death. He was the charismatic leader of the communist revolution and the dominant political figure from 1949 to 1976. His personal views and proclivities affected the lives of millions, given the extraordinary concentration of power in his hands.

Peng Dehuai (1898–1974): Born in Hunan Province, Peng was one of China's top communist military figures both before and after 1949. He commanded the Chinese forces in Korea and for most of the 1950s took charge of the day-to-day operations of the CCP's Military Affairs Commission. Peng clashed with Mao over various issues from the early 1940s through the 1950s. In what proved to be a turning point in the politics of the Mao era, Peng was purged at the Lushan plenum in August 1959 after delivering a strong critique of the mistakes of the Great Leap Forward. Peng received very rough treatment during the Cultural Revolution and died as a result of this persecution.

Peng Zhen (1902–1997): Born in Shanxi Province, Peng Zhen played key roles in the Beijing municipal Communist party leadership and in the political and legal affairs system until the Cultural Revolution. He was also a member of the CCP Politburo and Secretariat. Peng was one of the first victims of the Cultural Revolution. He was rehabilitated after Mao Zedong's death and for a period in the 1980s headed the legislature, the National People's Congress. Despite his advanced years and lack of any formal title, Peng remained a significant force in politics into the early 1990s. Although he remained worried about the impact of "bourgeois liberal" thinking in China, according to his official biography Peng "highly appraised" Deng's decision to speed up the pace of economic reform in early 1992. He died in Beijing on April 26, 1997.

Pu Yi (1906–1967): The last emperor of the Qing dynasty, Pu Yi was only five years old when the dynasty fell. In 1932 he became the head of the puppet government the Japanese established in Manchuria (Manchukuo).

Qianlong emperor (1711–1799): The greatest Chinese emperor after the Kangxi emperor, the Qianlong emperor occupied the dragon throne from 1736 to 1796, when he abdicated due to age. He expanded the empire through the conquests of Ili and Turkestan. The Qing reached its zenith and began to decline under the rule of the Qianlong emperor.

Qiao Shi (1924–): Born in Zhejiang Province, Qiao worked primarily in economic administration during the 1950s. From 1963 to 1983 he worked in the International Liaison Department of the CCP, concerned with foreign policy and contacts with the international communist movement. During the remainder of the 1980s Qiao held posts as head of the Organization Department of the CCP, as head of the General Office of the CCP, and as head of the political and legal affairs system. He then became head of the legislature, the National People's Congress; a member of the Standing Committee of the Politburo; and a vice premier of the State Council. In part because he was regarded as a possible rival to Jiang Zemin, Qiao was forced to step down from all his formal posts in 1997 and 1998.

Qin Shi Huang Di (259–210 B.C.): The first emperor of the short-lived Qin dynasty, Qin Shi Huang Di is widely regarded as China's first real emperor. Millions died under the exactions of his ruthless rule. He standardized weights and measures, created a national communications system, constructed major stretches of the Great Wall, and built a tomb of legendary grandeur. He also created the country's first nationwide bureaucracy. Mao Zedong occasionally remarked that he regarded himself as a modern Qin Shi Huang Di.

Rao Shushi (1903–1975): Born in Jiangxi Province, Rao was one of the major leaders of east China from 1949 to 1952. Rao then moved to Beijing, where he took charge of the CCP Organization Department. He was purged with Gao Gang in 1954, with whom he had allegedly conspired to obtain the top state and party posts under Mao Zedong.

Song Ping (1917–): Born in Shandong Province, Song held a number of posts after 1949 involved primarily with state economic planning. He headed the State Planning Commission from 1983 to 1987, at which time he became head of the CCP Organization Department. He was a conservative supporter of Chen Yun during the reform era. Song was a Politburo member from 1987 to 1992.

Sun Yat-sen (Sun Zhongshan) (1866–1925): Born in Guangdong Province, Sun organized the Guomindang and is generally regarded as the founding father of Republican China. Sun was the first Chinese revolutionary of international reputation. He served for only six weeks as the first president of the Republic of China. Sun's political thought in the form of the "Three People's Principles" has been the official guiding ideology of the Guomindang.

Tan Zhenlin (1902–1983): Born in Hunan Province, Tan served as party secretary in Zhejiang Province from 1949 to 1955 and then moved to Beijing, where he joined the CCP Secretariat in 1956 and the Politburo in 1958. He lost both memberships during the Cultural Revolution.

Tang Shengzhi (1890–?): Born in Hunan Province, Tang was a Guomindang military commander who in 1929 went to battle against forces loyal to Chiang Kai-shek. He was pardoned in 1931 but remained in the PRC after 1949, where he held minor government posts.

Tian Jiaying (?–1966): Tian served in Mao Zedong's personal office from the 1950s to the early 1960s. A disagreement with Mao over agricultural policy during the Great Leap Forward led to his dismissal. He committed suicide early in the Cultural Revolution.

Tian Jiyun (1929–): Born in Shandong Province, Tian has spent his career primarily in financial administration, first in Guizhou Province, then in Sichuan Province, and finally at the national level. He has held the posts of vice premier, member of the CCP Secretariat, and member of the Politburo. Tian stepped down as vice chairman of the National People's Congress in March 2003 and as a member of the Politburo in November 2002.

Tongzhi emperor (1856–1875): On the throne from 1861 until his death in 1875, the Tongzhi emperor was too young to exercise real power. But during his reign, talented government officials brought the Taiping, Nian, Northwest Moslem, and Southwest Moslem rebellions to an end and sought to revitalize the Confucian base of the dynasty. This effort, partially successful, has been dubbed the Tongzhi Restoration.

Wan Li (1916–): Born in Shandong Province, Wan served on the Beijing municipal CCP committee from 1958 to 1966 and 1974 to 1975. After terms as minister of railways and minister of agriculture, he joined the CCP Secretariat in 1980 and the Politburo in 1982. He then served as chairman of the legislature, the National People's Congress, from 1987 to 1993.

Wang Dongxing (1916–): Born in Jiangxi Province, Wang pursued a career in the security services, most notably as the man in charge of Mao Zedong's personal security detachment and then as the leader of the 8341 Division, which provided security for the entire top leadership. Wang served on the Politburo from 1977 to 1980. Generally considered a hard-liner loyal to Mao, he was removed by Deng Xiaoping as part of Deng's effort to sustain his reform initiatives.

Wang Guangmei (1922–): Born in the United States, Wang came from a prominent Tianjin family. Liu Shaoqi married her in 1948, shortly before the communist victory. Jiang Qing resented Wang's upper-class background and when Jiang gained power with the onset of the Cultural Revolution, she had Wang thrown in prison, where she languished in solitary confinement for nearly twelve years.

Wang Hongwen (1935–1992): Born in Jilin Province, Wang worked in security at an enterprise in Shanghai and catapulted to political power through his early leadership of one of the most prominent Shanghai Red Guard units during the initial stages of the Cultural Revolution. Wang served on the Politburo Standing Committee from 1973 to 1976, when he was arrested as a member of the Gang of Four, which also included Jiang Qing, Yao Wenyuan, and Zhang Chunqiao. Wang died in prison in Beijing, August 3, 1992.

Wang Jingwei (1883–1944): Born in Guangdong Province, Wang headed the "left Guomindang" during the Northern Expedition but later defected to the Japanese and headed one of their regional puppet governments in China.

Wang Zhen (1908–1993): Born in Hunan Province, Wang was a military man of peasant origin who delighted in discomfiting intellectuals with his crude manners and ready resort to violence. During the 1980s he became an important member of the conservative opposition to Deng Xiaoping's reform effort.

Wei Jianxing (1931–): Born in Zhejiang Province, Wei rose to national prominence in the 1980s, when he moved from Harbin municipality and became head of the CCP Organization Department (1984 to 1985). He then assumed leadership of the Ministry of Supervision (until 1998) and in 1992 became secretary of the CCP Central Discipline Inspection Commission (until 2002). He also gained positions on the CCP Secretariat and the Politburo in 1992. Wei was a member of the Politburo and its Standing Committee until November 2002.

Wei Jingsheng (1950–): Born in Beijing Municipality, Wei was a worker who became prominent during the Democracy Wall movement of 1978–79, when he wrote an essay calling for a "fifth modernization," democracy. He was sentenced in 1979 to fifteen years in prison for revealing state secrets to foreigners. Released six months early in 1993, he immediately began to criticize the government over human-rights issues. Twenty months of incommunicado detention without charge followed, then sentencing in 1995 to a further fourteen years in prison. In November 1997, Wei was released and exiled to the United States for health reasons.

Wen Jiabao (1942–): Born in Tianjin in 1942, Wen joined the CCP in 1965. During the Cultural Revolution, he worked for ten years with a geomechanics survey team in Gansu Province, serving first as a technician and later as a political instructor. He was promoted to deputy director of the Gansu Provincial Geological Bureau in 1981 and moved to the General Office of the Party's Central Committee in 1985. Wen became an alternate member of the Politburo in 1987 and a full member in 1997. In 1998, he was appointed vice premier, in charge of agriculture, finance and banking. He became a member of the Politburo Standing Committee in November 2002 and Premier of the State Council in March 2003.

Wu Bangguo (1941–): Born in Anhui Province, Wu studied engineering at Qinghua University. From 1967 to 1992 he worked in Shanghai in electronics and science and technology positions. He worked closely in Shanghai with Jiang Zemin and was a leading figure in the Shanghai Municipal CCP Committee from 1983 to 1992. Wu joined the CCP Politburo in 1992 and then became vice premier of the State Council with responsibility for state-owned enterprises. He joined the Standing Committee of the Politburo in November 2002 and became head of the National People's Congress in March 2003.

Wu De (1914–): Born in Hebei Province, Wu headed Beijing's municipal party committee from 1973 to 1978. On 5 April 1976, he ordered the forcible expulsion of thousands of demonstrators from Tiananmen Square. He held Politburo membership from 1973 to 1980, when he was removed as part of Deng Xiaoping's effort to sweep out conservative opposition to his reform initiatives.

Wu Peifu (1874–1939): Born in Shandong Province, Wu was an important northern warlord in the 1920s. He largely controlled the Beijing government until 1922. He suppressed railway workers on strike on the Beijing-Hankow railway in 1923, dealing a major blow to communist efforts to instigate revolution through worker organizations.

Wu Zetian (625–705): Through talent, intrigue, and ruthlessness, Wu Zetian was the only woman in Chinese history to become empress.

Wu Zhipu (1906?–Cultural Revolution): Wu was a key leader in Henan Province for the 1950s and a secretary of the CCP's central-south bureau from 1962 to 1967. He played a significant role in the movement toward communes in 1958 and encouraged Mao Zedong's most radical economic and political inclinations at the beginning of the Great Leap Forward.

Xianfeng emperor (1831–1861): The Xianfeng emperor ruled China from 1851 to 1861. During this time the country was plagued by the Taiping, Nian, Southwest Moslem, and Northwest Moslem rebellions, as well as by foreign pressures to implement fully the treaties signed at the conclusion of the Opium War.

Yan Xishan (1881–1960): Born in Shaanxi Province and a major warlord there, Yan joined with other northern warlords against Chiang Kai-shek at the end of the 1920s. Thereafter, he joined the Guomindang, serving in its National Military Council and other organs. He eventually became a presidential advisor to Chiang.

Yao Wenyuan (1931–?): Born in Zhejiang Province, Yao was an editor in Shanghai who achieved fame as a member of the Cultural Revolution Small Group in the late 1960s. His critique of Wu Han's play, *Hai Rui Dismissed from Office,* in late 1965 may be seen as the opening shot in the Cultural Revolution. He was purged and arrested in October 1976 as a member of the Gang of Four, which also included Jiang Qing, Wang Hongwen, and Zhang Chunqiao. Sentenced to twenty years, Yao was released in October 1996 and has subsequently died.

Ye Jianying (1897–1986): Born in Guangdong Province, Ye was one of China's ten military marshals. He held high PLA and party posts, at various times serving as the operational head of the CCP Military Affairs Commission and as a member of the Politburo. Ye was one of the very few top leaders to survive the Cultural Revolution unscathed. He protected Deng Xiaoping when Deng was purged in 1976, and he played key roles in the October 1976 arrest of the Gang of Four and in Deng's 1977–78 political comeback.

Ye Qun (?–1971): Ye was Lin Biao's wife. A powerful personality, she achieved considerable influence in the military during the Cultural Revolution years. Ye died in the plane crash in Outer Mongolia that also killed her husband, allegedly while both were fleeing to the Soviet Union in the wake of a failed attempt to assassinate Mao Zedong.

Ye Xuanping (1924–): Born in Guangdong Province, Ye is the son of Marshal Ye Jianying. Ye became a powerful leader of Guangdong Province in the mid-1980s and then was moved to a largely figurehead position in Beijing.

Yuan Shikai (1859–1916): Born in Henan Province, Yuan developed the most modern military forces in the late Qing dynasty. When rebellion broke out against the Qing in 1911, his machinations brought about the abdication of the emperor and the end of the dynastic system. Yuan soon became the president the Republic of China, and within a few years attempted to have himself declared emperor. The attempt failed, and Yuan died soon after.

Zeng Qinghong (1939–): Born in Jiangxi Province, Zeng is the son of former Minister Zeng Shan. Zeng's career brought him into close contact with Yu Qiuli, a major figure in China's petroleum sector during much of the Deng era. In 1984 Zeng shifted to Shanghai, where he worked very closely with Jiang Zemin. When Jiang moved to Beijing in May 1989, Zeng was the only staff member he brought with him. During the ensuing thirteen years Zeng played a vital role as political advisor to Jiang, rising to become a candidate member of the Politburo. Zeng became a member of the Politburo Standing Committee at the Sixteenth Party Congress in November 2002 and Vice President in March 2003.

Zhang Chunqiao (1917–1990s[?]): Born in Shandong Province, Zhang was a municipal official involved in cultural affairs in Shanghai at the start of the Cultural Revolution. He became a key figure in the radical group during the Cultural Revolution and was purged and arrested in October 1976 as a member of the Gang of Four, which also included Jiang Qing, Wang Hongwen, and Yao Wenyuan. Zhang is reported to have died in prison during the 1990s.

Zhang Xueliang (1901–2001): Born in Liaoning Province, Zhang was the son of warlord Zhang Zuolin. Zhang engineered the December 1936 kidnapping of Chiang Kaishek in order to force Chiang to focus his energies on stopping the Japanese encroachments into China. Zhang was placed under house arrest upon his release of Chiang, and he remained under a loose form of house arrest in Taiwan into the 1990s, when he moved to Hawaii.

Zhang Zuolin (1873–1928): Born in Liaoning Province, Zhang Zuolin was a powerful warlord in the 1920s. He was assassinated by the Japanese, who blew up the train on which he was riding.

Zhao Ziyang (1919–): Born in Henan Province, Zhao spent most of his pre–Cultural Revolution career in Guangdong Province. He suffered during the Cultural Revolution but then took command of Sichuan Province in the late 1970s. His successes in Sichuan catapulted him to national power, first as premier and then as general secretary of the CCP during the 1980s. In these positions, Zhao became a major architect of Deng Xiaoping's economic reforms. Zhao was purged in mid-1989, a political casualty of the Tiananmen movement and its suppression.

Zhou Enlai (1898–1976): Born in Zhejiang Province, Zhou was one of the outstanding figures in the Chinese communist leadership. He served as premier and, until 1958, as the PRC's foreign minister. His actual activities were varied, encompassing security as well as economics and foreign affairs. Chinese often liken Zhou to a willow tree— extremely durable but able to bend easily with the wind. Zhou was Mao Zedong's key colleague. He never challenged Mao head on. Rather, he played an essential role in turning Mao's wide-ranging ideas into actual programs and activities. In some instances, he used his power to tone down the excesses of Mao's initiatives.

Zhou Xiaozhou (1912–1966): Born in Hunan Province, Zhou spent his career during the 1950s in posts in Hunan. He had served as assistant to Mao Zedong for a period in Yan'an. Zhou was purged along with Peng Dehuai at the Lushan plenum in August 1959 for opposing the way the Great Leap Forward was being carried out.

Zhu De (1886–1976): Born in Sichuan Province, Zhu was, along with Mao Zedong, the most important military commander of the revolution before 1949. Considered the "grand old man" of the revolution, Zhu did not exercise great power after 1949, although he served as a member of the Politburo from 1934 until his death in 1976.

Zhu Rongji (1928–): Born in Hunan Province, Zhu had a career in the State Planning Commission and State Economic Commission until 1987. He was Shanghai's mayor from 1988 to 1992, during which time he established a reputation as an effective, open-minded economic administrator. A member of the Politburo Standing Committee, Zhu became premier in 1998 and forcefully promoted economic reform in that position. He stepped down from the Politburo Standing Committee in November 2002 and from his position as premier in March 2003.

Zou Jiahua (1927–): Born in Shanghai Municipality, Zou studied in Moscow in the early 1950s with Li Peng. He then had a career primarily engaged in the machine-building and related military-ordnance industries through the mid-1980s. Zou was a Politburo member from 1987 to 1998, and was also a vice premier of the State Council. He headed the State Planning Commission from 1989 to 1993. Zou retired as vice chairman of the Chinese legislature, the National People's Congress, in March 2003. He is a son-in-law of the late Marshal Ye Jianying.

APPENDICES

APPENDIX 1:

Full Text of Jiang Zemin's Report at the Sixteenth Party Congress

Comrades,

Now I would like to make a report to the congress on behalf of the Fifteenth Central Committee of the Communist Party of China (CPC).

The Sixteenth National Congress of the CPC is the first of its kind held by our Party in the new century. It is a very important congress convened by our Party in the new situation in which we have begun to take the third step of the strategic plan for socialist modernization.

The theme of the congress is to hold high the great banner of Deng Xiaoping Theory, fully act on the important thought of Three Represents, carry forward our cause into the future, keep pace with the times, build a well-off society in an all-round way, speed up socialist modernization and work hard to create a new situation in building socialism with Chinese characteristics.

As human society entered the 21st century, we started a new phase of development for building a well-off society in an all-round way and speeding up socialist modernization. The international situation is undergoing profound changes. The trends toward world multipolarization and economic globalization are developing amidst twists and turns. Science and technology are advancing rapidly. Competition in overall national strength is becoming increasingly fierce. Given this pressing situation, we must move forward, or we will fall behind. Our Party must stand firm in the forefront of the times and unite with and lead the Chinese people of all ethnic groups in accomplishing the three major historical tasks: to propel the modernization drive, to achieve national reunification and to safeguard world peace and promote common development, and in bringing about the great rejuvenation of the Chinese nation on its road to socialism with Chinese characteristics. This is a grand mission history and the era have entrusted to our Party.

I Work of the Past Five Years and Basic Experience of 13 Years

The five years since the Fifteenth National Congress of the CPC have been a period in which we have held high the great banner of Deng Xiaoping Theory and kept blazing new trails in a pioneering spirit, and a period in which we have continued to forge ahead triumphantly on the road to socialism with Chinese characteristics in spite of difficulties and risks.

At the Fifteenth National Congress, Deng Xiaoping Theory was established as the Party's guiding ideology, the Party's basic program for the primary stage of socialism was put forward, and the objectives and tasks for China's cross-century development were specified. Acting in the spirit of the congress, the Central Committee held seven plenary sessions at which it made decisions and plans on such major issues as agriculture and rural work, the reform and development of state-owned enterprises, the formulation of the Tenth Five-Year Plan (2001–2005) and the improvement of the Party's work style. Over the past five years, we have traversed an extraordinary course and scored tremendous achievements in reform, development and stability, domestic and foreign affairs and national defense and in running the Party, state and army.

The national economy has maintained a sustained, rapid and sound development. By pursuing the principle of stimulating domestic demand and adopting the proactive fiscal policy and the sound monetary policy in good time, we overcame the adverse effects the Asian financial crisis and world economic fluctuations had on China, and maintained a relatively rapid economic growth. The strategic adjustment of the economic structure has been crowned with success. The position of agriculture as the foundation of the economy has been strengthened. Traditional industries have been upgraded. High and new technology industries and modern services have gained speed. A large number of infrastructure projects in such areas as water conservancy, transportation, telecommunications, energy and environmental protection have been completed. Significant headway has been made in the large-scale development of China's western region. Economic returns have further improved. National revenue has kept growing. The Ninth Five-Year Plan (1996–2000) was fulfilled and the Tenth Five-Year Plan has seen a good start.

Reform and opening up have yielded substantial results. The socialist market economy has taken shape initially. The public sector of the economy has expanded and steady progress has been made in the reform of state-owned enterprises. Self-employed or private enterprises and other non-public sectors of the economy have developed fairly fast. The work of building up the market system has been in full swing. The macro-control system has improved constantly. The pace of change in government functions has been quickened. Reform in finance, taxation, banking, distribution, housing, government institutions and other areas has continued to deepen. The open economy has developed swiftly. Trade in commodities and services and capital flow have grown markedly. China's foreign exchange reserves have risen considerably. With its accession to the World Trade Organization (WTO), China has entered a new stage in its opening up.

Notable progress has been registered in improving socialist democracy and spiritual civilization. Continued efforts have been made to improve democracy and the legal system. New steps have been taken in political restructuring. The patriotic united front has grown stronger. Further progress has been made in the work relating to ethnic, religious and overseas Chinese affairs. Fresh progress has been made in keeping public order through comprehensive measures. Science, technology, education, culture, health, sports, family planning and other undertakings have moved ahead. The media and publicity work as well as ideological and moral education have kept improving. The people's cultural life has become increasingly rich and colorful.

New strides have been taken in strengthening national defense and army building. Efforts have been redoubled to make the People's Liberation Army more revolutionary, modernized and regularized. Our national defense capabilities and the army's defense and combat effectiveness have further improved. The army, the armed police and the militia have played an important role in defending and building up our motherland.

On the whole, the people have reached a well-off standard of living. The income of urban and rural residents has gone up steadily. The urban and rural markets have been brisk, and there has been an ample supply of goods. The quality of life of the residents has been on the rise, with considerable improvement in food, clothing, housing, transport and daily necessities. There has been marked progress in building the social security system. The seven-year program to help 80 million people out of poverty has been in the main fulfilled.

Fresh progress has been made in the great cause of national reunification. The Chinese Government has resumed the exercise of sovereignty over Macao. The principle of "one country, two systems" has been implemented and the basic laws of Hong Kong and Macao special administrative regions have been carried out to the letter. Hong Kong and Macao enjoy social and economic stability. Personnel, economic and cultural exchanges across the Taiwan Straits have kept increasing. The fight against "Taiwan independence" and other attempts to split the country has been going on in depth.

New prospects have been opened up in our external work. In light of the developments and changes in the international situation, we have adhered to the correct foreign policy and related principles. We have carried out both bilateral and multilateral diplomatic activities extensively and taken an active part in international exchanges and cooperation. China's international standing has risen still further.

Party building has been strengthened in an all-round way. All the Party members have steadily intensified their study of Deng Xiaoping Theory. We have put forward and expounded the important thought of Three Represents. Good results have been produced in the intensive education in the need to stress study, political awareness and integrity and in the study of the "Three Represents." An all-out endeavor has been made to build up the Party ideologically, organizationally and in work style. Our ideological and political work has been strengthened. New steps have been taken in the reform of the personnel system. The endeavor to build a clean and honest government and combat corruption has been going on in depth and yielding fresh notable results.

Facts prove that the major policy decisions taken by the Central Committee at and since the Fifteenth National Congress are correct and accord with the fundamental interests of the overwhelming majority of the people. Our achievements are the outcome of the united endeavor of the whole Party and the people of all ethnic groups of the country. They provide a more solid foundation for the future development of the cause of the Party and state.

We must be clearly aware that there are still quite a few difficulties and problems in our work. The income of farmers and some urban residents has increased only slowly. The number of the unemployed has gone up. Some people are still badly off. Things have yet to be straightened out in the matter of income distribution. The order of the market economy has to be further rectified and standardized. Public order is poor in some places. Formalism, the bureaucratic style of work, falsification, extravagance and waste are still serious problems among some leading cadres in our Party, and corruption is still conspicuous in some places. The Party's way of leadership and governance does not yet entirely meet the requirements of the new situation and new tasks. Some

Party organizations are feeble and lax. We must pay close attention to these problems and continue to take effective measures to solve them.

Our achievements over the past five years have been scored through reform and opening up, especially through our practice since the Fourth Plenary Session of the Thirteenth Central Committee in 1989. These 13 years have witnessed a highly volatile international situation and a magnificent upsurge of China's reform, opening up and modernization. From the late 1980s to the early 1990s, there occurred serious political disturbances in China, drastic changes in Eastern Europe and the disintegration of the Soviet Union. Socialism in the world suffered serious setbacks. China was faced with unprecedented difficulties and pressure in its efforts to develop the socialist cause. At this crucial historical juncture bearing on the destiny of the Party and state, the Party Central Committee relied firmly on all the comrades in the Party and the Chinese people of all ethnic groups and unswervingly adhered to the line prevailing since the Third Plenary Session of the Eleventh Central Committee, and thus successfully brought the overall situation of reform and development under control and safeguarded the great cause of socialism with Chinese characteristics. After Comrade Deng Xiaoping made remarks on his tour of the South, the Fourteenth National Congress decided to establish a socialist market economy as the goal of reform, thus ushering in a new stage for reform, opening up and the modernization drive. To develop a market economy under socialism is a great pioneering undertaking never tried before in history. It is a historic contribution of the Chinese Communists to the development of Marxism. It has given expression to our Party's tremendous courage to persist in making theoretical innovation and keeping pace with the times. The shift from the planned economy to the socialist market economy represented a new historic breakthrough in reform and opening up and brought about entirely new prospects for China's economic, political and cultural progress. After the demise of Comrade Deng Xiaoping, we held high the great banner of Deng Xiaoping Theory and made pioneering efforts to advance the cause of socialism with Chinese characteristics into the 21st century in an all-round way.

Over the past 13 years, with clearly defined objectives, we worked with one heart and one mind and scored historic achievements. In 2001, China's GDP reached 9.5933 trillion yuan, almost tripling that of 1989, representing an average annual increase of 9.3 percent. China came up to the sixth place in the world in terms of economic aggregate. On the whole, the people made a historic leap from having only adequate food and clothing to leading a well-off life. As is universally recognized, the 13 years have been a period in which China's overall national strength has risen by a big margin, the people have received more tangible benefits than ever before, and China has enjoyed long-term social stability and solidarity and had a good government and a united people. China's influence in the world has grown notably, and the cohesion of the nation has increased remarkably. The hard work of our Party and people and their great achievements have attracted worldwide attention and will surely go down as a glorious page in the annals of the great rejuvenation of the Chinese nation.

A review of these 13 years shows that we have traversed a tortuous course and that our achievements are hard won. We have responded confidently to a series of unexpected international events bearing on China's sovereignty and security. We have surmounted difficulties and risks arising from the political and economic spheres and from nature. We have gone through one trial after another and removed all kinds of obstacles, thus ensuring that our reform, opening up and modernization drive have been forging ahead in the correct direction like a ship braving surging waves. We have attained these successes by relying on the correct guidance of the Party's basic theory, line and program, on the high degree of unity and solidarity of the Party and on the tenacious work of the whole Party and the people of all ethnic groups around the country.

Here, on behalf of the CPC Central Committee, I wish to express our heartfelt thanks to the people of all our ethnic groups, the democratic parties, people's organizations and patriots from all walks of life, to our compatriots in the Hong Kong Special Administrative Region, the Macao Special Administrative Region and Taiwan as well as overseas Chinese, and to our foreign friends who care about and support China's modernization drive!

The practice of the past 13 years has helped us acquire a deeper understanding of what socialism is, how to build it, and what kind of Party to build and how to build it, and we have gained most valuable experience in this regard.

1. Uphold Deng Xiaoping Theory as our guide and constantly bring forth theoretical innovation. Deng Xiaoping Theory is our banner, and the Party's basic line and program are the fundamental guidelines for every field of our work. Whatever difficulties and risks we may come up against, we must unswervingly abide by the Party's basic theory, line and program. We should persist in arming the entire Party membership with Marxism-Leninism, Mao Zedong Thought and Deng Xiaoping Theory and using them to educate our people. We should continue to emancipate our minds, seek truth from facts, keep pace with the times and make innovations in a pioneering spirit. We should respect the creativity of the general public and test and develop the Party's theory, line, principles and policies in practice.

2. Keep economic development as the central task and solve problems cropping up on our way forward through development. Development is the fundamental principle. We must seize all opportunities to accelerate development. Development calls for new ideas. We should stick to the principle of expanding domestic demand and implement the strategy of national rejuvenation through science and education and that of sustainable development. While seeking speed, we should pay attention to structure, quality and efficiency, and while propelling economic development, we should take into consideration population, resources and the environment. On the basis of economic growth, we need to promote all-round social progress, constantly better people's lives and ensure that all the people share the fruits of development.

3. Persevere in reform and opening up and keep improving the socialist market economy. Reform and opening up are ways to make China powerful. We must press ahead with the reform in all areas resolutely. The reform must be promoted realistically, comprehensively and progressively with breakthroughs made in key areas and emphasis placed on institutional improvement and innovation. We should follow the orientation of reform toward the socialist market economy and make sure that the market forces play an essential role in the allocation of resources under the state's macroeconomic control. By both "bringing in" and "going out," we should actively participate in international economic and technological cooperation and competition and open wider to the outside world.

4. Adhere to the *Four Cardinal Principles** and develop socialist democracy. The Four Cardinal Principles are the very foundation on which we build our country. We must uphold leadership by the CPC and consolidate and improve the state system—a people's democratic dictatorship and the system of political power—the people's congresses. We should uphold and improve the system of multiparty cooperation and political consultation led by the Communist Party and the system of regional ethnic

* The *Four Cardinal Principles* are: to keep to the socialist road and to uphold the people's democratic dictatorship, leadership by the Communist Party, and Marxism-Leninism and Mao Zedong Thought.

autonomy. We should promote political restructuring, develop democracy, improve the legal system, rule the country by law, build a socialist state under the rule of law and ensure that the people exercise their rights as the masters of the country.

5. Attach equal importance to both material and spiritual civilization and run the country by combining the rule of law with the rule of virtue. Socialist spiritual civilization is an important attribute of socialism with Chinese characteristics. Basing ourselves on China's realities, we must carry forward the fine tradition of our national culture and absorb the achievements of foreign cultures in building socialist spiritual civilization. We should unceasingly upgrade the ideological and ethical standards as well as the scientific and cultural qualities of the entire people so as to provide a strong motivation and intellectual support for the modernization drive.

6. Ensure stability as a principle of overriding importance and balance reform, development and stability. Stability is a prerequisite for reform and development. We should take into full consideration the momentum of reform, the speed of development and the sustainability of the general public. Continued improvement of people's lives must be regarded as an important link in balancing reform, development and stability. We should press ahead with reform and development amidst social stability and promote social stability through reform and development.

7. Persevere in the Party's absolute leadership over the army and take the road of fewer but better troops with Chinese characteristics. The people's army is a staunch pillar of the people's democratic dictatorship. It should meet the general requirements of being qualified politically and competent militarily and having a fine style of work, strict discipline and adequate logistic support, with a view to enabling itself to win battles and never degenerate, paying attention to strengthening itself through science and technology and building itself into a more revolutionary, modernized and regularized army. We must ensure that the army is forever loyal to the Party, socialism, the motherland and the people.

8. Continue to unite with all forces that can be united with and increase the cohesion of the Chinese nation. We should hold high the banners of patriotism and socialism, strengthen the great solidarity of the people of all ethnic groups, and consolidate and develop the broadest possible patriotic united front. We need to strengthen our solidarity with the democratic parties and personages without party affiliation. We should handle well the work relating to ethnic minorities, religions and overseas Chinese. We should adhere to the principle of "one country, two systems" and bring into full play every positive factor in a common endeavor to accomplish the grand cause of national reunification and the great rejuvenation of the Chinese nation.

9. Pursue the independent foreign policy of peace, safeguard world peace and promote common development. We will, as always, attach paramount importance to our state sovereignty and security. We will develop friendly relations and cooperation with all other countries on the basis of the Five Principles of Peaceful Coexistence. We will oppose hegemonism and power politics and promote the establishment of a fair and rational new international political and economic order. In handling international affairs, we should observe and cope with the situation cool-headedly, adhere to the principle of mutual respect and seek common ground while shelving differences. We need to respect the diversity of the world, promote democracy in international relations and strive for a peaceful international environment and a good climate in areas around China.

10. Strengthen and improve the Party's leadership and propel the new great project of Party building. To run the state well, we must run the Party well first. To do this, we must be strict with the Party members. We must maintain the Party's nature and purposes, strengthen and improve Party building in the spirit of reform, enhance the

Party's art of leadership and governance, increase its capability of fighting corruption and guarding against degeneration and risks and make unremitting efforts to combat corruption. The Party must keep its flesh-and-blood ties with the people as well as its progressiveness, purity, solidarity and unity.

The above-mentioned ten principles constitute the basic experience the Party must follow as it leads the people in building socialism with Chinese characteristics. This experience and the historical experience gained by the Party since its founding can be summarized as follows: Our Party must always represent the development trend of China's advanced productive forces, the orientation of China's advanced culture and the fundamental interests of the overwhelming majority of the Chinese people. They are the inexorable requirements for maintaining and developing socialism and the logical conclusion our Party has reached through hard exploration and great practice.

II Implement the Important Thought of Three Represents in an All-Round Way

To open up new prospects for the cause of socialism with Chinese characteristics, we must hold high the great banner of Deng Xiaoping Theory and implement the important thought of Three Represents. As a continuation and development of Marxism-Leninism, Mao Zedong Thought and Deng Xiaoping Theory, this important thought reflects new requirements for the work of the Party and state arising from the changes in China and other parts of the world today. It is a powerful theoretical weapon for strengthening and improving Party building and promoting self-improvement and development of socialism in China. It is the crystallization of the Party's collective wisdom and a guiding ideology the Party must follow for a long time to come. Persistent implementation of the "Three Represents" is the foundation for building our Party, the cornerstone for its governance and the source of its strength.

The important thought of Three Represents has been put forward on the basis of a scientific judgment of the Party's historical position. Having gone through the revolution, reconstruction and reform, our Party has evolved from a party that led the people in fighting for state power to a party that has led the people in exercising the power and has long remained in power. It has developed from a party that led national reconstruction under external blockade and a planned economy to a party that is leading national development while the country is opening to the outside world and developing a socialist market economy. Keeping in mind the past, present and future of China and other parts of the world, we must accurately comprehend the characteristics of the times and the Party's tasks, scientifically formulate and correctly implement the Party's line, principles and policies, and study and settle questions concerning the promotion of China's social progress and the improvement of Party building. We should neither approach questions out of their historical context nor lose our bearings, and we should neither fall behind the times nor skip the stages, so as to ensure that our cause will advance from victory to victory.

The implementation of the important thought of Three Represents is, in essence, to keep pace with the times, maintain the Party's progressiveness and exercise the state power in the interest of the people. All Party members must be keenly aware of this basic requirement and become more conscious and determined in implementing this important thought.

1. To carry out the important thought of Three Represents, the whole Party must maintain the spirit of keeping pace with the times and blaze new trails for the development of the Marxist theory. Upholding the Party's ideological line, emancipating the

mind, seeking truth from facts and keeping pace with the times are decisive factors for our Party to retain its progressiveness and enhance its creativity. Keeping pace with the times means that all the theory and work of the Party must conform to the times, follow the law of development and display great creativity. Whether we can persist in doing this bears on the future and destiny of the Party and state.

Innovation sustains the progress of a nation. It is an inexhaustible motive force for the prosperity of a country and the source of the eternal vitality of a political party. The world is changing, China's reform, opening up and modernization drive are advancing and our people's great practice is progressing. All this urgently requires our Party to sum up new experience from practice, draw on the achievements of modern human civilization, broaden its fields of vision in theory and come up with new theses with the courage of the theory of Marxism. Only thus can our Party's ideology and theory guide the whole Party and the entire people forward and inspire them to push ahead the cause of building socialism with Chinese characteristics. Theoretical innovation based on practice precedes social development and changes. Bringing forth new ideas in institutions, science and technology, culture and other fields through theoretical innovation, exploring the way forward in practice, never becoming conceited and never slackening our effort—these are the ways of running the Party and state, which we should follow for a long time to come.

Innovation requires emancipating our minds, seeking truth from facts and keeping pace with the times. There is no limit to practice nor to innovation. We will surpass our predecessors, and future generations will certainly surpass us. This is an inexorable law governing social advancement. We must adapt ourselves to the progress of practice and test all things in practice. We must conscientiously free our minds from the shackles of the outdated notions, practices and systems, from the erroneous and dogmatic interpretations of Marxism and from the fetters of subjectivism and metaphysics. While upholding the basic tenets of Marxism, we must add new chapters of theory to it. While carrying forward the revolutionary tradition, we must acquire new experience. We should be good at seeking unity in thinking through the emancipation of our minds and guiding our new practice with the developing Marxism.

2. To carry out the important thought of Three Represents, it is essential for the Party to give top priority to development in governing and rejuvenating the country and open up new prospects for the modernization drive. A Marxist ruling party must attach great importance to the liberation and development of the productive forces. Without development, it would be impossible to maintain the progressiveness of the Party, give play to the superiority of the socialist system and make the people rich and the country strong. The progressiveness of the Party is concrete and historical, and it must be judged by whether the Party promotes the development of the advanced productive forces and culture in present-day China and works to safeguard and realize the fundamental interests of the overwhelming majority of the people. In the final analysis, it must be judged by the Party's role in propelling history forward.

In China, a large developing country with a backward economy and culture, where our Party is leading the people in the modernization drive, a good solution to the problem of development has a direct bearing on the trend of popular sentiment and the success of our cause. Shouldering the historical responsibility to propel the Chinese society, the Party must always keep a firm grip on development—the top priority for its governance and rejuvenation of the country. It must maintain its progressiveness and give play to the superiority of the socialist system by developing the advanced productive forces and culture and realizing the fundamental interests of the overwhelming majority of the people, speeding up all-round social progress and promoting the all-round development of people. So long as the Party firmly grasps this point, it will have thoroughly understood the aspirations of the people and the essence of the socialist modernization drive, and thus it will be able to keep implementing the important thought of Three Represents and consolidating its position as the ruling party and meet the requirement of making the country strong and the people rich.

Development requires that we always concentrate on economic growth, base ourselves on China's realities, conform to the trend of the times and continue to explore new ways to promote the progress of the advanced productive forces and culture. Development requires that we uphold and deepen the reform. It requires that we do away with all notions which hinder development, change all practices and regulations which impede it and get rid of all the drawbacks of the systems which adversely affect it. Development requires that we trust and rely on the people who are the motive force for pushing forward the advance of history. We will pool the wisdom and strength of the people of the whole country and concentrate on construction and development.

3. To carry out the important thought of Three Represents, it is essential to bring all positive factors into full play and bring new forces to the great cause of rejuvenating the Chinese nation. The interests of the overwhelming majority of the people and the initiative and creativity of the whole society and the entire nation are always the most decisive factors for advancing the cause of the Party and state. In the process of profound social changes in our country and the rapid development of the cause of the Party and state, it is vitally important to properly balance the interests of all quarters and fully mobilize and rally all positive factors.

With the deepening of reform and opening up and economic and cultural development, the working class in China has expanded steadily and its quality improved. The working class, with the intellectuals as part of it, and the farmers are always the basic forces for promoting the development of the advanced productive forces and all-round social progress in our country. Emerging in the process of social changes, entrepreneurs and technical personnel employed by non-public scientific and technological enterprises, managerial and technical staff employed by overseas-funded enterprises, the self-employed, private entrepreneurs, employees in intermediaries, free-lance professionals and members of other social strata are all builders of socialism with Chinese characteristics. We should unite with the people of all social strata who help to make the motherland prosperous and strong, encouraging their pioneering spirit, protecting their legitimate rights and interests and commending the outstanding ones in an effort to create a situation in which all people are well positioned, do their best and live in harmony.

We must respect work, knowledge, competent people and creation. This should be an important policy of the Party and state to be conscientiously implemented in society at large. We need to respect and protect all work that is good for the people and society. All work that contributes to the socialist modernization drive in China, physical or mental and simple or complicated, is glorious and should be acknowledged and respected. All investors at home or from overseas should be encouraged to carry out business activities in China's development. All legitimate income, from work or not, should be protected. It is improper to judge whether people are politically progressive or backward simply by whether they own property or how much property they own. But rather, we should judge them mainly by their political awareness, state of mind and performance, by how they have acquired and used their property, and by how they have contributed to the cause of building socialism with Chinese characteristics through their work. It is necessary to foster notions and form a business mechanism in conformity with the basic economic system in the primary stage of socialism and create a social environment in which people are encouraged to achieve something and helped to make a success of their careers, so as to unleash all the vitality contained in work, knowledge, technology, management and capital and give full play to all sources of social wealth for the benefit of the people.

In building socialism with Chinese characteristics, the fundamental interests of the people of the whole country are identical, on the basis of which concrete interest relations and internal contradictions can be adjusted. In the formulation and implementation of the Party's principles and policies, a basic point of departure is that we should represent the fundamental interests of the overwhelming majority of the people, and correctly reflect and take into account the interests of different groups of people, enabling the whole people to advance steadily toward the goal of common prosperity. We should protect the vitality for further growth of the developed regions, strong industries and people who have become rich first through hard work and lawful business operations and encouraging them to create social wealth. More importantly, we must pay great attention to less developed areas and the industries and people in straitened circumstances and show concern for them. In particular, we must see to it that the people in financial difficulties have subsistence allowances, and we must take effective measures to help them find jobs and improve their living conditions so that they will truly feel the warmth of our socialist society.

4. To carry out the important thought of Three Represents, it is essential to push forward Party building in a spirit of reform and instill new vitality in the Party. Attaching vital importance to and strengthening Party building is a magic weapon with which our Party has grown from a small and weak force to a large and strong one, risen in spite of setbacks and matured gradually in surmounting difficulties. As the historical experience of the Party over the past 80 years and more shows, the most important point is that we must build up the Party according to its political line, central task and general goal for building it with a view to enhancing its creativity, cohesion and fighting capacity.

Persisting in self-examination in compliance with the requirements of the times and pursuing self-improvement in a spirit of reform are the fundamental guarantee that our Party will always remain a Marxist party, will never be divorced from the people and will be full of vitality. We must be good at both reviewing our useful experience and learning lessons from our mistakes. We must be good at both leading the people ahead by putting forward and implementing the correct theory and line and acquiring the motivation for progress from the people's creations in practice and their desire for development. We must be good at both understanding and changing the objective world and organizing and guiding cadres and other Party members to strengthen their efforts to change their subjective world in practice. Bearing these requirements in mind, we must integrate adherence to the basic tenets of Marxism with efforts for theoretical innovation, maintenance of the fine tradition of the Party with promotion of the spirit of the times, and consolidation of the Party's class base with expansion of its mass base so that the Party serves as a strong core of leadership that is consolidated ideologically, politically and organizationally and always stands in the forefront of the times leading the people forward in solidarity.

All in all, the important thought of Three Represents is always in a process of development and progress. The whole Party must continue to emancipate the mind, come up with new ideas in respect of theory and create something new in practice. It must carry out the important thought of Three Represents in all endeavors of the socialist modernization drive and in all aspects of Party building so that it always advances with the times and shares weal and woe with the people.

Thanks to the joint efforts of the whole Party and the people of all ethnic groups, we have attained the objectives of the first two steps of the three-step strategy for China's modernization drive, and by and large, the people have become well-off. This is a great victory for the socialist system and a new milestone in the history of the development of the Chinese nation.

We must be aware that China is in the primary stage of socialism and will remain so for a long time to come. The well-off life we are leading is still at a low level; it is not all-inclusive and is very uneven. The principal contradiction in our society is still one between the ever-growing material and cultural needs of the people and the backwardness of social production. Our productive forces, science, technology and education are still relatively backward, so there is still a long way to go before we achieve industrialization and modernization. The dual structure in urban and rural economy has not yet been changed, the gap between regions is still widening and there are still quite a large number of impoverished people. China's population continues to grow, the proportion of the aged is getting larger, and the pressure on employment and social security is mounting. The contradiction between the ecological environment and natural resources on the one hand and economic and social development on the other is becoming increasingly conspicuous. We still feel pressure from developed countries as they have the upper hand in such fields as the economy, science and technology. The economic structure and managerial systems in other fields remain to be perfected. There are still some problems we cannot afford to overlook in improving democracy and the legal system as well as the ideological and ethical standards. We need to work hard over a long period of time to consolidate and uplift our current well-off standard of living.

An overview of the situation shows that for our country, the first two decades of the 21st century are a period of important strategic opportunities, which we must seize tightly and which offers bright prospects. In accordance with the development objectives up to 2010, the centenary of the Party and that of New China, as proposed at the Fifteenth National Congress, we need to concentrate on building a well-off society of a higher standard in an all-round way to the benefit of well over one billion people in this period. We will further develop the economy, improve democracy, advance science and education, enrich culture, foster social harmony and upgrade the texture of life for the people. The two decades of development will serve as an inevitable connecting link for attaining the third-step strategic objectives for our modernization drive as well as a key stage for improving the socialist market economy and opening wider to the outside world. Building on what is achieved at this stage and continuing to work for several more decades, we will have in the main accomplished the modernization program and turned China into a strong, prosperous, democratic and culturally advanced socialist country by the middle of this century.

III The Objectives of Building a Well-off Society in an All-round Way

—On the basis of optimized structure and better economic returns, efforts will be made to quadruple the GDP of the year 2000 by 2020, and China's overall national strength and international competitiveness will increase markedly. We will in the main achieve industrialization and establish a full-fledged socialist market economy and a more open and viable economic system. The proportion of urban population will go up considerably and the trend of widening differences between industry and agriculture, between urban and rural areas and between regions will be reversed step by step. We will have a fairly sound social security system. There will be a higher rate of employment. People will have more family property and lead a more prosperous life.

—Socialist democracy and the legal system will be further improved. The basic principle of ruling the country by law will be implemented completely. The political, economic and cultural rights and interests of the people will be respected and guaranteed in real earnest. Democracy at the grassroots level will be better practiced. People will enjoy a sound public order and live and work in peace and contentment.

—The ideological and ethical standards, the scientific and cultural qualities, and the health of the whole people will be enhanced notably. A sound modern national educational system, scientific, technological and cultural innovation systems as well as nationwide fitness and medical and health systems will take shape. People will have access to better education. We will make senior secondary education basically universal in the country and eliminate illiteracy. A learning society in which all the people will learn or even pursue life-long education will emerge to boost their all-round development.

—The capability of sustainable development will be steadily enhanced. The ecological environment will be improved. The efficiency of using resources will be increased significantly. We will enhance harmony between man and nature to push the whole society onto a path to civilized development featuring the growth of production, an affluent life and a sound ecosystem.

The objectives set at this congress for building a well-off society in an all-round way are objectives of comprehensive economic, political and cultural development of socialism with Chinese characteristics, objectives well geared to the efforts to speed up modernization. They tally with the national conditions, the realities of the modernization drive and the people's aspirations. They are of great significance. In order to attain the Party's objectives for the new stage in the new century, it is imperative to come up with new ideas for development, make new breakthroughs in reform, break new ground in opening up and take new moves in all fields of endeavor. All localities and departments must proceed from their actual conditions and take effective measures to attain the objectives. Places where conditions permit may develop faster and take the lead in accomplishing modernization by and large on the basis of building a well-off society in an all-round way. We are sure that after attaining the objectives of building a well-off society in an all-round way, our motherland will become stronger and more prosperous, the people will live a better and happier life, and socialism with Chinese characteristics will further demonstrate its great superiority.

IV Economic Development and Restructuring

In building a well-off society in an all-round way, it is of vital importance to take economic development as the central task and keep releasing and developing the productive forces. In light of the new trends in the economy, science and technology of the world and the requirements of our national economic development in the new period, we should undertake the following main tasks for economic development and reform in the first two decades of this century: to improve the socialist market economy, promote strategic adjustment of the economic structure, basically accomplish industrialization, energetically apply IT, accelerate modernization, maintain a sustained, rapid and sound development of the national economy and steadily uplift the people's living standards. In the first decade, we will accomplish all the objectives set in the Tenth Five-Year Plan and for the years up to 2010 so as to bring the economic aggregate, overall national strength and the people's living standards up to a much higher level and lay a solid foundation for even greater development in the second decade.

1. Take a new road to industrialization and implement the strategy of rejuvenating the country through science and education and that of sustainable development. It remains an arduous historical task in the process of our modernization drive to accom-

plish industrialization. IT application is a logical choice if industrialization and modernization of our country are to be accelerated. It is, therefore, necessary to persist in using IT to propel industrialization, which will, in turn, stimulate IT application, blazing a new trail to industrialization featuring high scientific and technological content, good economic returns, low resources consumption, little environmental pollution and a full display of advantages in human resources.

We must press ahead to optimize and upgrade the industrial structure so as to bring about an industrial pattern with high and new technology industries as the leader, basic and manufacturing industries as the kingpin and the service industry developing in all areas. We must give priority to the development of the information industry and apply IT in all areas of economic and social development. We must develop high and new technology industries to provide breakthroughs in stimulating economic growth. It is necessary to transform traditional industries with high and new technology and advanced adaptive technology and invigorate the equipment manufacturing industry. We should continue to strengthen infrastructure. We should accelerate the development of the modern service sector and raise the proportion of the tertiary industry in the national economy. We must correctly handle the relationships of development between the high and new technology industries and traditional industries, between capital-and-technology-intensive industries and labor-intensive industries and between virtual economy and real economy.

In taking a new road to industrialization, we must give play to the important role of science and technology as the primary productive force and pay close attention to improving the quality and efficiency of economic growth by relying on scientific and technological progress and raising the qualities of labor force. We must strengthen basic research and research in high technology, promote key technological innovation and systems integration so that technology will develop by leaps and bounds. We must encourage scientific and technological innovation and acquire key technology and independent intellectual property rights in key areas and a number of domains in frontier science and technology. We must deepen the reform of the administration systems of science, technology and education, strengthen the integration of science, technology and education with the economy, improve the service system for the development of science and technology and quicken the pace of translating research achievements into practical productive forces. We must press ahead with the building of a national innovation system. We must give play to the role of venture capital and develop a mechanism of capital operation and human capital pooling for promoting scientific and technological innovation and start-ups. We must improve the system of intellectual property rights protection. We must give top priority to sustainable development, adhere to the basic state policies of family planning and environmental and resources protection, keep the birthrate low and rationally develop and economically utilize all kinds of natural resources. We must lose no time in solving the problem of water shortages in some areas and build the south-to-north water diversion project. We should promote marine development and do well in the comprehensive improvement of land and resources. It is necessary to help the whole nation see the importance of environmental protection and do a good job of ecological conservation and improvement.

2. Make the rural economy flourish and speed up urbanization. A major task for building a well-off society in an all-round way is to make overall planning for urban and rural economic and social development, build modern agriculture, develop the rural economy and increase the income of farmers. We must strengthen the position of agriculture as the foundation of the economy, carry on the restructuring of agriculture and the rural economy, protect and raise the comprehensive grain production capacity, improve the system for ensuring the quality of farm produce and enhance the compet-

itiveness of agriculture in the market. We must push forward the industrialized operation of agriculture, better organize farmers in their access to the market and improve
the overall efficiency of agriculture. We must develop farm produce processing industry to boost the county economy. We must open up more rural markets and enliven the
distribution of farm produce by improving its market system.

It is an inevitable trend of industrialization and modernization for surplus rural
labor to move to non-agricultural industries and to cities and towns. It is essential to
raise the level of urbanization gradually and persist in the coordinated development of
large, medium and small cities and small towns along the path to urbanization with
Chinese characteristics. We should develop small towns on the basis of existing county
seats and of organic towns where conditions permit, make scientific planning and a
rational layout, integrating their development with the expansion of township and village enterprises and the rural service sector. All the institutional and policy barriers to
urbanization must be removed and the rational and orderly flow of rural labor guided.

We must adhere to the basic rural policies of the Party and keep stabilizing and
improving the two-tier management system that integrates unified with separate management on the basis of household contract management. Wherever conditions permit, the transfer of the contractual right of land can be carried out according to law
and on a voluntary and compensatory basis so as to develop scale operation step by
step. We must respect farmer households as market players and encourage innovation
in the rural management system. We must enhance the economic strength of the collectives. We should establish and improve a commercialized rural service system. We
must invest more in agriculture, give it more support and accelerate the progress of
agricultural science and technology and the building of rural infrastructure. We should
improve financial services in rural areas. We must continue with the reform in tax and
fees in rural areas to lighten the burdens of farmers and protect their interests.

3. Advance the development of the western region and bring about a coordinated
development of regional economies. The implementation of the strategy for the development of the western region bears on the overall situation of national development,
the ethnic unity and the stability in border areas. To lay a solid foundation and go
ahead in a down-to-earth manner, we must give priority to infrastructure and ecological environment improvement and strive for breakthroughs in a decade. We must
develop industries with local advantages and propel the development of key areas. We
should develop science, technology and education and train and make the best use of
all human resources. The state should provide the western region with greater support
in such areas as investment projects, tax policies and transfer payments, gradually build
up long-term and stable sources of funds for its development, improve the investment
environment, and guide foreign investment and domestic capital toward that region.
People there should further emancipate their minds, enhance their self-development
capabilities and explore a new path to accelerated development in reform and opening up.

The central region should redouble its efforts toward structural adjustment, giving
impetus to industrialized operation of agriculture, transforming traditional industries,
cultivating new economic growth points and speeding up industrialization and urbanization. The eastern region should quicken the pace of upgrading its industrial structure, develop modern agriculture, high and new technology industries and high
value-added processing and manufacturing industries and further develop the
outward-looking economy. We should encourage the special economic zones and the
Pudong New Area in Shanghai to spearhead, among other things, institutional innovation and greater openness. We should support the northeastern region and other old
industrial bases in accelerating their adjustments and transformation and support cities

and areas mainly engaged in natural resources exploitation in their efforts to develop alternative industries. We should support the old revolutionary base areas and areas inhabited by ethnic minorities in expediting their development. The state should give more support to main grain producing areas. The eastern, central and western regions should strengthen economic exchanges and cooperation to complement one another and secure common development so as to form a number of distinctive economic zones and belts.

4. Stick to and improve the basic economic system and deepen the reform of the state property management system. In line with the requirements of releasing and developing the productive forces, we must uphold and improve the basic economic system, with public ownership playing a dominant role and diverse forms of ownership developing side by side. First, it is necessary to consolidate and develop unswervingly the public sector of the economy. Expansion of the state sector and its control of the lifeline of the national economy is of crucial importance in displaying the superiority of the socialist system and reinforcing the economic strength, national defense capabilities and national cohesion. As an important component of the public sector, the collective sector of the economy plays a significant role in achieving common prosperity. Secondly, it is necessary to encourage, support and guide the development of the non-public sectors of the economy. The non-public sector of self-employed, private and other forms of ownership is an important component part of the socialist market economy. They play an important role in mobilizing the initiative of all quarters of the society to quicken the development of the productive forces. Thirdly, we must stimulate the development of the non-public sectors while keeping the public sector as the dominant player, incorporating both into the process of the socialist modernization drive instead of setting them against each other. All sectors of the economy can very well display their respective advantages in market competition and stimulate one another for common development.

Continuing to adjust the layout and structure of the state sector and reform the state property management system is a major task for deepening economic restructuring. We should give full play to the initiative of both the central and local authorities on the precondition of upholding state ownership. The state should make laws and regulations and establish a state property management system under which the Central Government and local governments perform the responsibilities of investor on behalf of the state respectively, enjoying owner's equity, combining rights with obligations and duties and administering assets, personnel and other affairs. The Central Government should represent the state in performing the functions as investor in large state-owned enterprises, infrastructure and important natural resources that have a vital bearing on the lifeline of the national economy and state security while local governments should represent the state in performing the functions as investors with regard to other state property. The Central Government and the provincial and municipal (prefectural) governments should set up state property management organizations. We should continue to explore systems and modes for managing state property effectively. Governments at all levels must strictly abide by the laws and regulations concerning the management of state property, persisting in the separation of government functions from enterprise management and separation of ownership from management so that enterprises can operate independently, assume sole responsibility for their profits or losses and preserve and increase the value of state property.

State-owned enterprises are the pillar of the national economy. We should deepen the reform of state-owned enterprises and further explore diversified forms for effectively realizing public ownership, especially state ownership. We should promote institutional, technological and managerial innovations in enterprises. Except for a tiny number of enterprises that must be funded solely by the state, all the others should introduce the joint-stock system to develop a mixed sector of the economy. Sources of investment must be diversified. The controlling shares in lifeline enterprises must be held by the state. Large and medium state-owned enterprises must continue their reform to convert themselves into standard companies in compliance with the requirements of the modern enterprise system and improve their corporate governance. Monopoly industries should carry out reforms to introduce competition mechanisms. We should form large internationally competitive companies and enterprise groups through market forces and policy guidance. We should give a freer rein to small and medium state-owned enterprises to invigorate themselves. We should deepen the reform of collective enterprises and give more support and help to the growth of the various forms of the collective sector of the economy.

We must give full scope to the important role of the non-public sector of self-employed, private and other forms of ownership of the economy in stimulating economic growth, creating more jobs and activating the market. We should expand the areas for the market access of domestic nongovernmental capital and adopt measures with regard to investment, financing, taxation, land use, foreign trade and other aspects to carry out fair competition. We should strengthen the supervision and administration of the non-public sectors according to law to promote their sound development. We should improve the legal system for protecting private property.

5. Improve the modern market system and tighten and improve macroeconomic control. We should give a fuller play to the basic role of the market in the allocation of resources and build up a unified, open, competitive and orderly modern market system. We should go ahead with reform, opening up, stability and development of the capital market. We should develop markets for property rights, land, labor and technology and create an environment for the equal use of production factors by market players. We must deepen the reform of the distribution system and introduce modern ways of distribution. We must rectify and standardize the order of the market economy and establish a social credit system compatible with a modern market economy. We must get rid of trade monopolies and regional blockades to allow free movement of goods and production factors on markets around the country.

We must improve the government functions of economic regulation, market supervision, social administration and public services, and reduce and standardize administrative procedures for examination and approval. We must stimulate economic growth, create more jobs, stabilize prices and maintain balance of international payments as the main macroeconomic control objectives. Stimulating domestic demand is an essential and long-standing factor underlying China's economic growth. We must stick to the policy of stimulating domestic demand and implement corresponding macroeconomic policies in light of actual needs. We must adjust the relationship between investment and consumption to raise the proportion of consumption in GDP gradually. We should improve the macroeconomic control system featuring the coordination of state planning and fiscal and monetary policies to give play to economic leverage. We should deepen the reform of the fiscal, taxation, banking, investment and financing systems. We should improve the budgetary decision-making and management system, step up the supervision of revenue and expenditures and intensify tax administration. We should carry out the reform steadily to deregulate interest rates to leave them to market forces, optimize the allocation of financial resources, strengthen regulation and prevent and defuse financial risks so as to provide better banking services for economic and social development.

6. Deepen the reform of the income distribution system and improve the social security system. Rationalizing the relations of income distribution bears on the imme-

diate interests of the general public and the display of their initiative. We should adjust and standardize the relations of distribution among the state, enterprises and individuals. We should establish the principle that labor, capital, technology, managerial expertise and other production factors participate in the distribution of income in accordance with their respective contributions, thereby improving the system under which distribution according to work is dominant and a variety of modes of distribution coexist. We should give priority to efficiency with due consideration to fairness, earnestly implementing the distribution policy while advocating the spirit of devotion and guarding against an excessive disparity in income while opposing equalitarianism. In primary distribution, we should pay more attention to efficiency, bringing the market forces into play and encouraging part of the people to become rich first through honest labor and lawful operations. In redistribution, we should pay more attention to fairness and strengthen the function of the government in regulating income distribution to narrow the gap if it is too wide. We should standardize the order of income distribution, properly regulate the excessively high income of some monopoly industries and outlaw illegal gains. Bearing in mind the objective of common prosperity, we should try to raise the proportion of the middle-income group and increase the income of the low-income group.

Establishing and improving a social security system compatible with the level of economic development constitutes an important guarantee for social stability and long-term peace and order in the country. We should stick to and improve the basic old-age pension and medical insurance systems for urban workers, combining socially pooled funds with personal contributions. We should improve the systems of unemployment insurance and subsistence allowances for urban residents. We should try various channels to raise and accumulate social security funds. Reasonable standards for social security benefits should be set in light of local conditions. We should develop social relief and welfare programs in urban and rural areas. Wherever conditions permit, we should try to establish systems of old-age pensions, medical insurance and subsistence allowances in rural areas.

7. Do a better job in opening up by "bringing in" and "going out." In response to the new situation of economic globalization and China's entry into the WTO, we should take part in international economic and technological cooperation and competition on a broader scale, in more spheres and on a higher level, make the best use of both international and domestic markets, optimize the allocation of resources, expand the space for development and accelerate reform and development by opening up.

We should expand trade in goods and services. We should implement the strategy of market diversification, bring into play our comparative advantages, consolidate our existing markets and open new ones in an effort to increase exports. We should sharpen the competitive edge of our goods and services for export by ensuring good quality. We should optimize our import mix and focus on bringing in advanced technology and key equipment. We should deepen the reform of the system of trade and economic relations with other countries, encouraging more enterprises to engage in foreign trade and improving relevant taxation systems and the trade financing mechanism.

We should attract more foreign direct investment and use it more effectively. We will open the service sector to the outside world step by step. We will utilize medium- and long-term foreign investment in many ways, combining it with the domestic economic restructuring and the reorganization and transformation of state-owned enterprises and encouraging multinational corporations to invest in agriculture and manufacturing and high and new technology industries. We should try to bring in from overseas large numbers of professionals and other intellectual resources in various areas. We should improve the environment for investment, grant national treatment to foreign investors and make relevant policies and regulations more transparent. Implementation of the strategy of "going out" is an important measure taken in the new stage of opening up. We should encourage and help relatively competitive enterprises with various forms of ownership to invest abroad in order to increase export of goods and labor services and bring about a number of strong multinational enterprises and brand names. We should take an active part in regional economic exchanges and cooperation. In opening wider to the outside world, we must pay great attention to safeguarding our national economic security.

8. Do everything possible to create more jobs and improve the people's lives. Employment has a vital bearing on the people's livelihood. The task of increasing employment is arduous now and will remain so for a long time to come. It is a long-term strategy and policy of the state to expand employment. Party committees and governments at all levels must take it as their major obligation to improve the business environment and create more jobs. We should open up more avenues for employment and develop labor-intensive industries. We should give policy support to enterprises that increase jobs or reemploy laid-off workers. We should help the general public to change their mentality about employment, introduce flexible and diverse forms of employment and encourage people to find jobs on their own or become self-employed. We should improve the system of pre-job training and employment services and raise workers' skills for new jobs. We should strengthen employment management in accordance with law, safeguard the legitimate rights and interests of workers, pay great attention to safety at work and protect the safety of state property and people's life.

The fundamental goal of economic development is to uplift the living standards and quality of life of the people. As the economy develops, we should increase the income of urban and rural residents, expand the scope of their consumption and optimize the consumption structure so as to meet the people's multifarious material and cultural needs. Further efforts should be made to develop public service facilities, better people's living environment and expand community services in order to make life easier for the people. We should establish a medical service and health care system that meets the requirements of the new situation. We should improve medical and health conditions in rural areas and the medical and health care for urban and rural residents. We should build up various programs to help the handicapped. We should intensify our efforts to fight poverty through development, build on the achievements we have scored in this regard, strive to accomplish the task of providing adequate food and clothing for the impoverished rural population and gradually enable them to lead a well-off life.

Accomplishing the tasks set for economic development and restructuring is of decisive significance to accelerating our socialist modernization. So long as the whole Party and the people of all ethnic groups work hard with one heart and one mind, we will definitely establish a mature socialist market economy and maintain a sustained, rapid and sound development of the national economy at the new stage in the new century.

V Political Development and Restructuring

Developing socialist democracy and establishing a socialist political civilization are an important goal for building a well-off society in an all-round way. Adhering to the Four Cardinal Principles, we must go on steadily and surely with political restructuring, extend socialist democracy and improve the socialist legal system in order to build a socialist country under the rule of law and consolidate and develop the political situation characterized by democracy, solidarity, liveliness, stability and harmony.

Our Party has always deemed it its duty to realize and develop people's democracy. Since the beginning of reform and opening up, we have pressed on with political restructuring and improved socialist democracy. The key to developing socialist democracy is to combine the need to uphold the Party's leadership and to ensure that the people are the masters of the country with the need to rule the country by law. Leadership by the Party is the fundamental guarantee that the people are the masters of the country and that the country is ruled by law. The people being the masters of the country constitutes the essential requirement of socialist democracy. Ruling the country by law is the basic principle the Party pursues while it leads the people in running the country. The CPC is the core of leadership for the cause of socialism with Chinese characteristics. Governance by the Communist Party means that it leads and supports the people in acting as the masters of the country and mobilizes and organizes them on a most extensive scale to manage state and social affairs and economic and cultural undertakings according to law, safeguarding and realizing their fundamental interests. The Constitution and other laws embody the unity of the Party's views and the people's will. All organizations and individuals must act in strict accordance with the law, and none of them are allowed to have the privilege to overstep the Constitution and other laws.

Political restructuring is the self-improvement and development of the socialist political system. It must help enhance the vitality of the Party and state, demonstrate the features and advantages of the socialist system, give full scope to the initiative and creativity of the people, safeguard national unity, ethnic solidarity and social stability and promote economic development and social progress. We must always proceed from our national conditions, review our experience gained in practice and at the same time learn from the achievements of political civilization of mankind. We should never copy any models of the political system of the West. We must concentrate on institutional improvement and ensure that socialist democracy is institutionalized and standardized and has its procedures.

1. Uphold and improve the systems of socialist democracy. It is essential to improve the systems of democracy, develop diverse forms of democracy, expand citizens' participation in political affairs in an orderly way, and ensure that the people go in for democratic elections and decision-making, exercise democratic management and supervision according to law and enjoy extensive rights and freedoms, and that human rights are respected and guaranteed. We should uphold and improve the system of people's congresses and ensure that the congresses and their standing committees exercise their functions according to law and that their legislation and policy decisions better embody the people's will. We should optimize the composition of the standing committees. We should uphold and improve the system of multiparty cooperation and political consultation under the leadership of the Communist Party. We should uphold the principle of "long-term coexistence, mutual supervision, treating each other with all sincerity and sharing weal and woe," step up our cooperation with the democratic parties and better display the features and advantages of the Chinese socialist system of political parties. We will ensure that the Chinese People's Political Consultative Conference (CPPCC) plays its role in political consultation, democratic supervision and participation in and deliberation of state affairs. We will consolidate and develop the broadest possible patriotic united front. We will fully implement the Party's policy toward ethnic minorities, uphold and improve the system of regional ethnic autonomy, consolidate and enhance socialist ethnic relations of equality, solidarity and mutual assistance and promote common prosperity and progress for all our ethnic groups. We will implement the Party's policy toward the freedom of religious belief, handle religious affairs according to law, encourage the adaptability of religions to the socialist

society and uphold the principle of self-administration and running religious affairs independently. We will conscientiously carry out the Party's policy toward overseas Chinese affairs.

Extending democracy at the grassroots level is the groundwork for developing socialist democracy. We will improve grassroots self-governing organizations, their democratic management system and the system of keeping the public informed of matters being handled, and ensure that the people directly exercise their democratic rights according to law, manage grassroots public affairs and programs for public good and exercise democratic supervision over the cadres. We will improve self-governance among villagers and foster a mechanism of their self-governance full of vitality under the leadership of village Party organizations. We will improve self-governance among urban residents and build new-type and well-managed communities featuring civility and harmony. We will uphold and improve the system of workers' conferences and other democratic management systems in enterprises and institutions and protect the legitimate rights and interests of workers.

2. Improve the socialist legal system. We must see to it that there are laws to go by, the laws are observed and strictly enforced, and law-breakers are prosecuted. To adapt to the new situation characterized by the development of a socialist market economy, all-round social progress and China's accession to the WTO, we will strengthen legislation and improve its quality and will have formulated a socialist system of laws with Chinese characteristics by the year 2010. We must see to it that all people are equal before the law. We should tighten supervision over law enforcement, promote the exercise of administrative functions according to law, safeguard judicial justice and raise the level of law enforcement so that laws are strictly implemented. We must safeguard the uniformity and sanctity of the legal system and prevent or overcome local and departmental protectionism. We will extend and standardize legal services and provide effective legal aid. We should give more publicity to the legal system so that the people are better educated in law. In particular, we will enhance the public servants' awareness of law and their ability to perform their official duties according to law. Party members and cadres, especially leading cadres, should play an exemplary role in abiding by the Constitution and other laws.

3. Reform and improve the Party's style of leadership and governance. This is a matter of overall significance to improving socialist democracy. Leadership by the Party mainly refers to its political, ideological and organizational leadership. The Party exercises leadership over the state and society by formulating major principles and policies, making suggestions on legislation, recommending cadres for important positions, conducting ideological publicity, giving play to the role of Party organizations and members and persisting in exercising state power according to law. Party committees, playing the role as the core of leadership among all other organizations at corresponding levels, should concentrate on handling important matters and support those organizations in assuming their responsibilities independently and making concerted efforts in their work. We will further reform and improve the Party's working organs and mechanisms. Acting on the principle that the Party commands the overall situation and coordinates the efforts of all quarters, we will standardize relations between Party committees on the one hand and people's congresses, governments, CPPCC committees and mass organizations on the other. We will support people's congresses in performing their functions as organs of state power according to law, in ensuring that the Party's views become the will of the state and that candidates recommended by Party organizations become leading cadres of the organs of state power through legal procedures, and in exercising supervision over them. We will support the government in fulfilling its legal functions and performing its official duties according to law. We will

support CPPCC committees in performing their functions by centering on the two major subjects of unity and democracy. We will strengthen the Party's leadership over trade unions, the Communist Youth League organizations, women's federations and other mass organizations and support them in working according to law and their own constitutions and acting as a bridge between the Party and the people.

4. Reform and improve the decision-making mechanism. Correct decision-making is an important prerequisite for success in all work. We will improve the decision-making mechanism by which decision-makers will go deep among the people and get to know how they are faring, reflect their will, pool their wisdom and value their resources, putting decision-making on a more scientific and democratic basis. Decision-making organs at all levels should improve the rules and procedures for taking major policy decisions, establish a system of reporting social conditions and public opinion, a system of keeping the public informed and a system of public hearings on major issues closely related to the interests of the people, perfect the expert consulting system and implement a verification system and a responsibility system in making policy decisions with a view to preventing arbitrary decision-making.

5. Deepen administrative restructuring. We should further change the functions of the government, improve the methods of management, introduce e-government, uplift administrative efficiency and reduce costs so as to form an administrative system featuring standardized behaviors, coordinated operation, fairness and transparency, honesty and high efficiency. We should standardize the functions and powers of the Central Government and local authorities according to law and properly handle relations between the departments directly under the Central Government and the local governments. Following the principle of simplification, uniformity and efficiency and meeting the requirements of coordination in decision-making, execution and supervision, we will continue to promote the restructuring of government departments, standardize their functions in a scientific manner, rationalize their set-ups, and optimize their composition in order to delimit the structures and sizes statutorily and solve the problems of too many levels, overlapping functions, overstaffing, divorce between powers and responsibilities and duplicate law enforcement. We will reform the management system of institutions in accordance with the principle of separating the functions of government from those of institutions.

6. Promote the reform of the judicial system. A socialist judicial system must guarantee fairness and justice in the whole society. In accordance with the requirements of judicial justice and strict law enforcement, we should improve the setups of judicial organs, the delimitation of their functions and powers and their management systems so as to form a sound judicial system featuring clearly specified powers and responsibilities, mutual coordination and restraint and highly efficient operation. We should institutionally ensure that the judicial and procuratorial organs are in a position to exercise adjudicative and procuratorial powers independently and impartially according to law. We should improve judicial proceedings and protect the legitimate rights and interests of citizens and legal persons. We should solve the problem of difficult enforcement of judgments. We should reform the working mechanisms of judicial organs and the management system of their human, financial and material resources and gradually separate their judicial adjudication and procuratorial work from their administrative affairs. We will tighten supervision over the judicial work and punish corruption in this field. We will build up a contingent of judicial personnel who are politically steadfast and professionally competent, have a fine style of work and enforce laws impartially.

7. Deepen the reform of the cadre and personnel system. Efforts should be made to form a vigorous personnel mechanism under which we can gather large numbers of

talented people, put them to the best use and get them prepared for both promotion and demotion, calling them to the service of the Party and state. In reforming and perfecting the cadre and personnel system and improving the system of public servants, we should focus on establishing a sound mechanism of selection, appointment, management and supervision, with a view to making it scientific, democratic and institutionalized. In the matter of cadre selection and appointment, Party members and ordinary people should have more right to know, to participate, to choose and to supervise. With regard to leading cadres of the Party and government, it is necessary to implement the system of fixed tenures, the system of resignation and the system of accountability for neglect of supervisory duty or the use of the wrong person. It is necessary to improve the system of giving cadres both positions and ranks and establish an incentive and guarantee mechanism for them. We should explore and improve the system of classified management of cadres and personnel in Party and government organs, institutions and enterprises. We should reform and improve the system of dual control over cadres. We should break with the notions and practices of overstressing seniority in the matter of selection and appointment, encourage the rational flow of trained people and create a sound environment which makes it possible for outstanding people to come to the fore in all fields.

8. Tighten the restraint on and supervision over the use of power. We should establish a mechanism for the exercise of power featuring reasonable structure, scientific distribution, rigorous procedures and effective restraint so as to tighten supervision over power in terms of decision-making, execution and other links and ensure that the power entrusted to us by the people is truly exercised for their benefits. We should focus on tightening supervision over leading cadres and especially principal ones, stepping up supervision over the management and use of human, financial and material resources. We should tighten internal supervision of leading groups and improve the procedures for deciding on important matters and the appointment or dismissal of cadres in important positions. We should reform and improve the system of Party discipline inspection and introduce and improve the system of inspection tours. We should give play to the role of judicial, administrative supervision and auditing organs and other functional departments. We should implement the system under which leading cadres report in various ways on their work and their efforts to perform their duties honestly, and improve the systems of reporting on important matters, of making inquiries and of democratic appraisal. We should conscientiously implement the system of making government affairs known to the public. We should tighten organizational and democratic supervision and give play to the supervisory function of the media.

9. Maintain social stability. To accomplish the heavy tasks of reform and development, we must have a harmonious and stable social climate for a long time to come. Party committees and governments at all levels should enthusiastically help the people solve practical problems they may confront in their work and life. They must carry out in-depth investigations and study, strengthen ideological and political work in light of different cases, and employ economic, administrative and legal means to handle the contradictions among the people properly, those involving their immediate interests in particular, so as to maintain stability and unity. It is essential to improve procuratorial, judicial and public security work, cracking down on criminal activities according to law, guarding against and punishing crimes committed by evil cult gangs and eliminating social evils so as to ensure the safety of the lives and property of the people. We must combine punishment and prevention, with emphasis on the latter, take comprehensive measures to maintain law and order and improve social management so as to keep public order. We must strengthen state security,

keeping vigilance against infiltrative, subversive and separatist activities by hostile forces at home and abroad.

Socialist democracy enjoys strong vitality and superiority. The CPC and the Chinese people have full confidence in the road to political development they have chosen and will press ahead with political development under socialism with Chinese characteristics.

VI Cultural Development and Restructuring

To build a well-off society in an all-round way calls for major efforts to develop socialist culture and spiritual civilization. In the present-day world, culture is interactive with economic and political activities, and its status and functions are becoming more and more outstanding in the competition in overall national strength. The power of culture is deeply rooted in the vitality, creativity and cohesion of a nation. All Party members must fully understand the strategic significance of cultural development and make socialist culture develop and flourish.

1. Keep the orientation of advanced culture firmly in hand. In contemporary China, to develop advanced culture means to develop national, scientific and popular socialist culture geared to the needs of modernization, of the world and of the future so as to enrich people's mental world and reinforce their mental strength. We must uphold Marxism-Leninism, Mao Zedong Thought and Deng Xiaoping Theory as our guidelines in the realm of ideology and have the important thought of Three Represents in command of the development of socialist culture. We must keep to the orientation of serving the people and socialism and the principle of letting a hundred flowers blossom and a hundred schools of thought contend and highlight the themes of the times while encouraging diversity. We should continue to arm people with scientific theory, provide them with correct media guidance, imbue them with lofty ideals, and inspire them with excellent works of literature and art. We must exert ourselves to develop advanced culture and support healthy and useful culture, changing what is backward and resisting what is decadent. Literary and art workers should go deep among the masses and into the thick of life so as to contribute to the people more works worthy of the times. The press, publishing, radio, film and television must give correct guidance to the public, and Internet web sites should serve as important fronts for spreading advanced culture. Basing ourselves on the practice of reform, opening up and modernization and keeping abreast of the latest developments in world culture, we must carry forward the fine tradition of our national culture, draw on the strong points of other nations and make innovations in content and form so as to enhance the attraction and appeal of socialist culture with Chinese characteristics.

2. Continue to carry forward and cultivate the national spirit. National spirit is the moral kingpin on which a nation relies for survival and development. Without an inspiring spirit and lofty character, it is impossible for a nation to stand proudly in the family of nations. For more than 5,000 years, the Chinese nation has evolved a great national spirit centering on patriotism and featuring unity and solidarity, love of peace, industry, courage and ceaseless self-improvement. This national spirit has been enriched in light of the requirements of the times and social development by the people under the leadership of our Party over along period of practice. Confronted with interaction of different thoughts and cultures in the world, we must take it as a crucial task in our cultural development to carry forward and cultivate the national spirit and incorporate it into our national education and the entire process of building spiritual civilization so that the entire people are always filled with an enterprising spirit.

3. Promote ideological and ethical progress. Ruling the country by law and ruling the country by virtue complement each other. It is necessary to establish a socialist ideological and ethical system compatible with the socialist market economy and the socialist legal standard and consistent with the traditional virtues of the Chinese nation. We must carry out intensive publicity and education in the Party's basic theory, line and program and in the important thought of Three Represents, and guide people in fostering a common ideal for socialism with Chinese characteristics, correct world outlook, views on life and values. We must carry out the Program for Improving Civic Morality, promote patriotism and, with serving the people at the core, collectivism as the principle and honesty as a priority, intensify education in social and professional ethics and family virtues and especially intensify the ideological and ethical improvement among youth so as to guide people in their pursuit of higher ideological and ethical standards on the basis of observing the basic code of conduct. We must strengthen and improve ideological and political work and encourage popular participation in building spiritual civilization.

4. Develop education and science. Education is the foundation for scientific and technological advancement and personnel training. Playing a vanguard role and having an overall bearing on the modernization drive, education must be placed on our development agenda as a strategic priority. We must carry out the Party's education policy that education should serve socialist modernization and the people and integrate itself with productive labor and social practice so as to train socialist builders and successors featuring an all-round development in morality, intelligence, physique and art. We should encourage innovation in education, deepen its reform, optimize its structure, allocate its resources rationally, raise its quality and management levels and promote quality-oriented education to cultivate hundreds of millions of high-quality workers, tens of millions of specialized personnel and a great number of top-notch innovative personnel. We should build up the ranks of teachers and raise their professional ethics and competence. We should continue to make nine-year compulsory education universal across the country, intensify vocational education and training, develop continued education and set up a system of life-long education. We should increase input in education, give more support to rural education, and encourage nongovernmental sectors to run schools. We should improve the state policy and system for aiding students in straitened circumstances. We should formulate a long-term program for scientific and technological development. We should step up the development of infrastructure for research. We should disseminate science and promote the scientific spirit. We must lay equal stress on social sciences and natural sciences and give full play to the important role of philosophy and other social sciences in economic and social development. It is essential to create an atmosphere in society at large favorable for respecting and promoting science, encouraging innovation and opposing superstition and pseudo-science.

5. Develop cultural undertakings and industry. In developing cultural undertakings and industry, it is imperative to meet the requirements of developing advanced culture and always place social effects in the first place. The state supports and protects public cultural undertakings and encourages them to enhance their vigor for self-development. We must continue to improve the policies and measures for the development of public cultural undertakings. We must give our support to the major news media and research institutions of social sciences of the Party and state, to the major cultural projects and art schools and troupes that are up to national standards and embody national characteristics, to the protection of major cultural heritage and outstanding folk arts, and to the cultural development in the old revolutionary base areas, areas inhabited by ethnic minorities, remote areas, impoverished areas and the central

and western regions of the country. We should strengthen cultural infrastructure and boost various types of popular culture. We should promote the reform and development of health and sports undertakings and carry on the nationwide fitness campaign to improve the physique of the entire people. We should make the 2008 Olympics a success. Developing the cultural industry is an important avenue to enriching socialist culture in the market economy and to meeting the spiritual and cultural needs of the people. It is essential to improve policies toward the cultural industry, support its development and enhance its overall strength and competitiveness.

6. Continue to deepen cultural restructuring. It is necessary to push forward cultural restructuring in light of the characteristics of the development of socialist spiritual civilization and laws governing it and in response to the needs of the growing socialist market economy. We must lose no time in working out overall planning for cultural restructuring. We must integrate the deepening of reform with structural adjustment and promotion of development and straighten out the relationship between the government and cultural enterprises and institutions. We must build up a legal system concerning culture and intensify macro-control. We should deepen the internal reform of cultural enterprises and institutions and gradually establish a management system and operational mechanism favorable to arousing the initiative of cultural workers, encouraging innovation and bringing forth more top-notch works and more outstanding personnel. In compliance with the principle of both enriching culture and intensifying management, we should improve the system of markets for cultural products and their management mechanism to create a social climate favorable for a flourishing socialist culture.

The Chinese civilization, extensive and profound, and with a long history behind it, has contributed tremendously to the progress of human civilization. We will surely have a new upsurge in building socialist culture and create an even more splendid advanced culture in the great struggle of the Chinese people in the contemporary era.

VII National Defense and Army Building

Strengthening our national defense is a strategic task in our modernization drive and an important guarantee for safeguarding our national security and unity and building a well-off society in an all-round way. We must uphold the principle of coordinated development of national defense and the economy and push forward the modernization of national defense and the army on the basis of economic growth.

The army must take Mao Zedong's military thinking and Deng Xiaoping's thinking on army building in the new period as the guide to action and fully implement the important thought of Three Represents. It must persist in taking the road of fewer but better troops with Chinese characteristics and become more revolutionary, modernized and regularized in compliance with the general requirements of being qualified politically and competent militarily and having a fine style of work, strict discipline and adequate logistic support and in close connection with the two historic objectives of being capable of winning battles and never degenerating.

The army should give first priority to ideological and political development in all its endeavors and retain the nature, quality and style of work worthy of a people's army. The Party's absolute leadership over the army is the eternal soul of the army. There must be no wavering in upholding the fundamental principle and system that the Party leads the people's army.

The army must implement the military strategic principle of active defense and raise its defense capabilities and combat effectiveness under high-tech conditions. In response to the trend of military changes in the world, it must carry out the strategy of building a strong army through science and technology and improve its qualities. It should attach strategic importance to education and training, carry on intensive science- and technology-related military training and strengthen the building of military academies and schools so as to bring up a large number of high-quality military personnel of a new type. It is necessary to innovate and develop military theories. Efforts should be made to accomplish the historical tasks of mechanization and IT application, thereby bringing about leapfrog development in the modernization of our army.

It is necessary to explore the characteristics and laws for running the army under the new historical conditions and press ahead with reforms in the building of national defense and the army. The formation and structure of the army must be optimized and the related policies and systems should be adjusted and improved. The army must be strict with itself and improve the system of military rules and regulations so as to raise the level of handling its affairs according to law. It is essential to persist in building the army through diligence and thrift and establishing and improving an integrated logistic support system for the three armed services, for both military and civilian purposes and for both peacetime and wartime. It is necessary to deepen the restructuring of defense-related science, technology and industry, combine military efforts with civilian support, establish and improve the mechanism of competition, appraisal, supervision and incentives and enhance the capabilities of independent innovation so as to speed up the development of defense-related science and technology as well as arms and equipment. It is necessary to improve the mobilization system for national defense, strengthen the militia and reserves and develop strategies and tactics of the people's war under high-tech conditions. The armed police should strive for all-round improvement and be loyal guards of the Party and the people forever.

Party organizations and governments at all levels and the people should be concerned with and support the building of national defense and the army. The army should support and take an active part in national construction. We should strengthen education in national defense to enhance the entire people's awareness of its importance. The government and the people should support the army and give preferential treatment to the families of servicemen and martyrs, and the army should support the government and cherish the people so as to consolidate the solidarity between the army and the government and between the army and the people.

VIII   "One Country, Two Systems" and Complete National Reunification

To achieve complete reunification of the motherland is a common aspiration of all sons and daughters of the Chinese nation both at home and abroad. We have successfully resolved the questions of Hong Kong and Macao and are striving for an early settlement of the question of Taiwan and for the accomplishment of the great cause of national reunification.

The return of Hong Kong and Macao to the motherland has enriched the concept of "one country, two systems" in both theory and practice. Facts prove that "one country, two systems" is a correct policy and has strong vitality. We will resolutely implement this policy and act in strict accordance with the basic laws of Hong Kong and Macao special administrative regions. We will render full support to the chief executives and governments of the two regions in their work and unite with people from all walks of life there in a joint effort to maintain and promote the prosperity, stability and development of Hong Kong and Macao.

We will adhere to the basic principles of "peaceful reunification" and "one country, two systems" and the eight-point proposal on developing cross-straits relations and advancing the process of peaceful national reunification at the present stage. We will work with our compatriots in Taiwan to step up personnel exchanges and promote economic, cultural and other interflows between the two sides and firmly oppose the Taiwan separatist forces. The basic configuration and development trend of the cross-straits relations remain unchanged. The desire of our Taiwan compatriots for peace, stability and development is growing stronger day by day. The splitting activities by the Taiwan separatist forces are unpopular.

Adherence to the one-China principle is the basis for the development of cross-straits relations and the realization of peaceful reunification. There is but one China in the world, and both the mainland and Taiwan belong to one China. China's sovereignty and territorial integrity brook no division. We firmly oppose all words and deeds aimed at creating "Taiwan independence," "two Chinas" or "one China, one Taiwan." The future of Taiwan lies in the reunification of the motherland. To conduct dialogue and hold negotiations on peaceful reunification has been our consistent position. Here we repeat our appeal: On the basis of the one-China principle, let us shelve for now certain political disputes and resume the cross-straits dialogue and negotiations as soon as possible. On the premise of the one-China principle, all issues can be discussed. We may discuss how to end the cross-straits hostility formally. We may also discuss the international space in which the Taiwan region may conduct economic, cultural and social activities compatible with its status, or discuss the political status of the Taiwan authorities or other issues. We are willing to exchange views with all political parties and personages of all circles in Taiwan on the development of cross-straits relations and the promotion of peaceful reunification.

We place our hopes on the people in Taiwan for the settlement of the Taiwan question and the realization of the complete reunification of China. Our compatriots in Taiwan have a glorious patriotic tradition and are an important force in developing cross-straits relations. We fully respect their life style and their wish to be the masters of our country. The two sides should expand mutual contacts and exchanges and work together to carry forward the fine tradition of the Chinese culture. As the direct links of mail, air and shipping services, and trade across the Taiwan Straits serve the common interests of the compatriots on both sides, there is every reason to take practical and positive steps to promote such direct links and open up new prospects for cross-straits economic cooperation.

"One country, two systems" is the best way for the reunification between the two sides. After its reunification with the mainland, Taiwan may keep its existing social system unchanged and enjoy a high degree of autonomy. Our Taiwan compatriots may keep their way of life unchanged, and their vital interests will be fully guaranteed. They will enjoy a lasting peace. Taiwan may then truly rely on the mainland as its hinterland for economic growth and thus get broad space for development. Our Taiwan compatriots may join the people on the mainland in exercising the right to administer the country and sharing the dignity and honor of the great motherland in the international community.

The 23 million Taiwan compatriots are our brothers and sisters of the same blood. No one is more eager than we are to resolve the Taiwan question through peaceful means. We will continue to implement the basic principles of "peaceful reunification" and "one country, two systems" and act on the eight-point proposal. We will work in utmost sincerity and do all we can to strive for a peaceful reunification. Our position of never undertaking to renounce the use of force is not directed at our Taiwan compatriots. It is aimed at the foreign forces' attempts to interfere in China's reunification and the Taiwan separatist forces' schemes for "Taiwan independence." To safeguard national unity bears on the fundamental interests of the Chinese nation. We Chinese people will safeguard our state sovereignty and territorial integrity with firm resolve. We will never allow anyone to separate Taiwan from China in any way.

China will be reunified, and the Chinese nation will be rejuvenated. The Taiwan question must not be allowed to drag on indefinitely. We are convinced that with the concerted efforts of all sons and daughters of the Chinese nation, the complete reunification of the motherland will be achieved at an early date.

IX The International Situation and Our External Work

Peace and development remain the themes of our era. To preserve peace and promote development bears on the well-being of all nations and represents the common aspirations of all peoples. It is an irresistible trend of history. The growing trends toward world multipolarization and economic globalization have brought with them opportunities and favorable conditions for world peace and development. A new world war is unlikely in the foreseeable future. It is realistic to bring about a fairly long period of peace in the world and a favorable climate in areas around China.

However, the old international political and economic order, which is unfair and irrational, has yet to be changed fundamentally. Uncertainties affecting peace and development are on the rise. The elements of traditional and non-traditional threats to security are intertwined, and the scourge of terrorism is more acutely felt. Hegemonism and power politics have new manifestations. Local conflicts triggered by ethnic or religious contradictions and border or territorial disputes have cropped up from time to time. The North-South gap is widening. The world is far from being tranquil and mankind is faced with many grave challenges.

No matter how the international situation changes, we will, as always, pursue the independent foreign policy of peace. The purpose of China's foreign policy is to maintain world peace and promote common development. We are ready to work with all nations to advance the lofty cause of world peace and development.

We stand for going along with the historical tide and safeguarding the common interests of mankind. We are ready to work with the international community to boost world multipolarization, promote a harmonious coexistence of diverse forces and maintain stability in the international community. We will promote the development of economic globalization in a direction conducive to common prosperity, draw on its advantages and avoid its disadvantages so that all countries, particularly developing countries, can benefit from the process.

We stand for establishing a new international political and economic order that is fair and rational. Politically all countries should respect and consult one another and should not seek to impose their will on others. Economically they should complement one another and pursue common development and should not create a polarization of wealth. Culturally they should learn from one another and work for common prosperity and should not exclude cultures of other nations. In the area of security, countries should trust one another and work together to maintain security, foster a new security concept featuring mutual trust, mutual benefit, equality and coordination, and settle their disputes through dialogue and cooperation and should not resort to the use or threat of force. We oppose all forms of hegemonism and power politics. China will never seek hegemony and never go in for expansion.

We stand for maintaining the diversity of the world and are in favor of promoting democracy in international relations and diversifying development models. Ours is a colorful world. Countries having different civilizations and social systems and taking different roads to development should respect one another and draw upon one another's strong points through competition and comparison and should develop side by side by seeking common ground while shelving differences. The affairs of each country should be left to the people of that country to decide. World affairs should be determined by all countries concerned through consultations on the basis of equality.

We stand for fighting against terrorism of all forms. It is imperative to strengthen international cooperation in this regard, address both the symptoms and root causes of terrorism, prevent and combat terrorist activities and work hard to eliminate terrorism at root.

We will continue to improve and develop relations with the developed countries. Proceeding from the fundamental interests of the people of all countries concerned, we will broaden the converging points of common interests and properly settle differences on the basis of the Five Principles of Peaceful Coexistence, notwithstanding the differences in social system and ideology.

We will continue to cement our friendly ties with our neighbors and persist in building a good-neighborly relationship and partnership with them. We will step up regional cooperation and bring our exchanges and cooperation with our surrounding countries to a new height.

We will continue to enhance our solidarity and cooperation with other third world countries, increase mutual understanding and trust and strengthen mutual help and support. We will enlarge areas of cooperation and make it more fruitful.

We will continue to take an active part in multilateral diplomatic activities and play our role in the United Nations and other international or regional organizations. We will support other developing countries in their efforts to safeguard their legitimate rights and interests.

We will continue to develop exchanges and cooperation with political parties and organizations of all countries and regions on the principles of independence, complete equality, mutual respect and noninterference in each other's internal affairs.

We will continue to carry out extensive people-to-people diplomacy, expand cultural exchanges with the outside world, enhance the friendship between peoples and propel the development of state-to-state relations.

The world is marching toward brightness and progress. The road is tortuous, but the future is bright. The forces for peace, justice and progress are invincible after all.

X Strengthen and Improve Party Building

In a large multi-ethnic developing country like ours, we must spare no efforts to strengthen and improve the Party's leadership and fully advance the great new undertaking of Party building if we are to rally the entire people to work heart and soul in building a well-off society in an all-round way and speed up the socialist modernization drive.

To strengthen and improve Party building, we must hold high the great banner of Deng Xiaoping Theory, implement the important thought of Three Represents in a comprehensive way and ensure that the Party's line, principles and policies fully reflect the fundamental interests of the people and the requirements of development of our times. We must adhere to the principle that the Party exercises self-discipline and is strict with its members, and further address the two major historical subjects of how to enhance the Party's art of leadership and governance and how to raise the Party's capacity to resist corruption, prevent degeneration and withstand risks. We must acquire an accurate understanding of social progress in contemporary China, and reform and improve the Party's way of leadership and governance and its leadership and working systems so that the Party will be full of vigor and vitality in its work. We must proceed with Party building ideologically, organizationally and in work style in parallel with institutional improvement, not only ensuring a good performance of our day-to-day work, but also tackling prominent issues in good time. Unyielding efforts will be made to ensure that our Party is forever the vanguard both of the Chinese working class and of the Chinese people and the Chinese nation as well as the core of leadership in building socialism with Chinese characteristics and that it always represents the development trend of China's advanced productive forces, the orientation of China's advanced culture and the fundamental interests of the overwhelming majority of the Chinese people.

1. Study and implement the important thought of Three Represents intensively and raise all Party members' level of the Marxist theory. The rise in the Party's ideological and theoretical level is an ideological guarantee for continued progress of the cause of our Party and state. We must highlight the Party's ideological and theoretical building. We must continue to arm all Party members with Marxism-Leninism, Mao Zedong Thought and Deng Xiaoping Theory and usher in a new upsurge in the study and implementation of the important thought of Three Represents. Party members and cadres, particularly senior and middle-rank cadres, should take the lead in studying and acting on the important thought of Three Represents. They should play an exemplary role in studying diligently, using their brains, emancipating their minds, keeping pace with the times and boldly engaging in practice and innovation. We will carry out an intensive education among all Party members in the history of development of Marxism and promote the truth-seeking and pioneering spirit. We will deepen our understanding of the laws on governance by the Communist Party, on building socialism and on development of human society and constantly enrich and develop Marxism.

2. Build up the Party's governing capacity and improve its art of leadership and governance. Faced with profound changes in the conditions of governance and social environment, Party committees and leading cadres at all levels must, in response to the requirements of the new situation and new tasks, acquire new knowledge, accumulate new experience and develop new abilities in practice, thus living up to the mission assigned to them and the full trust placed on them. They must view the world with broad vision, acquire a correct understanding of the requirements of the times and be good at thinking on a theoretical plane and in a strategic perspective so as to improve their ability of sizing up the situation in a scientific way. They must act in compliance with objective and scientific laws, address promptly the new situation and problems in reform and development, know how to seize opportunities to accelerate development and enhance their abilities of keeping the market economy well in hand. They must correctly understand and handle various social contradictions, know how to balance the relations among different interests, overcome difficulties and go on improving their ability of coping with complicated situations. They must enhance their awareness of law and know how to integrate the adherence to Party leadership and the people being the masters of the country with ruling the country by law and improve their abilities of exercising state power according to law. They must base themselves on the overall interests of the work of the entire Party and the whole country, firmly implement the Party's line, principles and policies, work creatively in light of realities and keep enhancing their ability of commanding the whole situation.

3. Adhere to and improve democratic centralism and enhance the Party's vitality, solidarity and unity. Democratic centralism is a system that integrates centralism on the basis of democracy with democracy under centralized guidance. Inner-Party democ-

racy is the life of the Party and plays an important exemplary and leading role in people's democracy. We should establish and improve an inner-Party democratic system that fully reflects the will of Party members and organizations, starting with the reform of the relevant systems and mechanisms on the basis of guaranteeing the democratic rights of Party members and giving priority to improving the systems of Party congresses and of Party committees. The system of Party congresses with regular annual conferences should be tried out in more cities and counties. We should explore ways to give play to the role of delegates when Party congresses are not in session. In accordance with the principle of collective leadership, democratic centralism, individual consultations and decision by meetings, we should improve the rules of procedure and decision-making mechanism within Party committees in order to give fuller play to the role of plenary sessions of Party committees. We need to reform and improve the inner-Party electoral system. We should establish and improve inner-Party information sharing and reporting systems and the system of soliciting opinions concerning major policy decisions. The centralization and unity of the Party and state are where the fundamental interests of the people of all ethnic groups lie. The whole Party and the entire nation must maintain a high degree of unity with regard to the guiding ideology, line, principles and policies and major questions of principle. All Party members must consciously abide by the principle that individual Party members are subordinate to the organization, that the minority is subordinate to the majority, that lower Party organizations are subordinate to the higher ones and that all the constituent organizations and members of the Party are subordinate to its National Congress and Central Committee. They must safeguard the authority of the Central Committee and ensure that its decisions are carried out without fail. Party organizations at all levels and all Party members, leading cadres in particular, must strictly abide by Party discipline. Under no circumstances should they be allowed to go their own ways in disregard of orders and prohibitions.

4. Build a contingent of high-caliber leading cadres and form an energetic and promising leadership. It is a matter of vital importance for maintaining prolonged stability of the Party and state to build a contingent of high-caliber leading cadres capable of assuming heavy responsibilities and withstanding the test of trials and tribulations, and especially to train a large number of outstanding leading cadres for the mission of running the Party, state and army in accordance with the principle of bringing up more revolutionary, younger, better educated and more professionally competent cadres. We should conscientiously implement the regulations on the selection and appointment of leading cadres and make a point of testing and identifying cadres in the practice of reform and development so as to promote to leading positions in good time those who are accredited with ability, integrity and outstanding performance and enjoy popular support. We should make greater efforts to train and select outstanding young cadres, helping them cultivate their Party spirit, pursue theoretical study and gain practical experience so that they will improve in all respects. We should do a better job of training and selecting women cadres, cadres from among ethnic minorities and non-Party cadres. We should continue to do well the work related to retired cadres. We should turn the leading bodies of the Party at all levels into staunch collectives that firmly implement the important thought of Three Represents mainly by improving their qualities, optimizing their composition, refining their work style and enhancing solidarity. We should train more and more successors to the cause of socialism with Chinese characteristics so that the cause of the Party and people will be carried forward.

5. Build the Party well at the primary level, reinforce its class foundation and expand its mass base. The primary organizations of the Party constitute its foundation

for doing all its work and building up its combat effectiveness. They should organize, motivate and practice the implementation of the important thought of Three Represents. We should, by focusing on the central task and serving the overall interests, broaden the fields of our endeavor, intensify our functions and expand the coverage of the Party's work so as to increase the rallying power and combat effectiveness of primary organizations. We should strengthen the building of village-level supporting organizations which rally around village Party organizations, and explore effective ways that will enable cadres to receive education regularly and farmers to get long-term tangible benefits. In order that state-owned and collective enterprises operate well, we must persistently rely on the working class wholeheartedly, and Party organizations in those enterprises should take an active part in the decision-making on major issues and give full play to their role as the political core. We should strengthen Party building in enterprises of the non-public sectors. Party organizations in enterprises must carry out the Party's principles and policies, and provide guidance to and supervise the enterprises in observing the laws and regulations of the state. They should exercise leadership over trade unions, the Communist Youth League and other mass organizations, rally the workers around them, safeguard the legitimate rights and interests of all quarters and stimulate the healthy development of the enterprises. We should attach great importance to Party building in communities, striving to bring about a new pattern in Party building in urban communities, with the focus on serving the people. We should intensify our efforts to establish Party organizations in mass organizations and intermediaries. We should fully carry out Party building in Party and government organs as well as schools, research institutions, cultural groups and other institutions.

Party members must play their vanguard and exemplary role, foster the lofty ideal of communism, fortify their conviction in socialism with Chinese characteristics and work hard to realize the Party's basic program for the current stage. We need to carry out Party-wide education to maintain the progressiveness of Party members mainly by putting the important thought of Three Represents into practice. We should recruit Party members mainly from among workers, farmers, intellectuals, servicemen and cadres, thus expanding the basic components and backbone of the Party. We should make a point of recruiting Party members from among those in the forefront of work and production and from among the prominent intellectuals and young people. We should admit into the Party advanced elements of other social strata who accept the Party's program and Constitution, work for the realization of the Party's line and program consciously and meet the qualifications of Party membership following a long period of test, in order to increase the influence and rallying force of the Party in society at large. We must, in light of the new situation, seek new mechanisms and methods for the management of Party membership.

6. Strengthen and improve the Party's style of work and intensify the struggle against corruption. The key to improving the Party's style of work lies in keeping the flesh-and-blood ties between the Party and the people. The biggest political advantage of our Party lies in its close ties with the masses while the biggest potential danger for it as a ruling party comes from its divorce from them. We must at all times and under all circumstances adhere to the Party's mass line, and to the purpose of serving the people heart and soul and regard the people's interests as the starting point and goal of all our work. We must carry forward the fine tradition and style of our Party, bearing in mind the fundamental principle that the Party is built for the public and that it exercises state power for the people. We must make effective efforts to resolve the outstanding issues in respect of the way of thinking, study and work of our Party, its style of leadership and its cadres' way of life and especially to prevent and overcome formalism and bureau-

cracy by acting on the principle of the *"eight do's" and "eight don'ts"** put forward by the Party Central Committee, by resorting to both educational and institutional means and by correctly conducting criticism and self-criticism. Closely following the new changes in social activities and carefully studying the new features of our mass work, we must strengthen and improve such work throughout the process of building the Party and political power. All Party members, primarily leading cadres at all levels, must do mass work well in light of the new situation and, by persuading, setting examples and providing services, unite and lead the masses in making progress.

To combat and prevent corruption resolutely is a major political task of the whole Party. If we do not crack down on corruption, the flesh-and-blood ties between the Party and the people will suffer a lot and the Party will be in danger of losing its ruling position, or possibly heading for self-destruction. Against the background of its long-term governance and China's opening up and development of the socialist market economy, the Party must be on full alert against corrosion by all decadent ideas and maintain the purity of its membership. Party committees at all levels must fully recognize the urgency as well as the protracted nature of the fight against corruption. They should enhance confidence, do a solid job, take a clear-cut stand and never waver in carrying on the fight in depth. We should work still harder to make sure that our leading cadres are clean, honest and self-disciplined, and see to it that major corruption cases are investigated and dealt with. Malpractices in departments and trades and services must be corrected. We must adhere to the principle of addressing both symptoms and root causes of corruption and taking comprehensive measures to rectify both while devoting greater efforts gradually to tackling the latter. We must strengthen education, develop democracy, improve the legal system, tighten supervision, make institutional innovation and incorporate counter-corruption in all our major policy measures so as to prevent and tackle corruption at its source. We must uphold and improve the leadership system and working mechanism against corruption and earnestly implement the responsibility system for improving the Party's work style and building clean government, in a concerted effort to prevent and punish corruption. Leading cadres, particularly senior ones, should play an exemplary role in exercising the power in their hands correctly. They must always be honest and upright and take the initiative to crack down on all forms of corruption. All corruptionists must be thoroughly investigated and punished without leniency.

So long as all Party comrades always maintain the vigor and vitality, dashing spirit and integrity as Communists and have the people at heart, the foundation of our Party's governance will remain rock solid.

Comrades,

To build a well-off society in an all-round way and create a new situation in building socialism with Chinese characteristics, it is essential, under the firm leadership of the CPC, to develop a socialist market economy, socialist democracy and an advanced socialist culture, keep the coordinated development of the socialist material, political

---

* The "eight do's" and "eight don'ts" are:
(1) Emancipate the mind and seek truth from facts; do not stick to old ways and make no progress.
(2) Combine theory with practice; do not copy mechanically or take to book worship.
(3) Keep close ties with the people; do not go in for formalism and bureaucracy.
(4) Adhere to the principle of democratic centralism; do not act arbitrarily or stay feeble and lax.
(5) Abide by Party discipline; do not pursue liberalism.
(6) Be honest and upright; do not abuse power for personal gains.
(7) Work hard; do not indulge in hedonism.
(8) Appoint people on their merits; do not resort to malpractice in personnel placement.

and spiritual civilizations, and bring about the great rejuvenation of the Chinese nation.

The CPC is deeply rooted in the Chinese nation. Since the very day of its founding, it has been the vanguard of the Chinese working class and also of the Chinese people and the Chinese nation, shouldering the grand mission of realizing the great rejuvenation of the Chinese nation. During the new-democratic revolution, our Party united and led the Chinese people of all ethnic groups in fulfilling the historic task of winning national independence and people's liberation, thus laying the groundwork for our great national rejuvenation. After the founding of New China, our Party creatively completed the transition from New Democracy to socialism, the greatest and most profound social transformation ever in China's history, and embarked on a socialist road and the historical journey to the great rejuvenation of the Chinese nation. Since the Third Plenary Session of its Eleventh Central Committee, our Party has found the correct road to socialism with Chinese characteristics, injecting new and greater vitality into our drive for national rejuvenation. Splendid prospects present themselves before the great cause of rejuvenation of the Chinese nation.

To build a well-off society in an all-round way, step up the socialist modernization drive and make socialist China a stronger and more prosperous country, thus contributing still more to the cause of human progress—this is a historical mission our Party must take on with courage. The fulfillment of this mission inevitably depends on the solidarity of the Party and that of the Chinese people of all ethnic groups. Solidarity means strength; solidarity means victory. After going through all the hardships and setbacks, our Party and people have gained rich experience and become increasingly mature. In the face of a world that is far from being tranquil and the formidable tasks before us, all Party members must be mindful of the potential danger and stay prepared against adversities in times of peace. We must be keenly aware of the rigorous challenges brought about by the ever-sharpening international competition as well as risks and difficulties that may arise on our road ahead. We must bear in mind the overall interests of our Party all the more deeply, cherish the solidarity all the more dearly and safeguard stability all the more firmly.

All Party comrades and the people of all ethnic groups of the country, let us rally closely around the Party Central Committee and work with one heart and one mind in a joint and unyielding effort to advance the cause of building socialism with Chinese characteristics and create a happier life and a better future for us all!

Xinhua News Agency November 17, 2002

CONSTITUTION OF THE COMMUNIST PARTY OF CHINA

Amended and adopted at the Sixteenth National Congress of the Communist Party of China on 14 November 2002

General Program

The Communist Party of China is the vanguard both of the Chinese working class and of the Chinese people and the Chinese nation. It is the core of leadership for the cause of socialism with Chinese characteristics and represents the development trend of China's advanced productive forces, the orientation of China's advanced culture and the fundamental interests of the overwhelming majority of the Chinese people. The realization of communism is the highest ideal and ultimate goal of the Party.

The Communist Party of China takes Marxism-Leninism, Mao Zedong Thought, Deng Xiaoping Theory and the important thought of Three Represents as its guide to action.

Marxism-Leninism brings to light the laws governing the development of the history of human society. Its basic tenets are correct and have tremendous vitality. The highest ideal of communism pursued by the Chinese Communists can be realized only when the socialist society is fully developed and very advanced. The development and improvement of the socialist system is a long historical process. So long as the Chinese Communists uphold the basic tenets of Marxism-Leninism and follow the road suited to China's specific conditions and chosen by the Chinese people of their own accord, the socialist cause in China will be crowned with final victory.

The Chinese Communists, with Comrade Mao Zedong as their chief representative, created Mao Zedong Thought by integrating the basic tenets of Marxism-Leninism with the concrete practice of the Chinese revolution. Mao Zedong Thought is Marxism-Leninism applied and developed in China; it consists of a body of theoretical principles concerning the revolution and construction in China and a summary of experience therein, both of which have been proved correct by practice; it represents the crystallized, collective wisdom of the Communist Party of China. Under the guidance of Mao Zedong Thought, the Communist Party of China led the people of all ethnic groups in their prolonged revolutionary struggle against imperialism, feudalism and bureaucrat-capitalism, winning victory for the new-democratic revolution and founding the People's Republic of China, a people's democratic dictatorship. After the founding of the People's Republic, it led them in carrying out socialist transformation, completing the transition from New Democracy to socialism, establishing the basic system of socialism and developing socialism economically, politically and culturally.

After the Third Plenary Session of the Eleventh Party Central Committee, the Chinese Communists, with Comrade Deng Xiaoping as the chief representative, summed up their experience, both positive and negative, emancipated their minds, sought truth from facts, shifted the focus of the work of the whole Party onto economic development and carried out reform and opening to the outside world, ushering in a new era of development in the cause of socialism, gradually formulating the line, principles and policies concerning the building of socialism with Chinese characteristics and expounding the basic questions concerning the building, consolidating and developing of socialism in China, and thus founding Deng Xiaoping Theory. Deng Xiaoping Theory is the outcome of the integration of the basic tenets of Marxism-Leninism with the practice of contemporary China and the features of the times, a continuation and development of Mao Zedong Thought under new historical conditions; it represents a new period of development of Marxism in China, it is Marxism of contemporary China and it is the crystallized, collective wisdom of the Communist Party of China. It is guiding the socialist modernization of our country from victory to victory.

Since the Fourth Plenary Session of the Thirteenth Party Central Committee and in the practice of building socialism with Chinese characteristics, the Chinese Communists, with Comrade *Jiang Zemin* as their chief representative, have acquired a deeper understanding of what socialism is, how to build it and what kind of a party to build and how to build it, accumulated new valuable experience in running the Party and state and formed the important thought of Three Represents. The important thought of Three Represents is a continuation and development of Marxism-Leninism, Mao Zedong Thought and Deng Xiaoping Theory; it reflects new requirements for the work of the Party and state arising from the changes in China and other parts of the world today; it serves as a powerful theoretical weapon for strengthening and improving Party building and for promoting self-improvement and development of socialism in China; and it is the crystallized, collective wisdom of the Communist Party of China. It is a guiding ideology that the Party must uphold for a long time to come. Persistent implementation of the "Three Represents" is the foundation for building our Party, the cornerstone for its governance and the source of its strength.

China is at the primary stage of socialism and will remain so for a long period of time. This is a historical stage which cannot be skipped in socialist modernization in China that is backward economically and culturally. It will last for over a hundred years. In socialist construction we must proceed from our specific conditions and take the path to socialism with Chinese characteristics. At the present stage, the principal contradiction in Chinese society is one between the ever-growing material and cultural needs of the people and the low level of production. Owing to both domestic circumstances and foreign influences, class struggle will continue to exist within a certain scope for a long time and may possibly grow acute under certain conditions, but it is no longer the principal contradiction. In building socialism, our basic task is to further release and develop the productive forces and achieve socialist modernization step by step by carrying out reform in those aspects and links of the production relations and the superstructure that do not conform to the development of the productive forces. We must uphold and improve the basic economic system, with public ownership playing a dominant role and diverse forms of ownership developing side by side as well as the system of distribution under which distribution according to work is dominant and a variety of modes of distribution coexist, encourage some areas and some people to become rich first, gradually eliminate poverty and achieve common prosperity, and continuously meet the people's ever-growing material and cultural needs on the basis of the growth of production and social wealth. Development is our Party's top priority in governing and rejuvenating the country. The general starting point and criterion for judging all our work should be how it benefits the development of the productive forces in our socialist society, adds to the overall strength of our socialist country and improves the people's living standards. The beginning of the new century marks China's entry into the new stage of development of building a well-off society in an all-round way and accelerating socialist modernization. The strategic objectives of economic and social development at the new stage in the new century are to consolidate and develop the well-off standard of living initially attained, bring China into a well-off society of a higher level to the benefit of well over one billion people by the time of the Party's centenary and bring the per capita GDP up to the level of moderately developed countries and realize modernization in the main by the time of the centenary of the People's Republic of China.

The basic line of the Communist Party of China at the primary stage of socialism is to lead the people of all our ethnic groups in a concerted, self-reliant and pioneering effort to turn China into a prosperous, strong, democratic and culturally advanced modern socialist country by making economic development our central task while adhering to the Four Cardinal Principles and persevering in the reform and opening up.

In leading the cause of socialism, the Communist Party of China must persist in taking economic development as the central task, making all other work subordinated to and serve this central task. We must lose no time in speeding up economic development, implement the strategy of rejuvenating the country through science and education and that of sustainable development, give full play to the role of science and technology as the primary productive force. We must take advantage of the advancement of science and technology to improve the quality of workers and work hard to push forward the economy with good results, high quality and high speed.

The Four Cardinal Principles—to keep to the socialist road and to uphold the people's democratic dictatorship, leadership by the Communist Party of China, and Marxism-Leninism and Mao Zedong Thought—are the foundation on which to build our country. Throughout the course of socialist modernization we must adhere to the Four Cardinal Principles and combat bourgeois liberalization.

Reform and opening up are the only way to make our country strong. We must carry out fundamental reform of the economic structure that hampers the development of the productive forces, and keep and improve a socialist market economy; we must also carry out corresponding political restructuring and reform in other fields. The opening up means all-dimensional opening up, both externally and internally. We must expand economic and technological exchanges and cooperation with other countries, make more and better use of foreign capital, resources and technologies, and assimilate and exploit the achievements of all other cultures, including all the advanced modes of operation and methods of management of developed countries in the West that embody the laws governing modern socialized production. We must be bold in blazing new trails in the practice of reform and opening up.

The Communist Party of China leads the people in promoting socialist democracy and building socialist political civilization. It keeps expanding socialist democracy, strengthens the socialist legal system, rules the country by law, builds a socialist country under the rule of law and consolidates the people's democratic dictatorship. The system of people's congresses and the system of multiparty cooperation and political consultation under the leadership of the Communist Party of China should continue. The Party should encourage the people to act as the masters of the country and take effective measures to protect the people's right to run the affairs of the state and of society and manage economic and cultural undertakings. It should encourage the free airing of views and establish and improve systems and procedures of democratic decision-making and supervision. State legislation and law enforcement should be strengthened so as to gradually put all work of the state on a legal footing. Comprehensive measures for keeping law and order should be taken to maintain the long-term social stability. Efforts must be made according to law to crack down on the criminal activities and criminals that endanger national security and interests, social stability and economic development. We should strictly distinguish between the two different types of contradictions—those between ourselves and the enemy and those among the people, so as to handle them properly.

The Communist Party of China leads the people in their efforts to build spiritual civilization as well as material and political civilizations and to combine ruling the country by law and ruling the country by virtue. Socialist spiritual civilization provides a powerful ideological driving force and intellectual support and helps create a good social climate for economic development, reform and opening up. It is essential to press ahead with education, science and culture, respect learning and talented people, raise the ideological, moral, scientific and educational levels of the entire nation, develop the fine national traditional culture, and develop a thriving socialist culture. It is essential to inspire the Party members and the people with the Party's basic line, patriotism, community spirit and socialist ideology, enhance their sense of national dignity, self-confidence and self-reliance, imbue the Party members with lofty ideals of communism, resist corrosion by capitalist and feudal decadent ideas and wipe out all social evils so that our people will have lofty ideals, moral integrity, a good education and a strong sense of discipline.

The Communist Party of China persists in its leadership over the People's Liberation Army and other people's armed forces, builds up the strength of the People's Liberation Army, and gives full play to its role in consolidating national defense, defending the motherland and participating in the socialist modernization drive.

The Communist Party of China upholds and promotes relations of equality, unity and mutual assistance among all ethnic groups in the country, upholds and constantly improves the system of regional ethnic autonomy, actively trains and promotes cadres from among ethnic minorities, and helps them with economic and cultural development in the areas inhabited by ethnic minorities so as to achieve common prosperity and all-round progress for all ethnic groups.

The Communist Party of China unites with all workers, farmers and intellectuals, and with all the democratic parties, personages without party affiliation and the patriotic forces of all ethnic groups in China in further expanding and fortifying the broadest possible patriotic united front embracing all socialist workers and all patriots who support socialism or who support the reunification of the motherland. We should constantly work to strengthen the unity of all the Chinese people, including our compatriots in *Hong Kong* and *Macao* special administrative regions and in *Taiwan* as well as overseas Chinese. We should accomplish the great task of reunifying the motherland in conformity with the principle of "one country, two systems."

The Communist Party of China stands for developing relations with other countries in order to bring about a favorable international environment for China's reform, opening up and modernization. In international affairs, it adheres to the independent foreign policy of peace, safeguarding China's independence and sovereignty, opposing hegemonism and power politics, defending world peace, and promoting human progress. It works to develop relations between China and other countries on the basis of the five principles of mutual respect for sovereignty and territorial integrity, mutual non-aggression, noninterference in each other's internal affairs, equality and mutual benefit, and peaceful coexistence. It strives for the constant development of good-neighborly relations between China and the surrounding countries and for the strengthening of the unity and cooperation between China and other developing countries. The Communist Party of China develops relations with communist parties and other political parties in other countries in accordance with the principles of independence, complete equality, mutual respect and noninterference in each other's internal affairs.

In order to lead the people of all ethnic groups in China in attaining the great goal of socialist modernization, the Communist Party of China must adhere to the Party's basic line in strengthening and improving Party building, persist in the principle that the Party exercises self-discipline and is strict with its members, and carry forward its fine tradition and style of work. It must constantly improve its art of leadership and governance, raise its ability to resist corruption, prevent degeneration and withstand risks, constantly strengthen its class foundation, expand its mass base and enhance its creativity, cohesion and combat effectiveness, so that it will stand forever in the forefront of the times and make itself a strong nucleus that can lead all the Chinese people in the unceasing march along the road of socialism with Chinese characteristics. In building the Party, we must be determined to meet the following four essential requirements:

First, adhering to the Party's basic line. The whole Party must achieve unity in thinking and in action with Deng Xiaoping Theory, the important thought of Three Represents and the Party's basic line and will persevere in doing so for a long time to come. We must integrate the reform and the open policy with the Four Cardinal Principles, carry out the Party's basic line in all fields of endeavor, implement in an all-round way the Party's basic program for the primary stage of socialism and combat all "Left" or Right erroneous tendencies, maintaining vigilance against Right tendencies and primarily against "Left" tendencies. We must intensify the building of leading bodies at all levels, selecting and promoting cadres who have scored outstanding achievements in their public service and have won the trust of the masses in the reform, opening up and the modernization drive, and train and cultivate millions of successors to the cause of socialism, thus ensuring organizationally the implementation of the Party's basic line and program.

Second, persevering in emancipating the mind, seeking truth from facts and keeping pace with the times. The Party's ideological line is to proceed from reality in handling all matters, to integrate theory with practice, to seek truth from facts, and to verify and develop the truth through practice. Party members must adhere to this ideological line, explore new ways, boldly experiment with new methods, go in for innovation, work creatively, constantly study new situations, review new experience and solve new problems, and enrich and develop Marxism in practice.

Third, persevering in serving the people wholeheartedly. The Party has no special interests of its own apart from the interests of the working class and the broadest masses of the people. At all times the Party gives top priority to the interests of the people, shares weal and woe with them and keeps in closest contact with them, and it does not allow any member to become divorced from the masses or place himself above them. The Party follows the mass line in its work, doing everything for the masses, relying on them in every task, carrying out the principle "from the masses, to the masses," and translating its correct views into conscious action of the masses. The biggest political advantage of our Party lies in its close ties with the masses while the biggest potential danger for it as a ruling party comes from its divorce from them. The Party's style of work and its maintenance of ties with the masses of the people are a matter of vital importance to the

Party, and the Party persistently opposes corruption, exerting great efforts to improve its style of work and make itself clean and honest.

Fourth, upholding democratic centralism. Democratic centralism is a combination of centralism on the basis of democracy and democracy under centralized guidance. It is the fundamental organizational principle of the Party and is also the mass line applied in the Party's political activities. Within the Party, democracy and the initiative and creativity of Party organizations at all levels as well as the vast number of Party members must be given full play. Correct centralism must be practiced so as to ensure concerted action in the whole Party and prompt and effective implementation of its decisions. The sense of organization and discipline must be strengthened, and all members are equal before Party discipline. Supervision over leading organs of the Party and over Party members holding leading positions must be strengthened and the system of inner-Party supervision constantly improved. In its internal political activities, the Party conducts criticism and self-criticism in the correct way, waging ideological struggles over matters of principles, upholding truth and rectifying mistakes. Diligent efforts must be made to create a political situation in which there are both centralism and democracy, both discipline and freedom, both unity of will and personal ease of mind and liveliness.

Leadership by the Party means mainly political, ideological and organizational leadership. The Party must meet the requirements of reform, opening up and the socialist modernization drive and strengthen and improve its leadership. Acting on the principle that the Party commands the overall situation and coordinates the efforts of all quarters, the Party must play the role as the core of leadership among all other organizations at the corresponding levels. It must concentrate on leading economic development, organize and coordinate all forces in a concerted effort to focus on economic development. The Party must practice democratic and scientific decision-making; formulate and implement the correct line, principles and policies; do its organizational, publicity and educational work well and make sure that all Party members play an exemplary and vanguard role. The Party must conduct its activities within the framework of the Constitution and other laws. It must see to it that the legislative, judicial and administrative organs of the state and the economic, cultural and people's organizations work with initiative and independent responsibility and in harmony. The Party must strengthen its leadership over the trade unions, the Communist Youth League organizations, the women's federations and other mass organizations, and give full scope to their roles. The Party must adapt itself to the march of events and changing circumstances, improving its system and style of leadership and raising its governing capacity. Party members must work in close cooperation with the vast number of non-Party people in the common endeavor to build socialism with Chinese characteristics.

CHAPTER I *Membership*

ARTICLE 1

Any Chinese worker, farmer, member of the armed forces, intellectual or any advanced element of other social strata who has reached the age of eighteen and who accepts the Party's Program and Constitution and is willing to join and work actively in one of the Party organizations, carry out the Party's decisions and pay membership dues regularly may apply for membership in the Communist Party of China.

ARTICLE 2

Members of the Communist Party of China are vanguard fighters of the Chinese working class imbued with communist consciousness.

Members of the Communist Party of China must serve the people wholeheartedly, dedicate their whole lives to the realization of communism, and be ready to make any personal sacrifices.

Members of the Communist Party of China are at all times ordinary members of the working people. Communist Party members must not seek personal gain or privileges, although the relevant laws and policies provide them with personal benefits and job-related functions and powers.

ARTICLE 3

Party members must fulfill the following duties:

(1) To conscientiously study Marxism-Leninism, Mao Zedong Thought, Deng Xiaoping Theory and the important thought of Three Represents, study the Party's line, principles, policies and decisions, acquire essential knowledge concerning the Party, obtain general, scientific and professional knowledge and work diligently to enhance their ability to serve the people.

(2) To implement the Party's basic line, principles and policies, take the lead in reform, opening up and socialist modernization, encourage the people to work hard for economic development and social progress and play an exemplary and vanguard role in production, work, study and social activities.

(3) To adhere to the principle that the interests of the Party and the people stand above everything else, subordinating their personal interests to the interests of the Party and the people, being the first to bear hardships and the last to enjoy comforts, working selflessly for the public interests and working to contribute more.

(4) To conscientiously observe the Party discipline, abide by the laws and regulations of the state in an exemplary way, rigorously guard secrets of the Party and state, execute the Party's decisions, and accept any job and actively fulfill any task assigned them by the Party.

(5) To uphold the Party's solidarity and unity, be loyal to and honest with the Party, match words with deeds, firmly oppose all factions and small-clique activities and oppose double-dealing and scheming of any kind.

(6) To earnestly engage in criticism and self-criticism, boldly expose and correct shortcomings and mistakes in work and resolutely combat corruption and other malpractices.

(7) To maintain close ties with the masses, disseminate the Party's views among them, consult with them when problems arise, keep the Party informed of their views and demands in good time and defend their legitimate interests.

(8) To promote new socialist ways and customs and advocate communist ethics. To step forward and fight bravely in times of difficulty or danger, daring to make any sacrifice to defend the interests of the country and the people.

ARTICLE 4

Party members enjoy the following rights:

(1) To attend relevant Party meetings, read relevant Party documents, and benefit from the Party's education and training.

(2) To participate in the discussion of questions concerning the Party's policies at Party meetings and in Party newspapers and journals.

(3) To make suggestions and proposals regarding the work of the Party.

(4) To make well-grounded criticism of any Party organization or member at Party meetings, to present information or charges against any Party organization or member concerning violations of discipline or the law to the Party in a responsible way, to demand disciplinary measures against such a member, or call for dismissal or replacement of any incompetent cadre.

(5) To participate in voting and elections and to stand for election.

(6) To attend, with the right of self-defense, discussions held by Party organizations to decide on disciplinary measures to be taken against themselves or to appraise their work and behavior; other Party members may also bear witness or argue on their behalf.

(7) In case of disagreement with a Party decision or policy, to make reservations and present their views to Party organizations at higher levels even up to the Central Committee, provided that they resolutely carry out the decision or policy while it is in force.

(8) To put forward any request, appeal, or complaint to higher Party organizations even up to the Central Committee and ask the organizations concerned for a responsible reply.

No Party organization, up to and including the Central Committee, has the right to deprive any Party member of the above-mentioned rights.

ARTICLE 5

New Party members must be admitted through a Party branch, and the principle of individual admission must be adhered to.

An applicant for Party membership must fill in an application form and be recommended by two full Party members. The application must be accepted at a general membership meeting of the Party branch concerned and approved by the next higher Party organization, and the applicant must undergo observation for a probationary period before being granted full membership.

Party members who recommend an applicant must make genuine efforts to acquaint themselves with the applicant's ideology, character, personal record and work performance and explain to each applicant the Party's program and Constitution, qualifications for membership and the duties and rights of members, and must make a responsible report to the Party organization on the matter.

The Party branch committee must canvass the opinions of persons concerned, inside and outside the Party, about an applicant for Party membership and, after establishing the latter's qualification following rigorous examination, submit the application to a general membership meeting for discussion.

Before approving the admission of applicants for Party membership, the next higher Party organization concerned must appoint people to talk with them, in order to get to know them better and help deepen their understanding of the Party.

In special circumstances, the Central Committee of the Party or the Party committee of a province, autonomous region or municipality directly under the Central Government may admit new Party members directly.

ARTICLE 6

A probationary Party member must take an admission oath in front of the Party flag. The oath reads: It is my will to join the Communist Party of China, uphold the Party's program, observe the provisions of the Party Constitution, fulfill a Party member's duties, carry out the Party's decisions, strictly observe Party discipline, guard Party secrets, be loyal to the Party, work hard, fight for communism throughout my life, be ready at all times to sacrifice my all for the Party and the people, and never betray the Party.

ARTICLE 7

The probationary period of a probationary member is one year. The Party organization should make serious efforts to educate and observe the probationary members.

Probationary members have the same duties as full members. They enjoy the rights of full members except those of participating in voting and elections and standing for election.

Upon the expiration of the probationary period of a probationary member, the Party branch concerned should promptly discuss whether he is qualified for full membership. A probationary member who conscientiously performs his duties and is qualified for full membership shall be granted full membership as scheduled; if continued observation and education are needed, the probationary period may be extended, but by no more than one year; if a probationary member fails to perform his duties and is found to be unqualified for full membership, his probationary membership shall be annulled. Any decision to grant a probationary member full membership, extend a probationary period, or annul a probationary membership must be made through discussion held by the general membership meeting of the Party branch concerned and approved by the next higher Party organization.

The probationary period of a probationary member begins from the day the general membership meeting of the Party branch admits him as a probationary member. The Party standing of a member begins from the day he is granted full membership on the expiration of the probationary period.

ARTICLE 8

Every Party member, irrespective of position, must be organized into a branch, cell or other specific unit of the Party to participate in the regular activities of the Party organization and accept supervision by the masses inside and outside the Party. Leading Party cadres must attend democratic meetings held by the Party committee or leading Party members' groups. There shall be no privileged Party members who do not participate in the regular activities of the Party organization and do not accept supervision by the masses inside and outside the Party.

ARTICLE 9

Party members are free to withdraw from the Party. When a Party member asks to withdraw, the Party branch concerned shall, after discussion by its general membership meeting, remove his name from the Party rolls, make the removal public and report it to the next higher Party organization for the record.

The Party branch shall try to educate the Party member who lacks revolutionary will, fails to fulfill the duties of a Party member, or is not qualified for membership and require him to correct his mistakes within the time. If he remains incorrigible after education, he should be persuaded to withdraw from the Party. The case shall be discussed and decided by the general membership meeting of the Party branch concerned and submitted to the next higher Party organization for approval. If the Party member being persuaded to withdraw refuses to do so, the case shall be submitted to the general membership meeting of the Party branch concerned for discussion to decide on the removal of his name from the Party rolls, after which the decision shall be submitted to the next higher Party organization for approval.

A Party member who fails to take part in regular Party activities, pay membership dues or do work assigned by the Party for six successive months without good reason is regarded as having given up membership. The general membership meeting of the Party branch concerned shall decide on the removal of such a person's name from the Party rolls and report it to the next higher Party organization for approval.

CHAPTER II *Organization System of the Party*

ARTICLE 10

The Party is an integral body organized under its program and Constitution on the principle of democratic centralism. The basic principles of democratic centralism as practiced by the Party are as follows:

(1) Individual Party members are subordinate to the Party organization, the minority is subordinate to the majority, the lower Party organizations are subordinate to the higher Party organizations, and all the constituent organizations and members of the Party are subordinate to the National Congress and the Central Committee of the Party.

(2) The Party's leading bodies at all levels are elected except for the representative organs dispatched by them and the leading Party members' groups in non-Party organizations.

(3) The highest leading body of the Party is the National Congress and the Central Committee elected by it. The leading bodies of local Party organizations are the Party congresses at their respective levels and the Party committees elected by them. Party committees are responsible, and report their work, to the Party congresses at their respective levels.

(4) Higher Party organizations shall pay constant attention to the views of lower organizations and the rank-and-file Party members, and solve in good time the problems they raise. Lower Party organizations shall report on their work to, and request instructions from, higher Party organizations; at the same time, they shall handle, independently and in a responsible manner, matters within their jurisdiction. Higher and lower Party organizations should exchange information and support and supervise each other. Party organizations at all levels should enable Party members to keep well informed of inner-Party affairs and to have as many opportunities as possible to involve themselves in them.

(5) Party committees at all levels function on the principle of combining collective leadership with individual responsibility based on division of labor. All major issues shall be decided upon by the Party committees after discussion in accordance with the principle of collective leadership, democratic centralism, individual consultations and decision by meetings. The members of the Party committees should earnestly perform their duties in accordance with the collective decisions taken and division of labor.

(6) The Party forbids all forms of personality cult. It is necessary to ensure that the activities of the Party leaders are subject to the supervision of the Party and the people, and at the same time to uphold the prestige of all the leaders who represent the interests of the Party and the people.

ARTICLE 11

The election of delegates to Party congresses and of members of Party committees at all levels should reflect the will of the voters. Elections shall be held by secret ballot. The lists of candidates shall be submitted to the Party organizations and voters for full deliberation and discussion. The election procedure in which the number of candidates nominated is greater than the number of persons to be elected may be used directly in a formal election or this procedure may be used first in a preliminary election in order to draw up a list of candidates for the formal election. The voters have the right to inquire about the candidates, demand a change or reject one in favor of another. No organization or individual shall in any way compel voters to elect or not to elect any candidate.

If any violation of the Party Constitution occurs in the election of delegates to a local Party congress or to Party congresses at the primary level, the Party committee at the next higher level, after investigation and verification, should decide to declare the election invalid and take appropriate measures. The decision shall be reported to the Party committee at the next higher level for checking and approval before it is formally announced and implemented.

ARTICLE 12

When necessary, the Central Committee of the Party and the local Party committees at all levels will convene conferences of delegates to discuss and decide on major problems that require timely solution. The number of delegates to such conferences and the procedure governing their election shall be determined by the Party committees convening them.

ARTICLE 13

The formation of a new Party organization or the dissolution of an existing one shall be decided upon by the higher Party organizations.

The Central Committee of the Party and the local Party committees at all levels may send out their representative organs.

When the congress of a local Party organization at any level or the congress of Party organization at the primary level is not in session, the next higher Party organization may, when it deems it necessary, transfer or appoint responsible members of that organization.

ARTICLE 14

When making decisions on important questions affecting the lower organizations, the leading bodies of the Party at all levels should, under normal circumstances, solicit opinions of the lower organizations. Measures should be taken to ensure that the lower organizations can exercise their functions and powers normally. Except in special circumstances, higher leading bodies should not interfere with matters that ought to be handled by lower organizations.

ARTICLE 15

Only the Central Committee of the Party has the power to make decisions on major policies of a nationwide character. Party organizations of various departments and localities may make suggestions with regard to such policies to the Central Committee, but shall not make any decisions or publicize their views outside the Party without authorization.

Lower Party organizations must firmly implement the decisions of higher Party organizations. If lower organizations consider that any decisions of higher organizations do not suit the specific conditions in their localities or departments, they may demand modification. If the higher organizations insist on their original decisions, the lower organizations must carry out such decisions and refrain from publicly voicing their differences, but retain the right to report to the next higher Party organization.

Newspapers, journals and other means of publicity run by Party organizations at all levels must disseminate the line, principles, policies and decisions of the Party.

ARTICLE 16

When discussing and making decisions on any matter, Party organizations must keep to the principle of subordination of the minority to the majority. A vote must be taken when major issues are decided on. Serious consideration should be given to the differing views of a minority. In case of controversy over major issues in which supporters of the two opposing views are nearly equal in number, except in emergencies where action must be taken in accordance with the majority view, the decision should be put off to allow for further investigation, study and exchange of opinions followed by another vote. Under special circumstances, the controversy may be reported to the next higher Party organization for a ruling.

When, on behalf of the Party organization, an individual Party member is to express views on major issues beyond the scope of the existing decisions of the Party organizations, the content must be referred to the Party organization for prior discussion and decision, or referred to the next higher Party organization for instructions. No Party member, whatever his position, is allowed to make decisions on major issues on his own. In an emergency, when a decision by an individual is unavoidable, the matter must be reported to the Party organization immediately afterwards. No leader is allowed to take decisions arbitrarily on his own or to place himself above the Party organization.

ARTICLE 17

The central, local and primary organizations of the Party must all pay great attention to Party building. They shall regularly discuss and examine the Party's work in publicity, education, organization and discipline inspection, its mass work and united front work. They must carefully study ideological and political developments inside and outside the Party.

CHAPTER III *Central Organizations of the Party*

ARTICLE 18

The National Congress of the Party is held once every five years and convened by the Central Committee. It may be convened before the normally scheduled date if the Central Committee deems it necessary or if more than one-third of the organizations at the provincial level so request. Except under extraordinary circumstances, the Congress may not be postponed.

The number of delegates to the National Congress of the Party and the procedure governing their election shall be determined by the Central Committee.

ARTICLE 19

The functions and powers of the National Congress of the Party are as follows:

(1) To hear and examine the reports of the Central Committee;

(2) To hear and examine the reports of the Central Commission for Discipline Inspection;

(3) To discuss and decide on major questions concerning the Party;

(4) To revise the Constitution of the Party;

(5) To elect the Central Committee; and

(6) To elect the Central Commission for Discipline Inspection.

ARTICLE 20

The powers and functions of the National Conference of the Party are as follows: to discuss and make decisions on major questions; and to replace members and elect additional members of the Central Committee and the Central Commission for Discipline Inspection. The number of members and alternate members of the Central Committee to be replaced or newly elected shall not exceed one-fifth of the respective totals of members and alternate members of the Central Committee elected by the National Congress of the Party.

ARTICLE 21

The Central Committee of the Party is elected for a term of five years. However, when the next National Congress is convened before or after its normally scheduled date, the term shall be correspondingly shortened or extended. Members and alternate members of the Central Committee must have a Party standing of five years or more. The number of members and alternate members of the Central Committee shall be determined by the National Congress. Vacancies on the Central Committee shall be filled by its alternate members in the order of the number of votes by which they were elected.

The Central Committee of the Party meets in plenary session at least once a year, and such sessions are convened by its Political Bureau.

When the National Congress is not in session, the Central Committee carries out its decisions, directs the entire work of the Party and represents the Communist Party of China in its external relations.

ARTICLE 22

The Political Bureau, the Standing Committee of the Political Bureau and the General Secretary of the Central Committee of the Party are elected by the Central Committee in plenary session. The General Secretary of the Central Committee must be a member of the Standing Committee of the Political Bureau.

When the Central Committee is not in session, the Political Bureau and its Standing Committee exercise the functions and powers of the Central Committee.

The Secretariat of the Central Committee is the working body of the Political Bureau of the Central Committee and its Standing Committee. The members of the Secretariat are nominated by the Standing Committee of the Political Bureau of the Central Committee and are subject to endorsement by the Central Committee in plenary session.

The General Secretary of the Central Committee is responsible for convening the meetings of the Political Bureau and its Standing Committee and presides over the work of the Secretariat.

The members of the Military Commission of the Central Committee are decided on by the Central Committee.

The central leading bodies and leaders elected by each Central Committee shall, when the next National Congress is in session, continue to preside over the Party's day-to-day work until the new central leading bodies and leaders are elected by the next Central Committee.

ARTICLE 23

Party organizations in the Chinese People's Liberation Army carry on their work in accordance with the instructions of the Central Committee. The political work organ of the Military Commission of the Central Committee is the General Political Department of the Chinese People's Liberation Army; the General Political Department directs Party and political work in the army. The organizational system and organs of the Party in the armed forces are prescribed by the Military Commission of the Central Committee.

CHAPTER IV *Local Organizations of the Party*

ARTICLE 24

The Party congress of a province, autonomous region, municipality directly under the Central Government, city divided into districts, or autonomous prefecture is held once every five years.

The Party congress of a county (banner), autonomous county, city not divided into districts, or municipal district is held once every five years.

Local Party congresses are convened by the Party committees at the corresponding levels. Under extraordinary circumstances, they may be held before or after their normally scheduled dates upon approval by the next higher Party committees.

The number of delegates to the local Party congresses at any level and the procedure governing their election are determined by the Party committees at the corresponding levels and should be reported to the next higher Party committees for approval.

ARTICLE 25

The functions and powers of the local Party congresses at all levels are as follows:

(1) To hear and examine the reports of the Party committees at the corresponding levels;

(2) To hear and examine the reports of the commissions for discipline inspection at the corresponding levels;

(3) To discuss and decide on major issues in the given areas; and

(4) To elect the Party committees and commissions for discipline inspection at the corresponding levels.

ARTICLE 26

The Party committee of a province, autonomous region, municipality directly under the Central Government, city divided into districts, or autonomous prefecture is elected for a term of five years. The members and alternate members of such a committee must have a Party standing of five years or more.

The Party committee of a county (banner), autonomous county, city not divided into districts, or municipal district is elected for a term of five years. The members and alternate members of such a committee must have a Party standing of three years or more.

When local Party congresses at various levels are convened before or after their normally scheduled dates, the terms of the committees elected by the previous congresses shall be correspondingly shortened or extended.

The number of members and alternate members of the local Party committees at various levels shall be determined by the next higher committees. Vacancies on the local Party committees at various levels shall be filled by their alternate members in the order of the number of votes by which they were elected.

The local Party committees at various levels meet in plenary session at least twice a year.

Local Party committees at various levels shall, when the Party congresses of the given areas are not in session, carry out the directives of the next higher Party organizations and the decisions of the Party.

Congresses at the corresponding levels, direct work in their own areas and report on it to the next higher Party committees at regular intervals.

ARTICLE 27

Local Party committees at various levels elect, at their plenary sessions, their standing committees, secretaries and deputy secretaries and report the results to the higher Party committees for approval. The standing committees of local Party committees at various levels exercise the powers and functions of local Party committees when the latter are not in session. They continue to handle the day-to-day work when the next Party congresses at their levels are in session, until the new standing committees are elected.

ARTICLE 28

A prefectural Party committee, or an organization analogous to it, is the representative organ dispatched by a provincial or an autonomous regional Party committee to a prefecture covering several counties, autonomous counties or cities. It exercises leadership over the work in the given region as authorized by the provincial or autonomous regional Party committee.

CHAPTER V *Primary Organizations of the Party*

ARTICLE 29

Primary Party organizations are formed in enterprises, rural areas, government departments, schools, scientific research institutes, communities, mass organizations, intermediaries, companies of the People's Liberation Army and other basic units, where there are at least three full Party members.

In primary organizations, primary Party committees and committees of general Party branches or Party branches are set up as the work requires and according to the number of Party members, subject to approval by the higher Party organizations. A primary Party committee is elected by a general membership meeting or a delegate meeting. The committee of a general Party branch or a Party branch is elected by a general membership meeting.

ARTICLE 30

A Primary Party committee is elected for a term of three to five years, while a general Party branch committee or a Party branch committee is elected for a term of two or three years. Results of the election of a secretary and deputy secretaries by a primary Party committee, general branch committee or branch committee shall be reported to the higher Party organizations for approval.

ARTICLE 31

The primary Party organizations are militant bastions of the Party in the basic units of society, where all the Party's work proceeds and they serve as the foundation of its fighting capacity. Their main tasks are:

(1) To disseminate and carry out the Party's line, principles and policies, the decisions of the Central Committee of the Party and other higher Party organizations, and their own decisions; to give full play to the exemplary, vanguard role of Party members, and to unite and organize the cadres and the rank of file inside and outside the Party to fulfill the tasks of their own units.

(2) To organize Party members to conscientiously study Marxism-Leninism, Mao Zedong Thought, Deng Xiaoping Theory, the important thought of Three Represents, the Party's line, principles, policies and decisions, acquire essential knowledge concerning the Party and obtain general, scientific and professional knowledge.

(3) To educate and supervise Party members, raise the overall quality of the Party membership, cultivate their Party spirit, ensure their regular participation in the activities of the Party organizations, make criticism and self-criticism, maintain and observe Party discipline, see that Party members truly fulfill their duties and protect their rights from encroachment.

(4) To maintain close ties with the masses, constantly seek their criticisms and opinions regarding Party members and the Party's work, safeguard the legitimate rights and interests of the masses and do effective ideological and political work among them.

(5) To give full scope to the initiative and creativeness of Party members and the masses and to discover, nurture and recommend fine, talented people from among Party members and the masses and encourage them to contribute their skills and learning to the reform, opening up and the socialist modernization drive.

(6) To educate and train the activists who apply for Party membership, attend to the routine work concerning the recruitment of new members and attach great importance to recruiting Party members from among those in the forefront of production and work and from among young people.

(7) To see to it that Party and non-Party cadres strictly observe the law and administrative discipline and the financial and economic statutes and personnel regulations of the state and that none of them infringe on the interests of the state, the collective or the masses.

(8) To encourage Party members and the masses to conscientiously resist unhealthy practices and wage resolute struggles against all illegal and criminal activities.

ARTICLE 32

The primary Party committees in communities, townships and towns and the Party organizations in villages and communities provide leadership for the work in their localities and assist administrative departments, economic institutions and self-governing mass organizations in fully exercising their functions and powers.

In a state-owned or collective enterprise, the primary Party organization acts as the political nucleus and works for the operation of the enterprise. The primary Party organization guarantees and supervises the implementation of the principles and policies of the Party and the state in its own enterprise and backs the meeting of shareholders, board of directors, board of supervisors and manager (factory director) in the exercise of their functions and powers according to law. It relies wholeheartedly on the workers and office staff, supports the work of the congresses of representatives of workers and office staff and participates in making final decisions on major questions in the enterprise. It works to improve its own organization and provides leadership over ideological and political work, efforts for cultural and ethical progress and the trade unions, the Communist Youth League and other mass organizations.

In a non-public economic institution, the primary Party organization carries out the Party's principles and policies, provides guidance to and supervises the enterprise in observing the laws and regulations of the state, exercises leadership over the trade union, the Communist Youth League organization and other mass organizations, rallies the workers and office staff around it, safeguards the legitimate rights and interests of all quarters and stimulates the healthy development of the enterprise.

In an institution where the administrative leaders assume full responsibility, the primary Party organization acts as the political nucleus. In an institution where the administrative leaders assume full responsibility under the leadership of the Party committee, the primary Party organization discusses and decides on major issues and at the same time ensures that the administrative leaders are able to fully exercise their functions and powers.

In offices of the Party or the state at all levels, the primary Party organizations assist the chief administrators in fulfilling their tasks and improving their work. They exercise supervision over all Party members, including the chief administrators who are Party members, but do not direct the work of their units.

CHAPTER VI *Party Cadres*

ARTICLE 33

Party cadres are the backbone of the Party's cause and public servants of the people. The Party selects its cadres according to the principle that they should possess both political integrity and professional competence, adheres to the practice of appointing people on their merits and opposes favoritism; it exerts genuine efforts to make the ranks of the cadres more revolutionary, younger in average age, better educated and more professionally competent.

The Party attaches great importance to education, training, selection and assessment of cadres, especially to the training and selection of outstanding young cadres. The Party actively promotes the reform of the cadre system.

The Party attaches great importance to the training and promotion of women cadres and cadres from among the ethnic minorities.

ARTICLE 34

Leading Party cadres at all levels must show exemplary performance in carrying out their duties as Party members prescribed in Article 3 of this Constitution and must meet the following basic requirements:

(1) Know Marxism-Leninism, Mao Zedong Thought and Deng Xiaoping Theory well enough to perform their duties, earnestly put the important thought of Three Represents into practice, try hard to analyze and solve practical problems with the stand, viewpoint and methods of Marxism, keep stressing study, political awareness and integrity, and be able to stand the test of all trials and tribulations.

(2) Have the grand ideal of communism and firm conviction in socialism with Chinese characteristics, firmly implement the Party's basic line, principles and policies, be determined to carry out the reform and opening to the outside world, devote themselves to the cause of modernization and work hard to start undertakings and make solid achievements in socialist construction.

(3) Persist in emancipating their minds, seeking truth from facts, keeping pace with the times and blazing new trails in a pioneering spirit; conduct earnest investigations and studies so as to be able to integrate the Party's principles and policies with the actual conditions in their localities or departments and work efficiently; tell the truth, do practical work, seek tangible results and oppose formalism.

(4) Be fervently dedicated to the revolutionary cause and imbued with a strong sense of political responsibility, have practical experience, and be qualified for leading posts in organizational ability, general education and vocational knowledge.

(5) Properly exercise the power invested in them by the people, handle matters according to law, be upright and clean and work diligently for the people, set an example by their own actions, work hard and live simply, maintain close ties with the masses, uphold the Party's mass line, conscientiously accept the criticism and supervision of the Party and the masses, exercise self-respect, self-examination, self-caution and self-motivation, combat bureaucratism, and fight against malpractices such as abuse of power for personal gain.

(6) Uphold the Party's system of democratic centralism, maintain a democratic style of work, take the overall situation into consideration, and be good at uniting and working with other comrades, including those who hold differing opinions.

ARTICLE 35

Party cadres should be able to cooperate with non-Party cadres, respect them and be open-minded in learning from their strong points.

Party organizations at all levels must be good at discovering and recommending talented non-Party cadres with practical learning for leading posts, and ensure that the latter enjoy authority commensurate with their posts and can fully play their roles.

ARTICLE 36

Leading Party cadres at all levels, whether elected through democratic procedure or appointed by a leading body, are not entitled to lifelong tenure, and they can be transferred from or relieved of their posts.

Cadres no longer fit to continue working due to old age or poor health should retire according to the regulations of the state.

CHAPTER VII *Party Discipline*

ARTICLE 37

Party discipline refers to the rules of conduct that must be observed by Party organizations at all levels and by all Party members. It is the guarantee that the unity and solidarity of the Party are safeguarded and that the tasks of the Party are accomplished. Party organizations must strictly observe and maintain Party discipline. A Communist Party member must conscientiously act within the bounds of Party discipline.

ARTICLE 38

Party organizations should criticize, educate or take disciplinary measures against members who violate Party discipline, depending on the nature and seriousness of their mistakes and in the spirit of "learning from past mistakes to avoid future ones, and curing the sickness to save the patient."

Party members who have seriously violated criminal law shall be expelled from the Party.

It is strictly forbidden in the Party to take any measures against a member that contravene the Party Constitution or the laws of the state, or to retaliate against or frame a member. Any offending organization or individual must be dealt with according to Party discipline and the laws of the state.

ARTICLE 39

There are five measures for enforcing Party discipline: warning, serious warning, removal from Party posts, probation within the Party, and expulsion from the Party.

The period for which a Party member is placed on probation shall not exceed two years. During that period, the Party member concerned has no right to participate in voting or elections or stand for election. A Party member who during that time truly rectifies his mistake shall have his rights as a Party member restored. Party members who refuse to mend their ways shall be expelled from the Party.

Expulsion is the ultimate Party disciplinary measure. In deciding on or approving an expulsion, Party organizations at all levels should study all the relevant facts and opinions and exercise extreme caution.

ARTICLE 40

Any disciplinary measure to be taken against a Party member must be discussed and decided on at a general membership meeting of the Party branch concerned, and reported to the primary Party committee concerned for approval. If the case is relatively important or complicated, or involves the expulsion of a member, it shall be reported to a Party commission for discipline inspection at or above the county level for examination and approval, in accordance with the specific situation. Under special circumstances, a Party committee or a commission for discipline inspection at or above the county level has the authority to decide directly on disciplinary measures to be taken against a Party member.

Any decision to remove a member or alternate member of the Central Committee or a local committee at any level from his posts within the Party, to place such a person on probation within the Party or to expel him from the Party must be approved by a two-thirds majority vote at a plenary meeting of the Party committee to which he belongs. In special circumstances, the decision may be taken first by the Standing Committee of the Political Bureau of the Central Committee or the standing committee of a local Party committee, pending confirmation at the plenary meeting of the Party committee. Such a disciplinary measure against a member or alternate member of a local Party committee is subject to approval by the higher Party committee.

A member or alternate member of the Central Committee who has seriously violated the criminal law shall be expelled from the Party on decision by the Political Bureau of the Central Committee; a member or alternate member of a local Party committee who has seriously violated criminal law shall be expelled from the Party on decision by the standing committee of the Party committee at the corresponding level.

ARTICLE 41

When a Party organization is deciding on a disciplinary measure against a Party member, it should investigate and verify the facts in an objective way. The Party member in question must be informed of a decision regarding any disciplinary measure to be taken and of the facts on which it is based. The person concerned must be given a chance to account for himself and speak in his own defense. If the member does not accept the decision, he can appeal, and the Party organization concerned must promptly deal with or forward his appeal, and must not withhold or suppress it. Those who cling to erroneous views and unjustifiable demands shall be educated by criticism.

ARTICLE 42

If a Party organization fails to uphold Party discipline, it must be investigated.

In case a Party organization seriously violates Party discipline and is unable to rectify the mistake on its own, the next higher Party committee should, after verifying the facts and considering the seriousness of the case, decide on the reorganization or dissolution of the organization, report the decision to the Party committee at the next higher level for examination and approval, and then formally announce and carry out the decision.

CHAPTER VIII *Party Organs for Discipline Inspection*

ARTICLE 43

The Party's Central Commission for Discipline Inspection functions under the leadership of the Central Committee of the Party. The Party's local commissions for discipline inspection at all levels and primary commissions for discipline inspection function under the dual leadership of the Party committees at the corresponding levels and the next higher commissions for discipline inspection.

The Party's commissions for discipline inspection at all levels serve a term of the same duration as the Party committees at the corresponding levels.

The Party's Central Commission for Discipline Inspection elects, in plenary session, its standing committee, secretary and deputy secretaries and reports the results to the Central Committee for approval. Local commissions for discipline inspection at all levels elect, at their plenary sessions, their respective standing committees, secretaries and deputy secretaries. The results of the elections are subject to endorsement by the Party committees at the corresponding levels and should be reported to the next higher Party committees for approval. The question of whether a primary Party committee should set up a commission for discipline inspection or simply appoint a discipline inspection commissioner shall be determined by the next higher Party organization in light of the specific circumstances. The committees of general Party branches and Party branches shall have discipline inspection commissioners.

The Party's Central Commission for Discipline Inspection shall, when its work so requires, accredit discipline inspection groups or commissioners to Party or state organs at the central level. Leaders of the discipline inspection groups or discipline inspection commissioners may attend relevant meetings of the leading Party organizations in the said organs as non-voting participants. The leading Party organizations in the organs concerned must support their work.

ARTICLE 44

The main tasks of the Party's commissions for discipline inspection at all levels are as follows: to uphold the Constitution and other statutes of the Party, to check up on the implementation of the line, principles, policies and decisions of the Party and to assist the respective Party committees in improving the Party's style of work and in organizing and coordinating the work against corruption.

The commissions for discipline inspection at all levels shall frequently provide education for Party members on their duty to observe Party discipline and adopt decisions for the upholding of Party discipline; they shall supervise Party members holding leading positions in exercising their power; they shall examine and deal with relatively important or complicated cases of violation of the Constitution or other statutes of the Party by Party organizations or Party members and decide on or rescind disciplinary measures against Party members involved in such cases; they shall deal with complaints and appeals made by Party members; and they shall guarantee the rights of Party members.

The commissions for discipline inspection at all levels shall report to the Party committees at the corresponding levels on the results of their handling of cases of special importance or complexity, as well as on the problems encountered. The local commissions for discipline inspection at all levels and primary commissions for discipline inspection shall also present such reports to the higher commissions.

If a commission for discipline inspection at any level discovers any violation of Party discipline by a member of the Party committee at the corresponding level, it may take the initial step of verifying the facts and, if it is necessary to put a case on file, it should report to the Party committee at the corresponding level for approval, and if a member of the standing committee of the Party committee is involved, it should first report to the Party committee at the corresponding level and then to the commission for discipline inspection at the next higher level for approval.

ARTICLE 45

Higher commissions for discipline inspection have the power to examine the work of the lower commissions and to approve or modify their decisions on any case. If decisions so modified have already been ratified by the Party committee at the corresponding level, the modification must be approved by the next higher Party committee.

If a local commission for discipline inspection or a primary commission for discipline inspection does not agree with a decision made by the Party committee at the corresponding level in dealing with a case, it may demand the commission at the next higher level to reexamine the case; if a local or primary commission discovers cases of violation of Party discipline by the Party committee at the corresponding level or by its members, and if that Party committee fails to deal with them properly or at all, it has the right to appeal to the higher commission for assistance in dealing with such cases.

CHAPTER IX *Leading Party Members' Groups*

ARTICLE 46

A leading Party members' group may be formed in the leading body of a central or local state organ, people's organization, economic or cultural institution or other non-Party unit. The group plays the role of the core of leadership. Its main tasks are: to see to it that the Party's line, principles and policies are implemented, to discuss and decide on matters of major importance in its unit, to do well in managing affairs concerning cadres, to unite with the non-Party cadres and the masses in fulfilling the tasks assigned by the Party and the state and to guide the work of the Party organization of the unit and those directly under it.

ARTICLE 47

The composition of a leading Party members' group is decided by the Party organization that approves its establishment. The group shall have a secretary and, if necessary, deputy secretaries.

A leading Party members' group must accept the leadership of the Party organization that approves its establishment.

ARTICLE 48

Party committees may be set up in state organs which exercise centralized leadership over their subordinate units. The Central Committee of the Party shall provide the specific procedure for their establishment and define their functions, powers and tasks.

CHAPTER X *Relationship between the Party and the Communist Youth League*

ARTICLE 49

The Communist Youth League of China is a mass organization of advanced young people under the leadership of the Communist Party of China; it is a school where a large number of young people learn about socialism with Chinese characteristics and about communism through practice; it is the Party's assistant and reserve force. The Central Committee of the Communist Youth League functions under the leadership of the Central Committee of the Party. The local chapters of the Communist Youth League are under the leadership of the Party committees at the corresponding levels and of the higher organizations of the League itself.

ARTICLE 50

Party committees at all levels must strengthen their leadership over the Communist Youth League organizations and pay attention to selecting and training League cadres. The Party must firmly support the Communist Youth League in the lively and creative performance of its work to suit the characteristics and needs of young people, and give full play to the League's role as a shock force and as a bridge linking the Party with great numbers of young people.

Those secretaries of League committees at or below the county level or in enterprises and institutions who are Party members may attend meetings of Party committees at the corresponding levels and meetings of their standing committees as non-voting participants.

CHAPTER XI *Party Emblem and Flag*

ARTICLE 51

The emblem of the Communist Party of China is a design of sickle and hammer.

ARTICLE 52

The flag of the Communist Party of China is a red flag highlighted by a golden Party emblem on it.

ARTICLE 53

The Party emblem and flag are the symbol and sign of the Communist Party of China. Party organizations at all levels and all Party members shall safeguard the sanctity of the Party emblem and flag. Party emblems and flags should be made and used according to regulations.

China's State Constitution

Adopted in 1982, with amendments in 1988, 1993, and 1999

Preamble

China is one of the countries with the longest histories in the world. The people of all nationalities in China have jointly created a splendid culture and have a glorious revolutionary tradition. Feudal China was gradually reduced after 1840 to a semi-colonial and semi-feudal country. The Chinese people waged wave upon wave of heroic struggles for national independence and liberation and for democracy and freedom. Great and earth-shaking historical changes have taken place in China in the 20th century. The Revolution of 1911, led by Dr Sun Yat-sen, abolished the feudal monarchy and gave birth to the Republic of China. But the Chinese people had yet to fulfil their historical task of overthrowing imperialism and feudalism. After waging hard, protracted and tortuous struggles, armed and otherwise, the Chinese people of all nationalities led by the Communist Party of China with Chairman Mao Zedong as its leader ultimately, in 1949, overthrew the rule of imperialism, feudalism and bureaucrat capitalism, won the great victory of the new-democratic revolution and founded the People's Republic of China. Thereupon the Chinese people took state power into their own hands and became masters of the country.

After the founding of the People's Republic, the transition of Chinese society from a new-democratic to a socialist society was effected step by step. The socialist transformation of the private ownership of the means of production was completed, the system of exploitation of man by man eliminated and the socialist system established. The people's democratic dictatorship led by the working class and based on the alliance of workers and peasants, which is in essence the dictatorship of the proletariat, has been consolidated and developed. The Chinese people and the Chinese People's Liberation Army have thwarted aggression, sabotage and armed provocations by imperialists and hegemonists, safeguarded China's national independence and security and strengthened its national defence. Major successes have been achieved in economic development. An independent and fairly comprehensive socialist system of industry has in the main been established. There has been a marked increase in agricultural production. Significant progress has been made in educational, scientific, cultural and other undertakings, and socialist ideological education has yielded noteworthy results. The living standards of the people have improved considerably. Both the victory of China's new-democratic revolution and the successes of its socialist cause have been achieved by the Chinese people of all nationalities under the leadership of the Communist Party of China and the guidance of Marxism-Leninism and Mao Zedong Thought, and by upholding truth, correcting errors and overcoming numerous difficulties and hardships.

The basic task of the nation in the years to come is to concentrate its effort on socialist modernization. Under the leadership of the Communist Party of China and the guidance of Marxism-Leninism and Mao Zedong Thought, the Chinese people of all nationalities will continue to adhere to the people's democratic dictatorship and follow the socialist road, steadily improve socialist institutions, develop socialist democracy, improve the socialist legal system and work hard and self-reliantly to modernize industry, agriculture, national defence and science and technology step by step to turn China into a socialist country with a high level of culture and democracy. The exploiting classes as such have been eliminated in our country. However, class struggle will continue to exist within certain limits for a long time to come. The Chinese people must fight against those forces and elements, both at home and abroad, that are hostile to China's socialist system and try to undermine it. Taiwan is part of the sacred territory of the People's Republic of China. It is the lofty duty of the entire Chinese people, including our compatriots in Taiwan, to accomplish the great task of reunifying the motherland. In building socialism it is imperative to rely on the workers, peasants and intellectuals and unite with all the forces that can be united. In the long years of revolution and construction, there has been formed under the leadership of the Communist Party of China a broad patriotic united front that is composed of democratic parties and people's organizations and embraces all socialist working people, all patriots who support socialism and all patriots who stand for reunification of the motherland. This united front will continue to be consolidated and developed. The Chinese People's Political Consultative Conference is a broadly representative organization of the united front, which has played a significant historical role and will continue to do so in the political and social life of the country, in promoting friendship with the people of other countries and in the struggle for socialist modernization and for the reunification and unity of the country. The People's Republic of China is a unitary multi-national state built up jointly by the people of all its nationalities. Socialist relations of equality, unity and mutual assistance have been established among them and will continue to be strengthened. In the struggle to safeguard the unity of the nationalities, it is necessary to combat big-nation chauvinism, mainly Han chauvinism, and also necessary to combat local-national chauvinism. The state does its utmost to promote the common prosperity of all nationalities in the country. China's achievements in revolution and construction are inseparable from support by the people of the world. The future of China is closely linked with that of the whole world. China adheres to an independent foreign policy as well as to the five principles of mutual respect for sovereignty and territorial integrity, mutual non-aggression, non-interference in each other's internal affairs, equality and mutual benefit, and peaceful coexistence in developing diplomatic relations and economic and cultural exchanges with other countries; China consistently opposes imperialism, hegemonism and colonialism, works to strengthen unity with the people of other countries, supports the oppressed nations and the developing countries in their just struggle to win and preserve national independence and develop their national economies, and strives to safeguard world peace and promote the cause of human progress. This Constitution affirms the achievements of the struggles of the Chinese people of all nationalities and defines the basic system and basic tasks of the state in legal form; it is the fundamental law of the state and has supreme legal authority. The people of all nationalities, all state organs, the armed forces, all political parties and public organizations and all enterprises and undertakings in the country must take the Constitution as the basic norm of conduct, and they have the duty to uphold the dignity of the Constitution and ensure its implementation.

CHAPTER I.

General Principles

ARTICLE 1.

The People's Republic of China is a socialist state under the people's democratic dictatorship led by the working class and based on the alliance of workers and peasants. The socialist system is the basic system of the People's Republic of China. Sabotage of the socialist system by any organization or individual is prohibited.

ARTICLE 2.

All power in the People's Republic of China belongs to the people. The organs through which the people exercise state power are the National People's Congress and the local people's congresses at different levels. The people administer state affairs and manage economic, cultural and social affairs through various channels and in various ways in accordance with the law.

ARTICLE 3.

The state organs of the People's Republic of China apply the principle of democratic centralism. The National People's Congress and the local people's congresses at different levels are instituted through democratic election. They are responsible to the people and subject to their supervision. All administrative, judicial and procuratorial organs of the state are created by the people's congresses to which they are responsible and under whose supervision they operate. The division of functions and powers between the central and local state organs is guided by the principle of giving full play to the initiative and enthusiasm of the local authorities under the unified leadership of the central authorities.

ARTICLE 4.

All nationalities in the People's Republic of China are equal. The state protects the lawful rights and interests of the minority nationalities and upholds and develops the relationship of equality, unity and mutual assistance among all of China's nationalities. Discrimination against and oppression of any nationality are prohibited; any acts that undermine the unity of the nationalities or instigate their secession are prohibited. The state helps the areas inhabited by minority nationalities speed up their economic and cultural development in accordance with the peculiarities and needs of the different minority nationalities. Regional autonomy is practised in areas where people of minority nationalities live in compact communities; in these areas organs of self-government are established for the exercise of the right of autonomy. All the national autonomous areas are inalienable parts of the People's Republic of China. The people of all nationalities have the freedom to use and develop their own spoken and written languages, and to preserve or reform their own ways and customs.

ARTICLE 5.

The state upholds the uniformity and dignity of the socialist legal system. No law or administrative or local rules and regulations shall contravene the constitution. All state organs, the armed forces, all political parties and public organizations and all enterprises and undertakings must abide by the Constitution and the law. All acts in violation of the Constitution and the law must be investigated. No organization or individual may enjoy the privilege of being above the Constitution and the law.

ARTICLE 6.

The basis of the socialist economic system of the People's Republic of China is socialist public ownership of the means of production, namely, ownership by the whole people and collective ownership by the working people. The system of socialist public ownership supersedes the system of exploitation of man by man; it applies the principle of 'from each according to his ability, to each according to his work.'

ARTICLE 7.

The state economy is the sector of socialist economy under ownership by the whole people; it is the leading force in the national economy. The state ensures the consolidation and growth of the state economy.

ARTICLE 8.

Rural people's communes, agricultural producers' co-operatives, and other forms of co-operative economy such as producers' supply and marketing, credit and consumers co-operatives, belong to the sector of socialist economy under collective ownership by the working people. Working people who are members of rural economic collectives have the right, within the limits prescribed by law, to farm private plots of cropland and hilly land, engage in household sideline production and raise privately owned livestock. The various forms of co-operative economy in the cities and towns, such as those in the handicraft, industrial, building, transport, commerical and service trades, all belong to the sector of socialist economy under collective ownership by the working people. The state protects the lawful rights and interests of the urban and rural economic collectives and encourages, guides and helps the growth of the collective economy.

ARTICLE 9.

Mineral resources, waters, forests, mountains, grassland, unreclaimed land, beaches and other natural resources are owned by the state, that is, by the whole people, with the exception of the forests, mountains, grassland, unreclaimed land and beaches that are owned by collectives in accordance with the law. The state ensures the rational use of natural resources and protects rare animals and plants. The appropriation or damage of natural resources by any organization or individual by whatever means is prohibited.

ARTICLE 10.

Land in the cities is owned by the state. Land in the rural and suburban areas is owned by collectives except for those portions which belong to the state in accordance with the law; house sites and private plots of cropland and hilly land are also owned by collectives. The state may in the public interest take over land for its use in accordance with the law. No organization or individual may appropriate, buy, sell or lease land, or unlawfully transfer land in other ways. All organizations and individuals who use land must make rational use of the land.

ARTICLE 11.

The individual economy of urban and rural working people, operated within the limits prescribed by law, is a complement to the socialist public economy. The state protects the lawful rights and interests of the individual economy. The state guides, helps and supervises the individual economy by exercising administrative control.

ARTICLE 12.

Socialist public property is sacred and inviolable. The state protects socialist public property. Appropriation or damage of state or collective property by any organization or individual by whatever means is prohibited.

ARTICLE 13.

The state protects the right of citizens to own lawfully earned income, savings, houses and other lawful property. The state protects by law the right of citizens to inherit private property.

ARTICLE 14.

The state continuously raises labour productivity, improves economic results and develops the productive forces by enhancing the enthusiasm of the working people, raising the level of their technical skill, disseminating advanced science and technology, improving the systems of economic administration and enterprise operation and management, instituting the socialist system of responsibility in various forms and improving organization of work. The state practises strict economy and combats waste. The state properly apportions accumulation and consumption, pays attention to the interests of the collective and the individual as well as of the state and, on the basis of expanded production, gradually improves the material and cultural life of the people.

ARTICLE 15.

The state practises economic planning on the basis of socialist public ownership. It ensures the proportionate and co-ordinated growth of the national economy through overall balancing by economic planning and the supplementary role of regulation by the market. Disturbance of the orderly functioning of the social economy or disruption of the state economic plan by any organization or individual is prohibited.

ARTICLE 16.

State enterprises have decision-making power in operation and management within the limits prescribed by law, on condition that they submit to unified leadership by the state and fulfill all their obligations under the state plan. State enterprises practise democratic management through congresses of workers and staff and in other ways in accordance with the law.

ARTICLE 17.

Collective economic organizations have decision-making power in conducting independent economic activities, on condition that they accept the guidance of the state plan and abide by the relevant laws. Collective economic organizations practise democratic management in accordance with the law, with the entire body of their workers electing or removing their managerial personnel and deciding on major issues concerning operation and management.

ARTICLE 18.

The People's Republic of China permits foreign enterprises, other foreign economic organizations and individual foreigners to invest in China and to enter into various forms of economic co-operation with Chinese enterprises and other economic organizations in accordance with the law of the People's Republic of China. All foreign enterprises and other foreign economic organizations in China, as well as joint ventures with Chinese and foreign investment located in China, shall abide by the law of the People's Republic of China. Their lawful rights and interests are protected by the law of the People's Republic of China.

ARTICLE 19.

The state develops socialist educational undertakings and works to raise the scientific and cultural level of the whole nation. The state runs schools of various types, makes primary education compulsory and universal, develops secondary, vocational and higher education and promotes pre-school education. The state develops educational facilities of various types in order to wipe out illiteracy and provide political, cultural, scientific, technical and professional education for workers, peasants, state functionaries and other working people. It encourages people to become educated through self-study. The state encourages the collective economic organizations, state enterprises and undertakings and other social forces to set up educational institutions of various types in accordance with the law. The state promotes the nationwide use of Putonghua (common speech based on Beijing pronunciation).

ARTICLE 20.

The state promotes the development of the natural and social sciences, disseminates scientific and technical knowledge, and commends and rewards achievements in scientific research as well as technological discoveries and inventions.

ARTICLE 21.

The state develops medical and health services, promotes modern medicine and traditional Chinese medicine, encourages and supports the setting up of various medical and health facilities by the rural economic collectives, state enterprises and undertakings and neighbourhood organizations, and promotes sanitation activities of a mass character, all to protect the people's health. The state develops physical culture and promotes mass sports activities to build up the people's physique.

ARTICLE 22.

The state promotes the development of literature and art, the press, broadcasting and television undertakings, publishing and distribution services, libraries, museums, cultural centres and other cultural undertakings, that serve the people and socialism, and sponsors mass cultural activities. The state protects places of scenic and historical interest, valuable cultural monuments and relics and other important items of China's historical and cultural heritage.

ARTICLE 23.

The state trains specialized personnel in all fields who serve socialism, increases the number of intellectuals and creates conditions to give full scope to their role in socialist modernization.

ARTICLE 24.

The state strengthens the building of socialist spiritual civilization through spreading education in high ideals and morality, general education and education in discipline and the legal system, and through promoting the formulation and observance of rules of conduct and common pledges by different sections of the people in urban and rural areas. The state advocates the civic virtues of love for the motherland, for the people, for labour, for science and for socialism; it educates the people in patriotism, collectivism, internationalism and communism and in dialectical and historical materialism; it combats the decadent ideas of capitalism and feudalism and other decadent ideas.

ARTICLE 25.

The state promotes family planning so that population growth may fit the plans for economic and social development.

ARTICLE 26.

The state protects and improves the living environment and the ecological environment, and prevents and controls pollution and other public hazards. The state organizes and encourages afforestation and the protection of forests.

ARTICLE 27.

All state organs carry out the principle of simple and efficient administration, the system of responsibility for work and the system of training functionaries and appraising their work in order constantly to improve quality of work and efficiency and combat bureaucratism. All state organs and functionaries must rely on the support of the people, keep in close touch with them, heed their opinions and suggestions, accept their supervision and work hard to serve them.

ARTICLE 28.

The state maintains public order and suppresses treasonable and other counter-revolutionary activities; it penalizes actions that endanger public security and disrupt the socialist economy and other criminal activities, and punishes and reforms criminals.

ARTICLE 29.

The armed forces of the People's Republic of China belong to the people. Their tasks are to strengthen national defence, resist aggression, defend the motherland, safeguard the people's peaceful labour, participate in national reconstruction, and work hard to serve the people. The state strengthens the revolutionization, modernization and regularization of the armed forces in order to increase the national defence capability.

ARTICLE 30.

The administrative division of the People's Republic of China is as follows: (1) The country is divided into provinces, autonomous regions and municipalities directly under the Central Government; (2) Provinces and autonomous regions are divided into autonomous prefectures, counties, autonomous counties and cities; (3) Counties and autonomous counties are divided into townships, nationality townships and towns. Municipalities directly under the Central Government and other large cities are divided into districts and counties. Autonomous prefectures are divided into counties, autonomous counties, and cities. All autonomous regions, autonomous prefectures and autonomous counties are national autonomous areas.

ARTICLE 31.

The state may establish special administrative regions when necessary. The systems to be instituted in special administrative regions shall be prescribed by law enacted by the National People's Congress in the light of the specific conditions.

ARTICLE 32.

The People's Republic of China protects the lawful rights and interests of foreigners within Chinese territory, and while on Chinese territory foreigners must abide by the law of the People's Republic of China. The People's Republic of China may grant asylum to foreigners who request it for political reasons.

CHAPTER II.

The Fundamental Rights and Duties of Citizens

ARTICLE 33.

All persons holding the nationality of the People's Republic of China are citizens of the People's Republic of China. All citizens of the People's Republic of China are equal before the law. Every citizen enjoys the rights and at the same time must perform the duties prescribed by the Constitution and the law.

ARTICLE 34.

All citizens of the People's Republic of China who have reached the age of 18 have the right to vote and stand for election, regardless of nationality, race, sex, occupation, family background, religious belief, education, property status, or length of residence, except persons deprived of political rights according to law.

ARTICLE 35.

Citizens of the People's Republic of China enjoy freedom of speech, of the press, of assembly, of association, of procession and of demonstration.

ARTICLE 36.

Citizens of the People's Republic of China enjoy freedom of religious belief. No state organ, public organization or individual may compel citizens to believe in, or not to believe in, any religion; nor may they discriminate against citizens who believe in, or do not believe in, any religion. The state protects normal religious activities. No one may make use of religion to engage in activities that disrupt public order, impair the health of citizens or interfere with the educational system of the state. Religious bodies and religious affairs are not subject to any foreign domination.

ARTICLE 37.

The freedom of person of citizens of the People's Republic of China is inviolable. No citizen may be arrested except with the approval or by decision of a people's procuratorate or by decision of a people's court, and arrests must be made by a public security organ. Unlawful deprivation or restriction of citizens' freedom of person by detention or other means is prohibited; and unlawful search of the person of citizens is prohibited.

ARTICLE 38.

The personal dignity of citizens of the People's Republic of China is inviolable. Insult, libel, false charge or frame-up directed against citizens by any means is prohibited.

ARTICLE 39.

The home of citizens of the People's Republic of China is inviolable. Unlawful search of, or intrusion into, a citizen's home is prohibited.

ARTICLE 40.

The freedom and privacy of correspondence of citizens of the People's Republic of China are protected by law. No organization or individual may, on any ground, infringe upon the freedom and privacy of citizens' correspondence except in cases where, to meet the needs of state security or of investigation into criminal offences, public security or procuratorial organs are permitted to censor correspondence in accordance with procedures prescribed by law.

ARTICLE 41.

Citizens of the People's Republic of China have the right to criticize and make suggestions to any state organ or functionary. Citizens have the right to make to relevant state organs complaints and charges against, or exposures of, violation of the law or dereliction of duty by any state organ or functionary; but fabrication or distortion of facts with the intention of libel or frame-up is prohibited. In case of complaints, charges or exposures made by citizens, the state organ concerned must deal with them in a responsible manner after ascertaining the facts. No one may suppress such complaints, charges and exposures, or retaliate against the citizens making them. Citizens who have suffered losses through infringement of their civil rights by any state organ or functionary have the right to compensation in accordance with the law.

ARTICLE 42.

Citizens of the People's Republic of China have the right as well as the duty to work. Using various channels, the state creates conditions for employment, strengthens labour protection, improves working conditions and, on the basis of expanded production, increases remuneration for work and social benefits. Work is the glorious duty of every able-bodied citizen. All working people in state enterprises and in urban and rural economic collectives should perform their tasks with an attitude consonant with their status as masters of the country. The state promotes socialist labour emulation, and commends and rewards model and advanced workers. The state encourages citizens to take part in voluntary labour. The state provides necessary vocational training to citizens before they are employed.

ARTICLE 43.

Working people in the People's Republic of China have the right to rest. The state expands facilities for rest and recuperation of working people, and prescribes working hours and vacations for workers and staff.

ARTICLE 44.

The state prescribes by law the system of retirement for workers and staff in enterprises and undertakings and for functionaries of organs of state. The livelihood of retired personnel is ensured by the state and society.

ARTICLE 45.

Citizens of the People's Republic of China have the right to material assistance from the state and society when they are old, ill or disabled. The state develops the social insurance, social relief and medical and health services that are required to enable citizens to enjoy this right. The state and society ensure the livelihood of disabled members of the armed forces, provide pensions to the families of martyrs and give preferential treatment to the families of military personnel. The state and society help make arrangements for the work, livelihood and education of the blind, deaf-mute and other handicapped citizens.

ARTICLE 46.

Citizens of the People's Republic of China have the duty as well as the right to receive education. The state promotes the all-round moral, intellectual and physical development of children and young people.

ARTICLE 47.

Citizens of the People's Republic of China have the freedom to engage in scientific research, literary and artistic creation and other cultural pursuits. The state encourages and assists creative endeavours conducive to the interests of the people made by citizens engaged in education, science, technology, literature, art and other cultural work.

ARTICLE 48.

Women in the People's Republic of China enjoy equal rights with men in all spheres of life, political, economic, cultural and social, and family life. The state protects the rights and interests of women, applies the principle of equal pay for equal work for men and women alike and trains and selects cadres from among women.

ARTICLE 49.

Marriage, the family, and mother and child are protected by the state. Both husband and wife have the duty to practise family planning. Parents have the duty to rear and educate their minor children, and children who have come of age have the duty to support and assist their parents. Violation of the freedom of marriage is prohibited. Maltreatment of old people, women and children is prohibited.

ARTICLE 50.

The People's Republic of China protects the legitimate rights and interests of Chinese nationals residing abroad and protects the lawful rights and interests of returned overseas Chinese and of the family members of Chinese nationals residing abroad.

ARTICLE 51.

The exercise by citizens of the People's Republic of China of their freedoms and rights may not infringe upon the interests of the state, of society and of the collective, or upon the lawful freedoms and rights of other citizens.

ARTICLE 52.

It is the duty of citizens of the People's Republic of China to safeguard the unity of the country and the unity of all its nationalities.

ARTICLE 53.

Citizens of the People's Republic of China must abide by the constitution and the law, keep state secrets, protect public property and observe labour discipline and public order and respect social ethics.

ARTICLE 54.

It is the duty of citizens of the People's Republic of China to safeguard the security, honour and interests of the motherland; they must not commit acts detrimental to the security, honour and interests of the motherland.

ARTICLE 55.

It is the sacred obligation of every citizen of the People's Republic of China to defend the motherland and resist aggression. It is the honourable duty of citizens of the People's Republic of China to perform military service and join the militia in accordance with the law.

ARTICLE 56.

It is the duty of citizens of the People's Republic of China to pay taxes in accordance with the law.

CHAPTER III.

The Structure of the State

SECTION 1. *The National People's Congress*

ARTICLE 57.

The National People's Congress of the People's Republic of China is the highest organ of state power. Its permanent body is the Standing Committee of the National People's Congress.

ARTICLE 58.

The National People's Congress and its Standing Committee exercise the legislative power of the state.

ARTICLE 59.

The National People's Congress is composed of deputies elected by the provinces, autonomous regions and municipalities directly under the Central Government, and by the armed forces. All the minority nationalities are entitled to appropriate representation. Election of deputies to the National People's Congress is conducted by the Standing Committee of the National People's Congress. The number of deputies to the National People's Congress and the manner of their election are prescribed by law.

ARTICLE 60.

The National People's Congress is elected for a term of five years. Two months before the expiration of the term of office of a National People's Congress, its Standing Committee must ensure that the election of deputies to the succeeding National People's Congress is completed. Should exceptional circumstances prevent such an election, it may be postponed by decision of a majority vote of more than two-thirds of all those on the Standing Committee of the incumbent National People's Congress, and the term of office of the incumbent National People's Congress may be extended. The election of deputies to the succeeding National People's Congress must be completed within one year after the termination of such exceptional circumstances.

ARTICLE 61.

The National People's Congress meets in session once a year and is convened by its Standing Committee. A session of the National People's Congress may be convened at any time the Standing Committee deems this necessary, or when more than one-fifth of the deputies to the National People's Congress so propose. When the National People's Congress meets, it elects a presidium to conduct its session.

ARTICLE 62.

The National People's Congress exercises the following functions and powers:

(1) To amend the Constitution;

(2) To supervise the enforcement of the Constitution;

(3) To enact and amend basic statutes concerning criminal offences, civil affairs, the state organs and other matters;

(4) To elect the President and the Vice-President of the People's Republic of China; (previously translated as Chairman and Vice-Chairman of the People's Republic of China—translator's note)

(5) To decide on the choice of the Premier of the State Council upon nomination by the President of the People's Republic of China, and to decide on the choice of the Vice-Premiers, State Councillors, Ministers in charge of Ministries or Commissions and the Auditor-General and the Secretary-General of the State Council upon nomination by the Premier;

(6) To elect the Chairman of the Central Military Commission and, upon his nomination, to decide on the choice of the other members of the Central Military Commission;

(7) To elect the President of the Supreme People's Court;

(8) To elect the Procurator-General of the Supreme People's Procuratorate;

(9) To examine and approve the plan for national economic and social development and the reports on its implementation;

(10) To examine and approve the state budget and the report on its implementation;

(11) To alter or annul inappropriate decisions of the Standing Committee of the National People's Congress;

(12) To approve the establishment of provinces, autonomous regions, and municipalities directly under the Central Government;

(13) To decide on the establishment of special administrative regions and the systems to be instituted there;

(14) To decide on questions of war and peace; and

(15) To exercise such other functions and powers as the highest organ of state power should exercise.

ARTICLE 63.

The National People's Congress has the power to recall or remove from office the following persons:

(1) The President and the Vice-President of the People's Republic of China;

(2) The Premier, Vice-Premiers, State Councillors, Ministers in charge of Ministries or Commissions and the Auditor-General and the Secretary-General of the State Council;

(3) The Chairman of the Central Military Commission and others on the commission;

(4) The President of the Supreme People's Court; and

(5) The Procurator-General of the Supreme People's Procuratorate.

ARTICLE 64.

Amendments to the Constitution are to be proposed by the Standing Committee of the National People's Congress or by more than one-fifth of the deputies to the National People's Congress and adopted by a majority vote of more than two-thirds of all the deputies to the Congress. Statutes and resolutions are adopted by a majority vote of more than one half of all the deputies to the National People's Congress.

ARTICLE 65.

The Standing Committee of the National People's Congress is composed of the following: The Chairman; The Vice-Chairmen; The Secretary-General; and Members. Minority nationalities are entitled to appropriate representation on the Standing Committee of the National People's Congress. The National People's Congress elects, and has the power to recall, all those on its Standing Committee. No one on the Standing Committee of the National People's Congress shall hold any post in any of the administrative, judicial or procuratorial organs of the state.

ARTICLE 66.

The Standing Committee of the National People's Congress is elected for the same term as the National People's Congress; it exercises its functions and powers until a new Standing Committee is elected by the succeeding National People's Congress. The Chairman and Vice-Chairmen of the Standing Committee shall serve no more than two consecutive terms.

ARTICLE 67.

The Standing Committee of the National People's Congress exercises the following functions and powers:

(1) To interpret the Constitution and supervise its enforcement;

(2) To enact and amend statutes with the exception of those which should be enacted by the National People's Congress;

(3) To enact, when the National People's Congress is not in session, partial supplements and amendments to statutes enacted by the National People's Congress provided that they do not contravene the basic principles of these statutes;

(4) To interpret statutes;

(5) To examine and approve, when the National People's Congress is not in session, partial adjustments to the plan for national economic and social development and to the state budget that prove necessary in the course of their implementation;

(6) To supervise the work of the State Council, the Central Military Commission, the Supreme People's Court and the Supreme People's Procuratorate;

(7) To annul those administrative rules and regulations, decisions or orders of the State Council that contravene the Constitution or the statutes;

(8) To annul those local regulations or decisions of the organs of state power of provinces, autonomous regions and municipalities directly under the Central Government that contravene the Constitution, the statutes or the administrative rules and regulations;

(9) To decide, when the National People's Congress is not in session, on the choice of Ministers in charge of Ministries or Commissions or the Auditor-General and the Secretary-General of the State Council upon nomination by the Premier of the State Council;

(10) To decide, upon nomination by the Chairman of the Central Military Commission, on the choice of others on the commission, when the National People's Congress is not in session;

(11) To appoint and remove the Vice-Presidents and judges of the Supreme People's Court, members of its Judicial Committee and the President of the Military Court at the suggestion of the President of the Supreme People's Court;

(12) To appoint and remove the Deputy Procurators-General and procurators of the Supreme People's Procuratorate, members of its Procuratorial Committee and the Chief Procurator of the Military Procuratorate at the request of the Procurator-General of the Supreme People's Procuratorate, and to approve the appointment and removal of the chief procurators of the people's procuratorates of provinces, autonomous regions and municipalities directly under the Central Government;

(13) To decide on the appointment and recall of plenipotentiary representatives abroad;

(14) To decide on the ratification and abrogation of treaties and important agreements concluded with foreign states;

(15) To institute systems of titles and ranks for military and diplomatic personnel and of other specific titles and ranks;

(16) To institute state medals and titles of honour and decide on their conferment;

(17) To decide on the granting of special pardons;

(18) To decide, when the National People's Congress is not in session, on the proclamation of a state of war in the event of an armed attack on the country or in fulfillment of international treaty obligations concerning common defence against aggression;

(19) To decide on general mobilization or partial mobilization;

(20) To decide on the enforcement of martial law throughout the country or in particular provinces, autonomous regions or municipalities directly under the Central Government; and

(21) To exercise such other functions and powers as the National People's Congress may assign to it.

ARTICLE 68.

The Chairman of the Standing Committee of the National People's Congress presides over the work of the Standing Committee and convenes its meetings. The Vice-Chairmen and the Secretary-General assist the Chairman in his work. Chairmanship meetings with the participation of the chairman, vice-chairmen and secretary-general handle the important day-to-day work of the Standing Committee of the National People's Congress.

ARTICLE 69.

The Standing Committee of the National People's Congress is responsible to the National People's Congress and reports on its work to the Congress.

ARTICLE 70.

The National People's Congress establishes a Nationalities Committee, a Law Committee, a Finance and Economic Committee, an Education, Science, Culture and Public Health Committee, a Foreign Affairs Committee, an Overseas Chinese Committee and such other special committees as are necessary. These special committees work under the direction of the Standing Committee of the National People's Congress when the Congress is not in session. The special committees examine, discuss and draw up relevant bills and draft resolutions under the direction of the National People's Congress and its Standing Committee.

ARTICLE 71.

The National People's Congress and its Standing Committee may, when they deem it necessary, appoint committees of inquiry into specific questions and adopt relevant resolutions in the light of their reports. All organs of state, public organizations and citizens concerned are obliged to supply the necessary information to those committees of inquiry when they conduct investigations.

ARTICLE 72.

Deputies to the National People's Congress and all those on its Standing Committee have the right, in accordance with procedures prescribed by law, to submit bills and proposals within the scope of the respective functions and powers of the National People's Congress and its Standing Committee.

ARTICLE 73.

Deputies to the National People's Congress during its sessions, and all those on its Standing Committee during its meetings, have the right to address questions, in accordance with procedures prescribed by law, to the State Council or the ministries and commissions under the State Council, which must answer the questions in a responsible manner.

ARTICLE 74.

No deputy to the National People's Congress may be arrested or placed on criminal trial without the consent of the Presidium of the current session of the National

People's Congress or, when the National People's Congress is not in session, without the consent of its Standing Committee.

ARTICLE 75.

Deputies to the National People's Congress may not be called to legal account for their speeches or votes at its meetings.

ARTICLE 76.

Deputies to the National People's Congress must play an exemplary role in abiding by the Constitution and the law and keeping state secrets and, in production and other work and their public activities, assist in the enforcement of the Constitution and the law. Deputies to the National People's Congress should maintain close contact with the units and people which elected them, listen to and convey their opinions and demands and work hard to serve them.

ARTICLE 77.

Deputies to the National People's Congress are subject to the supervision of the units which elected them. The electoral units have the power, through procedures prescribed by law, to recall the deputies whom they elected.

ARTICLE 78.

The organization and working procedures of the National People's Congress and its Standing Committee are prescribed by law.

SECTION 2. *The President of the People's Republic of China*

ARTICLE 79.

The President and Vice-President of the People's Republic of China are elected by the National People's Congress. Citizens of the People's Republic of China who have the right to vote and to stand for election and who have reached the age of 45 are eligible for election as President or Vice-President of the People's Republic of China. The term of office of the President and Vice-President of the People's Republic of China is the same as that of the National People's Congress, and they shall serve no more than two consecutive terms.

ARTICLE 80.

The President of the People's Republic of China, in pursuance of decisions of the National People's Congress and its Standing Committee, promulgates statutes; appoints and removes the Premier, Vice-Premiers, State Councillors, Ministers in charge of Ministries or Commissions, and the Auditor-General and the Secretary-General of the State Council; confers state medals and titles of honour; issues orders of special pardons; proclaims martial law; proclaims a state of war; and issues mobilization orders.

ARTICLE 81.

The President of the People's Republic of China receives foreign diplomatic representatives on behalf of the People's Republic of China and, in pursuance of decisions of the Standing Committee of the National People's Congress, appoints and recalls plenipotentiary representatives abroad, and ratifies and abrogates treaties and important agreements concluded with foreign states.

ARTICLE 82.

The Vice-President of the People's Republic of China assists the President in his work. The Vice-President of the People's Republic of China may exercise such parts of the functions and powers of the President as the President may entrust to him.

ARTICLE 83.

The President and Vice-President of the People's Republic of China exercise their functions and powers until the new President and Vice-President elected by the succeeding National People's Congress assume office.

ARTICLE 84.

In case the office of the President of the People's Republic of China falls vacant, the Vice-President succeeds to the office of President. In case the office of the Vice-President of the People's Republic of China falls vacant, the National People's Congress shall elect a new Vice-President to fill the vacancy. In the event that the offices of both the President and the Vice-President of the People's Republic of China fall vacant, the National People's Congress shall elect a new President and a new Vice-President. Prior to such election, the Chairman of the Standing Committee of the National People's Congress shall temporarily act as the President of the People's Republic of China.

SECTION 3. *The State Council*

ARTICLE 85.

The State Council, that is, the Central People's Government of the People's Republic of China, is the executive body of the highest organ of state power; it is the highest organ of state administration.

ARTICLE 86.

The State Council is composed of the following: The Premier; The Vice-Premiers; The State Councillors; The Ministers in charge of Ministries; the Ministries in charge of Commissions; The Auditor-General; and The Secretary-General. The Premier has overall responsibility for the State Council. The Ministers have overall responsibility for the respective ministries or commissions under their charge. The organization of the State Council is prescribed by law.

ARTICLE 87.

The term of office of the State Council is the same as that of the National People's Congress. The Premier, Vice-Premiers and State Councillors shall serve no more than two consecutive terms.

ARTICLE 88.

The Premier directs the work of the State Council. The Vice-Premiers and State Councillors assist the Premier in his work. Executive meetings of the State Council are composed of the Premier, the Vice-Premiers, the State Councillors and the Secretary-General of the State Council. The Premier convenes and presides over the executive meetings and plenary meetings of the State Council.

ARTICLE 89.

The State Council exercises the following functions and powers: (1) To adopt administrative measures, enact administrative rules and regulations and issue decisions and orders in accordance with the Constitution and the statutes; (2) To submit proposals to the National People's Congress or its Standing Committee; (3) To lay down the tasks and responsibilities of the ministries and commissions of the State Council, to exercise unified leadership over the work of the ministries and commissions and to direct all other administrative work of a national character that does not fall within the jurisdiction of the ministries and commissions; (4) To exercise unified leadership over the work of local organs of state administration at different levels throughout the country, and to lay down the detailed division of functions and powers between the Central Government and the organs of state administration of provinces, autonomous regions and municipalities directly under the Central Government; (5) To draw up and implement the plan for national economic and social development and the state budget; (6) To direct and administer economic work and urban and rural development; (7) To direct and administer the work concerning education, science, culture, public health, physical culture and family planning; (8) To direct and administer the work concerning civil affairs, public security, judicial administration, supervision and other related matters; (9) To conduct foreign affairs and conclude treaties and agreements with foreign states; (10) To direct and administer the building of national defence; (11) To direct and administer affairs concerning the nationalities and to safeguard the equal rights of minority nationalities and the right of autonomy of the national autonomous areas; (12) To protect the legitimate rights and interests of Chinese nationals residing abroad and protect the lawful rights and interests of returned overseas Chinese and of the family members of Chinese nationals residing abroad; (13) To alter or annul inappropriate orders, directives and regulations issued by the ministries or commissions; (14) To alter or annul inappropriate decisions and orders issued by local organs of state administration at different levels; (15) To approve the geographic division of provinces, autonomous regions and municipalities directly under the Central Government, and to approve the establishment and geographic division of autonomous prefectures, counties, autonomous counties and cities; (16) To decide on the enforcement of martial law in parts of provinces, autonomous regions and municipalities directly under the Central Government; (17) To examine and decide on the size of administrative organs and, in accordance with the law, to appoint, remove and train administrative officers, appraise their work and reward or punish them; and (18) To exercise such other functions and powers as the National People's Congress or its Standing Committee may assign it.

ARTICLE 90.

The ministers in charge of ministries or commissions of the State Council are responsible for the work of their respective departments and convene and preside over their ministerial meetings or commission meetings that discuss and decide on major issues in the work of their respective departments. The ministries and commissions issue orders, directives and regulations within the jurisdiction of their respective departments and in accordance with the statutes and the administrative rules and regulations, decisions and orders issued by the State Council.

ARTICLE 91.

The State Council establishes an auditing body to supervise through auditing the revenue and expenditure of all departments under the State Council and of the local governments at different levels, and those of the state financial and monetary organizations and of enterprises and undertakings. Under the direction of the Premier of the State Council, the auditing body independently exercises its power to supervise through auditing in accordance with the law, subject to no interference by any other administrative organ or any public organization or individual.

ARTICLE 92.

The State Council is responsible, and reports on its work, to the National People's Congress or, when the National People's Congress is not in session, to its Standing Committee.

Section 4. *The Central Military Commission*

ARTICLE 93.

The Central Military Commission of the People's Republic of China directs the armed forces of the country. The Central Military Commission is composed of the following: The Chairman; The Vice-Chairmen; and Members. The Chairman of the Central Military Commission has overall responsibility for the commission. The term of office of the Central Military Commission is the same as that of the National People's Congress.

ARTICLE 94.

The Chairman of the Central Military Commission is responsible to the National People's Congress and its Standing Committee.

Section 5. *The Local People's Congress and the Local People's Governments at Different Levels*

ARTICLE 95.

People's congresses and people's governments are established in provinces, municipalities directly under the Central Government, counties, cities, municipal districts, townships, nationality townships and towns. The organization of local people's congresses and local people's governments at different levels is prescribed by law. Organs of self-government are established in autonomous regions, autonomous prefectures and autonomous counties. The organization and working procedures of organs of self-government are prescribed by law in accordance with the basic principles laid down in Sections V and VI of Chapter Three of the Constitution.

ARTICLE 96.

Local people's congresses at different levels are local organs of state power. Local people's congresses at and above the county level establish standing committees.

ARTICLE 97.

Deputies to the people's congresses of provinces, municipalities directly under the Central Government, and cities divided into districts are elected by the people's congresses at the next lower level; deputies to the people's congresses of counties, cities not divided into districts, municipal districts, townships, nationality townships and towns are elected directly by their constituencies. The number of deputies to local people's congresses at different levels and the manner of their election are prescribed by law.

ARTICLE 98.

The term of office of the people's congresses of provinces, municipalities directly under the Central Government and cities divided into districts is five years. The term of office of the people's congresses of counties, cities not divided into districts, municipal districts, townships, nationality townships and towns is three years.

ARTICLE 99.

Local people's congresses at different levels ensure the observance and implementation of the Constitution, the statutes and the administrative rules and regulations in their respective administrative areas. Within the limits of their authority as prescribed by law, they adopt and issue resolutions and examine and decide on plans for local economic and cultural development and for development of public services. Local people's congresses at and above the county level examine and approve the plans for economic and social development and the budgets of their respective administrative areas, and examine and approve reports on their implementation. They have the power to alter or annul inappropriate decisions of their own standing committees. The people's congresses of nationality townships may, within the limits of their authority as prescribed by law, take specific measures suited to the peculiarities of the nationalities concerned.

ARTICLE 100.

The people's congresses of provinces and municipalities directly under the Central Government, and their standing committees, may adopt local regulations, which must not contravene the Constitution, the statutes and the administrative rules and regulations, and they shall report such local regulations to the Standing Committee of the National People's Congress for the record.

ARTICLE 101.

At their respective levels, local people's congresses elect, and have the power to recall, governors and deputy governors, or mayors and deputy mayors, or heads and deputy heads of counties, districts, townships and towns. Local people's congresses at and above the county level elect, and have the power to recall, presidents of people's courts and chief procurators of people's procuratorates at the corresponding level. The election or recall of chief procurators of people's procuratorates shall be reported to the chief procurators of the people's procuratorates at the next higher level for submission to the standing committees of the people's congresses at the corresponding level for approval.

ARTICLE 102.

Deputies to the people's congresses of provinces, municipalities, directly under the Central Government and cities divided into districts are subject to supervision by the units which elected them; deputies to the people's congresses of counties, cities not divided into districts, municipal districts, townships, nationality townships and towns are subject to supervision by their constituencies. The electoral units and constituencies which elect deputies to local people's congresses at different levels have the power, according to procedures prescribed by law, to recall deputies whom they elected.

ARTICLE 103.

The standing committee of a local people's congress at and above the county level is composed of a chairman, vice-chairmen and members, and is responsible, and reports on its work, to the people's congress at the corresponding level. The local people's congress at and above the county level elects, and has the power to recall, anyone on the standing committee of the people's congress at the corresponding level. No one on the standing committee of a local people's congress at and above the county level shall hold any post in state administrative, judicial and procuratorial organs.

ARTICLE 104.

The standing committee of a local people's congress at and above the county level discusses and decides on major issues in all fields of work in its administrative area; supervises the work of the people's government, people's court and people's procuratorate at the corresponding level; annuls inappropriate decisions and orders of the people's government at the corresponding level; annuls inappropriate resolutions of the people's congress at the next lower level; decides on the appointment and removal of functionaries of state organs within its jurisdiction as prescribed by law; and, when the people's congress at the corresponding level is not in session, recalls individual deputies to the people's congress at the next higher level and elects individual deputies to fill vacancies in that people's congress.

ARTICLE 105.

Local people's governments at different levels are the executive bodies of local organs of state power as well as the local organs of state administration at the corresponding level. Local people's governments at different levels practise the system of overall responsibility by governors, mayors, county heads, district heads, township heads and town heads.

ARTICLE 106.

The term of office of local people's governments at different levels is the same as that of the people's congresses at the corresponding level.

ARTICLE 107.

Local people's governments at and the above the county level, within the limits of their authority as prescribed by law, conduct the administrative work concerning the economy, education, science, culture, public health, physical culture, urban and rural development, finance, civil affairs, public security, nationalities affairs, judicial administration, supervision and family planning in their respective administrative areas; issue decisions and orders; appoint, remove and train administrative functionaries, appraise their work and reward or punish them. People's governments of townships, nationality townships and towns carry out the resolutions of the people's congress at the corresponding level as well as the decisions and orders of the state administrative organs at the next higher level and conduct administrative work in their respective administrative areas. People's governments of provinces and municipalities directly under the Central Government decide on the establishment and geographic division of townships, nationality townships and towns.

ARTICLE 108.

Local people's governments at and above the county level direct the work of their subordinate departments and of people's governments at lower levels, and have the power to alter or annul inappropriate decisions of their subordinate departments and people's governments at lower levels.

ARTICLE 109.

Auditing bodies are established by local people's governments at and above the county level. Local auditing bodies at different levels independently exercise their power to supervise through auditing in accordance with the law and are responsible to the people's government at the corresponding level and to the auditing body at the next higher level.

ARTICLE 110.

Local people's governments at different levels are responsible, and report on their work, to people's congresses at the corresponding level. Local people's governments at and above the county level are responsible, and report on their work, to the standing committee of the people's congress at the corresponding level when the congress is not in session. Local people's governments at different levels are responsible, and report on their work, to the state administrative organs at the next higher level. Local people's governments at different levels throughout the country are state administrative organs under the unified leadership of the State Council and are subordinate to it.

ARTICLE 111.

The residents' committees and villagers' committees established among urban and rural residents on the basis of their place of residence are mass organizations of self-management at the grass-roots level. The chairman, vice-chairmen and members of each residents' or villagers' committee are elected by the residents. The relationship between the residents' and villagers' committees and the grass-roots organs of state power is prescribed by law. The residents' and villagers' committees establish committees for people's mediation, public security, public health and other matters in order to manage public affairs and social services in their areas, mediate civil disputes, help maintain public order and convey residents' opinions and demands and make suggestions to the people's government.

SECTION 6. *The Organs of Self-Government of National Autonomous Areas*

ARTICLE 112.

The organs of self-government of national autonomous areas are the people's congresses and people's governments of autonomous regions, autonomous prefectures and autonomous counties.

ARTICLE 113.

In the people's congress of an autonomous region, prefecture or country, in addition to the deputies of the nationality or nationalities exercising regional autonomy in the administrative area, the other nationalities inhabiting the area are also entitled to appropriate representation. The chairmanship and vice-chairmenships of the standing committee of the people's congress of an autonomous region, prefecture or county shall include a citizen or citizens of the nationality or nationalities exercising regional autonomy in the area concerned.

ARTICLE 114.

The administrative head of an autonomous region, prefecture or county shall be a citizen of the nationality, or of one of the nationalities, exercising regional autonomy in the area concerned.

ARTICLE 115.

The organs of self-government of autonomous regions, prefectures and counties exercise the functions and powers of local organs of state as specified in Section V of Chapter Three of the Constitution. At the same time, they exercise the right of autonomy within the limits of their authority as prescribed by the Constitution, the law of regional national autonomy and other laws, and implement the laws and policies of the state in the light of the existing local situation.

ARTICLE 116.

People's congresses of national autonomous areas have the power to enact autonomy regulations and specific regulations in the light of the political, economic and cultural characteristics of the nationality or nationalities in the areas concerned. The autonomy regulations and specific regulations of autonomous regions shall be submitted to the Standing Committee of the National People's Congress for approval before they go into effect. Those of autonomous prefectures and counties shall be submitted to the standing committees of the people's congresses of provinces or autonomous regions for approval before they go into effect, and they shall be reported to the Standing Committee of the National People's Congress for the record.

ARTICLE 117.

The organs of self-government of the national autonomous areas have the power of autonomy in administering the finances of their areas. All revenues accruing to the national autonomous areas under the financial system of the state shall be managed and used independently by the organs of self-government of those areas.

ARTICLE 118.

The organs of self-government of the national autonomous areas independently arrange for and administer local economic development under the guidance of state plans. In developing natural resources and building enterprises in the national autonomous areas, the state shall give due consideration to the interests of those areas.

ARTICLE 119.

The organs of self-government of the national autonomous areas independently administer educational, scientific, cultural, public health and physical culture affairs in their respective areas, sort out and protect the cultural legacy of the nationalities and work for the development and prosperity of their cultures.

ARTICLE 120.

The organs of self-government of the national autonomous areas may, in accordance with the military system of the state and concrete local needs and with the approval of the State Council, organize local public security forces for the maintenance of public order.

ARTICLE 121.

In performing their functions, the organs of self-government of the national autonomous areas, in accordance with the autonomy regulations of the respective areas, employ the spoken and written language or languages in common use in the locality.

ARTICLE 122.

The state gives financial, material and technical assistance to the minority nationalities to accelerate their economic and cultural development. The state helps the national autonomous areas train large numbers of cadres at different levels and specialized personnel and skilled workers of different professions and trades from among the nationality or nationalities in those areas.

SECTION 7. *The People's Court and the People's Procuratorates*

ARTICLE 123.

The people's courts in the People's Republic of China are the judicial organs of the state.

ARTICLE 124.

The People's Republic of China establishes the Supreme People's Court and the local people's courts at different levels, military courts and other special people's courts. The term of office of the President of the Supreme People's Court is the same as that of the National People's Congress; he shall serve no more than two consecutive terms. The organization of people's courts is prescribed by law.

ARTICLE 125.

All cases handled by the people's courts, except for those involving special circumstances as specified by law, shall be heard in public. The accused has the right of defence.

ARTICLE 126.

The people's courts shall, in accordance with the law, exercise judicial power independently and are not subject to interference by administrative organs, public organizations or individuals.

ARTICLE 127.

The Supreme People's Court is the highest judicial organ. The Supreme People's Court supervises the administration of justice by the local people's courts at different levels and by the special people's courts; people's courts at higher levels supervise the administration of justice by those at lower levels.

ARTICLE 128.

The Supreme People's Court is responsible to the National People's Congress and its Standing Committee. Local people's courts at different levels are responsible to the organs of state power which created them.

ARTICLE 129.

The people's procuratorates of the People's Republic of China are state organs for legal supervision.

ARTICLE 130.

The People's Republic of China establishes the Supreme People's Procuratorate and the local people's procuratorates at different levels, military procuratorates and other special people's procuratorates. The term of office of the Procurator-General of the Supreme People's Procuratorate is the same as that of the National People's Congress; he shall serve no more than two consecutive terms. The organization of people's procuratorates is prescribed by law.

ARTICLE 131.

People's procuratorates shall, in accordance with the law, exercise procuratorial power independently and are not subject to interference by administrative organs, public organizations or individuals.

ARTICLE 132.

The Supreme People's Procuratorate is the highest procuratorial organ. The Supreme People's Procuratorate directs the work of the local people's procuratorates at different levels and of the special people's procuratorates; people's procuratorates at higher levels direct the work of those at lower levels.

ARTICLE 133.

The Supreme People's Procuratorate is responsible to the National People's Congress and its Standing Committee. Local people's procuratorates at different levels are responsible to the organs of state power at the corresponding levels which created them and to the people's procuratorates at the higher level.

ARTICLE 134.

Citizens of all nationalities have the right to use the spoken and written languages of their own nationalities in court proceedings. The people's courts and people's procuratorates should provide translation for any party to the court proceedings who is not familiar with the spoken or written languages in common use in the locality. In an area where people of a minority nationality live in a compact community or where a number of nationalities live together, hearings should be conducted in the language or languages in common use in the locality; indictments, judgments, notices and other documents should be written, according to actual needs, in the language or languages in common use in the locality.

ARTICLE 135.

The people's courts, people's procuratorates and public security organs shall, in handling criminal cases, divide their functions, each taking responsibility for its own work, and they shall co-ordinate their efforts and check each other to ensure correct and effective enforcement of law.

CHAPTER IV.
The National Flag, the National Emblem and the Capital

ARTICLE 136.

The national flag of the People's Republic of China is a red flag with five stars.

ARTICLE 137.

The national emblem of the People's Republic of China is Tian'anmen in the centre illuminated by five stars and encircled by ears of grain and a cogwheel.

ARTICLE 138.

The capital of the People's Republic of China is Beijing.

Amendments to the Constitution

AMENDMENT ONE
Approved on April 12, 1988, by the Seventh NPC at its 1st Session

1. Article 11 of the Constitution shall include a new paragraph which reads: "The State permits the private sector of the economy to exist and develop within the limits prescribed by law. The private sector of the economy is a complement to the socialist public economy. The State protects the lawful rights and interests of the private sector of the economy, and exercises guidance, supervision and control over the private sector of the economy."

2. The fourth paragraph of Article 10 of the Constitution, which provides that "no organization or individual may appropriate, buy, sell or lease land or otherwise engage in the transfer of land by unlawful means," shall be amended as: "no organization or individual may appropriate, buy, sell or otherwise engage in the transfer of land by unlawful means. The right to the use of land may be transferred according to law."

AMENDMENT TWO
Approved on March 29, 1993, by the Eighth NPC at its 1st Session

3. The last two sentences of the seventh paragraph of the Preamble which reads "The basic task of the nation in the years to come is to concentrate its effort on socialist modernization. Under the leadership of the Communist Party of China and the guidance of

Marxism-Leninism and Mao Zedong Thought, the Chinese people of all nationalities will continue to adhere to the people's democratic dictatorship and follow the socialist road, steadily improve socialist institutions, develop socialist democracy, improve the socialist legal system and work hard and self-reliantly to modernize industry, agriculture, national defense and science and technology step by step to turn China into a socialist country with a high level of culture and democracy," shall be amended as: "China is at the primary stage of socialism. The basic task of the nation is, according to the theory of building socialism with Chinese characteristics, to concentrate its effort on socialist modernization. Under the leadership of the Communist Party of China and the guidance of Marxism-Leninism and Mao Zedong Thought, the Chinese people of all nationalities will continue to adhere to the people's democratic dictatorship and follow the socialist road, persevere in reform and opening to the outside, steadily improve socialist institutions, develop socialist democracy, improve the socialist legal system and work hard and self-reliantly to modernize industry, agriculture, national defense and science and technology step by step to turn China into a socialist country with prosperity and power, democracy and culture."

4. At the end of the tenth paragraph of the Preamble, add "The system of multi-party cooperation and political consultation led by the Communist Party of China will exist and develop in China for a long time to come."

5. Article 7 which reads "The State economy is the sector of socialist economy under ownership by the whole people; it is the leading force in the national economy. The State ensures the consolidation and growth of the State economy," shall be changed to: "The State-owned economy, that is, the socialist economy under ownership by the whole people, is the leading force in the national economy. The State ensures the consolidation and growth of the State-owned economy."

6. The first item of Article 8 which reads "Rural people's communes, agricultural producers' cooperatives, and other forms of cooperative economy such as producers', supply and marketing, credit and consumers' cooperatives, belong to the sector of socialist economy under collective ownership by the working people. Working people who are members of rural economic collectives have the right, within the limits prescribed by law, to farm plots of cropland and hilly land allotted for private use, engage in household sideline production and raise privately-owned [sic] livestock," shall be amended as: "Rural household-based contract responsibility system with remuneration linked to output, and other forms of cooperative economy such as producers', supply and marketing, credit and consumers' cooperatives, belong to the sector of socialist economy under collective ownership by the working people. Working people who are members of rural economic collectives have the right, within the limits prescribed by law, to farm plots of cropland and hilly land allotted for private use, engage in household sideline production and raise privately-owned livestock."

7. Article 15 which reads "The State practices economic planning on the basis of socialist public ownership. It ensures the proportionate and coordinated growth of the national economy through overall balancing by economic planning and the supplementary role of regulation by the market.

Disturbance of the orderly functioning of the social economy or disruption of the State economic plan by any organization or individual is prohibited," shall be changed to: "The state has put into practice a socialist market economy. The State strengthens formulating economic laws, improves macro adjustment and control and forbids according to law any units or individuals from interfering with the social economic order."

8. Article 16 which reads "State enterprises have decision-making power in operation and management within the limits prescribed by law, on condition that they submit to unified leadership by the State and fulfil their obligations under the State plan. State enterprises practice democratic management through congresses of workers and staff and in other ways in accordance with the law," shall be revised as: "Stated-owned enterprises have decision-making power in operation and management within the limits prescribed by law. State-owned enterprises practise democratic management through congresses of workers and staff and in other ways in accordance with the law."

9. Article 17 which reads "Collective economic organizations have decision-making power in conducting independent economic activities, on condition that they accept the guidance of the State plan and abide by the relevant laws.

Collective economic organizations practice democratic management in accordance with the law, with the entire body of their workers electing or removing their managerial personnel and deciding on major issues concerning operation and management," shall be amended as: "Collective economic organizations have decision-making power in conducting independent economic activities, on condition that they abide by the relevant laws. Collective economic organizations practice democratic management, elect or remove their managerial personnel and decide on major issue concerning operation and management according to law."

10. The item of Article 42 which reads "Work is the glorious duty of every able-bodied citizen. All working people in State enterprises and in urban and rural economic collectives should perform their tasks with an attitude consonant with their status as masters of the country. The State promotes socialist labor emulation, and commends and rewards model and advanced workers. The state encourages citizens to take part in voluntary labor," shall be amended as: "Work is the glorious duty of every able-bodied citizen. All working people in State-owned enterprises and in urban and rural economic collectives should perform their tasks with an attitude consonant with their status as masters of the country. The State promotes socialist labor emulation, and commends and rewards model and advanced workers. The State encourages citizens to take part in voluntary labor."

11. Article 98 which reads "The term of office of the people's congresses of provinces, municipalities directly under the Central Government and cities divided into districts is five years. The term of office of the people's congresses of countries, cities not divided into districts, municipal districts, townships, nationality townships and towns is three years," shall be revised as: "The term of office of the people's congresses of provinces, municipalities directly under the Central Government, counties, cities and municipal districts is five years. The term of office of the people's congresses of townships, nationality townships and towns is three years."

AMENDMENT THREE
Approved on March 15, 1999, by the Ninth NPC at its 2nd Session

The original text of paragraph seven in the Preamble of the Constitution is: "Both the victory of China's new-democratic revolution and the successes of its socialist cause have been achieved by the Chinese people of all nationalities under the leadership of the Communist Party of China and the guidance of Marxism-Leninism and Mao Zedong Thought, and by upholding truth, correcting errors and overcoming numerous difficulties and hardships. China is currently in the primary stage of socialism. The basic task of the nation is to concentrate its effort on socialist modernization in accordance with the theory of building socialism with Chinese characteristics. Under the leadership of the Communist Party of China and the guidance of Marxism-Leninism and Mao Zedong Thought, the Chinese people of all nationalities will continue to adhere to the people's democratic dictatorship, follow the socialist road, persist in reform and opening-up [sic], steadily improve socialist institutions, develop socialist democracy, improve the socialist legal system and work hard and self-reliantly to modernize industry, agriculture, national defense and science and technology step by step to turn China into a powerful and prosperous socialist country with a high level of culture and democracy."

It is revised into: "Both the victory of China's new-democratic revolution and the successes of its socialist cause have been achieved by the Chinese people of all nationalities under the leadership of the Communist Party of China and the guidance of Marxism-Leninism and Mao Zedong Thought, and by upholding truth, correcting errors and overcoming numerous difficulties and hardships. China will stay in the primary stage of socialism for a long period of time. The basic task of the nation is to concentrate its efforts on socialist modernization by following the road of building socialism with Chinese characteristics. Under the leadership of the Communist Party of China and the guidance of Marxism-Leninism, Mao Zedong Thought and Deng Xiaoping Theory, the Chinese people of all nationalities will continue to adhere to the people's democratic dictatorship, follow the socialist road, persist in reform and opening-up, steadily improve socialist institutions, develop a socialist market economy, advance socialist democracy, improve the socialist legal system and work hard and self-reliantly to modernize industry, agriculture, national defense and science and technology step by step to turn China into a powerful and prosperous socialist country with a high level of culture and democracy." One section is added to Article Five of the Constitution as the first section: "The People's Republic of China practices ruling the country in accordance with the law and building a socialist country of law."

The original text of Article Six of the Constitution is: "The basis of the socialist economic system of the People's Republic of China is socialist public ownership of the means of production, namely, ownership by the whole people and collective ownership by the working people." "The system of socialist public ownership supersedes the system of exploitation of man by man; it applies the principle of 'from each according to his ability, to each according to his work'."

It is revised into: "The basis of the socialist economic system of the People's Republic of China is socialist public ownership of the means of production, namely, ownership by the whole people and collective ownership by the working people. The system of socialist public ownership supersedes the system of exploitation of man by man; it applies the principle of 'from each according to his ability, to each according to his work'." "During the primary stage of socialism, the State adheres to the basic economic system with the public ownership remaining dominant and diverse sectors of the economy developing side by side, and to the distribution system with the distribution according to work remaining dominant and the coexistence of a variety of modes of distribution."

The original text of the first section in Article Eight of the Constitution is: "The rural household-based output-related contracted responsibility system and other forms of the cooperative economy such as producers', supply and marketing, credit and consumers' cooperatives belong to the sector of the socialist economy under collective ownership by the working people. Working people who are members of rural economic collectives have the right, within the limits prescribed by law, to farm plots of cropland and hilly land allotted for private use, engage in household sideline production and raise privately owned livestock."

It is revised into: "Rural collective economic organizations practice the double-tier management system that combines unified and separate operations on the basis of the household-based output-related contracted responsibility system. Various forms of the cooperative economy in rural areas such as producers', supply and marketing, credit and consumers' cooperatives belong to the sector of the socialist economy under collective ownership by the working people.

Working people who are members of rural economic collectives have the right, within the limits prescribed by law, to farm plots of cropland and hilly land allotted for private use, engage in household sideline production and raise privately owned livestock."

The original text of Article 11 of the Constitution is: "The individual economy of urban and rural working people, operating within the limits prescribed by law, is a complement to the socialist public economy. The State protects the lawful rights and interests of the individual economy." "The State guides, helps and supervises the individual economy by exercising administrative control." "The State permits the private economy to exist and develop within the limits prescribed by law. The private economy is a complement to the socialist public economy. The State protects the lawful rights and interests of the private economy, and guides, supervises and administers the private economy."

It is revised into: "Individual, private and other non-public economies that exist within the limits prescribed by law are major components of the socialist market economy." "The State protects the lawful rights and interests of individual and private economies, and guides, supervises and administers individual and private economies."

The original text of Article 28 of the Constitution is: "The State maintains public order and suppresses treasonable and other counter-revolutionary activities; it penalizes actions that endanger public security and disrupt the socialist economy and other criminal activities, and punishes and reforms criminals."

It is revised into: "The State maintains public order and suppresses treasonable and other criminal activities that endanger State security; it penalizes actions that endanger public security and disrupt the socialist economy and other criminal activities, and punishes and reforms criminals." (Update in 1999)

Notes

PREFACE

1. "Blue" because of the color of the clothing most Chinese of the time wore.

CHAPTER 1

1. For example, attitudes and mores of American society in the early seventeenth century as portrayed by Wood (1991), chap. 1, paralleled to a remarkable extent those of Chinese society of the same period.

2. Quoted from the "Debate on Salt and Iron," as excerpted in Ebrey (1981), pp. 24–25.

3. Siu (1990).

4. Cf. Unger (1996); Tu (1991).

5. Translation from Cranmer-Byng (1962), pp. 338–40. The most complete examination of the Macartney mission is in Peyrefitte (1992).

6. Hymes (1966) tries to determine the actual mobility into the elite through careful study of Fu-chou in the Sung dynasty. He demonstrates that there was somewhat less upward mobility than is commonly asserted.

7. Watson (1988).

8. Link (1992).

9. The only female ruler in Chinese history was the empress Wu Zetian (r. 690–705).

10. Fairbank (1953); Fairbank (1968).

11. Peyrefitte (1992) conveys the practical consequences of this in vivid detail.

12. Rawski, (1996); Fletcher, "Ch'ing Inner Asia;" Fletcher, "The Heyday of the Ch'ing Order."

13. Whitney (1970). Addition information on Manchu governance of the Qing is available in: Crossley (1997); Elliott (2001); and Rawski (1998).

14. Waldron (1989).

15. An extraordinary sense of the life and times of Qin Shi Huangdi is provided in a novel: Levi (1985). Western punishments of that era were equally cruel.

16. See, for example, Balazs (1964).

17. Johnston (1996).

18. See, for example, Wright (1964). Bartlett (1991) uses a different definition of "inner" and "outer" court.

19. Two books highlight different views on this issue during the Qing dynasty. Bartlett (1991) argues that the administrative system carved out substantial independence from the emperor's control; Kuhn (1990) argues in favor of more unbounded imperial power.

20. Morse (1966) presents both the formal system and its warts.

21. This practice, called the *xiangyue* system, is described in Hsiao (1960).

22. On government administration, see Ch'u (1969).

23. Naquin and Rawski (1987).

24. Naquin and Rawski (1987).

25. On the gentry, see Ch'u (1969), chap. 10, and Ho (1962).

26. Ho (1962).

27. Wolf contribution to Wolf and Witke (1975).

28. Fried (1953).

29. See, for example, Melby (1968), the Chinese civil war memoir of an American diplomat.

30. Nathan (1985).

31. Rowe (1984); Rowe (1989).

32. See, e.g., the travel accounts as late as the 1920s of Franck (1923).

33. Detailed in Naquin and Rawski (1987).

34. Elvin (1973).

35. The two key studies in this debate are Kang (1986) and Perkins (1969).

36. These questions are reviewed and evaluated in Little (1989).

37. Skinner (1964–65); Skinner (1977).

38. Actually, eight fully formed regions and one, the northeast, that was only partially in evidence. By the period of the PRC, the ninth region is also fully formed.

39. Naquin and Rawski (1987) describe the distinctive traits of each of these macroregions during the late Qing.

40. For the scholar, the major difficulty is that the historical data available are presented in terms of administrative boundaries, and for most issues it is extremely difficult to reconstitute all information according to the boundaries of regional systems. Whitney (1970) provides additional information both on revenue sources and on reasonable ways of dividing China into distinctive regions.

41. Naquin and Rawski (1987).

42. Skinner has developed his argument in a series of publications. The one most pertinent to this point is Skinner (1977), pp. 275–352.

43. Shue (1988); Balazs (1964).

44. Balazs (1964).

45. Wittfogel (1957).

46. Tong (1991).

47. Naquin and Rawski (1987), p. 25.

48. Hummel (1967).

49. For a fascinating self-portrait of this great figure, see Spence (1974).

50. Perry (1980).

51. Michael (1966–71); Chu (1966); Jen (1973).

52. More broadly on this, see Kuhn (1970).

53. Wright (1966).

54. Kennedy (1987); Barraclough (1967).

55. These products included opium, imported primarily by the British, who grew it in

Bengal, India, and shipped it to China to earn money to pay for tea, silks, and other items destined for the British market. By 1820 annual opium shipments to China totaled about ten thousand chests (one chest contained 133 pounds of opium). The figure grew to forty thousand chests by 1838 and fifty to sixty thousand by 1860.

56. This cycle is detailed in Teng and Fairbank (1963).

57. In reality, even the types of concessions made at the conclusion of the Opium War largely mirrored those made in 1835 to the Kokand Khanate in Inner Asia: Fletcher, "The Heyday of the Ch'ing Order."

58. Classic studies of this dynamic include Fairbank (1953) and Teng and Fairbank (1963).

59. Smith (1978).

60. Teng and Fairbank (1963).

61. A magisterial treatment that carries the story forward well into the twentieth century is given by Wang (1966).

62. Fairbank (1953); Murphey (1970).

63. Beasley (1972); Beckmann (1962); Fairbank, Reischauer, and Craig (1973); Lockwood (1954).

64. Oksenberg and Goldstein (1974); Lieberthal chapter in Harding (1984).

65. Lieberthal (1977).

66. See the discussions of this in Wright (1966), Eastman (1974), and Dirlik (1975).

67. Cf. Kuo essay in Fairbank and Liu (1978).

68. Hao essay in Twitchett and Fairbank (1978); Hsiao (1975); Kwong (1984).

69. Tan (1955).

70. For a wide-ranging, excellent series of essays on this reform decade, see Wright (1968).

71. Young (1977).

CHAPTER 2

1. Young (1977).

2. Gillin (1967).

3. Chi (1969); Pye (1971); Sutton (1980).

4. Wang (1966).

5. Young (1977).

6. Wang (1966).

7. Spence (1981); Witke chapter in Young (1973).

8. Chow (1960) presents a magisterial treatment of this movement.

9. North (1952).

10. Chu (1992); Tine (1989); Dickson (1997); Dickson and Chao (2002).

11. Schiffrin (1970).

12. Schwartz (1964).

13. Harrison (1972).

14. Eastman (1974).

15. A vivid dramatization is provided by Malraux (1934). Differing analytical frameworks are provided in Isaacs (1938) and Schwartz (1964).

16. For differing interpretations of this period, see Wilbur (1984) and Isaacs (1938).

17. Wakeman (2003) provides fascinating details on one of the key figures in this effort.

18. Young (1977). On the anticommunist terror and the CCP's counterefforts, see Byron and Pack (1992).

19. Bergere in Howe (1981); Lieberthal (1980).

20. Eastman (1974).

21. Some held on in the cities until 1932–33, and a very few remained after that. Byron and Pack (1992) provide a vivid description of the increasingly difficult threat those in Shanghai faced.

22. Pu Yi (1979).

23. One of the most important resulting developments was the student-led December Ninth movement in 1936: Klein (1976).

24. Byron and Pack (1992) attribute the CCP's stance to pressures from Moscow, where Stalin was worried about Japanese advances on the Asian mainland.

25. Chi (1982).

26. Tuchman (1970).

27. Vivid portrayals are provided in the accounts of two eyewitnesses: Fairbank (1982); and T. H. White (1978).

28. Details are provided in Whitson (1973).

29. Lieberthal (1980).

30. On the politics of this period, see Pepper (1978). See also Tien (1972) and Bianco (1971).

31. There are numerous histories of the Chinese communist movement before 1949. Two of the more complete are Harrison (1972) and Guillermaz (1972).

32. Bennett (1976).

33. Skocpol (1979) emphasizes this central idea.

34. On Peng Pai, another key figure, see Hofheinz (1977).

35. See, for example, Schram (1963) and Schram (1966).

36. Mao (1965a), pp. 24, 28 (quotation changes sequence of sentences in the original).

37. Schwartz (1964) and Isaacs (1938) give differing assessments, with Isaacs feeling that the CCP would have been wise to break with the GMD and form its own organs of power before April 1927.

38. Urban uprisings, encouraged by Moscow, continued into 1930. All of them failed.

39. Erbaugh (1992) analyzes the role of the Hakka minority in the Chinese communist movement.

40. Byron and Pack (1992).

41. Kim chapter in Barnett (1969).

42. A detailed explanation of the communists' 1950 land-reform law that embodies these distinctions is provided in *Renmin shouce* (1951), pp. *ch'en* 32–43.

43. Belden (1949) provides first-hand accounts of these types of efforts in the 1940s.

44. Details are provided in Van Slyke (1967).

45. Mao, vol. 2, pp. 79–194.

46. Erbaugh (1992).

47. Salisbury (1985) provides a detailed and vivid account of the rigors of the Long March.

48. Barnett (1967) discusses the special status of the Long March cadres.

49. Snow (1961), pp. 215–16. See also Salisbury (1985), among many sources on the Long March.

50. Braun's Chinese name was Li De.

51. Byron and Pack (1992) provide information on Wang's stay in Moscow and his initial efforts once he returned to China.

52. Both sides of this equation are presented in Peck (1967).

53. Van Slyke (1967).

54. The final straw was a GMD attack on Communist New Fourth Army forces that had penetrated south of the Yangtze River: Harrison (1972).

55. Belden (1949); Selden (1971); Van Slyke (1968).

56. Lifton (1961).

57. Belden (1949) describes life in several of these base areas.

58. Selden (1971).

59. Byron and Pack (1992) and Vladimirov (1975) provide good details.

60. Levine (1987) details developments in this region from 1945 to 1948.

61. Pepper (1978).

62. Lieberthal (1980).

63. Lieberthal (1971).

64. E.g., Guillermaz (1972).

65. Pepper (1978) provides detailed information on the "third force" possibilities.

66. See, e.g., Solinger (1977).

67. The author has heard this statement made by various high-ranking PRC officials.

68. A. Goldstein (1991); Teiwes (1990).

69. Teiwes (1990).

CHAPTER 3

1. Anarchism, though, had been an early influence on the communist movement: Dirlik (1991).

2. See, e.g., MacFarquhar, Cheek, and Wu (1989).

3. Li (1994).

4. Bernstein (1984); Becker (1996).

5. Lieberthal (1971).

6. Lardy and Lieberthal (1983).

7. Bennett (1976) provides a systematic overview of this phenomenon.

8. Schram (1966).

9. Siu (1990).

10. *Mao Zedong sixiang wan sui!* (1969), p. 195.

11. Van Slyke (1967).

12. Van Slyke (1968).

13. Pepper (1978).

14. Coble (1980).

15. For this reason, sources for the information provided in this brief description generally are given in Chapters 6 and 7, rather than here.

16. The Politburo elected in November 2002 is unusual in having nine members of its Standing Committee.

17. Wu (1992).

CHAPTER 4

1. A. Goldstein (1991).

2. Teiwes (1990) makes this case in detail with respect to the first major purge of top officials after 1949: the 1953–54 Gao Gang–Rao Shushi affair.

3. Central work conferences are detailed in Chang (1970) and Lieberthal and Dickson (1989).

4. Mao (1977).

5. Text of this speech is in Mao, vol. 3 (1965), pp. 361–75.

6. Riskin (1987).

7. On Sino-Soviet relations see Barnett (1977), Clubb (1971), and Dittmer (1992); on Mao's trip see Goncharov, Lewis, and Xue (1993).

8. Cohen (1990).

9. On the Korean War and Sino–U.S. relations, see *inter alia:* Chen (2001); Cohen (1990); Gaddis (1978); Grasso (1987); Hoyt (1990); Hunt (1987); Hunt (1992); Kalicki (1975); Stueck (1981); Zhang (1992); and Goncharov, Lewis, and Xue (1993).

10. Whiting (1960); Goncharov, Lewis, and Xue (1993).

11. Barnett (1964); Lieberthal (1980).

12. Teiwes chapter in MacFarquhar and Fairbank (1987), reprinted in MacFarquhar (1993).

13. Friedman, Pickowicz, and Selden (1991).

14. Friedman, Pickowicz, and Selden (1991); Schurmann (1971).

15. Lieberthal (1980).

16. Lieberthal (1980); Montell (1954); Barnett (1964); Teiwes in MacFarquhar (1993); Teiwes (1979).

17. Lieberthal (1980).

18. Wu (1993); on thought reform during these early post-1949 years more generally, see Lifton (1961).

19. Borisov and Koloskov (1975); Naughton chapter in Lieberthal and Lampton (1992); Perkins (1966). The Naughton essay explains the enormous importance of the technology transfers involved in this Soviet aid program. On the economic planning system in China, see Lyons (1987).

20. Shue (1980).

21. Yeh chapter in Treadgold (1967).

22. Teiwes chapter in MacFarquhar and Fairbank (1987), reprinted in MacFarquhar (1993); Schurmann (1971).

23. Li (1994); Salisbury (1992).

24. Teiwes chapter in MacFarquhar (1993).

25. For details of this process in the southwest, see Solinger (1977).

26. The definitive study to date is Teiwes (1990).

27. On field armies and their relations to civilian politics, see Whitson with Huang (1973), Whitson (1973), and Swaine (1992).

28. Oksenberg (1974).

29. The most complete analysis of this tension is Lee (1991).

30. On the reasons for launching the Great Leap, see Lieberthal chapter in MacFarquhar and Fairbank (1987), reprinted in MacFarquhar (1993); and MacFarquhar (1983).

31. Text in Mao (1977).

32. The text of Khrushchev's speech is available in Khrushchev (1970), pp. 559–618.

33. The second session met in May 1958. This is the only CCP Congress to have met in two sessions.

34. The officially released version of this speech is in Mao (1977).

35. MacFarquhar (1974).

36. For examples in various units, see Chang (1991), Wu (1993), and Yue and Wakeman (1985).

37. Their experience in the camps, from which many of the survivors did not emerge until 1979, is typified by Wu (1993).

38. Donnithorne (1967); Lardy (1978); Schurmann (1971).

39. Schurmann (1971).

40. *Mao Zedong sixiang wan sui!* (1969).

41. Joffe (1971).

42. L. T. White III (1978) details this phenomenon in Shanghai.

43. Skinner (1965).

44. There are numerous accounts of the Lushan conference and plenum. See, e.g., MacFarquhar (1983), Li (1989), and Domes (1985).

45. See the plenum communiqué in Bowie and Fairbank (1962), pp. 533–35.

46. Becker (1996).

47. America suffered about three thousand deaths from terrorism on September 11, 2001.

48. Numerous writings describe and analyze the Great Leap Forward. See, e.g., Bachman (1991), Lieberthal chapter in MacFarquhar (1993), MacFarquhar (1983), and Solomon (1971).

49. Walder (1986) analyzes the resulting situation in the urban state enterprises.

50. Specifically, Mao engaged in polemics with Moscow via letters exchanged by the respective central committees that China published. The texts of these are available in Griffith (1967).

51. Naughton (1988).

52. Baum and Teiwes (1968).

53. Lewis and Xue (1988) provide the best available account of China's development of the atomic bomb.

54. Lee (1991).

55. Harding (1981); Joffe (1971).

56. See, e.g., Harding in MacFarquhar and Fairbank (1991), reprinted in MacFarquhar (1993).

57. Kang's control over the civilian security forces is suggested in Byron and Pack (1992).

58. Andrew Walder examines this policy and its effects within the factory in Walder (1986).

59. Lampton (1977).

60. Nelsen (1981).

61. See, e.g., Yue and Wakeman (1985), and Chang (1991).

62. Salisbury (1992), among other sources.

63. Chinese and foreign scholars have never fully been able to explain the extent to which Mao was able to provoke sadistic violence among the population. One of the more serious attempts at explanation is in White (1989). See also Thurston (1988).

64. Dittmer (1974).

65. Numerous accounts by former Red Guards detail the horrors they inflicted. See, e.g., Liang and Shapiro (1983), Yue and Wakeman (1985), Chang (1991), and Thurston (1991).

66. Text available in *Chinese Communist Party Documents* (1968), pp. 33–54.

67. Chang (1970); Lieberthal and Dickson (1989).

68. Walder (1978).

69. Bernstein (1977).

70. Gottlieb (1977); Lieberthal (1978).

71. Text of the 1969 Party Constitution is available in *Peking Review,* 30 April 1969, pp. 36–39.

72. For details, see Naughton chapter in Lieberthal et al. (1991).

73. Nelsen (1981).

74. There are numerous accounts of the Cultural Revolution in various localities and schools. For details of developments at Peking University, see Yue and Wakeman (1985); for Qinhua University, see Hinton (1972); for the high-school level, see Bennett and Montaperto (1972).

75. Bernstein (1977).

76. Whitson and Huang (1973).

77. MacFarquhar chapter in MacFarquhar and Fairbank (1991), reprinted in MacFarquhar (1993).

78. There is no certainty about the actual events leading to Lin's demise. The view presented here is the official Beijing version, but it may not be accurate. See MacFarquhar chapter in MacFarquhar (1993).

79. Detailed in Li (1994).

80. MacFarquhar provides a good overview in his chapter in MacFarquhar (1993).

81. Lieberthal (1977).

82. MacFarquhar chapter in MacFarquhar (1993).

83. Harding (1993); Solomon (1981).

84. On Mao's tactics, see Oksenberg chapter in Wilson (1977); on Mao's dealings with those in Group One (as his personal office was designated), see Li (1994).

85. For systematic analysis of this issue, see Harding (1981).

86. For various thoughts about the encapsulation of peasant society, see Oi (1989), Shue (1988), and Siu (1989).

87. Walder (1986).

88. The first eight categories referred to negative class labels such as landlords and rightists.

CHAPTER 5

1. Oksenberg and Yeung (1977).

2. On this period, see MacFarquhar chapter in MacFarquhar (1993), Garside (1981), Lieberthal (1978), and Fingar (1980).

3. Lampton, *Paths to Power*, focused on Ji and Chen as possible successors to Mao.

4. Text of the communiqué announcing these appointments is in *FBIS* [Foreign Broadcast Information Service], 22 August 1977, pp. D2–10.

5. Sources provided in Lieberthal and Dickson (1989), p. 246.

6. In March 1978 Deng also assumed his former government post as a vice premier of the State Council.

7. Text of Hua's speech is available in *FBIS*, 22 August 1977, pp. D11–46.

8. This, for example, occurred in rural policy during the shift from people's communes to family farming in 1979–84: Kelliher (1992).

9. Bonavia (1989); Franz (1988).

10. The major sources for Deng's political tactics from 1977 through the 1980s are Harding (1987), Hamrin (1990), MacFarquhar chapter in MacFarquhar (1993), Baum (1993), and Fewsmith (1994).

11. Ruan (1994); Schoenhals (1991).

12. Yang Zhong Mei (1988).

13. Ho and Hueneman (1984).

14. Pepper (1990).

15. Text of Hua's proposal is in *Peking Review*, 7 March 1978, pp. D1–38.

16. Yang Zhong Mei (1988).

17. Seymour (1980).

18. The "communiqué" of the plenum is available in *Peking Review*, 9 December 1978, pp. 6–16.

19. The positions cited are the major ones held before their respective purges.

20. The full text of Wei's declaration is available in Seymour (1980), pp. 47–69.

21. Wei was eventually paroled in late 1993, just six months shy of serving his full sentence. He did not change his views while in prison, and his outspoken comments after his release led to his rearrest in early 1994. China released him again and exiled him to the United States in 1997.

22. Bachman (1985); Lardy and Lieberthal (1983).

23. Ruan (1994) provides an insider's account of the politics of this period.

24. Yang Zhong Mei (1988) provides a political biography of Hu.

25. For graphic details, see Chang (1991).

26. Shambaugh (1984) provides a political biography of Zhao.

27. Fewsmith (1994).

28. On the retrenchment policy in the urban sector, see Solinger (1991).

29. See Shirk (1993).

30. Toffler (1980).

31. The reform effort is analyzed in terms of policy cycles in Baum (1993) and Hamrin (1990). Fewsmith (1994) views the oscillations in the reforms more as a function of the struggle for power at the top of the system, given the rules of the game there.

32. A voluminous literature exists on the Tiananmen demonstrations and their aftermath. Perhaps the best documentary collection in English on this movement and its background is Oksenberg, Sullivan, and Lambert (1990).

33. For three interesting interpretations of this dynamic, see Manion's Introduction in Oksenberg, Sullivan, and Lambert (1990); Pye (1990); and Esherick and Wasserstrom (1990).

34. Manion's Introduction to Oksenberg, Sullivan, and Lambert (1990).

35. Representative documents are in Oksenberg, Sullivan, and Lambert (1990).

36. Nathan and Link (2001) provides purported transcripts of key leadership meetings from throughout this crisis.

37. Text of Deng's remarks appear in Oksenberg, Sullivan, and Lambert (1990), pp. 376–82.

38. Baum (1993) provides information on Deng's "southern journey" and its aftermath through mid-1993.

39. Because the political history of the Deng era is detailed in Baum (1993), Hamrin (1990), Harding (1987), and Fewsmith (1994) and is summed up above, the specific political events of this period are not footnoted in this section.

40. Halpern chapter in Lieberthal and Lampton (1992).

41. Oksenberg, Sullivan, and Lambert (1990).

42. Nathan and Link (2001).

43. Nathan and Gilley (2002) provide details.

44. Qiao resigned to conform to the new retirement norm; Jiang (who was already seventy) promised to step down from the Politburo after one final five-year term.

45. Li (2001).

46. Nathan and Gilley (2002).

47. Li (2001).

48. Manion (1993) presents the most comprehensive analysis of the 1980s efforts to retire revolutionary cadres. See also the Manion chapter in Lieberthal and Lampton (1992).

49. Chinese figures in different sources on the number of "state and party cadres," the number of "leading officials," and the number of "people in leading bodies" seem to vary by large numbers. Very likely, there are definitional issues at play that are produc-

ing these seemingly large variances, but the net result is that gross statistics are difficult to compare across different studies.

50. Burns (1989).

51. Cui and Wang (n.d.). This volume, published on the mainland, provides no date and no place of publication. It also, like virtually all such volumes published in China, provides no information on the method used to generate the numbers.

52. Cui and Wang (n.d.), p. 25.

53. Cui and Wang (n.d.), p. 24.

54. Yang (1991).

55. Liu (1991), p. 31.

56. Detailed in Li (2001).

57. Li (2002) provides data to support this point.

58. Li and White (1991); White and Li (1990); Li (2002).

CHAPTER 6

1. Related in Salisbury (1992).

2. Two very good analyses of the Stalinist system are in Bialer (1980) and Fainsod (1965).

3. Specifically, as of the end of 2000 China had 50,769 administrative units of "township" rank, but 5,902 of these were urban street organizations: *Xingzheng* (2001).

4. The boundaries of at least some of the units at all levels below the Center have changed at various times since 1949.

5. All known meetings through 1986 of the national bodies discussed in this chapter are detailed in Lieberthal and Dickson (1989).

6. This body is also called the Military Commission in some sources. On this commission, see Nelsen (1981), Swaine (1992), and Shambaugh (2002).

7. Name changed to "Information" in 1998.

8. Li (1993).

9. Tanner in Potter (1993); Tanner (1994).

10. Lubman (1999); Peereomboom (2002).

11. On Discipline Inspection until the Cultural Revolution, see Schurmann (1971); on the situation under Deng, see Sullivan (1984).

12. Lieberthal and Oksenberg (1988).

13. Reductions of about 50 percent at the provincial level and 20 percent at the city, county, and township levels were also completed by the end of 2002. In most cases above the county level, however, nearly all individuals who lost their jobs in the streamlining effort were placed in other positions and thus did not lose their livelihoods. Chan and Drewry (2001) provides an overview of this process at the Center. See also Brodsgaard (2002).

14. Specifically, Chongqing has a population of 30,900,000 and encompasses eighteen counties and four municipalities with county rank, among other bodies. Sichuan after the loss of Chongqing has a population of 83,290,000: *Xingzheng* (2001). Beijing made this change in order to achieve better coordination of the many activities connected with construction of the mammoth Three Gorges dam, whose reservoir at its comple-

tion in 2009 will run for more than three hundred miles from near the eastern boundary of Sichuan to Chongqing city itself.

15. *Xingzheng* (2001).

16. Teiwes (1979).

17. Liaoning province as of 2002, for example, was testing a pension system that, if successful, would be utilized elsewhere.

18. Kim (2002) provides details.

19. Some of the results are analyzed in: Cheung, Chung, and Lin (1998).

20. The exception is Anhui. The other six are: Sichuan-Chongqing, Jiangxi, Hunan, Hubei, Henan, and Guangxi.

21. *Zhongguo nongye* (2002), Charts 9 and 12.

22. Brodsgaard (2002).

23. *Xingzheng* (2001).

24. Ibid.

25. *Zongguo nongye* (2002), Chart 2.

26. On "residents committees," see Townsend.

27. Walder (1986).

28. Lieberthal and Oksenberg (1988). This was less the case in the countryside, where the village head played a key broker role between the village and the higher levels of the commune organization: Oi (1989); Shue (1988); Friedman, Pickowicz, and Selden (1991).

29. The "floating" population refers to rural migrants to cities who lack permanent urban residence rights. See Solinger, "China's Urban Transients," and Solinger, "The Chinese Work Unit."

30. As of 2000, a total of 90.12 million people had moved from the countryside to cities and towns. An additional 30.95 million had moved within the countryside. Web site of the State Statistical Bureau, September 10, 2002.

31. Lu and Perry (1997) provide a good overview of the history of the *danwei* system and its recent changes.

32. Xinhuashe, July 29, 2002 (in Chinese) reports that China has formed 10,000 community committees in cities across the land that employ a total of 50,000 cadres on the state payroll, 36,000 full-time and 57,000 part-time service staff, and 540,000 volunteers. It also notes a parallel development of community-level party organizations.

33. Lieberthal chapter in Lieberthal and Lampton (1992).

34. Lieberthal and Oksenberg (1988).

35. Shirk chapter in Lieberthal and Lampton (1992).

36. The official position on Mao's "mistakes" is contained in the "Resolution on Certain Questions in the History of Our Party . . ." adopted in June 1981: "Resolution on Certain Questions . . ." (1981).

37. Schell (1984).

38. Watson chapter in Lieberthal et al. (1991).

39. Wong (1991).

40. Chongqing Municipality, as noted earlier, was split off from Sichuan province in order to provide an administrative unit that could in a focused way cope with the

forced migration attendant upon the construction of the Three Gorges dam. The municipality was given administrative control over almost all of eastern Sichuan province and also gained the bureaucratic rank of a province.

41. For the history of the negotiations over this dam project, see Lieberthal and Oksenberg (1988).

42. Salisbury (1992).

43. Bernstein (1984).

44. Even in the late 1950s, roughly 70 percent of the Chinese Communist party members were illiterate: Dickson (1994).

45. On central work conferences, see Chang (1970) and Lieberthal and Dickson (1989).

46. Partial documentation is in MacFarquhar, Cheek, and Wu (1989).

47. Lieberthal (1978); Wu (1970).

48. Lee (1991).

49. Huang (1996).

50. Halpern chapter in Lieberthal and Lampton (1992).

51. Jacobson and Oksenberg (1990).

52. Halpern chapter in Lieberthal and Lampton (1992).

53. Gill and Mulvenon (2002); Glaser and Saunders (2002); Shambaugh, "China's International Relations Think Tanks."

54. Lynch; Li Xiaoping (2002).

55. Liu Binyan, who was one of China's best known investigative reporters, provides details on this dynamic in Liu (1992).

56. Harding (1981).

57. Sullivan (1984).

58. That is, more than $180 billion per year: Hu Angang (2002).

59. Lieberthal and Oksenberg (1988).

60. Economy (2003).

61. A substantial literature addresses this question in various ways. See, for example, Whyte (1992), Pye (1991), Perry (1994), Zha (1996), Unger and Chan (1995), Shue (1994), and Neville (1996).

62. Tanner and Green (2002).

63. Oksenberg and Tong (1991); Kim (2002).

64. Kim (2002). This is presented in detail in Chapter 8.

65. *Caijing* (2002).

CHAPTER 7

1. A massive literature discusses various aspects of the Qing governing structure and practice. See Morse (1966) for an interesting description of the dynamics of the overall Qing governmental system.

2. This conceptualization comes from Lieberthal and Oksenberg (1988).

3. Mao, for example, attacked Bo Yibo early in the Cultural Revolution in part by criticizing how much meat Bo's family consumed during the famine of the early 1960s.

4. Mao (1977).

5. Li (1994) provides numerous examples of this attitude.

6. Li (1994).

7. Salisbury (1992).

8. Salisbury (1992).

9. Li (1994) provides a powerful, detailed description of Mao in his last days.

10. Chen Yun, Li Xiannian, and Bo Yibo had worked primarily in economic policy making; Peng Zhen had headed the Beijing municipal party apparatus and, more important, had held the top post in the "political and legal system" (described in the text below), which coordinated work in the civilian coercive bureaucracies such as the police, court system, and prison labor system; Wang Zhen's ties were primarily to the military.

11. Hamrin chapter in Lieberthal and Lampton (1992) provides an insightful analysis of the dynamics of appointments in the top power elite.

12. Pye (1980).

13. Fewsmith (1994), Fewsmith (2001).

14. Discussion of the *mishu* system is based on Li and Pye (1992) and numerous interviews on the topic with Chinese officials.

15. Mao's tolerance of even these individuals had its limits, though. He became disillusioned with Tian Jiaying and persecuted him. Tian committed suicide early in the Cultural Revolution.

16. Li (1994) provides the best available overview of the security system for China's leaders.

17. The first edition of this book described (on pp. 192–194) a third element, the *kou*, at the very peak of the political system. Interviews suggest that this terminology fell out of favor in the mid-1990s, reflecting the evolution of the system toward greater decentralization and institutionalization. The *kou* originally embodied the notion that one top leader assumed centralized control of each major functional part of the political system. By the late 1990s, the leadership felt this terminology resonated too much with the personalized politics of the more revolutionary phase of the Chinese system.

18. The most extensive available analysis of the "leadership small group" structure is the Hamrin chapter in Lieberthal and Lampton (1992). This section draws from Hamrin and from interviews the author has conducted with Chinese officials.

19. This is the official translation for an office whose Chinese name is Zhongyang jigou bianzhi weiyuanhui.

20. Luo is a "state councilor," which carries the same rank as a vice premier.

21. Barnett first introduced Western scholars to the notion of the *xitong*. As Barnett notes, Chinese officials use this term in two ways: to refer to a group of functionally related bureaucracies (e.g., the "finance and economics *xitong*"); and to refer to the bureaucratic hierarchy under one ministry or commission (e.g., the "information ministry *xitong*"): Barnett (1967). The discussion here refers only to the former use of the term.

22. *Xingzheng* (2001), p. 1. The county level figure includes 1,503 counties, 116 autonomous counties, 49 banners, 3 autonomous banners, 2 special districts, one forestry district, and 787 county level districts of higher level cities. The township level figure includes 20,312 *zhen*, 23,199 *xiang*, and 1356 national minority *xiang*.

23. Mao Zedong as Chairman of the CCP stood above the party. Deng Xiaoping did

not take on the general secretary role after Mao died, preferring to put others on the front line of managing the CCP itself.

24. Interviews indicate that the CCP governing bureaucracy lost about 20 percent of the positions in its roster during the effort to reduce the size of the governing apparatus in 1998–2002. This target was not announced publicly, and no breakdown of the alleged 20 percent reduction is available.

25. Barnett (1967) provides details of the personnel dossier system. White (1989) analyzes the tensions this system engendered.

26. The Chinese term for nomenklatura is *zhiwu mingcheng biao,* "job title list."

27. Lynch (1999).

28. Whyte (1974) provides background on these.

29. Paine chapter in Lieberthal and Lampton (1992); Pepper (1990).

30. Xinhuashe (in Chinese), August 22, 2002.

31. Fainsod (1965).

32. Tanner chapter in Mulvenon (2002).

33. Cohen (1968).

34. Schurmann (1971).

35. The most complete description of the Chinese gulag is in Wu (1992).

36. Wu (1992). One analyst estimates that 3.5 million had been detained over the years in the reform through labor system (where a citizen can be held for up to four years on the basis of an administrative decision without benefit of trial), with about three hundred thousand detainees in this system as of 2002: Hung (2002).

37. See, e.g., Bao (1973).

38. Wang Ruowang (1991) provides a graphic account of the fate of a leading Shanghai official arrested by the Public Security Bureau.

39. Byron and Pack (1992).

40. *Zhonghua Renmin Gongheguo sheng . . .* (1989).

41. Chan and Drewry (2001).

42. Good analyses of various dimensions of the military system and its connections with the civilian apparatus include Joffe (1971), Joffe (1987), Nelson (1981), Shambaugh (2002), Swaine (1992), Whitson (1973), and Whitson with Huang (1973).

43. This conceptualization is explored in the Pollack chapter in Lieberthal and Lampton (1992).

44. The fullest statement of this argument is Whitson with Huang (1973).

45. Swaine (1992) carries the analysis up to the early 1990s, detailing the changes in the field armies and their role in the system under the reforms.

46. Nelsen (1981).

47. The number of military regions has varied from thirteen before the Cultural Revolution to eleven in the 1970s and early 1980s, to seven since the mid-1980s.

48. Shambaugh (2002).

49. Barnett (1967).

50. The five hundred thousand figure is from Brodsgaard (2002).

51. This story is traced in the Hamrin chapter in Lieberthal and Lampton (1992).

52. Hamrin and Zhao (1995) provides details.

53. Burns (1987); Burns, *The CCP Nomenklatura System*; Burns (1994).

54. Burns (1994).

55. A key exception is, of course, the economic elites who are emerging in the rapidly growing private sector.

56. Lieberthal and Oksenberg (1988).

57. Lieberthal chapter in Lieberthal and Lampton (1992).

58. Barnett provides an extensive description of "Party life" in Barnett (1967); see also Townsend (1969).

CHAPTER 8

1. State Statistical Bureau (1991), p. 277.

2. Lynch (1999).

3. Oi (1994); Whiting (2001).

4. Lardy (1983), Zhou (1996), Zweig (1997).

5. Ash (1992).

6. O'Brien and Li chapter in Goldman and MacFarquhar (1999); Choate (1997); O'Brien and Li (2000).

7. Pei (2002).

8. Donnithorne (1967).

9. Oksenberg and Tong (1991); Wong (1991); World Bank, *Revenue Mobilization*; Kim (2002).

10. The most thorough overview of the forces shaping the evolution of the fiscal system under the reforms is Kim (2002).

11. Maruya (1992). With Guangdong as with other provinces, the financial relationship was more complex than the tax arrangement alone reveals. Beijing also gave Guangdong extraordinary policy concessions to enable it to attract foreign investment, primarily from Hong Kong. This contributed greatly to Guangdong's roughly 20 percent annual economic growth. Beijing also, though, forced Guangdong to purchase central government bonds that it then did not redeem, amounting to imposing a non-tax tax on the province. And Beijing manipulated the financial flows of the largest SOEs in the province, further affecting the real resources available to the province, as opposed to the Center.

12. Oksenberg and Tong (1991).

13. World Bank Transition Economics Division (December 1993), p. 7.

14. Wong (1991).

15. World Bank Transition Economics Division (December 1993), p. 7.

16. On interprovincial financial transfers via the Center under the reforms, see Sehrt (1999).

17. He and Heuneman (1984).

18. Lardy, *Foreign Trade*; Lardy (2002); Pearson (1991).

19. Accurate Taiwan figures are not available, but especially since 1999 Taiwan investment in the mainland has been massive.

20. Lardy (2002).

21. Naughton (1996).

22. Naughton (1990).

23. World Bank (1990a).

24. Xinhuashe (in Chinese), August 25, 2002.

25. Lieberthal and Oksenberg (1988).

26. Naughton (1996)

27. Liu Ping (2001).

28. Donnithorne (1967).

29. Sehrt (1999)

30. Yang (2002).

31. Solinger (1996) provides a good example. See also Shirk (1994).

32. OECD (2002).

33. *Guoji* (2002).

34. *Jinan* (2002).

35. "Completely indigenous Chinese firms" means firms that are not foreign-invested and are not producing on foreign license. Only a very few such firms, such as Haier in white goods, Huawei in telecoms, Konka in TVs, and Galantz in microwave ovens have become internationally competitive on a basis other than cheap labor.

36. Growth accelerated to 8 percent in 2002.

37. Lardy (2002) provides an excellent overview and analysis.

38. Lardy (2002).

CHAPTER 9

1. Vaclav Smil provides an overview of the parlous state of China's environment in Smil (1993).

2. Hertsgaard.

3. World Bank (1997).

4. World Bank (1991).

5. Biers (1994).

6. World Bank (1997).

7. Kyng (2003).

8. Smil (1997).

9. Cannon and Jenkins (1990).

10. Yi (1989) and World Bank (1997).

11. Luk and Whitney (1993); Lieberthal and Oksenberg (1988).

12. Nuclear power is not discussed here because it does not depend on natural resource distribution. China has a very modest civilian nuclear power effort, with one plant at Daya Bay in Guangdong and another near Shanghai. China has no plans to make nuclear power a major component of its energy system. This distinguishes the PRC from Japan, South Korea, and Taiwan, all of which make extensive use of nuclear power.

13. World Bank (1985) and World Bank (1997).

14. World Bank (1997).

15. Shapiro (2001) provides a wide-ranging exposition of the environmental consequences of the Maoist era.

16. Yeh chapter in Treadgold (1967).

17. The Halpern chapter in Lieberthal and Lampton (1992) discusses the externality issue. See also Donnithorne (1967). This is a well-known phenomenon in socialist economic systems.

18. Personal communication from the foreign expert to the author.

19. *New York Times*, 19 July 1994; Ross (1988); "Scientists Warn of Resource Shortages" (1992); "New Strategy for Environmental Protection" (1988).

20. Ross (1980).

21. Smil (1993); Turner (2002).

22. See Ross chapter in Oksenberg and Economy (1999). This played a role in raising environmental consciousness in the USSR in the 1980s: Economy (1994).

23. Jahiel (1994).

24. Turner (2002).

25. Some analysts are anticipating the number of vehicles on China's roads to increase from 12 million in 1997 to 49 million in 2010. Turner (2002).

26. Personal observation by the author.

27. "Environment and Development" (1992); Jahiel (1994); Ross (1988); Smil (1993).

28. Qu and Li (1990).

29. Jahiel (1994); Ross (1987); Ross (1988).

30. Turner (2002).

31. Jahiel (1994) provides a detailed analysis of the fee system and its consequences.

32. Jahiel (1994).

33. Lieberthal and Oksenberg (1988).

34. Qu and Li (1990).

35. This is true even in very water-short areas of North China: Smil (1993).

36. Jahiel (1994) provides examples.

37. D. Li (1993).

38. World Bank (2001).

39. This formed a major plank of the opposition to the North American Free Trade Agreement and later to globalization itself in the 1990s.

40. Smil (1993).

41. Turner (2002).

42. Kyng (2003).

43. Economy (2004).

CHAPTER 10

1. See, for example Friedman, Pickowicz, and Selden (1991), Oi (1989), Shue (1988), and Siu (1989).

2. Townsend (1969) provides details.

3. See the exchange between Walder and Womack: Walder (1991) and Womack (1991) (quotation in text is from Womack, p. 314) for a discussion of this issue in state enterprises. The discussion grows out of Walder (1986).

4. E.g., Perry (1993).

5. The Cheek chapter in Wasserstrom and Perry (1992) uses the notion of traditional intellectuals as priests.

6. Mao, vol. 3 (1965), pp. 69–98.

7. Kyng (2003); Siu (1990) presents a nuanced treatment of the changing role of intellectuals from the imperial era to the present in her introductory essay.

8. See, e.g., Wu (1993).

9. Liang and Shapiro (1983).

10. For an extensive treatment of this and related issues, see Thurston (1988).

11. E.g., Pye (1980), Pye (1988), and Pye (1992); Solomon (1971). Nathan (1993) questions the empirical validity of such statements about the distinctiveness of China's political culture.

12. For example, when in 1976 the author visited the site of the first Chinese Communist Party Congress in Shanghai, he offered to provide a copy of a master's thesis written about that Congress by Chen Gongbo, who had been in attendance and later went to Columbia University. The exhibit guide responded curtly that Chen had become a renegade and therefore that his writings were of no historical interest.

13. The most striking example is the 1974 campaign to "criticize Lin Biao and Confucius," during which many younger Chinese learned about the rudiments of Confucian teachings.

14. Link (1992) provides a subtle, sensitive explication of this phenomenon.

15. One intellectual commented to the author in 1980, "I can forgive the communists anything else, but I can never forgive them for making my children despise intellectuals."

16. White (1989); Barnett (1967).

17. These examples are obtained from interviews.

18. Goodman chapter in Goldman and MacFarquhar (1999).

19. *Financial Times* (December 28, 2002).

20. Feuchtwang chapter in Perry and Seldon (2000).

21. Schechter (2001).

22. "New Qigong Film" (1991); Lou and Huang (1990); Cui (1989); "Qigong—Popularity Is Rising" (1988).

23. The Shue chapter in Migdad, Kohli, and Shue (1994) examines this in several rural locations. See also: Economy (2003).

24. Kaye (1993); "Hong Kong: Secret Societies Rampant . . ." (1992); "Wang Zhen Decries Loss of Party Influence" (1991); Cheung (1990); "Nanjing Paper . . ." (1987); "Threat from Secret Societies . . ." (1986).

25. Solinger (1999); Lee (2002).

26. Lee (2002). See also Lee chapter in Perry and Selden (2000).

27. Based on author's interviews with participants in the meeting.

28. Interview with the author.

29. Background details are provided in the Solinger chapter in Rosenbaum (1992).

30. Leung (1993).

31. The incident in Jilin came to the attention of higher officials and then received local publicity. Based on the author's interview of a foreign visitor who read the local press reporting on this incident. Numerous other examples of such petty despotism can be found in: Perry and Selden (2000); and Shambaugh (2000).

32. On the Organic Law and its implementation, see O'Brien (1994); Lawrence (1994); O'Brien and Li chapter in Goldman and MacFarquhar (1999); Coate (1997); Manion (1997). Rozelle (1994) details how extensive the authority of government officials remains in many Chinese villages.

33. O'Brien and Li (1995); C. K. Lee (2002).

34. Madsen (1993); Solinger (1993); Zhou (1993); Perry (1993); Rosenbaum (1992); Wasserstrom and Perry (1992); Wakeman (1993); Rowe (1993); Shen (1992); McCormick, Su, and Xiao (1992), among others.

35. Lubman (1999).

36. Unger and Chan (1995); White, Howell, and Shang (1996).

37. The Solinger chapter in Rosenbaum (1992) explores this interaction regarding the state and merchants in a nuanced way. See also the contributions to Perry and Selden (2000) and Goldman and MacFarquhar (1999).

38. Huang (1993).

39. China differed from most third-world countries in that it had a strong state and a weak society: Migdal (1988). On the application of this idea to Maoist China, see Kelliher (1992).

40. Li Peilin (2003) provides basic data.

41. Li Peilin (2003).

42. Peerenboom (2002).

43. Inglehart, Basanez, and Moreno (1998).

44. Lubman (1999).

45. Pei chapter in Perry and Selden (2000); Peerenboom (2002).

46. Peerenboom (2002).

47. Tanner (2002). Wu (1992); Seymour and Anderson (1998). Reform through education can be extended for a fourth year.

48. Nathan (1985).

49. Lubman (1999).

50. Cohen (1965).

51. On the issue of class in Maoist China, see Kraus (1981).

52. Li Cheng (2001).

53. Khan et al. (1992); Khan and Riskin (2001).

54. Khan and Riskin (2002).

55. Khan et al. (1992); Khan and Riskin (2001).

56. Khan et al. (1992), pp. 1041–42.

57. Khan et al. (1992); Khan and Riskin (2001).

58. Khan and Riskin (2001).

59. Khan et al. (1992).

60. For an excellent treatment of the impact of the rural reforms on women, see the Kelkar chapter in Agarwal (1988).

61. During the Cultural Revolution, this brigade became a widely heralded model of the spirit of hard struggle and self-reliance, due to its success in springing back from natural disaster without relying on government assistance. Salisbury (1992) provides behind-the-scenes information on the politics of the Dazhai model.

62. Good sources on the position of women under the Chinese communists during the Maoist era include: Andors (1983); Johnson (1983); and Davin's chapter in Afshar (1991).

63. See Bauer et al. (1992).

64. Kahn and Riskin (2001).

65. "Symposium on Rural Family Change" (1992); Judd (1990); Bridges (1991); Kahn and Riskin (2001).

66. On the birth-control program, see Zhang (1992); Yang and Zhang (1992); Peng (1990).

67. Norman (1993); "Slaughtering the Innocents" (1993); Andersen (1993).

68. Li Peilin (2003).

69. "Four Sentenced to Death" (1993); Kahn (1993); Mirsky (1992); "Hong Kong: Officials Fight . . ." (1991).

70. Lee and Kleinman (2002).

71. Davis (1992); C. K. Lee (2002).

72. Blecher (2002); Li Peilin (2003).

73. Bernstein and Lu (2000); Bernstein and Lu (2003).

74. Goldman and Perry (2002).

75. See, e.g., Chan (2001); C. K. Lee (1998).

CHAPTER 11

1. MacFarquhar (1991); Chang (2001).

2. Yan (1992).

3. Friedman (1994).

4. Jiang (2002).

5. This is a central thesis of Zheng (1994).

6. Oi (1994); Whiting (2001).

7. Zheng (1994).

8. Naughton explores this in his chapter in Lieberthal and Lampton (1992).

9. Oi (1994) details this at the township level.

10. Lieberthal and Lampton (1992) explores this issue systematically.

11. Lynch (1999).

12. Jiang (2002).

13. The other two Sixteenth Politburo Standing Committee members are Hu Jintao, who alone among its pre–Sixteenth Congress members remained on the Politburo Standing Committee, and Zeng Qinghong, who rose from an alternate member of the Fifteenth Politburo.

14. Walder (1986); Whyte (1974).

15. Abnett (2002); Bottelier (2002); Cassidy (2002); Lardy (2002).

16. Jiang (2002), in Appendix 2.

17. Oi (2003).

18. Economy (2004).

19. Dreyer (1976); Goldstein (1997).

20. Lawrence (2000); Bakshi (2002); Gao (2002); Pan (2002).

21. Goldstein (1997).

22. Clough (1978).

23. Freeman (1998).

24. Chao and Myers (1998); Dickson (1997).

25. Chu and Lin (2001).

26. Christensen chapter in Ellings and Friedberg (2001).

27. Lardy (2002).

28. Blecher (2002) finds that this argument has had a meaningful impact among urban workers.

29. Disagreement among knowledgeable specialists on China over fundamental aspects of the country's institutional strength and political stability is highlighted in the series of essays under "Changing of the Guard" (2003).

30. This amplifies on Lieberthal (2003).

Bibliography of Sources Cited in the Text

Abnett, William. "China and Compliance with World Trade Organization Commitments: The First Six Months," in *China's WTO Accession: The Road to Implementation*. Seattle: NBR Special Report No. 3 (November 2002), pp. 5–22.

Afshar, Haleh, ed. *Women, Development, and Survival in the Third World*. London: Longman, 1991.

Agarwal, Bina, ed. *Structures of State Patriarchy: State, Community, and Household in Modernizing Asia*. London: Zed Books, 1988.

"Alongside China's Official Exchanges, Booming Illegal Stock Market Operates." *Wall Street Journal* (Eastern edition), 2 June 1993, p. A11.

Andersen, John W., and Molly Moore. "Murdered at Birth for Being Female." *Toronto Star*, 4 April 1993, p. A1.

Amnesty International. *Political Imprisonment in the People's Republic of China*. London: Amnesty International, 1978.

———. *China: Violations of Human Rights*. London: Amnesty International, 1984.

Andors, Phyllis. *The Unfinished Liberation of Chinese Women, 1949–1980*. Bloomington: Indiana University Press, 1983.

Armstrong, Tony. *Breaking the Ice: Rapprochement between East and West Germany, the United States and China, and Israel and Egypt*. Washington, D.C.: United States Institute of Peace Press, 1993.

Ash, Robert. "The Agricultural Sector in China: Performance and Policy Dilemmas during the 1990s." *China Quarterly* 131 (September 1992): 545–76.

Ash, Robert, and Y. Y. Kueh. "Economic Integration within Greater China: Trade and Investment Flows between China, Hong Kong, and Taiwan." *China Quarterly* 136 (December 1993): 711–45.

Atlantic Council and National Committee on U.S.–China Relations. *United States and China Relations at a Crossroads*. Washington, D.C., and New York: Atlantic Council and National Committee on U.S.–China Relations, 1993.

Bachman, David M. *Chen Yun and the Chinese Political System*. Berkeley and Los Angeles: University of California Press, 1985.

———. *Bureaucracy, Economy, and Leadership in China: The Institutional Origins of the Great Leap Forward*. New York: Cambridge University Press, 1991.

———. "The Limits to Leadership in China." In *The Future of China*. NBR Analysis, vol. 3, no.3 (August 1992), pp. 23–35. Seattle: National Bureau of Asian Research, 1992.

Bakshi, Jyostna. "Shanghai Cooperation Organization Before and After September 11," *Strategic Analysis* 26:2 (April–June 2002).

Balazs, Etienne. *Chinese Civilization and Bureaucracy.* New Haven, Conn.: Yale University Press, 1964.

Bao, Ruo-wang. *Prisoner of Mao.* New York: Coward, McCann and Geoghegan, 1973.

Barnett, A. Doak. *Communist China: The Early Years, 1949–1955.* New York: Praeger, 1964.

————. *Cadres, Bureaucracy, and Political Power in Communist China.* New York: Columbia University Press, 1967.

————. *China and the Major Powers in East Asia.* Washington, D.C.: Brookings Institution, 1977.

Barnett, A. Doaked. *Chinese Communist Politics in Action.* Seattle: University of Washington Press, 1969.

Barraclough, Geoffrey. *An Introduction to Contemporary History.* New York: Penguin, 1967.

Bartlett, Beatrice. *Monarchs and Ministers.* Berkeley and Los Angeles: University of California Press, 1991.

Bauer, John, Wang Feng, Nancy Riley, and Xiaohua Zhao. "Gender and Inequality in Urban China." *Modern China* (July 1992): 333–70.

Baum, Richard. *Prelude to Revolution: Mao, the Party, and the Peasant Question, 1962–1966.* New York: Columbia University Press, 1975.

————. *Burying Mao.* Princeton, N.J.: Princeton University Press, 1994.

Baum, Richard, and Frederick Teiwes. *Ssu-Ch'ing: The Socialist Education Movement of 1962–1966.* Berkeley and Los Angeles: University of California Press, 1968.

Beasley, W. G. *The Meiji Restoration.* Stanford: Stanford University Press, 1972.

Becker, Jasper. *Hungry Ghosts.* New York: Free Press, 1996.

Beckman, George M. *The Modernization of China and Japan.* New York: Harper & Row, 1962.

Belden, Jack. *China Shakes the World.* New York: Monthly Review Press, 1949.

Bennett, Gordon A. *Yundong: Mass Campaigns in Chinese Communist Leadership.* Berkeley: University of California, Center for Chinese Studies, 1976.

Bennett, Gordon A., and Ronald Montaperto. *Red Guard: The Political Biography of Dai Hsiao-Ai.* Garden City, N.Y.: Anchor, 1972.

Bernstein, Thomas P. *Up to the Mountains and Down to the Villages: The Transfer of Youth from Urban to Rural China.* New Haven, Conn.: Yale University Press, 1977.

————. "Stalinism, Famine, and Chinese Peasants—Grain Procurement during the Great Leap Forward." *Theory and Society* 13, no. 3 (1984): 339–77.

Bernstein, Thomas, and Xiaobo Lu. "Taxation Without Representation: Peasants, The Central and Local States in Reform China." *China Quarterly* 163 (September 2000): 742–63.

————. *Taxation Without Representation in Contemporary Rural China.* New York: Cambridge University Press, 2003.

Bialer, Seweryn. *Stalin's Successors: Leadership, Stability, and Change in the Soviet Union.* Cambridge: Cambridge University Press, 1980.

Bianco, Lucien. *Origins of the Chinese Revolution, 1915–1949.* Stanford: Stanford University Press, 1971.

Biers, Dan, "China's Rush to Boost Industry Causing Disastrous Pollution." Associated Press, 28 April 1994.

Blecher, Marc. "Hegemony and Workers' Politics in China," *China Quarterly* (June 2002): 283–303.

Bonavia, David. *Deng.* Hong Kong: Longman, 1989.

Borisov, O. B., and B. Y. Koloskov. *Sino-Soviet Relations, 1945–1970.* Translated by Yuri Shirokov. Moscow: Progress Publishers, 1975.

Bottelier, Pieter. "Implications of WTO Membership in China: State-Owned Banks and the Management of Public Finances," *Journal of Contemporary China* (August 2002): 397–412.

Bowie, Robert K., and John K. Fairbank. *Communist China, 1955–1959.* Cambridge, Mass.: Harvard University Press, 1962.

Bridges, William P., Moshe Semoyonov, and Richard E. Barret. "Female Labor Participation in Urban and Rural China." *Rural Sociology* 56 (Spring 1991): 1–21.

Brodsgaard, Kjeld Erik. "Institutional Reform and the *Bianzhi* System in China." *China Quarterly* (June 2002): 361–86.

Bunce, Valerie. *Do Leaders Make a Difference?* Princeton, N.J.: Princeton University Press, 1981.

Burns, John P. "China's Nomenklatura System." *Problems of Communism* 36 (September–October 1987): 36–51.

———. "Chinese Civil Service Reform: The 13th Party Congress Proposals." *China Quarterly* 120 (December 1989): 739–70.

———. *The Chinese Communist Party Nomenklatura System: A Documentary Study of Party Control of Leadership Selection.* Armonk, N.Y.: M. E. Sharpe, 1989.

———. "Strengthening Central CCP Control of Leadership Selection: The 1990 Nomenklatura." *China Quarterly* 128 (June 1994): 458–91.

Byron, John, and Robert Pack. *Claws of the Dragon.* New York: Simon and Schuster, 1992.

Caijing (Finance). 5 August 2002 article by Hu Yifan.

Cannon, Terry, and Alan Jenkins. *The Geography of Contemporary China: The Impact of Deng Xiaoping's Decade.* New York: Routledge, 1990.

Cassidy, Robert. "Trade in Services in China: Implementing the WTO," in *China's WTO Accession: The Road to Implementation.* Seattle: NBR Special Report No. 3 (November 2002), pp. 23–45.

Chan, Anita. *China's Workers Under Assault.* Armonk, N.Y.: M. E. Sharpe, 2001.

Chan, Anita, Richard Madsen, and Jonathan Unger. *Chen Village: The Recent History of a Peasant Community in Mao's China.* Berkeley and Los Angeles: University of California Press, 1984.

Chan, Che-po, and Gavin Drewry, "The 1998 State Council Organizational Streamlining: Personnel Reduction and Change of Government Function," *Journal of Contemporary China* 10, no. 29 (November 2001): 553–72.

Chang, Gordon H. *Friends and Enemies: The United States, China, and the Soviet Union, 1948–1972.* Stanford: Stanford University Press, 1990.

Chang, Gordon. *The Coming Collapse of China.* New York: Random House, 2001.

Chang, Jung. *Wild Swans: Three Daughters of China*. New York: Simon and Schuster, 1991.

Chang, Parris. "Research Notes on the Changing Loci of Decision in the CCP." *China Quarterly* 44 (October–December 1970): 169–94.

"Changing of the Guard," *Journal of Democracy* 14:1 (January 2003): 5–81.

Chao, Linda and Raymond H. Myers. *The First Chinese Democracy: Political Life in the Republic of China on Taiwan*. Baltimore: Johns Hopkins University Press, 1998.

Cheesman, Bruce. "China—South Korea: A Case of Pure Mathematics." *Asian Business* 28 (October 1992): 16.

Chen, Jian. *Mao's China and the Cold War*. Chapel Hill and London: University of North Carolina Press, 2001.

Chen, Jie. *Ideology in U.S. Foreign Policy*. Westport, Conn.: Praeger, 1992.

Chesneaux, Jean. *The Chinese Labor Movement, 1919–1927*. Stanford: Stanford University Press, 1968.

Cheung, Peter T. Y., Jae Ho Chung, and Zhirmin Lin, eds. *Provincial Strategies of Economic Reform in Post-Mao China*. Armonk, N.Y.: M. E. Sharpe, 1998.

Cheung, Tai Ming. "Fighting the Good Fight: Underground Church Reaps the Fruits of Religious Boom." *Far Eastern Economic Review* 149 (5 July 1990): 39–41.

Chi, Hsi-Sheng. *The Chinese Warlord System: 1916–1928*. Washington, D.C.: American University Center for Research in Social Systems, 1969.

———. *Nationalist China at War: Military Defeats and Political Collapse, 1937–1945*. Ann Arbor: University of Michigan Press, 1982.

China Statistical Information and Consultancy Service. *China Statistical Yearbook, 1991*. Beijing: China Statistical Information and Consultancy Service, 1991.

Choate, Allen C. "Local Governance in China: An Assessment of Villagers Committees." The Asia Foundation, Working Paper No.1, February 1997.

Chow, Ts'e-tung. *The May Fourth Movement: Intellectual Revolution in Modern China*. Cambridge, Mass.: Harvard University Press, 1960.

Ch'u, Tung-tsu. *Local Government in China Under the Ch'ing*. Stanford: Stanford University Press, 1969.

Chu, Wen-djang. *The Moslem Rebellions in Northwest China*. Paris: Mouton, 1966.

Chu, Yun-han. *Crafting Democracy in Taiwan*. Taipei: Institute for National Policy Research, 1992.

Chu, Yun-han, and Jih-wen Lin, "Political Development in Twentieth Century Taiwan," *China Quarterly* No. 165 (March 2001): 102–29.

Clough, Ralph. *Island China*. Cambridge, Mass.: Harvard University Press, 1978.

Clubb, O. Edmund. *China and Russia: The Great "Game."* New York: Columbia University Press, 1971.

Coble, Parks M. *The Shanghai Capitalists and the Nationalist Government, 1927–1937*. Cambridge, Mass.: Council on East Asian Studies, Harvard University, 1980.

Cohen, Jerome A. *The Criminal Process in the People's Republic of China, 1949–1963: An Introduction*. Cambridge, Mass.: Harvard University Press, 1968.

Cohen, Paul. *Reform in Nineteenth-Century China*. Cambridge, Mass.: East Asian Research Center, Harvard University, 1976.

Cohen, Warren I. *America's Response to China: A History of Sino-American Relations.* New York: Columbia University Press, 1990.

"Corrupt Officials Expelled from Party." *Beijing Review* 36 (12 July 1993): 5.

Cranmer-Byng, J. L., ed. *An Embassy to China.* London: Longman, 1962.

Crossley, Pamela Kyle. *The Manchus.* Cambridge, Mass.: Blackwell Publishers, 1997.

Cui, Lili. "Qigong on Qinghua Campus." *Beijing Review* 32 (24 April 1989): 24–26.

Cui Wunian and Wang Junxian. *Zhongguo ganbu jiegou di bianqian* (Changes in the structure of China's cadres). N.p., n.d.

Davis, Deborah. "China's Social Welfare: Policies and Outcomes." *China Quarterly* 119 (September 1989): 577–97.

———. "Job Mobility in Post-Mao Cities: Increases in the Margins." *China Quarterly* 132 (December 1992): 1062–85.

Deng Xiaoping. *Selected Works of Deng Xiaoping, 1975–1982,* v. 2. Beijing: Foreign Languages Press, 1984.

———. *Selected Works of Deng Xiaoping, 1983–1992,* v. 3. Beijing: Foreign Languages Press, 1993.

Dickson, Bruce. "The Adaptability of Leninist Parties: A Comparison of the Chinese Communist Party and the Kuomintang." Ph.D. diss., University of Michigan, 1994.

———. *Democratization in China and Taiwan: The Adaptability of Leninist Parties.* New York: Oxford University Press, 1997.

Dickson, Bruce, and Chien-min Chao, eds. *Assessing the Lee Teng-hui Legacy in Taiwan's Politics: Democratic Consolidation and External Relations.* Armonk, N.Y.: M. E. Sharpe, 2002.

Dirlik, Arif. "The Ideological Foundations of the New Life Movement." *Journal of Asian Studies* 34:4 (August 1975): 945–80.

———. *Anarchism in the Chinese Revolution.* Berkeley and Los Angeles: University of California Press, 1991.

"Disciplining Party Members." *Beijing Review* 33 (29 January 1990): 6–7.

Dittmer, Lowell. *Liu Shao-ch'i and the Chinese Cultural Revolution.* Berkeley and Los Angeles: University of California Press, 1974.

———. *Sino-Soviet Normalization and Its International Implications, 1945–1990.* Seattle: University of Washington Press, 1992.

Dittmer, Lowell, and Samuel S. Kim, eds. *China's Quest for National Identity.* Ithaca, N.Y.: Cornell University Press, 1993.

Domes, Jurgen. *Peng Te-huai: The Man and the Image.* London: C. Hurst and Co., 1985.

Donnithorne, Audrey. *China's Economic System.* New York: Praeger, 1967.

Dreyer, June T. *China's Forty Millions.* Cambridge, Mass.: Harvard University Press, 1976.

Eastman, Lloyd E. *The Abortive Revolution: China under Nationalist Rule, 1927–1937.* Cambridge, Mass.: Harvard University Press, 1974.

Ebrey, Patricia, ed. *Chinese Civilization and Society.* New York: Free Press, 1981.

Eckstein, Alexander. *Communist China's Economic Growth and Foreign Trade: Implications for U.S. Policy.* New York: McGraw-Hill, 1966.

———. *China's Economic Revolution.* Cambridge: Cambridge University Press, 1977.

Economy, Elizabeth. "Domestic Reforms and International Regime Formation: China, the USSR, and Global Climate Change." Ph.D. diss., University of Michigan, 1994.

————. *The River Runs Black: The Environmental Challenge to China's Future.* Ithaca: Cornell University Press; 2004.

Ellings, Richard and Aaron Friedberg, eds. *Strategic Asia: Power and Purpose, 2001–2002.* Seattle: National Bureau of Asian Research, 2001.

Elliott, Mark C. *The Manchu Way: The Eight Banners and Ethnic Identity in Late Imperial China.* Stanford: Stanford University Press, 2001.

Elvin, Mark. *The Pattern of the Chinese Past.* Stanford: Stanford University Press, 1973.

"Environment and Development: A World Issue." *Beijing Review* 35 (8 June 1992): 18–20.

Erbaugh, Mary S. "The Secret History of the Hakkas: The Chinese Revolution as a Hakka Enterprise," *China Quarterly* 132 (December 1992): 937–68.

Esherick, Joseph W. *Lost Chance in China: The World War II Despatches of John S. Service.* New York: Vintage, 1974.

Esherick, Joseph W., and Jeffrey N. Wasserstrom. "Acting Out Democracy: Political Theater in Modern China." *Journal of Asian Studies* 49 (November 1990): 835–65.

Fainsod, Merle. *How Russia Is Ruled.* Cambridge, Mass.: Harvard University Press, 1965.

Fairbank, John K. *Trade and Diplomacy on the China Coast: The Opening of the Treaty Ports, 1842–1854.* Stanford: Stanford University Press, 1953.

————. *Chinabound: A Fifty-Year Memoir.* New York: Harper and Row, 1982.

Fairbank, John K., ed. *The Chinese World Order.* Cambridge, Mass.: Harvard University Press, 1968.

Fairbank, John K., and Kwang-ching Liu, eds. *The Cambridge History of China.* Vol. 10. New York: Cambridge University Press, 1978.

Fairbank, John K., Edwin O. Reischauer, and Albert M. Craig. *East Asia.* Boston: Houghton Mifflin, 1973.

FBIS [Foreign Broadcast Information Service]. *China Daily Report.* Arlington, Va.

Fewsmith, Joseph. *Dilemmas of Reform in China: Political Conflict and Economic Debate.* Armonk, N.Y.: M. E. Sharpe, 1994.

————. *Elite Politics in Contemporary China.* Armonk, N.Y.: M. E. Sharpe, 2001.

Findlay, Christopher C. *Policy Reform, Economic Growthand China's Agriculture.* Paris: Development Centre, Organization for Economic Cooperation and Development, 1993.

Fingar, Thomas. *China's Quest for Independence: Policy Evolution in the 1970s.* Boulder: Westview Press, 1980.

Fletcher, Joseph. "Ch'ing Inner Asia c. 1800," *The Cambridge History of Modern China,* vol. 10. Edited by John K. Fairbank and Kwang-ching Liu. New York: Cambridge University Press, 1978, pp. 35–106.

————. "The Heyday of the Ch'ing Order in Mongolia, Sinkiang, and Tibet," in *The Cambridge History of Modern China,* vol. 10. Edited by John K. Fairbank and Kwang-ching Liu. New York: Cambridge University Press, 1978, pp. 351–408.

"Four Sentenced to Death for Women, Children Racket." Agence France Press, 15 November 1993.

Franck, Harry A. *Wandering in North China.* New York: Century Co., 1923.

Franz, Uli. *Deng Xiaoping.* Boston: Harcourt Brace Jovanovich, 1988.

Freeman, Chas. W., Jr. "Preventing War in the Taiwan Strait." *Foreign Affairs* 77:4 (July–August 1998): 6–11.

Fried, Morton. *The Fabric of Chinese Society.* New York: Praeger, 1953.

Friedman, Edward. "Reconstructing China's National Identity: A Southern Alternative to Mao-era Anti-imperialist Nationalism." *Journal of Asian Studies* (February 1994): 67–91.

Friedman, Edward, Paul G. Pickowicz, and Mark Selden. *Chinese Village, Socialist State.* New Haven, Conn.: Yale University Press, 1991.

Gaddis, John L. *Containment: Documents on American Policy and Strategy, 1945–1950.* New York: Columbia University Press, 1978.

Gamble, Sidney D. *Ting Hsien: A North China Rural Community.* Stanford: Stanford University Press, 1954.

Gao, Qiufu, "Terrorist Forces Resurge in Central Asia," *Beijing Review,* 22 August 2002.

Gao, Yuan. *Born Red: A Chronicle of the Cultural Revolution.* Stanford: Stanford University Press, 1987.

Garside, Roger. *Coming Alive: China after Mao.* New York: McGraw-Hill, 1981.

Garver, John W. *China's Decision for Rapprochement with the United States, 1968–1974.* Boulder: Westview Press, 1982.

———. "China's Push through the South China Sea: The Interaction of Bureaucratic and National Interests." *China Quarterly* 132 (December 1992): 999–1028.

———. *Foreign Relations of the People's Republic of China.* Englewood Cliffs, N.J.: Prentice-Hall, 1993.

Gill, Bates, and James Mulvenon, "Chinese Military-Related Think Tanks and Research Institutions." *China Quarterly* 171 (September 2002): 617–24.

Gillin, Donald G. *Warlord: Yen Hsi-shan in Shansi Province 1911–1949.* Princeton, N.J.: Princeton University Press, 1967.

Glaser, Bonnie and Philip Saunders, "Chinese Foreign Policy Research Institutes: Evolving Roles and Increasing Influence." *China Quarterly* (September 2002): 597–616.

Goldman, Merle. *Literary Dissent in Communist China.* New York: Atheneum, 1971.

———. *China's Intellectuals: Advise and Dissent.* Cambridge, Mass.: Harvard University Press, 1981.

Goldman, Merle, and Roderick MacFarquhar, eds. *The Paradox of China's Post-Mao Reforms.* Cambridge, Mass.: Harvard University Press, 1999.

Goldman, Merle, and Elizabeth Perry. *Changing Meanings of Citizenship in Modern China.* Cambridge, Mass.: Harvard University Press, 2002.

Goldstein, Alice, and Sidney Goldstein. "Population Movement, Labor Force Absorption, and Urbanization in China." *Annals of the American Academy of Political and Social Science* 476 (November 1984): 90–110.

Goldstein, Avery. *From Bandwagon to Balance-of-Power Politics.* Stanford: Stanford University Press, 1991.

Goldstein, Melvin. *The Snow Lion and the Dragon.* Berkeley: University of California Press, 1997.

Goldstein, Steven M. *Minidragons: Fragile Economic Miracles in the Pacific.* Boulder: Westview Press, 1991.

Goncharov, Sergei N., John W. Lewis, and Litai Xue. *Uncertain Partners*. Stanford: Stanford University Press, 1993.

Goodspeed, Peter. "China's Peasants Get Restless; Rural Protests Send Shock Waves through Beijing Urbanized Elite." *Toronto Star.* 11 July 1993, p. F2.

Gottlieb, Thomas M. *Chinese Foreign Policy: Factionalism and the Origins of the Strategic Triangle*. Santa Monica: Rand Corporation, 1977.

Granick, David. "Multiple Labor Markets in the Industrial State Enterprise Sector." *China Quarterly* 126 (June 1991): 269–89.

Grasso, June. *Truman's Two China Policy: 1948–1950*. Armonk, N.Y.: M. E. Sharpe, 1987.

Grieder, Jerome B. *Hu Shih and the Chinese Renaissance: Liberalism in the Chinese Revolution, 1917–1937*. Cambridge, Mass.: Harvard University Press, 1970.

Griffith, William E. *Sino-Soviet Relations, 1964–1965*. Cambridge: MIT Press, 1967.

Guillermaz, Jacques. *A History of the Chinese Communist Party*. New York: Random House, 1972.

Guoji jinrong bao (International Financial News), 29 August 2002.

Haggard, Stephen. *Pathways from the Periphery: The Politics of Growth in the Newly Industrializing Countries*. Ithaca, N.Y.: Cornell University Press, 1990.

Hallenberg, Jan. *Foreign Policy Change: United States Foreign Policy toward the Soviet Union and the People's Republic of China, 1961–1980*. Stockholm: University of Stockholm Press, 1984.

Hamrin, Carol Lee. *China and the Challenge of the Future: Changing Political Patterns*. Boulder: Westview Press, 1990.

Hamrin, Carol Lee, and Suisheng Zhao, eds. *Decision-making in Deng's China: Perspectives from the Insiders*. Armonk, M.Y.: M.E. Sharpe, 1995.

Harding, Harry, *Organizing China: The Problem of Bureaucracy 1949–1976*. Stanford: Stanford University Press, 1981.

———. *China's Second Revolution: Reform after Mao*. Washington, D.C.: Brookings Institution, 1987.

———. "The Concept of 'Greater China': Themes, Variations, and Reservations." *China Quarterly* 136 (December 1993a): 660–86.

———. *A Fragile Relationship: The United States and China Since 1972*. Washington, D.C.: Brookings Institution, 1993b.

Harding, Harry, ed. *China's Foreign Relations in the 1980s*. New Haven, Conn.: Yale University Press, 1984.

Harris, Lillian Craig. "Xinjiang, Central Asia, and the Implications for China's Policy in the Islamic World." *China Quarterly* 133 (March 1993): 111–29.

Harrison, James Pinckney. *The Long March to Power*. New York: Praeger, 1972.

Hertsgaard, Mark. "Our Real China Problem." *Atlantic Monthly* 280 (November 1997): 96–98.

Hinton, William. *Hundred Day War: The Cultural Revolution at Tsinghua University*. New York: Monthly Review Press, 1972.

———. *The Great Reversal: The Privatization of China*. New York: Monthly Review Press, 1990.

Ho, Ping-ti. *The Ladder of Success in Imperial China: Aspects of Social Mobility, 1368–1911*. New York: Science Editions, 1964.

Ho, Sam P., and Ralph W. Hueneman. *China's Open Door Policy: The Quest for Foreign Technology and Capital.* Vancouver: University of British Columbia Press, 1984.

Hofheinz, Roy, Jr. *The Broken Wave.* Cambridge, Mass.: Harvard University Press, 1977.

"Hong Kong: Officials Fight 'Losing War' against Slave Trade." *FBIS* (12 December 1991): 29.

"Hong Kong: Secret Societies 'Rampant' Throughout." *FBIS* (14 May 1992): 29.

Howe, Christopher, ed. *Shanghai: Revolution and Development in an Asian Metropolis.* Cambridge: Cambridge University Press, 1981.

Howellpearson, Martin. "The New Chinese Superstate." *Global Finance* 6, no. 2 (February 1992): 56–59.

Hoyt, Edwin Palmer. *The Day the Chinese Attacked: Korea 1950; The Story of the Failure of America's China Policy.* New York: McGraw-Hill, 1990.

Hsiao, Kung-Chuan. *Rural China: Imperial Control in the Nineteenth Century.* Seattle: University of Washington Press, 1960.

———. *A Modern China and a New World: K'ang Yu-wei, Reformer and Utopian.* Seattle: University of Washington Press, 1975.

Hu, Angang. "Enormous Corruption Black Hole: Public Revelation of the Various Types of Economic Losses Due to Corruption" (in Chinese), *Zhongguo guoqing fenxi yanjiu baogao* (Research report on analysis of China's national conditions), issue no. 5, 2002. Beijing: Guoqing yanjiu zhongxin, March 8, 2002.

Huang, Philip. " 'Public Sphere'/' Civil Society' in China? The Third Realm Between State and Society." *Modern China* (April 1993): 216–40.

Huang, Yasheng. "Web of Interests and Patterns of Behavior of Chinese Local Economic Bureaucracies and Enterprises during the Reforms." *China Quarterly* 123 (September 1990): 431–58.

Huang, Yasheng. "The Statistical Agency in China's Bureaucratic System: A Comparison with the Former Soviet Union." *Communist and Post-Communist Studies* 29 (March 1996): pp. 59–75.

Hucker, Charles O. *China's Imperial Past: An Introduction to Chinese History and Culture.* Stanford: Stanford University Press, 1975.

"Human Rights in China." *Beijing Review* 34, no. 44 (4–10 November 1991): 8–45.

Hummel, Arthur W. *Eminent Chinese of the Ch'ing Period.* Taipei: Ch'eng-Wen Publishing Company, 1967.

Hunt, Michael H. *Ideology and US Foreign Policy.* New Haven, Conn.: Yale University Press, 1987.

———. "Beijing and the Korean Crisis, June 1950–June 1951." *Political Science Quarterly* 107 (Fall 1992): 453–78.

Hyer, Eric. "China's Arms Merchants: Profits in Command." *China Quarterly* 132 (December 1992): 1101–18.

Hymes, Robert. *Statesmen and Gentlemen: The Elite of Fu-chou, Chiang-hsi, in Northern and Southern Sung.* New York: Cambridge University Press, 1966.

Inglehart, Ronald, Miguel Basanez, and Alejandro Moreno. *Human Values and Beliefs: A Comparative Sourcebook.* Ann Arbor: University of Michigan Press, 1998.

"Irrational Rationing: Chaotic Shenzhen Share Issue Reveals Basic Flaws." *Far Eastern Economic Review* 155 (20 August 1992): 65.

Isaacs, Harold R. *The Tragedy of the Chinese Revolution*. London: Secker and Warburg, 1938.

Jacobson, Harold K., and Michel Oksenberg. *China's Participation in the IMF, the World Bank, and the GATT: Toward a Global Economic Order*. Ann Arbor: University of Michigan Press, 1990.

Jahiel, Abigail. "Policy Implementation under 'Socialist Reform': The Case of Water Pollution Management in the People's Republic of China." Ph.D. diss., University of Michigan, 1994.

Jefferson, Gary H., and Thomas G. Rawski. "Unemployment, Underemployment, and Employment Policy in China's Cities." *Modern China* 18 (January 1992): 42–71.

Jen, Yu-wen. *The Taiping Revolutionary Movement*. New Haven, Conn.: Yale University Press, 1973.

"Jiang Declares War on Corruption." *Beijing Review* 36 (6 September 1993): 5–6.

Jiang, Zemin. "Report at the Sixteenth Party Congress." 2002. Available at www.16con gress.org.cn/english/features/49007.htm.

"Jiangsu Province Social Services Aid Agriculture." *FBIS* (12 December 1990): 45.

Jinan wanbao (Jinan evening news), 30 July 2002.

Joffe, Ellis. *Party and Army Professionalism and Political Control in the Chinese Officer Corps, 1949–1964*. Cambridge, Mass.: Harvard University Press, 1971.

———. *The Chinese Army after Mao*. Cambridge, Mass.: Harvard University Press, 1987.

Johnson, Kay. *Women, the Family, and Peasant Revolution in China*. Chicago: University of Chicago Press, 1983.

Johnston, Alastair I. "Independence through Unification: On the Correct Handling of Contradictons across the Taiwan Straits." *Contemporary Issues 2*. Cambridge: Fairbank Center for East Asian Research, May 1993.

———. *Cultural Realism: Strategic Culture and Grand Strategy in Chinese History*. Princeton, N.J.: Princeton University Press, 1995.

Jones, Peter. *China and the Soviet Union*. London: Longman, 1985.

Judd, Ellen R. " 'Men Are More Able': Rural Women's Conceptions of Gender and Agency." *Pacific Affairs* 63 (Spring 1990): 40–61.

Kahn, Joseph. "Buying, Selling of Women on Rise in China." *Vancouver Sun*, 30 May 1993, p. B3.

Kalicki, J. H. *The Pattern of Sino-American Crises: Political-Military Interactions in the 1950s*. London: Cambridge University Press, 1975.

Kang, Chao. *Man and Land in China*. Stanford: Stanford University Press, 1986.

Karp, Jonathan. "The Vietnam Option: Taiwan Directs Investment Flows Away from China." *Far Eastern Economic Review* 154 (31 October 1991): 70–71.

Kaye, Lincoln. "Religious Groundswell: Underground Churches Lead Christian Revival." *Far Eastern Economic Review* 156 (21 January 1993): 13.

Kelliher, Daniel. *Peasant Power in China: The Era of Rural Reform, 1979–1989*. New Haven, Conn.: Yale University Press, 1992.

Kennedy, Paul. *The Rise and Fall of the Great Powers*. New York: Random House, 1987.

Khan, Azizur Rahman, Keith Griffin, Carl Riskin, and Renwei Zhao. "Household Income and Its Distribution in China." *China Quarterly* 132 (December 1992): 1029–61.

Khan, Azizur Rahman, and Carl Riskin, *Inequality and Poverty in China in the Age of Globalization*. New York: Oxford University Press, 2001.

Khrushchev, Nikita S. *Khrushchev Remembers*. Boston: Little, Brown, 1970.

Kim, Heung-Kyu. "The Political Capacity of Beijing Still Matters: Political Leadership and Institutionalization of Fiscal Systems during the Period of Economic Decentralization in China, 1979–1997." Ph.D. diss., University of Michigan, 2002.

Kipnis, Andrew. *Producing Guanxi: Sentiment, Self and Subculture in a North China Village*. Durham, N. C.: Duke University Press, 1997.

Kirby, William. *Germany and Republican China*. Stanford: Stanford University Press, 1984.

Kissinger, Henry. *White House Years*. Boston: Little, Brown, 1979.

Klein, Donald. *Rebels and Bureaucrats: China's December 9ers*. Berkeley and Los Angeles: University of California Press, 1976.

Korzec, Michael. *Labour and the Failure of Reform in China*. New York: St. Martin's, 1992.

Kraus, Richard. *Class Conflict in Chinese Socialism*. New York: Columbia University Press, 1981.

Kristof, Nicholas D. "China's Newest Partner: South Korea." *New York Times*, 5 April 1993, pp. D1–D2.

Kuhn, Philip A. *Rebellion and Its Enemies in Late Imperial China*. Cambridge, Mass.: Harvard University Press, 1970.

———. *Soulstealers: The Chinese Sorcery Scare of 1768*. Cambridge, Mass.: Harvard University Press, 1990.

Kwong, Luke. *A Mosaic of the Hundred Days: Personalities, Politics, and Ideas of 1898*. Cambridge, Mass.: Harvard University Press, 1984.

Kyng, James. "China's Water Project Heralds Market Prices," *Financial Times*. February 20, 2003, p. 7.

Lam, Willy Wo-Lap. "Jiang Urges Huge Grain Store System." *South China Morning Post*, 16 June 1993, p. 10.

Lampton, David M. *The Politics of Medicine in China: The Policy Process, 1949–1977*. Boulder: Westview Press, 1977.

———. *Paths to Power: Elite Mobility in Contemporary China*. Ann Arbor: University of Michigan, Center for Chinese Studies, 1986.

———. *A Relationship Restored: Trends in U.S.–China Educational Exchanges, 1978–1984*. Washington, D.C.: National Academy Press, 1986.

Lardy, Nicholas R. *Economic Growth and Distribution in China*. Cambridge: Cambridge University Press, 1978.

———. *Agriculture in Modern China's Economic Development*. New York: Cambridge University Press, 1983.

———. "China Growing Economic Role in Asia." In *The Future of China*. NBR Analysis, vol. 3, no. 3 (August 1992), pp. 5–12. Seattle: National Bureau of Asian Research.

———. *Foreign Trade and Economic Reform in China, 1978–1990*. New York: Cambridge University Press, 1992.

———. *China in the World Economy*. Washington, D.C.: Institute for International Economics, 1994.

————. *Integrating China Into the Global Economy.* Washington, D.C.: Brookings Institution, 2002.

Lardy, Nicholas R., and Kenneth Lieberthal. *Chen Yun's Strategy for China's Development: A Non-Maoist Alternative.* Armonk, N.Y.: M. E. Sharpe, 1983.

Lawrence, Susan V. "Democracy, Chinese Style." *Australian Journal of Chinese Affairs* 32 (July 1994): 61–70.

————. "Where Beijing Fears Kosovo." *Far Eastern Economic Review* 163:36 (September 2000), 23–24.

Lee, Ching Kwan. *Gender and the South China Miracle.* Berkeley: University of California, 1998.

————. "The Force of Law and the Post-Socialist Subject: An Ethnographic Study of the State and New Industrial Labor in China." University of Michigan. Unpublished paper, 2002.

Lee, Hong Yung. *From Revolutionary Cadres to Technocrats in Socialist China.* Berkeley and Los Angeles: University of California Press, 1991.

Lee, Sing and Arthur Kleinman. "Suicide as Resistance in Chinese Society." In *Chinese Society: Change, Conflict, and Resistance.* Edited by Mark Selden and Elizabeth Perry. New York: Routledge, 2000. pp. 221–240.

Leung, Julia. "As Zhu Preaches Austerity, Boom Town Throws a Party." *Asian Wall Street Journal,* 3 January 1994.

Levi, Jean. *The Chinese Emperor.* New York: Harcourt Brace Jovanovich, 1985.

Levine, Steven I. *Anvil of Victory: The Communist Revolution in Manchuria, 1945–1948.* New York: Columbia University Press, 1987.

Lewis, John W., Di Hua, and Litai Xue. "Beijing's Defense Establishment: Solving the Arms Export Enigma." *International Security* 15, no. 4 (Spring 1991).

Lewis, John W., and Litai Xue. *China Builds the Bomb.* Stanford: Stanford University Press, 1988.

Li, Cheng. *China's Leaders: The New Generation.* New York: Roman and Littlefield Publishers, 2001.

Li, Cheng, and Lynn T. White III. "China's Technocratic Movement and the World Economic Herald." *Modern China* 17 (July 1991): 342–88.

Li, David D. "The Chinese State-Owned Enterprise Under Reform." Unpublished paper presented at the American Economic Association Annual Meeting, Boston, December 1993.

Li, Peilin. "Dangqian Zhongguo shehui fazhan de wenti he xin qushi" (Issues and new trends in contemporary China's social development), in *Shehui xinshi fenxi yu yuce* (Analysis of the social situation and forecasts), edited by Ping Huang. Beijing: Chinese Academy of Social Sciences, 2002.

Li, Rui. *Lushan Huiyi Shilu* (Record of the Lushan Conference). Beijing: Chunqiu Chubanshe, 1989.

Li, Wei. "The General Office System: A Crucial Integrative Mechanism of China's Bureaucracy." Unpublished manuscript, 1993.

————. "The Security Service for Chinese Central Leaders." Unpublished manuscript, 1994.

Li, Wei, and Lucian Pye. "The Ubiquitous Role of the *Mishu* in Chinese Politics." *China Quarterly* 132 (December 1992): 913–36.

Li, Xiaoping. " 'Focus' (*Jiaodian Fangtan*) and the Changes in the Chinese Television Industry," *Journal of Contemporary China* 11, no. 30 (February 2002): 17–34.

Li, Zhisui, with Anne Thurston. *The Private Life of Chairman Mao.* New York: Random House, 1994.

Liang, Heng, and Judith Shapiro. *Son of the Revolution.* New York: Alfred A. Knopf, 1983.

Lieberthal, Kenneth. "Mao vs. Liu? Policy Toward Industry and Commerce, 1946–1947," *China Quarterly* 47 (July / September 1971): 494–520.

———. "The Foreign Policy Debate in Peking as Seen through the Allegorical Articles." *China Quarterly* 71 (September 1977): 528–54.

———. *Central Documents and Politburo Politics in China.* Ann Arbor: University of Michigan, Center for Chinese Studies, 1978a.

———. "The Politics of Modernization." *Problems of Communism* 27, no. 3 (May–June 1978b): 1–17.

———. *Sino-Soviet Conflict in the 1970s: Its Evolution and Implications for the Strategic Triangle* (Rand report R-2342-NA). Santa Monica,: Rand Corporation, 1978c.

———. *Revolution and Tradition in Tientsin, 1949–1952.* Stanford: Stanford University Press, 1980.

———. "The Future of Hong Kong." *Asian Survey* (July 1992): 666–82.

———. "China in 2033," *China Business Review* 30:2 (March-April 2003).

Lieberthal, Kenneth, and Bruce J. Dickson. *A Research Guide to Central Party and Government Meetings in China, 1949–1986.* Armonk, N.Y.: M. E. Sharpe, 1989.

Lieberthal, Kenneth, Joyce Kalgren, Roderick MacFarquhar, and Frederic Wakeman, Jr., eds. *Perspectives on Modern China: Four Anniversaries.* Armonk, N.Y.: M. E. Sharpe, 1991.

Lieberthal, Kenneth, and David M. Lampton, eds. *Bureaucracy, Politics and Decision Making in Post-Mao China.* Berkeley and Los Angeles: University of California Press, 1992.

Lieberthal, Kenneth, and Michel Oksenberg. *Policy Making in China: Leaders, Structures, and Processes.* Princeton, N. J.: Princeton University Press, 1988.

Lieberthal, Kenneth, and C. K. Prahalad. "Multinational Corporate Investment in China." *China Business Review* 16, no.2 (March–April 1989): 47–49.

Lifton, Robert Jay. *Thought Reform and the Psychology of Totalism.* New York: W. W. Norton, 1961.

Link, Perry. *Evening Chats in Beijing: Probing China's Predicament.* New York: Norton, 1992.

Little, Daniel. *Understanding Peasant China: Case Studies in the Philosophy of Social Science.* New Haven, Conn.: Yale University Press, 1989.

Liu, Binyan. *People or Monsters and Other Stories and Reportage from China after Mao.* Bloomington: Indiana University Press, 1992.

Liu, Junlin. "Make Efforts to Strengthen Further Building of Cadres' Ranks." *Guangming ribao,* 14 July 1991. Translated in *FBIS/China Daily Report* (30 July 1991): 31–33.

Liu, Ping. "China Lifts Government Control on Prices on Great Part of Goods," *China Economic News* 29 (30 July 2001): 2–4.

Lo, T. Wing. *Corruption and Politics in Hong Kong and China.* Philadelphia: Open University Press, 1993.

Lockwood, William W. *The Economic Development of Japan: Growth and Structural Change, 1868–1938.* Princeton, N.J.: Princeton University Press, 1954.

Lord, Bette Bao. *Legacies: A Chinese Mosaic.* New York: Alfred A. Knopf, 1990.

Lou, Xinya, and Junjie Huang. "Qigong Series Off the Press." *Beijing Review* 33 (8 January 1990): 46.

Lu, Hsün, *Ah Q and Other Selected Stories.* Westport, Conn.: Greenwood Press, 1971.

Lu, Xiaobo and Elizabeth Perry, eds. *Danwei: The Changing Chinese Workplace in Historical and Comparative Perspective.* Armonk, N.Y.: M. E. Sharpe, 1997.

Lubman, Stanley. *Bird in a Cage: Legal Reform After Mao.* Stanford: Stanford University Press, 1999.

Luk, Shiu-hung, and Joseph Whitney, eds. *Megaproject: A Case Study of China's Three Gorges Project.* Armonk, N.Y.: M. E. Sharpe, 1993.

Luo, Qi, and Christopher Howe. "Direct Investment and Economic Integration in the Asia Pacific: The Case of Taiwanese Investment in Xiamen." *China Quarterly* 136 (December 1993): 746–69.

Lynch, Daniel. *After the Propaganda State: Media, Politics, and Thought Work in Reformed China.* Stanford: Stanford University Press, 1999.

Lyons, Thomas. *Economic Integration and Planning in Maoist China.* New York: Columbia University Press, 1987.

———. "Planning and Interprovincial Coordination in Maoist China." *China Quarterly* 121 (March 1990): 36–60.

MacFarquhar, Roderick. *The Origins of the Cultural Revolution 1: Contradictions among the People, 1956–1957.* New York: Columbia University Press, 1974.

———. *The Origins of the Cultural Revolution 2: The Great Leap Forward 1958–1960.* New York: Columbia University Press, 1983.

———. "The Anatomy of Collapse." *New York Review of Books,* 26 September 1991.

MacFarquhar, Roderick, ed. *The Politics of China, 1949–1989.* New York: Cambridge University Press, 1993.

MacFarquhar, Roderick, Timothy Cheek, and Eugene Wu. *The Secret Speeches of Chairman Mao.* Cambridge, Mass.: Harvard University Press, 1989.

MacFarquhar, Roderick, and John K. Fairbank, eds. *Cambridge History of China.* Vol. 14. New York: Cambridge University Press, 1987.

———, eds. *Cambridge History of China.* Vol. 15. New York: Cambridge University Press, 1991.

Madsen, Richard. "The Public Sphere, Civil Society and Moral Community: A Research Agenda for Contemporary Chinese Studies." *Modern China* 19 (April 1993): 183–98.

Malraux, André. *Man's Fate.* New York: Vintage, 1934.

Manion, Melanie. "Cadre Recruitment and Management in the People's Republic of China." *Chinese Law and Government* 17:3 (Fall 1984): 3–128.

———. *Retirement of Revolutionaries in China: Public Policies, Social Norms, Private Interests.* Princeton, N. J.: Princeton University Press, 1993.

———. "The Electoral Connection in the Chinese Countryside," *American Political Science Review* (December 1996): pp. 736–48.

Mann, Susan. *Local Merchants and the Chinese Bureaucracy, 1750–1950.* Stanford: Stanford University Press, 1987.

Mao Zedong. *Selected Works of Mao Zedong,* vol. 1. Beijing: Foreign Languages Press, 1965.

———. *Selected Works of Mao Tse-tung,* vol. 2. Peking: Foreign Languages Press, 1965.

———. *Selected Works of Mao Tse-tung,* vol. 3. Peking: Foreign Languages Press, 1965.

———. *Selected Works of Mao Tse-tung,* vol. 4. Beijing: Foreign Languages Press, 1967.

———. *Selected Works of Mao Zedong,* vol. 5. Beijing: Foreign Languages Press, 1977.

———. *Writings of Mao Zedong: 1949–1976,* vol. I. Armonk, N.Y.: M. E. Sharpe, 1986.

Mao Zedong sixiang wan sui! (Long live Mao Zedong Thought!) N.p., 1969.

Marshall's Mission to China, December 1945–1947: The Report and Appended Documents. Arlington, Va.: University Publications of America, 1976.

Maruya, Toyojiro. "The Development of the Guangdong Economy and Its Ties with Beijing." *China Newsletter* 96 (January–February 1992): 2–10.

Massey, Joseph. "301: The Successful Resolution." *China Business Review* 19, no. 6 (November–December 1992): 9–11.

McCormick, Barret L., Shaozhi Su, and Xiaoming Xiao. "The 1989 Democracy Movement: A Review of the Prospects for Civil Society in China." *Pacific Affairs* 65 (Summer 1992): 182–1993.

McCullough, David G. *Truman.* New York: Simon and Schuster, 1992.

Melby, John F. *Mandate of Heaven.* Toronto: University of Toronto Press, 1968.

Michael, Franz. *The Taiping Rebellion.* 3 vols. Seattle: University of Washington Press, 1966–1971.

Migdal, Joel S. *Strong Societies and Weak States.* Princeton, N.J.: Princeton University Press, 1988.

Migdal, Joel Samuel Atul Kohli, and Vivienne Shue, eds. *State Power and Social Forces: Domination and Transformation in The Third World.* New York: Cambridge University Press, 1994.

Mirsky, Jonathan. "China: Bartered Brides." *Ottawa Citizen,* 5 October 1992, p. D12.

Montell, Sherwin. "The San-fan Wu-fan Movement in China." In *Papers on China,* vol. 8. Cambridge, Mass.: Harvard University Press, 1954.

Morse, Hosea Ballou. *The Trade and Administration of the Chinese Empire.* Taipei: Ch'eng-Wen Publishing Company, 1966.

Mulvenon, James, ed. *The People's Liberation Army as an Organization.* Santa Monica: RAND Corporation, 2002.

Murphey, Rhoads. *The Treaty Ports and China's Modernization: What Went Wrong.* Ann Arbor: University of Michigan, Center for Chinese Studies, 1970.

"Nanjing Paper Attacks Secret Societies, Sects." *FBIS* (18 February 1987): 5.

Naquin, Susan, and Evelyn Rawski. *Chinese Society in the Eighteenth Century.* New Haven, Conn.: Yale University Press, 1987.

Nathan, Andrew J. *Chinese Democracy.* New York: Alfred A. Knopf, 1985.

———. "China's Path from Communism." *Journal of Democracy* 4, no. 2 (April 1993a): 30–42.

———. "Is Chinese Culture Distinctive?" *Journal of Asian Studies* 52 (November 1993b): 923–36.

Nathan, Andrew J., and Perry Link, eds. *The Tiananmen Papers.* New York: Public Affairs, 2001.

Nathan, Andrew J., and Bruce Gilley, *China's New Rulers: The Secret Files.* New York: *New York Review Books*, 2002.

Naughton, Barry. *Growing Out of the Plan: Chinese Economic Reform, 1978–1993.* Cambridge: Cambridge University Press, 1996.

———. "The Third Front: Defense Industrialization in the Chinese Interior." *China Quarterly* 115 (September 1988): 351–86.

———. "China's Experience with Guidance Planning." *Journal of Comparative Economics* 14 (1990): 743–67.

Nelsen, Harvey W. *The Chinese Military System: An Organizational Study of the Chinese People's Liberation Army,* 2nd ed. Boulder: Westview Press, 1981.

Nevill, Christopher. "Private Business Associations in China." *China Journal* (July 1996): 25–43.

"New Achievements in Social Services in 1992." *FBIS* (3 February 1993): 18.

"New Qigong Film." *Beijing Review* 34 (1 July 1991): 41–42.

"New Strategy for Environmental Protection: Putting a Price on Resources." *Beijing Review* 31 (22 August 1988): 32–34.

Norman, Matthew. "When Being Female Is a Deadly Crime." *Evening Standard,* 26 September 1993, p. 55.

North, Robert C. *Kuomintang and Chinese Communist Elites.* Stanford: Stanford University Press, 1952.

O'Brien, Kevin, and Li Lianjiang, "The Politics of Lodging Complaints in Rural China." *China Quarterly* 143 (September 1995): 756–783.

———. "Implementing Political Reform in China's Villages." *Australian Journal of Chinese Affairs* 32 (July 1994): 33–60.

———. "Accommodating Democracy in a One-Party State: Introducing Village Elections in China." *China Quarterly* 162 (June 2000): 465–89.

Ogata, Sadako M. *Normalization with China: A Comparative Study of U.S. and Japanese Processes.* Berkeley: University of California, Institute of East Asian Studies, 1988.

Oi, Jean. *State and Peasant in Contemporary China: The Political Economy of Village Government.* Berkeley and Los Angeles: University of California Press, 1989.

———. *Rural China Takes Off: Incentives for Reform.* Berkeley: University of California Press, 1999.

———. "State and Peasants on the Eve of the Sixteenth Party Congress: The Economic and Political Costs of Peasant Burdens." Paper presented at the "New Leadership, New China?" conference, Hoover Institution, 24–25 January 2003.

Oksenberg, Michel, and Steven Goldstein. "China's Political Spectrum." *Problems of Communism* 23 (March–April 1974): 1–13.

Oksenberg, Michel, and James Tong. "The Evolution of Central-Provincial Fiscal Relations in China, 1971–1984: The Formal System." *China Quarterly* 125 (March 1991): 1–32.

Oksenberg, Michel, and S.C. Yeung. "Hua Kuo-feng's Pre-Cultural Revolution Hunan Years, 1949–1966: The Making of a Political Generalist." *China Quarterly* 69 (March 1977): 3–54.

Oksenberg, Michel, Lawrence Sullivan, and Marc Lambert, eds. *Beijing Spring, 1989.* Armonk, N.Y.: M. E. Sharpe, 1990.

Oksenberg, Michel, and Elizabeth Economy, eds. *China Joins the World: Progress and Prospects.* New York: Council on Foreign Relations, 1999.

Organisation for Economic Co-operation and Development. *China in the World Economy: The Domestic Policy Challenges* (synthesis report). Paris: OECD Publications, 2002.

Overholt, William H. *The Rise of China.* New York: Norton, 1993.

Pan, Guang. "China–Central Asia–Russia Relations and the Role of the SCO in the War on Terrorism" *SIIS Journal* (Shanghai Institute of International Affairs Journal) 9:2 (May 2002).

Pearson, Margaret. *Joint Ventures in the People's Republic of China: The Control of Foreign Direct Investment under Socialism.* Princeton, N.J.: Princeton University Press, 1991.

Peck, Graham. *Two Kinds of Time.* Boston: Houghton Mifflin, 1967.

Peerenboom, Randall. "Let One Hundred Flowers Bloom, One Hundred Schools of Thought Contend: Debating Rule of Law in China." *Michigan Journal of International Law* 23:3 (Spring 2002): 471–544.

———. *China's Long March Toward the Rule of Law.* Cambridge: Cambridge University Press, 2002a.

Pei, Minxin. "China's Governing Crisis." *Foreign Affairs* (September–October 2002): 96–109.

Peng, Peiyun. "Population Problems and Countermeasures." *Beijing Review* 33 (7 May 1990): 20–24.

Pepper, Suzanne. *Civil War in China.* Berkeley and Los Angeles: University of California Press, 1978.

———. *China's Education Reform in the 1980s: Policies, Issues and Historical Perspectives.* Berkeley: University of California, Center for Chinese Studies, 1990.

Perkins, Dwight. *Market Control and Planning in Communist China.* Cambridge, Mass.: Harvard University Press, 1966.

———. *Agricultural Development in China, 1368–1968.* Chicago: Aldine, 1969.

Perkins, Dwight, ed. *Rural Development in China.* Baltimore: Johns Hopkins University Press, 1984.

Perry, Elizabeth J. *Rebels and Revolutionaries in North China, 1985–1945.* Stanford: Stanford University Press, 1980.

———. "China in 1992: An Experiment in Neo-Authoritarianism." *Asian Survey* 33 (January 1993): 12–21.

———. "Trends in the Study of Chinese Politics: State-Society Relations," *China Quarterly* 139 (September 1994): 704–13.

———. "Shanghai's Strike Wave of 1957." *China Quarterly* 137 (March 1994): 1–27.

Perry, Elizabeth J., and Mark Selden, eds. *Chinese Society: Change, Conflict and Resistance.* New York: Routledge, 2000.

Petrov, Vladimir. *Soviet-Chinese Relations 1945–1970.* Bloomington: Indiana University Press, 1975.

Peyrefitte, Alain. *The Immobile Empire.* New York: Alfred A. Knopf, 1992.

Potter, Pitman B., ed. *Domestic Law Reforms in Post-Mao China.* Armonk, N.Y.: M. E. Sharpe, 1993.

Powell, Simon. *Agricultural Reform in China: From Communes to Commodity Economy, 1978–1990.* Manchester: Manchester University Press, 1992.

Pu Yi, Aisin-Gioro. *From Emperor to Citizen.* Peking: Foreign Languages Press, 1979.

Pye, Lucian. *Warlord Politics: Conflict and Coalition in the Modernization of Republican China.* New York: Praeger, 1971.

———. *The Dynamics of Factions and Consensus in Chinese Politics: A Model and Some Propositions.* Santa Monica: Rand Corporation, 1980.

———. *The Mandarin and the Cadre.* Ann Arbor: University of Michigan, Center for Chinese Studies, 1988.

———. "Tiananmen and Chinese Political Culture: The Escalation of Confrontation from Moralizing to Revenge." *Asian Survey* 30 (April 1990): 331–47.

———. "The State and the Individual." *China Quarterly* 127 (September 1991): 443–62.

———. *The Spirit of Chinese Politics.* Cambridge, Mass.: Harvard University Press, 1992.

"Qigong—Popularity Is Rising." *Beijing Review* 31 (14 November 1988): 32–35.

Qu, Geping, and Woyen Lee, eds. *Managing the Environment in China.* Dublin: Tycooly International, 1984.

Qu, Geping, and Jinchang Li. *An Outline Study on China's Population—Environmental Issues.* Beijing: National Environmental Protection Agency, 1990.

Rawski, Evelyn S. "Presidential Address: Reenvisioning the Qing: The Significance of the Qing Period in Chinese History." *Journal of Asia Studies* 55:4 (November 1996): 829–50.

———. *The Last Emperors: A Social History of Qing Imperial Institutions.* Berkeley: University of California Press, 1998.

Renmin shouce (People's Handbook). Beijing, 1951.

"Resolution on Certain Questions in the History of Our Party since the Founding of the People's Republic of China." *Beijing Review* 27 (6 July 1981): 10–39.

Riskin, Carl. *China's Political Economy: The Quest for Development Since 1949.* Oxford: Oxford University Press, 1987.

Riskin, Carl, Renwei Zhao, and Shi Li, eds. *China's Retreat From Equality: Income Distribution and Economic Transition.* Armonk, N.Y.: M.E. Sharpe, 2001.

Rosenbaum, Arthur Lewis, ed. *State and Society in China.* Boulder: Westview Press, 1992.

Ross, Lester. "Forestry Policy in China." Ph.D. diss., University of Michigan, 1980.

———. *Environmental Law and Policy in the People's Republic of China.* New York: Quorum, 1987.

———. *Environmental Policy in China.* Bloomington: Indiana University Press, 1988.

"Rotten to the Core: Monopoly of Power Leads to Rampant Corruption." *Far Eastern Economic Review* 156 (16 September 1993): 16–17.

Rowe, William T. *Hankow: Commerce and Society in a Chinese City, 1796–1889.* Stanford: Stanford University Press, 1984.

———. *Hankow: Conflict and Community in a Chinese City, 1796–1895.* Stanford: Stanford University Press, 1989.

————. "The Problem of 'Civil Society' in Late Imperial China." *Modern China* (April 1993): 139–57.

Rozelle, Scott. "Decision Making in China's Rural Economy: The Linkages between Village Leaders and Farm Households." *China Quarterly* 137 (March 1994): 99–124.

Ruan, Ming. *The Empire of Deng.* Boulder: Westview Press, 1994.

Salisbury, Harrison E. *The Long March: The Untold Story.* New York: Harper & Row, 1985.

————. *The New Emperors: China in the Era of Mao and Deng.* Boston: Little, Brown, 1992.

Sander, Henny, and Jonathan Friedland. "Investment: Think Twice." *Far Eastern Economic Review* 156, no. 36 (9 September 1993): 46–49.

Saunders, Harold, et al. *Tibet: Issues for Americans.* New York: National Committee on U.S.–China Relations, 1993.

Schechter, Danny. *Falun Gong's Challenge to China: Spiritual Practice or Evil Cult?* New York: Akashic Books, 2001.

Schell, Orville. *To Get Rich Is Glorious: China in the Eighties.* New York: Pantheon, 1984.

Schiffrin, Harold Z. *Sun Yat-Sen and the Origins of the Chinese Revolution.* Berkeley and Los Angeles: University of California Press, 1970.

Schoenhals, Michael. "The 1978 Truth Criterion Controversy." *China Quarterly* 126 (June 1991): 243–68.

————. "Selections from *Propaganda Trends,* Organ of the CCP Central Propaganda Department." *Chinese Law and Government* 24, no. 4 (Winter 1991–1992): 5–93.

Schram, Stuart R. *The Political Thought of Mao Tse-Tung.* Middlesex: Penguin, 1963.

————. *Political Leaders of the Twentieth Century: Mao Tse-Tung.* Baltimore: Penguin, 1966.

Schurmann, Franz. *Ideology and Organization in Communist China.* 2d ed. Berkeley and Los Angeles: University of California Press, 1971.

"Scientists Warn of Resource Shortages." *Beijing Review* 35 (18 May 1992): 7.

Schwartz, Benjamin I. *Chinese Communism and the Rise of Mao.* Cambridge, Mass.: Harvard University Press, 1964.

Sehrt, Kaja (1999). "Banks vs. Budgets: Credit Allocation in the People's Republic of China, 1984–1997." Ph.D. diss., University of Michigan, 1998.

Selden, Mark. *The Yenan Way in Revolutionary China.* Cambridge, Mass.: Harvard University Press, 1971.

Seymour, James D. *The Fifth Modernization: China's Human Rights Movement, 1978–1979.* Stanfordville, N.Y.: Human Rights Publishing Group, 1980.

————. *China's Satellite Parties.* Armonk, N.Y.: M. E. Sharpe, 1987.

Seymour, James D., and Richard Anderson. *New Ghosts Old Ghosts: Prison and Labour Reform Camps in China.* Armonk, N.Y.: M. E. Sharpe, 1998.

Shambaugh, David. *The Making of a Premier: Zhao Ziyang's Provincial Career.* Boulder: Westview Press, 1984.

————. "Introduction: The Emergence of 'Greater China.'" *China Quarterly* 136 (December 1993): 653–59.

————. "China's International Relations Think Tanks: Evolving Structure and Process." *The China Quarterly* 171 (September 2002): 575–96.

————. *Modernizing China's Military: Progress, Problems, and Prospects.* Berkeley and London: University of California Press, 2002b.

Shambaugh, David, ed. *Is China Unstable?* Armonk, N.Y.: M.E. Sharpe, 2000.

Shapiro, Judith. *Mao's War Against Nature.* Cambridge: Cambridge University Press, 2001.

Shen, Tong. "Will China Be Democratic?" *World Affairs* 154 (Spring 1992): 139–54.

Sheng, Kang. *The Claws of the Dragon.* New York: Simon and Schuster, 1992.

Shirk, Susan L. "Recent Chinese Labor Policies and the Transformation of Industrial Organization in China." *China Quarterly* 88 (December 1981): 575–93.

————. *The Political Logic of Economic Reform in China.* Berkeley and Los Angeles: University of California Press, 1993.

————. *How China Opened Its Door: The Political Success of the PRC's Foreign Trade and Investment Reforms.* Washington, D.C. : Brookings Institution, 1994.

Shue, Vivienne. *Peasant China in Transition: The Dynamics of Development toward Socialism, 1949–1956.* Berkeley and Los Angeles: University of California Press, 1980.

————. *The Reach of State.* Stanford: Stanford University Press, 1988.

Siu, Helen F., *Agents and Victims in South China: Accomplices in Rural Revolution.* New Haven, Conn.: Yale University Press, 1989.

Siu, Helen F., ed. *Furrows: Peasants, Intellectuals, and the State.* Stanford: Stanford University Press, 1990.

Skinner, G. W. "Marketing and Social Structure in Rural China." *Journal of Asian Studies* 24, no. 1 (Nov. 1964): 3–43; 24, no. 2 (Feb. 1965): 195–228; 24, no. 3 (May 1965): 363–99.

————. *The City in Late Imperial China.* Stanford: Stanford University Press, 1977.

Skocpol, Theda. *States and Social Revolutions.* Cambridge: Cambridge University Press, 1979.

"Slaughtering the Innocents." *South China Morning Post,* 26 September 1993, p. 54.

Smil, Vaclav. *The Bad Earth: Environmental Degradation in China.* Armonk, N.Y.: M. E. Sharpe, 1984.

————. *China's Environmental Crisis.* Armonk, N.Y.: M. E. Sharpe, 1993.

————. *Environmental Problems in China: Estimates of Economic Cost.* Honolulu: East-West Center, 1997.

Smith, Richard. *Mercenaries and Mandarins: The Ever Victorious Army in Nineteenth Century China.* Millwood, N.Y.: KTO, 1978.

Snow, Edgar. *Red Star over China.* New York: Grove, 1961.

Solinger, Dorothy J. *Regional Government and Political Integration in Southwest China, 1949–1954: A Case Study.* Berkeley and Los Angeles: University of California Press, 1977.

————. *From Lathes to Looms: China's Industrial Policy in Comparative Perspective, 1979–1982.* Stanford: Stanford University Press, 1991.

————. "China's Transients and the State: A Form of Civil Society." *Politics and Society* 21 (March 1993): 91–122.

————. "China's Urban Transients in the Transition from Socialism and the Collapse of the Communist 'Urban Public Goods Regime,' " *Comparative Politics* 27 (January 1995): 127–46.

———. "The Chinese Work Unit and Transient Labor in the Transition from Socialism," *Modern China* 21 (April 1995): 155–83.

———. "Despite Decentralization: Disadvantage, Dependence, and Ongoing Central Power in the Inland—The Case of Wuhan," *China Quarterly* 45 (March 1996): 1–34.

———. *Contesting Citizenship in Urban China.* Berkeley: University of California Press, 1999.

Solomon, Richard H. *Mao's Revolution and the Chinese Political Culture.* Berkeley and Los Angeles: University of California Press, 1971.

Solomon, Richard H., ed. *The China Factor: Sino-American Relations and the Global Scene.* Englewood Cliffs, N.J.: Prentice-Hall, 1981.

Spector, Stanley. *Li Hung-Chang and the Huai Army: A Study in Nineteenth-Century Chinese Regionalism.* Seattle: University of Washington Press, 1964.

Spence, Jonathan. *Emperor of China: Self-Portrait of K'ang Hsi.* New York: Alfred A. Knopf, 1974.

———. *Death of Woman Wang.* New York: Viking, 1978.

———. *The Gate of Heavenly Peace.* New York: Penguin, 1981.

Starr, John Bryan, and Nancy Anne Dyer. *Post-Liberation Works of Mao Zedong: A Bibliography and Index.* Berkeley and Los Angeles: University of California Press, 1976.

"State Instituting Social Services for Retirees." Foreign Broadcast Information Service (27 October 1993): 40.

State Statistical Bureau. *China Statistical Yearbook, 1990.* New York: Praeger, 1991.

———, *China Statistical Yearbook, 2002.* Beijing: China Statistics Press, 2002.

Stueck, William Whitney. *The Road to Confrontation: American Policy Toward China and Korea, 1947–1950.* Chapel Hill: University of North Carolina Press, 1981.

Sullivan, Lawrence R. "The Role of Control Organs in the Chinese Communist Party, 1977–1983." *Asian Survey* 24 (June 1984): 597–617.

Sun, Yan. "Chinese Protests of 1989: The Issue of Corruption." *Asian Survey* 31 (August 1991): 762–82.

Sutter, Robert G. *China Watch: Sino-American Reconciliation.* Baltimore: Johns Hopkins University Press, 1978.

Sutton, Donald S. *Provincial Militarism and the Chinese Republic.* Ann Arbor: University of Michigan Press, 1980.

Swain, Jon. "Beijing Reasserts Control as Economic Unrest Mounts." *Sunday Times,* 4 July 1993.

Swaine, Michael. *The Military and Political Succession in China* (RAND Report R-4254-AF). Santa Monica: Rand Corporation, 1992.

"Symposium on Rural Family Change." *China Quarterly* 130 (June 1992): 317–91.

T'an, Chester C. *The Boxer Catastrophe.* New York: Columbia University Press, 1955.

Tanner, Murray Scot. "The Erosion of Central Party Control of Lawmaking." *China Quarterly* 138 (March 1994): 381–403.

Tanner, Murray Scot, and Eric Green. "Central-Local Relations and State Coercive Power: Decentralized Policing, Social Control, and 'Rule of Law' in China." Unpublished paper, 2002.

Tanner, Murray Scot, and Michael J. Feder. " 'Family Politics,' Elite Recruitment and Succession in Post-Mao China." *Australian Journal of Chinese Affairs* 30 (July 1993): 89–120.

Tawney, R. H. *Land and Labor in China*. Boston: Beacon, 1966.

Teiwes, Frederick C. *Elite Discipline in China: Coercive and Persuasive Approaches 1950–1953*. Canberra: Australian National University Press, 1978.

———. *Politics and Purges in China*. White Plains, N.Y.: M. E. Sharpe, 1979.

———. *Politics at Mao's Court: Gao Gang and Party Factionalism in the Early 1950s*. Armonk, N.Y.: M. E. Sharpe, 1990.

Teng, Ssu-Yu, and John K. Fairbank. *China's Response to the West: A Documentary Survey 1839–1923*. New York: Atheneum, 1963.

Terrill, Ross. *A Biography: Mao*. New York: Harper & Row, 1980.

"Text of the 14th CPC Congress Political Report." Foreign Broadcast Information Service (8 October 1992): 1–20.

"Threat From 'Secret Societies' Examined." Foreign Broadcast Information Service (16 July 1986): K1.

"Through the Roof: Shenzhen Takes Steps to Curb Property Speculation." *Far Eastern Economic Review* 154 (24 October 1991): 75–76.

Thurston, Anne F. *Enemies of the People*. Cambridge, Mass.: Harvard University Press, 1988.

———. *A Chinese Odyssey: The Life and Times of a Chinese Dissident*. New York: Scribner's, 1991.

———. "The Dragon Stirs." *Wilson Quarterly* (Spring 1993): 10–15.

Tien, Hung-Mao. *Government and Politics in Kuomintang China 1927–1937*. Stanford: Stanford University Press, 1972.

———. *The Great Transition: Political and Social Change in the Republic of China*. Stanford: Stanford University Press, 1989.

Tien, H. Yuan, Tianlu Zhang, Yu Ping, Jingneng Li, and Zhongtang Liang. "China's Demographic Dilemmas." *Population Bulletin* 47 (June 1992): 1–44.

Toffler, Alvin. *The Third Wave*. New York: Morrow, 1980.

Tong, James. *Disorder Under Heaven: Collective Violence in the Ming Dynasty*. Stanford: Stanford University Press, 1991.

Townsend, James R. *Political Participation in Communist China*. Berkeley and Los Angeles: University of California Press, 1969.

Treadgold, Donald W., ed. *Soviet and Chinese Communism: Similarities and Differences*. Seattle: University of Washington Press, 1967.

Tsai, Kellee. *Back-Alley Banking: Private Entrepreneurs in China*. Ithaca, N. Y.: Cornell University Press, 2002.

Tsou, Tang. *America's Failure in China, 1949–1950*. Vol. 1. Chicago: University of Chicago Press, 1963a.

———. *America's Failure in China, 1949–1950*. Vol. 2. Chicago: University of Chicago Press, 1963b.

Tu, Weiming. "Cultural China: The Periphery as Center." *Daedalus* 120 (Spring 1991): 1–32.

Tuchman, Barbara. *Stilwell and the American Experience in China 1911–1945*. New York: Macmillan, 1970.

Turner, Jennifer L. "The Dirty Burden: The Costs and Challenges of Environmental Degradation in China," in *Economics and National Security: The Case of China*, edited by

Kent H. Butts and Edward L. Hughes. Carlisle, Pa.: U.S. Army War College, 2002, pp. 331–52.

Twitchett, Denis, and John K. Fairbank, eds. *Cambridge History of China.* Vol. 11. New York: Cambridge University Press, 1978.

Unger, Jonathan, and Anita Chan. "China, Corporatism, and the East Asian Model." *Australian Journal of Chinese Affairs* 33 (January 1995): 29–53.

Unger, Jonathan, ed. *Chinese Nationalism.* Armonk, N.Y.: M.E. Sharpe, 1996.

Van Slyke, Lyman P. *The United Front in Chinese Communist History.* Stanford: Stanford University Press, 1967.

———. *The Chinese Communist Movement.* Stanford: Stanford University Press, 1968.

Vladimirov, Petr P. *The Vladimirov Diaries: Yenan, China, 1942–1945.* Garden City, N.Y.: Doubleday, 1975.

Vogel, Ezra F. *Japan as Number One: Lessons for America.* New York: Harper & Row, 1980.

———. *One Step Ahead in China: Guangdong under Reform.* Cambridge, Mass.: Harvard University Press, 1989.

———. *The Four Little Dragons: The Spread of Industrialization in East Asia.* Cambridge, Mass.: Harvard University Press, 1991.

Wakeman, Frederic, Jr. "The Civil Society and Public Sphere Debate." *Modern China* 19 (April 1993): 108–38.

Walder, Andrew G. *Chang Ch'un-Ch'iao and Shanghai's January Revolution.* Ann Arbor: University of Michigan Press, 1978.

———. *Communist Neo-Traditionalism: Work and Authority in Chinese Industry.* Berkeley and Los Angeles: University of California Press, 1986.

———. "Reply to Womack." *China Quarterly* 126 (June 1991): 333–39.

Waldron, Arthur. *The Great Wall of China: From History to Myth.* New York: Cambridge University Press, 1989.

Wang, Ruowang. *Hunger Trilogy.* Armonk, N.Y.: M. E. Sharpe, 1991.

Wang, Y. C. *Chinese Intellectuals and the West, 1872–1949.* Chapel Hill: University of North Carolina Press, 1966.

"Wang Zhen Decries Loss of Party Influence." Foreign Broadcast Information Service (12 March 1991): 32.

Wank, David L. "The Institutional Processes of Market Clientalism: *Guanxi* and Private Business in a South China City." *China Quarterly* 147 (September 1996): 820–38.

———. *Commodifying Communism: Business, Trust and Politics in a Chinese City.* Cambridge: Cambridge University Press, 1999.

Wasserstrom, Jeffrey, and Elizabeth Perry, eds. *Popular Protest and Political Culture in Modern China.* Boulder: Westview Press, 1992.

Watson, James L. *Death Ritual in Late Imperial and Modern China.* Berkeley and Los Angeles: University of California Press, 1988.

———."Hong Kong, 1997, and the Transformation of South China: An Anthropological Perspective." Contemporary Issues 1. Cambridge, Mass.: Harvard University, Fairbank Center for East Asian Research, May 1993.

White, Gordon. "State and Market in China's Labour Reforms." *Journal of Developmental Studies* 24 (July 1988): 180–202.

White, Gordon, Jude Howell, and Xiaoyuan Shang. *In Search of Civil Society: Market Reform and Social Change in Contemporary China.* Oxford: Clarendon Press, 1996.

White, Lynn T., III. *Careers in Shanghai.* Berkeley and Los Angeles: University of California Press, 1978.

———. *Policies of Chaos: The Organizational Causes of Violence in China's Cultural Revolution.* Princeton, N.J.: Princeton University Press, 1989.

White, Lynn T., III. *Unstately Power: Local Causes of China's Economic Reforms.* Vol. I. Armonk, N.Y.: M.E. Sharpe, 1998.

White, Lynn T., III, and Cheng Li. "Elite Transformation and Modern Change in Mainland China and Taiwan: Empirical Data and the Theory of Technocracy." *China Quarterly* 121 (March 1990): 1–35.

White, Theodore H. *In Search of History.* New York: Harper & Row, 1978.

Whiting, Allen S. *China Crosses the Yalu.* Stanford: Stanford University Press, 1960.

Whiting, Susan. *Power and Wealth in Rural China: The Political Economy of Institutional Change.* New York: Cambridge University Press, 2001.

Whitney, Joesph B. R. *China: Area, Administration, and Nation Building.* Chicago: University of Chicago, Department of Geography, Research Paper No. 123, 1970.

Whitson, William W. *The Military and Political Power in China in the 1970s.* New York: Praeger, 1972.

———. *Chinese Military and Political Leaders and the Distribution of Power in China, 1956–1971* (RAND report R-1091-DOS/ARPA). Santa Monica, Calif.: Rand Corporation, 1973.

Whitson, William W., and Chen-hsia Huang. *The Chinese High Command: A History of Communist Military Politics, 1927–1971.* New York: Praeger, 1973.

Whyte, Martin King. *Small Groups and Political Rituals in China.* Berkeley and Los Angeles: University of California Press, 1974.

———. "Urban China: A Civil Society in the Making?" in *State and Society in China,* edited by Arthur Rosenbaum. Boulder: Westview Press, 1992, pp. 77–102.

Wich, Richard. *Sino-Soviet Crisis Politics.* Cambridge, Mass.: Harvard University, Council on East Asian Studies, 1980.

Wilbur, C. Martin. *The Nationalist Revolution in China, 1923–1928.* New York: Cambridge University Press, 1984.

Wilson, Dick, ed. *Mao Tse-tung in the Scales of History: A Preliminary Assessment.* Cambridge, Mass.: Harvard University Press, 1977.

Wittfogel, Karl A. *Oriental Despotism: A Comparative Study of Total Power.* New Haven, Conn.: Yale University Press, 1957.

Wolf, Margery, and Roxanne Witke, eds. *Women in Chinese Society.* Stanford: Stanford University Press, 1975.

Womack, Brantly. "Transfigured Community: Neo-traditionalism and Work Unit Socialism in China." *China Quarterly* 126 (June 1991): 313–32.

Wong, Christine. "Central-Local Relations in an Era of Fiscal Decline: The Paradox of Fiscal Decentralization in China." *China Quarterly* 128 (December 1991): 691–715.

Wood, Gordon. *The Radicalism of the American Revolution.* New York: Random House, 1991.

World Bank. *China: The Energy Sector.* Washington, D.C.: World Bank, 1985.

————. *China: Between Plan and Market.* Washington, D.C.: World Bank, 1990.

————. *Revenue Mobilization and Tax Policy.* Washington, D.C.: World Bank, 1990.

————. *Efficiency and Environmental Impact of Coal Use in China.* Washington, D.C.: World Bank, 1991.

————. *The East Asian Miracle: Economic Growth and Public Policy.* New York: Oxford University Press, 1993a.

————. *China Updating Economic Memorandum: Managing Rapid Growth and Transition.* Washington, D.C.: World Bank, 1993b.

————. *Clear Water, Blue Skies.* Washington, D.C.: World Bank, 1997.

————. *China: Air, Land and Water: Environmental Priorities for a New Millennium.* Washington, D.C.: The World Bank, 2001.

World Bank Transition Economics Division. *Transition.* Washington, D.C.: World Bank Transition Economics Division.

Wright, Arthur. *Confucianism and Chinese Civilization.* New York: Atheneum, 1964.

Wright, Mary C. *The Last Stand of Chinese Conservatism: The T'ung-chih Restoration, 1862–1874.* Rev. ed. Stanford: Stanford University Press, 1966.

Wright, Mary C., ed. *China in Revolution: The First Phase, 1900–1913.* New Haven, Conn.: Yale University Press, 1968.

Wu, Hongda Harry. *Laogai: The Chinese Gulag.* Boulder: Westview Press, 1992.

Wu, Naitao. "An Open System: Ensuring An Honest Government." *Beijing Review* 33 (29 January 1990): 6–7.

Wu, Ningkun. *A Single Tear: A Family's Persecution, Love, and Endurance in Communist China.* New York: Atlantic Monthly Press, 1993.

Wu, Silas H. L. *Communication and Imperial Control in China: Evolution of the Palace Memorial System, 1693–1735.* Cambridge, Mass.: Harvard University Press, 1970.

Xingzheng qu hua jiance 2001 (Brief volume on administrative divisions 2001). Tianjin: Xinhuashe (New China News Agency). Zhongguo ditu chubanshe, 2001.

Yan, Jiaqi. *Lianbang Zhongguo gouxiang* (Conception of a federal China). Hong Kong: Mingbao Publishing Company, 1992.

Yang, C. K. *Chinese Communist Society: The Family and the Village.* Cambridge, Mass.: MIT Press, 1959.

Yang, Dali. "Anti-Corruption and Public Management Reforms in China." Unpublished paper, 2002.

Yang, Jisheng. "Bloated State Administrative Institutions." *Qunyan* 8 (7 August 1991): 23–34. Translated in Foreign Broadcast Information Service/*China Daily Report* (29 August 1991): 39–31.

Yang, Xiaobing. "Taiwan Steps Up Mainland Investment." *Beijing Review* 31 (24 October 1988): 42.

Yang, Xiaobing, and Lei Zhang. "China's Population Policy." *Beijing Review* 35 (13 April 1992): 17–20.

Yang, Zhong Mei. *Hu Yao Bang: A Chinese Biography.* Armonk, N.Y.: M. E. Sharpe, 1988.

Yi, Z. "Population Policies in China: New Challenge and Strategies," in *An Aging World: Dilemmas and Challenges for Law and Social Policy,* edited by J. M. Eekelaar and D. Pearl. Oxford: Clarendon, 1989.

Young, Earnest. *The Presidency of Yuan Shih-Kai.* Ann Arbor: University of Michigan Press, 1977.

Young, Marilyn B., ed. *Women in China.* Ann Arbor: University of Michigan, Center for Chinese Studies, 1973.

Yue, Daiyun, and Carolyn Wakeman. *To the Storm: The Odyssey of a Revolutionary Chinese Woman.* Berkeley and Los Angeles: University of California Press, 1985.

Zagoria, Donald. *The Sino-Soviet Conflict 1956–1961.* Princeton N.J.: Princeton University Press, 1962.

Zha, Jianying. "China's Pop Culture in the 1990s," in *China Briefing,* edited by William Joseph. Boulder: Westview Press, 1996. pp. 109–50.

Zhang, Shu Guang. *Deterrence and Strategic Culture: Chinese-American Confrontations, 1949–1958.* Ithaca, N.Y.: Cornell University Press, 1992.

Zheng, Yongnian. "The Making of a Federal System: Quasi Corporatism and the Rise of Local Power in China." Ph.D. diss., Princeton University, 1994.

Zhongguo nonye laodongli jiuye ji liudong zhuangkuang (The state of affairs of employment and circulation of China's rural labor force). Beijing: State Statistical Bureau Publishing Company, 2000.

Zhonghua Renmin Gongheguo sheng zizhiqu zhishushi dang zheng chun jiguan zuzhi jigou, gai yao (Outline of the organizational structure of the Party, government, and mass organizations of the provinces, autonomous regions, and directly administered cities of the PRC). Beijing: China Personnel Publishing Company, 1989.

Zhou, Kate Xiao. *How the Farmers Changed China: Power of the People.* Boulder, Colo.: Westview Press, 1996.

Zhou, Xuegang. "Unorganized Interest and Collective Action in Communist China." *American Sociological Review* 58 (February 1993): 54–73.

Zweig, David. *Agrarian Radicalism in China, 1968–1981.* Cambridge, Mass.: Harvard University Press, 1989.

———. *Freeing China's Farmers: Rural Restructuring in the Reform Era.* Armonk, N.Y.: M.E. Sharpe, 1997.

Zweig, David, with Chen Changgui. *China's Brain Drain to the United States: Views of Overseas Chinese Students and Scholars in the 1990s.* Berkeley: University of California, Institute of East Asian Studies, 1995.

Index